Learning and Behavior

A Contemporary Synthesis

Learning and Behavior
A Contemporary Synthesis

Mark E. Bouton
University of Vermont

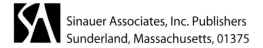
Sinauer Associates, Inc. Publishers
Sunderland, Massachusetts, 01375

The Cover
Flowering, 1934, 199
Paul Klee
Oil on primed canvas, 81.5 × 80 cm
Kunstmuseum Winterhur, Legat Clara und Emil Friedrich-Jezler
© 2006 Artists Rights Society (ARS), New York/VG Bild-Kunst, Bonn

Sinauer Associates, Inc.
23 Plumtree Road
Sunderland, MA 01375
U.S.A.

FAX 413-549-1118
publish@sinauer.com, orders@sinauer.com

Library of Congress Cataloging-in-Publication Data

Bouton, Mark E.
  Learning and behavior: a contemporary synthesis / Mark Bouton.
    p. cm.
  Includes bibliographical references and index.
  ISBN-13: 978-0-87893-063-0 (hardcover : alk. paper)
 1. Learning, Psychology of. 2. Cognition. 3. Conditioned response. I.
Title.

BF318.B675 2007
153.1'5—dc22

20060255377

6 5 4 3 2 1

For Suzy, Lindsay, and Grace
And for my mother and father

Table of Contents

6 Are the Laws of Conditioning General?   185

7 Behavior and Its Consequences   223

8 How Stimuli Guide Instrumental Action   267

Preface

I wrote this book because I love the field it describes. Learning Theory is part of a long and distinguished tradition in experimental psychology that is still producing new and valuable insights. Whenever I attend conferences or scientific meetings, I often meet people from other specialty areas (clinical psychologists, behavioral neuroscientists, and social psychologists, for example) who want to know more about what is going on in the field. The explanation is that basic principles of learning have deep connections with what many—if not all—psychologists study and do.

This text describes the principles of learning and behavior by emphasizing the intellectual context in which the important ideas and topics were developed. In addition to explaining the important facts and theories and describing the latest research, the book tries to honor where the facts and theories *came from*. This is a field that builds cautiously and rigorously. A historical narrative provides a good way for students to see how a science develops, progresses, and matures—and in the end, how everything is interconnected. I think it also keeps things interesting. Although my discussion is usually focused on laboratory experiments and the ideas that led to and followed them, I also often stop to discuss why an idea is relevant to the world outside the laboratory. The Table of Contents is full of places where we stop to catch our breath and ask, "what does it all mean"? The goal is to identify and reinforce the big ideas. It's the big ideas, rather than the details, that students working in other areas need to know and be ready to apply.

The book starts simply, and builds. Chapter 1 begins with a short history—what the field is currently about, how it got this way, and what it can offer to our general understanding of psychology and behavior in the real world. Chapter 2 then turns to the functions of both instrumental and Pavlovian learning. I believe that evolution and the functional analysis of learning are important and intrinsically interesting, and by the end of the second chapter, the text has covered a wide range of examples of learning without finding it necessary to use technical terms. Chapter 3 then examines the nuts and bolts of Pavlovian learning; the basic facts that one needs to know before applying it to phenomena in the world outside of the lab, and in order to understand it theoretically. This chapter concludes with an introduction to several crucial phenomena (blocking, contingency learning, and relative validity) that suggest that "information value" is important in Pavlovian learning. The "informational value" idea is interesting, has applied value, and was central to subsequent developments in the field.

Chapter 4 follows with an explanation of the modern theories of conditioning beginning with the Rescorla-Wagner model. I have found that students feel especially rewarded when they master this material, and I have done my best to cover it as clearly and incrementally as possible. I believe that if students are not introduced to current theories of conditioning, they are at a disadvantage if they want to apply the field to other parts of psychology or to the world at large. Moreover, the development of these theories tells another good story that illustrates how a science moves forward over time. Chapter 5 then complements Chapter 4 by exploring how learning is translated into behavior; it reviews work on remembering and forgetting, extinction, occasion setting, and behavior systems, for example. In many ways, Chapters 4 and 5 provide the theoretical heart of the book. In Chapter 6, I consider the challenge (first provided by the discovery of taste aversion learning) that such a theoretical heart, established so carefully in the lab, might not generalize that well to other examples of learning. This chapter takes the reader through more important learning phenomena, and then ultimately examines conditioning in honeybees and categorization and causal learning in humans. Again, the analysis of ideas—and their development and interconnectedness—takes center stage.

The last four chapters cover voluntary behavior—that is, behavior that is represented in instrumental or operant conditioning. After some discussion of the classic ideas of early theorists like Guthrie and Tolman, Chapter 7 considers work that followed Skinner's analysis and covers how behavior is related to its consequences. Once again, the emphasis is on how research builds and interconnects. Chapter 8, which covers stimulus control and animal cognition, begins with a fairly extensive discussion of categorization in pigeons, and then presents some basic generalization and discrimination phenomena that are necessary tools for understanding the more complex topics. From there, the narrative turns to topics from an information-processing perspective and then on to the cognition of timing and spatial learning. Once again, there is a story here that illustrates how different topics and phenomena are linked, and how simple, common principles often apply. Chapter 9 turns to the motivation of instrumental behavior, a topic that is fascinating and important—but is rarely considered in its own right in contemporary textbooks on learning and behavior. The final chapter provides what I believe is the current "synthetic" approach to instrumental behavior. It tells a story about avoidance learning, learned helplessness, misbehavior in appetitive learning, and the contemporary "cognitive" analysis of instrumental learning. This all provides a vehicle to reconsider and integrate many of the most important themes presented in previous chapters: evolution, cognition, motivation, and the interrelations between Pavlovian and operant learning. I hope this chapter will allow the reader to walk away from the book with a review and integration of the different topics firmly situated in his or her mind.

Acknowledgments

The project has been in the works for a long time. I would like to thank Peter Farley, until recently at Sinauer Associates, who first proposed that I write a book on Learning and then had the patience (and kindness) to wait for it. I would also like to acknowledge two teachers I have had the very good fortune to know: Roger M. Tarpy taught my first Learning course, got me interested in designing experiments, and gave me a reading list one summer that created a lifelong addiction. My other teacher was the late Robert C. Bolles, a wonderful scholar, humorist, and friend. Bob wanted me to write the book, and I wish he had been here to see it in the end. Anyone familiar with his work will see my debt to him, although I am also fond of the many things I have put in the book with which he would have (playfully) disagreed. Both Bob and Roger were master textbook writers—and had an ability to make students believe they had something to contribute.

The book also benefited from of chapter reviews written by respected researchers in the field: Andy Baker, Bernard Balleine, Bob Boakes, Michael Fanselow, Greg Fetterman, Karen Hollis, Vin LoLordo, Peter Lovibond, Peter Urcuioli, and Ben Williams. Needless to say, the warts that remain are my fault and not theirs. At Sinauer Associates, Graig Donini kept the project moving forward, and Sydney Carroll and Laura Green kept the production clean, accurate, and on track. Joan Gemme and Christopher Small are responsible for the clarity of the art and the wonderful design and "feel" of the book. At the University of Vermont, Angela Conner, Paula Rudolph, and most recently Lindsay Bouton helped with many library, database, and referencing tasks. I should also acknowledge a brilliant year I had at the Center for Advanced Study in the Behavioral Sciences (Stanford), where many early chapters were thought through and drafted. My writing was supported by the Center, and has been supported less directly over the years by the National Science Foundation and by the National Institute of Mental Health, which have supported my laboratory research, as well as the American Psychological Association, which provided staff support when I edited the *Journal of Experimental Psychology: Animal Behavior Processes*.

Most of all, I want to thank the many students in my classes who have tried their best to teach me how to explain this material. I hope that future students will enjoy reading the book as much as I enjoyed writing it.

Mark E. Bouton
Burlington, Vermont
September, 2006

Media & Supplements

Companion Website (www.sinauer.com/bouton)

The *Learning and Behavior* companion website (available free of charge) includes study resources to help students review the content of each chapter and test their understanding of the concepts presented in the textbook. The site contains the following elements:

- Chapter outlines
- Chapter summaries
- Key terms
- Glossary
- Online quizzes (20 questions per chapter)

FOR INSTRUCTORS

Instructor's Resource CD

Presentation Resources

The *Learning and Behavior* IRCD includes all of the textbook figures (both art and photos) and tables in electronic format. All images are provided in both JPEG (high- and low-resolution versions) and ready-to-use PowerPoint® presentations. The figures have all been formatted for optimal projection in the classroom.

Instructor's Manual & Test Bank, Rene Verry, Millikin University

The *Learning and Behavior* Instructor's Manual & Test Bank includes the following resources to aid instructors in planning and assessment:

- Detailed learning objectives
- Chapter outlines
- Key terms
- Class discussion and critical thinking exercises
- Suggested additional resources for lecture/course development
- 60 multiple choice test questions
- 10 or more short answer test questions

Computerized Test Bank

Also included on the Instructor's Resource CD is Brownstone's Diploma exam-creation software. This software allows instructors to easily create exams from the bank of test questions provided, import their own questions, format exams for print, and administer secure online exams.

Online Quizzing

Instructors can determine both the content and the availability of the companion website's online quizzes. Quizzes can be used in either review mode (always available to students, results given immediately) or assigned mode (specific availability, results released by the instructor). In addition, custom quizzes can be created using any combination of default questions and the instructor's own questions.

Learning and Behavior

A Contemporary Synthesis

Chapter One Outline

Philosophical Roots

    Are people machines?

    Associations and the contents of the mind

Biological Roots

    Reflexes, evolution, and early comparative psychology

    The rise of the conditioning experiment

A Science of Learning and Behavior

    John B. Watson

    B. F. Skinner

    Edward C. Tolman

    Computer and brain metaphors

    Human learning and animal learning

Tools for Analyzing Learning and Behavior

    Learning about stimuli and about behavior

    Crows foraging at the beach

    Kids at play

    People using drugs

    Relations between S, R, and S*

Summary

1

Learning Theory:
What It Is and How It Got This Way

MOST PEOPLE HOLDING THIS BOOK are at least a little familiar with Learning Theory. The topic is often mentioned in many survey and introductory courses in psychology. It is also part of the popular culture—cartoonists have mined it very well (Figure 1.1). My goal in this first chapter is to give you some more information about what the field is really like, why it is useful, and how it got to be what it is today.

Psychology's interest in learning does not need much introduction, because there is little doubt that learning is crucial in our lives. You have been learning in school since you were about 5 years old. But learning is even more pervasive and important than that—it is truly happening all the time. As you walked to class, you learned something about the route, the people you encountered along the way, and so forth. On trips to the library, you probably also learned where to find the periodicals, the areas where things are quiet, and the areas where your friends will be. When you get up in the morning, you already know where to find the coffee, how to create the perfect mix of hot and cold water in the shower, and where to find your jacket if it looks like it is cold outside. The fact is, learning is always in progress—always helping us adapt to our environment. "Much like the law of gravity, the laws of learning are always in effect" (Spreat & Spreat, 1982).

Figure 1.1 How the layman views Learning
Theory. (From ScienceCartoonsPlus.com.)

"PERHAPS, DR. PAVLOV, HE COULD BE
TAUGHT TO SEAL ENVELOPES."

Not so easy for many people to understand are the *methods* psychologists often use to study learning. This book is really about the field in which scientists investigate learning by studying the behavior of animals like rats and pigeons in laboratories equipped with mazes and Skinner boxes. Nowadays, these methods are applied to a range of topics that might surprise you. For example, Watanabe, Sakamoto, & Wakita (1995) used them to ask how pigeons learn to categorize works of art—specifically, paintings by Monet and Picasso. Other experimenters (e.g., Crombag & Shaham, 2002) have used them to study how behavior reinforced by taking drugs like heroin and cocaine can be treated and still be vulnerable to relapse. These topics, and many others that are connected with them, will be covered throughout this book. But for now, I want to note that how psychologists first came to see experiments with animals in learning laboratories—as connected to the world at large—is itself a rather interesting and colorful story. The main purpose of this chapter is to relate that story, and to tell you how **Learning Theory** (what I sometimes call the field that investigates learning and behavior principles by studying animals learning in the lab) got started and evolved into what it is today. A second purpose is to give you a frame of reference for understanding the rest of the book as well as the field's usefulness outside the laboratory. I decided to write the book because I think that Learning Theory is as central to understanding human and animal behavior as it ever was. Fortunately, I like to talk about it, too.

The story of how things became this way really started a few hundred years ago, when philosophers were worrying about the nature of human nature and the nature of the human mind. As time went on, modern science began to mature, and the questions and issues were put into a scientific perspective. By the 1800s, biology was beginning to provide some rather interesting new answers. There was a startling new idea: People had evolved. Learning Theory as we know it today actually was launched in the 1880s and 1890s, when people set out to study a major implication of the theory of evolution—namely, that the human mind had evolved. Let's start the story by taking a look at some of the early ideas about human nature and the human mind.

Philosophical Roots

Are people machines?

In the 1600s, science underwent a major renaissance. Thanks to scientists like Galileo and Newton, there was an exciting new understanding of mechanics—how physical things like planets or billiard balls move and interact. Craftspeople began to make better and better machines (Figure 1.2). For example, clocks became more intricate and accurate. By the 1600s the kind of clock one can still see in the village squares in Europe—with dolls chasing animals or ringing bells on the hour and so forth—were fairly common. It was probably inevitable that people began comparing themselves to these early robots and mechanical devices. Are humans simply complex machines? What makes us different from the dolls that dance and whir every hour on the hour? Nowadays, we are more likely to compare ourselves to computers. But in those days, mechanical devices reigned supreme. Is it possible to understand human action from mechanical principles?

One person who famously considered these questions was **René Descartes** (1596–1650; Figure 1.3A); he also came up with a famous answer. He said, in effect, that human beings are indeed like machines—but only partly so. Like other philosophers before him, Descartes distinguished between the human mind and body. He suggested that the body was an extension of the physical world, a machine that is governed by physical principles, like dolls and clockworks. But, every human also has a mind—a spiritual, godlike thing that is the source of free will and all voluntary behavior. The mind is what makes humans more than mere machines. It also separates humans from animals. Animals are pure body, without mind and without free will: their actions are governed by simple mechanical principles.

Descartes did more than merely suggest the mind-body distinction. He also proposed a mechanistic principle that was supposed to explain the body's activity, **reflex action**. For every action of the

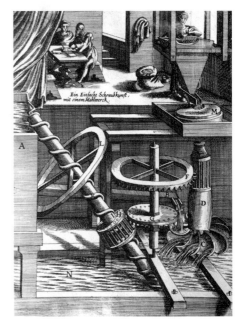

Figure 1.2 Illustration from a machinery book first published in 1661 devoted to pumps, presses and printing, and milling machinery by the Nuremberg architect Böckler. (Illustration © Timewatch Images/Alamy.)

(A) (B)

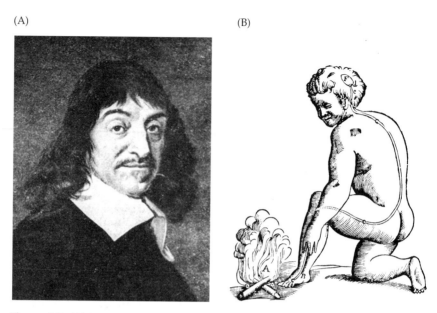

Figure 1.3 (A) René Descartes, who wondered whether humans were machines, and (B) came up with the concept of reflex action. (A, image courtesy of National Library of Medicine; B, illustration reproduced in Boakes, 1984.)

body, there is a stimulus that makes it happen (see Figure 1.3B). The child puts her hand in a fire, and the fire causes her hand to withdraw. The doctor drops the hammer on your knee, and your leg moves. There is a simple, automatic connection between stimulus and response. Descartes suggested that the stimulus agitated "animal spirits" that traveled up the nerves (basically, hollow tubes) and made the muscles swell. (Remember, this was 1637.) But the larger idea that a reflex connects a stimulus and response went on to have an enormous impact on biology and psychology.

For all the importance of reflex action in human behavior, according to Descartes, the mind still ruled—it could always intervene and modify a reflex. However, other thinkers were not as shy about claiming that all human behavior follows scientific principles. For example, **Thomas Hobbes** (1588–1679) argued that even the mind follows physical laws. He suggested that all human thought and action is governed by **hedonism**—the pursuit of pleasure and avoidance of pain. (This principle, familiar to most college students, is what reinforcement theory is really all about.) There was also **Julien de la Mettrie** (1709–1751), who saw more similarity between humans and animals than Descartes did. Once, while de la Mettrie had a fever, he realized that the body actually affects the mind. Fevers can affect your thoughts and so can wine or coffee. De la Mettrie's book was entitled *Man a Machine* (1748). By the 1700s the idea that human nature, and perhaps the human mind, could be understood by scientific principles was launched and on its way.

(A)

(B)

Figure 1.4 Two famous British Empiricists: (A) the English philosopher, John Locke, who founded the school of empiricism, and (B) David Hume, a Scottish philosopher and historian. Both believed that the mind is an empty, passive thing that receives and associates sense impressions. (A, image courtesy of National Library of Medicine; B, image © Classic Image/Alamy.)

Associations and the contents of the mind

At roughly the same time, a group of philosophers in Britain was thinking about the things the mind contains. Collectively, these philosophers are now known as the **British Empiricists**. Two of the most famous were **John Locke** (1632–1704) (Figure 1.4A) and **David Hume** (1711–1776) (Figure 1.4B). Of course, the mind as we know it is full of ideas. The point the Empiricists emphasized was that all ideas and knowledge are built up entirely from experience—a view known as "empiricism." Thus, according to Locke, the mind is a blank slate (**tabula rasa**) at birth, ready to be written on by experience. It is obvious that an empiricist view is important in the psychology of learning; it gives us a reason to investigate how experience shapes and changes us.

The British Empiricists took a very **atomistic** approach to the contents of the mind; they believed that the mind receives only simple sensations, and that these simple inputs are combined to build up all complex ideas. For example, Locke argued that when you see an apple, you actually see a collection of sense impressions—an apple is red, round, and shiny. With experience, these impressions are combined to form the complex idea of an apple. Hume emphasized the importance of **associations** between ideas. If we eat the apple, it might taste crisp and sweet. These impressions become further associated with the apple's visual properties; you can begin to see the complexity of the idea of an apple. But the complexity is built up out of simple parts—complicated ideas and trains of thought are constructed from simple sense impressions and the associations between them.

Figure 1.5 Immanuel Kant, according to whom the mind is an active thing that molds experience in part according to inborn assumptions. (Image courtesy of National Library of Medicine.)

Not surprisingly, later Empiricists (sometimes known as Associationists) wrote more about how associations are formed and how they operate—the so-called laws of association. Hume himself argued that the "contiguity" between ideas is important; two ideas will be associated if they occur closely together in time. The associationists also argued that impressions will become associated if they are similar, if they are lively, if the impressions are "dwelt upon" for increasing amounts of time, and if they have occurred together recently. With more and more laws of association, you can see that a fairly complete theory of learning and memory began to take shape. In fact, we will see that many of these ideas are still a part of learning theory. Even our interest in learning itself stems from our belief that experience is important. And you can often see an atomistic, associationist bias as well. Many researchers study learning in situations where animals have an opportunity to associate simple events. Out of this, more complex things are expected to emerge.

There has almost always been an alternative to empiricism, though. Some call it **rationalism** (e.g., Bower & Hilgard, 1981). This point of view is often associated (sorry!) with **Immanuel Kant** (1724–1804) (Figure 1.5), a German philosopher who had a different perspective on the content and activity of the mind. Kant agreed with the empiricists that a lot of knowledge comes from experience—but not all of it, he argued. In contrast to the Empiricists, Kant believed that some things do exist in the mind before experience writes on it. The mind has an inherent set of assumptions or ideas called "a prioris" that help mold and organize experience. For example, we know that objects have substance. We also know that things happen in space and in time. We also know causality, that is, that some things cause other things to happen. According to Kant, experience does not make us think this way. The mind comes into the world prepared to do it. The mind is not a blank slate, as Locke would have it, but more like a floppy disk for a computer (Bolles, 1993): Before anything useful can be written on it, it has to be formatted, given a structure. Otherwise the computer can't read it.

The influence of both empiricism and rationalism can still be seen in modern research. For example, in several places in this book we will discuss how animals like rats quickly learn to "dislike" and reject a food if they become sick a few hours after first ingesting it. This phenomenon ("taste aversion learning," see Chapter 2) had a profound influence on theories of learning when it was first noticed in the 1960s (see especially Chapter 6). One reason is that, although the rat is quick to associate a flavor with illness, he is not so ready to associate a sound or a light or even a texture with the illness (e.g., Domjan & Wilson, 1972; Garcia & Koelling, 1966; see Chapter 2). To put it casually, it is as if when the rat gets sick, he exercises the a priori assumption that "It must have been something I ate." Rats behave as if they blame taste over other cues for illness even when they are only one day old (Gemberling & Domjan, 1982). At this age, experience has not had much time to write on the rat pup's tabula rasa. Thus, the bias seems to be inborn, much the way Kant would have expected it. But while Kant would have assumed that God designed the rat to "think" this way, today we assume that evolution had a hand in it; evolution has important effects on learning (e.g., Chapters 2, 6, and 10). This point brings us to the other major input to modern learning theory, namely, the input from biology.

Biological Roots

Reflexes, evolution, and early comparative psychology

As relevant as the philosophical roots may be, the most direct impetus to Learning Theory was biology. By the middle of the 1800s, physiologists were making impressive progress figuring out how reflexes work. Descartes (himself a philosopher and mathematician) had convinced everyone that reflex action was important; but from roughly the 1750s onward, biologists really began to make significant scientific progress. They were discovering how organized reflexes are. They were also discovering that electricity (itself a new discovery) is involved in reflex action. They were even beginning to estimate the speed of neural transmission.

In 1866, Ivan Sechenov (1829–1905), a physiologist from Russia who had studied reflexes with all the great European scientists, put many of these ideas together. He wrote a book entitled *Reflexes of the Brain*. In it, he argued that mental processes could be analyzed in terms of physiological mechanisms—namely, the ones involved in reflexes. Thoughts, he argued, are responses—reflexive responses to stimuli. He noted that when going to sleep at night, he might think of the Emperor of China. In the daytime, if he happened to lie down in bed, he might automatically think of the Emperor again. His book also emphasized inhibition, a new reflex phenomenon discovered in the 1800s. A reflex could be bottled up and inhibited, waiting to be triggered by some tiny stimulus. In fact, emerging science on the reflex could go a long way toward explaining behavior and mental activity. Mental activity was going to be cracked by modern biology.

Another source of input arrived in the middle of the 1800s: **Charles Darwin** (1809–1882) (Figure 1.6A). Darwin, of course, was the Englishman who traveled around the world taking notes on all the plants and animals he encountered. In 1859, he described the theory of evolution in his book, *On the Origin of Species by Means of Natural Selection*. The theory was discussed and debated in Britain throughout the 1800s. But it is so important to us now that it is almost impossible to overstate it. All life has evolved through natural selection. There is continuity between humans and animals. Humans and animals are alike in their struggle for survival.

The theory of evolution changed the way people see life and also the relationships between humans and animals. One of the most remarkable implications of the idea is that maybe the human mind—the thing that was sup-

(A)

(B)

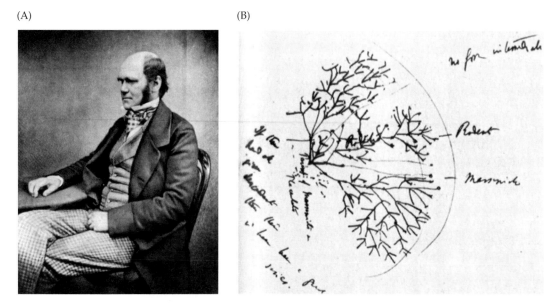

Figure 1.6 (A) Charles Darwin, at about age 45, when he was writing *On the Origin of Species by Means of Natural Selection*. (B) A drawing from one of Darwin's notebooks; he correctly saw evolution as a bush, and not a single line going from simple organisms to complex ones. (A, image reproduced in Boakes, 1984; B, diagram reproduced in Boakes, 1984.)

posed to separate humans from animals—had itself evolved. Darwin addressed the idea in a second book, *The Descent of Man and Selection in Relation to Sex* (1871). But the idea of evolution was mostly pursued in the late 1800s by a group of English scientists now known as the **early comparative psychologists**. Their goal was to trace the evolution of the mind by studying the mental lives of animals. George Romanes (1848–1894) went about collecting examples of animal behavior—often stories about pets reported by their owners—and made inferences about the kinds of mental abilities they represented or required. Romanes saw himself as a kind of geologist looking at the strata of a layered fossil record. Much of his thinking was based on the idea that evolution works as a linear progression, from the simple to the complex. In fact, as Darwin himself recognized (Figure 1.6B), evolution does not create a single line of progress but a rich set of branches on a complex bush.

Another early comparative psychologist, C. Lloyd Morgan (1852–1936), was much more conservative about the mental abilities he attributed to animals (Figure 1.7A). For example, while Romanes attributed all sorts of mental abilities to dogs, Morgan emphasized how slowly his own fox terrier, Tony (Figure 1.7B), had learned to open the latch of a gate. Morgan also tested Tony's spatial abilities. He threw a long stick over a fence and sent Tony to retrieve it. There was a gap between pickets in the fence of about 6

(A)   (B)

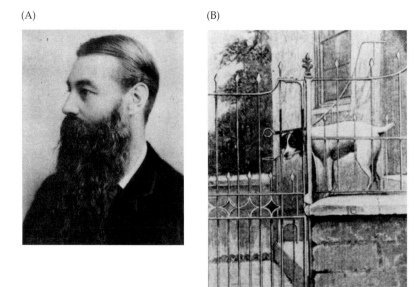

Figure 1.7 (A) C. Lloyd Morgan, the early comparative psychologist. (B) Morgan's dog, Tony, a clever animal who nonetheless probably learned things incrementally. (A, image from http://www-dimat.unipv.it/gnoli/lloyd-morgan2.jpg; B, image reproduced in Boakes, 1984.)

inches. Did Tony understand the spatial relationship and try to fit the stick through the gap longways? No—Tony barely got the problem right after many repetitions over several days. When Morgan repeated the experiment with a stick with a crook in it, Tony caught the crook repeatedly as he tried to force it through the gap. Eventually the crook broke off when Tony grabbed the stick at that end. A man who happened to be walking by at that moment commented, "Clever dog that, sir; he knows where the hitch do lie." "The remark was the characteristic outcome of two minutes' chance observation," Morgan wrote (Morgan, 1894, p. 258). There is a message here. Some of the most remarkable things we see animals do may actually be built up slowly from fairly laborious and simple processes. A certain amount of skepticism is appropriate.

Morgan is best known for his "law of parsimony," better known as **Morgan's Canon**. Put simply, the Canon states that an example of behavior should not be explained by a complex, high-level mental process if it can be explained with a simpler one. Morgan thought we should be stingy—parsimonious—with how we explain behavior. This idea is still with us today. In many ways, Learning Theory is merely a continuation of the grand tradition started by the early comparative psychologists. For example, later in this book (see Chapter 8) you will see that a part of the field devoted to studying animal cognition is expressly interested in studying the hypothetical mental processes in animals. But we are still very much interested in arriving at the simplest possible explanation of complex examples of behavior.

The rise of the conditioning experiment

Morgan and many of his contemporaries became interested in studying animal learning as a way of understanding the animal mind. **Edward L. Thorndike** (1874–1949) was another early comparative psychologist who was interested in exactly this (Figure 1.8A). In 1898, Thorndike published his doctoral dissertation, which was on the subject of the intelligence of cats. To study cat intelligence, Thorndike examined how they learned in an apparatus called a puzzle box (see Figure 1.8B). The puzzle box was made of wood and chicken wire. The cat was put in the box, and had to learn to open a latch inside to get out and get at some food that was located nearby. Thorndike's cats learned this problem fairly well, but they seemed to learn it slowly and gradually. In addition, Thorndike was unable to convey the "idea" of how to open the latch to several cats by moving their paws so as to open the latch. A simple (parsimonious) explanation was possible. When the cats got fed after getting out of the box, the food strengthened a simple association between the situation (S) and the latch-opening response (R). That is all that

(A)

(B)

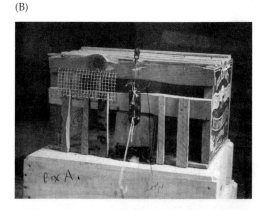

Figure 1.8 (A) Edward Thorndike. (B) Two of the puzzle boxes Thorndike used to study the intelligence of cats. (A, photograph courtesy of National Library of Medicine; B, photographs from Manuscripts and Archives, Yale University Library.)

was necessary to explain the gradual learning Thorndike observed from the puzzle box: the gradual "stamping in" of an S-R association.

A few years later, Thorndike (1911) saw that his mechanism for explaining learning in cats was also a good way to understand learning in other animals—and people, in general. He proposed the **law of effect**. When a response is followed by satisfaction (as is provided by food), an S-R connection is strengthened. When it is followed by discomfort (as would be provided by, say, a mild shock), the S-R association is weakened. Thorndike went on to have a great career as an educational psychologist. But the puzzle box experiments and the law of effect launched a very significant part of modern learning theory that I will return to later in this chapter.

Meanwhile, there was more going on in Russia, the home of Sechenov and a country steeped in the tradition of studying the biology of the reflex. **Ivan Pavlov** (1849–1936), who was a celebrated physiologist, was also beginning to study learning in animals (Figure 1.9A). Pavlov had begun his distinguished career investigating the reflexes of digestion. When we digest food, we secrete various gastric juices, some enzymes from the pancreas, and a hormone (insulin) that helps the body's cells absorb nutrients. We also salivate. In experiments with dogs, Pavlov showed how many of these responses were coordinated by the nervous system. His studies were so important that in 1904 he won a Nobel Prize in Medicine for them. He was the first physiologist, and the first Russian, to win a Nobel Prize.

Several years before he won the Nobel Prize, though, Pavlov also began to understand the importance of other kinds of digestive reflexes—namely

(A)   (B)

Figure 1.9 (A) Ivan Pavlov. (B) Pavlov's classical conditioning set-up. Today, classical conditioning is viewed as an important behavioral phenomenon (it gives neutral cues the power to elicit behavior) and as a method for studying associative learning—how organisms learn to associate events in the world. (A, photograph courtesy of National Library of Medicine; B, photograph © Bettman/Corbis.)

learned ones (Figure 1.9B). In 1897, at about the time that Thorndike was also studying learning in his cats in America, Pavlov's student Stefan Wolf-sohn was studying salivation in dogs. Dogs salivate to food introduced to the mouth, of course. But after the food has been put in the mouth a few times, the dog soon begins to salivate merely at the sight of food. The dog has learned to drool to a signal of food. Pavlov and his students called this a "psychic reflex." We now know it as a **conditioned reflex**.

In the usual textbook version of Pavlov's simplest experiment, Pavlov (or a student) would ring a bell, and then present some food to a dog. With a few bell-food pairings, the dog would begin to drool to the sound of the bell in anticipation of the food. Pavlov understood that this kind of learning was an important principle of behavior. It was another kind of reflex that helped the animal get ready to digest an upcoming meal. But he also saw the conditioning experiment as a way to study the animal's brain. Psychic, learned reflexes of the brain were the way someone could learn to think of the Emperor of China every time he lay down on a bed. Conditioning was a way to study the psychological process of learning, eventually working it out in physiological terms.

Pavlov arrived at his interest in learning from a route that was different from the one traveled by Thorndike and the other early comparative psychologists. He was interested in the reflex, while the comparative psychologists were interested in evolution. Significantly, both of these great traditions in biology converged on the fundamental importance of learning and the conditioning experiment at around the turn of the twentieth century.

A Science of Learning and Behavior

John B. Watson

At about this time, psychology in America was deeply influenced by a school of thought known as **structuralism**. The goal of structuralists was to analyze the structure of the mind. Their method was introspection; researchers looked into their own minds and described what they saw there. Intuitively, introspection may seem like a good way to study the mind, but it has extremely serious problems. For one thing, how do we know that the mind's contents are all conscious and available to our introspections? Equally important, what are we going to do if two introspectors disagree? For example, I might claim that all thoughts are connected to mental images, and you might claim that you have thoughts that are "imageless" (the idea of imageless thought was an actual controversy). Who is right? Who is the better introspector? Ultimately, a dispute between two introspectors would have to be settled by an authority: We would have to appeal to what other, wiser (and more powerful) introspectors might say. The problem with introspection is that the facts can only be settled by authority. And that is a very big problem. "Facts" must be open to falsification, or there can be no progress beyond the mere opinions of the powerful people. A science must have results that can be confirmed or disconfirmed by any investigator.

In 1913, John B. Watson (1878–1958) (Figure 1.10), a professor of comparative psychology at Johns Hopkins University, published an article that became known as a behaviorist manifesto. According to Watson's paper, the problem with psychology was that it had become too subjective. Debates about imageless thought could go on (and go nowhere) for hundreds of years. There was also little information of any practical value that could be taken from this kind of research. Instead, Watson argued that the field of psychology should include the study of something objective and available to all: *behavior*. Behavior is something that everyone can see, and any claim about it can be easily confirmed or falsified.

Watson's call for the study of behavior was a challenge to introspection, although his version of behaviorism was crude by modern standards (see below). Watson argued that thought was nothing more than muscle twitches in the throat. He doubted the existence of dreams—perhaps because he claimed to have never personally experienced them (Bolles, 1979). But his point about objectivity is still valid and important, and his behaviorist movement changed psychology forever. Today, psychologists can set about studying mental processes, but they typically do *not* do it by introspecting: they link their hypothetical mental processes to behavioral output that can be studied and measured objectively.

Figure 1.10 John B. Watson, the great American behaviorist. Watson's point was that psychological science must concern itself with observable things, such as behavior. (Photograph courtesy of the Alan Mason Chesney Medical Archives of The Johns Hopkins Medical Institutions.)

The conditioning experiment was central to Watson's vision of a scientific psychology (Watson, 1916). One of his most famous experiments (Watson & Rayner, 1920) was a conditioning experiment with a little boy named Albert B. (known today as "Little Albert," in contrast to Freud's famous case, "Little Hans"). Albert was an 11-month old boy whose mother was a wet-nurse in a local hospital in Baltimore. In their experiment, Watson and Rayner showed Albert a white rat, and as he reached out to touch it, they frightened him with a loud noise. After a few trials, Albert began to react with fright each time the rat was given to him. An emotional response, fear, had been conditioned in Albert, just like the salivary response had been conditioned in Pavlov's dog. Moreover, Albert's new fear of the rat generalized to other furry things, such as a rabbit and a fur coat. Watson and Rayner's paper poked fun at Freud's analysis of phobias, which were based on unresolved Oedipal complexes and the like. They had found an alternative source of emotional problems. Twenty years later, when Albert checks into a psychiatric clinic because of his fear of furry things, the local psychoanalyst will make him improve his relationship with his dad. But you and I know that it was simply a conditioning experience. Unfortunately, Albert was removed from the laboratory before Watson and Rayner had a chance to decondition his fear. Of course, Albert's conditioning experience was not really very traumatic. But this experiment still has an impact today in the sense that we still suspect a role for conditioning in many emotional disorders that begin with exposure to panic or trauma (e.g., Bouton, Mineka, & Barlow, 2001; Eysenck, 1979; Mineka, 1985; Mineka & Zinbarg, 2006).

Watson was a flamboyant character. Unfortunately, his career as a psychologist ended in scandal when someone discovered that he and his research assistant, Rosalie Rayner, were having an affair. Watson was forced to resign from the university, and he eventually joined the J. Walter Thompson advertising agency, where his interest in empirical work—in this case, market research—paid off very well. By 1924, he was one of four vice presidents in the company (Boakes 1984).

Outside of academia, Watson continued to write about psychology. One of his most famous books, *Behaviorism* (1924), was full of colorful, impassioned claims. His emphasis on learning is illustrated by the lines from this book that you have probably seen many times before:

> Give me a dozen healthy infants, well-formed, and my own specified world to bring them up in and I'll guarantee to take any one at random and train him to become any type of specialist I might select—doctor, lawyer, artist, merchant-chief and, yes, even beggar-man and thief, regardless of his talents, penchants, tendencies, abilities, vocations, and race of his ancestors. (Watson, 1924, p. 104.)

A nice sentiment, though perhaps a little overstated; the right environment can make the world better for anyone, regardless of race or station of birth. In truth, Watson was not quite as naive as this sentence suggests. It is always quoted out of context. The very next sentence in the book is:

> I am going beyond my facts and I admit it, but so have the advocates of the contrary and they have been doing it for many thousands of years. (Watson, 1924, p. 104.)

Watson was essentially a campaigner; he was out to change the world. Although his early ideas have been steadily transformed over the years, his emphases on behavior and on learning are still a very important part of psychology today. In fact, his view that psychology should rely on objective evidence and that it should be useful has inspired many research psychologists ever since.

B. F. Skinner

Watson's call to behaviorism was followed by a great deal of discussion about what it actually takes to be scientific about behavior. One of the most important writers on this subject was **B. F. Skinner** (1904–1990), who developed a type of behaviorism that is called **radical behaviorism** today (Figure 1.11A). Skinner was actually an English major, not a psychology major, and he began thinking about behaviorism after he had finished college. In his early papers on the subject (e.g., Skinner, 1931, 1935), he considered our old friend—the reflex. He noted that one meaning of the reflex is that it describes an empirical relationship between two events: given the stimulus, a response is also likely to occur. People in his day also gave the reflex

(A)

(B)

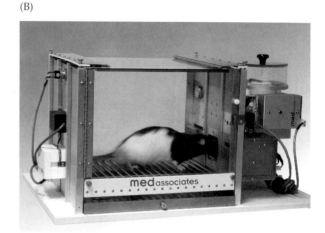

Figure 1.11 (A) B. F. Skinner. (B) A modern "Skinner box." Although the rat is free to press the lever to its left as often as it likes, the behavior is still controlled by its consequences (i.e., presentation of the food pellet). (A, photograph courtesy of National Library of Medicine; B, courtesy of Med Associates.)

an additional meaning—the physiological reflex arc. The physiological concept introduced a new set of events between the stimulus (S) and the response (R); a sensory neuron must respond to S and then fire a motor neuron that excites muscle and makes R. Talking about these physiological events does not change the basic empirical relationship between S and R. Instead, Skinner suggested, it merely introduces a new set of things that need to be explained. How does the sensory neuron fire? How does it excite the motor neuron? What physiological events actually make the muscle move? To explain these things, we must study other sciences, like physiology and molecular biology. The physiological reflex introduces a large number of new questions. It has taken us away from behavior. Psychologists, the radical behaviorist claims, should therefore stick to the simple empirical correlation between S and R.

The same argument can be made about mentalistic events we might want to stick between stimulus and response. For sure, concepts like short-term memory and attention are interesting, but introducing them merely introduces new things that have to be explained. Skinner did not deny that people have nervous systems or that they experience private events they call cognitions. But at best these things merely introduce new questions that need to be answered. At worst they masquerade as useful explanations (what does it really mean to say that the child responded because she had an insight?). The new concepts don't add anything useful, and they do not change the basic relationship between S and R. There is a very important message here. Your behavior is not caused by another little person living inside your head. It is lawfully related to the environment. Skinner's views are widely held today by a number of active scientists and practitioners known as "behavior analysts" (or "Skinnerians").

Skinner is important to our story for many reasons, and we will return to him later in this book. One of the most important things he did was to contribute a method: He designed the first **Skinner box** (see Figure 1.11B). (Skinner didn't name it that; Clark Hull did.) In the 1920s and 1930s, it was common to study the behavior of rats in mazes. Mazes are useful and interesting, but using them is labor-intensive, because an experimenter must hover near them until the rat gets from the start to the goal. Skinner was interested in gadgets, and eventually he closed the rat up in a small box and gave him a little lever to operate. When the lever was closed, another gadget delivered a food pellet to a cup attached inside the box to the wall nearby. Not surprisingly, the rat learned to press the lever to get the food pellet. If pellets were made contingent on lever-pressing, the rat would press the lever many times in an hour.

This arrangement is now known as the **operant experiment**, and it has become an extremely important tool for research. The rat's lever-press response is called an **operant** because it operates on the environment. The food pellet, which increases the rate of responding when it is made a consequence of the response, is called a **reinforcer**. Nearly everyone is familiar with the operant experiment; rats in boxes have been in magazine cartoons since at least the 1950s. But there is a fundamental insight here that is easy to miss. In the operant experiment, the rat is put in the box for a period of time in which it can press the lever *whenever it wants to*. The situation was different for the cat in Thorndike's puzzle box. The cat had only one opportunity at a time to respond: Once out of the puzzle box, it had to wait for Thorndike to set up another trial. In contrast, the rat in the Skinner box is free to make the response over and over, as often as it likes. Or it can curl up and sleep in the corner if it so decides. Lever pressing is purely voluntary. In this sense, the operant experiment captures an important characteristic of behavior in the world outside the laboratory: Within certain constraints, you and I are free to do more or less what we want when we want to. Skinner's insight was this: What we call "free," or "voluntary" behavior, like responding in the Skinner box, is still lawfully related to the environment. It increases or decreases according to its payoff. Operant, "voluntary" behavior is controlled by its consequences and it can be studied using the Skinner box.

In fact, the operant experiment exposes a new kind of empirical correlation between behavior and environmental events. The operant response is lawfully related to its **consequences**. We know this because we can present the food pellet in different ways. For instance, if we present a pellet every time the rat presses the lever, responding will happen at a high rate. But if we stop presenting pellets, the lever-pressing will stop. The operant's correlation with its consequences is somewhat different from the correlation in the traditional Descartes-and-Pavlov reflex in which the child withdraws her hand from the fire, or the dog salivates to the sound of the bell. In these cases, the response is **elicited** by an **antecedent** stimulus. It is a response to

TABLE 1.1 The operant-respondent distinction

Respondent	Operant
Controlled by antecedents	Controlled by consequences
"Elicited"	"Emitted"

an event that precedes it; this sort of behavior is a **respondent**. Unlike operant behavior, which is controlled by its consequences, respondent behavior is controlled by its antecedents. I have just described Skinner's **operant-respondent distinction** (Table 1.1).

Skinner's radical behaviorism seeks out empirical correlations between behavior and environmental events. It finds two very broad types: Some behaviors are controlled by their consequences (operant behaviors) and others are controlled by their antecedents (respondent behaviors). The system does not predict that certain types of behavior (barking, drooling, writing, drawing) will be operant or respondent; every new empirical relationship is open to discovery. We must figure out whether any particular behavior is controlled by something that precedes it or follows it. The operant-respondent distinction is extremely useful in the clinic, because it provides a simple way to discover how to control behavior. If a child who screams in public is brought to a behavior analyst, the analyst will look at the behavior's antecedents and also look at its consequences. Either one can be manipulated. If changing the consequences changes the behavior, we have an operant. If changing the antecedents changes the behavior, then we have a respondent. Either way, the behavior analyst wins because the behavior has been brought under control to the benefit (hopefully) of everyone. The basic system is so simple that it can be readily applied to any new situation. It has, with very positive effects. The radical behavioristic approach that Skinner began has done a great deal of good in the world.

Edward C. Tolman

It may surprise you to learn that you do not have to be a Skinnerian to be a behaviorist. There is at least one other brand of behaviorism, and I believe it has been adopted in one form or another by every field of scientific psychology. Like Skinner's approach, this one was developed in the 1920s and 1930s while people were discussing what it takes to be scientific about behavior. This version differs from radical behaviorism in that it accepts unobservable events in the explanation of behavior—provided they are used rigorously and carefully. The approach, often called **operational behaviorism**, got its start with **Edward C. Tolman** (1886–1959), an early behaviorist who spent his career at the University of California, Berkeley (Figure 1.12).

Tolman described his perspective in several articles, although one of the most important was a paper he published in 1938 (Tolman, 1938). I will illustrate the idea using an example by Miller (1959). The upper part of Figure 1.13 shows a series of empirical correlations one can easily gather in the lab-

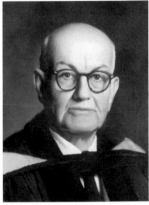

Figure 1.12 Edward C. Tolman was the learning theorist who developed "operational behaviorism," which made it acceptable to explain behavior with unobservable constructs (like motivation or cognition), provided they are specifically linked to observable input and output. (Photograph courtesy of University of California, Berkeley.)

oratory. A rat's drinking increases if it is deprived of water, fed dry food, or injected with a salt solution. So does lever-pressing for water in a Skinner box, and so on. The list of stimuli and responses could be expanded easily, of course. A nest of arrows would accumulate, getting bigger and more complicated with each new discovery.

The relationship can be simplified by using what Tolman (1938) called an **intervening variable** (another term we often use is **theoretical construct,** e.g., Bolles, 1975). The idea is illustrated by adding "thirst" between all the Ss and Rs as shown at the bottom of Figure 1.13. In this scheme, the things that we manipulate (input, at left) affect thirst; thirst in turn produces the behavioral effects described (output, at right). The thing

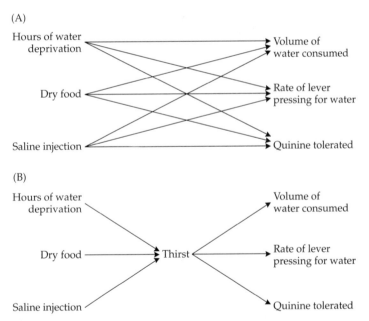

Figure 1.13 A theoretical construct like "thirst" is not directly observable, but it simplifies the explanation of behavior. (A) A set of empirical relations between experimental manipulations (left) and behaviors (right). (B) A simpler set of relations with "thirst." In this diagram, notice that thirst is linked to the empirical world on both the input side and the output side. The linkages are crucial because they make the system falsifiable and therefore scientific. (After Miller, 1959.)

called "thirst" is not directly observable; it is inferred from its effects on behavior. Nonetheless, it is reasonable to use it if we are careful to link it to several effects it has on behavior, and to the operations that are supposed to increase or decrease it. This is important. Invoking "thirst" would have no use in explaining behavior if we had no understanding of (a) how it comes about, and (b) how it affects behavior.

In principle, the scheme presented in the lower part of Figure 1.13 can be tested and proven wrong. For example, if a given number of hours of water deprivation leads to more lever- pressing than a given amount of consumed dry food, it should also lead to more water consumption, and acceptance of more quinine. If these predictions were disconfirmed, we would have to consider other schemes. The use of well-specified intervening variables is scientific, because the structure can be tested and falsified.

Using intervening variables also has advantages. For one thing, it simplifies the picture by reducing the messy number of empirical S-R correlations. It also suggests new hypotheses and relationships that stimulate new research. One of Tolman's points was that we always use theoretical constructs, and so do other sciences (gravity and atomic structure, for example, are important in physics even though they are inferred rather than observed directly). We just have to use them scientifically, by making sure they are "anchored" in the empirical world of stimuli and responses. Nearly every part of psychology has adopted the operational behavioristic framework. Thus, a social psychologist may study stereotypes and prejudice, but these terms are really only useful if they are operationally defined. Cognitive psychologists play the same game—working memory, semantic memory, and attention are not directly observable, but they are useful when they are linked to behavior.

Another pioneer in the use of intervening variables was **Clark L. Hull** (1884–1952). Hull (1943, 1952) presented a highly systematic theory of behavior that had a large impact in the 1940s and 1950s. Today, although many of Hull's ideas have been disconfirmed, his theory still stands as a brilliant example of how theoretical constructs can be used. The theory described a number of theoretical constructs that were carefully anchored on both the antecedent side and consequent side. Their interactions were also specified. For example, two of Hull's hypothetical constructs were Drive and Habit. Drive was the motivation caused by biological need (hunger, thirst, etc.); it was mostly influenced by being deprived of something important. Habit was learning; it was mostly influenced by the number of times the behavior had been reinforced. Based on empirical research (Perin, 1942; Williams, 1938), Hull concluded that Drive and Habit multiplied to influence performance. As we will see in later chapters, Hull's theory was different from Tolman's approach in important ways, but it was similar in its emphasis on intervening variables and the relations between motivation and learning. It is perfectly acceptable to build a science of behavior using unobservable things in our explanations. Tolman's perspective is with us today, and while we consider a great deal of research from the radical behaviorist perspective, this approach is generally accepted in this book.

Computer and brain metaphors

After World War II, there were further changes in how psychologists began to think about behavior. During the war, many psychologists helped design military equipment with an eye toward making it easy for people to operate. They often worked with engineers who were interested in information technology—for example, how information is transmitted over telephone lines. Psychologists began to think of people as processors of information. With the rise of the computer in the 1950s and 1960s, this perspective became more deeply ingrained. The idea was that people might operate like computers do, executing programs as they handle information. By the 1960s, it was becoming clear that computers could be programmed to solve problems and do other impressive tasks that humans do (e.g., Newell & Simon, 1961). The computer analogy was off and running in what we now know as cognitive psychology.

How people think about behavior has always been influenced by the technology of the times—remember how important the spirit of mechanism was to Descartes and the development of the reflex concept. The computer provides an extremely rich and compelling metaphor. The basic computer receives input (e.g., from a keyboard or from another computer on the Web), and eventually turns this information into output. It first transforms the input into a code of simple on-off electrical charges. It then processes this kind of information, performing calculations on it, transferring it to the monitor screen, and so forth, all while executing commands. Some of the information is stored in a temporary memory that is lost forever if the computer is switched off before the information is stored on the hard drive or a memory stick. If we looked inside the machine, we would find that all the work is being done by a central processor that manipulates the codes and symbols in a sequence. It is all very logical. The computer does much more than simply connect things, like a stimulus and a response, the way an old-fashioned telephone switchboard does.

The computer is the inspiration behind what is known as the **information processing** approach in cognitive psychology. Figure 1.14 presents an example of the "standard model" of cognition (Simon & Kaplan, 1989); the figure is actually based on a model proposed by Atkinson and Shiffrin (1971). The system emphasizes several theoretical constructs that intervene between stimulus (environmental input) and response. Each is devoted to processing information. The system receives sensory input from the external world, and this input is processed into different forms at different points in the sequence. It enters the sensory registers, which very briefly store it as raw visual or auditory input. If attention is paid to it, the information is transferred into short-term memory, where, if it is rehearsed enough, it eventually gets put into long-term memory. The influence of the computer analogy is clear. This approach to human information processing and memory has dominated the field for many years.

The computer metaphor is still important in psychology. But it cannot really tell the whole story. One problem is that it has surprisingly little to

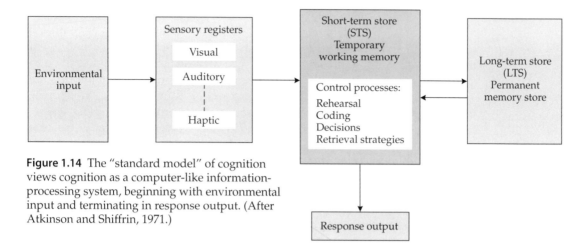

Figure 1.14 The "standard model" of cognition views cognition as a computer-like information-processing system, beginning with environmental input and terminating in response output. (After Atkinson and Shiffrin, 1971.)

say about learning—it mainly tells us about symbol manipulation. Another problem is that, although the standard model makes sense as a series of hypothetical constructs, it is not likely that the brain is really organized this way. Neurons in the brain operate fairly slowly, somewhere in the range of milliseconds. In contrast, computer components operate in the range of nanoseconds—about a million times faster (Rumelhart, 1989). There is an actual limit to the number of steps that the brain can perform in sequence in a task that takes a person a second or so to complete. This sort of calculation suggests that the brain must perform many operations in parallel—it must do more than one thing at a time—rather than in sequence, the way the typical computer operates.

Therefore, a somewhat different perspective began to emerge in the 1980s. It is often called **connectionism**, although it is also referred to as **parallel distributed processing** or **neural networks** (e.g., Rumelhart & McClelland, 1986a,b). The perspective represents a shift away from the computer metaphor and back to a brain metaphor. The basic idea is that cognition can be understood as a network of connections between units that look a little bit like neurons. Figure 1.15 illustrates a simple network, with just a few of these units, or "nodes." Each node is connected to each of the other nodes. If one node is activated, the activation travels to the connected nodes depending on the strength of the individual connections. You can imagine a large number of nodes being activated, and their activation transferring to other nodes through a multitude of connections that all get excited in parallel.

As an example, a network like the one in Figure 1.15 can recognize dogs and cats and discriminate them from other objects, such as bagels (e.g., McClelland & Rumelhart, 1985). Here is how it works. Each of the nodes is activated when a particular item is present in the environment. In our example, each node may respond to a particular feature of a dog. One node responds to ears, another node to a tongue, another node to a tail, etc. These dog features are strongly connected so that they tend to activate one another

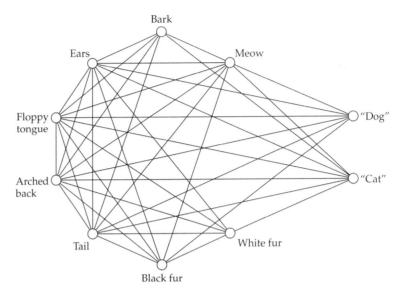

Figure 1.15 The "connectionist" point of view is that cognition results from a brain-like set of nodes (or units) and their interconnections. The diagram illustrates the concepts of dog and cat. Each concept is a set of features (floppy tongue, ears, bark) that are associated with many other features. When a new dog appears, at least some of the features become activated and further activate other features, depending on the strength of the interconnections. Concept learning requires the association of many features. (After McClelland & Rumelhart, 1985.)

when they are present. The nest of associations will also activate to a large extent when some, but not all, of the features are present. In this way, the network will respond "dog" with even a partial input. But it will not respond "cat" unless cat features are input. There is no reference to long-term memory, short-term memory, or template matching. The memory of "dog" is represented in the multiple connections.

Networks like the one shown in Figure 1.15 have a number of advantages. For one thing, it is easy to see how they learn. When the network is first exposed to different dogs, it associates the various features that occur together on each trial. Each of the corresponding connections is increased a little when features occur together, and decreased when they do not. (In fact, connection strengths can be either positive or negative, with the result that negative connections "inhibit" the connected nodes and vice versa.) After the connections have been learned, the net can respond to new dogs and discriminate them from cats, even if the new dogs or cats don't have all of the crucial features or even if some of the nodes or the connections were to disappear or die. The connectionist approach has so many advantages that some people assumed that it was a new "paradigm" that would replace the information processing approach in cognitive psychology. In truth, it did not. But the connectionist approach is now widely represented in cognitive science. Clearly, it is consistent with many of the earliest ideas (reflex, associationism, parsimony) that led to Learning Theory.

Human learning and animal learning

People sometimes get the impression that the computer metaphor (the information-processing approach) and, to some extent, the brain metaphor (the connectionist approach) are mostly relevant to the study of human, but not animal, learning. They sometimes guess that the information-processing approach replaced the kind of Learning Theory that was practiced by Pavlov, Thorndike, Skinner, Tolman, and Hull. They are incorrect. The truth is that the computer and brain metaphors are also important in Learning Theory (which has advanced considerably since the days of Skinner, Tolman, and Hull), and that what we know about human and animal learning has shown that they are really rather similar. Thanks to some important discoveries made in animal learning in the late 1960s (described in Chapters 3 and 4), animal learning researchers began to recognize that the information-processing approach could help us to understand classical conditioning (e.g., Wagner, 1976, 1978). It became routine to discuss attention, rehearsal, memory storage, and memory retrieval in explaining even the simple kind of learning shown by Pavlov's dogs—provided the terms were anchored carefully. Conditioned stimuli are now regarded as cues that retrieve memories of unconditioned stimuli; perhaps classical conditioning laws govern retrieval cues (e.g., Bouton, 1994a). Starting in the 1970s (e.g., Hulse, Fowler, & Honig, 1978), researchers also began to study traditionally "cognitive" topics in animals, such as short-term memory, memory codes, spatial memory, and timing, using sophisticated versions of the basic methods used in operant conditioning experiments (see Chapter 8). At the same time, animal learning researchers never lost the idea that complex behaviors (and now complex cognitions, see Figure 1.15) can be built out of simple associations or connections—the end product of conditioning. The conceptual separation between human and animal learning and memory may be more apparent than real. As the influential cognitive psychologist John R. Anderson (1995) has noted, "much current research on animal learning has a strong cognitive [information-processing] orientation, and there has been a resurgence of more behavioristic learning theories in research on human memory" (p. 4).

What, then, *are* the differences between the research literatures on human and animal learning? First, animal learning has kept its original interest in behavior. We may study topics like short-term memory, but the ultimate goal is usually to understand how it makes sense of behavior; this book adopts the view that our knowledge of behavior and learning would be incomplete without them. Second, animal learning researchers are often still rather stingy about the number of theoretical constructs they use—following Lloyd Morgan, the goal is still a parsimonious explanation. Third, research in animal learning typically asks questions about how we process, cope with, and remember things linked to motivationally significant events (like food, drugs, painful events, illness, etc.). In contrast, human learning research is often concerned with memory for material that is less emotion-ally charged and biologically significant, like word lists, sentences, and pic-tures. Perhaps because of this, topics covered in animal learning often seem more obviously connected to adaptation and evolution; learning is funda-mentally viewed as a way for organisms to adapt to their environments (see Chapter 2).

The most obvious difference between human and animal learning and memory, however, is the species that are studied. Earlier parts of this chap-ter reviewed how the interest in learning in animals originally came about. But when all is said and done, is there still a point to studying learning in animals? The answer is "yes." Learning can be studied in animals because most psychologists believe that there are fundamental, general processes that are represented in many species. (We will address this issue in many places in the book—especially Chapter 6.) This approach also offers simplicity. For example, an understanding of learning in a rat or pigeon is not complicated by the subject trying to figure out what the experimenter is trying to test and behaving accordingly (the so-called "demand characteristics" of human experiments). In addition, the prior knowledge and experience of animal subjects, as well as their genetic backgrounds, can be controlled precisely. As Tolman (1945) once quipped, "Let it be noted that rats live in cages: they do not go on binges the night before one has planned an experiment," (p. 166). Animal experiments offer simplicity and rigorous experimental control.

In animals one can also study the effects of certain events or procedures that could not be studied in humans. For instance, we can study how unpleasant emotions, like fear, are learned, or how strong hunger and other forms of motivation affect behavior and learning. One can also study the physiological bases of learning and memory in experiments on animals, and there is excellent work in behavioral neuroscience that investigates the brain mechanisms behind many of the fundamental processes of animal learning (e.g., see Balleine, 2005; Fanselow & Poulos, 2005; Schultz, 2006). The causal connections between brain processes and behavioral output can be difficult to study in humans. The behavioral study of learning in animals provides an important bridge between the neurosciences and psychology.

This is not to say that anything goes. Research with animals (like research with humans) is regulated by law and by rigorous ethical principles. Since the mid-1980s, animal research projects conducted at every U.S. college, uni-versity, and research institution has been reviewed by committees made up of scientists along with ordinary people from the lay community. The stress connected with certain procedures—such as fear and hunger—is kept to the minimum level that is necessary to study the problem. For example, elec-tric shock applied to the floor of a cage is often used to study fear in rats. The shocks used are as weak as possible; they can cause a mild "fear" in the rat, but they typically cause only a mild tingling to the human hand. In a similar way, the hunger used in animal learning research may be no more intense than what animals may experience in the wild (e.g., Poling, Nickel, & Alling, 1990). There have been unmistakable gains due to animal research (e.g., see Domjan & Purdy, 1995; Miller, 1985), and many will be featured in this book.

To summarize, the study of learning in animals is a method that allows scientists to study processes involved in learning and memory across species. Human learning and animal learning are complementary approaches to the same problem. The impact of the historical ideas traced in earlier parts of this chapter—the reflex, associationism, and the evolution of the mind—are clearly visible in modern animal learning theory and in cognitive psychology.

Tools for Analyzing Learning and Behavior

Learning theory provides a way to think about almost any example of behavior. It provides a kind of lens through which behavior can be viewed. The lens is the modern legacy of all of the early theorists we have reviewed in this chapter. It starts, first, by recognizing the role of two fundamental forms of learning in nearly any situation, and second, by recognizing that these forms of learning interact. Later chapters in this book will break the framework down into more detail and study its component parts. To appreciate what is coming, it is worth noting how the basic tools will work together.

Learning about stimuli and about behavior

Soon after John B. Watson's time, researchers began to settle on two basic "paradigms" of learning. One of them—the one investigated by Pavlov—is now known as **classical conditioning**. In modern times, there are two major reasons why classical conditioning is considered important. First, it is fundamental to adaptation, because it is the way animals learn to anticipate and deal with upcoming biologically significant events. The sound of Pavlov's bell did not just elicit drooling—it elicited a whole system of responses and behaviors that are organized to get the dog's system ready for food. (This idea is considered further in Chapters 2 and 5.) Second, notice that after conditioning has occurred, the dog behaves as if it has learned to associate the sound of the bell with food. Classical conditioning represents a situation in which the animal learns to associate stimuli in its environment. Classical conditioning is therefore used as a method for investigating how animals learn about stimuli. For this reason, I will sometimes call it **stimulus learning**.

The other basic paradigm is the result of Thorndike and Skinner's research. It is now called **instrumental conditioning** or **operant conditioning**. This kind of learning is also very important in behavior because, as we have already seen, it allows animals to do things that lead to good consequences. It also lets them learn to stop doing things that lead to bad consequences. Notice that the rat lever-pressing in the Skinner box to get food is behaving as if it has learned the connection between the act and the outcome. In modern terms, operant conditioning gives us a method for investigating how animals learn about the relations between behaviors and their consequences. I will therefore sometimes call it **response learning**.

Classical and operant conditioning have usually been studied separately. This is mainly for analytic reasons—it is easiest to investigate them by studying them apart from one another. But this has led psychologists to use different terms and vocabularies to describe them, and the different terms help create an unnecessary and artificial boundary between them. For now, I think it is important to understand that in the natural world, classical and operant conditioning are always working together. To help emphasize this, I will use some terms introduced by Bolles (1972a; see also Jenkins, 1977) that can describe either of them, and indeed any situation in which an organism is learning and behaving. The terms may seem a little abstract at first, but their abstractness is exactly the property that makes it possible to use them in any situation.

Here they are: In classical conditioning, the animal behaves as if it learns to associate a stimulus (S) with a biologically significant event (S*). In Pavlov's experiment, the sound of the bell was S and the food was S*. "S" is pronounced "Ess," and "S*" is pronounced "Ess star." The star (*) merely means that the event is biologically significant; in principle, S* can be anything significant, like food, shock, illness, a drug, or a copulation—depending upon the situation or experiment. Similarly, S might describe the sound of a bell, a light, the sight of a rat, a friend, or a room—again depending on the situation or the experiment. I will often refer to classical conditioning as **S-S* learning**, because the organism behaves as if it learns to associate an S and an S* (see Chapter 3).

In many ways, operant conditioning is a similar affair. In this case, the animal behaves as if it learns to associate a behavior or response (R) with a biologically significant event (S*). In Skinner's experiment, the lever-press was R and the food pellet was S*. In Thorndike's puzzle box experiments, moving the latch was R and the tasty fish was S*. I will often refer to operant conditioning as **R-S* learning**, because the organism behaves as if it has associated an R with an S*.

Classical and operant conditioning boil down to S-S* and R-S* learning. Both kinds of learning can occur whenever an organism encounters a biologically significant event (S*).

One difference between classical and operant conditioning is *what* the animal appears to learn: In classical conditioning, the animal mainly learns about stimuli, and in operant conditioning it mainly learns about behavior. (I am simplifying here.) Classical and operant conditioning also differ in the procedures used to study them. In a classical conditioning experiment, the experimenter controls when the crucial events—S and S*—occur. The subject responds, but the response has no effect on whether S* is delivered or not. In contrast, in the operant or instrumental situation, the subject's behavior is essential—"instrumental"—for producing S*. A difference between the two learning paradigms, then, is whether the subject's behavior controls the delivery of S*.

But again, the distinction is largely academic. Outside the laboratory, stimulus learning and response learning are almost inseparable. Every time an S* is associated with behavior, it can also be associated with stimuli that are also present, and vice versa. Behavior is a combined result of stimulus learning and response learning. Let us consider a few examples.

Crows foraging at the beach

Reto Zach (1978, 1979) watched crows feeding on whelks (large marine snails) (Figure 1.16) on a beach in British Columbia. The birds behaved in a way that was remarkable and efficient. At low tide, they poked around near the water among the whelks that tended to collect there. After lifting and then rejecting one or two whelks, apparently on the basis of their weight, each bird finally selected a large one and flew off with it to a favorite rocky location near cliffs at the back of the beach. Once there, the crow flew up to a height of a little over 5 meters and dropped the whelk on the rocks below. After a few attempts, the whelk shell broke, and the bird ate the tasty animal that was living inside.

There are several aspects of the crow's foraging behavior that are interesting. The birds tended to confine their foraging to low tide, when the

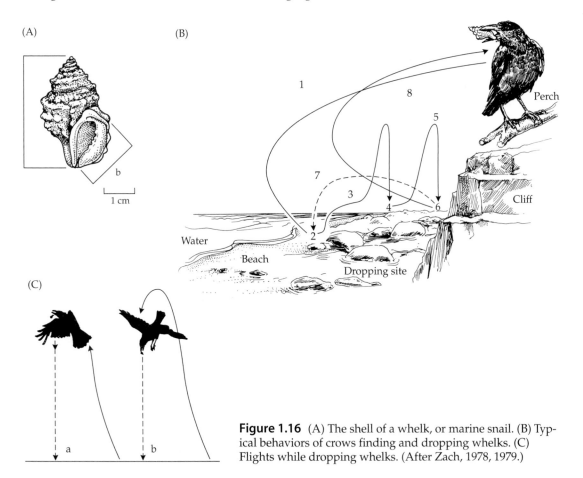

Figure 1.16 (A) The shell of a whelk, or marine snail. (B) Typical behaviors of crows finding and dropping whelks. (C) Flights while dropping whelks. (After Zach, 1978, 1979.)

whelks were most plentiful. They also took only the largest whelks, which Zach showed were the ones whose shells broke most easily when dropped. By selecting the largest whelks, the birds didn't waste energy trying to break whelk shells that would not break easily. The birds also had different favorite dropping locations. And before dropping their whelks, each bird flew to an optimal height that both minimized effort and maximized the probability that the whelk shell would break upon impact. Thus, the birds found and broke whelk shells in the most efficient possible way.

The behavior almost seems miraculous. It also seems quite intelligent and complex. Learning Theory gives us a fruitful way to think about how the birds do it. The crow fundamentally learns about various stimuli at the beach, and about its behavior, through stimulus and response learning. The first thing to notice is that there are several behaviors involved: The bird approaches the water, lifts and rejects some whelks, and after accepting one, the bird flies to a favorite site and drops the whelk onto the rocks from a specific height. Each of these behaviors is an operant that is reinforced by the payoff of gaining access to the animal inside. At the same time, the bird has also probably learned about stimuli in its environment. It may have learned that low tide signals whelks on the beach. It has also learned that whelk shells hide tasty animals—the whelk shell, along with the beach itself, are signals for food. And whelks of a large size and weight are the most likely to lead to reinforcement—more examples of stimulus learning. And as it flies off to the favorite dropping site, the bird uses cues to get there. The dropping site itself is associated with a reward, and that is why the bird may repeatedly visit the same site again and again. We can begin to understand the entire sequence by first breaking it down into components of stimulus learning and response learning.

Kids at play

The framework is useful for understanding behavior in virtually any setting. For example, when small children are out playing, all of their activities (playing with toys, drawing or painting, interacting with other children) are in principle governed by stimulus learning and response learning, which are constantly in operation. The child's choice of which activity to engage in is influenced by each behavior's reinforcing value or pay-off (see Chapter 7). And how small children actually learn to do the things they do is not trivial. A child who has learned to blow bubbles could have first associated the bubble container with fun and excitement (stimulus learning); this alone might generate interest and pleasure if a bubble bottle were to appear at a birthday party. And, of course, further learning to dip the wand in the soap, to bring the wand to the lips, and to actually blow are all examples of operant behaviors that are learned and perfected through response learning. The pleasure provided by this (or any other) activity will be further associated with the situation (e.g., a friend's house or the arrival of Uncle Bob)—more stimulus learning that will further influence behavior. Response learning and stimulus learning are always happening in combination and influencing behavior everywhere.

Learning about stimuli and responses starts very early in life (e.g., Lipsitt, 1990). Even very young babies quickly learn to suck on pacifiers that deliver a sweet solution. They also learn that sucking in the presence of certain pictures leads to the sweet solution while other pictures do not (e.g., Lipsitt, 1990). They suck mostly when the right pictures are shown. Sucking is an operant behavior, controlled by its consequences. The pictures also signal when the relation is in force. But the pacifier itself, and also the pictures, are directly associated with the sweet solution. Presumably, through stimulus learning, they generate excitement, and possibly also some of the sucking.

Carolyn Rovee-Collier has studied how babies 2–6 months of age learn and remember (e.g., Rovee-Collier, 1987, 1999). She and her students visit babies' homes and conduct experiments while the baby is in its crib. They mount a bouncing mobile on the crib directly above the baby. While the baby is on its back, the experimenter loops one end of a ribbon around the baby's ankle and the other end around the mobile (Figure 1.17A). Now, when the baby kicks, the mobile jiggles—and the babies are delighted with this. They quickly learn to kick their feet to shake the mobile, and they can remember this when they are tested later. This scenario, like so many others, involves both response- and stimulus-learning. The kicking response is an operant associated with movement of the mobile; but the mobile itself—and bumper and other stimuli around the walls of the crib—are also associated with the movement and the activity. Babies forget over time, of course, but they forget more slowly as they get older. Older babies (6–18 months old) can be tested with a different arrangement in which pressing a lever causes a minia-

(A)

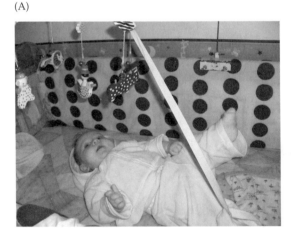

(B)

Figure 1.17 Children learning in Carolyn Rovee-Collier's experiments. (A) By kicking its foot, the very young baby moves the mobile to make it jiggle. (B) By pressing the lever, the somewhat older baby (6 months and older) makes the train move along its track. (Photographs courtesy of C. Rovee-Collier.)

ture toy train to move around a track (Figure 1.17B). There is little change in how learning and remembering work in these situations, and there is no obvious change in performance when the baby learns to talk. Rovee-Collier has concluded that "infants' memory processing does not fundamentally differ from that of older children and adults" (Rovee-Collier, 1999, p. 80).

People using drugs

Stimulus learning and response learning are also extremely useful in understanding drug-taking in humans (e.g., Stolerman, 1992). There is no question that drugs are biologically significant events (S*s), and that they can be powerful reinforcers. Drugs may reinforce drug-taking because they cause euphoria, or perhaps because they reduce anxiety. In either case, people can thus learn to acquire drugs and take them through simple response learning. (As we saw at the start of the chapter, drug-taking can actually be studied in rats, which will learn to press levers in a Skinner box if it leads to a drug injection.) Notice, though, that every time a drug is taken, the person can also associate it with the stimuli that are present at the same time—that is, the drug also provides an S* in a classical conditioning trial. Drug users associate both behaviors and stimuli with drugs. Both types of learning have major implications for how we think about drug abuse (e.g., Bevins & Bardo, 2004; Siegel, 1989; Stewart, de Wit, & Eikelboom, 1984; Stolerman, 1992). For example, one result of being presented with a cue associated with a drug is that it may elicit a withdrawal-like effect, or a general expectancy of the effects of getting high, that further motivates the operant behavior that produces it. As we will see, one important effect of stimulus learning is that it is supposed to motivate operant behavior (see Chapter 9).

I will return to the question of drug-taking in several subsequent chapters. Now that you know that drugs can be seen as reinforcers, you may see that it would be useful to know more about how reinforcers work. You may want to know how they maintain behavior, how different ways of scheduling reinforcers might influence behavior, and under what conditions pairing of a behavior and an S* produce learning and under what conditions it does not. Similarly, it would be useful to know how S-S* learning works, what conditions lead to it, and what conditions discourage it. You may want to learn more about what kinds of things are actually learned in S-S* learning: Do we respond to drug signals with excitement or other physiological responses? You may also want to know how knowledge about stimuli (S-S* learning) and knowledge about behavior (R-S* learning) influence one another. And, of course, if these kinds of learning are involved in drug abuse, you may want to know how to get rid of them. Learning theory gives us a handle on all of these questions. All of this (and more) is what this book is all about.

Relations between S, R, and S*

Panel A of Figure 1.18 puts all of the above examples together into a single description. The panel illustrates the idea that any situation involving bio-

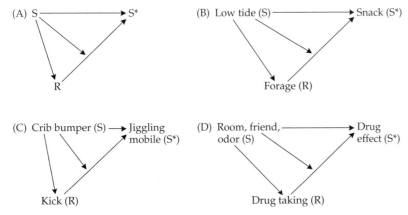

Figure 1.18 (A) S, R, and S* describe any example of behavior, and therefore help us to understand them. (B) Foraging crows learn to forage (R) in the presence of low tide (S) to get a tasty whelk snack (S*). (C) A baby learns to kick (R) in the presence of a particular crib bumper (S) in order to jiggle the mobile (S*). (D) A person takes a drug (R) in the presence of many stimuli, like a room, a friend, or an odor (S) in order to receive the drug's effect (S*).

logically significant events (S*) involves an opportunity to associate S* with both behavior (R) and with stimuli (S) present in the environment. We study S-S* learning, as well as its effects on behavior, when we study classical conditioning. We study R-S* learning, and its own effects, when we study operant conditioning. By now, it should be easy to relate almost any example of behavior to this general framework. The S, R, and S* scheme can apply to any situation as easily as it applies to foraging crows, bubble-blowing children, and drug abusers.

Panel A in Figure 1.18 also illustrates two other links besides R-S* and S-S*. In one, we learn that stimuli actually signal an association between a behavior and a significant event. This is what S's connection with the R-S* association portrays. For the foraging crow (Figure 1.18B), low tide signals that "foraging now pays" in addition to directly signaling the presence of food. For the baby in her crib (Figure 1.18C) the crib bumper signals that kicking will now jiggle the mobile. For the drug user (Figure 1.18D), a street corner might signal that "drug buying will bring drugs" in addition to being directly associated with drugs. This kind of learning also has an important influence on behavior. Here, the stimulus "sets the occasion" for the operant behavior (Skinner, 1938).

In the final link, we may learn a direct association between stimuli and response (S-R) so that the stimulus can elicit the response reflexively. Many psychologists think that this kind of association becomes important after a great deal of repetition and practice; as a behavior becomes "habitual," the situation may come to elicit it automatically. The behavior becomes "automatized" (e.g., Schneider & Shiffrin, 1977). Because of the early influence of the reflex concept, psychologists for the first 50 years of the twentieth century often assumed that S-R connections were the major basis of all learning. Nowadays, however, psychologists are open to a possible role for every one of the simple connections presented in Figure 1.18 (e.g., Rescorla, 1991; see also Chapter 10).

The scheme sketched in Figure 1.18 can be applied to almost any example of behavior you may encounter. Try thinking about how it helps you to understand your own behavior and the behavior of your friends. The framework can be surprisingly useful—it is worth the exercise. This book is organized so that the different types of learning represented here are discussed in a sequence. We will begin by talking about the similarities between S-S* and R-S* learning. Then we will ask how S-S* learning functions and how it works. There will be some surprises along the way, because Pavlovian conditioning is not what most people think it is (Rescorla, 1988b). We will eventually turn to R-S* learning, and the relationships between S-S* and R-S* learning, as we consider some interesting topics in animal cognition and motivation. Ultimately, we'll put the pieces back together and think about how the whole thing operates. The journey isn't short. But it is perhaps the most important part of a story that started with Descartes, Locke, Darwin, and the early comparative psychologists.

Summary

1. In the 1600s, philosophers began to wonder whether humans are machines that operate according to scientific laws. Descartes' distinction between mind and body held that only the body is controlled by such laws. Specifically, the human body (and all animal behavior) is controlled by reflex action.

2. Later philosophers suggested that even the mind is governed by scientific laws. The British Empiricists (e.g., Locke and Hume) argued that the mind is a tabula rasa at first, with knowledge being written on it by experience. Complex ideas are built up from simple associations, following several laws of association. Rationalists (e.g., Kant) differed from the empiricists in supposing that the mind is not initially empty, but starts with certain a priori assumptions with which it actively molds experience.

3. Meanwhile, in the 1800s biologists were beginning to learn more about the physiology of reflexes and reflex action. According to thinkers like Sechenov, even human thoughts could be understood as reflexes of the brain. By the turn of the twentieth century, all of this set the stage for Pavlov's pioneering work on learned "psychic" reflexes. Processes of major significance could now be studied with conditioning experiments.

4. In the mid-1800s, Darwin's theory of evolution emphasized the fact that humans and animals are alike. The early comparative psychologists began to study one of its most astonishing implications—that even the human mind

has evolved. To do this, they studied the behavior of animals in an attempt to identify the cognitive processes they possess. Ultimately, parsimonious principles won out. Thorndike's experiments on cat intelligence led to the conclusion that learning could generally be understood by knowing how reinforcers stamp in S-R associations. Thorndike's work also encouraged interest in conditioning experiments.

5. John B. Watson rescued psychology from the morass of introspection by proposing behavior as its subject matter. The main advantage of studying behavior is that everyone can see it; the facts therefore do not merely depend on what the most powerful people believe or introspect. Watson was also empiricistic, and saw a central role for learning. Like others before and after him, he also saw the reflex as an abstract thing, so that learned reflexes in animal conditioning experiments were directly relevant to the reflexes he saw in humans in the real world.

6. At least two forms of behaviorism emerged after Watson. Skinner's radical behaviorism set out to study the empirical relationships between observable events, such as stimuli and responses. This approach identified two types of behavior: respondents, which are behaviors elicited by events that precede them, and operants, which are behaviors that are controlled by their consequences.

7. In contrast, Tolman's operational behaviorism uses unobservable theoretical constructs (or "intervening variables") to help explain behavior. These constructs are useful provided they are carefully anchored to things that can be manipulated and measured objectively. The main idea of operational behaviorism—that unobservable constructs are useful and scientifically valid if they are systematically linked to behavioral output—is accepted today by most parts of scientific psychology.

8. After World War II, psychologists began using the computer as a metaphor for human nature, and this led to the information processing approach. In the 1980s, the connectionist approach began to use networks of neurons in the brain as its inspiration and metaphor. Both approaches are accepted and used today by modern students of learning in animals.

9. Modern Learning Theory accepts an overarching framework that can be used to analyze any example of human or animal behavior. Behaviors (R) typically occur in the presence of stimuli (S) and precede significant events (S*), like reinforcers. There are several possible relations that can be learned between S, R, and S*, and each can occur and play a powerful role. S-S* learning is studied with the methods of classical conditioning, which we will see has many surprising features and consequences. R-S* learning is studied with the methods of operant conditioning and is also fundamentally important. S may also signal the R-S* relation, may be connected directly with R, or may motivate behavior based on the R-S* relation. This book will consider what we know about each of these kinds of learning and their interrelationships.

Key Terms

Learning Theory
René Descartes
reflex action
Thomas Hobbes
hedonism
Julien de la Mettrie
British Empiricists
John Locke
David Hume
tabula rasa
atomistic
association
rationalism
Immanuel Kant
Charles Darwin
early comparative psychologists
Morgan's Canon
Edward L. Thorndike
law of effect
Ivan Pavlov
conditioned reflex
structuralism
B. F. Skinner
radical behaviorism
Skinner box

operant experiment
operant
reinforcer
consequence
elicited
antecedent
respondent
operant-respondent distinction
Edward C. Tolman
operational behaviorism
intervening variable
theoretical construct
Clark L. Hull
information processing
connectionism
parallel distributed processing
neural networks
classical conditioning
stimulus learning
instrumental conditioning
operant conditioning
response learning
S-S* learning
R-S* learning

Chapter Two Outline

Evolution and Behavior
> Natural selection
> Adaptation in behavior
> Fixed action patterns
> Innate behavior

Adaptation in Instrumental Conditioning
> The law of effect
> Reinforcement
> Shaping

Adaptation in Classical Conditioning
> Signals for food
> Territoriality and reproduction
> Fear
> Conditioning with drugs as S*s
> Sign tracking

Other Parallels between Signal and Response Learning
> Extinction
> Timing of S*
> Size of S*
> Preparedness

Summary

Chapter

2

Learning and Adaptation

IN THE LAST CHAPTER, WE SAW HOW RESEARCHERS eventually came to emphasize two basic forms of animal learning: classical conditioning in which animals learn to associate stimuli with S*s, and operant (or instrumental) conditioning in which they learn to associate behaviors with S*s. In later chapters, we will take a look at how these kinds of learning actually operate. But before we do, it is worth asking *why* they are so prevalent and important. The main reason is that both kinds of learning give humans and other animals a way to adapt to their changing environments. This rather simple idea has some surprisingly interesting implications. In the first sections of this chapter, I will consider some of the adaptive functions of behavior and learning. In the last part of the chapter, I will show that, largely because of their overlap in function, both classical and operant conditioning follow similar rules. As we discuss all of this, I hope you will begin to appreciate the surprisingly wide range of behavior that is influenced by classical and operant conditioning, and why they are worth knowing and thinking about.

Let's start with the idea that learning is mainly a way in which animals adapt to their environments. To be more specific, it is a way they can adapt *through experience*. It is interesting to observe that this kind of adaptation nicely complements another, more famous, adaptation process: evolution by natural selection.

Evolution and Behavior

Natural selection

Consider the story of how a population of moths (pepper moths) changed color from black-and-white speckled to more purely black as England became industrialized during the 1800s (see Kettlewell, 1956, for a review). During this period, air pollution began to darken the trees, turning them from speckled white to black. As a result, predatory birds found it easier to spot light moths that were resting on the trees, and light moths were eaten more readily than dark moths. The more conspicuous, lighter moths were gradually eliminated (see also Howlett & Majerus, 1987; and recent studies with blue jays by Bond & Kamil, 1998 and 2002—discussed in Chapter 8—for further evidence of such a process). The dark moths survived, passed their dark genes on to offspring, and the dark offspring in turn survived. Over generations, the population of moths became darker; in fact, the moths appeared to have adjusted to the new, darker, environment. No force or higher intelligence was necessary to make these insects turn from speckled white to black. Instead, lighter moths were simply at a disadvantage, and lighter pigmentation was eliminated from the population. This, of course, is an example of evolution through **natural selection**, a process that is also illustrated and supported by studies of finches on the Galápagos Islands (e.g., Grant & Grant, 2002). For example, after a major drought, the supply of edible seeds decreased dramatically, leaving only tough, difficult-to-crack seeds. Only birds with larger beaks could eat them, and there was an increase in the average beak size of birds in the next few generations.

In evolution, the bottom line is reproductive success. If the dark moths (or finches with sturdy beaks) survived to live longer lives, but failed to produce offspring and create a new generation, the process would have gone nowhere. In the long run, the winners in evolution are the individuals who pass their genes along to the next generation. These individuals are "fit"; the term **fitness** describes an animal's ability to produce offspring that will reproduce in the next generation. Evolutionary thinking has increasingly focused on the organism's ability to propagate its genes (e.g., Hamilton, 1964; Williams, 1966). To paraphrase E. O. Wilson (1975), the organism is essentially the gene's way of making more genes. For an entertaining and insightful discussion of these issues, I recommend Richard Dawkins' book, *The Selfish Gene* (Dawkins, 1989). For now, it is mainly important to remember that natural selection works because individuals with adaptive traits are more likely to reproduce and be represented in future generations.

Adaptation in behavior

For the moths in industrialized England, being dark had clear survival value. There was some initial genetic variation in this trait, and the blacker genes then survived. Blackness was represented in the next generation because blackness was inherited. If behaviors are likewise linked to genes, then they could likewise evolve through natural selection. This is the main idea of

ethology, the study of the adaptiveness and evolution of behavior. Like coloration or body parts, behaviors themselves may evolve.

Because of their interest in the evolution of behavior, ethologists study behavior as it occurs in nature. Only then can its adaptation to the environment be understood. The actual evolution of a behavior is not possible to observe, because behavior (unlike bones) does not leave fossils. Despite this, ethologists have worked out a number of interesting methods for making inferences about how behavior has evolved (e.g., see Alcock, 2005; Barash, 1982; McFarland, 1993). Sometimes a plausible evolutionary path can be put together by comparing the behavior of related species. For example, Kessel (1955) studied the evolution of an interesting aspect of courtship behavior in empidid flies. In some species, the male gives an empty silk balloon to the female during courtship. Where did this behavior come from? In related species, the male might give a juicy insect to the female, which she eats during mating. In other species, the prey item is adorned in silk; in still others, the prey item is wrapped completely. Kessel suggested that these simpler and more common behaviors evolved into the unusual behavior of the male empidid fly presenting an empty balloon to the female.

More typically, ethologists work out the evolution of a behavior by evaluating its possible benefit or survival value. In the case of the simplest empidid fly, the male may benefit from bringing a prey item to his mate because it gives her something to eat during courtship besides him! The "evaluative approach" (Barash, 1982) is most powerful when real evidence is obtained that confirms the hypothetical benefit to the animal. This point was made beautifully by Niko Tinbergen, one of the most important of the early ethologists. While studying black-headed gulls in the 1950s, he noticed that parent birds were quick to remove broken eggshells from the nest once their chicks had hatched. He hypothesized that this behavior was adaptive because the egg shells were white on the inside, and broken ones lying around the nest would be easy for predators to detect. By removing the broken eggshells, the parents were protecting their young. To test the idea, Tinbergen (1963) conducted experiments in which eggs were strewn around a field, with broken egg shells lying near some of the eggs. The eggs were subject to predation from crows and other gulls. Consistent with his hypothesis, the eggs that were near broken egg shells were eaten more often than eggs that were not (Figure 2.1). The experiments established a clear payoff for eggshell removal by gull parents.

Tinbergen's hypothesis was also supported by the comparison of black-headed gulls with other species. Ester Cullen (1957) compared the behavior of the black-headed gull with the behavior of the kittiwake, a closely related species. Unlike the black-headed gull, which nests in large colonies on the ground, the kittiwake nests on steep cliffs, where its eggs and chicks are less bothered by natural predators. Interestingly, kittiwakes do not practice eggshell removal. They also do not perform other antipredator behaviors practiced by black-headed gulls, such as alarm calling when predators are in the area or predator "mobbing." (In mobbing, a group of gulls gather and

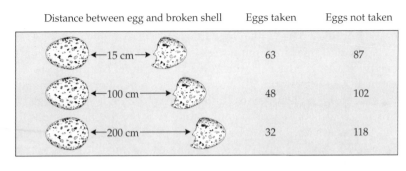

Distance between egg and broken shell	Eggs taken	Eggs not taken
←15 cm→	63	87
←100 cm→	48	102
←200 cm→	32	118

Figure 2.1 Eggshell removal in herring gulls. Predators are more likely to spot eggs and eat them if they are near a broken eggshell. There is thus an evolutionary "payoff" for removing eggshells from the nest. (After Tinbergen, 1963.)

screech loudly at the predator to drive it away.) By studying related species in different environments, we can understand how behavior has adapted to those environments. Unrelated species in similar environments can also be compared (see Alcock, 2005). This sort of study provides interesting insights into how behavior evolves and adapts an animal to its environment.

Fixed action patterns

When ethologists examine the behavior of animals in the natural world, they often uncover what Konrad Lorenz called **fixed action patterns**. Fixed action patterns are fixed behavior sequences that are triggered by stimuli known as **releasers** or **sign stimuli**. They are supposed to have several characteristics. Furthermore, fixed action patterns are highly stereotyped (they do not vary between individuals or between occasions when one individual performs them). They also depend on initial triggering only. And, most important, they are not supposed to depend on learning; this means that they appear in their typical form when the animal first performs them. Fixed action patterns are supposed to be built into the genes—innate—just as morphological characteristics such as wings and eye color are.

One of the most impressive examples of a fixed action pattern is cocoon-building behavior in the spider *Cupiennius salei* (Eibl-Eibesfeldt, 1970). The female first spins the base of the cocoon, and then its walls; after depositing the eggs inside, she closes the top. Remarkably, the sequence always takes about 6400 movements. This is true even if the cocoon is destroyed halfway through the task—the spider keeps going where she left off. If the glands producing the cocoon's threads fail to function (as they did at least once when hot lights used in filming the process dried them out), the spider still performs the whole sequence. After initial triggering, the sequence just keeps on going. A fixed action pattern does not depend on feedback once it is set in motion.

Eibl-Eibesfeldt (1970, 1979, 1989) discussed a number of possible fixed action patterns in humans. For example, humans from every culture that have been studied (from Western Europe to Papua New Guinea to Samoa)

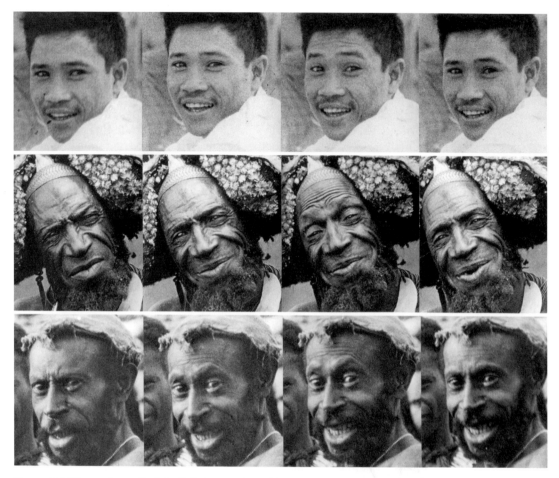

Figure 2.2 The eyebrow flash in Bali (top row) and Papua New Guinea (middle and bottom rows). The sequences shown occurred in well under 2 seconds. (From Eibl-Eibesfeldt, 1970.)

appear to smile. They also flash their eyebrows at the beginning of friendly social greetings (Figure 2.2). The fact that eyebrow flashing and smiling are so stereotyped and appear to occur over such a wide range of cultures (with learning environments that presumably differ quite substantially) suggests to Eibl-Eibesfeldt that they may be innate fixed action patterns.

Innate behavior

In truth, the "innateness" of fixed action patterns is more often assumed than really proven. Even a learned behavior can be highly stereotyped if crucial features of the environment are similar enough between individuals. In the strict sense, it is surprisingly difficult to prove that a behavior is "innate." Ethologists once thought that a behavior's innateness could be proven by running "deprivation experiments" in which they raised the animal from birth in an environment that lacked experiences that are assumed necessary for the behavior to be learned. If the behavior still emerged during development, then it must be innate. Unfortunately, deprivation experiments can never be conclusive, because an experimenter can never deprive an animal of all experience; after all, it is never possible to know for sure that the animal has been deprived of all the right experiences.

There are better methods to study innateness. In **artificial selection** experiments, researchers study whether behaviors can be passed from generation to generation by only allowing animals that show a specific behavior to interbreed. Many behaviors have been selected this way (e.g., Cade, 1981; Hirsch, 1963). For psychologists, some of the best-known work of this type was conducted by Tryon (1942), who ran rats in mazes and separately mated those that learned quickly and those that did not. Offspring of "bright" parents were bright, offspring of "dull" parents were dull, and the difference between the lines increased over succeeding generations. Although the results suggest that maze-brightness and -dullness can be inherited, the difference between lines also appeared to depend on the kind of environment in which the rats were raised. Cooper and Zubek (1958) found that rats of the bright and dull lines differed when they were raised in "normal" laboratory cages. But when they were raised in either enriched or impoverished cages, the difference between bright and dull rats disappeared. The expression of genetic potential in behavior may often interact with the type of experience offered by particular environments.

For many reasons, then, the term "innate" is probably best used to refer only to behaviors that have no obvious basis in learning (McFarland, 1993). Interestingly, even behaviors that meet this definition can be modified to some extent by experience over time. For example, we will soon see that classical conditioning allows "innate" behavior to be evoked by cues that merely *signal* sign stimuli. Conditioning thus allows innate behaviors to be released by a wider range of stimuli. Innate behavior can also be modified by instrumental conditioning. For example, Tinbergen and Perdeck (1950) showed that herring gull chicks peck at their parents' beaks in order to make them regurgitate food, which the chicks then eat with some enthusiasm. The chicks' pecking appears immediately after hatching and is highly similar between birds. It is also released only by highly specific sign stimuli. Hailman (1967) noticed that the similar pecking of young laughing gulls became more accurate and efficient as the birds grew older. Part of this is due to maturation, but part of it is also due to the fact that some forms of the response are more successful than others in producing food—in other words, the behavior is affected by response learning.

Experience can modify "innate" behaviors in still other ways. One very common feature of behavior is that it often shows **habituation**. When a sign stimulus is presented repeatedly, the strength of the response often declines. For example, young birds are initially frightened when a shadow flies over them, but the fear response decreases with repeated exposure to the shadow

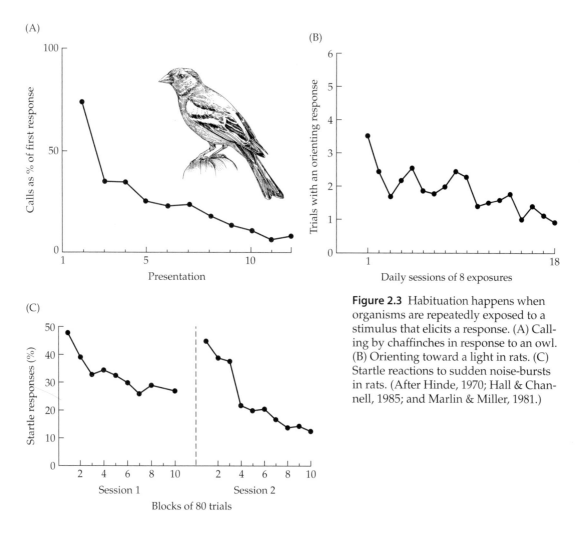

(A)

Calls as % of first response

(B)

Trials with an orienting response

Presentation

Daily sessions of 8 exposures

(C)

Startle responses (%)

Session 1   Session 2

Blocks of 80 trials

Figure 2.3 Habituation happens when organisms are repeatedly exposed to a stimulus that elicits a response. (A) Calling by chaffinches in response to an owl. (B) Orienting toward a light in rats. (C) Startle reactions to sudden noise-bursts in rats. (After Hinde, 1970; Hall & Channell, 1985; and Marlin & Miller, 1981.)

(e.g., Schleidt, 1961). Mobbing behavior likewise decreases with repeated exposure to the eliciting stimulus (e.g., Hinde, 1970; Figure 2.3). A rat will orient to a light the first few times it is presented, but this orienting response likewise declines with repeated presentation. And many organisms are startled by presentation of a sudden burst of noise; if the noise is presented repeatedly, the startle response also becomes habituated (e.g., Davis, 1970; Groves & Thompson, 1970; Marlin & Miller, 1981). Habituation is extraordinarily common across species, situations, stimuli, and behaviors, and we will consider it again at other places in this book (see Chapters 4 and 9). It presumably prevents the animal from wasting time and energy on behaviors that are not necessarily functional. It is another way that experience changes even innate behavior.

An animal with completely inflexible behavior would not be able to adjust to changes in its environment. Animals therefore often benefit from having some ability to learn. On the other hand, learning can sometimes carry serious costs. For example, a mouse would clearly benefit from innately recognizing and defending itself against a predator the first time one is encountered; a failure to respond correctly on Trial 1 would likely mean the end of the game (e.g., Bolles, 1970; Edmunds, 1974; Hirsch & Bolles, 1980). Innate behaviors are there the first time the animal needs them. Evolution by natural selection allows behaviors to adapt across generations of animals. Learning, on the other hand, allows behaviors to adapt through experience within an animal's own lifetime.

Adaptation in Instrumental Conditioning

Thanks to instrumental conditioning, animals learn to perform behaviors that increase their fitness. Food, water, and sex are classic rewards that reinforce learning; it is no coincidence that they are also important for reproductive success. The importance of other S*s is less obvious. Humans are social animals that depend on mutual cooperation; this is presumably why social stimuli such as smiles and approval seem to serve as such powerful rewards. Consider the relationship between a parent and a baby. The baby needs an adult's help to get by; but in an evolutionary sense, the parent also gains fitness by helping the child (related genes survive). Accordingly, the parent reinforces appropriate behavior in the infant with social and comfort rewards. On the other hand, the infant also controls reinforcers that keep her parents attentive; for example, she smiles when she feels satisfied. (Any parent of a 2-month-old will tell you how pleasing—and reinforcing—an infant's smile is.) The smile promotes bonding and reinforces nurturing behavior. The point is that instrumental conditioning is organized here so that both parties get the things they need in order to survive and thrive.

The adaptive nature of instrumental conditioning is also illustrated by a bit of animal behavior I mentioned in the last chapter: Zach's (1978, 1979) study of crows foraging on the beach in British Columbia. Recall that the crows select only large whelks from the beach and then drop them onto preselected rocks from a height of a little over 5 meters. Zach (1979) actually performed some calculations that suggest that the crows had arrived at an optimal solution to eating whelks. The crows learned to choose only whelks whose shells tend to break easily (the big whelks), and the crows tend to drop the whelks from a height that balances the energetic cost of lifting them against the height necessary to break their shells. In this example, animals learned a complex behavior that seems almost perfectly in tune with the environment. Thanks to learning, the crow's behavior is beautifully adapted to the task of feeding on whelks.

The law of effect

In instrumental conditioning, we are always concerned with the relationship between a behavior (R) and a biologically significant event (S*). At an extremely general level, it is easy to show that this learning allows adapta-

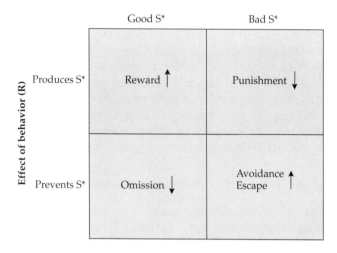

Figure 2.4 The Law of Effect. Inside each cell is the type of learning that results from each combination of an effect of behavior (left) and a type of S* (top). Arrows indicate whether behavior increases or decreases in strength.

tion to the environment. S*s can be either good or bad (that is, having a positive or negative survival value), and Figure 2.4 shows that behaviors can produce or prevent either type of S*. The most famous relation, of course, is the one in which a behavior produces a good S*, such as food, water, or a mate. When a behavior produces a good S*, the behavior usually increases in strength. This is called **reward learning**.

In other cases, behaviors can lead to S*s that are bad or painful. Here, behavior decreases in strength. The effect and the procedure are both known as **punishment**; the bad S* in this case is called a **punisher**. Punishment is quite common, and it can have powerful effects on behavior.

There are two other fundamental behavior-S* relations. When a behavior prevents a bad S*, the behavior increases in strength; this is **avoidance** learning. If a behavior terminates a nasty S* that is already present, it will also increase; this is **escape** learning. The final cell in the table in Figure 2.4 describes a situation in which a behavior prevents the occurrence of a good S*. This relation is sometimes called **omission** training. Not surprisingly, this sort of arrangement usually causes a decrease in the strength of the response.

Figure 2.4 illustrates that instrumental behavior increases or decreases depending on its effect on the environment. As you may remember from Chapter 1, this general rule is called the **law of effect**. (Many other versions of the law emphasize only the reward and punishment cells of the table in Figure 2.4.) The law reminds us that instrumental learning generally works so that animals will maximize benefits (good S*s) and minimize costs (bad S*s). It does not tell us *how* behavior comes to increase or decrease in strength in the various cells (see Figure 2.4); that will be the subject of later chapters. For now, I would only suggest that the law of effect may be just about as beautiful as anything found in nature. If you wanted to create an animal that would be able to adapt to its environment, this is undoubtedly how you would design it.

Reinforcement

We use the term **reinforcement** to describe a situation in which a relation between an R and an S* increases the strength of the response. Reinforcement means strengthening. Both reward learning and avoidance (or escape) learning involve a strengthening of behavior. Since reward learning involves a positive (or good) S*, it is often known as **positive reinforcement**. Since avoidance and escape learning involve a negative (or bad) S*, they are examples of **negative reinforcement**. Notice that the term "negative" describes the badness of the S*, and not its effect on behavior. Negative reinforcement is not the same as punishment.

Shaping

Brand new behaviors can be added to an animal's repertoire through a process called **shaping**. In shaping, behaviors that initially do not exist emerge when approximations of them are reinforced. Many students learn about shaping when they are given a rat in a psychology lab course and are asked to teach it to press a lever in a Skinner box in order for the rat to get a food reward. There is always an immediate difficulty because the rat does not press the lever at first; it is impossible to deliver a reinforcer after a behavior that never happens. The trick is to reinforce closer and closer approximations of the lever-press response. Typically, the student first delivers food to the rat when the rat is anywhere near the lever. Being in the vicinity of the lever therefore increases in frequency, and once it is happening fairly often, the student requires the rat to actually position itself above the lever to earn the next pellet. Once the animal is hovering over the lever, it is more likely that the lever will pressed accidentally. Usually it is, and as a result, food pellets are delivered automatically, the rat begins to lever-press at a steady rate, and the student is able to go out and seek reinforcers of his or her own. By reinforcing successive approximations of the response, it is possible to increase the likelihood of the response so that simple reward learning can take over.

Shaping is quite familiar in humans. For instance, a baby is presumably taught to say *mommy* and *daddy* through such a process. Parents tend to reinforce approximations of these words (*ma* or *da-da*) when they occur, with praise, smiling, and so forth. At the same time, other inappropriate versions are not reinforced. Gradually, the words are spoken with better and better clarity. Explicit shaping techniques have also been used with autistic and developmentally disabled people. For example, Lovaas (1967) has developed techniques for shaping speech in autistic children. Wolf, Risley, and Mees (1964) taught an autistic boy to wear his glasses by reinforcing approximations of this with food (and cues associated with food) over breakfast and at other times when the boy was hungry.

Shaping can be described in a slightly more formal way. Suppose that a rat initially learns to press a lever with an average of about 20 grams of force. Usually, the rat will make a number of presses with forces greater than and less than 20 grams. A possible distribution is illustrated in Figure 2.5 (curve

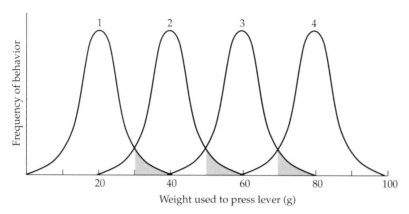

Figure 2.5 Shaping introduces new behaviors. Initially, a rat might press a lever with an average of 20 grams of force (1). By reinforcing successive approximations of a heavier response (shaded areas), new behaviors are introduced while others are extinguished (2 through 4).

1). Notice that a response of 80 grams does not occur at this point. It would be possible to shape that response by reinforcing only extreme scores (the shaded area of the distribution). This causes the distribution to shift to the right, because responses with a weight below the new requirement are not reinforced and become "extinguished." Responses greater than the new requirement also tend to occur, because the rat is not very precise; his responses tend to generalize to different values, a phenomenon known as "induction." At this stage, a new requirement can be introduced, and the distribution again shifts accordingly. The process is repeated until an 80-gram response, which originally had no strength, is performed quite regularly. By reinforcing successive approximations of the 80-gram response, a new behavior is added to the rat's repertoire.

Figure 2.5 could easily be modified to describe learning in high jumpers and pole vaulters, who are being reinforced to jump higher and higher. Of course, the principles of shaping also apply to other behaviors that do not line up so conveniently on a single dimension. The point is, by selectively reinforcing some behaviors and not others, the distribution of behavior can change so that new acts are introduced. Acquisition of any complex behavior could follow the kind of principle illustrated in Figure 2.5.

Shaping does not require a coach or a teacher. It can happen more haphazardly in the natural environment. Consider again Zach's crows as they forage on whelks. At the beginning, a crow might dig among whelks and find one whose shell has been cracked open by waves as they crash on the rocks. The snack might reinforce continued digging by the crow among the whelks. This could increase the likelihood that a whelk is lifted, its shell cracks, and lifting behaviors increase, until one is lifted to a higher point, and an optimum height is reached. Alternatively, a crow digging among the whelks could fly away with a whelk to escape being pestered by another crow. The whelk could drop and break its shell, causing the behavior to be repeated, and differential reinforcement would shape the final solution. A variety of scenarios are possible. The point is that shaping does not require the forethought of a teacher; it occurs all the time in the natural world. It naturally allows the animal to adapt to its environment.

Shaping actually works like evolution by natural selection. In fact, Figure 2.5 could have been taken from a textbook illustrating the natural selection of a trait over generations of animals. If we put "darkness of moths" on the *x*-axis, we would have a graph of the moths-becoming-darker-in-industrialized-England problem we considered earlier. In this case, the distribution would shift over generations because extremes of the distribution have successful offspring; the offspring have a higher distribution of their own. (By the way, shaping and evolution don't just select directionally; for example, they could just as easily select against the extremes of the frequency distribution, etc.) Both evolution and instrumental conditioning involve processes of extinction and shifts in distributions. The parallel has been noted many times before (e.g., Staddon & Simmelhag, 1971). As B. F. Skinner liked to note in the latter part of his career, both natural selection and operant conditioning involve "selection by consequences" (Skinner, 1981). In evolution, the consequence is reproductive success. In instrumental conditioning, the consequence is an S*. By giving animals the ability to learn through instrumental conditioning, nature has given them an extremely important way to continue to adapt their behavior to their environment.

Adaptation in Classical Conditioning

Classical conditioning provides a second way that learning allows adaptation. The point is similar to the one I just made about instrumental conditioning. By learning that a signal predicts an S*, an animal is often able to make a response to the signal before the S* actually happens. In this way, the conditioned response can allow the animal to prepare for the upcoming S* (Domjan, 2005; Hollis, 1982, 1997). Let's take a look at some examples.

Signals for food

First consider Pavlov's original experiment with drooling dogs. It is very easy to overlook the fact that the response that occurs to the signal—salivation—functions to help the dog digest the food, S*. By drooling before food enters the mouth, the dog gets ready to break down the food more readily and digest it more efficiently. It is also easy to miss the fact that salivation was only *part* of what the dog was probably doing in Pavlov's experiment—just a kind of tip of the iceberg. Pavlovian signals for food also elicit many other anticipatory, functional responses: gastric juices begin to flow, enzymes from the pancreas are secreted, and the hormone insulin—needed to get nutrients from the blood into the body's cells—is secreted. Each of these is part of a whole constellation of responses that together can help the dog digest the anticipated food. True to this idea, animals that are given signals for their meals, and therefore have the opportunity to learn to respond this way, are better at gaining nutrients from the meal (Powley, 1977; Woods & Strubbe, 1994).

Classical conditioning also helps animals identify and avoid foods that contain poisonous substances. Rats eat many meals a day, very opportunistically, and they need to learn about all the new foods they find and eat. Some foods may contain poisons that can make the animal sick, and, as I mentioned in Chapter 1, Pavlovian learning provides a way in which they can learn to avoid these foods. In the 1960s, some important experiments by John Garcia and his associates established that rats will learn to reject food flavors that are associated with illness (e.g., Garcia & Koelling, 1966; Garcia, Ervin, & Koelling, 1966). If the rat is given a novel flavor (like vinegar) in a drink, and then made sick (usually with exposure to a drug), it will quickly come to reject the vinegar flavor when it is again offered. The rat learns an "aversion" to the vinegar flavor, and this phenomenon is known as **taste aversion learning**. Taste aversion learning takes the form of a learned rejection of a flavor (S) that is associated with gastric illness (S*).

John Garcia

Humans learn taste aversions, too (e.g., Garb & Stunkard, 1974; Logue, 1985; see also Lamon, Wilson, & Leaf, 1977). I know two or three people who will not go near tequila because of a conditioning experience they had during late adolescence. Tequila is a liquor with a pungent flavor that is sometimes consumed at parties in a way that almost guarantees a taste aversion learning trial (alcohol poisoning). As a consequence of tasting the stuff before and getting sick, my friends have acquired a strong dislike for the flavor of tequila. Taste aversion has many interesting features (see Chapter 6), but for now you can see that it functions to help humans and other animals learn about—and stay away from—bad food and drink.

The "dislike" we learn for foods associated with illness is complemented by a kind of "liking" that is learned for foods associated with good things. Rats will learn to prefer a neutral flavor (like vanilla) if it is associated with the sweet taste of sucrose or saccharin (Fanselow & Birk, 1982). They may also learn to like flavors associated with their recovery from illness (Zahorik & Maier, 1969) and flavors that are associated with nutrients that are important to them, such as calories (e.g., Bolles, Hayward, & Crandall, 1981; Capaldi, Campbell, Sheffer, & Bradford, 1987; Mehiel & Bolles, 1984; Sclafani, 1995). Interestingly, the preference rats learn for flavors associated with calories is affected by how hungry or satiated they are. When the rat is food deprived, it has a stronger preference for a flavor that has been associated with calories than when it is satiated (Fedorchak & Bolles, 1987; see also Fedorchak & Bolles, 1988). By allowing us to learn to like the tastes of foods that contain useful, positive S*s, classical conditioning once again helps us adapt to our environment. Through it we learn to respond appropriately to foods we have experienced before.

Territoriality and reproduction

Feeding is one example of a behavior that is clearly important to survival and fitness. But other kinds of behavior are also important. Through sexual

Karen Hollis

behavior, animals propagate their genes, and through aggression, they defend their resources. Not surprisingly, classical conditioning is involved in these situations, and it is not difficult to see how important it is to the animal's fitness.

Karen Hollis (e.g., 1990) has done some fascinating work on conditioning in the blue gourami (*Trichogaster trichopterus*), a freshwater fish native to southeast Asia and Africa. Male gouramis establish their territories at about the time of the monsoons. They then defend them aggressively against other males, but will allow females to enter and deposit eggs in nests the males have made within the territory. Hollis has shown the advantages of conditioning in both territorial aggression and sexual behavior. In one set of experiments (Hollis, 1984), two males were housed at opposite ends of an aquarium but were never allowed to see each other. Over several days, one of them received trials in which a light was turned on before a rival male was presented (actual fighting between the fish was prevented by a glass barrier). This was meant to establish the light as a Pavlovian cue or signal for the rival male. The other member of the pair received the same lights and exposure to a rival, but these never occurred together in time. Over trials, the signal came to elicit aggressive displays in the first fish. But the interesting test came when the two fish—on opposite sides of the aquarium—met each other for the first time. For both fish, the light was presented just before the encounter. As Figure 2.6 shows, the fish whose light had previously signaled the arrival of another male showed more aggressive biting and tailbeating. Had they actually been allowed to mix, the fish that had the light signal would have won the fight. There was a clear value to having a light signal the approach of a rival before the fight.

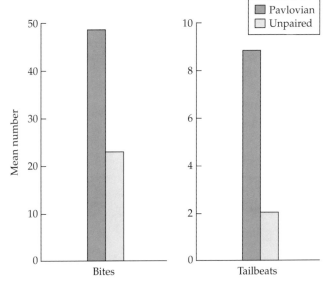

Figure 2.6 When a male blue gourami receives a Pavlovian cue signaling a rival male, he exhibits more aggressive biting and tailbeating. The signal gets the male ready for territorial defense. (After Hollis, 1984.)

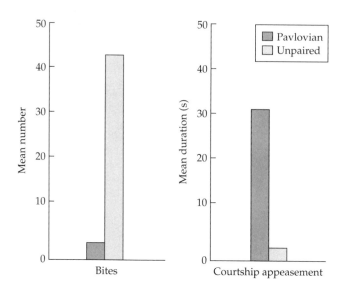

Figure 2.7 When a male blue gourami receives a Pavlovian cue signaling the presence of a female, aggressive biting is reduced and time in a courtship appeasement posture is increased. The signal gets the male ready for courtship. (After Hollis et al., 1989.)

When a female instead of a male enters the territory, the male gourami needs to switch from aggression to a sexy mood. In fact, after some initial aggressive displaying, males in their natural environment do eventually perform a behavior that brings the entering female toward the nest. This behavior can also be conditioned. For example, in another experiment (Hollis, Cadieux, & Colbert, 1989) male-female pairs saw each other regularly for several days. For some pairs, each exposure was signaled by a red light. Other pairs received similar exposures to one another, and similar lights, but exposures and lights were never paired. In a crucial test, all fish received their signals immediately before an encounter. The signal had a clear effect on the males. When the red light had previously signaled a female, it reduced the male's aggressive biting, and increased the time he spent in a courtship appeasement posture (Figure 2.7). There was less of an effect on the females (not shown), although there were other signs that they had learned a signal-mate relationship. The point of these results, though, is that a signal for a mate (as opposed to a rival) prepares the male for reproduction rather than fighting. Amazingly, males that anticipate the arrival of a female this way before copulation also spend more time nest building, spawn quicker, and produce more young than males without the signal (Hollis, Pharr, Dumas, Britton, & Field, 1997). This effect of the signal on actual reproductive success is a dramatic illustration of how conditioning can enhance fitness.

Conditioning of reproductive behavior has been shown in a number of species (Domjan & Hollis, 1988). Michael Domjan and his collaborators did some related work with Japanese quail (*Coturnix coturnix japonica*) (see Domjan, 1994, 1997 for reviews). Males of this species readily learn about stimuli that signal an opportunity to mate. In some experiments (Domjan, Lyons, North, & Bruell, 1986), a red light came on before the male was allowed to copulate with a female that had been released into his cage. A control group

Figure 2.8 A male Japanese quail learns to approach a Pavlovian signal (in this case, a light) that is associated with access to a female. (After Domjan et al., 1986.)

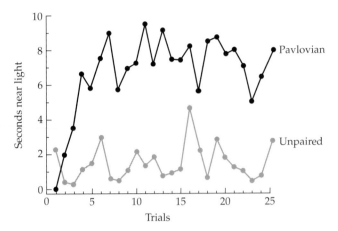

had the same exposure to the light and copulation, but the two events were never paired together. The first group of males quickly learned to approach and stay in the vicinity of the light when it was turned on (Figure 2.8). They were also quicker to grab and mount the female when she was presented. Once again, the signal prepared the male for presentation of the female. Males that receive a signal may actually release more spermatozoa than do control males during copulation (Domjan, Blesbois, & Williams, 1998).

Other experiments indicate that male Japanese quail also learn about the characteristics of the birds they copulate with. For example, when a brown male copulates with a buff-colored female, the male learns to strongly prefer them in the sense that they approach buff-colored females more often than nonbuff-colored females (Nash & Domjan, 1991). In this case, the birds learn to associate the features of the female with copulation (Crawford & Domjan, 1993; Domjan, Akins, & Vandergriff, 1992). Interestingly, there is less evidence of sexual conditioning in the female quail, partly because females seem to be much less interested than males in staying near a member of the opposite sex (Domjan & Hall, 1986)! The difference may be consistent with different behavioral strategies shown by the two sexes. Male Japanese quail benefit from multiple copulations, because each copulation may increase their reproductive success. The same is not true for females; they produce eggs only periodically and fertilize them with sperm stored from an earlier encounter (Domjan, personal communication). Females in this species may therefore maximize their reproductive success with fewer sexual encounters (see Trivers, 1972). Conditioning may play a role primarily where it is most likely to enhance fitness.

Fear

In other situations, animals are confronted with signals for danger. In the laboratory, a signal may be paired with a brief but painful electric shock. Because of conditioning, the signal comes to arouse a complex set of behavioral and physiological responses that we know as "fear." The constellation of responses includes a number of changes in heart rate, blood pressure, and respiration that prepare the animal to defend itself (see Hollis, 1982).

In rodents, one of the main responses to a cue associated with electric shock is "freezing"—the animal stops in its tracks (e.g., Blanchard & Blanchard, 1969; Bouton & Bolles, 1980); see Chapter 10. Although other behaviors, like running away, are available to frightened rats, freezing appears to be the dominant response (Fanselow & Lester, 1988). Rodents freeze when they encounter natural predators (e.g., weasels, cats, and gopher snakes), and being very still has a definite payoff; mice that freeze in the presence of a predator are less likely to be attacked and killed than those that do not (Hirsch & Bolles, 1980). Freezing may reduce predation because predators tend to respond to movement; alternatively, it may cause a predator to pay less attention to the prey, or remove releasers for predation (Suarez & Gallup, 1981). Freezing is an adaptive response to danger signals, because it helps the animal to prepare for a dangerous encounter.

The fear system elicited by danger signals has other adaptive components. In addition to the effects just described, a signal for electric shock induces a state of analgesia. That is, the frightened rat becomes less sensitive to pain (see Fanselow, 1985, for a review). Often, the analgesia is caused by the release of endorphins—natural opiates in the body that can deaden pain. For example, Fanselow and Baackes (1982) showed that rats were less likely to nurse a wounded paw when they were tested in the presence of a signal for electric shock. This suppression was reduced if the rats were injected with naltrexone, a drug that blocks endorphin-induced analgesia. Rats also show a similar analgesia caused by endorphins when they are confronted by a cat (Lester & Fanselow, 1985) or the odor of rats that have been stressed by exposure to an electric shock (Fanselow, 1985). Bolles and Fanselow (1980; see Chapter 10) noted that defense against a predator would be compromised if a wounded animal were to feel pain and consequently limp or lick a wound. Classically conditioned signals for shock allow the animal to prepare for a defensive encounter, because they evoke a whole constellation of adaptive physiological and behavioral responses.

Conditioning with drugs as S*s

Classical conditioning can readily occur with drugs as S*s. This is because any time a drug is ingested, there is an opportunity to associate it (S*) with cues (Ss) that are present at the time. (Drugs are also powerful reinforcers in the instrumental conditioning sense; animals will learn to press levers to get many of the drugs that are abused by humans [e.g., Young & Herling, 1986].) In humans, the places where drugs are taken, the people with whom drugs are taken, or the stimuli involved in drug-taking rituals may presumably be learned as signals for the drug. Classical conditioning can occur anywhere, and the conditioned response is once again adaptive.

Shepard Siegel discovered an important feature of the response acquired in such situations (see Siegel, 1989, for an especially good review). In Pavlov's famous dog experiment, the response (salivation) learned to the

Shepard Siegel

Figure 2.9 The development of drug tolerance (A) can be due to the conditioning of a compensatory conditioned response (B). The learned response becomes stronger after each drug exposure. The observed effect of the drug is its direct effect (a) minus the conditioned response (b). Pavlovian learning is always possible when we are exposed to biologically significant events (S*s).

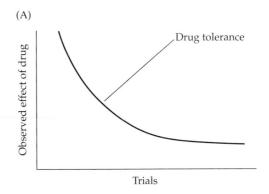

(A)

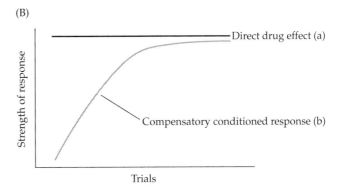

(B)

signal (ringing of a bell) was the same as the one elicited by S* (also salivation). With drug S*s, however, the response to the signal often looks very different from the one elicited by S*. Often it is the opposite, and it functions to cancel the upcoming effect of the drug. This makes adaptive sense, because a dose of a drug can cause an organism to be out of balance. The response functions (again) to preserve equilibrium, or prepare the organism for the upcoming stimulus. In conditioning with drugs, one often observes the acquisition of a **conditioned compensatory response**.

Consider morphine, an opiate that is related to other abused drugs like heroin. Morphine is often given to patients to reduce their pain; thus, one effect of the drug is analgesia. However, this effect typically habituates; the analgesic effect decreases a little with each exposure to the drug (Figure 2.9A). The decrease in the drug effect is called **drug tolerance**. Siegel (1975) proposed that this tolerance might result from classical conditioning. Each time the drug is taken, it could become more strongly associated with environmental cues. If the resulting response to the environmental cues were compensatory (Figure 2.9B), it would subtract from the drug's simple effect. As conditioning increased over trials, the response would begin to reduce the drug's effect.

There is now an impressive amount of evidence for the role of conditioning in drug tolerance. For example, if tolerance is really due to a response elicited by signals for the drug, it should disappear if the drug is tested without those cues. Experiments have confirmed that tolerance to several drugs might work this way. In one of the earliest experiments with morphine (Siegel, 1975), one group of rats received morphine injections in one room (Room A), while another group of rats received the same injections in a different room (Room B). The drug's analgesic effect was tested by putting a subject rat on a "hot plate"—a plate that is heated to an uncomfortable, but not damaging, temperature. In a few seconds, the rat usually lifted and licked its paws, and if it took a long time to do so, it was probably not feeling pain. After tolerance had developed in Siegel's experiment, both groups were tested with the drug in Room A. The two groups had received the same number of previous injections of the drug, but one of the groups now received it in Room A for the first time. As you can see in Figure 2.10, this group showed little tolerance; it was as if they were receiving the drug for the first time. A similar loss of tolerance with a change of contexts has been reported with alcohol (e.g., Crowell, Hinson, & Siegel, 1981; Mansfield & Cunningham, 1980), barbiturates (e.g., Hinson, Poulos, & Cappell, 1982), amphetamines (Poulos, Wilkinson, & Cappell, 1981), and at least one benzodiazepine tranquilizer (midazolam) (King, Bouton, & Musty, 1987). In addition, I will introduce in the next few chapters far more subtle conditioning effects that have been reported in morphine tolerance (Siegel, 1989).

It is sometimes possible to measure the compensatory response directly. If morphine's effect is to reduce pain, perhaps the learned response that develops in the presence of the drug cues is the opposite: an increase in sensitivity to pain. Siegel (1975) demonstrated exactly that. Rats received morphine injections in either Room A or Room B. Then they were tested *without the drug* in Room A. (Siegel substituted an inert injection of saline for the drug.) When no drug was expected in Room A (because it had previously been delivered in Room B), the latency to lift the paw was about 9.1 seconds. But when the drug was expected in Room A, the latency to respond was significantly shorter (4.4 seconds). In a room associated with morphine, the rat appears to be more sensitive to pain.

The learning of a compensatory response is clearly adaptive. For example, tolerance to a drug can protect an organism from possible overdose. This fact has clear implications for drug abuse. If tolerance to drugs occurs as a result of compen-

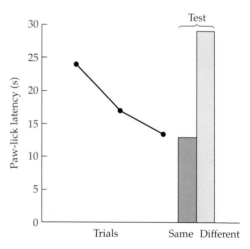

Figure 2.10 Tolerance to morphine's analgesic effect develops quickly over trials (left). Tolerance is present as long as morphine is tested in the presence of cues that have been associated with the drug (Same), but it is lost if the drug is tested in the presence of different cues (Different). Such findings have important implications for understanding drug overdose. (After Siegel, 1975.)

satory response conditioning, then an abuser will be especially vulnerable to overdose in a new context. Some survivors of heroin overdose have actually reported taking the drug under novel circumstances when they overdosed (Siegel, 1984; see also Siegel & Ramos, 2002). But data from self-reports are not entirely reliable, because a subject's memory might be faulty or because he or she might not have noticed other details that could have contributed to the overdose. The most compelling evidence comes from experiments with rats (Siegel, Hinson, Krank, & McCully, 1982; see also Melchior, 1990; Vila, 1989). Siegel et al. (1982) gave two groups of rats 15 doses of heroin in one room. A control group received none. At the end of the experiment, all rats were given a large dose of heroin. A very large percentage of the control subjects—for whom this was the first exposure to heroin—died (96%). A smaller percentage (32%) of drug-exposed subjects, who were tested in the heroin room, died (another example of tolerance). Most important, tolerant rats given the lethal dose in an environment that was different from the one in which they had received the previous injections were about twice as likely to die (64% died) as the animals injected in the usual environment. Outside of the Pavlovian signal of the drug, the rat lost the protection provided by the compensatory response.

There are several points to this discussion involving the role of conditioning in drug tolerance. First, it should be clear that research on conditioning has important implications for human behavior outside the laboratory. Second, you may now see that the response one observes to signals for S*s is not necessarily the same as one observes to S*s (this issue will be considered again in more detail in Chapter 5). The usual cultural stereotype of Pavlov's drooling-dog experiment is an oversimplification. Finally, the important work of Siegel and his collaborators provides yet another illustration of the main theme of this chapter. By being able to anticipate S*, the body can deal more optimally with S*. Classical conditioning fundamentally functions to allow us to adapt to our environment.

Sign tracking

It is possible to describe behavior that results from classical conditioning in a much more general way. Broadly speaking, classical conditioning affects behavior in a manner that complements the law of effect in instrumental conditioning (see Figure 2.4). We can once again classify S*s as good or bad according to survival value. Figure 2.11 describes the four possible relations between an S and a good or bad S*. The table is similar to the table constructed for instrumental conditioning (see Figure 2.4), except we are now concerned with Ss instead of Rs. Another difference is that the term "predict" replaces "produce," because the S in this table does not necessarily cause S* the way the R (in the table in Figure 2.4) does in instrumental conditioning. Nonetheless, Ss and Rs can both predict the occurrence or nonoccurrence of S*s.

When a signal predicts a good S*, animals often begin to approach the signal. This tendency is known as **sign tracking**. The term was originally used to describe the fact that pigeons that receive a brief illumination of a plastic

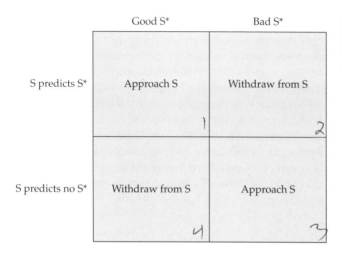

	Good S*	Bad S*
S predicts S*	Approach S	Withdraw from S
S predicts no S*	Withdraw from S	Approach S

Figure 2.11 Sign tracking in Pavlovian learning. Inside each cell is the type of behavior that results from each different combination of S and S*.

disk just before presentation of food will learn to approach and peck the disk when it is illuminated (Brown & Jenkins, 1968; Hearst & Jenkins, 1974). But all sorts of animals will tend to approach signals for all sorts of good S*s; for example, honeybees will approach visual cues associated with sucrose (see Bitterman, 1988, 1996, for reviews), and rats will tend to approach cues associated with food (e.g., Karpicke, Christoph, Peterson, & Hearst, 1977). Chicks will also tend to approach and snuggle with cues for warmth (Wasserman, 1973), and don't forget the male Japanese quail (see Figure 2.8). In fact, you can think of the rat's tendency to learn to "like" flavors associated with good S*s (discussed above) as a kind of approach response; it can also be considered a type of sign tracking.

When signals instead predict bad S*s, animals tend to withdraw from them. Rats will stay away from cues and places associated with an electric shock (e.g., Karpicke, Christoph, Peterson, & Hearst, 1977; Odling-Smee, 1975), and presumably so will humans. Taste aversion learning is also an example of the same general response tendency: Association of a flavor with illness makes the animal withdraw from (and reject) the flavor. This general tendency is sometimes known as **negative sign tracking**. The term describes the behavior (withdrawal) rather than the nature of S*.

Interestingly, if a signal predicts a decrease in the probability of a bad S*, animals will tend to approach it. Rats will approach a location that predicts freedom from shock (Leclerc & Reberg, 1980). In a similar way, rats will tend to approach and like flavors that have been associated with feeling better, the so-called medicine effect (Zahorik & Maier, 1969).

The final cell in the table in Figure 2.11 describes a situation in which a signal predicts a decrease in the probability of a good S*. One way to think of this sort of cue is that it has frustrating effects: A good S* that is otherwise likely to happen is now less likely to occur. Somewhat understandably, animals will tend to withdraw from this sort of signal. Pigeons will move away from an illuminated disk if it predicts a decrease in the probability of food (e.g., Hearst & Franklin, 1977). Rats will also stay away from boxes associated with the absence of expected food (e.g., Daly, 1969).

As we have already seen, Pavlovian signals have many effects in addition to these gross approach and withdrawal tendencies. But notice that these general tendencies, like the law of effect in instrumental conditioning, have a nice function. They may help ensure that animals continue to make contact with good S*s and stay away from bad ones. In a sense, signals that animals learn about through classical conditioning guide behavior in a way that is highly consistent with the response rule represented in instrumental conditioning's law of effect. Once again, if you wanted to create an animal that would be able to adapt to its environment, you would probably consider designing it in this way.

Other Parallels between Signal and Response Learning

Given the similar functions of instrumental and classical conditioning, it is not surprising that they are each sensitive to very similar variations in S*. It is now widely believed that both types of learning follow similar general rules or laws (e.g., Dickinson, 1980; Mackintosh, 1983; Rescorla, 1987). We will examine this issue in more detail in Chapter 10. For now, I will describe four important parallels between them that flow directly from the idea that instrumental and classical conditioning are both designed to optimize the animal's interactions with S*s.

Extinction

In either instrumental or classical conditioning, responding remains high as long as R or S continues to produce or predict S*. However, if S* is dropped from the situation, responding will decline. Pavlov first noticed that once the dog was salivating to the sound of the bell, the salivation response declined if the bell was rung several times without food. In instrumental conditioning, a rat that has been trained to bar-press for a food reward will stop bar-pressing if the reward is no longer presented. Both the procedure of withholding S* after conditioning and the decline in responding that results from that procedure are called **extinction**. Figure 2.12 shows examples of extinction in both instrumental and classical conditioning.

Extinction is an extremely important fact in conditioning and learning; you find it almost as often as you find acquisition itself. (Learning that results from the pairings of R or S with S* is often called **acquisition** to contrast it with extinction.) Extinction is intimately involved in shaping—when reinforcers are applied for specific behaviors, behaviors that are not reinforced are eliminated. In fact, extinction is a crucial process in behavior change. Thanks to extinction, an animal will stop foraging in a particular location or patch if the payoff for foraging drops to zero. Extinction allows the animal to continue to adapt to a changing environment.

Extinction is an important tool in the clinic, because clinical psychologists are often interested in eliminating behaviors that cause problems for

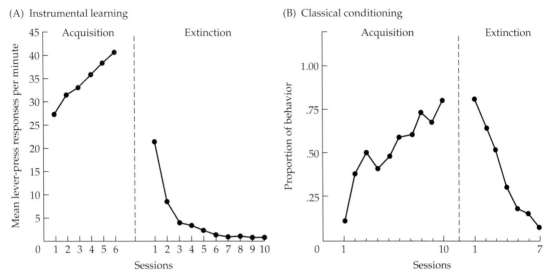

Figure 2.12 Extinction occurs in either instrumental or classical conditioning when S* is no longer delivered after the R or S. (A) After an instrumental (operant) lever-press response is learned (acquisition), rats stop lever-pressing when reward is withheld (extinction). (B) When an auditory cue is paired with food, rats show an excited "head jerk" response (acquisition), which then declines when food is no longer presented (extinction). (A, after Nakajima, Tanaka, Urushihara, & Imada, 2000; B, after Bouton & Peck, 1989.)

the client. For example, a child may be referred to a psychologist because the child keeps acting out and disrupting his or her class. One treatment strategy would be to identify the events that reinforce this behavior (e.g., attention or peer approval) and then eliminate them. By withholding the reinforcers that maintain it, the behavior will theoretically decline. Extinction is also often the method of choice in treating classically conditioned phobias and anxiety disorders. A client's fear of insects, for example, can be treated by exposing the client over and over to the feared stimulus without an aversive consequence (e.g., Wolpe, 1958; Stampfl & Levis, 1967). Such **exposure therapy** is one of the most effective treatments used in reducing learned fears (e.g., Barlow, 2002; Marks, 1978).

It is tempting to conclude that extinction involves destruction of the original learning. However, it is fairly easy to show that a great deal of the original learning actually remains after extinction (Bouton, 1991, 1994a, 2004). One example was provided long ago by Pavlov. If extinction occurs on one day, and then we wait some period of time before the signal is presented again, the response often recovers to some extent. This effect is known as **spontaneous recovery**: An extinguished response can recover with the passage of time. Spontaneous recovery happens in both instrumental and classical conditioning. In both cases, withholding S* causes a decrease in performance, but this does not necessarily reflect a loss of what was originally learned. What an animal does is not always a direct reflection of what it "knows": It is always important to distinguish between learning and performance. This distinction will come up in many ways and in many different chapters.

Extinction is different from two other processes that also make behavior decrease in strength. Extinction appears to be similar to habituation (see Figure 2.3) in that both effects involve a decline in behavior due to repeated exposure to a stimulus. The most important difference between the two processes is that extinction is a decline in a learned behavior, whereas the behavior in habituation is not learned. Extinction is also different from forgetting. When something is forgotten, it is lost because of the simple passage of time. In extinction, behavior is lost because of direct experience with R or S now disconnected from S*. Forgetting and extinction will be discussed in more detail in Chapter 5.

Timing of S*

Since both instrumental and classical conditioning allow the animal to adapt to an upcoming S*, it is not surprising that both types of learning depend on when the critical events (R and S* or S and S*) occur in time. As a general rule, the closer two events occur together, the more likely the animal will behave as if the two events were associated. Learning is best when the events are contiguous, a fact that was appreciated by the British Empiricists, such as Locke, Hume, and others (see Chapter 1).

Instrumental conditioning works best when the behavior is followed immediately by S*. People experienced with the shaping of behaviors in either animals or humans know that a delay of a few seconds can ruin the effects of a reinforcer. We are always engaging in a stream of different activities. If the reinforcer is delivered even a few seconds after a target response, it is likely that some other behavior will be reinforced instead. Timing of S* is also very important in punishment. For best results, the punisher must be applied quickly. Figure 2.13 illustrates the effect on performance of introducing a delay between the response and reinforcers and punishers.

Timing is also important in classical conditioning. As a general rule, the animal will respond more to S if S has preceded S* by only a short delay. One of the most interesting facts about classical conditioning is that while this rule is always true, the intervals between S and S* that allow learning differ quite a bit for different instances of conditioning. For example, in fear conditioning, a rat will learn to be afraid of a tone even if the tone goes off tens of seconds before an electric footshock (S*) is presented. Apparently, intervals of much longer than this prevent much learning from occurring. In contrast, when rats are learning taste aversions, a delay of several hours between the flavor (S) and getting sick (S*) still allows learning to occur. The discrepancy is consistent with the view that taste aversion learning is adapted to allow animals to learn about slow-acting poisons. I will examine some implications of this view in Chapter 6. For now, however, it is important to notice that even in taste aversion learning, conditioning is still better the closer that S and S* occur together in time (Figure 2.14).

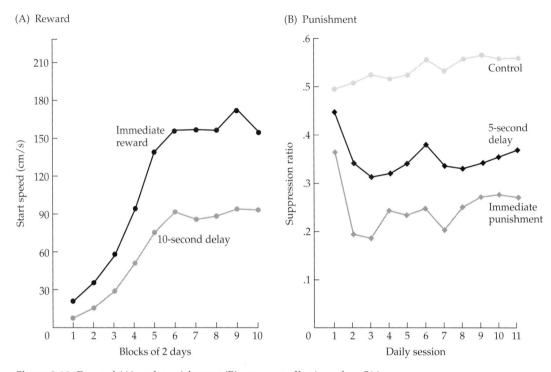

Figure 2.13 Reward (A) and punishment (B) are most effective when S* is presented immediately after the response—rather than delayed. (After Capaldi, 1978; Church, 1969.)

One way to think of the effects of S* timing on learning is that learning is designed to uncover the probable "causes" of S* (e.g., Dickinson, 1980). Instrumental conditioning works so that animals will repeat behaviors that cause good S*s (reward learning) and stop doing behaviors that cause bad S*s (punishment); an act that precedes an S* by a relatively brief time interval is more likely to have caused S* than an act that occurred more remotely in time. A similar argument works in classical conditioning. The rat learns to be afraid of a tone that is a plausible signal (or cause) of a footshock. It might also reject a flavor that has preceded illness by an hour or two; once again timing is important, but here it is likely that a food consumed an hour or two ago contained a poison that is the cause of the present illness. All types of learning are sensitive to the interval between R or S and S* because causes of S* tend to happen recently in time. Notice that we are merely thinking about what learning is designed to do; it is not necessary to believe that the animal is consciously or actively seeking causes. Nevertheless, in learning, timing of S* is (almost) everything.

Size of S*

Behavior resulting from instrumental and classical conditioning is also strongly affected by the size or value of S*. In general, the bigger (or longer

(A) Fear conditioning in rats

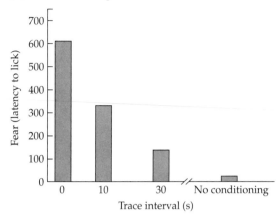

Trace interval (s)

(B) Autoshaping in pigeons

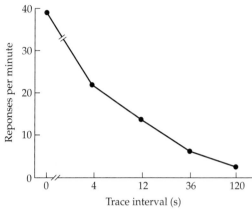

Trace interval (s)

Figure 2.14 Classical conditioning is better when the interval between S and S* is minimal. (A) Fear conditioning in rats, where a tone was paired with an electric shock that was delayed by 0, 10, or 30 seconds. (B) Autoshaping in pigeons, where pigeons were presented an illuminated disk for 12 seconds that was then followed by food after various intervals. Note the log scale on the x-axis. (C) Flavor aversion learning in which rats received a drink of saccharin either alone (Control) or followed by X-irradiation (which made them sick) after various delays. In the test, rats were given a choice between saccharin and water. Notice that the intervals permitting learning depend on the example of conditioning—taste aversion learning works well when *hours* intervene between S and S*. (A, after Marlin, 1981; B, after Lucas, Deich, & Wasserman, 1981; C, after Smith & Roll, 1967.)

(C) Taste aversion in rats

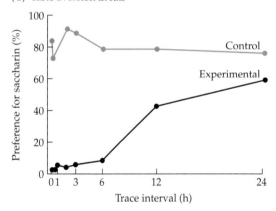

Trace interval (h)

or more intense) the S*, the more powerful its impact on behavior. This is a direct effect of the fact that the function of either instrumental or classical conditioning is to optimize interactions with S*—the bigger the S*, the more of it there is to interact with.

With few exceptions, larger positive S*s, lead to stronger overall behavior. For example, rats will run down alleyways at faster and faster speeds when larger and larger rewards await them at the end (e.g., Bower, 1961; Crespi, 1942; Figure 2.15). These sorts of results are consistent with the general belief that people will work harder and more productively for larger rewards. Similarly, the stronger an aversive S* is, the stronger its punishing effect will be (e.g., Azrin, 1960; Camp, Raymond, & Church, 1967). As a first approximation, your intuitions about how the size of S* affects behavior is accurate: Instrumental action is directly affected by the size of S*.

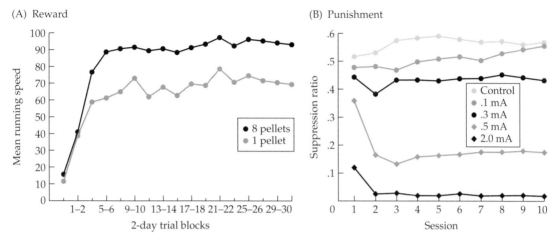

Figure 2.15 Bigger S*s cause better response learning. (A) Reward learning in rats in a runway. (B) Punishment of lever-pressing in rats with different intensities of electric shock. (A, after Bower, 1961; B, after Camp et al., 1967.)

Consistent with the theme of this chapter, the bigger the S*, the more responding one also observes in classical conditioning. Larger positive S*s produce stronger appetitive behaviors (e.g., Holland, 1979; Morris & Bouton, 2006); similarly, larger negative S*s produce stronger fears (e.g., Annau & Kamin, 1961; Holland, 1979; Morris & Bouton, 2006; Figure 2.16). The size of S* has potent effects on behavior that results from both response and stimulus learning.

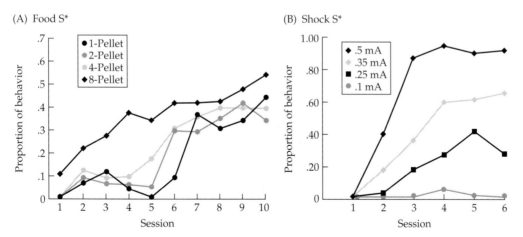

Figure 2.16 Bigger S*s cause better stimulus learning, too. (A) Classical conditioning with a food S*. When an auditory cue signals food, rats show an excited "head jerk" response. (B) Conditioning with an electric footshock S*. Rats freeze in the presence of a cue signaling an electric shock. (A, after Morris & Bouton, 2006; B, after Holland, 1979.)

Preparedness

Signal and response learning are also alike in that some combinations of events are learned more readily than others. Animals behave as if evolution has "prepared" them to associate certain events or stimuli.

This idea owes itself most importantly to the pioneering work of John Garcia. In one of the most important papers published on classical conditioning, Garcia and Koelling (1966) examined the rat's ability to associate two types of Ss (a taste stimulus or an audiovisual stimulus) with two types of S*s (an illness or an electric shock). In the conditioning trials, rats drank a flavored solution from a water bottle; at the same time, every time their tongue lapped at the drinking spout, it caused a click and a flash of light (Figure 2.17). (The audiovisual stimulus is known as "bright-noisy water.") Rats in different groups then received either an electric footshock or nausea after exposure to this complex stimulus. Finally, the rats were tested with either the taste or the bright-noisy water alone.

The results were striking. The rats that were made ill during conditioning showed a strong rejection of taste, but little rejection of bright-noisy water. Conversely, the rats that received an electric footshock during conditioning showed the opposite pattern: They rejected bright-noisy water but not taste. Similar results have been obtained when taste and auditory cues were given to separate groups during conditioning (Domjan & Wilson, 1972). It is not possible to claim that the two Ss differed in salience; each was associated better than the other with one of the S*s. Similarly, it is not possible to say that the S*s differed in their salience; each was associated better than the other with one of the Ss. What matters is the specific *combina-*

(A)

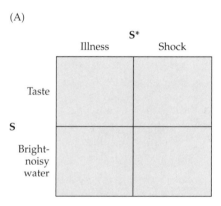

(B)

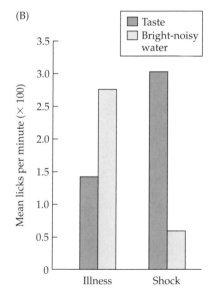

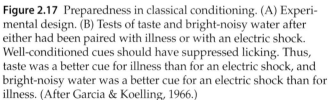

Figure 2.17 Preparedness in classical conditioning. (A) Experimental design. (B) Tests of taste and bright-noisy water after either had been paired with illness or with an electric shock. Well-conditioned cues should have suppressed licking. Thus, taste was a better cue for illness than for an electric shock, and bright-noisy water was a better cue for an electric shock than for illness. (After Garcia & Koelling, 1966.)

tion of S and S*. When sick, the rat behaves as if it thinks "It must have been something I ate" (see Chapter 1).

As I mentioned in the last chapter, the rat's tendency to associate tastes with illness (and external cues with shock) appears to be built-in at birth. In an ingenious experiment, Gemberling and Domjan (1982) showed essentially the same pattern of results in rats that received conditioning when they were only one day old. Rats of this age have both their ears and eyes closed, and so it was not possible to use audiovisual cues. Gemberling and Domjan (1982) therefore substituted texture (a rough cloth or the slippery interior of a milk carton) for the bright-noisy water. Compatible results were obtained; preparedness is evident before much experience with various kinds of stimuli can have an impact. The idea that the associative predilection is inborn is also supported by the fact that the bobwhite quail—a bird that feeds during the daytime and swallows seeds whole—appears to associate illness with visual cues more readily than with taste (Wilcoxon, Dragoin, & Kral, 1971).

The rat's tendency to associate illness with taste seems to make sense from an evolutionary perspective. Rats are omnivores whose diet varies quite a lot; they feed opportunistically and mostly at night. Foods can usually be identified by flavor, and the rat must be able to learn about and identify the foods that contain slow-acting poisons. Given this scenario, rats that were able to avoid flavors associated with poisons would have a selective advantage over rats that could not make the same association (e.g., Rozin & Kalat, 1971).

Preparedness also appears to influence instrumental conditioning, where the reward sometimes fails to increase the desired behavior. Keller and Marian Breland made a career of shaping animals to do interesting things for television cameras (among other things). Keller Breland had been a student of B. F. Skinner's. However, in a classic paper, the Brelands (Breland & Breland, 1961) documented some entertaining difficulties that they had encountered while training animals to do certain things. For example, they once tried to train a pig for a bank commercial to put a wooden coin in a piggy bank. Unfortunately, despite intensive and heroic efforts, the pig never learned to put the coin in the bank—instead, it began rooting the coin around the floor of the pigpen with its snout. The Brelands noted that rooting is one of the pig's natural foraging behaviors. (I will return to intrusions of this sort of "misbehavior" in Chapter 10.) In a similar vein, Bolles (e.g., 1972b) noted that, although it is easy to train a rat to press a lever for food, it is much more difficult to teach it to perform the same response to avoid shock. Stevenson-Hinde (1973) showed that young male chaffinches learned a pecking response more readily when they got food as a reward than when the reward was a tape recording of an adult chaffinch singing. (Adult song was effective at reinforcing the birds to perch on a twig.)

Sara Shettleworth performed some of the most systematic research on preparedness in a series of studies with golden hamsters (e.g., Shettleworth, 1975, 1978; Shettleworth & Juergensen, 1980). When each of several natural behaviors was followed by a food reward, dramatically different results

Sara Shettleworth

Figure 2.18 Preparedness in instrumental conditioning. Some of the hamster's natural behaviors are easier to associate with food than are other behaviors. The left part of the graph shows acquisition and the right part shows extinction. See text for definitions. (After Shettleworth, 1975.)

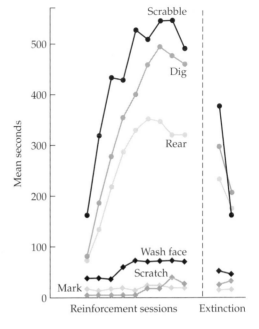

were obtained. For example, rearing in the middle of the test arena, rearing while moving the paws rapidly at the walls ("scrabbling"), and digging in the sawdust on the floor all increased when paired with a food reward. But face washing, scratching, and scent marking behaviors did not (Figure 2.18). The same behaviors also differed in how easily they were punished by an electric shock (Shettleworth, 1978), although the success of punishment was not completely predictable from the success of reinforcement with a food reward. In principle, different R-S* combinations may fail to produce learning for any of a variety of reasons (see Domjan, 1983, for a review). But the available evidence suggests that certain combinations of Rs and S*s are learned more readily than others.

Does preparedness exist in humans? Yes, probably. Humans that have survived the tequila ritual I mentioned earlier tend to associate the flavor of tequila—and not the friends or the shot glass that were also present—with alcohol poisoning. ("It must have been something I drank.") As is the case with most anecdotal evidence, though, other interpretations of this are also possible—for example, the flavor of tequila may merely be the most novel and distinctive of the available cues. Nonetheless, other data do suggest preparedness in humans. Seligman (1971) noted that snake and spider phobias are especially prevalent in the clinic; this may suggest preparedness in human fear-learning, because snakes and spiders are presumably no more likely to be paired with pain than are knives or electrical outlets. In laboratory experiments, people do associate an electric shock more readily with fear-relevant stimuli (slides of snakes, spiders, or angry faces) than with fear-irrelevant stimuli (flowers, mushrooms, or happy faces) (Öhman, Dimberg, & Ost, 1985; see Öhman & Mineka, 2001, for one review). (Interestingly, monkeys also associate fearful experiences, excited by the sight of another monkey acting fearfully, with snake or crocodile models—but not with flowers or toy bunnies [Cook & Mineka, 1989, 1990].) People with a strong fear of snakes or spiders also overestimate their correlation with shock in experiments in which shocks are equally associated with relevant and irrelevant stimuli (Tomarken, Mineka, & Cook, 1989). Susan Mineka (1992) has suggested that these tendencies may reflect the influence of "evolutionary memories" that, along with other cognitive biases shown by fearful subjects, have an important impact on human emotional disorders. Not all combinations of Ss and S*s or Rs and S*s are equally learnable. It is useful to view human learning and behavior—like that of other animals—within its evolutionary context.

Summary

1. Behaviors may be selected by evolution if they have survival value. Such behaviors are innate in the sense that they have no obvious original basis in learning.

2. Evolution is a process that allows adaptation between generations; learning, on the other hand, is a process that allows adaptation within an animal's lifetime.

3. Through instrumental conditioning, animals learn to increase their contact with good S*s (S*s with positive survival value) and decrease their contact with bad S*s (S*s with negative survival value). The law of effect describes this state of affairs. Behaviors increase if they produce good S*s (reward learning) or prevent bad S*s (avoidance or escape learning). They decrease if they produce bad S*s (punishment) or prevent good S*s (omission). The term "reinforcement" means strengthening; it is used to describe either reward learning (positive reinforcement) or avoidance and escape learning (negative reinforcement).

4. Shaping allows new behaviors to be added to an animal's repertoire. In shaping, new behaviors emerge because successive approximations of the behavior are differentially reinforced. Shaping does not necessarily require a teacher, and it resembles natural selection in the sense that behavior is selected by its consequences.

5. In classical conditioning, animals learn to respond to signals for S*. The response is adaptive because it helps the animal optimize its interaction with the upcoming S*. Signals for food evoke responses that help the animal digest the meal and identify good and bad food sources. Signals for rivals and for mates evoke responses that prepare the animal for a fight or a sexual encounter. Danger signals evoke a constellation of physiological and behavioral responses that allow the animal to defend itself against the impending aversive S*. Conditioning with drug S*s allows the learning of adaptive responses, like the compensatory conditioned response, that help an animal maintain equilibrium.

6. Through classical conditioning, animals also learn to approach signals for good S*s as well as those that predict the absence of bad S*s; they also with-

draw from signals that predict the presence of bad S*s or the absence of good S*s. This tendency is called sign tracking, and it complements the law of effect in helping animals to increase or decrease their contact with events that have either positive or negative survival value.

7. Extinction occurs in both instrumental and classical conditioning. It is a decline in responding that occurs when S* no longer follows the signal or behavior that previously predicted it. Extinction allows the animal to continue to adapt as the environment changes. It is also useful in reducing unwanted behaviors in the clinic.

8. Classical and instrumental conditioning are both sensitive to the timing and the magnitude of S*. Learning is best when S* follows the signal or the behavior quickly and when S* is large or intense.

9. Evolution may prepare animals to associate some events more readily than others. Such "preparedness" is evident in both classical and instrumental conditioning. This phenomenon was discovered in aversion learning experiments: Taste is a good signal for illness but a bad one for an electric shock, while audiovisual cues are bad signals for illness but good cues for shock.

Key Terms

natural selection
fitness
ethology
fixed action patterns
releaser
sign stimuli
artificial selection
habituation
reward learning
punishment
punisher
avoidance
escape
omission
law of effect

reinforcement
positive reinforcement
negative reinforcement
shaping
taste aversion learning
conditioned compensatory response
drug tolerance
sign tracking
negative sign tracking
extinction
acquisition
exposure therapy
spontaneous recovery
preparedness

Chapter

3

The Nuts and Bolts of Conditioning

CHAPTER 2 EXAMINED WHY IT MAKES SENSE that classical and instrumental conditioning should occur and why they are so important. We also had a chance to look at many different examples of these two fundamental forms of learning. One of the themes was that they have similar functions. This new chapter begins by asking a different kind of question: How do these types of learning actually work? This is the question that has interested most of the researchers who have gone into the lab to study learning.

This chapter takes an initial look at the mechanisms of classical conditioning. As we get into this type of learning, it is worth remembering that conditioning experiments are designed to create a well-controlled situation that is *representative* of associative learning in general. By studying learning in a relatively simple system, we hope to arrive at principles that may describe associative learning in general. (I will consider some challenges to this idea in Chapter 6.) Don't forget that the modern view is that classical conditioning and instrumental learning reflect similar learning processes. In both, animals behave as if they have learned to associate events (either Ss or Rs) with S*s. It makes sense to first consider classical conditioning because it is often easier to study: The experimenter can present S and S* whenever he or she wants to. (In instrumental conditioning, R occurs at the whim of the subject and is not entirely under the experimenter's control.) If we can be precise about presenting Ss and S*s, we may hope to arrive at some fairly precise laws that describe the learning processes represented in both classical and instrumental conditioning.

As we dig a little deeper into conditioning, I hope you will appreciate that, although it looks a little simple, it is not very simple-minded. By the end of this chapter, you may begin to realize that conditioning is probably not what you think it is (Rescorla, 1988b).

The Basic Conditioning Experiment

Pavlov's experiment

Pavlov's infamous experiment itself simplified some observations made by Wolfsohn, an associate of Pavlov's who was working in Pavlov's laboratory (Boakes, 1984). Wolfsohn was studying how the dog salivated in response to a number of different things that were put into its mouth. Perhaps not surprisingly, the dog salivated in response to things like sand and pebbles as well as food. Wolfsohn noticed that, after sand had been put in the dog's mouth a few times, the sight of the sand alone was enough to cause some salivation. The dog had learned about sand; it had associated the visual features of sand with the fact that it causes salivation. Most objects consist of a number of features (visual cues, tactile sensations, etc.) that can be associated when we learn about the object. Object-learning is an example of associative learning.

To study the phenomenon more thoroughly, it was useful to design a procedure in which the initially neutral cue (the sight of the sand) could be separated from the stimulus (sand in the mouth) that actually caused the salivation. Separating the neutral and causal stimuli was the beginning of the conditioning experiment that we know so well today in which a ringing bell and food are paired on each of a number of conditioning trials.

Pavlov developed the procedure, discovered many of its most important effects, and introduced the terms that are still used to describe it. These terms may seem unnecessarily confusing at first, but they are a kind of "necessary evil" if you want to read and think more about classical conditioning. The idea was to create a neutral description of the experiment that could be used to describe *any* experiment on any example of conditioning. Pavlov noticed that the biologically significant stimulus, food, had the power to elicit salivation unconditionally. That is, drooling to food did not depend on (i.e., was not conditional on) the dog having been through the experiment. Because of this, the food is known as the **unconditional stimulus**, or **US**. (In early translations of Pavlov's work, the term unconditio*ned* was used instead of unconditio*nal*.) Because the drooling response to food was not conditional on the experiment, drooling to the food was similarly known as the **unconditional response**, or **UR**. These terms are summarized in Figure 3.1.

The sound of a bell comes to elicit salivation as a result of the conditioning experience; its control over the response is "conditional" on the conditioning experience. The ringing bell is therefore known as the **conditional stimulus**, or **CS**. (Once again, early translations of Pavlov had this as conditio*ned* stimulus, a term that is also still used today.) The response to the sound

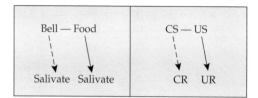

Figure 3.1 The crucial events in Pavlov's famous experiment (left) and the terms we now use to describe them (right). Pavlov invented the terms, which are not pretty, but are widely used today because scientists need a consistent language to discuss all examples of classical conditioning.

of a bell itself—also conditional on the conditioning experience—is naturally known as the **conditional response**, or **CR**.

Pavlov actually used an interesting variety of cues as conditional stimuli—his dogs learned to salivate to things like bubbling noises, whistles, metronomes, and rotating discs. Early on, Pavlov also established that conditioning with one CS could often **generalize** to other similar CSs. Thus, after conditioning with a tone of a certain pitch, animals will also respond to other CSs of similar pitch. (Responding to similar cues is called **generalization**.) Pavlov actually covered a lot of important and interesting ground in his work. But for better or worse, one of his most lasting contributions is the vocabulary that is still used to describe conditioning experiments. It is worth rehearsing the terms US, UR, CS, and CR a little bit before you read anything in the modern literature on classical conditioning.

What is learned in conditioning?

Explanations of conditioning have usually assumed that the subject learns an association between two of the events in the experiment. The main controversy has been which two events? When psychologists in America first became interested in conditioning in the early twentieth century, they assumed that the dog learned to associate the bell with salivation (the CS with the UR). The bell and drooling to the food occurred together in time, and since the reflex is all about connections between stimulus and response, it was natural to assume that there was an S-R association, or **S-R learning**. Pavlov himself, however, had actually taken a different view. He assumed that the dog came to associate the bell and food, and that the bell eventually elicited drooling because it had been associated with the food (Figure 3.2). For Pavlov, the ringing bell became a substitute for the food in controlling the drooling reflex; his idea is known today as the **stimulus substitution** theory. The crucial association was between two stimuli: **S-S learning**.

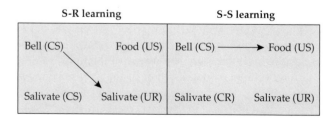

Figure 3.2 Two associations can be learned in a classical conditioning experiment. At left, the organism might associate a stimulus (the CS) and a response (the drooling UR)—so-called S-R learning. At right, the organism might associate a stimulus (the CS) with another stimulus (the US)—so-called S-S learning.

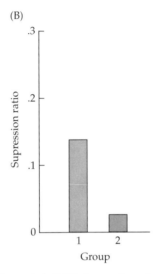

(A)

Group	Phase 1	Phase 2	Test
1	L — Klaxon	Klaxon, klaxon, ...	L?
2	L — Klaxon	—	L?

(B)

Figure 3.3 (A) Design of Rescorla's (1973a) experiment suggesting that rats associate CS and US in Pavlovian conditioning experiments. In the experiment, a light (L) was paired with a loud klaxon in two groups of rats. This caused the conditioning of fear to the light. In the next phase, the klaxon was presented over and over again to Group 1 so that fear of it became habituated. When the light was tested in both groups it also elicited less fear in Group 1. (B) Results of testing. The measure of conditioning is the suppression ratio—less fear is indicated by a *higher* ratio. (After Rescorla, 1973a.)

Research that has followed suggests that the association is most often S-S, and although both S-S and S-R learning are possible, most experiments suggest that the animal has learned to associate the CS with the US (e.g., see Rescorla, 1978). For example, in one experiment with rats, Robert Rescorla (1973a) conditioned a fear of a light (L) by pairing the light with the sound of a klaxon—a very loud stimulus that arouses fear. After fear conditioning was complete, one group of rats received repeated exposure to the klaxon alone in a second phase (Figure 3.3). The exposure habituated the rats' fear of the klaxon; at the end of this phase, the klaxon no longer frightened the rats. A control group did not receive habituation. At the end of the experiment, both groups were tested for their fear of the light. The rats for which the klaxon had been habituated were less afraid of the light.

Why should habituation of the klaxon cause fear of the *light* to change? The klaxon was never paired with the light again after fear of it had been habituated. Rescorla argued that learning in the first phase must have been

S-S: The rats first learned to associate the light with the klaxon. As a result, the light aroused fear because it activated a representation of the klaxon in memory. The habituation phase then taught the rats that the klaxon was not all that bad after all. During testing, the light activated the *modified* klaxon representation, and the rats experienced less fear. Similar results have been produced in several other situations (e.g., Holland, 1990a; 2005; Holland & Rescorla, 1975a; Holland & Straub, 1979; Rescorla, 1974). According to modern thinking about classical conditioning, conditioning typically produces an association between the CS and the US, although S-R learning does sometimes occur (e.g., Rizley & Rescorla, 1972; see also Chapter 10).

Variations on the basic experiment

There are two variations on the simple conditioning experiment that further allow a CS to elicit a response even though it has never been directly associated with a US. Once a CS has been fairly well conditioned, the CS itself can serve as a "US" and support new conditioning. The effect, known as **second-order** (or **higher-order**) **conditioning**, is illustrated in Figure 3.4. In this example, a light CS is first paired with a food US until the light elicits a conditioned response quite reliably. Then, in the second phase, a new CS (a tone, T) is now paired with the light. As a result of these trials, the tone now elicits a CR, even though it has never been paired directly with a US. This phenomenon has been shown in several conditioning arrangements (e.g., Rescorla, 1980).

Figure 3.4 also illustrates a related phenomenon that is easy to confuse with second-order conditioning. In **sensory preconditioning**, two conditional stimuli are first paired, and then one is separately associated with a US. In the illustration, a tone and a light are paired in an initial phase. Then, the light is separately associated with food. In a third test phase, the experimenter tests the subject's response to the *tone*. In this arrangement, the tone will elicit a CR. Like second-order conditioning, sensory preconditioning suggests that conditioning can occur even when the CS is not paired directly

Second-order conditioning

Phase 1	Phase 2	Test
L — Food	T — L	T?

Sensory preconditioning

Phase 1	Phase 2	Test
T — L	L — Food	T?

Figure 3.4 Second-order conditioning and sensory preconditioning. Both are important because they are ways organisms can come to respond to a CS (in this case a tone, T) that has never been directly paired with the US (food).

with a US. In fact, one of the interesting things about sensory preconditioning is that the target CS (the tone) is also never paired with the response
it eventually evokes. In second-order conditioning, the tone could be associated with a response elicited by the light, but in sensory preconditioning
the same two stimuli are paired before the light ever has a reason to elicit
the CR. Because of this, sensory preconditioning is often thought to be a case
of pure S-S learning.

These phenomena provide ways that stimuli can control conditioned
responding without ever being paired directly with a US. Generalization,
second-order conditioning, and sensory preconditioning can expand the
range of stimuli that can affect behavior even after a fairly specific conditioning experience. They are worth keeping in mind when you consider how
behaviors, like some fear responses that might be seen in a clinic, can arise
through simple conditioning (for related discussions, see Mineka, 1985, and
Davey, 1992).

Methods for Studying Classical Conditioning

It is useful to think broadly about conditioning so that you get into the practice of applying laboratory findings to behavior in the real world. But when
scientists investigate the specific details of conditioning, it is important to
have a standard set of methods that can be used by different investigators
working in different laboratories. That way, researchers know that they are
studying the same problem, which makes it easier to arrive at an agreement
on important details. Classical conditioning research has focused on several
standard examples of conditioning that are often referred to as **conditioning preparations**. The range of responses studied reinforces the point that
conditioning controls many different types of behavior in many different
species.

Eyeblink conditioning in rabbits

One important conditioning preparation involves the eyeblink reflex in rabbits. In this method, rabbits are initially habituated to mild restraint in a
stock that keeps them in one place (Figure 3.5). The stock can then be put in
a soundproof enclosure that reduces extraneous noise and light. The rabbit is then exposed to brief (typically about one-half second) tones and light
CSs that are paired with USs that consist of either a puff of air to the cornea
of the eye or a mild electric shock (usually about a tenth of a second) delivered near the eye. These cause the rabbit to blink. And, after a number of
trials, the rabbit begins to blink in response to the CS (see Figure 3.5). The
response that many investigators actually measure is closure of the nictitating membrane—a third inner eyelid rabbits have that sweeps across the
eyeball when the rabbit blinks. The eyeblink conditioning method was
developed and promoted by Isadore Gormezano and his associates, who
did an impressive amount of work uncovering the variables that affect the
conditioning (e.g., Gormezano, Kehoe, & Marshall, 1983).

(A)

(B)

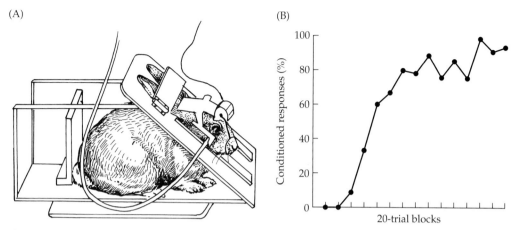

Figure 3.5 Eyeblink conditioning in rabbits. (A) The experimental set-up for measuring nictitating membrane conditioning. (B) Typical acquisition curve. (A, after Gormezano et al., 1983; B, after Weidemann and Kehoe, 2005.)

The eyeblink CR is easy to measure and observe. Conditioning proceeds so that, with more and more pairings of the CS and US, the CS comes to elicit the eyeblink just before the US is about to occur. An interval of about four-tenths of a second between the onset of the CS and the onset of the US is about optimal for getting good eyeblink responding to the CS. With typical procedures, the conditioned response itself begins to happen regularly after a few hundred CS-US pairings. One of the attractive features of the eyeblink method is that the conditioned response is simpler than the types of responses that are measured in other conditioning preparations (see below). This simplicity, plus the fact that so much systematic behavioral research has been done with the eyeblink method, has made it possible for significant headway to be achieved in understanding the neural basis of conditioning and learning (e.g., Christian & Thompson, 2003; Gormezano, Prokasy, & Thompson, 1987; Steinmetz, 1996; Steinmetz, Gluck, & Solomon, 2001; Thompson, 1986; Thompson & Krupa, 1994).

Fear conditioning in rats

Classical conditioning has been thought to control emotional responses ever since John B. Watson and the early days of behaviorism. Recall that Watson and Rayner (1920) showed that Albert, a one-year old infant in a daycare setting, learned to be afraid of a white rat when the rat was paired with the banging of a steel rail. Watson and Rayner showed that Albert acquired a fear of the rat that generalized to other white furry objects. Conditioning is still widely assumed to be a basis for the learning of fears and phobias.

In the laboratory, fear conditioning is now typically conducted with rats as the subjects rather than as the conditional stimuli. A time-honored method is known as **conditioned suppression** or the **conditioned emotional response**

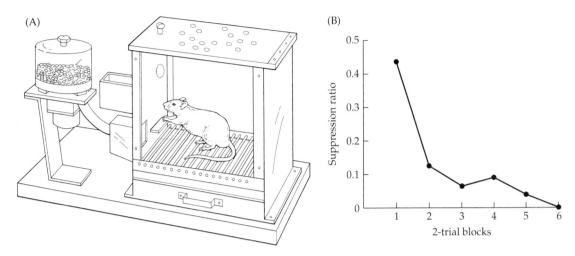

Figure 3.6 Conditioned suppression in rats. (A) The experimental set-up. (B) Typical acquisition curve. The measure of conditioning is the suppression ratio (see text for further explanation). (After Hall, Prados, and Sansa, 2005.)

(CER) technique. The rat is first trained to press a bar in a standard Skinner box for a food reward (Figure 3.6). Then, after the rat is pressing the bar at a regular rate, the experimenter presents a light or tone or noise CS, and this stimulus is paired with a brief (0.5 second) and mild electric shock delivered through the floor of the box. (The typical shock feels like a tingling sensation to a human's hand). The lever-press response has nothing to do with the presentation of the CS or US. However, after the CS has been paired with shock several times, the rat will stop pressing when the CS is turned on. The extent to which bar-pressing is suppressed by presentation of the CS is a measure of conditioned fear. Often, the rat stops bar-pressing because the CS elicits freezing (e.g., Bouton & Bolles, 1980), which has become an important measure of conditioning in its own right (e.g., Kim & Fanselow, 1992; Maren & Fanselow, 1998; Rudy & O'Reilly, 1999).

In the conditioned suppression situation, researchers use a standard technique to express the extent to which the CS suppresses the bar-press response. First, they count the number of bar presses made during the CS and during an equal time period just before the CS (often called the "pre-CS period"). Then they calculate a **suppression ratio** by taking the CS count and dividing it by the sum of responses made during the pre-CS period and the CS. The ratio has a value of 0.5 when the CS does not change the bar-press rate, but it goes down to zero as the CS becomes more and more effective at suppressing the bar-press rate (see Figure 3.6).

In this method, the CS durations are relatively lengthy, ranging from 30 seconds to three minutes. In typical procedures, conditioning appears to be quite strong after only four to eight conditioning trials (see Figure 3.6); it is fairly easy to show significant learning after only one CS-US pairing. Conditioning can also occur when CS and US are separated by many seconds (e.g., Kamin, 1965). The picture is somewhat different from the one presented in eyeblink conditioning. Nonetheless, it is interesting to observe that the basic variables that affect the strength of conditioning are similar in the two methods.

Conditioned suppression has been an important method for several reasons. Fear conditioning continues to have implications for cognitive-behavioral treatments of anxiety in clinical psychology (e.g., Bouton, 2002; Bouton et al., 2001; Mineka, 1985, 1992). In addition, as we will see in Chapter 9, conditioned emotions are worth studying because they play a role in motivating instrumental behavior. Finally, a number of conditioning's most important phenomena were first discovered and investigated with conditioned suppression. This method was first used by W. K. Estes and B. F. Skinner (1941), but in the 1960s it became an important method for studying conditioning thanks to the work of Leon Kamin (e.g., 1965; 1969) and Robert Rescorla (e.g., 1968b).

Autoshaping in pigeons

In the previous chapter, I noted that animals approach signals for good unconditional stimuli—a conditioned behavior known as "sign tracking." The first systematically investigated example of sign tracking is known as **autoshaping**. Brown and Jenkins (1968) were faced with the task of getting a group of pigeons to learn to peck a plastic disk on the wall in order to get food (Figure 3.7). (Pecking at the disk is recorded by a device that is a lot like a telegraph key—hence, the disk is usually known as a "key.") Instead

(A)

(B)

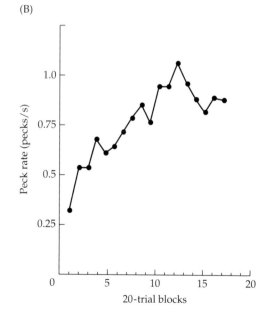

Figure 3.7 Autoshaping in pigeons. (A) The experimental set-up. (B) Typical acquisition curve. (After Balsam and Payne, 1979.)

of shaping the response by reinforcing successive approximations, Brown and Jenkins merely illuminated the key for 8 seconds, and then gave food to the pigeons. After about 45 such pairings of the "keylight" and food, the birds began pecking the key when it was lit. The pecking response was shaped automatically, and ever since, pecking behavior created this way by experimenters has been known as autoshaping. Nowadays, pigeons can be shown complex visual stimuli generated by computer and presented on TV screens attached to the wall (e.g., George & Pearce, 1999, 2003; see also Chapter 8). Autoshaped pecks at the stimuli on the screen can be detected, for example, by photocells.

The interesting thing about the autoshaped pecking response is that the bird does not have to peck the key to get the food. The arrangement is Pavlovian; the food is presented whether or not the bird pecks the key. It is almost as if the bird cannot resist pecking the food signal. This sort of conclusion is suggested almost humorously by several results. For example, the key can be placed at the end of a long box with food that is made available for a few seconds from a hopper positioned some distance away. If illumination of the key is paired with food, the bird will approach and peck the key even though it prevents getting back to the hopper in time to get the food (Hearst & Jenkins, 1974). We will consider other data like this in Chapter 10. Since the 1970s, autoshaping in pigeons has been used as a method for investigating how animals associate signals with food (e.g., Locurto, Terrace, & Gibbon, 1981).

With typical procedures, autoshaping develops after about 40 CS-US pairings. Pigeons will associate the keylight with food when the food is separated from the keylight by as much as 6–12 seconds (Balsam, 1984; Kaplan, 1984; Lucas et al., 1981). In terms of the number of trials to acquisition as well as the delay permitted between CS and US, autoshaping falls somewhere between eyeblink and fear conditioning.

Taste aversion learning in rats

As described in Chapter 2, rats will come to reject a flavor that is associated with the injection of a drug that makes them nauseated. Here, the flavor stimulus (e.g., saccharin) is a CS, while the drug injection is a US. Taste aversion learning is one of the more rapid and robust examples of classical conditioning. Under the right conditions, a strong aversion can be learned after only one conditioning trial. Also, as discussed in the previous chapter, aversions can be learned when the CS and US (flavor and injection) are separated by up to several hours (see Figure 2.14). These features of taste aversion learning (among others) led many investigators to conclude that taste aversions are a unique and highly specialized form of learning (e.g., Rozin & Kalat, 1971; Seligman, 1970). There is no question that some things appear to make taste aversion learning special; we will consider the question more carefully in Chapter 6. However, many have argued that including taste aversions in the list of Pavlovian learning systems is not only reasonable but has invigorated—and provided important insights into—the general principles of classical conditioning (e.g., Domjan, 1983).

One attraction to taste aversion learning is that it appears to be an example of how animals learn about foods. By understanding taste aversions, one can begin to understand how animals come to select and avoid certain foods. Taste aversions also have important applications outside the laboratory. For example, some of the drugs that are used to treat cancer are toxic and cause severe nausea. Cancer patients undergoing treatment can lose their appetite; indeed, loss of appetite and malnourishment may be a significant factor in death due to cancer (Morrison, 1976). Ilene Bernstein showed that children entering a Seattle clinic to get chemotherapy would learn an aversion to a novel ice cream they ate a few minutes before treatment (Bernstein, 1978; see also Bernstein & Webster, 1980). The aversion required an actual pairing of the ice cream with the chemotherapy treatment and was specific to the ice cream that was eaten before the treatment. Taste aversion learning—or something like it—appears to play a significant role in chemotherapy situations (see Burish, Levy, & Meyerowitz, 1985).

Things that Affect the Strength of Conditioning

A number of factors affect whether or not conditioning occurs when CSs and USs are presented, or more usually, how good the conditioning is that results after this type of presentation. Let's review several of the basic variables that affect how well classical conditioning is learned. Some of these variables were introduced in the last chapter.

Time

Time is a fundamentally important factor in classical conditioning. This makes sense from the functional perspective developed in the last chapter—other things being equal, animals should be sensitive to the closeness with which CS and US occur in time. However, this is only one of the ways in which classical conditioning is sensitive to time.

As a rule of thumb, conditioning works best when the CS occurs *before* the US; the CS must signal that a US is about to happen. (I use "rule of thumb" to describe a decent, but not totally infallible, rule to go by.) Figure 3.8 describes a number of ways in which CS and US can be presented in time. In **delay conditioning**, the CS comes on and then ends with presentation of the US. This is an excellent way to produce conditioning, although the amount of conditioning will decrease if the interval of CS-onset to US-onset exceeds some value. This interval depends on the conditioning preparation; in eyeblink conditioning, for example, the optimal interval between CS- and US-onset is four-tenths of a second, with little conditioning occurring at all when the interval exceeds 2 or 3 seconds (Gormezano, Kehoe, & Marshall, 1983; Smith, 1968). In conditioned suppression, an interval of 180 seconds is quite effective (e.g., Kamin, 1965).

Another arrangement is **trace conditioning**, where the CS and US are separated by a gap (the "trace interval"). Trace conditioning gets its name from the idea that some neural "trace" of the CS, rather than the CS itself, is paired

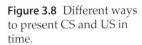

Figure 3.8 Different ways to present CS and US in time.

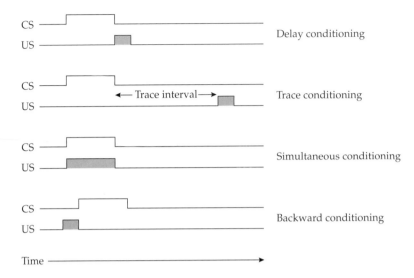

with the US. Trace procedures can produce good learning, but conditioning gets worse as the trace interval increases (e.g., Balsam, 1984; Smith, Coleman, & Gormezano, 1969; see Chapter 2). The most obvious reason why conditioning decreases with longer trace intervals is that the animal may begin to forget the CS over longer and longer gaps in time (cf. Wagner, 1981). There are other reasons too. For instance, with longer trace intervals the animal might not discriminate the trace interval (which soon ends in the US) from the interval of time that occurs between trials (which does not end in a US). To test this possibility, a second stimulus can be presented during either the trace interval or the interval between trials (the so-called **intertrial interval**). Either stimulus will increase the conditioning that develops to the CS (Bolles et al., 1978; Kaplan & Hearst, 1982).

A third way to arrange the CS and US in time is to present them both simultaneously. This is **simultaneous conditioning**. Since the CS does not really signal that the US is about to occur in this arrangement (by definition, the US is already happening), simultaneous conditioning is often believed to yield weak conditioning. The arrangement does cause weaker conditioning than a delay procedure with a short CS-US interval (Heth, 1976), but John J. B. Ayres and his associates have shown that the simultaneous procedure can often produce surprisingly good conditioning (e.g., Burkhardt & Ayres, 1978; Mahoney & Ayres, 1976). Most responses that are used to measure conditioning are performed because they help the animal deal with an *upcoming* US, and this may lead us to underestimate the amount of learning that really does occur with a simultaneous procedure (Matzel, Held, & Miller, 1988). As usual, it is useful to distinguish what a subject does (i.e., its performance) from what it actually knows (i.e., its learning).

The final arrangement shown in Figure 3.8 gets the name **backward conditioning** from the fact that the CS follows, rather than precedes, the US in time.

The backward procedure usually does not produce as much conditioned responding as forward pairings of the CS and US, although you often do get some responding (e.g., Ayres, Haddad, & Albert, 1987). The rule of thumb I gave you above seems to handle this result nicely: If the CS signals anything, it signals the interval before the next trial—that is, a period with no US (Moscovitch & LoLordo, 1968). In fact, the subject often treats a backward CS as a signal for "no US" (a conditioned inhibitor, see below), although the reason for this is a matter of controversy. One possibility is that it signals a period of no US. Another is that it is associated most directly with a reaction to the *offset* of the US (e.g., Solomon & Corbit, 1974; Wagner, 1981; see Maier, Rapaport, & Wheatley, 1976). In fear conditioning, for example, the onset of a shock US can arouse fear, while its offset may elicit something like relief. A backward CS may appear to signal "no US" because it is associated with relief (see Chapter 4).

Another well-known effect of time in conditioning is illustrated in Figure 3.9. Conditioning is better if the conditioning trials are spread out in time (**spaced-trials** procedure) than if they occur close together in time (**massed-trials** procedure). There are several reasons why spaced trials may cause better conditioning than massed trials. One idea is that learning requires that the subject "rehearse" the CS and US together in memory for awhile after each conditioning trial (e.g., Wagner, Rudy, & Whitlow, 1973). A new trial could interrupt rehearsal of the last one if it occurs too soon (see Chapter 4 for other, related possibilities). Another interesting finding, though, is that if the time between trials and the time in the CS are both increased by the same factor, there may be no benefit to spacing the trials. For example, if they are both tripled, as in the lowest line in Figure 3.9, the subject can perform poorly, as if the trials are massed (e.g., Gibbon et al., 1977; see also Holland, 2000; Lattal 1999). John Gibbon, Peter Balsam, and Randy Gallistel have suggested that the success of conditioning depends on the ratio between the time between trials and time in the CS; the ratio is bigger when time between trials is increased (see Figure 3.9, line 1 versus line 2), but not if the time in the CS and the time between trials are both multiplied by the same factor (see Figure 3.9, line 1 versus line 3; e.g., Gibbon & Balsam, 1981; Gallistel & Gibbon, 2000).

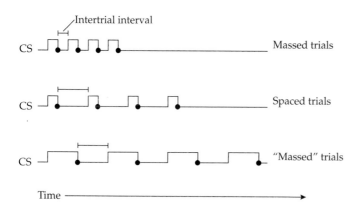

Figure 3.9 Trial spacing in Pavlovian conditioning. Bullets (•) indicate presentation of a US. Conditioning is better when trials are spaced rather than massed in time (line 2 versus line 1). However, time is relative. If the duration of the CS and the time between the trials are both multiplied by the same factor, there is no benefit to trial spacing; that is, conditioning would be about the same in lines 1 and 3.

Novelty of the CS and the US

Conditioning occurs most rapidly if the CS and US are new to the subject when conditioning first begins. Exposure to either stimulus before they are paired during conditioning can interfere with learning.

Exposure to the CS before conditioning can reduce how quickly animals learn about it. The finding that "preexposure" to the CS can interfere with conditioning is called **latent inhibition** (e.g., Lubow, 1973). The more exposures to the CS, the more interference one observes with conditioning (e.g., Siegel, 1969). The simplest explanation begins by assuming that the subject must pay attention to the CS in order for conditioning to occur. If you were exposed to a ringing bell repeatedly at the start of an experiment, you might initially pay attention to it, but your initial attention might decrease—habituate—with more and more exposures. During preexposure, the subject may come to pay less and less attention to the CS; preexposure might habituate an attentional response to the CS that is necessary for good conditioning to occur.

A related effect happens with preexposure to the US. Repeated exposure to the US alone before conditioning can reduce its effectiveness as a US (e.g., Randich & LoLordo, 1979). The effect is called the **US preexposure effect**: Exposure to the US before conditioning has occurred can retard subsequent conditioning. Once again, the more preexposure, the worse the conditioning is later. Habituation may be involved again. By presenting the US repeatedly before conditioning, you may habituate some effect of the US that is necessary for good conditioning.

Latent inhibition and the US preexposure effect have significant implications for learning in the real world. Consider the conditioning of fears and phobias. Because of latent inhibition, a person is less likely to learn to associate familiar stimuli with a traumatic event—instead, more conditioning will occur to novel stimuli. Similarly, a less novel (or more familiar) traumatic US might be less effective at causing fear conditioning. In addition to their practical value in understanding real-world conditioning, both latent inhibition and the US preexposure effect have been important in shaping theories of conditioning, as we will see in Chapter 4.

Intensity of the CS and the US

I mentioned in the last chapter that conditioning is better—or the strength of the conditioned response is stronger—the stronger or more "intense" the US. For example, stronger footshocks yield stronger fear conditioning (Annau & Kamin, 1961; Morris & Bouton, 2006). In conditioning, the stronger the US, the better the results. Intensity of the US—or the US's magnitude—roughly determines the upper limit of learning.

The intensity of the CS is also important. Thus, a quiet bell or noise or tone is less effective than a louder one. Conditioning theorists often speak of the "salience" of the CS—the louder or brighter the CS, the more salient it is. Roughly speaking, salient CSs are especially attention-grabbing. This may explain why they are more effective in conditioning.

There are limitations to the effect of CS intensity, though. Imagine trying to condition a dog to salivate to the sound of a very loud fire bell. The ringing fire bell is a more intense stimulus than the quietly ringing bell Pavlov usually used, but it is quite doubtful that the dog would salivate more to the ringing fire bell because the sound would also be startling and frightening. Turning it on would frighten the dog, and perhaps make the bell quite poor at eliciting a drooling reflex. More intense CSs are not always better than weaker CSs in conditioning experiments, because strong stimuli often elicit responses of their own. Therefore, salient—but not overpowering—stimuli are the most effective as CSs in conditioning experiments.

Pseudoconditioning and sensitization

The fact that CSs can elicit responses of their own can actually complicate how one interprets the results of conditioning experiments. The problem is especially important if the CS naturally elicits a response that looks like the response that is supposed to be conditioned. For example, if presenting a light caused the subject to blink its eye before any conditioning, it would be difficult to separate blinking that resulted from conditioning from this natural blinking to the light.

The problem is actually more subtle than this. Suppose we run a subject who receives a number of pairings of a light CS and an airpuff US in a simple eyeblink conditioning experiment. If blinking to the CS started at zero and then increased on each trial, we might feel safe concluding that the subject was learning to associate the CS and the US. Unfortunately, there are two processes besides true conditioning that might make the subject respond more and more to the CS. A careful experimenter always needs to separate these counterfeit processes from true conditioning.

One counterfeit process is appropriately known as **pseudoconditioning**. Pseudoconditioning is an increase in responding to the CS that might occur *because of mere exposure to the US*. For example, suppose that you yourself are the subject in our eyeblink experiment. One of the things about the strange experience I have subjected you to is that you repeatedly get a little blast of air to the eye. It is conceivable that you would blink more and more to any sudden stimulus, including a flash of light (the CS) because of your repeated experience with the airpuff. That is, simple exposure to the airpuff alone might be enough to make you blink to the flash of light, even if the light and puff had never been associated. This is pseudoconditioning—an increase in responding to the CS that occurs because of exposure to the US, rather than to true conditioning.

To make things worse, there is a second process that can cause responding to a CS and be mistaken for true conditioning. **Sensitization** is slightly different from pseudoconditioning: it is an increase in responding to the CS that can occur because of mere exposure to the *CS*. In the eyeblink experiment, you might be inclined to blink more and more to a flash of light because you have merely received the light before. (Sensitization is the opposite of habituation; both effects can occur [e.g., Groves & Thompson, 1970].)

This effect will also need to be distinguished from blinking at the flash of light that happens because you have associated it with the airpuff.

Experimenters can use control groups to help reduce their concerns about pseudoconditioning and sensitization. Since pseudoconditioning is due to exposure to the US alone (airpuff, in our example), a group could be given the same exposures to the US alone, and then tested for a response to the CS. If the conditioning group responded more to the CS, the difference could not be due to pseudoconditioning. Similarly, since sensitization is due to exposure to the CS alone, a group could be given the same exposures to the CS. If the conditioning group again responded more to the CS, the difference could not be due to sensitization.

Pseudoconditioning and sensitization are possible in any conditioning experiment. Ilene Bernstein recognized this in the taste aversion learning experiment with children receiving chemotherapy that I mentioned earlier (Bernstein, 1978). Bernstein noticed that the drugs used to treat cancer often make people very nauseated; she also knew that cancer patients often lose their appetite for food. Could chemotherapy be conditioning taste aversions to the patients' food? To find out, Bernstein ran an experiment on taste aversion learning in children who came to a clinic to receive chemotherapy. The experimental group received a novel ice cream (Mapletoff, a combination of maple and marshmallow flavoring) before receiving a drug that was known to make them nauseated. When they next returned to the clinic, they were given a choice between eating another dish of Mapletoff and playing a game. The children rejected Mapletoff and chose instead to play the game (Figure 3.10).

Had the children learned an aversion to Mapletoff? One possibility is that they rejected it because of pseudoconditioning: The fact that they had been made ill before could have decreased their interest in any ice cream. To check, Bernstein included a group that received the same kind of chemotherapy—but no Mapletoff—on the experimental visit. (They played with a toy instead.) These children did not reject Mapletoff during the subsequent test; in fact, a majority chose it over the game. The rejection shown by the experimental group was therefore not due to pseudoconditioning. Was the rejection due to sensitization? In this case, sensitization would be a loss of preference for Mapletoff after a simple exposure to it. To check, Bernstein included a second control group that received the Mapletoff on the "conditioning" day, but did not receive a drug that made them sick. These children did not reject Mapletoff ice cream on the subsequent test either; the rejection by the experimental subjects was not due to sensitization. By testing con-

Figure 3.10 Design and results of Bernstein's (1978) experiment on taste aversion learning in children receiving chemotherapy.

Events paired on conditioning day	Percent choosing Mapletoff on test day
Mapletoff — Treatment	21%
Toy — Treatment	67%
Mapletoff — No treatment	73%

trol groups for both pseudoconditioning and sensitization, Bernstein was able to conclude that the rejection of Mapletoff in her experimental subjects was due to the explicit combination of Mapletoff and chemotherapy—this was true aversion conditioning.

It is possible to control for both pseudoconditioning and sensitization in a single control group that receives as many CSs and USs as the experimental group but in a way that does not allow conditioning. Some possibilities are to present the CS and US separated by an amount of time that does not support conditioning, or in a backward manner, or randomly in time. It would be a mistake, though, to assume that subjects don't learn anything with these procedures (see the next sections). Nevertheless, the methods still control for pseudoconditioning and sensitization if they give the subjects equal exposure to the CS and the US.

Conditioned Inhibition

We have been talking about the kind of conditioning that occurs when CSs are associated with USs. There is another type of conditioning, however, that occurs when CSs are associated with the absence of USs. The earliest work on this kind of learning was once again done by Pavlov. Because he was a physiologist (rather than a psychologist), Pavlov saw this second type of conditioning as an example of a process that is known to exist in the nervous system: inhibition. Pavlov's neuroscientific vocabulary is retained today. Thus, when a CS is associated with a US, we speak of conditioned **excitation**. But when a CS is associated with the *absense* of a US, we speak of conditioned **inhibition**. CSs with conditioned excitation and inhibition are known as conditioned **excitors** and **inhibitors**, respectively.

Conditioned inhibition is as fundamental to modern research as conditioned excitation. Excitation and inhibition are thought to be opposites. For example, in fear conditioning, an excitor (a CS paired with shock) excites a fear or anxiety state when it is presented. Conversely, an inhibitor (a CS associated with no shock) inhibits fear, signals safety, or causes "relief." In situations where the US is food, an excitor (a CS paired with food) elicits a state of appetitive excitement. In contrast, an inhibitor (associated with no food) might inhibit that state and cause frustration. Excitation and inhibition are both motivationally significant (see Chapter 9).

Pavlov first encountered inhibition when he studied extinction. You will remember that extinction happens when a CS that has been paired with a US is subsequently presented repeatedly without the US. The conditioned response is gradually lost, but Pavlov knew it was not "unlearned"; he and his students had observed spontaneous recovery and other phenomena. This meant to Pavlov that the conditioned reflex must have been inhibited in extinction. Inhibition developed in extinction and opposed or subtracted from the original excitatory reflex. For some reason, it was more "labile" than excitation so that it was lost when time passed or when some distraction occurred.

How to detect conditioned inhibition

It is easy to recognize a conditioned excitor when you find one: The subject responds to the CS as if it expects a US. It is more difficult to recognize a conditioned inhibitor, though. This is because a signal for "no US" will not necessarily cause a behavior that is different from the behavior elicited by a stimulus that signals nothing at all. Detecting or measuring conditioned inhibition is therefore a rather indirect business.

There are two methods used to measure inhibition (Rescorla, 1969b; Williams, Overmier, & LoLordo, 1992). Both capitalize on the fact that inhibition and excitation are viewed as opposites. The first method is known as a **summation test**. In it, the inhibitor is presented together with a conditioned excitor. A true inhibitor will inhibit the response elicited by the excitor: There will be less responding when the excitor is combined with an inhibitor than when the excitor is presented alone (Figure 3.11). When the excitor is combined with a neutral stimulus, there should be less of a decrease in responding. (Some loss may occur, though, if the animal does not generalize completely from the excitor to the novel test compound.)

Excitors and inhibitors behave as if an excitor has a positive value and an inhibitor has a negative value. The rule of thumb is that when they are put together, they tend to summate, so that adding a negative cue (the inhibitor) subtracts from the effect of the positive cue (the excitor). Consistent with this scenario, when two excitors are put together, the response to the compound is more than to either cue alone (e.g., Reberg, 1972; see Figure 3.11). Be careful, however. Excitors and inhibitors do not literally add to one another. Instead, we are usually interested in knowing that some stimuli cause more or less responding, so-called **ordinal predictions**. The results shown in Figure 3.11 provide an ordering of the stimuli: Two excitors will cause more responding than one excitor alone, and an inhibitor and an excitor will cause less responding than the excitor alone.

A second method for measuring conditioned inhibition is the **retardation-of-acquisition test**. If a conditioned inhibitor is converted into an excitor by pairing it with a US, responding develops to the CS very slowly—the

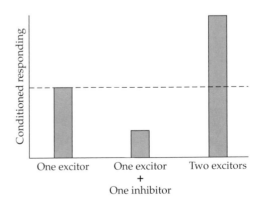

Figure 3.11 Hypothetical effects of presenting an excitor alone (left), the excitor together with an inhibitor (middle), and the excitor together with another excitor (right). As a rule of thumb, CSs "summate" when they are presented together. Inhibitors subtract from excitors, as if they have a negative value.

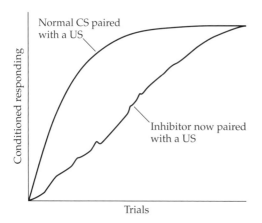

Figure 3.12 Hypothetical effects of pairing an inhibitor with a US. Acquisition of conditioned responding is slower ("retarded") with an inhibitor than with a CS that has not received any previous training.

acquisition of responding is "retarded" (Figure 3.12) compared to when the US is paired with a normal CS. This makes sense when you realize that a signal for no US is being turned into the opposite polarity—or a signal for the US. The results of retardation tests must be regarded with caution, though, because other things besides inhibition can cause retarded acquisition. A CS may look like a conditioned inhibitor in this sort of test if the animal has merely learned not to pay attention to it—a possibility that should be kept separate from inhibition. In fact, retardation has even been observed when the CS is actually a very weak excitor (Hall & Pearce, 1979). Because of this, researchers interested in investigating inhibition should probably use it only together with the summation test.

Sometimes the measurement of inhibition is less tricky. In **bidirectional response systems**, a response can go either above or below its baseline level; directional changes in the baseline response may correspond to excitation or inhibition. For example, resting heart rate might increase when a fear excitor is presented but decrease when a fear inhibitor is presented. Similarly, in autoshaping, pigeons will approach excitors and withdraw from inhibitors (e.g., Hearst & Franklin, 1977; Kaplan & Hearst, 1982). In these cases it is less difficult to know an inhibitor when you have one—it evokes a change from baseline that is opposite to the one evoked by an excitor.

How to produce conditioned inhibition

Conditioned inhibition can be acquired in several different ways (see LoLordo & Fairless, 1985). As a rule of thumb (remember, these are not infallible!), it develops when a CS occurs and signals no US. One method is known as **differential inhibition** or **discriminative inhibition**. One CS (call it A) is repeatedly paired with a US, while another CS (call it X) is repeatedly presented without a US on other trials. Not surprisingly, the animal will come to respond to A but not to X. The subject discriminates between the two stimuli. Often, X becomes a conditioned inhibitor. In fact, excitation and inhibition are thought to be conditioned in most basic discrimination procedures.

A second method is the **conditioned inhibition** procedure. (Like many effects in conditioning, the term describes both a result and a procedure.) In this case, one CS (A) is paired with a US, and on other trials it is presented together with a second stimulus (X). (A and X presented together make up a **compound CS**.) The compound AX stimulus is then presented without a US. Not surprisingly, subjects will respond when A is presented by itself but will learn to not respond to AX. Casually speaking, X signals a trial when A will not be followed by a US. And interestingly enough, if X is removed and tested by itself, the subject treats it as if it signals no US—it has the properties of a conditioned inhibitor. The conditioned inhibition procedure is thought to be one of the most fundamental and effective ways to condition inhibition.

Other methods involve presenting a CS (X) alone and then presenting a US far away from it in time. The CS and US are never paired; in fact, they are "unpaired," and the method is sometimes called the **explicitly unpaired** procedure. Since the CS and US are negatively "correlated" in time, the procedure is sometimes described as **negative correlation**. In this case, X sometimes acquires inhibition too.

In some cases, inhibition can actually develop even when a CS always ends in a US. In **inhibition of delay**, a US is presented at the end of a lengthy CS. With many conditioning trials, the animal behaves as if the early part of the CS signals a period of no US (e.g., Rescorla, 1967a; Rosas & Alonso, 1997). A final method is one I mentioned previously—backward conditioning (see Figure 3.8). Here, the CS occurs after the US. As I described above, this procedure sometimes establishes the CS as a signal for no US— that is, as a conditioned inhibitor. Some theories now assume that backward conditioning is one of the most fundamental ways to produce inhibition.

Two methods that do NOT produce true inhibition

I warned you above that the notion that inhibition develops when a CS is associated with no US, was no better than a rule of thumb. This is correct, of course; the rule is fallible. There are at least two situations in which a CS can be presented without a US where the CS does not acquire the properties of a conditioned inhibitor.

Recall that "latent inhibition" refers to the situation in which a CS is preexposed—without a US—on a number of trials before conditioning begins. Preexposure to the CS makes it difficult to convert the CS into an excitor when it is subsequently paired with the US. (Astute readers will recognize this as a retardation-of-acquisition test.) Despite this result, and indeed, despite the very term "latent inhibition," simple preexposure does not cause the CS to acquire true inhibition. A CS that is simply preexposed before conditioning begins fails the summation test. That is, the CS does not inhibit responding when it is presented together with an excitor (e.g., Reiss & Wagner, 1972; Rescorla, 1971). As noted above, preexposure to the CS may cause the animal to pay less attention to the same CS later. This does not necessarily mean that the animal learns that the CS signals "no US." One idea is that, *to acquire true inhibition, a CS must occur without a US when that US is otherwise expected* (e.g., Wagner & Rescorla, 1972).

Ironically, given Pavlov's original discoveries, another place in which a CS is associated with no US—and does not acquire true inhibition—is extinction. To meet today's definition of inhibition, an extinguished CS would need to pass both summation and retardation tests. Reberg (1972) arranged the following summation test: Two CSs were separately paired with a US; then one was extinguished by presenting it alone—over and over. At the end of this phase, Reberg presented the two stimuli together in compound. If the extinguished CS had become an inhibitor, he expected it to subtract from responding to the other cue. Instead, it *increased* responding to the other cue. If anything, the extinguished CS was still an excitor after extinction.

Other experimenters have run the retardation test. For example, rabbits received conditioning with a CS, then extinction, and then a reconditioning phase (Napier, MacCrae & Kehoe, 1992). If the CS had become an inhibitor in extinction, it should be slow to acquire responding in the reconditioning phase. Napier et al. found exactly the opposite: Reconditioning was very rapid. In fact, rapid reconditioning is often observed after extinction (but see Bouton, 1986). Once again, if anything, an extinguished CS looks like an excitor rather than an inhibitor. This fact has interesting implications that we will discuss later (see Chapter 5). For now, however, it seems clear that a CS does not become a conditioned inhibitor after extinction because the CS fails both the summation and retardation tests.

Information Value in Conditioning

To the uninitiated, conditioning looks like an awfully straightforward example of learning. When a CS and a US occur together in time, it just isn't that surprising that an animal will learn to associate them. What is all the fuss about? In many ways, the modern era of conditioning research began in the late 1960s when several discoveries came along that shattered some cherished intuitions about conditioning. Each discovery suggested that conditioning does not automatically happen when a CS and a US are paired—CS-US pairings are not enough to guarantee learning. Instead, conditioning only occurs if the CS provides information about the upcoming US. It is not possible to appreciate this idea without talking about the experiments that encouraged it—so let us look at them.

CS-US contingencies in classical conditioning

One line of research was begun by Robert Rescorla while he was a graduate student at the University of Pennsylvania (Rescorla, 1966, 1967b, 1968b). Rescorla (1968) presented a series of tone CSs to his subjects. He also presented brief shock USs. These were scheduled in different ways for different groups of subjects. For one group (Group 1), the shock US was scheduled to occur with a probability of .4 whenever a CS occurred; as shown in Figure 3.13, this means two out of every five CSs were paired with a shock. At the end of several sessions of this training, Rescorla found that the rats

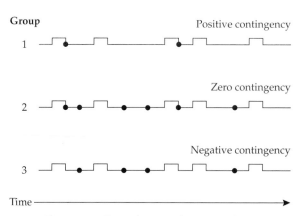

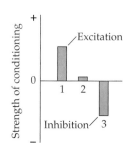

Figure 3.13 Procedure used in Rescorla's experiments demonstrating the importance of CS-US contingency in conditioning. In Group 1, the probability of the US (indicated with bullets) is greater when the CS is on than when the CS is off. Here the contingency between CS and US is positive, and excitatory conditioning to the CS is observed. In Group 2, the probability of the US is the same whether the CS is on or off. Here there is no contingency between CS and US, and this produces no conditioning even though the CS and US are paired together many times. In Group 3, the probability of the US when the CS is on is less than the probability of the US when the CS is off. Here the contingency between CS and US is negative, and inhibitory conditioning of the CS is observed.

were quite afraid of the CS. When the probability of the US was .4 in the CS, the rats had learned quite a lot.

A second group (Group 2) received the same CSs and the same USs (within the CSs) as the first group. As illustrated in Figure 3.13, the subjects in this group thus received the same number of pairings between CS and US as the first group. However, the second group also received shocks when the CS was not on. Rescorla scheduled these extra USs so that they occurred with the same probability as those scheduled in the CS. That is, the probability of a shock was .4 in both the presence and the absence of the tone. The tone was then tested after several sessions of this sort of training. Amazingly, the subjects in Group 2 acted as if they had no knowledge that the CS and the US were associated—they showed no fear of the tone. This result was quite impressive because the second group had had the same number of CS-US pairings as the first group. Evidently, *pairings of a CS and a US were not sufficient to produce conditioning*. In this arrangement, the CS provided no new information about the occurrence of the US. To get conditioning, the CS had to predict an increase in the probability of the US.

Rescorla also ran a third group (Group 3) that received the same exposures to the tone CS. This group also received the shocks in the absence of the CS that the second group had received, but it did not receive any shocks during the CS. For this group, the onset of the CS did signal a change in the probability of the US—in this case, it signaled a *decrease* in the likelihood of the US. Perhaps not surprisingly, and given what you have read in the previous section, the rats treated this CS as a safety signal—that is, a conditioned inhibitor for shock.

For several reasons, Rescorla's experiment initiated a profound change in the way we conceptualize conditioning. To emphasize the point, Group 2's lack of learning indicated that CS-US pairings were not the cause of conditioning; to produce conditioning, the CS must actually signal an increase or decrease in the probability of the US. CS-US pairings are not good enough to produce conditioning; the CS must be informative about the US.

The second implication of Rescorla's results is that excitation and inhibition can be regarded as two ends of the same continuum. An excitor (like the tone in Group 1) is a CS that signals an *increase* in the probability of a US; an inhibitor (like the one in Group 3) signals a *decrease* in its probability. The fundamental difference is the nature of the relationship, or **contingency**, between the two events. In a **positive contingency** between the CS and the US, the US is more probable when the CS is on than when it is off. This is the condition of Group 1; excitation was learned with a positive contingency. In a **negative contingency**, the US is less probable when the CS is on than when it is off. This is the condition of Group 3; inhibition was learned with a negative contingency. Group 2's treatment falls in between. For this group, the US is equally probable when the CS is on and when it is off. There is *no contingency* between the CS and the US. The fact that nothing was learned here suggests that the lack of a contingency describes a sort of zero point, with excitation and inhibition being created by positive and negative contingencies on either side of it.

One warning is in order about this set of circumstances. It is tempting to conclude that Rescorla's subjects literally learned (and understood) the contingency between the CS and the US. Presumably, this would require some fairly sophisticated mental machinery. In point of fact, learning researchers have never really supposed this (see Papini & Bitterman, 1990). Instead, a CS-US contingency simply describes a relationship between CS and US that will allow excitation or inhibition to be learned. Neither excitation nor inhibition requires that the subject really calculate a contingency or correlation coefficient in its head. We will return to the question of how positive and negative contingencies lead to excitation and inhibition in the next chapter.

Blocking and unblocking

Leon Kamin (1968, 1969) reported some equally interesting experiments with rats in conditioned suppression. The design of one of his experiments is shown in Figure 3.14. There were three phases. In the first phase, one of the groups received 16 trials in which a noise CS (N) was paired with a footshock US (Shock). This was enough training to produce considerable responding whenever the noise was presented. In the second phase, this group received 8 further trials in which a light (L) was added to the noise to make a compound CS (LN). A second group received the same 8 pairings of the light and noise compound and the shock US, but the noise had not been conditioned before. In a third phase, Kamin simply tested condition-

Leon Kamin

Figure 3.14 (A) Design of Kamin's blocking experiment. Both Group 1 and Group 2 received an equal number of pairings of the light (L) and noise (N) compound with shock in Phase 2. But for Group 1, the noise had previously been associated with shock, making the light a redundant predictor of shock. Prior conditioning with the noise "blocked" conditioning with the light. (B) Results of the test trials. The measure is the suppression ratio—less conditioning is indicated by a *higher* ratio. (After Kamin, 1969.)

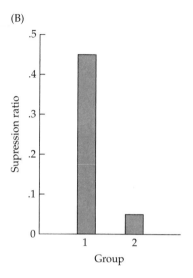

(A)

Group	Phase 1	Phase 2	Test
1	16 N — Shock	8 LN — Shock	L?
2	—	8 LN — Shock	L?

(B)

ing to the light by presenting it alone (L). Both groups had received 8 pairings of the light with the shock. If pairings of light and shock were all that was required to induce conditioning, then the groups should not have differed in their conditioning to the light.

What Kamin found was very different and very interesting. The results are also shown in Figure 3.14. The group that had received the light combined with the noise showed good conditioning. But the group that had the light combined with a noise that had previously been conditioned, showed *no evidence of learning at all with the light*. Prior conditioning with the noise is said to have "blocked" conditioning of the light. This result is called the **blocking** effect.

Blocking is important because it again suggests that conditioning does not simply happen because CS and US are paired. Kamin suggested that the blocking group didn't need to learn much about the light because the noise already predicted the shock. In effect, the light was redundant to the noise in predicting shock. The experiment thus suggests that learning only occurs when the CS provides *new* information about the US. When it doesn't predict anything new, relatively little learning occurs.

Kamin reported a second result that further supported this interpretation. If learning occurs when a CS predicts something new, perhaps the rat will learn about the light if the light is made to predict something new during the second phase. The design of this next experiment is shown in Figure 3.15. As before, one group received N-shock training followed by LN-shock. When

(A)

Group	Phase 1	Phase 2	Test
1	N — Shock	LN — Shock	L?
2	N — Shock	LN — SHOCK!!	L?
3	N — SHOCK!!	LN — SHOCK!!	L?

(B)

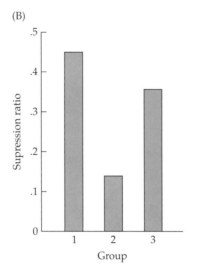

Figure 3.15 (A) Design of Kamin's unblocking experiment. For Groups 1 and 3, the light was redundant to the noise in predicting shock, and the noise blocked conditioning to the light. But for Group 2, when the light was added to the noise, it signaled an increase in the intensity of the shock—this allowed conditioning of the light, or "unblocking." (B) Results of the test trials with the light. Less conditioning is indicated by a *higher* supression ratio. (After Kamin, 1969.)

the light was tested alone, blocking was again observed. A second group received the same N-shock conditioning in the first phase, but in the second phase—when the light was added to the noise—the compound was paired with a stronger shock (SHOCK!!). Here, the light did predict something new, and as predicted, the rats learned about it fine. A final group received the same LN compound trials with the larger shock, but previously the noise had been associated alone with the same larger shock. In this case, the light did not predict anything new, and once again blocking was observed. The results of this experiment and the previous one suggest an interesting new idea about conditioning. As in Rescorla's contingency experiment, pairings of a CS and a US (light and shock) were not sufficient to produce conditioning. Instead, learning occurred in Kamin's experiments only if the CS predicted something *new*.

My students at the University of Vermont are familiar with another example of the blocking effect, once I point it out to them. Since the university is about 30 minutes south of the Canadian border, nearly all of the students have visited Canada at least once. They may also have handled a little Canadian paper money while there. The basic monetary unit, of course, is the dollar (worth only a little less than the American dollar at this writing), but each of the different Canadian bills ($5, $10, $20) is printed with both a number and a *color* that correspond to the dollar amount. The interesting thing is that few of my American students can remember the color of, say, the Canadian $10 bill. One possible reason is that we have had a lot of training in America in which the number printed on the bill is associated with its value (what the bill can buy). In Canada, number and color are both printed on the bill, but the color is redundant to the number. The cues are analogous to the light and noise in Kamin's blocking experiment—prior learning with numbers blocks learning about colors.

(A) Conditioning

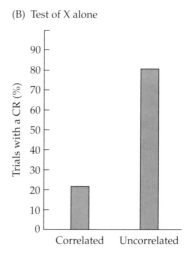

Group Correlated	Group Uncorrelated
AX — US	AX — US
AX — US	AX — No US
BX — No US	BX — US
BX — No US	BX — No US

(B) Test of X alone

Figure 3.16 (A) Design of the "relative validity" experiment. Groups Correlated and Uncorrelated had the same number of X-US pairings (for both groups, X was paired with the US half the time X was presented). However, for the Correlated group, there was a better predictor of US (or no US) also present on each trial (stimuli A and B, respectively). In contrast, for the Uncorrelated Group, stimulus X was no worse than A or B at predicting US (or no US)—all CSs were paired with the US half the time they were presented. When X was later tested alone (B), X was much better conditioned in the Uncorrelated Group. (After Wagner et al., 1968.)

Relative validity in conditioning

A similar theme was picked up by Allan Wagner, who was running a number of experiments similar to Kamin's at Yale University. In one type of experiment (Wagner et al., 1968), a blocking-like effect was shown under especially interesting conditions. The design of the experiment is shown in Figure 3.16. There were two groups. For both groups, a CS (called X) occurred on every trial; half the time it was presented together with a stimulus (called A), and half the time it was presented together with a different stimulus (called B). For one of the groups (Group Correlated), AX was always paired with a US, while BX always occurred without a US. For the other group (Group Uncorrelated), AX and BX were each paired with the US only half the time. The question is, how much would the different groups learn about X? For both groups, X was paired with the US half the time (this is ordinarily enough to produce plenty of conditioning). For both groups, X was also presented with A or B half the time. The difference is that, for Group Correlated, stimulus A was a perfect predictor of the US, and stimulus B was a perfect predictor of no US. X was not as useful as A or B at predicting the outcomes of the trials. For Group Uncorrelated, though, the situation was different. Here, stimuli A and B were both imperfect predictors of the US—like X itself, each was paired with the US half the time. For Group Uncorrelated, X was no better or worse than stimulus A or B at predicting the outcomes of the trials. (In fact, because X was present on all the trials with the US, it was arguably a little better than A or B.)

The main results are shown in Figure 3.16B. There was more conditioning to X in Group Uncorrelated than in Group Correlated. In Group Correlated, there was little learning about X. (There was a lot of learning about

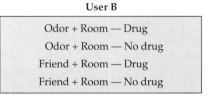

User A	User B
Odor + Room — Drug	Odor + Room — Drug
Odor + Room — Drug	Odor + Room — No drug
Friend + Room — No drug	Friend + Room — Drug
Friend + Room — No drug	Friend + Room — No drug

Figure 3.17 In the real world, conditioning probably always occurs with compounded CSs, and the results may be surprising. For example, two hypothetical drug users might take a drug 50% of the time they are in a particular room. Half of the time an odor is also present, and half of the time a friend is present. Despite similar histories of drug use, according to the results of the relative validity experiment (see Figure 3.16), User A will eventually crave the drug in the presence of the odor, but not in the room alone, or in the presence of the friend. In contrast, User B will experience strong drug cravings whenever he is in the room, or in the presence of the odor, or with the friend. The laws of conditioning are always at work—and perhaps more subtle than we often realize.

stimuli A and B.) Apparently, the subject learned about the best predictors of the US—and effectively ignored X. Conditioning is a little like a competition in which the best predictors win the prize.

The relative validity experiment is not a purely academic exercise. In the world outside the laboratory, conditioning probably always involves compounded cues. Figure 3.17 illustrates two fictional histories of drug use for two drug users. In the last chapter, I presented evidence suggesting that conditioning may be involved in drug dependence. Let us assume that drug craving is elicited by cues that are associated with the drug. If we want to understand what conditioning research really has to say about drug dependence, we must acknowledge that natural conditioning probably involves the conditioning of compounded cues, and that the amount of conditioning acquired by any one cue will depend on how well it competes with other cues.

In the arrangement shown in Figure 3.17, a room is paired with a drug on 50% of the trials for both drug users. Therefore, both drug users have the same number of room-drug pairings. But for the first drug user (User A), an odor is always present on trials when the drug is taken, and a friend is always present on trials when the drug is not taken. You may notice that User A's drug history is exactly like Group Correlated's treatment in the Wagner et al. (1968) experiment. Based on that experiment, we would expect that the odor would acquire the most conditioning, and block conditioning of the room. For the second user (User B), the situation is like Group Uncorrelated. For this person, all the cues—room, odor, and friend—are equally correlated with the drug; they are each paired with the drug 50% of the time. In this case, the three stimuli will each acquire some conditioning. Drug cravings will be controlled by completely different cues for the two users, even though they have had very similar experiences with the drug and the conditioned stimuli. This experiment has not actually been run with drug USs, but in principle, you may begin to see what experiments on information value in conditioning may actually say about real-world experiments. Users receiving the same number of exposures to the drug, the odor, the friend, and the room may differ substantially in which cues control drug dependence.

It is not a bad exercise to construct this kind of a scenario for any of the effects that I have described in this chapter. Conditioning research has implications for real life, but it is more subtle, and more interesting, than many people think it is.

Summary

1. Pavlov's basic conditioning experiment provides a method for studying how organisms associate events that occur together in time. Today, it is generally believed that subjects learn to associate the CS and the US.

2. Second-order conditioning, sensory preconditioning, and generalization each provide ways in which stimuli that have never been directly associated with a US can elicit a conditioned response.

3. Most modern research on classical conditioning uses one of several basic methods. These include eyeblink conditioning in rabbits, fear conditioning in rats, autoshaping in pigeons, and taste-aversion learning in rats. The conditioning that is observed in each of these systems has some unique characteristics, but it is interesting that the same laws of learning still generally apply.

4. The success of conditioning depends on several factors. The timing of the CS and US is important; for best conditioning, the CS should precede the US, and should occur relatively close to it in time. Also, conditioning is more successful if conditioning trials are spaced apart rather than massed together. Conditioning is also best when the CS and the US are both novel and relatively intense or salient.

5. Researchers need to distinguish between responding to a CS that results from true conditioning and responding that results from pseudoconditioning or sensitization. Control groups that receive equivalent exposure to the CS and US are usually used for this purpose.

6. Conditioned excitors are CSs that predict a US; conditioned inhibitors are CSs that predict a decrease in the probability of a US. Inhibitors have effects on behavior that generally oppose the effects of excitors. To detect inhibition, it is often necessary to run summation and retardation-of-acquisition tests.

7. Conditioned inhibition results from several different procedures, including differential inhibition, conditioned inhibition, explicit unpairing (or negative correlation), and inhibition of delay. Latent inhibition and extinction do not produce CSs that satisfy the modern definition of inhibition—for example, they fail summation tests.

8. Conditioning is *not* an automatic result of pairing a CS and a US. Research on CS-US contingencies, blocking, and relative validity each indicate that CS-US pairings are not sufficient to cause learning. Instead, the CS must provide nonredundant information about the occurrence of the US for learning to occur. This idea has stimulated some important advances in our understanding of how conditioning works, some of which will be discussed in the next chapter.

Key Terms

unconditional stimulus (US)
unconditional response (UR)
conditional stimulus (CS)
conditional response (CR)
generalization
S-R learning
stimulus substitution
S-S learning
second-order (or higher-order)
   conditioning
sensory preconditioning
conditioning preparations
conditioned suppression
conditioned emotional response
   (CER)
suppression ratio
autoshaping
delay conditioning
trace conditioning
intertrial interval
simultaneous conditioning
backward conditioning
spaced trials
massed trials

latent inhibition
US preexposure effect
pseudoconditioning
sensitization
excitation
inhibition
excitor
inhibitor
summation test
ordinal predictions
retardation-of-acquisition test
bidirectional response systems
differential inhibition
discriminative inhibition
conditioned inhibition
compound CS
explicitly unpaired
negative correlation
inhibition of delay
contingency
positive contingency
negative contingency
blocking
relative validity

Chapter Four Outline

Chapter

4

Theories of Conditioning

THE PRECEDING CHAPTERS were full of so many facts that by now it must be getting difficult to keep them straight. Here is a possible solution: What you need is a theory. Theories are useful in organizing and integrating facts. For example, in the last chapter we considered the effects on conditioning of how the CS and US are presented in time (see Figure 3.8). You could memorize the separate facts: that delay conditioning is better than simultaneous conditioning, that simultaneous conditioning is better than backward conditioning, and so on. Or you could organize them with a summary: Learning is best when the CS can signal the US. The summary is a theoretical idea. It is relatively easy to remember, and from the summary, you can reassemble the facts.

This chapter focuses on theories of conditioning—some much more systematic ideas about how associative learning, as it is studied in conditioning, actually works. The development of these theories is sometimes thought to be one of the most important achievements in learning research in the last several decades. The theories will probably look a little woolly at first, but they are not as difficult as you might think, and they are even a little fun to play with. The theories are worth the trouble because they have many implications for understanding human and animal behavior, and they are practical because they may help simplify and organize the facts for you. When you walk away from this book, if all you remember is a good theory, you will be able to reconstruct a reasonable approximation of many of the facts.

Theories do more than just simplify and organize—they are usually created to *explain* things. What we need is a tool that will help explain how animals and humans behave as if they have learned to associate CSs and USs or responses and reinforcers. We need to know how contingencies and information value get translated into knowledge and behavior. We need to know why novelty of the US or CS is so important in allowing learning to occur. By the end of this chapter, we will be able to explain and integrate these disparate facts.

Theories are also important because they stimulate research, which is a harder point to appreciate. Basically, if we want to know whether an explanation is right or wrong, we need to run experiments to *test* it. A theory is only testable if its predictions can be proved wrong—in other words, it must be "falsifiable." Good theories are always constructed so that they can be falsified; if they cannot be proved false, we usually aren't interested in them. Good theories therefore lead to research. Right or wrong, they can increase our knowledge.

This chapter begins with a theory that time has judged outstanding on all of these criteria: It simplified the facts, it explained things in a clear and unambiguous way, and it was extremely testable. The theory has stimulated much research, and it is safe to say that we wouldn't know as much about conditioning as we do today if the theory hadn't been formulated. It is a theory originally published in two important papers by Robert Rescorla and Allan Wagner (Rescorla & Wagner, 1972; Wagner & Rescorla, 1972). In these papers, they tried to explain some of the exciting conditioning results that had been emerging at the time, such as the effects of information value in learning. You will remember from the last chapter that these findings challenged most views of learning, which tended to see conditioning as a pretty boring and passive affair. Although findings like blocking and contingency learning suggested that information value was important in conditioning, the meaning of the term "information value" was fuzzy and vague. One goal of the Rescorla-Wagner model was to pin it down. The model began by providing a very concrete account of simple conditioning.

The Rescorla-Wagner Model

The Rescorla-Wagner model is all about surprise. It assumes that learning occurs on a conditioning trial only if the US is surprising. This idea was first suggested by Kamin's blocking and unblocking effects (1968, 1969)—learning to a light did not occur if the US was already signaled by another CS. The signal made the US predicted, and not surprising. In reality, there is an element of surprise any time learning does occur. Think about the very first conditioning trial when a CS is first paired with a US. Because nothing signals the US, it is surprising, and we get some learning. But as conditioning trials proceed, the CS will come to predict the US, and the US will

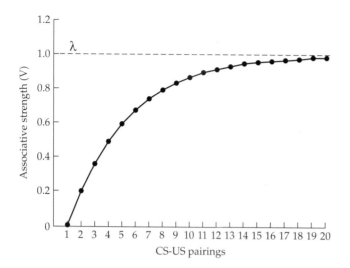

Figure 4.1 The growth of associative strength (V) to a CS as a function of CS-US pairings. The curve approaches an asymptote set by λ.

become less and less surprising. At some point during training, the CS will predict the US perfectly, and at this point no further learning will occur. An upper limit to learning is reached when the US is no longer surprising.

These ideas are illustrated in Figure 4.1. The figure shows the growth of "associative strength," the strength of the CS's (hypothetical) association with the US, over trials. Note that with each trial, there is an increase or jump in associative strength. On early conditioning trials, the jumps are large; that is, each trial causes a relatively large increase in associative strength. But the jumps decrease in size as learning progresses, until the learning curve approaches its upper limit, or "asymptote." Rescorla and Wagner suggested that the size of each jump depends on how surprising the US is on the corresponding trial. On early trials, when the US is surprising, we get a big jump. But on later trials, when the CS has come to predict the US, the US is not surprising, and we get no further jumps. Surprise decreases as learning approaches its limit. Once the CS predicts the US, the US is not surprising, and no further learning occurs.

Rescorla and Wagner gave "associative strength" a shorter name. They called it V, for predictive value. They suggested that V increases on each trial until the CS predicts the US perfectly, at which point V reaches an upper limit of conditioning that the US will allow. The asymptote—the upper limit of the curve—is called λ (lambda). The asymptote is determined by the magnitude of the US. On any given trial, the change in associative strength can be determined by a very simple equation:

$$\Delta V = \alpha\beta(\lambda - V)$$

The symbol Δ (delta) means change; α and β are fractions (they have values between 0 and 1) that relate to the salience of the CS and US, respectively, which we will discuss shortly. The key is the quantity in parentheses, λ – V. This quantity describes the **surprisingness of the US**. λ is the US term; it

(A)

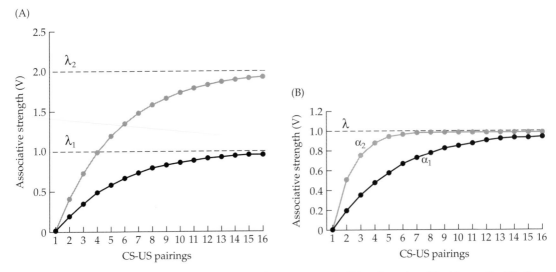

(B)

Figure 4.2 (A) The effect of US magnitude (λ) on learning. The bigger the US, the higher the asymptote. (B) The effect of CS salience (α) on learning. The more salient (i.e., intense) the CS, the faster the learning approaches the asymptote—which is still determined by US magnitude (λ).

Robert Rescorla

Allan Wagner

stands for the US. V is the learning term; it describes how well the CS is associated with, and thus predicts, the US. The difference between the two terms corresponds to how much bigger the US is than what the CS predicts, and is thus a surprise. As the value of V gets bigger, the CS becomes a better and better predictor of the US, and the difference ($λ – V$) gets smaller and smaller until no further changes in associative strength occur.

Figure 4.2A illustrates how the picture changes if we use USs of different magnitudes. The model assumes that larger USs mean larger λs. The bigger the λ, the higher the asymptote that learning reaches. This is consistent with the effects of US magnitude described in the last chapter—the bigger the better. Figure 4.2B illustrates what happens as we look at CSs with different saliences. Salience affects α, a fraction with a value between 0 and 1. On each trial, the quantity multiplies the surprise factor in the equation; therefore, the bigger the α, the bigger the size of each jump. Note that α affects how quickly the learning curve approaches its maximum, but it does not affect the maximum itself. That is always set by λ, the magnitude of the US.

Thus far the model is merely a description of the learning curve (see also Bush and Mosteller, 1955). But Rescorla and Wagner added a simple twist that had far-reaching implications. They proposed that the degree to which the US is predicted on a trial depends, not on any single CS, but on *all* the CSs that are present on that trial. Thus, if two CSs are presented together in a compound, they *both* contribute to predicting the US. To capture this idea, Rescorla and Wagner suggested that the extent to which the US is predicted is described by the *sum* of the V values of all stimuli present on a given trial. Thus:

$$\Delta V = \alpha\beta(\lambda - \Sigma V)$$

where Σ means "sum of." The key is really the difference between λ and the summed value of all stimuli present on the trial. With this simple equation, one can go a remarkably long way in describing and predicting the results of conditioning experiments.

Blocking and unblocking

Let's first return to Kamin's blocking effect. In the blocking experiment, a noise and a US were first paired, and then a light-noise compound was paired with the same US. No learning occurred to the light. The model's account of this effect is simple and "elegant"—a term we use to mean "disarmingly simple and pretty." During conditioning in the first phase, the noise acquires a positive V value. In fact, Kamin conditioned it to about the asymptote. Let us assume that Kamin used a US with a λ equal to 1. At the end of the first phase then, the rat has learned that the associative strength of the noise (V_N) is:

$$V_N = 1.0$$

During the second phase, conditioning trials continue, but a light is now added to the noise. To find out what the model predicts will happen to the light, we simply plug numbers into the equation:

$$\Delta V_L = \alpha\beta(\lambda - \Sigma V)$$

where ΣV will equal the *total* associative strength on these trials, or the values of both the noise and the light:

$$\Delta V_L = \alpha\beta[\lambda - (V_N + V_L)]$$

Since the light is new to the rat, the light has no associative strength, and its initial V value $(V_L) = 0$. I will also assume that $\alpha\beta = .2$. Putting these numbers into the equation, we get:

$$\Delta V_L = .2\,[1.0 - (1.0 + 0)] = 0$$

The model predicts no change in associative strength (ΔV) to the light. Note that this occurs because there is no surprise on the compound trials—the quantity $\lambda - \Sigma V$ equals 0. The model is loyal to the "surprise" interpretation of blocking.

Kamin's unblocking result was equally important. In that experiment, Phase 1 conditioning occurred as before so that the noise was first associated with a shock. Then, on the crucial compound trials when light was added, the intensity of the US was increased. The increased US led to learning about the light. The model accounts for this following the same strategy used in blocking. The key here is that the larger US in the second phase has a bigger λ value.

As before, let us assume that the noise is first conditioned to a V value equal to 1; that is, it is originally conditioned to the asymptote. Now, on the compound trials we solve for ΔV_L, as before:

$$\Delta V_L = \alpha\beta[\lambda - (V_N + V_L)]$$

But now we have a new and larger US that will support more conditioning than the previous US. Since we used a value of 1 before, we must use a larger number this time. I will use a value of 2, but any number greater than 1 will do:

$$\Delta V_L = .2\ [2.0 - (1.0 + 0)] = +.20$$

The model correctly predicts an increase in associative strength to the light on the first trial when the US intensity is increased in Phase 2 of the blocking design.

The numbers I used in the model above are somewhat arbitrary; this works very well as long as one sticks to certain rules. In particular, one must be consistent in assigning λ values. The rule, again, is that larger USs require larger λs. But note that, because the numbers plugged into the equations are arbitrary, the numbers that result must be arbitrary too. The model is not designed to predict the numbers of drops a dog salivates, the amount of time a rat spends freezing, or the number of times a pigeon pecks a keylight. Instead, the model answers questions like "which group will acquire more conditioning?" It predicts how to rank order groups. In the illustration of blocking and unblocking, we did not arrive at a value of "fear" (or conditioned suppression) in Kamin's rats. What we found was that increasing the US in Phase 2 (the unblocking procedure) will produce more conditioning than using the same US (the blocking procedure).

Extinction and inhibition

The model provides a ready account of extinction. It uses the same equation as before—the only difference is that presenting the CS with no US is the same as running conditioning trials with a *US of zero intensity*. In keeping with the US magnitude rule, we now use 0 as the value for λ. Suppose we have paired our noise with the US enough times that the CS has a V = 1. Now, when extinction trials begin, we introduce a new value for λ, 0. So:

$$\Delta V_N = .2\ [0 - 1] = -.2$$

Because ΔV solves to a negative number, the model predicts that V will decrease on the extinction trial. On the next trial, we insert a reduced value for V; ultimately, V will decrease on each trial until there is no more surprise and it approaches a new asymptote of 0. This is shown in Figure 4.3. The animal adjusts its "expectation" so as to accurately predict the new trial outcome. The model assumes that V returns to a value of 0 during extinction.

The only new idea is that when a trial involves no US, we simply use a λ value of 0 in the original equation. This trick has important implications for conditioned inhibition. One of the easiest ways to train inhibition is Pavlov's conditioned inhibition paradigm. Here, a light might be paired

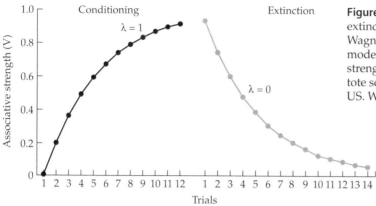

Figure 4.3 Conditioning (left) and extinction (right) in the Rescorla-Wagner model. In extinction, the model assumes that associative strength approaches a new asymptote so that the CS now predicts no US. When there is no US, $\lambda = 0$.

with a US, but paired with no US when it is compounded with a noise: The noise becomes an inhibitor. The model predicts this readily, and believe it or not, you already have all the information you need to know!

The easiest way to understand conditioned inhibition is to break Pavlov's experiment down into the two phases shown in Figure 4.4. During Phase 1, assume that the light is paired with the US enough to acquire some associative strength. In fact, let's assume it reaches the asymptote, with a value of λ or 1. In the second phase, we then add the noise to the light, and "pair" this compound with no US. To see the model's prediction of what will happen on the first compound trial, we use the usual equation to solve for ΔV_N:

$$\Delta V_N = \alpha\beta[\lambda - (V_L + V_N)]$$

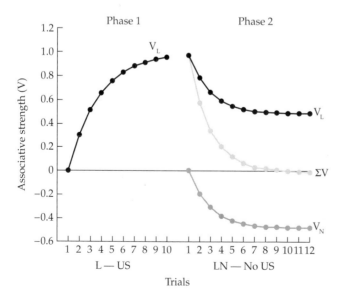

Figure 4.4 The conditioning of inhibition in the Rescorla-Wagner model. At left, a light CS is associated with a US; its associative strength therefore approaches a value of $\lambda = 1$. In the next phase, the light is compounded with a noise CS and the compound is presented without a US (LN — No US). The value of λ is now 0; therefore, the sum of the associative strengths of L and N (ΣV) will approach 0 over trials in the second phase. This requires that V_L decrease a bit from 1 and that V_N decrease from 0. When V of a CS goes below 0, it becomes an inhibitor.

Remember that trials with no US have a λ of 0 (a US of zero magnitude). Furthermore, in this example we have trained the light to have a value of V = 1. Thus:

$$\Delta V_N = \alpha\beta \, [0 - (1 + 0)] = -.2$$

The model predicts that the noise will decrease in strength. But since it starts with a value of 0, it will have to decrease below zero; therefore, V_N will become *negative*. This is how the model defines inhibition: An inhibitor is a CS with a negative V value.

Given this information, the picture of conditioning is now complete. Conditioned inhibitors have negative V values while excitors have positive V values. The system preserves the idea that excitation and inhibition are at opposite ends of one continuum (e.g., Rescorla, 1967b). It also allows for the known effects of compounding excitors and inhibitors that we discussed in Chapter 3. Recall that performance to compound stimuli is usually a function of the sum of the elements—excitors add to one another, but inhibitors subtract. By giving exitors and inhibitors positive and negative numbers, the model preserves this idea. Basically, performance to a compound stimulus will be the summed value of the compounded CSs, or in terms of the model, ΣV.

Figure 4.4 actually shows that the values of both the noise and the light will change during the Phase 2 compound trials. This is because both elements in the compound are paired with some surprise, and therefore both may change. To solve for changes to V_L, we follow the usual rules. In fact, the equations and the numbers we enter into them are the same as that for the noise. So just as V_N decreases, so does V_L. The main difference is that, while the decreases in V_N make the neutral stimulus drop to a value less than 0, the decreases in V_L bring it down from the value of 1, learned during the first phase.

A closer look at Figure 4.4 actually reveals an interesting—and clinically relevant—further prediction. Note that as the compound extinction trials continue, there is a point at which the model predicts no further changes to V_N or V_L. In the long run, an *infinite* number of compound trials beyond those shown above will lead to no further decrease in the V values. If we were interested in extinguishing fear to a phobic stimulus like the light, this is relevant, because it tells us that certain extinction procedures will not be effective in making the excitor truly neutral (V_L never reaches 0). Basically, the rule is this: If an inhibitor is presented in compound with the excitor during extinction, the inhibitor may "protect" the excitor from total associative loss. The prediction of **protection from extinction** has been confirmed in experiments by Rescorla (2003) and Soltysik et al. (1983). It is clinically relevant; clinicians may extinguish excitors in the presence of cues that can become inhibitory during exposure therapy. If we were to eventually test the excitor on its own—away from the influence of the inhibitor—we would observe fear performance again. This is a possible reason for relapse.

To understand the prediction, it is helpful to remember that the Rescorla-Wagner equation embodies the concept of surprise. In the illustration, both

V_L and V_N decrease until their *combined* predictive value—ΣV—equals zero. At this point, the inhibitory noise predicts "no US" about as much as the excitatory light predicts the US. The two predictions cancel each other out, and the compound therefore predicts nothing. When nothing occurs at the end of the trial, there is no surprise, and no change in associative strength occurs.

Protection from extinction has an interesting flip side. Just as presenting an inhibitor in compound with an excitor can "protect" the excitor from associative loss in extinction, presenting another excitor can facilitate it! Suppose we ran another experiment so that a light and a buzzer were initially conditioned to have V values of 1. For one group, we then put the light and buzzer together and present the compound without the US. According to the equation, the loss in V_L should be:

$$\Delta V_L = \alpha\beta[\lambda - (V_L + V_B)]$$

In the next equation, I have already substituted the V values of the light and buzzer for ΣV. Using a λ value of 0 for these extinction trials, the equation solves to:

$$\Delta V_L = .2\ [0 - (1 + 1)] = -.4$$

What does the resulting number mean? Essentially, the decrease caused by the light and buzzer together will be greater than if the light were extinguished *alone*. If a second group received extinction trials with the light only (no buzzer) the result would be:

$$\Delta V_L = .2\ [0 - (1)] = -.2$$

The model thus predicts a greater decrease when an excitor is extinguished in compound with another excitor. The prediction was confirmed by Wagner, Saavedra, and Lehmann (see Wagner, 1971) and by Rescorla (2000). The point is this: If you want extinction trials to be truly effective, put your CS in compound with other excitors (not inhibitors) during extinction.

Other new predictions

The fun thing about the Rescorla-Wagner model is that odd predictions practically jump out of it once you learn to play with it. It is worth a try—you might like it!

The top line of Figure 4.5A illustrates an experiment run by Kremer (1978; see also Lattal & Nakajima, 1998; Rescorla, 1970) that would not have seemed very interesting before the Rescorla-Wagner model. During the first phase of this experiment, a light and a noise were separately paired with the US on many trials. This allowed the value of each stimulus to approach the asymptote. In the second phase, Kremer put them together in compound and continued to pair them with the US. What does the model predict? It is actually somewhat unusual in that it predicts that both the light and the noise will *lose* associative strength, even though they continue to be paired with the US!

To understand the prediction, we merely use the same tools we have used before. Assume that both light and noise are conditioned to the asymptote

(A)

Phase 1	Phase 2	Test
L — Shock, N — Shock	LN — Shock	L?, N?
L — Shock, N — Shock	LNX — Shock	X?

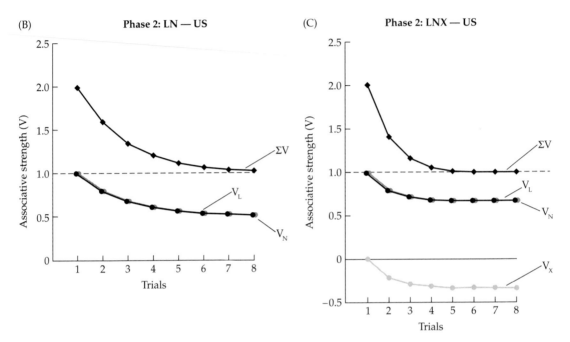

(B) **Phase 2: LN — US**

(C) **Phase 2: LNX — US**

Figure 4.5 "Overexpectation" of the US. (A) Designs of Kremer's (1978) two experiments. (B) Rescorla-Wagner predictions for what will happen when the compound LN is paired with a US after L and N have each been separately associated with the US and learning has reached the asymptote ($V_L = V_N = \lambda = 1$). In Phase 2, the summed strengths of L and N (ΣV) "overexpects" the US, and ΣV will therefore decrease over trials until its value is equal to λ. This requires that the associative strengths of L and N decrease. (C) Rescorla-Wagner predictions for a similar experiment in which a CS that starts with a value of 0 associative strength (CS X) is added to the compound. The model predicts that X will become an inhibitor (its value will drop below 0)—even though it is always paired with the US.

in Phase 1. If we used our usual US with a value of $\lambda = 1$, then at the asymptote both V_L and V_N would equal 1. To predict changes that will occur during Phase 2, we use the usual equation. For now, let's focus on the noise:

$$\Delta V_N = \alpha\beta[\lambda - (V_L + V_N)]$$

We continue to use the same US as before, with its λ value of 1.0. Given the V values for light and noise that were established during the first phase, the numbers come to:

$$\Delta V_N = .2\,[1.0 - (1.0 + 1.0)] = -.2$$

The noise's associative strength will therefore decrease during this phase! In effect, the noise and light together "overpredict" the US, and the noise's associative strength is reduced accordingly. This surprising prediction was confirmed by Kremer (1978), and also by Lattal and Nakajima (1998), and Rescorla (1970). It is known as the **overexpectation effect**.

In fact, both noise and light will decrease in strength during the second phase; this is because both stimuli are present on these trials, and both—in principle—are subject to the same forces. Figure 4.5B actually illustrates the model's prediction for both stimuli during Phase 2. Notice that the value of neither stimulus returns to 0; do you see why? It is because the changes will stop occurring only when the *summed* values of the noise and light (ΣV) equals λ (1.0). At this point, what is predicted (ΣV) and what actually occurs (λ) are perfectly in line with one another. Once these quantities are equal, there is no more surprise and no further changes will occur.

Kremer (1978) actually took the model a step further. In another experiment (see Figure 4.5A, second row), he ran the same Phase 1 but added a new, almost perverse, twist when he began Phase 2: Instead of only presenting light and noise with the US, Kremer added a *third* CS, X, with no previous training. This stimulus was completely neutral at the beginning of Phase 2. The model makes a cool prediction here: Even though X is always paired with a US, the model predicts that it should become a conditioned inhibitor!

Arriving at the prediction is easy. As before, light and noise are both trained to an asymptote value of $\lambda = 1.0$. The US in Phase 2 is the same, and thus also has a λ value of 1.0. The new stimulus, X, starts with a value of zero, because it is a new stimulus with no previous history of conditioning. The only new trick is that ΣV now requires summing the V values of all three stimuli: L, N, and X. To find out what happens to X, we expand on the familiar equation, so that:

$$\Delta V_X = \alpha\beta[\lambda - (V_L + V_N + V_X)]$$

Substituting the numbers from above, the equation becomes:

$$\Delta V_X = .2\ [1 - (1 + 1 + 0)] = -.2$$

The model predicts that X's value will decrease (as L and N did in Kremer's previous experiment). However, since X starts at 0, the decrease will drive X into the realm of negative numbers; it will thus become a conditioned inhibitor. Kremer (1978) confirmed this prediction in a conditioned suppression experiment with rats.

Figure 4.5C shows the changes predicted with all three stimuli used during Phase 2. We now see that our previous description of a conditioned inhibitor as a stimulus that "predicts no US" is not quite right. In this experiment, X was always paired with a US; so, how can we say it predicts no US? A better description may be that an inhibitor signals that an upcoming US is not as strong as other cues on the trial predict it to be. For many people, the symbols and numbers of the model are actually easier to comprehend and remember than the verbal description.

Let's pause and take stock of what we've learned thus far. In our discussion of the Rescorla-Wagner model, chaos has practically broken loose. Kamin's early work told us that CS-US pairings are not sufficient to cause learning, but that turns out to be only part of the story. CS-US pairings can actually reduce associative strength—or even cause conditioned inhibition. And, extinction trials may not always be sufficient to cause extinction or to produce conditioned inhibition. The model has given us a glimpse of a brave new world. The research stimulated by the Rescorla-Wagner model shook up our previous understanding of—and common intuitions about—Pavlovian conditioning. In fact, the model has helped to change the way we think about this deceptively simple learning process.

CS-US contingencies

The model also offered a precise way to think about the experiments suggesting a role for a CS-US contingency in conditioning (e.g., Rescorla, 1966, 1967b, 1968b; see Chapter 3). It also clarified their connection with other findings on information value. The procedures used in these experiments are summarized again in Figure 4.6. Remember that a negative CS-US contingency—where the US is more probable without the CS than with it—leads to inhibitory conditioning of the CS, while a zero CS-US contingency leads to zero learning. As noted by Papini and Bitterman (1990), one superficial explanation of these findings has been embraced by some textbooks: Perhaps the animal learns or directly appreciates the correlation between the CS and the US. However, as was suggested in the last chapter, there are less grandiose ways to think about what is learned in the contingency experiment. The Rescorla-Wagner model offers one of these explanations.

The model explains contingency effects in a remarkably straightforward way. Rescorla and Wagner pointed out that the CS and US are not presented in a vacuum in the contingency experiment. Instead, they always occur together with stimuli that are always present in the background. These background stimuli could include odors or sounds or visual aspects of the room, apparatus, or box that the subject is in while it is exposed to the CS and US. Such stimuli are called **contextual stimuli**, or **context**, and we must always presume that the animal can learn about these cues in addition to

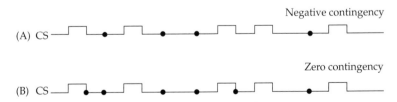

Figure 4.6 (A) A negative contingency between CS and US (the US is less probable in the presence of the CS than in its absence). (B) Zero contingency between CS and US (the US is equally probable in the presence and absence of the CS).

the ordinary CS. In fact, there is good evidence that animals and humans do learn to associate these background stimuli with the CS or US during conditioning. The key idea was that these contextual stimuli may serve as a single, long-lasting CS that is present whenever the CS and US are presented. When the US is presented in the absence of the CS, it is therefore paired with the context. And, whenever the CS itself is presented, *it is always presented in compound with the context.*

Once we recognize the presence of contextual stimuli, all sorts of things begin to happen. First, consider the negative contingency situation as it is sketched in Figure 4.6A. The model tells us that there are (basically) two kinds of trials during the session: (1) trials when the CS is presented (but these are really CS-context compound trials), and (2) trials during the intervals between CSs, when the context is presented alone. In the negative contingency case, the CS-context compound is not paired with the US, but the context is paired with the US on its own. If we call the CS "X" and the context "A," then we see that the negative contingency case is a new example of Pavlov's venerable conditioned inhibition paradigm:

$$A - US, AX - No\ US$$

We have already seen that the model has no trouble accounting for inhibition developing in this situation (see Figure 4.4).

The zero contingency case (see Figure 4.6B) boils down to a very similar argument. Once again there are two kinds of trials: those in which the CS and context occur together, and those in which the context occurs alone. Here, however, the CS-context compound is sometimes paired with the US. What are we to make of this? In the long run, the two trial types can be thought of as AX-US and A-US, respectively; to simplify, the zero contingency case boils down to another example of the blocking paradigm. On trials when the CS is paired with the US, the US is not surprising because it is already predicted by the context.

By pointing to the possible role of contextual cues, the model provides an elegant description of contingency experiments (see Rescorla, 1972). Furthermore, its account of these effects was tested and supported (e.g., Baker, 1977; Dweck & Wagner, 1970; Rescorla, 1972). The strategy was to use one of several methods to reduce contextual conditioning that occurred during contingency training. When this was done, the effects changed accordingly. For example, when contextual conditioning is reduced during negative contingency training, little inhibition is acquired by the CS (Baker, 1977).

The effects of CS-US contingency remains an active research question to this day, however. There are other ways to view contingency effects (e.g., Gallistel & Gibbon, 2000; Gibbon & Balsam, 1981; Miller & Schachtman, 1985; see Durlach, 1989, for one review). For example, **comparator theories** also propose that contingency effects result from conditioning of the context (Gibbon & Balsam, 1981; Miller & Schachtman, 1985), but they give that conditioning a different role. Once again, the subject mainly learns two things: that the CS and US are associated, and that the context and US are

Ralph R. Miller

associated. (The CS and context are also associated, but this can be ignored for now.) These CS-US and context-US associations are then compared to determine the level of responding to the CS. If the CS's association with the US is weaker than the context's association with the US, the animal will not respond to the CS. In the zero contingency case, the CS's strength is the same as the context's strength, and no responding is observed. In the case of a negative contingency, the CS's strength is weaker than the context. Notice that the animal makes the crucial comparison after all the learning has already occurred. The comparison thus determines performance, not actual learning about the CS. One unique prediction of this view is that changing the strength of the context's association *after* CS conditioning is finished should modify responding to the CS. If the context's strength is weakened after either type of conditioning (for example by extinguishing it), the subject should respond more to the CS. This type of prediction has been confirmed by a number of experiments in Ralph Miller's laboratory (Kasprow, Schachtman, & Miller, 1987; Schachtman et al., 1987; see also Matzel, Brown, & Miller, 1987; but see Holland, 1999). Unfortunately, the complementary prediction that strengthening the context should weaken responding to a CS has not been confirmed (e.g., Miller, Hallam, & Grahame, 1990). Nonetheless, an extension of comparator theory (Denniston, Savastano, & Miller, 2001) has attempted to address this issue and has made a number of quite striking new predictions that have been confirmed in the Miller laboratory (e.g., Blaisdell et al., 1998; Friedman et al., 1998; Urcelay & Miller, 2006).

Interestingly, nearly all the views of the effects of contingency have proposed a role for conditioning of the context. In fact, beginning with the Rescorla-Wagner model's account of contingency effects, the role of context in conditioning in general has become an active area of research (e.g., Balsam & Tomie, 1985; Bouton & Nelson, 1998b). We will look at some more of this research later in this chapter, and in the next chapter as well. To a large extent, a considerable amount of knowledge gained in this area would have been delayed if it had not been for the Rescorla-Wagner model.

Summary: What does it all mean?

The Rescorla-Wagner model provides a very successful account of compound conditioning. Not only is it good at providing a parsimonious account of the results of compound conditioning experiments, but, by pointing to the possible general role of context, it emphasizes that conditioning probably always involves the conditioning of compounds. In a way, this is one of the most important messages to take home about the Rescorla-Wagner model. The general point is that (1) conditioning always involves compound stimuli, and (2) the increment or decrement in conditioning to any individual element depends importantly on what the other elements of the compound predict. Models like the Rescorla-Wagner model begin to give us a sophisticated handle on the probable complexity of learning in the real world.

Some Problems with the Rescorla-Wagner Model

Although the Rescorla-Wagner model is a powerful theory, in many ways it is only a first step toward a complete account of conditioning. The model has several well-known shortcomings (e.g., Miller, Barnet, & Grahame, 1995).

The extinction of inhibition

The Rescorla-Wagner model makes another prediction that runs counter to all intuitions. It concerns how we might extinguish learned inhibition. The model claims that, if a conditioned inhibitor is merely presented in extinction trials without a US ($\lambda = 0$), such trials should remove inhibition. On these trials, the inhibitor—with its negative V value—should lose its value until it returns to zero. That is:

$$\Delta V_N = .2 \, [0 - (-1)] = +.2$$

The inhibitor should "gain" strength—or more precisely, lose its negative value until it reaches zero. The prediction is interesting, because our intuitions about inhibition seem to predict the opposite. Why should presenting a CS signaling no US, without a US, get rid of its signal value? Here our intuitions turn out to be more accurate than the model. Repeated presentations of an inhibitor without the US do not decrease inhibition (e.g., DeVito & Fowler, 1986; Witcher & Ayres, 1984; Zimmer-Hart & Rescorla, 1974); related predictions also failed (e.g., Baker, 1974). This sort of result suggests that there may be something wrong with the way the Rescorla-Wagner model treats inhibition. Perhaps inhibition isn't exactly the symmetrical opposite of excitation, as the model implies by giving excitors and inhibitors positive and negative numbers separated by the central value of zero.

Latent inhibition

In the last chapter, we saw that if a subject is preexposed to a CS before conditioning begins, conditioned responding appears relatively slowly during a conditioning phase. The problem is that the model has no way of accounting for this effect. During the preexposure trials, no US occurs and no US is expected. There is no basis for expecting a change in the value of V, or indeed, a change in anything. Latent inhibition is considered to be an extremely important effect, and this failure is viewed as a serious shortcoming of the Rescorla-Wagner model.

Another look at blocking

The blocking effect is central to the Rescorla-Wagner model's emphasis on the surprisingness of the US. Blocking is said to occur because the US is ineffective—it has been rendered unsurprising. But during the 1970s, a series of experiments by Nicholas Mackintosh and his associates raised some questions about this account (see Mackintosh, 1978, for a review).

Consider the experiment sketched in Figure 4.7 (Mackintosh & Turner, 1971). Both groups received initial conditioning with a noise CS until the

(A)

Group	Phase 1	Phase 2	Phase 3	Test
1	N — Shock	—	LN — SHOCK!!	L?
2	N — Shock	LN — Shock	LN — SHOCK!!	L?

(B)

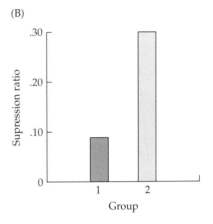

Figure 4.7 (A) Design of the experiment by Mackintosh and Turner (1971). (B) Results of the test trials. Exposure to LN-shock trials in Phase 2 made it more difficult to learn about the light in Phase 3. Remember that with the suppression ratio, lower scores indicate more conditioning. (B, after Mackintosh & Turner, 1971.)

asymptote was reached. Later (Phase 3), they received an LN compound CS paired with a larger shock. Based on Kamin's results, L should have acquired some conditioning—it predicted something new. The difference between the groups, however, occurred in between Phases 1 and 3. A control group (Group 1) received nothing, but the experimental group (Group 2) received several trials in which the LN compound CS was paired with the original US. By now you know exactly what the Rescorla-Wagner model predicted here. If N had already been conditioned to the asymptote, there should have been no change in the value of V for either CS. The model predicted nothing would happen during Phase 2. In fact, the groups shouldn't have differed in this experiment.

What makes this experiment interesting, though, is that the groups did differ in how much conditioning they eventually acquired to the light. As shown in Figure 4.7B, the control group did learn about the light—pairing the compound CS with a larger shock in Phase 3 allowed learning to happen because of unblocking. But the unblocking effect was missing in the experimental group. Evidently, the LN-shock trials had caused something to happen that interfered with the learning that was subsequently possible in Phase 3. Mackintosh and Turner (1971) suggested that during Phase 2, the animals recognized that L was a redundant predictor of shock. Because of its redundancy, they learned to pay less attention to it. Therefore, during Phase 3 there was no learning to the light because the rats had already begun to ignore it.

Results like these suggest a second important thing that might occur in the blocking experiment. The Rescorla-Wagner model merely emphasizes that the US is ineffective because it is not surprising. But the Mackintosh and Turner result suggests that animals may learn to ignore redundant predictors of the US. Mackintosh recognized that this could provide a completely different explanation of blocking. Blocking may have occurred because the learning mechanism may have detected the redundancy of the noise and then tuned it out. Instead of emphasizing the ineffectiveness of the US (the approach taken by the Rescorla-Wagner model), it is possible to emphasize the ineffectiveness of the *CS*. Let us look at how attention to the CS could affect conditioning.

The Role of Attention in Conditioning

Nicholas Mackintosh

It seems obvious that learning only happens if we are paying proper attention. In fact, there is simply too much information going on in the environment for a subject to take notice of—and attend to—at any one time. Several British psychologists have been interested in the fact that this sort of factor must be important—even in simple conditioning. The basic idea is that the amount of associative strength that is learned on any conditioning trial depends on how much attention is paid to the CS. In addition, the attention paid to a CS depends in part on how well the CS predicts its consequences.

The Mackintosh model

Mackintosh presented a model of attention and conditioning that was considered an alternative to the Rescorla-Wagner model (Mackintosh, 1975a). The basic idea is that the amount of attention a subject will pay to a CS depends on how well the CS predicts a US. If the CS is a good predictor of a US, then the subject will pay attention to it. But if the CS is no better at predicting the US than other CSs that are also present on a trial, then attention to it will decline. The subject attends to stimuli in its environment if those stimuli are useful in predicting biologically significant events.

Mackintosh put this plausible idea into the familiar vocabulary. Conditioning trials were assumed to result in increases or decreases in associative strength according to the equation:

$$\Delta V = \alpha\beta(\lambda - V)$$

But conditioning trials also cause changes in attention to the CS, which Mackintosh linked to the term α. The effects of αs of different sizes were already illustrated in Figure 4.2. If α (attention to the CS) is high, the amount of learning that occurs on any trial will be high. If α is low, the amount of learning will be low. Notice also that if α is 0—that is, if there is no attention paid to the CS—then the equation will solve to a value of 0, and there will be no learning at all to the CS on that trial.

Mackintosh (1975a) argued that α increased to a given CS on a conditioning trial if the CS was the best predictor of the US on that trial. In contrast, α to a CS decreased if the CS was no better than the others at predicting the US. (It is not necessary to consider the equations that represented these ideas.) As conditioning proceeds, the subject pays more and more attention to the best predictor of the US, and less and less attention to the weaker predictors.

One advantage of Mackintosh's model was that it explained latent inhibition. When the CS is presented without a US during the preexposure phase, the value of α to the CS was predicted to go down. The CS is no better than background contextual cues at predicting no US. When the CS is paired with the US in a second phase, the value of α starts quite low, making the increments in associative strength that happen on any trial quite small.

Naturally enough, the Mackintosh model also handled effects like the Mackintosh and Turner result (1971) (see Figure 4.7). During the second phase of that experiment, the experimental group (Group 2) received a light-noise compound that was paired with shock. On the first trial, the subject attended to both the CSs, and some learning to each CS did occur. But the noise had already been established as a good predictor of the US in the first phase. Its α value therefore remained high. But on Trial 1, the light was recognized as a worse predictor of the US, and because of that, the value of α for the light CS decreased. As a result, by the time Phase 3 came around, the value of α to the light was low enough to interfere with good learning in that phase.

The Mackintosh model's explanation of blocking is different from that of the Rescorla-Wagner model. According to the former, the US was perfectly capable of causing learning to both the light and the noise; the important thing was that, after the first compound trial, the animal paid less attention to the light. Since it takes one trial to learn which CSs are the best predictors, the value of α can only change after the first conditioning trial. In contrast to the Rescorla-Wagner model, the Mackintosh model thus predicted normal learning about the noise on the first blocking trial. Mackintosh (1975b) reported normal learning to the noise on the first trial (consistent with his prediction). On the other hand, others have reported fairly complete blocking on the first trial, in support of the Rescorla-Wagner prediction (e.g., Balaz, Kasprow, & Miller, 1982).

Unfortunately, Mackintosh's idea that attention should increase for good predictors has not always fared very well (see LePelley, 2004, for one review). Figure 4.8 shows an experiment by Hall and Pearce (1979). One group

(A)

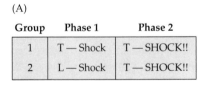

Group	Phase 1	Phase 2
1	T — Shock	T — SHOCK!!
2	L — Shock	T — SHOCK!!

(B)

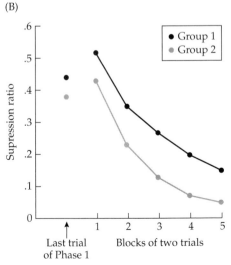

Figure 4.8 (A) Design of experiment by Hall and Pearce (1979). (B) Results of conditioning during Phase 2. Group 1, which had previously learned to associate the CS with a small shock, was slower to learn about it in Phase 2—even though the shock had previously been a good predictor of a US. (B, after Hall & Pearce, 1979.)

received 66 initial conditioning trials with a tone and a weak shock before conditioning with a stronger shock in a second phase. A second group received conditioning with different shocks in the two phases, but for this group, the tone CS was not used until the second phase. We are interested in the rate of conditioning to the tone in the second phase. According to Mackintosh, Group 1 should learn especially quickly: During Phase 1, the tone was established as a good predictor of a US, and the value of α upon entering Phase 2 should be very high. At the start of Phase 2, the animals should be paying a great deal of attention to the tone, and should therefore learn about it very rapidly.

John Pearce

What Hall and Pearce found, however, was quite striking. Instead of causing rapid conditioning, conditioning of the tone in Phase 1 caused the animals to learn about it more slowly during Phase 2! The initial learning caused **negative transfer** with learning in Phase 2, which is a phenomenon known as **Hall-Pearce negative transfer**. If the value of α had in fact changed for the CS during Phase 1, we must assume—quite contrary to Mackintosh— that it actually *decreased* as the CS became a good predictor of the US. Mackintosh had convinced everyone that attention to the CS is important in classical conditioning, but his rules for how attention changes as a function of conditioning did not appear to be quite right.

The Pearce-Hall model

Pearce and Hall therefore proposed their own rule for how attention changes during the conditioning of a CS (Pearce & Hall, 1980). Their idea contrasts sharply with that of Mackintosh, although it seems just as plausible intuitively. (This is a good argument against trusting your intuitions in psychology.) They suggested that an animal should not waste mental effort paying attention to a CS whose meaning is already well understood. Instead, mental effort—attention— should be applied to those CSs whose meanings aren't yet understood. Once the subject has learned what the CS predicts, it should pay less attention to it. Responding to the CS will tend to occur automatically (see Schneider & Shiffrin, 1977; Bargh & Chartrand, 1999), without the animal paying much further attention.

Like Mackintosh, Pearce and Hall represented attention with the symbol, α. However, in their model, the value of α on any given trial was determined by how surprising the US was on the preceding trial. (If the US is surprising, the CS isn't well understood, and this increases attention on the next trial. The quantity $\lambda - \Sigma V$ was used again to represent the degree of surprise.) If the US was surprising, say, on Trial 22, then the value of α would be high on Trial 23. In contrast, if the US was not surprising on Trial 22, the value of α would be low on the next trial. The size of α's value on any particular trial further determined how much would be learned on that trial.

Geoffrey Hall

To test these ideas, Kaye and Pearce (1984) ran some experiments in which rats were conditioned with a small light CS mounted on the wall several inches above the floor of the conditioning chamber. When the light was turned on, the rats would move near it and sometimes touch it with their noses and

(A)

(B)

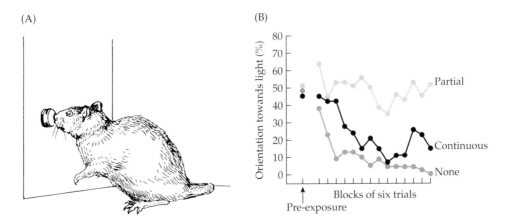

Figure 4.9 (A) A rat orienting toward a light CS. (B) Orienting to the light CS in an experiment in which the light was paired with a US on every trial (Continuous), never paired with the US (None), or paired with a US unpredictably 50% of the time (Partial). Consistent with the Pearce-Hall model, the rat oriented less to the CS when it always predicted the US or nothing. But it continued to orient when the outcome was uncertain from trial to trial. (B, after Kaye & Pearce, 1984.)

paws. If the rats performed this orienting behavior, it seemed reasonable to suppose that they were paying attention to the light. Figure 4.9 shows how this response changed during conditioning. Group Continuous received a condensed milk US each time the light was turned on. Initially, orienting to the light was high (the rats oriented when the stimulus was novel), but it declined over conditioning—as if the animal paid less and less attention to the light. The second group, Group None, received no milk after each presentation of the light. Here again, orienting to the CS declined; it was perfectly good at predicting nothing. The most interesting group was Group Partial. For these rats, the milk US was presented on a random half of the trials, but none was presented on the other half. Mixing up US and no US trials meant that each outcome was always somewhat surprising—the model predicted that the value of α would remain high. And, as Figure 4.9 indicates, that is exactly what Kaye and Pearce found. The results of several experiments like this one suggest that orienting to the light is a function of how surprising the US is on preceding trials (e.g., Wilson, Boumphrey, & Pearce, 1992).

These results support the model's explanations of Hall-Pearce negative transfer (see Figure 4.8) and latent inhibition. With enough conditioning trials in Phase 1, the CS becomes a perfect predictor of the US. The US becomes unsurprising, and the value of α at the beginning of Phase 2 should be very low. Therefore, on the first trial of Phase 2, little learning is possible. Ultimately, the negative transfer effect comes about because the animal has paid less and less attention to the CS as he has come to know more and more about it. The same mechanism explains latent inhibition. When the CS is presented over and over in the first phase, the lack of a US on those trials is not surprising. The natural amount of attention paid to a novel CS was predicted to decrease (Group None in Figure 4.9B). The rule did a nice job accounting for both problems and made some new predictions, too (e.g., Hall & Pearce, 1982).

The Pearce-Hall model also makes a number of other predictions. Surprisingly, many of them are quite similar to predictions made by Mackintosh's model. For example, blocking is supposed to work because the value of α becomes very low after the first compound trial—the US is not surprising on Trial 1. Once again, blocking should only occur after a minimum of two compound trials, but I already mentioned that blocking is evident after only one trial. Neither Mackintosh nor Pearce and Hall wanted that result to happen. We are living in an imperfect world. More likely, the world is nearly perfect, and our models just haven't gotten there yet. But the Pearce-Hall model, and the research connected with it, is important in telling us how attention to the CS might change during conditioning.

Summary: What does it all mean?

Some of the Rescorla-Wagner model's shortcomings have been addressed by noting that animals must pay attention to CSs in order to learn about them. From a purely practical perspective, it is useful to remember that learning depends on attention. If attention is low, pairings of a CS and a US may not be sufficient to cause learning. The important thing to know, however, is that attention itself depends on previous learning. Both the Mackintosh and Pearce-Hall models brought us a step forward in understanding how attention operates (see LePelley, 2004, for a recent integration). Attention changes according to how well unconditioned stimuli have been predicted by conditioned stimuli on a previous learning trial. According to the Pearce-Hall model, you pay attention to a cue on Trial 2 only if you didn't predict the right outcome on Trial 1.

Short-Term Memory and Learning

Attention has been an important concept in cognitive psychology for many years. It is usually placed in the information-processing model of memory that became popular in psychology beginning in the late 1950s, which I mentioned briefly in Chapter 1 (e.g., Broadbent, 1958; Atkinson & Shiffrin, 1971). Interestingly, we can think about conditioning quite profitably using the same kinds of concepts and terms.

A simple version of this system is shown in Figure 4.10. According to it, stimuli from the environment first enter sensory memory—a hypothetical memory store that briefly holds visual and auditory information as literal images or echoes. If the stimuli are attended to, they enter another hypothetical store known as **short-term memory**. You are no doubt familiar with short-term memory. Casually speaking, it is the space where thinking occurs. It represents the kind of memory involved when you remember a telephone

Figure 4.10 The standard model of cognition or information processing. An item can be primed in short-term memory through two routes: (1) It can enter from the external world (via sensory memory); this is known as "self-generated priming"; or (2) It can be retrieved from long-term memory; this is known as "retrieval-generated priming."

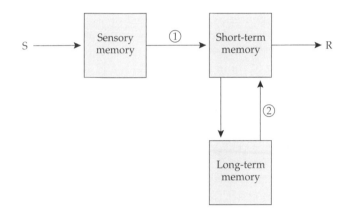

number between looking it up in the phone book and actually dialing the telephone. Information in short-term memory doesn't last very long unless you rehearse it—the telephone number is lost if you don't keep repeating it to yourself. Short-term memory is also said to have a limited capacity. You can demonstrate this by shouting random numbers at your roommate as he or she moves from phone book to telephone. (Please don't mention where you got this idea.) Your roommate can't hold all the numbers in memory at once, and your shouting will essentially knock the numbers out; short-term memory is brief and fairly small.

What we have been calling learning usually involves storage of information in **long-term memory**. Long-term memory is very different from short-term memory. For one thing, information stored here lasts almost indefinitely. It also has an enormous capacity. Notice this the next time you are in a trivia contest or play the game, Trivial Pursuit®. Even if you don't play with world-class players, it is impressive to see how much trivial information people seem to retain throughout their lifetimes. In point of fact, animals also remember conditioning for quite awhile (e.g., Gleitman, 1971; Hendersen, 1985; see Chapter 5). When a CS-US association is learned, we assume it has been stored in something like long-term memory.

The key idea is that storage of information from the environment in long-term memory depends on the whole preceding chain of events. Stimuli must enter the system, must be attended to, and must be processed somehow in short-term memory. Theorists often emphasize the short-term memory step. If information isn't processed sufficiently there, it simply won't get transferred to long-term memory.

In the 1970s, Allan Wagner (1976, 1978) used this framework to extend the Rescorla-Wagner model. In doing so, he more than doubled the range of facts that it explained. He kept the crucial concept of surprise. He suggested that a surprising event gets extensive processing in short-term memory and that increases its chances of being stored in long-term memory. Surprise is easy to conceptualize in the information-processing framework. Casually speaking, an event is surprising if you aren't already thinking about it. Within the information-processing system, an event is surprising only if it is not already present in short-term memory. Learning depends on the event being surprising, but surprise is reduced if the event is already present in short-term memory when the event actually happens.

An event that is already present in short-term memory before it happens is said to be primed in short-term memory. **Priming** reduces surprise. The numbered arrows in Figure 4.10 show that there are two ways stimuli can enter short-term memory—this means there are two ways that items can be primed. In arrow 1, a stimulus enters short-term memory from the external world via sensory memory. If an event is presented, it primes itself in short-term memory. This is known as **self-generated priming**. In arrow 2, the item is called up out of long-term memory through a process known as memory retrieval. A second way an item can be primed, then, is by a retrieval cue pulling it out of long-term memory. Remember that we now believe that CSs retrieve memory representations of the US (see Chapter 3). In the information processing system, presenting a CS will pull the US out of long-term memory and prime it in short-term memory. This is known as **retrieval-generated priming**. Surprise can be reduced in two ways: A retrieval cue can call the item up out of long-term memory, or a recent presentation of the event can also prime it.

Priming of the US

Now consider blocking, the finding that originally caused all of this interest in surprise. In Phase 1 of the blocking experiment, a noise is associated with a US. When the noise is presented, it then retrieves the US representation from long-term memory and puts it into short-term memory. In Phase 2, when light and noise are presented together, the noise immediately primes the US into short-term memory. When the US happens at the end of the trial, it is therefore not surprising. Blocking is the classic example of retrieval-generated priming.

The new model suggests new possibilities. Most importantly, it suggests that the surprisingness of the US should also be reduced by self-generated priming. W. S. Terry, a graduate student working in Wagner's laboratory, investigated this (Terry, 1976). Rabbits received eyeblink conditioning with two CSs—A and B. Trials with A and B were intermixed. Four seconds before each A-US trial, Terry presented the US. Trials with B were not preceded by a US. Terry predicted that the US before the A-US pairing would prime the US in short-term memory, making its occurrence with A less surprising. What he found was consistent with this: The rabbits learned more slowly about A than about B.

In another experiment, Terry presented a distracting click and vibration between the priming US and the A-US pairing. The click and vibration allowed the rabbit to learn quite well about A. Terry suggested that these stimuli entered short-term memory and knocked the US out after it had been primed—at the end of the A-US trial; the US was therefore surprising again. The situation is like your shouting of numbers at your roommate when he or she is about to dial a telephone number. Short-term memory has a limited capacity—especially, perhaps, in bunnies. Wagner's ideas about short-term memory, priming, and the surprisingness of the US were nicely confirmed by Terry's experiments.

Priming of the CS

The Rescorla-Wagner model emphasized the surprisingness of the US. The priming model expanded on this by giving us both retrieval-generated and self-generated priming. But even more interesting, it claimed that surprisingness of the *CS* was equally important. Learning depends on the joint processing of CS and US in short-term memory. If surprisingness of the US is important in determining processing, then it is only natural to believe that surprisingness of the CS is also important.

This idea gave Wagner a handle on one of the problems that the Rescorla-Wagner model could not deal with: latent inhibition. According to the newer model, exposure to the CS before conditioning should reduce its surprisingness; latent inhibition happens because the CS becomes less surprising. Since Wagner had become quite specific about the mechanisms of surprise, this idea led to new ideas about latent inhibition, which should come about because of either self-generated or retrieval-generated priming.

The role of self-generated priming has been investigated in several experiments. Figure 4.11 describes a taste-aversion experiment by Best, Gemberling, and Johnson (1979) (see also Kalat & Rozin, 1973). The first group of rats received vinegar 30 minutes before they were made ill with lithium chloride—let's assume that these events occurred at 4:00 and 4:30 in the afternoon. A second group received the same treatments at 4:00 and 4:30, but they also received a taste of vinegar earlier, at noon. Consumption of vine-

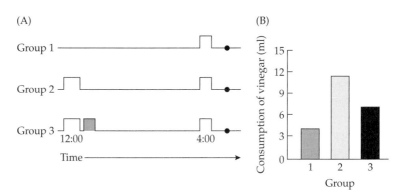

Figure 4.11 (A) Timeline of the experiment by Best, Gemberling, and Johnson (1979). Group 2 received a priming taste of vinegar 4 hours before it was paired with illness (•). Group 3 received the same prime, but then a distracting vanilla taste shortly thereafter. (B) Results indicated that the prime reduced conditioning of an aversion to vinegar, but that the distractor reduced the priming effect. (B, after Best, Gemberling, & Johnson, 1979.)

gar was tested two days later (Figure 4.11B). The second group acquired a weaker aversion than the first group; preexposure to vinegar at noon reduced its conditionability later.

You have probably guessed how the priming model explains this result. The first exposure primed vinegar in short-term memory, making it less surprising at 4:00. This interpretation is a slight stretch because it assumes that priming in "short-term memory" lasts at least 4 hours—a considerably longer interval than your short-term memory for telephone numbers probably lasts. Nonetheless, many features of taste aversion learning suggest that flavor memories do in fact last a surprisingly long time. (Similar experiments in my own lab have shown that the rat's memory for a priming tone CS is gone in under 4 minutes [Sunsay, Stetson, & Bouton, 2004]). Now consider the third group in Best et al.'s taste aversion experiment. This group received the same exposures to vinegar at noon and 4:00 p.m., but they also received a "distractor" exposure to a novel vanilla flavor soon after the first exposure to vinegar. This distractor allowed the rats to learn about vinegar again. Subsequent experiments showed that vanilla presented instead at 3:00 was at least as effective at increasing the aversion to vinegar. The argument is that, because of short-term memory's limited capacity, the vanilla knocked the vinegar representation out, making the vinegar surprising again. The result and interpretation are consistent with Terry's (1976) experiments on self-generated priming of the US described above.

In truth, most experiments on latent inhibition involve a gap of 24 hours or so between preexposure to the CS and the beginning of conditioning. This is presumably much longer than self-generated priming will last. But Wagner's model contains a second mechanism that easily accounts for this phenomenon: The CS may also be less surprising because of retrieval-generated priming. Once again we note that learning does not occur in a vacuum; rather, it occurs in contexts. During the preexposure phase, the CS may become associated with contextual cues. The animal may be returned to its home cage overnight. But as long as the context-CS association is not forgotten, on return to the same context the next day the context will retrieve the CS and prime in short-term memory, which would make the CS less surprising. Latent inhibition may result from the context causing retrieval-generated priming.

A simple way to test this is to preexpose the CS in one context (e.g., conditioning box A) and then pair the CS and US in a completely different context (e.g., conditioning box B). If this is done, box B cannot prime the memory of the CS; the CS should therefore be conditioned at an ordinary rate. This prediction has been widely tested and confirmed (e.g., Hall & Channell, 1985; Lovibond, Preston, & Mackintosh, 1984; Swartzentruber & Bouton, 1986). If CS preexposure and conditioning occur in different—rather than the same—contexts, conditioning occurs at a more rapid rate. A change of context between preexposure and conditioning reduces latent inhibition.

The effect of context in latent inhibition is more consistent with Wagner's model than the attention models considered in the previous section (Mackintosh, 1975a; Pearce & Hall, 1980). Neither of those models predicts that a context switch would have such an important effect on latent inhibition. Interestingly, a context switch also reduces the Hall-Pearce negative transfer effect (Swartzentruber & Bouton, 1986). That effect can also result from the context becoming associated with CS, thereby making it less surprising. The fact that context is important in both of these phenomena suggests that Wagner's retrieval-generated priming mechanism may have a role in both effects. It seems the short-term memory model of conditioning is promising indeed.

Habituation

In Chapter 2, we first encountered habituation, a common finding in studies of behavior and learning. Repeated exposure to a stimulus usually leads to a decline in strength of the response it originally elicited. Wagner's priming model provided a novel and highly testable explanation of even this phenomenon. If we assume that the response evoked by the stimulus results from its surprisingness, then habituation may result from the decrease in surprise. With repeated exposure, it may become less and less surprising. As usual, the model indicates that surprise can be reduced by either self-generated priming or retrieval-generated priming. Wagner's priming model allowed, for possibly the first time, full integration of habituation with other aspects of animal learning.

J. W. Whitlow (1975), then a graduate student in Wagner's laboratory, examined the idea that habituation resulted from self-generated priming. He exposed rabbits to 1-second tones; these initially caused a vasoconstriction response in the ear. The rabbits were actually exposed to a jumbled series of high- and low-pitched tones presented 60 seconds apart. Half the time, tones were preceded by a tone of the same pitch. Half the time, tones were preceded by a tone of a different pitch. According to the priming model, presenting a tone would prime it in short-term memory, making it less surprising for a little while. This should have made the tone less surprising; but it should not have made a different tone less surprising. As shown in Figure 4.12, there was less vasoconstriction (surprise?) when a tone had been preceded by itself, rather than by a different tone. But when a distracting stimulus was presented in between, there was less difference between the same and different conditions. These results are consistent with the idea that habituation here was caused, in part, by self-generated priming in short-term memory.

An even more provocative idea is that habituation could be due to retrieval-generated priming. Something beyond self-generated priming is necessary, because habituation can often last quite a long time between exposures (e.g., Leaton, 1974). The idea, again, is that during exposure to the stimulus, the animal might form an association between the stimulus and the background context. When brought back to that context, the context would retrieve the stimulus from long-term to short-term memory, reducing its surprisingness. A clear prediction is that habituation should be "context-specific"; that is, a change of context between repeated exposure and a final test should make it impossible for the test context to cause priming. This prediction has now been tested in several species and with several methods

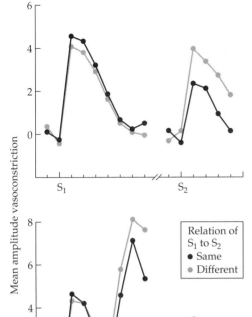

Figure 4.12 Results of Whitlow's (1975) experiment on the effects of self-generated priming on habituation. In the upper panel, a tone presented in the second position (S_2) is preceded by either the same stimulus or a different stimulus (S_1); notice that there is a bigger response to S_2 when the preceding stimulus was different. In the lower panel, when a distractor stimulus (D) was presented between S_1 and S_2, the difference between the same and different conditions disappeared. The distractor knocked the tone presented at S_1, out of short-term memory. (After Whitlow, 1975.)

for studying habituation. Unfortunately, the prediction (and other related ones) has *not* been confirmed in most experiments (e.g., Baker & Mercier, 1982; Churchill, Remington, & Siddle, 1987; Hall & Channell, 1985; Leaton, 1974; Marlin & Miller, 1981), although relatively recent results suggest that habituation of some responses might be more context-specific than others (Jordan, Strasser, & McHale, 2000). For the most part, however, habituation in one context transfers quite well to other contexts.

The trouble confirming context-specific habituation has implications that go beyond habituation itself. For example, the priming model argues that latent inhibition happens because preexposure to the CS habituates the surprisingness of CS. Hall and Channell (1985) ran a latent inhibition experiment using a small light CS mounted high on the wall—much like Kaye and Pearce (1984) did in the experiment described earlier (see Figure 4.9). During preexposure, orienting to the CS habituated as expected. When the context was changed, habituation remained. But when the CS was then paired with the US, the latent inhibition effect was lost. This outcome suggests that habituation and latent inhibition may result from separable processes; one (latent inhibition) is context-specific and the other (habituation) is not. Although Wagner's model was correct in predicting that latent inhibition would be lost with a change of context, it might not have pegged the right reason. We will return to this issue in the next chapter.

Summary: What does it all mean?

The short-term memory model expanded on the surprise idea first built into the Rescorla-Wagner model. Surprise became more than a mathematical quantity—it depended on whether an event is already represented in short-term memory, and it could be reduced by either of two priming mechanisms. The theory pointed for the first time to the surprisingness of the CS as well as the US, and it integrated habituation with other aspects of learning. In fact, since processing of the CS in short-term memory is analogous to paying attention to the CS, the priming model was able to handle many of the attentional effects proposed by Mackintosh, and Pearce and Hall. It integrated a very large amount of information. The model wasn't perfect, but it certainly was impressive.

By the mid-to-late 1970s, classical conditioning was being interpreted from an explicitly "cognitive" framework. Due in large part to Wagner's model, it became conventional to speak of the role of short-term memory, retrieval, and rehearsal when discussing conditioning. Wagner's model showed how this sort of account could be rigorous, and its power convinced people of the fruitfulness of a cognitive approach. Conditioning is now thought to depend crucially on how memories are processed in short-term memory.

Nodes, Connections, and Conditioning

Another way to think about long-term memory is to focus on the associations that are hypothetically stored there. As we saw in the previous chapter, it is useful to assume that conditioning results in an association between representations of the CS and US. Figure 4.13 shows an association between

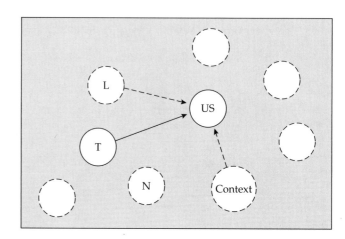

Figure 4.13 Long-term memory as a place full of memory nodes (represented as circles) that may be associated with one another. Associations (or connections) are represented here as arrows.

a tone and a shock represented in long-term memory. In the figure, the tone-shock association exists in memory alongside all sorts of other representations. For instance, there is a representation of a light and a noise, which may or may not also be associated with shock. In modern parlance, the memory representations—which are activated when the stimuli are presented in the real world—are known as **nodes**. The associations between nodes, which vary in strength due to learning, are often known as connections. A whole set of interconnected nodes is known as a network. As we saw in Chapter 1, the "neural network" or "connectionist" framework became popular in psychology in the 1980s (e.g., McClelland & Rumelhart, 1985), and there will be more to say about it in Chapter 6. For now, think of the connectionist framework as an expansion of the way we began to think about conditioning in Chapter 3. When a CS is presented, its node is activated, and activation travels down existing associations to activate other nodes.

Activation of a node is only temporary, and is thus analogous to being in short-term memory. Notice that a node will be activated either (1) when the item occurs in the external world, or (2) when another node associated with it has been activated. These two means of activation are the same as putting the item in short-term memory through (1) self-generated priming and (2) retrieval-generated priming, respectively. Accordingly, in the 1980s Wagner and his associates began putting the short-term memory model into this connectionist framework (Mazur & Wagner, 1982; Wagner, 1981; Wagner & Brandon, 1989, 2001). In important ways, the model was the same as before, but the new version expanded the model's scope and power even further. It is now the single most complete account of conditioning and associative learning that is available.

Wagner's "SOP" model

Wagner's (1981) new version of the model is known as **SOP**, which stands for **standard operating procedures** or "sometimes opponent process." The name doesn't describe the model very well, although Chapter 9 will have more to say about "opponent processes." But the name stuck—so what can be said? The new approach accepts the idea that a CS or US node becomes activated when the stimulus is presented in the real world. But the model assumes that activation has two levels of intensity, both of which are illustrated in the top part of Figure 4.14. When a CS or a US is presented, its node is first activated to a state called **A1**. A1 is a high level of activation and is analogous to an item being in focal attention. The node stays in this state only briefly. It soon decays to a lower level of activation, known as **A2**, which is analogous to an item being in peripheral attention. The node stays in A2 for a somewhat longer period of time but then eventually returns to the **inactive** state where it remains indefinitely until the node is activated again. This is a fixed chain of events. Once the node is in A1, it always decays to A2, and from there it always becomes inactive. Once the node is in A2, it must always become inactive before it can go to A1 again; it cannot go directly from A2 to A1.

Figure 4.14 Activation of a memory node in SOP theory. (A) When the stimulus is presented, the node goes into A1, decays to A2, and then becomes inactive again. (B) Activation of the node actually depends on the proportion of elements within the node that individually go from A1, to A2, and then inactive. Some elements decay more quickly than others; activation of the node really reflects the proportion of elements in A1 or A2 at any given time.

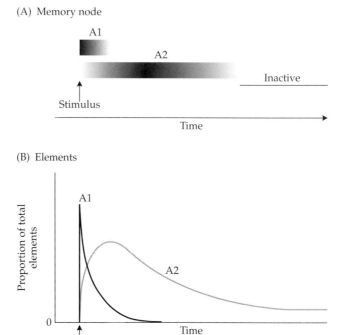

Three other ideas complete the picture of how SOP operates. First, an association will be formed between two nodes (like a CS and a US) only if they are both activated to a state of focal activation—A1—at the same time. This is like having them rehearsed together in short-term memory; as we saw before, this is what allows learning to happen on conditioning trials. Second, once the CS and US are associated, the direct activation of the CS node will now activate the US node—but not to its highest level of activation. The CS activates the US node *only to the level of A2*. This makes sense: A memory activated by a retrieval cue (and put in A2) is never quite as vivid as the real thing (in A1). Third, each node is actually made up of a large set of elements that are activated when the node is said to be activated. It is technically the node's elements that go to A1, decay to A2, and then become inactive again. When I say that a node is in A1 or A2 at a particular time, what I really mean is that a large proportion of the node's elements are in that state at that time (see Figure 4.14B).

Let us stop for a moment and consider what these ideas can do. When a CS and a US occur together on a conditioning trial, the CS and US nodes are in A1 together for a while; the strength of the association between them will consequently increase a little bit. The association will get stronger and stronger with each conditioning trial. As the association becomes stronger, the CS becomes better and better at activating elements in the US node on each trial—but only to the level of A2. Notice what this will do. The fact that the CS activates elements in the US node to A2 will now prevent them from going to A1 when the US actually occurs on the trial (remember, you cannot go directly from A2 to A1). In the long run, the US becomes less and less effective at causing new increments in conditioning because it is already expected and not surprising (it is in A2 and cannot go to A1). We've seen this idea before. As a consequence, there is less and less of an increase in associative strength on each trial, and the usual learning curve with an asymptote is observed (see Figure 4.1).

The same ideas explain the priming effects that were so new and important to the short-term memory model (pp. 125–128). Remember that priming a stimulus in short-term memory made it less surprising and therefore less available for learning. In SOP, priming a stimulus puts the corresponding memory node in A2; this prevents it from going back to A1. In self-generated priming (e.g., Terry, 1976; Best et al., 1979; Sunsay et al., 2004), presenting a CS or a US just before a conditioning trial puts it briefly in A1, but it soon decays to A2. If the node is still in A2 when the stimulus is presented on the next conditioning trial, it cannot go back to A1, and excitatory learning cannot occur. In retrieval-generated priming, presenting a retrieval cue puts the associated node in A2. Once again, the retrieved stimulus cannot be put in A1 while it is in A2, and excitatory learning cannot occur (e.g., Kamin, 1969). Distractors can knock primed information out of short-term memory (see Figures 4.11 and 4.12) because only a limited number of nodes in the entire memory system can be active at any one time. The familiar ideas about memory and surprise are all found in SOP in a new form. The model builds on the successes of the earlier models.

The SOP model also does much more than the earlier models. One of the most famous factors that affect the strength of conditioning is the timing of the CS and US (see Chapter 3). Believe it or not, none of the theories we have discussed so far can explain this fundamental effect. But SOP does—one of the most important things to know about SOP is that it explains the effects of time on conditioning. The top panel of Figure 4.15 shows activity in a CS node and a US node when the US occurs soon after the CS. In this arrangement, the CS and US nodes are simultaneously in the A1 state for a good period of time—and conditioning will therefore occur. However, if US presentation is delayed, fewer elements of the CS would be in the A1 state, and less conditioning will occur (see Figure 4.15, middle panel). Because individual elements vary in how quickly they decay, the proportion of CS elements that are in A1 gradually decreases as time goes by; the model therefore predicts smooth trace interval functions like the ones shown in Figure 2.14.

Backward conditioning, where the US is presented before the CS, illustrates another important feature of SOP. Here the US is in A2 when the CS is put into A1. These are the conditions that will cause an inhibitory CS-US association to be formed. To state it more clearly, *an inhibitory association will develop if the CS node is in A1 at the same time the US node is in A2.* Backward conditioning can therefore lead to conditioned inhibition. But notice that inhibitory conditioning will actually depend on the precise timing of US

Figure 4.15 Activity in a CS node and US node when the US occurs soon after the CS (top), longer after the CS (middle), and before the CS (bottom). These conditions describe delay conditioning, trace conditioning, and backward conditioning, respectively.

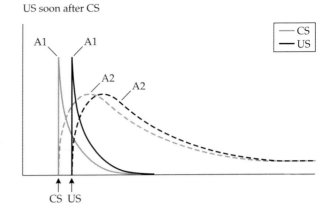

US soon after CS

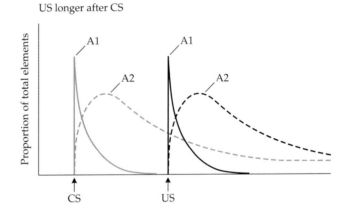

US longer after CS

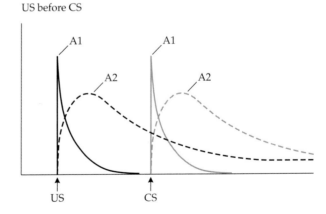

US before CS

and CS. If there is too long a gap between US and CS, the US node will have decayed from A2 to the inactive state before the CS is presented; neither inhibition nor excitation will be learned. And notice that, if the CS follows the US very closely in time, the US may still be in A1 when the CS is put in

A1, which would lead to excitatory backward conditioning. In SOP, timing is (almost) everything. In contrast, the previous models had ignored the effects of time.

SOP's inhibition principle also explains how inhibition is learned during compound conditioning. Remember that, in the traditional "conditioned inhibition" procedure, one CS (A) is paired with a US, and on other trials it is presented with another stimulus (X) without the US. X becomes a conditioned inhibitor. Interestingly, this is entirely consistent with SOP's inhibitory learning principle. Thanks to conditioning on the A-US trials and on the nonreinforced compound trials (AX — No US), A will activate the US node to the A2 state. X is thus presented at the same time the US node is in A2. These are the conditions for inhibitory learning—X is in A1 while the US node is in A2. SOP explains why backward conditioning and the conditioned inhibition procedure both produce inhibitory conditioning. I hope that you can see that SOP addresses a truly remarkable range of conditioning data.

Sensory versus emotional US nodes

Eight years after SOP was first introduced, Wagner and his colleague Susan Brandon expanded the model in an important new direction. They noted that USs often have emotional as well as sensory qualities (Wagner & Brandon, 1989; see also Konorski, 1967). For example, when a rabbit receives a shock US near the eye, the shock arouses an *affect* or emotion, such as fear; but the rabbit also perceives that the shock was delivered specifically to the left eye. Similarly, if you are nearly hit by a car while riding your bicycle, you may experience a strong emotional reaction, but you might also notice the color and the make of the car that nearly got you. An expanded version of SOP called "AESOP," for "affective extension of SOP," assumes that a US presentation actually activates two US nodes: a sensory node that corresponds to the stimulus's specific sensory qualities, and an "emotive" node that corresponds to its affective qualities. During conditioning, the CS becomes associated with *both* of these nodes in parallel (Figure 4.16), and they each control a different response. Both associations are learned according to the rules described above. That is, presentation of CS and US cause the CS and the emotive and sensory US nodes to first go to A1, then A2, and then to inactive. The two associations are learned when the CS node and the corresponding US node are in the A1 state at the same time. The only difference is that the emotive node is assumed to move between the A1, A2, and inactive states more slowly than the sensory node. This is consistent with your bike-riding experience: The emotional effects of that near-accident on your bike tend to persist much longer than the sensory experience does.

Consider a rabbit in an eyeblink experiment in which the CS is paired with a US delivered near the left eye. As the association between the CS and the emotional US node strengthens during conditioning, presentation of the CS begins to activate the emotional

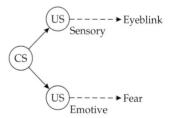

Figure 4.16 AESOP envisions parallel associations between the CS and sensory and emotive US nodes. When these nodes are activated by the CS, they cause different conditioned responses.

node, which evokes fear responses. At the same time, as the association between the CS and the sensory node becomes stronger, the CS activates the sensory node. This causes the rabbit to blink its left eye when the CS is presented. (The fact that the response is so specific to the left eye—not the right one—is consistent with the idea that it is specific to a sensory aspect of the US.) Both kinds of responses happen when the CS activates the corresponding US node to A2. But since the emotive node stays in A2 much longer than the sensory node, the fear state persists longer than the eyeblink. The model acknowledges the fact that CSs don't really evoke only one response; in fact, they may elicit multiple responses in parallel. Emotive and sensory conditioning are not completely independent, though. The theory also proposes that the emotive response will invigorate the sensory response (see Chapter 5).

Now return your thoughts once more to backward conditioning. Here the US precedes the CS. When the US is presented, both the sensory and emotive US nodes will go immediately into A1 and then decay to A2. However, the decay will be far quicker for the sensory node. Given this circumstance, it should be possible to present the CS at a point in time where the sensory node has moved to A2 while the emotive node is still in A1. Do you see what this predicts? The sensory association that results should be inhibitory—the CS is associated with the sensory node in A2. But the emotive association should be excitatory—the CS is associated with the emotive node in A1. Thus, the CS should inhibit the eyeblink CR at the same time it excites fear. This rather striking prediction is consistent with results reported by Tait and Saladin (1986) and McNish, Betts, Brandon, and Wagner (1997).

AESOP acknowledges that USs have multiple qualities that we learn about in a parallel fashion. This is generally consistent with what we know about the brain, which has separate systems that process different aspects of events in parallel. The distinction between emotive and sensory conditioning is also important to keep in mind when we apply conditioning theories to the real world. For example, one of the major symptoms of posttraumatic stress disorder (PTSD) is that patients typically "reexperience" both sensory impressions and emotional responses that are associated with a very traumatic event in their lives (e.g., Conway, 2005; Ehlers, Hackmann, & Michael, 2004). Sensory and emotive conditioning may play a role in this phenomenon. For example, a friend of mine (who happens to be an expert on autobiographical memory) once told me of an acquaintance who was in an accident in which the train he was riding was derailed. Because the train was powered by electric wires overhead, a bright blue flash occurred as the train was disconnected and careened off the tracks. Although the man survived, to this day an encounter with a bright blue flash (e.g., the light on top of a police car) evokes in him both visual memories of images surrounding the accident (activation of associated sensory nodes?) and an emotional response (activation of the associated emotional node?). That is, the CS has both sensory and emotional effects. Interestingly, according to AESOP, since the emotional effect of the accident lasted longer than the sensory effect, a large number of CSs that both preceded and followed the train going off the rails might be able to evoke an emotional response. AESOP's distinction between emotional and sensory aspects of conditioning also yields other predictions that have been tested and confirmed (e.g., Betts, Brandon, & Wagner, 1996).

Elemental versus configural CS nodes

Most recently, Wagner and Brandon have expanded their thinking about what goes on in the CS node when it is activated (Wagner, 2003; Wagner & Brandon, 2001). Their new ideas were largely stimulated by the work of John Pearce, the theorist who was 50% responsible for the Pearce-Hall model discussed above (Pearce & Hall, 1980). Beginning in the late 1980s and continuing to this day (e.g., Pearce, 1987, 1994, 2002), Pearce and his students have emphasized certain facts about conditioning that no theory discussed so far can handle. One of the simplest is a phenomenon that Pavlov discovered and called **external inhibition** (Pavlov, 1927). Suppose a subject is conditioned so that CS A is paired repeatedly with a US. Simple enough—A will gain in associative strength until it reaches an asymptote. But now, after conditioning A, let's present it together with a new, untrained stimulus, B. Conditioning with A is now followed by tests of AB. Even though B has zero associative strength, the addition of B somehow reduces the response to A (e.g., Pavlov, 1927). Intuitively, it occurs because the tested stimulus (CS AB) is different from the one that was associated with the US (CS A). There is imperfect generalization from A to AB. Adding B to A causes "generalization decrement." Surprisingly, the models we have considered so far do not explain or predict this basic phenomenon. In each of them, A has acquired associative strength, but because B has none, it should have no effect on responding to A.

Pearce (1987, 1994) has explained this kind of result by assuming that the organism will respond to the entire set of stimuli present on a conditioning trial as if it has been presented as a single stimulus. In the first phase of the external inhibition experiment, the animal learns to associate A and the US. But when presented with the compound (AB), the animal simply responds to this stimulus to the extent it is *similar* to the previously conditioned one. Pearce suggests that the similarity between two stimuli (like A and AB) is roughly the percentage of stimuli they share in common. Since A is 50% of the stimuli in AB, the similarity between A and AB is 50%. To predict the relative amount of responding one would receive when presented with AB after conditioning of A, you simply multiply the associative strength of A by the similarity between A and AB (50%). The theory thus explains external inhibition. It also predicts the exact same effect if AB is first conditioned and then A is tested alone. Here again, the organism is tested with a CS that has 50% in common with the stimulus that was conditioned in Phase 1. Pearce has shown that a full quantitative model using this idea at its core can explain many of the basic facts of conditioning, such as blocking, conditioned inhibition, and so forth.

Pearce's approach is called a **configural theory** because it assumes we learn about the entire set or "configuration" of stimuli that are presented on any

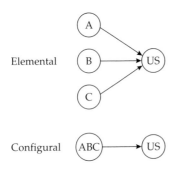

Elemental

Configural

Figure 4.17 Organisms might learn about either elemental or configural CS nodes when a compound CS (ABC) is associated with a US.

trial. When a compound made of several CSs (like A, B, and C) is paired with the US, the approach claims that we learn a single association between "ABC" and the US. This is illustrated in Figure 4.17. In contrast, the theories we have previously considered are all **elemental theories** because they assume that each of the separate elements in a compound (A, B, and C) are individually associated with the US (also illustrated in Figure 4.17). According to Pearce, this is wrong—we don't learn all of those separate associations. We learn a single association between ABC and the US, and then respond to other stimuli depending on how similar they are to ABC.

The Pearce model stimulated lots of experiments that confirmed many new predictions. It is especially good at explaining discriminations in which organisms learn to respond differently to CSs when they are presented alone and when they are combined. For example, in **positive patterning**, two CSs are paired with the US when they are presented together, but not when they are presented alone (AB+, A–, B–). The animal learns to respond to AB, but not to A or B presented separately. Conversely, in **negative patterning**, CSs are paired with the US when they are presented alone, but not when they are combined (A+, B+, AB–). Here animals learn to respond to A and B presented separately, but not when they are combined in the compound. The negative patterning discrimination would be impossible to learn if animals could only learn separate associations to the elements A and B—these would summate when A and B are combined, forever (and incorrectly) producing more responding to AB than to A or B! For this reason, the negative patterning discrimination is considered a classic case that proves the existence of configural cues. In the Pearce model, A and B each acquire excitation, and the AB configuration acquires inhibition that offsets the excitation that generalizes to it from A and B.

Pearce's model also predicts other new results that other models do not (see Pearce, 2002, Pearce & Bouton, 2001 for reviews). For example, think about an animal learning to discriminate between stimulus A and stimuli A and B combined (A+, AB–). It seems obvious that this discrimination will be easier than one in which a third CS (C) is added to both types of trials (AC+, ABC–). Intuitively, AC and ABC are more similar and should be harder to discriminate; in the model, they share a larger percentage of elements. Pearce and Redhead (1993) confirmed that this is the case (see also Redhead & Pearce, 1995). Amazingly, elemental models of conditioning do not predict this simple finding. They seem to underestimate the importance of the similarity between compounds that are associated with US and no US.

The success of the Pearce model has tempted many researchers to abandon the idea that organisms associate each element separately in favor of a configural approach. However, Wagner and Brandon have recently shown that an elemental theory like SOP can explain most of the new findings (Wagner, 2003; Wagner & Brandon, 2001). To put it simply, they suggest that activity in the CS node fundamentally changes when the CS is presented along with another stimulus. Consider your perception of musical notes. If you strike middle C on a piano, it sounds one way when you hit the key alone, but another way when you strike it along with the notes E or E-flat. (E and E-flat along with C create the sounds of a major chord and minor chord, respectively.) The extra note seems to change the quality of the original note. SOP now supposes that something like this happens when CSs are presented together in compounds—especially when they are from the same sensory modality. Remember that the model actually assumes that each CS node is made up of a lot of little elements. Each time CS A is presented, it activates a number of elements in the corresponding node. Some of these elements are activated whenever A is presented. But another set of elements are activated when A is presented with a second stimulus, like B. These new elements *replace* some of the elements that are activated when A is presented alone. In this way, when B is added to A, the compound AB does not activate all the elements in A that were associated with the US when A was paired with the US alone. Adding B to A thus weakens the conditioned response. That is how external inhibition can be explained by an elemental theory.

Some interesting research has contrasted SOP's new "replaced elements" conception with Pearce's configural approach. For example, Brandon, Vogel, and Wagner (2000) studied eyeblink conditioning in two groups of rabbits. As illustrated in Figure 4.18, one group received conditioning with CS A alone,

(A)

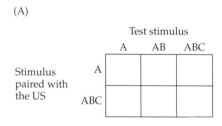

(B)

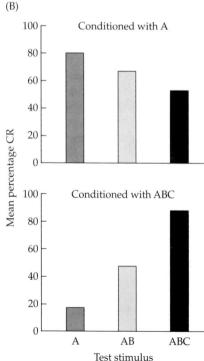

Figure 4.18 (A) Design and (B) results of the experiment by Brandon, Vogel, & Wagner (2000). Adding B and C to A after conditioning of A has less effect than removing B and C after conditioning of ABC. (B, after Brandon, Vogel, & Wagner, 2000.)

while another group received conditioning with the compound ABC. The three CSs were a light, a tone, and a vibrotactile stimulus—all from different sensory modalities. Once conditioning in both groups reached its maximum, all rabbits received tests with A, AB, and ABC. How much would conditioning from the first phase generalize to the new test stimuli? Notice that the group trained with A alone had CSs *added* during testing (AB and ABC include added CSs), whereas the group conditioned with ABC had CSs *removed* from the compound during testing (AB and A dropped C and B). According to Pearce (1987, 1994), either adding or removing CSs should have the same effect: No matter how you slice it, A and ABC share 33% of their elements, so the same drop in responding should occur when rabbits conditioned with A are tested with ABC, and rabbits conditioned with ABC are tested with A. But the "replaced elements" conception suggests a possible difference. After conditioning with A, adding new elements should cause a drop in responding because the new stimuli replace some of the elements activated by A. But subtracting CSs should be an even bigger deal. The reason is that SOP (like all elemental models since Rescorla-Wagner) assumes that, when the compound ABC is conditioned, A, B, and C will each compete with one another for association with the US. Each would acquire one-third of the available associative strength. (For example, in the Rescorla-Wagner model, all three CSs must share λ.) Therefore, dropping B from ABC should remove about 33% of conditioned responding, and dropping BC from ABC should remove a whopping 66%. There should be a huge effect of removing CSs from a conditioned compound, but possibly a much smaller effect from adding them to a single CS.

The results of the test trials are shown in Figure 4.18B. Consistent with the replaced-elements idea, adding stimuli to A caused a smaller drop in responding then removing stimuli from ABC. Only the replaced elements idea can explain this. Other differences in the effects of adding or removing CSs have been reported (González, Quinn, & Fanselow, 2003; Rescorla, 1999a). At present, a "replaced elements" version of elemental theory appears to work better than a configural theory.

Summary: What does it all mean?

Nowadays, "SOP theory" means the original model (Wagner, 1981) expanded to include sensory and emotional US nodes (i.e., AESOP) (Wagner & Brandon, 1989) and replaceable elements in the CS nodes (Wagner, 2003; Wagner & Brandon, 2001). Even from the beginning, SOP was the most comprehensive account of Pavlovian learning available. It is really quite impressive what it can now do. SOP provides a way to combine the compound conditioning effects addressed in the Rescorla-Wagner model, the attention and priming effects addressed in the Mackintosh, Pearce-Hall, and short-term memory models, and it does all this while also providing a good account of the effects of time, emotional and sensory aspects of conditioning, and stimulus configuration and generalization. In a way, the SOP model provides the overall scientific "paradigm" (Kuhn, 1962) in which almost all contemporary research on Pavlovian learning can be described and understood.

Some researchers worry that the model's scope and complexity might make it difficult to falsify. I am not particularly convinced by this argument. For example, we have just seen that it is possible to design new experiments that test the model's ideas and assumptions. Furthermore, some complexity may be necessary to explain conditioning, which looks awfully simple at first but actually has a wonderful richness, depth, and complexity to it. The fact is, SOP can explain, organize, and integrate an impressively broad range of findings in Pavlovian learning, one of the most subtle and thoroughly investigated problems in psychology.

Summary

1. Theories of conditioning have made steady progress. Since the early 1970s, they have been able to account for an increasingly wide and sophisticated range of effects that have been discovered in classical conditioning.

2. The Rescorla-Wagner model is built on the idea that learning depends on the surprisingness of the US. If the US is perfectly predicted on a conditioning trial, then it is not surprising, and no learning will occur on that trial. If the US is not predicted accurately, there is surprise, and the CSs present on the trial either gain or lose associative strength accordingly. The associative strengths of all CSs present on a trial add together to determine what is predicted.

3. The Rescorla-Wagner model assumes that excitors are CSs that acquire a positive associative strength during conditioning. Inhibitors are CSs that acquire a negative strength. To explain the effects of zero and negative contingencies between CS and US (which cause no learning and inhibition, respectively), the model assumes that background contextual stimuli acquire associative strength and then influence the CS as any other CS would.

4. Research stimulated by the Rescorla-Wagner model makes it clear that conditioning is not a simple-minded matter of associating two events that are paired. Pairing a CS and US is not always good enough to cause learning; under some conditions, pairing a CS with a strong US can actually reduce associative strength or even cause the learning of conditioned inhibition. Conversely, presenting a CS without a US does not necessarily result in extinction or conditioned inhibition. Learning on any conditioning trial depends crucially on the associative strength of all cues present on the trial.

5. Despite its successes, the Rescorla-Wagner model has several shortcomings. It incorrectly predicts that inhibition will be lost if an inhibitor is presented without a US. It does not explain latent inhibition. And it also fails to predict results which suggest that blocking may result at least partly from the animal learning not to pay attention to redundant predictors of the US.

6. The Mackintosh and Pearce-Hall models propose that learning is always influenced by the animal's attention to the CS. The amount of attention paid to a CS changes over trials; in fact, it is controlled by previous learning. According to the Pearce-Hall model, animals will still attend to a CS on Trial 2 only if the US was poorly predicted on Trial 1.

7. Wagner's short-term memory model expanded on the Rescorla-Wagner model by proposing that learning is determined by the surprisingness of both

the US *and* the *CS* on a conditioning trial. Either stimulus is not surprising if it has been "primed" in short-term memory. Priming occurs (1) if the stimulus has been presented recently (self-generated priming), or (2) if a memory of the stimulus has been retrieved from long-term memory by a stimulus previously associated with it (retrieval-generated priming). Contextual cues associated with the CS or US can cause retrieval-generated priming.

8. The short-term memory model explains habituation by proposing that a stimulus becomes less surprising with repeated exposure. Self-generated and retrieval-generated priming should both play a role, although the implication that habituation should be lost with a change of context has not been confirmed.

9. During conditioning, the subject may learn an association between nodes in long-term memory that correspond to the CS and US. Wagner's SOP model proposes that the nodes can be activated to two levels of intensity: A1, which roughly corresponds to focal awareness; and A2, which corresponds to peripheral awareness. When a stimulus is presented, its node is briefly activated to A1; from there it decays to A2. An association is formed between two stimuli only if they are both in A1 at the same time. SOP makes most of the predictions made by the short-term memory model, but it accounts for even more phenomena, such as the crucial effects of CS and US timing on conditioning.

10. AESOP, a more recent extension of SOP, proposes that USs have both "sensory" and "emotive" nodes. Activation of these nodes evokes different kinds of responses. Emotive nodes control emotional responses, and once activated, they take more time to decay than do sensory nodes.

11. The most recent extension of SOP further proposes that activation of the CS node is different when the CS is presented alone or along with other stimuli. This allows the theory to explain certain "configural" effects in which organisms respond differently when the CS is presented alone versus being presented in a compound with other stimuli.

12. Although conditioning theories will continue to change and advance, SOP theory (with its more recent extensions) is a powerful theory that can account for many of the most important effects in Pavlovian learning.

Key Terms

surprisingness of the US
protection from extinction
overexpectation effect
contextual stimuli
context
comparator theories
negative transfer
Hall-Pearce negative transfer
short-term memory
long-term memory
priming
self-generated priming

retrieval-generated priming
nodes
standard operating procedures (SOP)
A1
A2
inactive
external inhibition
configural theory
elemental theories
positive patterning
negative patterning

Chapter

5

Whatever Happened to Behavior Anyway?

THE LAST CHAPTER WAS FULL OF DETAILS about how information is processed and stored in memory during Pavlovian learning (stimulus learning). Theories of conditioning were covered in some detail because they help to explain the conditions that lead to learning, and how learning actually proceeds. Experiments on classical conditioning actually provide some of the most systematic information psychologists have on how basic learning processes operate. But it is also worth asking how all the "knowledge" that is learned in conditioning (e.g., associative strength, a CS-US association, etc.) eventually gets translated into behavior. Historically, that was what the field of Learning was all about; since the days of John Watson it has been interested in generating principles of behavior. But somewhat ironically, you might have noticed that, except for one or two sections, Chapter 4 was fairly quiet about behavior. For the most part, conditioning theories focus on the learning process itself, rather than on the critical changes in behavior that learning ultimately results in. To steal a quote from Edwin Guthrie, a learning theorist from the 30s and 40s, modern conditioning theories have "left the rat lost in thought." The present chapter is designed to help restore a little balance. While Chapter 4 addressed the learning process in Pavlovian conditioning, Chapter 5 will discuss performance processes, or how stimulus learning gets translated into behavior.

The chapter considers the issue several ways. We begin with the idea that, in order to influence performance, learned information must be remembered, activated, or retrieved. We will therefore look a little deeper at factors that govern memory and memory retrieval—the initial step in translating learning back into performance. In a way, the question is: After learning has occurred, what is necessary for conditioned responding to be evident at all? The discussion then leads us into a related topic that has figured prominently in conditioning research since the 1980s—the so-called "modulation" of learned CS-US associations (e.g., Swartzentruber, 1995). This topic is concerned with the fact that responding to a CS can be influenced by other cues in the background that "set the occasion" for the response—perhaps the way cues are sometimes thought to control operant responses (see Chapter 1). Finally, in the last section of the chapter, we will consider what determines the actual form of the behavior the CS evokes. That is, when conditioned responding is evident, what does it look like, and why? This section will return us to some issues that we first discussed in Chapter 2, where we saw that signals for biologically significant S*s evoke a wide range of interesting behaviors that are generally organized to get us ready for S*. We need to dig a little deeper into how all that actually works.

As usual, I hope you discover some other interesting effects and phenomena as we learn what we can about performance processes. Let us start the story by first considering retrieval and remembering, and their rather interesting opposite—forgetting.

Memory and Learning

How well is conditioning remembered?

Once Pavlovian learning has occurred, it can influence performance for a long time. That is, a CS that undergoes conditioning at one point in time can still evoke a conditioned response long into the future. In this sense, animals appear to remember conditioning for impressive intervals. For example, Robert Hendersen (1985) paired a CS with either a mild, medium, or strong electric shock in different groups of rats. He then tested their memory for conditioning either 1 day or 60 days later by presenting the CS and measuring how much fear it still evoked. Fear was indexed by the extent to which the CS suppressed licking water from a tube. (If you think a 60-day interval is not very long, consider the fact that the rats were probably only about 90 days old at the start of the experiment.) Figure 5.1 shows the results. The memory of conditioning was almost perfect after the 60-day "retention interval." That is, there was no evidence that the rats forgot anything between the 1- and 60-day intervals. The rats even behaved as if they rather accurately remembered the intensity of the shock that had been associated with the CS. The results are consistent with other results suggesting that conditioning—with either aversive or appetitive USs—can be retained surprisingly well over time (e.g., Gale et al., 2004; Gleitman, 1971; Hoffman, Selekman, & Fleshler, 1966).

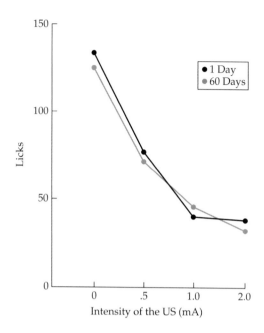

Figure 5.1 Conditioned fear 1 day and 60 days after conditioning. The measure of conditioning was suppression of water-licking—a variation on the conditioned suppression procedure. Regardless of the intensity of the US used in conditioning, there was virtually no forgetting after 60 days. (After Hendersen, 1985.)

This is not to say that conditioning is always remembered perfectly. Animals do sometimes forget details about the CS or the US. For example, over time the animal is more likely to respond to stimuli that are different from the original CS. That is, they begin to generalize more to other stimuli (e.g., Perkins & Weyant, 1958; Thomas & Lopez, 1962). It is as if the animal's memory of the CS becomes a little fuzzy over time. The animal's memory of the US can become a little fuzzy too; they may also increasingly generalize between different USs (Hendersen, Patterson, & Jackson, 1980). This type of forgetting of the details of stimuli (or stimulus attributes), which occurs in both animals and humans, has some interesting implications (see Riccio, Richardson, & Ebner, 1984; Riccio, Rabinowitz, & Axelrod, 1994). For example, it is surprising to think that forgetting can actually result in an increase in responding to untrained stimuli. Although the memory of conditioning seems surprisingly durable (see Figure 5.1), subtle forms of forgetting do occur.

It is also true that some forms of conditioning are forgotten more quickly than others. For example, Hendersen (1978) and Thomas (1979) found that fear inhibition can be forgotten faster than fear excitation (the kind of memory tested in Figure 5.1). For example, Hendersen (1978) conditioned fear inhibition to a light (X) using the A+, AX– procedure, where A was paired with a shock US and the AX compound was not. A tone (B) was also paired with the shock on other trials. Both 1 day and 35 days later, the light was then tested for its ability to inhibit fear of the tone. The results are shown in Figure 5.2. Excitation was retained very well—as in the above example. But inhibition was markedly reduced; after 35 days, CS X did not inhibit fear of CS B. Inhibition thus seems to be more sensitive to the effects of time

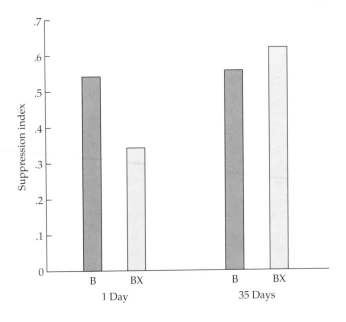

Figure 5.2 Conditioned inhibition is forgotten over time. The inhibitor (X) lost some of its ability to inhibit fear of an excitor (B) 35 days—as opposed to 1 day—after conditioning. In the "suppression index" used here, more fear is higher on the scale. (After Hendersen, 1978.)

than is excitation. The fact that fear inhibition is forgotten more quickly than fear excitation may explain why fear and anxiety may sometimes seem to emerge "out of the blue" over time. If an emotional memory is learned but inhibited, and the inhibition fades more quickly than the excitation, then inhibited fears and anxieties may gradually appear in behavior.

Other kinds of learning also seem to be forgotten relatively easily, and researchers have been able to develop some nice methods to study how and why organisms do forget (see Spear, 1978, for a review). For instance, Gordon, Smith, and Katz (1979) trained rats to run from a white compartment to a black compartment in a box during a flashing light to avoid receiving a shock. (This is actually an instrumental learning task, although we will see in Chapters 9 and 10 that Pavlovian learning probably plays a powerful role.) Four days after the rats had learned to jump from the white compartment to the black compartment, they received memory testing—they were returned to the white compartment and tested for their latency to run to the black compartment. No shocks were presented during the test. Time to run to the black compartment increased from less than a second at the end of training to about 10 seconds during testing, four days later. This increase in latency suggests a lot of forgetting occurred during the 4 days between tests.

The group of rats that forgot is shown at left in Figure 5.3. What makes the experiment interesting, though, is the behavior of the other groups shown in the figure. These rats received "reminder" treatments sometime before the final test. The idea was to find a way to reduce the forgetting that otherwise occurred after four days. The reminder consisted of bringing the rats back to the experimental room and putting them in the white compartment (with the flashing light) for 15 seconds. Different groups received this treatment at different inter-

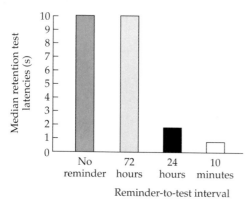

Figure 5.3 Forgetting can be reduced by a reminder. All groups were tested four days (96 hours) after avoidance learning. High latencies indicate forgetting. There was substantial forgetting in the group that received no reminder before the test. But if a reminder was presented either 24 hours or 10 min before the test, memory performance was markedly improved. (After Gordon, Smith, & Katz, 1979.)

vals before the test. Amazingly, it improved memory performance quite dramatically if it was performed either 10 minutes or 24 hours before the test (see Figure 5.3, rightmost bars). However, presenting the reminder 72 hours before testing was not effective—presumably, the rats forgot all over again. But the effectiveness of the reminder treatment illustrates a very important point about memory: Forgotten memories can be triggered by reexposure to part of the original learning situation. This is often called **memory reactivation**.

You have undoubtedly had similar experiences, such as remembering an old boyfriend or girlfriend when, later in life, you got a whiff of their aftershave or perfume. Or you might have suddenly thought of something you did in the sixth grade when you heard an old song on the radio. In the animal lab, if fear learning is forgotten, it can be reactivated by reexposure to the original shock US (e.g., Campbell & Jaynes, 1966; Spear & Parsons, 1976; see Spear, 1978, for a review). These effects all indicate that forgetting can occur even though information is still stored in the brain somewhere. When forgetting happens, the information is often still available, but not accessible or successfully retrieved.

Causes of forgetting

There are at least three reasons why forgetting might occur. One possibility is that the memory trace might literally fade away or "decay" over time. This potential cause of forgetting is known as **trace decay**. At first glance, it seems quite plausible as a cause of forgetting, because it seems difficult to believe that the brain stores memory traces forever. On the other hand, reactivation effects like the ones we just considered (see Figure 5.3) suggest that memories are often surprisingly intact even after long periods of time (Gordon et al., 1979; Spear & Parsons, 1976). The fact that reminders can often jog forgotten memories indicates that memories can be forgotten without necessarily becoming decayed or destroyed. Memory theorists have therefore tended to emphasize two other reasons why people and animals forget. Interestingly, these other causes of forgetting do not necessarily imply that the memory decays at all over time.

The next possible cause of forgetting is **interference** (e.g., McGeoch, 1932; Postman & Underwood, 1973). Put simply, memory for information learned at one point in time can be hurt when conflicting information is learned at some other point in time. The conflicting information somehow interferes with access to the target information. There are two types of interference. If the interfering information is learned *before* the target information is learned, we have **proactive interference**—the memory interference works "proactively," or forward, in time. When the interfering information is learned *after*, rather than before, the target information, we have **retroactive interference**—interference that works "retroactively," or backward, in time. To illustrate, people can be brought into the lab and given two lists of words (List 1 and List 2) to memorize. The experimenter can then ask them to remember either the first or the second list (e.g., Barnes & Underwood, 1959; Briggs, 1954; Postman, Stark, Fraser, 1968). In proactive interference, List 1 interferes with memory for List 2. In retroactive interference, List 2 interferes with memory for List 1.

In the long run, memories may be forgotten over time because time permits the accumulation of interference. For example, competing information learned during the retention interval could easily cause forgetting (retroactive interference). Indeed, conflicting information given to people after they have witnessed crimes or traffic accidents can hurt the accuracy of eyewitness testimony (e.g., Belli & Loftus, 1996; Loftus, 1979). In addition, because proactive interference tends to increase over time (e.g., Postman et al., 1968), information learned earlier would also increasingly yield forgetting as time passes. The subject of interference dominated research on human learning and memory for several decades until roughly the close of the 1960s (e.g., Postman & Underwood, 1973), and it is still widely seen as a powerful source of forgetting (e.g., Mensink & Raiijmakers, 1988).

A third major source of forgetting is **retrieval failure**. The idea here is that information may remain available in memory, but is forgotten if you can't retrieve it. A memory is a little like a book at the library. It might be in the stacks somewhere, but it will be lost if you don't know where to find (retrieve) it. To get good memory retrieval, the conditions present during memory testing need to be as similar as possible to those that were present during learning. That is, the **context** must be as similar as possible. For example, in an experiment that was similar to the one shown in Figure 5.3, Gordon, McCracken, Dess-Beech, and Mowrer (1981) trained rats to run from white to black compartments during the flashing light to avoid receiving a mild electric shock. In this case, the training occurred in one of two distinctive rooms that differed in size, lighting, and odor. Testing then occurred in either the same room (Room 1) or the other room (Room 2), 24 hours later. The results are shown in Figure 5.4. There was a clear loss in performance when testing happened in Room 2. The authors suggested that the rats failed to retrieve the pertinent information because of the difference in context. In either rats or humans, performance during memory tests can be worse when the test is conducted in a context that is different from the one in which learning originally occurred (see Bouton, 1993, for a review).

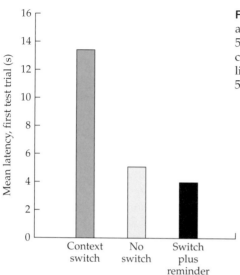

Figure 5.4 Forgetting also happens after a context change, and this can also be reduced by a reminder. As in Figure 5.3, high latencies suggest forgetting; the context switch caused forgetting, but this was reduced with a reminder like that used to ameliorate forgetting over time (see Figure 5.3). (After Gordon et al., 1981.)

The third group of rats shown in the figure received a reminder treatment similar to the one we discussed earlier. A few minutes before the test in the "different" context (Room 2), rats in this group were placed for 15 seconds in a white box similar to the avoidance apparatus' start box. As the figure suggests, this treatment once again improved performance during the test. The point is this: Forgetting that is caused by either the passage of time (see Figure 5.3) or a context change (see Figure 5.4) can be alleviated by a reminder treatment. This is exactly the kind of result that suggests that forgetting—in either case—occurs because of retrieval failure.

As mentioned above, similar effects have been shown in humans. In a famous experiment, Godden and Baddeley (1975) showed that scuba divers who learned a word list while either on land or underwater remembered the list better when they were tested in the same context—that is, they remembered best while either dry or wet (respectively), but not vice versa. Smith (1979) also found that students remember word lists better in the physical room where the lists were first learned; a switch to another room reduced that memory. Here, forgetting was reduced when the participants were instructed to think about the room in which they had learned the list. However, it is important to note that context-dependent memory effects are not always obtained in humans (see Smith, 1988; Smith & Vela, 2001, for more information). This turns out to be true in animals, too. Simple, classically conditioned excitatory conditioning very often transfers to new contexts, just as it is often remembered well over time (see Bouton, 1993).

In summary, the passage of time can lead to forgetting for several reasons. The target memory might decay; similar information learned before or after the target memory is learned might cause interference; or the memory may become more difficult to retrieve. In the latter case, the passage of time may lead to changes in the internal or external context that leads to a mismatch between the learning and the testing contexts (Bouton, 1993; Bouton, Nelson, & Rosas, 1999; Gordon et al., 1981; Spear, 1978). Of these possible causes of forgetting, interference and retrieval failure are now considered the most prevalent and important. In fact, retrieval failure may play a role in many situations where learned information or knowledge is not evident in behavior (e.g., Miller, Kasprow, & Schachtman, 1986).

Remembering, forgetting, and extinction

One situation where interference and retrieval may be important is that of extinction (Bouton, 1991, 1993, 2004). Although every model of conditioning we discussed in Chapter 4 has an explanation of extinction, it is not clear that any of these models get it quite right. For example, the Rescorla-Wagner model assumes that extinction trials (trials with no US) are basically conditioning trials with a US of zero intensity. Because of this, extinction should eventually make the CS's associative strength return to zero (see Figure 4.3). That is, the model assumes that extinction destroys the original learning. This is a bit simplified, as we will see in a moment. But there is a possible problem here. You already know that extinction does not destroy the original learning: As mentioned in Chapter 2, Pavlov discovered spontaneous recovery—the phenomenon in which the response returns when time passes after extinction. For spontaneous recovery to occur, the original learning could not have been destroyed. If it was, how could behavior ever return? Pavlov suggested that extinction creates inhibition, which he assumed was more labile, or fragile, then excitation. Some of the models that followed the Rescorla-Wagner model, such as the Pearce-Hall model and SOP theory, went on to accept the idea that the CS acquires inhibition during extinction (see below). But they did not try to explain why the passage of time causes spontaneous recovery. Theories of conditioning do not explain one of the world's most famous extinction effects.

I have personally been doing research on extinction for a number of years and have suggested that one way to go forward would be to combine theories of conditioning with the memory principles that were just discussed above (e.g., Bouton, 1991, 1993, 2004). Spontaneous recovery is just one of *several* effects indicating that extinction does not destroy the original learning. There are also important context effects. For example, Figure 5.5A illustrates a phenomenon known as the **renewal effect** (e.g., Bouton & King, 1983). Rats first received CS-shock pairings in one context, Context A. (The contexts were separate Skinner boxes located in different rooms of the lab; they had different visual, tactile, and odor features.) In a second phase, the rats then received extinction (trials on which the CS was presented without shock) in either the same context (Group Ext-A, for "extinction in Context A") or in a second context (Group Ext-B, for "extinction in Context B"). The results (see Figure 5.5B) indicated that suppression evoked by the CS gradually extinguished during this extinction phase. But interestingly, even though Group Ext-B was receiving the CS in a context that was different

(A)

Group	Phase 1	Phase 2	Test
Ext-A	A: T — Shock	A: T — No shock	A: T?
Ext-B	A: T — Shock	B: T — No shock	A: T?
NE	A: T — Shock	—	A: T?

Figure 5.5 (A) Design of the experiment by Bouton and King (1983). (B) Results during extinction (left) and testing (right). Suppression was "renewed" when the CS was tested in the conditioning context (Context A) after extinction in Context B. (After Bouton and King, 1983.)

(B)

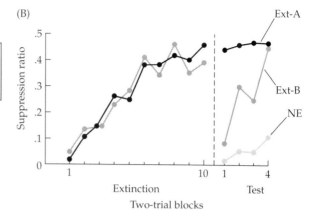

from the one in which conditioning had occurred, this change in context had no effect on the rate of extinction. Groups Ext-A and Ext-B showed the same amount of suppression throughout extinction. This finding is consistent with what I mentioned above—simple conditioned excitation is often remembered well regardless of the context in which the CS is tested, just as it is remembered well over time (see Figure 5.1).

But now consider the effects of changing the context *after extinction*. In the final phase, all of the rats were returned to Context A and tested there with the CS. This meant that Group Ext-B now received the CS in a context that was different from the one in which extinction had occurred—in fact, the original conditioning context. As Figure 5.5B indicates, the return to Context A caused a strong recovery—or "renewal"—of suppression in this group. Extinction in Context B hadn't destroyed the original learning, although Group Ext-B showed less suppression than a control group that had received no extinction (Group NE). This experiment, along with others that followed, demonstrates that extinction performance can be relatively specific to the context in which it is learned (see Bouton, 2002, 2004, for recent reviews). One can also create renewal by just removing the subject from the context of extinction, without returning it to the original conditioning context (e.g., Bouton & Ricker, 1994). Extinction performance thus depends at least in part on being in the extinction context.

In principle, the renewal effect illustrated in Figure 5.5 is actually consistent with the Rescorla-Wagner model. If you think about it, Context B could become a conditioned inhibitor during extinction—it is combined with the CS on no-US trials in extinction, and this could give the context inhibitory associative strength (see Chapter 4, and especially Figure 4.4). Bouton and King (1983) therefore tested Context B for inhibition, and surprisingly, it failed all the tests (see also Bouton & Swartzentruber, 1986). This, combined with other evidence, suggests that even though responding to the CS is suppressed in the extinction context, the context does not work through simple inhibitory conditioning (see Bouton, 1991, 1993, for reviews). What, then, is going on?

Figure 5.6 Associations that a tone CS (T) might have after extinction. In conditioning, the CS was associated with a US; in extinction, a new inhibitory association was formed (—|). Activation of this inhibitory association suppresses activation of the US node; however, to activate the inhibition, one must have input from the extinction context as well as the tone. Outside the extinction context, inhibition isn't activated, and responding is expected to return. (After Bouton and Nelson, 1994.)

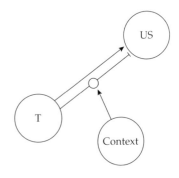

Perhaps the context serves as a cue that retrieves something like the *meaning* of the CS—that is, the CS's current relationship with shock. (For example, after extinction, the CS signals no shock.) And if extinction doesn't destroy the original CS-US association, then an extinguished CS actually has two available meanings: "The tone means shock," as well as "the tone means no shock." The CS is thus ambiguous—like an ambiguous word. And, further like an ambiguous word, *its current meaning depends on the current context.* To illustrate, your response to someone shouting "Fire!" might be very different when you are in a crowded movie theater as opposed to a shooting gallery at the county fair. As effects like the renewal effect suggest, responding an extinguished CS can also depend on the context in which it occurs.

To put this all together, Figure 5.6 illustrates some plausible associations that might exist after responding to a CS has been extinguished. During conditioning, the CS is associated with the US, and as we have seen before, the CS therefore evokes a response because it activates the US node or representation. During extinction, this association is not destroyed. Instead, the CS acquires a second, inhibitory association with the US. As noted above, this idea is actually built into both the Pearce-Hall model and SOP theory, which were both introduced in Chapter 4. For example, in SOP, the CS activates the US node to A2 on each trial of extinction; you may remember that this is exactly the condition that allows a CS to acquire inhibition! The new inhibitory association is gradually acquired in extinction, and it gradually suppresses the conditioned response by inhibiting the US node—which would otherwise be activated by the original excitatory association. After extinction, the CS thus has two associations or meanings; one that excites the US node and one that inhibits it.

The context's role is also presented in Figure 5.6. Notice that the context node connects with another node on the CS's inhibitory association. This second node activates the final inhibitory association, but only if *both* the CS and the right context are present. This means that when the CS is presented in the extinction context, the inhibitory link will be activated, and the animal will not respond to the CS. But when the CS is presented outside the extinction context, the inhibitory link will not be activated, and renewed responding (the renewal effect) will occur. After extinction, conditioned responding is always "on" unless the extinction context is present to help switch it "off." Notice that the excitatory association does not require a context for activation. This is consistent with the common result, illustrated in Figure 5.5B, that conditioning is less hurt by changing the context than extinction performance is.

Another point is that "context" is provided by many types of background cues (e.g., Bouton, 1993; Bouton & Swartzentruber, 1991). One example is the room or Skinner box in which the experiment takes place—the most common definition of "context." Another example, however, is the internal "state" produced by drugs. When fear extinction is conducted in the presence of a state provided by an anxiety-reducing drug (e.g., valium, librium, or alcohol), a renewal effect occurs when a rat is tested without the drug (Bouton, Kenney, & Rosengard, 1990; Cunningham, 1979). The animal is afraid of the CS again. Thus, a drug can also play the role of context. In addition, a context change may be created by the passage of time. As time goes by, certain internal body states and external stimuli are likely to change. Extinction may thus be specific to the context of a particular time. According to this idea, spontaneous recovery—the recovery of responding that occurs when time elapses after extinction—is the renewal effect that happens when the CS is tested outside of extinction's **temporal context** (e.g., Bouton, 1993). Thus, both spontaneous recovery and renewal occur because the animal fails to retrieve inhibition outside an extinction context. Consistent with this idea, both effects are reduced if the animal is given a reminder treatment that reminds it of extinction just before the test (Figure 5.7) (Brooks

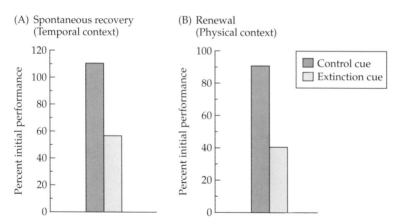

Figure 5.7 Spontaneous recovery (A) and the renewal effect (B) can both be reduced by presentation of a cue that reminds the animal of extinction. Analogous to what we saw in Figures 5.3 and 5.4, reminders reduce the failure to retrieve extinction caused by either the passage of time or a context change. Amount of responding in the test is expressed as the percent of responding that was achieved at the end of conditioning. (Data from Brooks & Bouton, 1993, 1994; figure after Bouton, 1994a.)

& Bouton, 1993, 1994). I hope you see the clear parallel with experiments on the effects of remembering and forgetting described in Figures 5.3 and 5.4.

These ideas might have implications for clinical psychologists, because extinction is thought to be the basis of exposure therapies (see Chapter 2) that are designed to reduce certain behavioral problems like anxiety disorders that may be caused by conditioning. The renewal effect and spontaneous recovery may both provide reasons for **relapse** after therapy (e.g., Bouton, 1988, 2002; Bouton & Swartzentruber, 1991). Thus, the effects of extinction therapy may tend to diminish if the context is changed after a therapy session, or if time is allowed to elapse. Therapists should be careful about performing extinction in a unique context, like an unusual office or while the patient is under the influence of a drug. Instead, they should try to ensure that their treatments will be retrieved in contexts where the original problem is most troublesome to their clients, either by conducting exposure in a similar context or by arming them with skills or cues that will help them retrieve extinction when conditions make relapse likely (for more discussion of these issues, see Bouton, 2001, 2002).

These ideas are consistent with some interesting clinical research. Fears in humans can indeed be reduced by exposure to the feared stimulus, but the fear may be renewed in a different context. For example, Mystkowski, Craske, and Echiverri (2002) gave students who reported being afraid of spiders a session in which the students were exposed to a tarantula in a context provided by either a room in a lab or a patio outdoors. This reduced their fear. The students were later tested in the same or different contexts; they reported more distress when they were tested in a different context, suggesting they experienced a renewal of fear (see also Mystkowski, Craske, Echiverri, & Labus, 2006). Renewal has also been reported in humans given extinction exposure to alcohol cues. Collins and Brandon (2002) gave undergraduate social drinkers several exposures to the sight and odor of beer in a distinctive room. These repeated exposures caused a reduction in their salivation and urge to drink in the presence of the beer cues. But when tested in a different room, both responses (salivation and the urge to drink) were renewed. Interestingly, this renewal effect was reduced if the participants were given a cue that reminded them of extinction—as in the animal experiments summarized in Figure 5.7. Renewal has also been reported after the extinction of cigarette cues (Thewissen, Snijders, Havermans, van den Hout, & Jansen, 2006). And, in an experiment that was mentioned way back in Chapter 1, Crombag and Shaham (2002) found that rats that lever-pressed for an intravenous mixture of heroin and cocaine in one context, and then had the behavior extinguished in a second context, showed a powerful renewal of lever-pressing when they were returned to the original context. All of these results suggest that the renewal effect is clinically relevant and may be obtained under a range of circumstances.

There are other effects besides spontaneous recovery and renewal that indicate that extinction does not destroy the original learning (e.g., see Bouton, 2002, 2004). For example, if the US is presented on its own after extinction, it can cause responding to the CS to return when the CS is tested later (e.g., Bouton, 1984; Bouton & Bolles, 1979; Bouton & King, 1983; Delamater, 1997; Rescorla & Heth, 1975). This effect is called **reinstatement**. Reinstatement occurs because the new US presentations condition the context, and this conditioning triggers fear of the CS when the CS is tested in the same context (e.g., Bouton, 1984; Bouton & Bolles, 1979; Bouton & King, 1983). Once again, extinction doesn't destroy the original learning, and the response one observes depends on the animal's knowledge about the context. Still another effect is **rapid reacquisition** (e.g., Napier, Macrae, & Kehoe, 1992; Ricker & Bouton, 1996). In this case, the conditioned response can sometimes return very quickly when CS-US pairings are repeated after extinction. One explanation is that recent conditioning trials are another part of the context in which the CS was originally conditioned. Resuming CS-US pairings after extinction thus returns the organism to the conditioning context—and causes a renewal effect (e.g., Bouton, Woods, & Pineno, 2004; Ricker & Bouton, 1996). For a more complete explanation of these effects and their applications to clinical phenomena see Bouton (2002).

In summary, I have just described an approach to extinction that combines conditioning theory with two of the memory mechanisms described earlier in this chapter. First, the learning involved in extinction reduces conditioned performance by creating a form of retroactive interference. Second, that interference is controlled by retrieval by the extinction context. In the proper context, an interfering memory is retrieved; in the wrong context, it is not. These characteristics of extinction may have practical implications for understanding relapse after exposure therapy.

Other examples of context, ambiguity, and interference

It is worth noting that a CS may acquire more than one association in a number of conditioning paradigms. Table 5.1 lists several of these effects. For example, consider **counterconditioning**. In this procedure, a CS is associated with one US (e.g., shock) in one phase (Phase 1) and then a different CS (e.g., food) in a second phase (Phase 2). As in extinction, learning from the second phase interferes retroactively with performance from the first phase. And often, Phase 1 learning interferes with Phase 2 performance as the Phase 2 pairings proceed. Counterconditioning was proposed as the theoretical idea behind "systematic desensitization" of simple phobias (Wolpe, 1958). In systematic desensitization, patients are gradually exposed to CSs they are afraid of while the patients are in a state of relaxation. This can be a very effective way to reduce anxiety or fear. The idea is to substitute a new response (e.g., relaxation) for an old one (e.g., anxiety) by pairing the stimulus with the new response. But like extinction, context and ambiguity might also be involved.

Consistent with this idea, spontaneous recovery and renewal effects both occur after counterconditioning (Bouton & Peck, 1992; Peck & Bouton, 1990).

TABLE 5.1 Some paradigms involving ambiguity, interference, and retrieval

Paradigm	Phase 1	Phase 2
Extinction	CS+	CS–
Counter-conditioning		
Aversive–appetitive	CS — Shock	CS — Food
Appetitive–aversive	CS — Food	CS — Shock
Verbal interference	List 1	List 2
Latent inhibition	CS–	CS+
Hall–Pearce negative transfer	CS — Shock	CS — SHOCK!!!

Source: After Bouton, 1993.

As in extinction, the Phase 2 treatment does not necessarily destroy the association learned in Phase 1. The first association remains available, and returns to performance with context change over the passage of time.

The other paradigms listed in Table 5.1 are also affected by context and time. Spontaneous recovery and context effects—in particular renewal effects—have been observed in all of them (e.g., Bouton, 1993). In fact, latent inhibition is worth considering again in this light. In Chapter 4, we saw that latent inhibition is often explained by assuming that CS-processing becomes habituated during the first phase. However, the role of habituation may be overrated. We saw that latent inhibition is reduced when the context is changed after preexposure to the CS, while habituation usually is not affected (e.g., Hall & Channell, 1985). Such results suggest that habituation and latent inhibition are not always connected; in a new context, the organism seems to recognize the CS (and thus continues to show habituation to it) but might not remember what it means. Instead of only habituating, the animal might learn that the CS means nothing of consequence (e.g., Bouton, 1993). This type of learning may then depend on the context. Gordon and Weaver (1989) found that, when latent inhibition was reduced by a context switch, it could be restored if a retrieval cue (a noise that had been featured during preexposure) was presented before the test. Thus, latent inhibition looked like it was forgotten with a context switch. This is another example of interference that may depend on the context for retrieval.

Kraemer and Roberts (1984) first reported a finding that is consistent with this view. Figure 5.8 presents a follow-up experiment by Aguado, Symonds, and Hall (1994). Two groups of rats received preexposure to a saccharin drink before a trial on which the saccharin was paired with illness. These groups were labeled "LI," for latent inhibition training. The two control groups ("Cont") received no latent inhibition exposure to saccharin before the same conditioning trial. Then, the saccharin aversion was tested either 2 days or 12 days after conditioning. At the 2-day interval, a large latent inhibition effect was evident; the Latent Inhibition group showed a weaker aversion than the two control groups, but at the 12-day interval, latent inhibition was

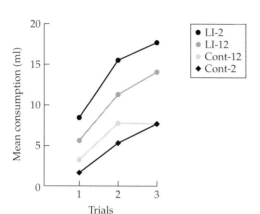

Figure 5.8 The effects of time after latent inhibition. In this taste aversion experiment, rats were tested for their consumption of the flavor either 2 days or 12 days after conditioning. The groups received either preexposure to the CS (LI, for latent inhibition) or no preexposure to the CS (Cont, for control). Remember that a taste aversion reduces consumption and is represented as a low score on the y-axis. At 12 days, the latently inhibited aversion had become stronger. (After Aguado et al., 1994.)

reduced. Latent inhibition (like extinction) thus appears to go away over time. This result suggests that preexposure to the CS does not necessarily cause a failure to learn about the CS. Instead, preexposure might temporarily interfere with the expression of that knowledge in performance. Note that this is the same idea we just considered for extinction. Both effects result from an interference effect that is lost with context change or a passage of time.

One challenge for this explanation of latent inhibition is that it has never been clear what the animal actually learns about the CS during the preexposure phase. We know that latent inhibition is not the same as conditioned inhibition (see Chapter 3), so it would be wrong to think that a preexposed CS predicts "no US" in the same way a true inhibitor does. Maybe animals actively seek reinforcers that will satisfy their current needs—hungry rats might seek food, while thirsty rats seek water. If a rat is hungry or thirsty, a CS preexposed without the reinforcer might be encoded as irrelevant for finding food or water (Killcross & Balleine, 1996). The animal might learn that the CS is not useful for predicting a particular goal. Alternatively, the animal might learn that the CS is just an intermittent feature of a particular context (see Gluck & Myers, 1993).

Regardless of what is actually learned in latent inhibition, the main point is that the interference paradigms described in Table 5.1 have a great deal in common. Information from both phases can be learned and retained, and performance is determined by the extent to which either is retrieved. Interference and memory retrieval are important determinants of performance in classical conditioning.

Summary

Classical conditioning can have long-lasting effects on behavior, although certain types of information (about the CS or the US) may be forgotten over time. When forgetting occurs, it is often caused by either interference or retrieval failure. Interference and retrieval are worth adding to the various learning mechanisms we discussed in Chapter 4 for a complete understanding of Pavlovian learning. Extinction is a good illustration. The learning of something new during extinction causes retroactive interference—the first-learned association is not destroyed but becomes less accessible, and performance goes away. But extinction (and the interference it causes) seems especially dependent on the context for retrieval. This means that if the CS is presented in a different context, the original CR can recover or return (spontaneous recovery or renewal). And the same principles may work in other interference paradigms besides extinction. Interference and retrieval are important processes that influence whether the CR is observed. A blending of memory and conditioning concepts thus helps us understand how learning is translated into performance.

The Modulation of Behavior

We have just seen that the context is important in controlling responding to the CS after extinction and other interference paradigms. If the extinguished CS is presented in the context where extinction was learned, extinction performance (i.e., not responding to the CS) is observed. But if the CS is presented outside the extinction context, responding may be renewed. One way to look at this state of affairs is that the context **modulates** responding to the CS. After extinction, it appears to turn responding to the CS off. Interestingly, it doesn't seem to work as a simple inhibitor—that is, a CS with a negative V value or inhibitory association with the US. Researchers have begun to realize that modulation effects like this may operate quite often in Pavlovian learning.

Occasion setting

In the early 1980s, several findings began to suggest that a CS can influence behavior in ways that are not captured by theories like the ones described in Chapter 4 (e.g., Ross & Holland, 1981; see early reviews by Holland, 1985; Jenkins, 1985; Rescorla, 1985). Those theories are extremely good at explaining how a CS can enter into associations with a US, but we now know that a CS sometimes works in a way that does not depend on its direct association with the US. To use the language promoted by Peter Holland (see also Moore, Newman, & Glasgow, 1969), who borrowed Skinner's description of how cues influence operant behavior (Skinner, 1938; see Chapters 1 and 7), a CS can sometimes modulate responding to another CS by "setting the occasion for" the conditioned response. When it does, the CS is known as an **occasion setter**.

Simply put, you can think of an occasion setter as a *cue that provides information about whether another CS will be paired with a US*. Research on occasion setting has usually focused on the discrimination procedures shown in Table 5.2. In the **feature-positive discrimination**, the subject receives a mixture of tri-

TABLE 5.2 Procedures that generate occasion setting

Feature–positive discrimination	L → T+, T–
Feature–negative discrimination	T+, L → T–

als in which a CS (e.g., a tone) is presented with a US ("+") and trials in which it is presented without the US ("–"). A second CS (e.g., a light) is set up so that it precedes the tone on the positive trials. Its presence allows the animal to learn to respond only on the positive trials. The **feature-negative discrimination** is the logical reverse. Here again, there are positive and negative trials, but this time the light signals the negative trials—the ones where the US does not occur. In either type of discrimination, the light is called a **feature stimulus**, while the tone is called the **target stimulus**. There is some method to the madness in the labeling. When the feature (the light) signals positive trials, we have a feature-positive discrimination. When the feature signals the negative trials, we have a feature-negative discrimination. The target is a "target" in the sense that it is the focus of the experimenter's attention—we want to know whether or not the animal responds to it on positive and negative trials.

Animals learn these discriminations pretty easily—that is, they quickly learn to respond only on the positive trials (Figure 5.9). This should not really surprise you. Discriminations like this are easy to explain by the models described in Chapter 4. Let's think about how they do it. "Feature-negative discrimination" is just another name for Pavlov's conditioned inhibition procedure. As we saw in Chapter 4, in the Rescorla-Wagner model (for example) the animal should associate the target tone CS with the US on the positive trials. (That is, the tone should gain a positive V value.) The animal should also learn inhibition to the light CS on the negative trials, when the light is combined with the tone and presented without the US. (The light

Feature-positive discrimination

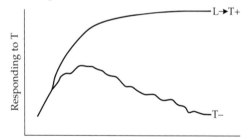

Feature-negative discrimination

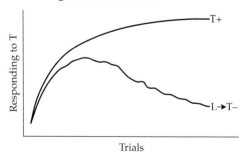

Figure 5.9 Responding to the tone CS during conditioning in a feature-positive and a feature-negative discrimination.

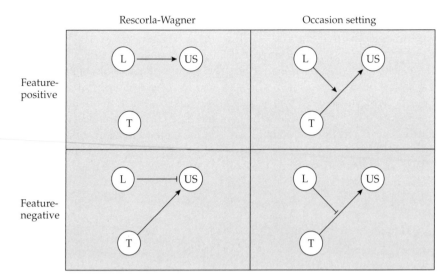

Figure 5.10 Associations that might form during feature-positive and feature-negative discriminations learned the Rescorla-Wagner way or the occasion-setting way. L is the feature CS (a light), and T is the target stimulus (e.g., a tone). Inhibition is indicated by a blocked line (—|).

should gain a negative V value.) The resulting state of affairs is illustrated in the lower left panel of Figure 5.10, which shows tone and light nodes with their corresponding excitatory and inhibitory associations with the US. When the tone target is presented alone, the subject responds because the tone node excites the US node. But when the tone is presented with the light feature, the feature's inhibitory association inhibits activation of the US node; therefore, the animal won't respond. That is all it takes to learn a feature-negative discrimination "the Rescorla-Wagner way."

The feature-positive discrimination is also reasonably simple. According to the Rescorla-Wagner model, the target tone would gain some associative strength on the positive trials, but two factors work against this. First, the target loses some associative strength every time it occurs without the US on the negative trials. Second—and more important—on positive trials, its boost in associative strength must be shared with the feature light CS, which is also present. Because the feature is never presented without the US, it is a more informative predictor of the US. In Rescorla-Wagner terms, the light's associative strength will never decline, and it will *block* any possible boost in strength to the target CS on the positive trials. Therefore, after feature-positive discrimination training, the feature—and not the target—should have a strong association with the US. This state of affairs is illustrated in the upper left portion of Figure 5.10. When the tone is presented alone, there is no association with the US, and therefore no conditioned responding. In contrast, when the tone is presented with the light, the light activates the US node, and this causes conditioned responding. The successful "solution" of the feature-positive discrimination occurs because the animal simply associates the US with the light. That is all there is to the Rescorla-Wagner way. It is a powerful and simple explanation of the feature-positive discrimination.

Unfortunately, learning doesn't always work this way. Instead, sometimes the light feature appears to influence responding by modulating the target's association with the US—as illustrated in the righthand panels of Figure 5.10. In these cases, the light feature is more than a simple excitor or inhibitor—it does not merely have an excitatory or inhibitory association with the US. Instead, *it theoretically works by influencing the association between the target tone and the US.* In the feature-positive discrimination (see Figure 5.10, top right), the light feature activates the tone's whole association with the US. If it does this, it is a **positive occasion setter**. In the feature-negative discrimination (see Figure 5.10, lower right), the light can inhibit the tone's association with the US. If it does this, it is a **negative occasion setter**. In either case, the light feature "sets the occasion" for the target-US association.

Three properties of occasion setters

How in the world do we know all this? One way is to look carefully at the form of the response that develops as the discrimination is learned. Ross and Holland (1981) took advantage of an earlier discovery by Holland (e.g., 1977) that will be discussed in more detail later in this chapter. Holland found that rats respond in different ways to light and tone CSs when these cues are associated with food pellets. When a light signals a food pellet, it evokes a behavior known as "rearing," where the rat stands up on its hind paws. In contrast, when a tone CS signals a food pellet, rearing behavior is not evoked. Instead, the rat jerks its head around in a rather excited manner. Holland called this type of response "head jerk behavior." Thus, the "form" of the conditioned response depends on whether a light CS or a tone CS has been associated with food.

Now consider what the rat might do during compound light-tone trials in the feature-positive discrimination. If the rat learns the Rescorla-Wagner way (see Figure 5.10, upper left), there should be a strong light-food association, but no tone-food association because the light has blocked learning about the tone. Since the tone has been blocked, no responding is expected on trials when the tone is presented alone. But when the light is added on the light-tone compound trials, responding will occur because the light has been directly associated with food. Now, here is the important idea: Since a light associated with food elicits rearing (as was just noted), we should therefore expect the rat to rear to the light-tone compound. This makes sense if the rat has merely associated the light CS with food—the Rescorla-Wagner way. But if the rat has learned the occasion-setting way (see Figure 5.10, upper right), the light should cause a different behavior. Here, it is supposed to modulate the tone's own association with food. Since the tone's association with food causes head-jerking, the light should allow the tone to evoke the head-jerk response. The rat should therefore head-jerk

Figure 5.11 Responding to the light-tone combination after serial (left) or simultaneous (right) feature-positive training. In the serial group, the responding was actually to the tone alone after presentation of the light. The serial procedure caused occasion setting—the light turned on head-jerk responding to the tone. The simultaneous procedure, in contrast, merely allowed the light to be associated with the US (indicated by rearing). (Data from Ross & Holland, 1981; figure after Holland, 1992.)

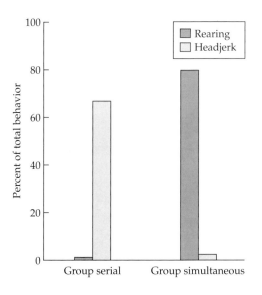

(indicating tone-food association), not rear (indicating light-food association), when it is presented with the light-tone compound. By looking at the form of the response on the compound trials, we can determine if the rat has learned the occasion-setting way or the Rescorla-Wagner way.

Ross and Holland (1981) found evidence of occasion setting—that is, the rat head-jerked, rather than reared, in the presence of the light-tone compound (see Figure 5.11, left side). Thus, the light was basically turning on the tone's control of behavior. Interestingly, Ross and Holland found this result when they used a "serial" compound conditioning procedure. In a serial procedure, the light and tone are presented in a series—the light is presented (and then turned off) before the tone is presented on the compound trials. With the serial procedure, the rats learned the occasion-setting way—the light modulated head-jerking behavior to the sound of the tone. In contrast, after a more traditional "simultaneous" procedure in which the light and tone went on and off at the same time whenever they occurred together, the rats appeared to learn the Rescorla-Wagner way—that is, the animals learned a simple light-food association. They reared (and did not head-jerk) during the compound stimulus (see Figure 5.11, right side). The serial feature-positive discrimination led the light to activate the tone-food association (occasion setting), whereas the simultaneous procedure led to simple light-food learning. The difference is subtle and mind-boggling. (I will try to explain this phenomenon in the section below entitled, "What is learned in occasion setting?")

Rescorla (1985) soon reported similar results with pigeons in autoshaping. As you already know, in this method the pigeon pecks at a key on the chamber wall when illumination of the key (keylight) is associated with food. In Rescorla's experiments, the keylight was the target CS, and a diffuse noise was the feature in a feature-positive discrimination. The noise was audible for 15 seconds, and the keylight came on during the final five seconds of the noise. On these trials, the keylight was paired with food; on other trials, there was no noise, and the keylight occurred without food. The noise itself did not elicit any keypecking—that behavior was only elicited by the keylight. But the noise allowed the keylight to elicit pecking when the noise came on with the light. Once again, a feature allowed a target CS to control responding. Somehow, during feature-positive training, the noise came to set the occasion for pecking at the keylight.

In the long run, a careful analysis of the form of conditioned response thus indicates that the feature is not controlling behavior through a direct association with food. Instead, it modulates the target's own association. This kind of result, on response form, provides the first crucial line of evidence of occasion setting. But there are at least two other results that describe special properties of occasion setters. As before, they both suggest that a feature in a feature-positive or a feature-negative discrimination might not influence behavior through its direct association with the US.

The second line of evidence is that an occasion setter will still modulate responding to the target if we modify its direct association with the US. For example, if a feature from a feature-positive discrimination were merely being associated with food, then presenting it repeatedly alone (extinction) should reduce its influence. However, such extinction of a positive occasion setter does not eliminate its impact (e.g., Rescorla, 1986). Analogous results with negative occasion setters can be even stranger. In a feature-negative discrimination, the negative feature turns off responding to the target. So what should happen if we were to pair the negative feature with a US and turn it into an excitor—a CS with a direct and positive association with the US? A simple inhibitor's power to turn off responding to a target should be abolished, and that appears to be true (Holland, 1984). But if the feature is a negative occasion setter, it is still able to inhibit responding to the target, even after we associated it directly with the US (Holland, 1984)! An occasion setter's power thus seems quite separate from its direct association with the US.

The third line of evidence for occasion setting is this: We have already seen that excitors and inhibitors usually summate when they are combined. That is, when an inhibitor is combined with an excitor, it reduces performance to the excitor, and when an excitor is combined with another excitor, it increases performance to it (see Figure 3.11). Things do not work this way in the world of occasion setting (e.g., Holland, 1986, 1989b). Specifically, if we test an occasion setter's effect on a new CS, it typically does not influence responding to the new CS at all. (A "new CS" means a CS that is different from the target that was in the original feature-positive or feature-negative discrimination.) There is an important exception, though. If the new CS has been a target in a separate feature-positive or feature-negative discrimination, then the occasion setter will influence responding to the new CS (e.g., Lamarre & Holland, 1987; Rescorla, 1985). There is something rather special about what is learned about both the feature and the target in an occasion-setting discrimination. This issue will be considered further after first pausing for breath and reviewing what you have just learned.

What does it all mean?

To summarize, occasion setters are features from serial feature-positive and feature-negative discriminations that allow animals to discriminate positive from negative trials. But they do this in a way that is not predicted by conditioning theories. Occasion setters have at least three unexpected properties: (1) They modulate the behavior that is otherwise evoked by the target, (2) they are not affected much by changing their direct associations with the US, and (3) they do not always affect responding to new stimuli.

These differences are important because they seem to lie outside the scope of the conditioning theories we discussed in Chapter 4; they tell us that stimuli can do more than enter into simple associations. Thus, there is more to the psychology of learning than simple associative strength. But these differences also have practical implications. For example, occasion setting may be involved outside the laboratory, wherever conditioning occurs. Consider drug addiction: The heroin abuser no doubt encounters many different cues that are potentially associated with their drug of choice (Siegel & Ramos, 2002). It is possible that the main CS for the drug is something like the proximate cue of the needle piercing the flesh. More remote cues that precede the prick of the needle—like room cues or the sight of the needle and paraphernalia—might function as occasion setters that set the occasion for the CS-drug relationship. If we wanted to eliminate the abuser's habit, we might try to extinguish the room cues or the paraphernalia cues by presenting them over and over without the drug. But if the cues are occasion setters, that treatment may be ineffective because, as we have just seen, occasion setters are not affected by simple extinction (Rescorla, 1986). Similar arguments apply to the treatment of phobias and anxiety disorders (e.g., see Bouton, 1988). Fear of a CS may be a problem in one particular context; therefore, a natural approach would be to extinguish the context. However, if the context acts as an occasion setter, simple extinction won't eliminate its impact (e.g., Bouton & Swartzentruber, 1986). For practical as well as theoretical reasons, it would be good to understand exactly how occasion setting works.

What is learned in occasion setting?

One way to address this question is to ask what the organism actually learns in occasion setting. One clue comes from the procedures that produce it. As noted above, occasion setting is mainly learned in "serial" discriminations in which the feature is presented before the target. (Simultaneous discriminations create features that have the properties expected of ordinary excitors or inhibitors.) In a serial procedure, the target provides information about "when" the US is going to happen; in contrast, the occasion setter uniquely signals "whether or not" the US is going to follow the target (e.g., Bouton, 1997; see also Holland, 1992). Maybe this is the major difference—

occasion setters might signal "whether" the US will happen, and the target might signal "when" it will occur.

This is not a bad rule of thumb, but it doesn't quite get to the heart of the matter. In the serial discrimination procedure, the extra interval of time between the feature coming on and the US being delivered probably also makes the feature a weaker signal for the US. Remember that conditioning is usually weaker the longer the interval between CS and US. Perhaps a weak feature-US association is what somehow allows occasion setting. Consistent with this idea, Holland (1989a) found that occasion setting can actually be learned in simultaneous procedures if the feature is less salient than the target. When a dim light feature was combined with a very loud tone target, for example, occasion setting developed. Thus, the bottom line may be that *occasion setting will occur when a weak feature signals reinforcement or nonreinforcement of a stronger target.*

Rescorla (1988a) suggested why things might work this way. When the target is strong, it will quickly develop a strong association with the US because it competes more effectively with the feature for conditioning—that is, it gets a bigger boost in associative strength every time the compound is paired with the US. Therefore, on trials when the target occurs *without* the US, there is a bigger surprise, and a bigger inhibitory adjustment. Strangely enough, if you remember what was previously said about extinction (e.g., see Figure 5.6), this might mean that the strong target would wind up with more inhibition as well as more excitation. This inhibition may play a key role—occasion setting appears to develop when the procedure allows lots of inhibition to develop to the target (see Rescorla, 1988a). And the occasion setter might work by somehow modulating that inhibition (e.g., Swartzentruber & Rescorla, 1994).

To capture this idea, Figure 5.12 assumes that the target CS (T) in a feature-positive and feature-negative discrimination gains both an excitatory and an inhibitory association with the US (Bouton & Nelson, 1998a). It is like an extinguished CS (see Figure 5.6) in that excitatory and inhibitory

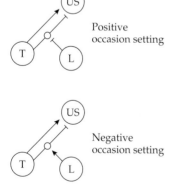

Positive
occasion setting

Negative
occasion setting

Figure 5.12 Occasion setters modulate inhibition to the target CS. During feature-positive and feature-negative discrimination learning, the target CS (T) acquires both excitation and inhibition—as we saw in extinction (e.g., see Figure 5.6). The occasion setter (L) works by either inhibiting or activating the target's inhibitory association with the US.

associations are gradually learned when the target is paired with the US, and presented without the US, respectively. As the figure illustrates, the occasion setter (L) now works by *modulating the target's inhibitory association* (Bouton & Nelson, 1998a; Swartzentruber & Rescorla, 1994; see also Schmajuk, Lamoureux, & Holland, 1998). This means (somewhat strangely!) that a positive occasion setter actually inhibits the target's inhibition, whereas a negative occasion setter excites the target's inhibition. You might notice that the negative occasion setter is basically working the same way the context works in extinction (see Figure 5.6)—both the occasion setter and the context activate a CS's inhibitory association. The parallel is not surprising, because the context in extinction may function as a negative occasion setter (e.g., Bouton, 2004). Bouton and Nelson (1998a) have further suggested that activation of the target's inhibitory association—like activation of an extinguished CS's inhibitory association—might also depend on input from the context. Thus, in negative occasion setting, the target CS, the occasion setter, and the context might *all* need to be present to activate the final inhibitory link (see Bouton & Nelson, 1998a, for the evidence). The main point is that occasion setters seem to operate by modulating the target CS's inhibition. This begins to explain why occasion setters only influence new target CSs that have been in an occasion setting discrimination (see the bottom of p. 165). Presumably, those CSs also have an inhibitory association on which the occasion setter can have its effect.

Configural conditioning

Another idea about what is learned in occasion setting is that the feature-target compound creates a **configural cue** that acquires associative strength (e.g., Kehoe & Gormezano, 1980; Pearce, 1987, 1994; Wagner, 2003; Wagner & Brandon, 2001; Woodbury, 1943). This idea was introduced in the last chapter: When two or more CSs are combined, they can create a new stimulus—a so-called configural cue—that becomes associated with the US (see Figure 4.17 for an illustration). In this view, when feature and target cues are combined in feature-positive or feature-negative discriminations, they would create a unique stimulus that would gain excitation or inhibition, and control conditioned responding accordingly. If things worked this way, it would not be surprising to find that extinguishing the feature cue on its own, or perhaps pairing it with the US, might do little to change responding to the feature-target compound—we haven't done anything to the configural cue! You may recognize this as property number 2 of occasion setting (see above). The point is that occasion setting might somehow boil down to the conditioning of configural cues.

Does this sort of approach handle all the facts of occasion setting? It does quite well with many of them (see Holland, 1992). But the clearest configural conditioning model (Pearce's model, introduced in Chapter 4) makes incorrect predictions in a number of places that would take far too much space to describe here (see Holland, 1992; see also Bouton & Nelson, 1994, 1998a). Most research on occasion setting has taken an elemental, rather than a configural, approach. But as research on the problem continues in the future, configural accounts will need to be kept in mind.

Other forms of modulation

Occasion setting is not the only example of performance to one stimulus being modulated by another stimulus. Ordinary CSs can also exaggerate or potentiate the strength of URs or CRs that are elicited by other stimuli. For example, rats startle more vigorously to a sudden burst of noise if the noise burst is presented during a fear CS (e.g., Brown, Kalish, & Farber, 1951). Conditioned fear elicited by the CS "potentiates" the startle response (see Davis, 1992, for a review), and this phenomenon is known as **fear potentiated startle**. Similar effects occur in humans (e.g., Lang, 1995). I am reminded of the moment of panic I once felt when I heard a sudden rattle while hiking in rattlesnake country. It was only the sound of some fishing tackle breaking loose in a plastic box I was carrying. Fear, apprehension, or anxiety can potentiate defensive reflexes elicited by other stimuli. Fear of a CS thus modulates the startle response.

Potentiated startle effects are addressed in Wagner and Brandon's (1989) AESOP theory (see Chapter 4). Remember that their "affective extension" of SOP theory argued that CSs enter into associations with both emotional and sensory aspects of the US. The emotive association elicits emotional responses directly when it is activated by a CS, but it can also modulate other responses. Brandon, Wagner, and their colleagues have studied such effects in rabbits. They conditioned fear to a 30-second CS by pairing it with an electric shock US delivered near the rabbit's eye. Brief, 1-second CSs will elicit an eyeblink CR when they are paired with this US, but the 30-second stimulus does not—it only elicits fear or anxiety. Nonetheless, the conditioned fear stimulus will potentiate an eyeblink UR to the shock near the eye or a startle response elicited by an airpuff to the ear (e.g., Brandon, Bombace, Falls, & Wagner, 1991; McNish, Betts, Brandon, & Wagner, 1997). It will also potentiate an eyeblink CR that is elicited by a second brief CS (e.g., Brandon & Wagner, 1991). This form of modulation is different from occasion setting, because it does appear to result from a direct association between the modulating CS and the US.

Summary

Modulation processes like the ones we have been discussing are probably fairly common in conditioning. Thus, the performance one observes to a CS always depends to some extent on other stimuli in the background. Occasion setting and other types of modulation make good functional sense: They presumably allow cues that are somewhat remote in time from the US to control responses that are timed quite well to deal with the US, and they are important in determining the performance that results in Pavlovian conditioning.

Understanding the Nature of the Conditioned Response

So far we have been worried about how a learned association is translated into behavior, but we have said little about the actual nature or form of the behavior itself that results. What does the organism do when the CS-US association has been properly modulated or retrieved? It is interesting to observe that this issue has become a fundamental problem in learning theory only relatively recently. In earlier years, when learning was assumed to involve connecting the CS with the UR, it was very clear what the behavior should be that resulted from conditioning. It should be the same as the unconditional response to the US (see Chapter 3). Even in the stimulus substitution view, which held that the fundamental "content" of learning was S-S rather than S-R, the nature of the response was also clear. If the CS merely came to substitute for the US as a kind of surrogate, then the response to the CS after conditioning should also be the same as the UR.

Two problems for stimulus substitution

In the 1970s, two kinds of findings came along that raised big questions about stimulus substitution. First, researchers discovered that the form of the CR is not just determined by the UR; *the CR is also influenced by the nature of the CS*. Remember that peculiar finding discovered by Holland (1977) that was used in occasion setting research and that I promised to return to: Rats jerk their heads to auditory CSs associated with food pellets, but they rear to visual CSs associated with the same unconditioned stimulus and, therefore, the same unconditioned response.

Timberlake and Grant (1975) reported results that were equally striking. They used the presentation of a rat to signal a food pellet to other rats. A rat was gently fastened to a platform that could swivel through a door and into the conditioning chamber. Presentation of the rat this way was paired with food pellets over a series of conditioning trials. What kind of conditioned response do you think was learned by the subject rats? Salivation, or perhaps a little gnawing on the CS rat? Not at all. When presentation of the CS rat was followed by a food pellet, the subject rats began engaging in social contact with it. They approached, licked, groomed, and crawled over the CS rat. Subjects that received a CS rat unpaired with food showed little of these behaviors—the contact behaviors thus depended on associating the CS rat with food. And subjects that received conditioning with a wood block CS (mounted on the platform instead of a rat) didn't show social contact behaviors either. What seemed to be occurring was an increase in food-related social behaviors directed at the CS. Rats naturally tend to feed with groups of other rats; they live in colonies and take their meals socially. Hamsters, which are more solitary, do not show the same social effects when run in the same type of experiment (Timberlake, 1983). Stimuli that naturally support social behavior increasingly elicit contact when they are paired with food. Something about the nature of the CS selects US-related behaviors that are appropriate to the CS. This is a long way from stimulus substitution.

The second kind of finding that challenged stimulus substitution was discovered when drugs were used as unconditioned stimuli. The charge was led by Shepard Siegel, whose experiments were discussed in Chapter 2. To remind you, remember that injection of morphine causes analgesia—a reduction in sensitivity to pain. When morphine is paired with a CS, though, the CR seems to be a *compensatory response*; the CS evokes an increase in sensitivity to pain (e.g., Siegel, 1975). Other research suggests a similar pattern for the body-temperature effects of alcohol. Alcohol causes a drop in body temperature unconditionally, while CSs associated with it cause an increase in body temperature (e.g., Mansfield & Cunningham, 1980). The CR and UR again seem to be opposites, which is hardly consistent with stimulus substitution.

Compensatory responses are not restricted to drug USs. For example, in Chapter 2 we also saw that a painful shock US can condition an endogenous analgesia—an opposite response, once again (e.g., Fanselow & Baackes, 1982). Similarly, rats exposed to cold temperatures gradually learn to compensate; their body temperature shows less change with repeated exposure. Interestingly, this effect is connected with classical conditioning—when the context is changed, the animal loses its cold tolerance (e.g., Kissinger & Riccio, 1995), perhaps because it loses the compensatory response. Woods (1991) has noted that similar compensatory processes are involved in digesting meals. Although food is clearly necessary for survival, a big meal can actually disturb the body's equilibrium. Cues that are associated with meals may therefore elicit conditioned compensatory responses that get the animal ready to cope with the intake of food.

Siegel himself has become interested in a phenomenon in color vision known as the **McCollough effect** (McCollough, 1965; e.g., see Siegel & Allan, 1998). The phenomenon is illustrated in Figure 5.13. Humans can be shown alternating pictures of a black vertical grid superimposed on a colored (e.g., blue) background and a horizontal grid on another color (e.g., yellow) background. After multiple exposures of each, a test picture with both vertical and horizontal grids on white can then be shown. Thanks to the earlier exposures, the subject now sees the opposite color on the two grids (yellow on vertical and blue on horizontal). These are essentially conditioned visual afterimages. Although other ways of explaining this effect have been proposed (e.g., Dodwell & Humphrey, 1990), a strong case can be made for a conditioning-like process in which the grids are CSs, the colors are USs, and the conditioned response is opposite to the original US. For example, blocking and overshadowing effects can be observed with compounded vertical

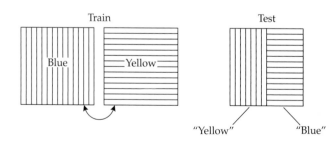

Figure 5.13 The McCollough effect. During testing with vertical or horizontal grids previously associated with blue or yellow colors (for example), you see the opposite color.

and diagonal grids (Siegel, Allan, & Eissenberg, 1994). All this adds up to something rather important: Conditioning processes seem to be operating everywhere, and compensatory, US-opposite conditioned responses are not uncommon in human and animal behavior.

These two challenges to stimulus-substitution have stimulated thinking about the nature of the conditioned responding in several important ways. Let's consider the compensatory CR first, and then return to the fact that the CS can also influence the form of the CR.

Understanding conditioned compensatory responses

One point to make about the compensatory response is that it suggests the functional nature of the conditioned response. As argued in Chapter 2, the CR fundamentally serves to allow the animal to adapt to the upcoming US (Hollis, 1982, 1997). Thus, the CRs that develop during conditioning might be the ones that are best in helping the organism get ready for the US. This perspective represents a shift in how we think about the impact of conditioning on behavior. Now, we see the result of conditioning as a set of behaviors evoked by the CS that allow the animal to optimize its interaction with the US. However, this perspective is rather broad and not very precise about predicting the actual form the CR will take.

Another approach is to take a harder look at the nature of the unconditioned response. Consider SOP theory again. Recall that presentation of a US is supposed to initiate a standard sequence of events. The US node is first put into its focally active state, A1, and then it decays to its peripherally active state, A2, before it becomes inactive again. It seems possible that these two levels of activation can sometimes control different responses. If this were the case, we should see a "response" to the US that is actually a sequence of two responses: one corresponding to A1, and a second corresponding to A2. The important thing is that, according to the theory, the CS will come to activate the US node into *A2*. Thus, the response elicited by the CS should be the second response—not the first—in the sequence initiated by the US.

Paletta and Wagner (1986) noted that a morphine injection first suppresses a rat's general activity (causing sedation). But eventually this suppression gives way to a rebound effect in which activity is actually elevated above baseline. This sequence is shown in Figure 5.14. If these two responses correspond to A1 and A2, then the SOP prediction is clear: CS-morphine pairings should allow the CS to evoke elevated activity when it is tested on its own. This was confirmed in a second experiment (see Figure 5.14, inset). Rats received morphine injections in either the test apparatus (m-e) or the home cage (m-hc). A control group received saline in the experimental apparatus (s). In the test shown, the animals were injected with saline in the test box. When the box was associated with morphine, hyperactivity—a compensatory response—was observed. But SOP would see the compensatory response as consistent with, not opposite to, the UR. The trick is to analyze the UR in more detail and recognize that the CR will match the second com-

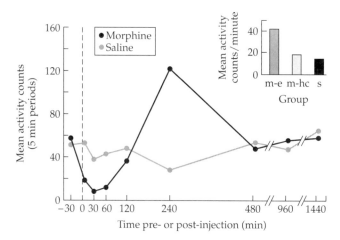

Figure 5.14 Activity after morphine or saline injections. After morphine, activity first decreased (A1) and then increased (A2) above normal. When morphine was associated with a unique box or environment (m-e in the inset), the box elicited an increase in activity—as if it was activating the morphine US's A2 response. (Data from Paletta & Wagner, 1986; figure after Wagner & Brandon, 1989.)

ponent. In many cases, we will find that A1 and A2 control the same responses rather than different responses. Here we would not observe a biphasic unconditional reaction like the one shown in Figure 5.14, and we would not expect a conditioned compensatory response.

In a very important paper, Eikelboom and Stewart (1982) described another way to think about the UR. Their approach was physiological; we must recognize that presenting a US causes a whole multitude of physiological reactions or responses. Eikelboom and Stewart noted that, for a "response" to be a UR in the usual sense, *the response must be mediated by the central nervous system*—that is, it must be caused by neural activity in the brain or the spinal cord. This seems rather obvious, in a way. As shown in the top part of Figure 5.15, classic responses to typical USs used in condi-

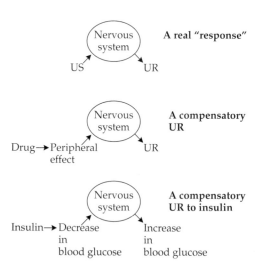

Figure 5.15 Making sense of compensatory conditioned responses. A real "response" to a US is the reaction of the nervous system (top). However, sometimes a drug US can have a peripheral effect that stimulates the nervous system to compensate (middle). The peripheral effect can be mistaken for a UR—but it actually stimulates the nervous system to compensate, which is the true UR. This phenomenon is illustrated by the effect of insulin (bottom). When the UR is compensatory, so is the CR.

tioning experiments are always mediated by the nervous system. To put it a little loosely, the US provides input to the brain, and the brain reacts to it.

Eikelboom and Stewart noted that the definition of the UR gets confused when we consider the effects of drug USs. Drugs can produce many "responses" that we can measure. Some are mediated by the central nervous system in the classic way described at the top of Figure 5.15, but others are not. For example, consider the effects of injecting insulin. (Insulin is a hormone, not a drug, but it illustrates the point very clearly.) The effect of insulin that is usually measured (Siegel, 1972) is a drop in the level of blood glucose. This effect (at least when the insulin dose is small), occurs because the hormone promotes glucose uptake into the cells (and out of the blood). It is a direct effect—the brain has nothing to do with it. It is not really an unconditioned response in the same sense of Pavlov's original UR. We might therefore expect it to be something different.

The drop in blood glucose is actually a new stimulus that the nervous system now reacts to. A sudden drop in blood glucose can be dangerous; it is detected by the brain, which now responds in a way that is designed to cope and adapt. Here, then, is where the compensatory response comes from: It is the brain's unconditional response to a peripheral input, a drop in blood glucose. It is a UR. Seen this way, the compensatory CR that develops over conditioning trials is just like any other CR. It does resemble the UR, properly defined, and stimulus substitution is preserved. As you have probably guessed, conditioning experiments with small doses of insulin tend to lead to the compensatory conditioning of elevated blood glucose (Siegel, 1972; Woods & Shogren, 1972).

This approach recognizes that compensatory responses are not the only outcome of conditioning with drug USs. When those responses are caused by neural activity, the CR will look the same as the UR. When the "responses" are direct peripheral effects, they stimulate a compensation by the nervous system, and we observe something that looks like a drug-opposite effect. The Eikelboom-Stewart perspective also allows some drugs to show conditioned sensitization effects—that is, conditioning may sometimes cause an increase in a drug-like response to the CS. This might cause a response when the CS is tested alone, or it might cause an enhanced response to the US when the CS is tested in the presence of the CS. Recent research has identified a number of conditioned sensitization effects with drugs (e.g., Stewart, 1992; see also Robinson & Berridge, 1993).

Furthermore, drugs may have multiple effects on the body, some of which may be nervous-system mediated, and others of which may not be. The approach predicts that a single drug may condition responses that both mimic and compensate for URs. For example, injections of atropine cause both pupil dilation and a drying of the mouth. The first effect is mediated by the brain, while the second effect is not—atropine suppresses activity at the salivary glands, which presumably initiates a brain reaction designed to compensate. True to the Eikelboom-Stewart perspective, pupil dilatation and salivation can be conditioned at the same time (Korol, Sletten, & Brown,

1966). The first looks like normal conditioning, while the second is a compensatory response. All this makes sense when one considers how the drug actually interacts with the nervous system.

Ramsay and Woods (1997) noted that it is idealistic to think that one can always identify a simple CR or UR in a drug-conditioning experiment. Drugs have so many effects that any given "response" we measure (blood glucose level, body temperature, etc.) is actually bound to be a complex product of a very large number of ongoing physiological processes. It may therefore be impossible to identify the crucial UR and CR. It may also be difficult to know what the crucial "stimulus" is that the nervous system actually detects and reacts to. Given the enormous complexity involved, the best one may do to predict the direction the CR will take is to look carefully at the body's response on a drug's first presentation. If the body seems to react by compensating so that the drug's effect seems to weaken as the drug concentration in the system is increasing (so-called acute tolerance), then compensatory effects will be conditioned. On the other hand, if the effect of the drug is still increasing as the drug's concentration in the system begins to subside (so-called acute sensitization), then conditioned sensitization effects may be observed.

A complete understanding of the effects of conditioning with drug USs will require a sophisticated understanding of many physiological processes. On the other hand, a complete understanding of how physiological processes maintain the body's equilibrium may likewise require a sophisticated understanding of conditioning. Several writers have noted that learning processes like those in Pavlovian conditioning probably play a widespread role in helping the body regulate equilibrium or homeostasis (e.g., Dworkin, 1993; Ramsay & Woods, 1997).

Conditioning and behavior systems

Other sorts of biological processes—in this case, ethological ones—have been used to help understand why the form of the CR depends on the nature of the CS (e.g., Timberlake & Grant, 1975). Conditioning is now thought to engage whole **behavior systems**—sets of behaviors that are organized around biological functions and goals (e.g., Timberlake, 1994, 2001; Timberlake & Silva, 1995). Encountering food USs during conditioning makes a whole system of feeding behaviors possible. These might include behaviors such as foraging, chasing, hoarding, food-handling, etc. Sexual USs likewise engage a sexual behavior system (which might include various search behaviors as well as copulation responses), frightening USs may engage a defensive behavior system, and so on. In each case, animals have ways of responding to particular USs that have developed through evolution and/or prior learning. Ultimately, presentation of a US in a conditioning experiment will enable a whole potential system of such behaviors, just as it would in the organism's natural world.

Once a behavior system is engaged, stimuli in the environment provide "support" (Tolman, 1932) for particular behaviors in the same sense that a

William Timberlake

hallway makes it possible to walk and a swimming pool makes it possible to swim. A CS may determine the CR in this way. Thus, a small moving object that signals food might support and elicit chase behaviors, whereas a diffuse noise might mainly activate search behaviors. You have already been given a glimpse of the behavior-system account of Timberlake and Grant's discovery that rats, used as signals for food, support social responding. Since the rat is a social feeder, rats come to display certain social behaviors toward one another when they are hungry and/or expecting food. When a rat signals food, the feeding system is engaged, and the signal thus evokes the corresponding social contact behaviors. There are presumably no such behaviors in the hamster's solitary feeding system, and consequently, hamster CSs do not evoke social behavior (Timberlake, 1983).

William Timberlake, one of the main theorists working in this area, has described a feeding behavior system in the rat that is illustrated in Figure 5.16 (e.g., Timberlake, 1983, 1994, 2001; Timberlake & Silva, 1995). You can think of the system as an exhaustive set of behaviors available to the rat that generally have the function of finding and consuming food. Like earlier models from ethology (e.g., Baerends, 1976; Tinbergen, 1951), the system is hierarchically organized so that higher functions have a number of more specific behaviors and functions that subserve them. At the highest level, the system has "modes" that correspond to the system's biggest functions or goals: the search for—and consumption of—food. But within these modes there are "modules" that correspond to more specific subfunctions; for example, "general search" has different modules of travel, investigate, and chase, and each of these has corresponding responses and actions. Each

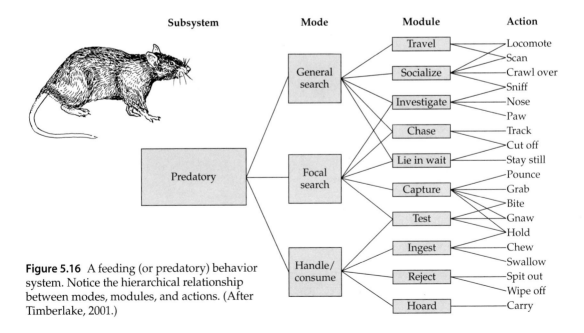

Figure 5.16 A feeding (or predatory) behavior system. Notice the hierarchical relationship between modes, modules, and actions. (After Timberlake, 2001.)

mode, module, and behavior also has its own support stimuli. For example, hunger and the onset of nightfall (when rats normally feed) are stimuli that might support and initiate the general search mode. These cues would therefore initiate any of the associated modules and actions organized around the function of finding food. If an animal in the general search mode were then to encounter a Pavlovian cue for food, the animal might change to the focal search mode, with new modules and new behaviors organized around the function of actually procuring food. Finally, when food itself is encountered, the animal might switch to a handling/consuming mode with modules and behaviors organized around the handling and ingesting of food. These types of behaviors can be elicited when a rolling ball bearing is used to signal food—the rat chases it, handles it, and chews it (e.g., Timberlake, Wahl, & King, 1982). At any point, behavior is jointly selected by the current mode and by the environmental stimuli that support it.

A related system for antipredator defense in the rat has been developed by Michael Fanselow (e.g., Fanselow, 1989, 1994; Fanselow & Lester, 1988; see also Bolles & Fanselow, 1980). In this system, behavior is organized around the function of avoiding being eaten by another animal. In this case, the stimulus that switches the rat between modes is the likelihood that the rat will encounter a predator. Fanselow has called this likelihood **predatory imminence**. When the rat first leaves its nest or burrow, predatory imminence is probably low—the rat is not likely to encounter a predator at this time. At this point, the animal will enter a "pre-encounter" mode in which it might engage in different behaviors (e.g., nest maintenance, meal pattern organization, etc.) that are organized to prevent detection by a predator. When the rat actually detects a predator nearby, it enters the "post-encounter" mode in which it primarily freezes and becomes analgesic (see Chapter 2)—this is "fear." If and when the predator is actually about to attack, however, the animal enters a "circa-strike" mode; here the behaviors (fighting, threat display, jump attack) are active and presumably designed for escape. Different defensive behaviors are thus organized around their function. Each is elicited by different support stimuli. Interestingly, different brain areas also correspond with and control different modes (e.g., Fanselow, 1994).

Michael Domjan (e.g., 1994, 1997, 1998) has likewise presented a model of a sexual behavior system in the Japanese quail. Some of this research was mentioned in Chapter 2. Like the feeding system, the sexual system involves a general search mode, a focal search mode, and a consummatory mode—in this case, actual copulatory behavior. Initially, an animal might engage in a general search mode. Interestingly, long-duration CSs that are paired with copulation after they have been on for 20 minutes seem to support such a mode by evoking pacing behavior (Akins, Domjan, & Gutierrez, 1994; see below). In contrast, conditioning with a localized light or a stuffed toy dog as a CS engages focal search: The birds approach the stimulus. Actual copulatory responding, however, does not occur unless the CS is a model of a real female, prepared by a taxidermist, which contains plumage and other

Michael Domjan

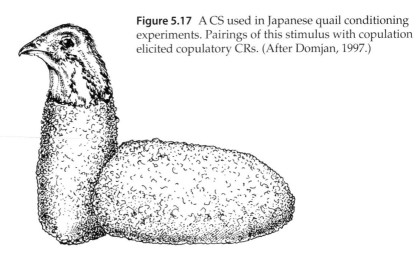

Figure 5.17 A CS used in Japanese quail conditioning experiments. Pairings of this stimulus with copulation elicited copulatory CRs. (After Domjan, 1997.)

features of a female quail (e.g., Domjan, Huber-McDonald, & Holloway, 1992; Figure 5.17). Interestingly, conditioning at one step in the sequence may modulate responding in the next step. For example, although a light CS elicits approach and not copulation, it does make latency to copulate quicker when the female US is introduced. Similarly, males that have associated the test context with copulation are more likely to copulate with a partial model of a female than are birds that have had equivalent copulatory experience elsewhere (Domjan, Greene, & North, 1989). Some of the features of the quail's sexual system are summarized in Figure 5.18. The figure emphasizes the fact that different types of CSs may engage different modes (and therefore different CRs), and that CSs (and the modes they evoke) can also potentiate behavior elicited at the next point in the sequence.

Behavior systems are usually thought to be organized in time—that is, cues that are remote in time from the US tend to support behaviors—like search behaviors—that are different from cues that are more immediate, which often support consumption. This idea led Akins et al. (1994) to a nice prediction in sexual conditioning (see also Akins, 2000). Although it is common to think that increasing the interval between the onset of the CS and

Figure 5.18 Summary of conditioning in the male Japanese quail behavior system (e.g., Domjan, 1997, 1998). Different types of CSs engage different modes and evoke different CRs. If the bird is in the focal search mode, this also potentiates the consummatory CR.

Copulation = US/UR

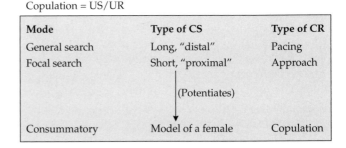

Mode	Type of CS	Type of CR
General search	Long, "distal"	Pacing
Focal search	Short, "proximal"	Approach
	(Potentiates)	
Consummatory	Model of a female	Copulation

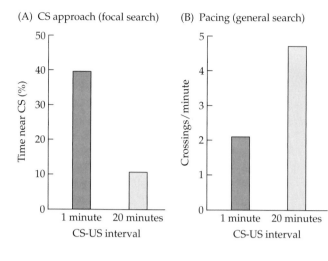

Figure 5.19 Short and long CSs that end in the same US will elicit different CRs. Male Japanese quail were given conditioning with either a 1- or 20-minute CS. The 1-minute CS elicited approach behaviors (A). Although the 20-minute CS elicited very little approach, it elicited a great deal of pacing (B), which the 1-minute CS did not. (After Akins et al., 1994.)

the onset of the US (the CS-US interval) will decrease the strength of conditioning, Akins et al. realized that CSs with different temporal relations to the US might support different modes in the sexual system. In one experiment, they compared the effects of 1- and 20-minute CSs that were paired with copulation with a female. When approach to the CS was considered, there was less responding with the 20-minute CS (see Figure 5.19A). This is the usual effect of lengthening the CS-US interval. But when they considered the amount of pacing back and forth in the test cage, the reverse relationship was obtained—there was more pacing with the longer, 20-minute CS-US interval (see Figure 5.19B). If Akins et al. had only measured approach, they would have concluded that the longer CS-US interval merely led to weaker conditioning. But more correctly, it influenced the qualitative nature of the CR: Pacing behavior may be linked to general search rather than focal search. Timberlake et al. (1982) also found qualitative changes in how a rat behaved toward the ball bearing, depending on the CS-US interval. These results are not consistent with the simpler view, tacitly accepted in previous chapters, that the amount of time between CS and US merely influences the strength of conditioning. The behavior systems approach provides an important complement to our understanding of conditioning.

What does it all mean?

Once again, it is easy to lose the forest for the trees. What does all this information about conditioning in animals tell us about learning and behavior in humans? Perhaps the main point is that behavior systems theory gives us a useful way to think about the nature of behavior that results from conditioning. For one thing, it is important to remember that CSs don't elicit a simple unitary reflex. Instead, they evoke whole systems—or constellations—of behavior. At a theoretical level, they do this by engaging pre-organized modules and modes, which are functionally organized to help the organism deal with (or cope with) the US. Different kinds of CSs can support different kinds of CRs, and this depends on both their qualitative nature and duration. The cultural stereotype of Pavlovian conditioning—Pavlov's dog drooling in response to a ringing bell—is really only the tip of the iceberg.

A few years ago I had the opportunity to develop this line of thinking with two clinical psychologists, David Barlow and Susan Mineka (Bouton, Mineka, & Barlow, 2001). Barlow is a well-known clinical scientist who has devoted his career to understanding anxiety disorders (e.g., Barlow, 2002). Mineka is also a respected clinical psychologist, although she was originally also trained as a researcher in Learning Theory (you might remember some of her experiments on fear conditioning from Chapter 2). The three of us were interested in understanding **panic disorder**, a very common anxiety disorder in which people experience intense, out-of-the-blue panic attacks and then come to fear these attacks. For people who develop panic disorder, the panic attacks become worse and worse, and the fear of having another one becomes debilitating. Many people with the disorder also develop **agoraphobia**—literally a "fear of the market place"—in which they become afraid of leaving the house and going to public places.

Although fear conditioning is widely thought to contribute to anxiety disorders, there has been much confusion about how it might contribute to panic disorder (e.g., McNally, 1990, 1994). Nonetheless, there can be little doubt that something as emotionally potent as a spontaneous panic attack can serve as a powerful US (and UR) that can cause fear conditioning. CSs associated with panic can thus come to arouse fear. However, based on what we know about the usual organization of behavior systems, we should probably expect different kinds of modes to come into play. As summarized in Figure 5.20, we might think that relatively long-duration or "distal" cues—such as a shopping mall or other locations where a panic attack might eventually occur—provide CSs that support a "preparatory" mode and CRs that get the system ready for the next panic attack. The CR elicited by such cues is what we know as "anxiety," a sense of apprehension or worry. In contrast, close-up CSs that are proximally associated with panic might support a different CR—actual panic conditioned responses, which are much more intense. Unlike anxiety, panic CRs might be designed to deal with a pow-

Figure 5.20 Summary of a behavior-system account of panic disorder in humans (Bouton, 2005; Bouton et al., 2001). CSs of different durations or temporal proximity to a panic attack may engage different modes and evoke different CRs (anxiety or panic). Anxiety may also potentiate the panic CR.

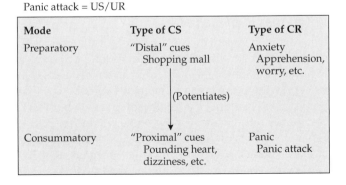

Panic attack = US/UR

Mode	Type of CS	Type of CR
Preparatory	"Distal" cues Shopping mall	Anxiety Apprehension, worry, etc.
	↓ (Potentiates)	
Consummatory	"Proximal" cues Pounding heart, dizziness, etc.	Panic Panic attack

erful emotional event that is already in progress. You can see the clear connection with the "pre-encounter" and "circa-strike" behaviors suggested by Fanselow and Lester (1988).

One type of proximal CS that is often associated with panic is "interoceptive" (or internal) cues generated by the panic attack itself. That is, patients that have repeated panic attacks might learn to associate internal cues that are part of the onset of panic (feeling dizzy or a sudden pounding of the heart, etc.) with the rest of the panic attack. Conditioning of such early onset cues is reasonably well-known (e.g., Kim, Siegel, & Patenall, 1999; see also Goddard, 1999). They provide one reason why panic attacks get worse and worse with repeated exposures: Onset cues begin to elicit panic and, thus, fan the fire more quickly. A second reason that panic attacks become worse is highlighted in Figure 5.20: Based on what we know about other behavior systems, the preparatory mode elicited by distal cues (anxiety) should be expected to potentiate panic CRs and URs (e.g., Brandon et al., 1991; Brandon & Wagner, 1991; Domjan et al., 1989). That is, the presence of conditioned anxiety should exacerbate panic (e.g., Barlow, 1988, 2002; Basoglu, Marks, & Sengun, 1992). The parallels between the sexual conditioning system (see Figure 5.18) and the panic system (see Figure 5.20) are hopefully clear (see also Bouton, 2005).

Our conceptualization of panic disorder (Bouton et al., 2001) also used other information presented in this chapter to help demystify the role of conditioning. For example, some critics of a conditioning approach have wondered why a CS like a pounding heart does not elicit panic in the context, say, of athletic exercise, or why extinction exposure to the CS without panic during exercise does not eliminate its tendency to cause panic in other situations. One answer is that the loss of responding that occurs in extinction can be expected to be specific to the context where it is learned—as we saw earlier (e.g., see Figure 5.5). Thus, although panic in response to the CS of feeling a pounding heart may extinguish in the context of exercise, extinction in that context will not abolish the CS's ability to elicit panic in other contexts, such as in a crowded bus or at a shopping mall. The fact that excitatory conditioned responses generalize more across contexts than does extinction may be a reason why many behavior disorders are so persistent.

Thus, the trees do make a forest. As you go through this book, I hope you will see that Learning Theory really does provide a set of powerful tools for understanding behavior and behavior problems outside the laboratory.

Conclusion

Conditioning influences both physiological and behavioral processes, and the nature of the CR depends on organized systems that operate at both of these levels. The physiological responses that will be evoked by a CS depend on interactions between processes that function overall to maintain equilibrium. Behavioral responses evoked by the CS depend on behavioral processes that are organized to help animals cope with motivationally significant events. In either case, what one measures in a conditioning experiment is now recognized as a kind of tip of the iceberg—Pavlov's dog was doing much more than just drooling. To understand the form of the responses evoked by a CS, one must understand the biological function that the system might serve in the animal's natural environment (e.g., Holland, 1984).

Summary

1. Conditioning can be remembered very well over time. The forgetting that occurs can often be alleviated by reminder treatments, which suggests that forgetting does not necessarily mean a permanent loss from the memory store. Two major causes of forgetting are: interference in which something learned at some other point in time interferes with the target memory, and retrieval failure in which the target memory is not accessed because the context has changed.

2. Extinction phenomena involve both of these processes. Extinction itself results from retroactive interference rather than destruction of the original CS-US association. However, extinction performance depends a great deal on the context for retrieval. When the context is changed after extinction, extinction is not retrieved, and a recovery of responding known as the "renewal effect" occurs.

3. The passage of time theoretically causes a change of context. Spontaneous recovery is therefore the renewal effect that occurs when the temporal context changes after extinction. Spontaneous recovery and the renewal effect can both be alleviated by cues that remind the subject of extinction. Other paradigms that involve interference may involve similar retrieval principles—one example is counterconditioning; another example might be latent inhibition.

4. Stimuli can "set the occasion for" a target CS's association with the US. Occasion setting often arises in serial feature-positive and feature-negative discriminations. Occasion setters differ from ordinary CSs in at least three ways: (1) They influence the behavior that is controlled by the target, (2) they are not affected by changing their direct associations with the US, and (3) they do not influence performance to all CSs.

5. The target CS in occasion setting has properties that are similar to an extinguished CS. That is, the target CS seems to have both excitatory and inhibitory associations with the US that result from reinforcement and nonreinforcement, respectively. Occasion setters appear to operate by modulating the target's inhibitory association with the US.

6. The conditioned response to the CS is not really the same as the unconditioned response to the US. Sometimes the two appear to be opposites, with the CR compensating for the UR. The nature of the CS also influences the form of the CR.

7. "Responses" are things that are generated by the central nervous system. True URs must therefore be produced by the brain and/or the spinal cord. Drug USs often have peripheral physiological effects that masquerade as a real response. Instead, these are stimuli that cause a compensatory reaction

from the nervous system. This compensatory UR leads to the conditioning of a compensatory CR.

8. Conditioning enables whole "behavior systems" that are functionally organized to deal with the US. The behavior that results from classical conditioning is therefore quite rich and variable. Different types of CSs may support different components of the behavior system. This is why both the qualitative nature of the CS and the length of the CS-US interval are important in determining the form of the CR.

Key Terms

memory reactivation
trace decay
interference
proactive interference
retroactive interference
retrieval failure
renewal effect
temporal context
relapse
reinstatement
rapid reacquisition
counterconditioning
modulate
occasion setter

feature-positive discrimination
feature-negative discrimination
feature stimulus
target stimulus
positive occasion setter
negative occasion setter
configural cue
fear potentiated startle
McCollough effect
behavior systems
predatory imminence
panic disorder
agoraphobia

Chapter Six Outline

Everything You Know Is Wrong

Special Characteristics of Flavor Aversion Learning

    One-trial learning

    Long-delay learning

    Learned safety

    Hedonic shift

    Compound potentiation

    Summary

Some Reasons Why Learning Laws May Be General

    Evolution produces both generality and specificity

    The generality of relative validity

Associative Learning in Honeybees and Humans

    Conditioning in bees

    Category and causal learning in humans

    Some disconnections between conditioning and human category and causal learning

    Causes, effects, and causal power

Conclusion

Summary

Chapter

6

Are the Laws of Conditioning General?

WE HAVE BEEN DISCUSSING EXPERIMENTS run in animal learning laboratories as if these experiments mean something for the world at large. Our discussion has accepted what people like Watson and Thorndike first told us we could assume: that the rules of learning that govern the behavior of a rat or pigeon in a Skinner box generalize to other examples of animal and human behavior. We have been using terms like CS and US (or R, S, and S*) quite abstractly—they are meant to stand for a very broad range of things and events. Is this safe? Can we really think of different CSs or different responses as abstract and more or less interchangeable? To some extent, you already know we can. The laws of learning we have studied so far have been widely applied to problems in clinical psychology (e.g., O'Donohue, 1998; Mineka & Zinbarg, 2006), and in the last chapter we saw some further examples of how principles derived from laboratory research on extinction can predict the effects of exposure treatments in humans (see pp. 152–157). But this chapter takes a deeper look at the question. There are reasons to wonder whether the laws of learning we have been discussing so far are always as general as we have assumed them to be.

Everything You Know Is Wrong

In fact, the idea that the laws of learning are general was strongly challenged during the late 1960s and early 1970s, when several remarkable discoveries came along and revolutionized our thinking about the psychology of learning. This was the period when blocking, contingency effects, relative validity effects, and so on began a new era of the study of classical conditioning (see Chapters 3 and 4). There were many other things going on at the time as well. One of the most important was the serious investigation of taste aversion learning in which animals learn to reject a flavor when it is associated with illness. The phenomenon seemed extremely special and unique. Once taste aversion learning was accepted as a fact that learning theorists had to deal with, it also fundamentally changed the way they thought about learning. To me, the story is fascinating in part because I think it was mixed up in the fact that the 1960s and 1970s were also a period in which big changes were occurring in society: The United States was deeply involved in a highly protested war in Vietnam, the civil rights movement and the Great Society were underway, and the sexual revolution was in progress. Lots of accepted truths were being rejected and overturned. To quote a comedy group that was active at the time (the Firesign Theater), it was as if "everything you know is wrong."

Taste aversion learning has been mentioned in every one of the preceding chapters. The reason is simple: It has provided many insights into learning and behavior. But what makes it so crucial in the history of learning theory? Reports of taste aversion learning date back at least to the 1950s (Garcia, Kimledorf, & Koelling, 1955), but when John Garcia first forced it upon the scientific community in the 1960s in several important papers (e.g., Garcia, Ervin, & Koelling, 1966; Garcia & Koelling, 1966), there were two things that seemed almost unbelievable about it. First, as we saw in Chapter 2, rats appeared to associate the flavor with illness over extraordinarily long intervals of time—even several hours (see Chapter 3). This result, known as **long-delay learning**, was completely unheard of in earlier work in animal learning. In fact, some very rigorous experiments with rats in runways had indicated that learning was extremely difficult if the interval between the response and reward delivery was longer than a few seconds (e.g., Grice, 1948; see Renner, 1964, Tarpy & Sawabini, 1974, for reviews). Consistent with this, eyeblink conditioning shows optimal learning when the trace interval between CS and US is less than a second or so. Viewed in this context, the fact that a rat could associate a flavor and a bout of illness that followed it by several hours was nothing short of stunning. It suggested a *qualitative* difference between flavor aversion learning and other types of associative learning.

The second thing about taste aversion learning that rocked the boat was that some of the earliest reports suggested that only certain combinations of CS and US could be learned. Flavors paired with illness worked great; but when flavor was paired with electric footshock, or an audiovisual cue was paired with illness, there was little evidence of learning (Garcia & Koelling, 1966; see pp. 66–69). As I pointed out before, it wasn't that the flavor was an unusually salient CS, or that the illness was an unusually potent US. Something about the *combination* of the two was crucial in determining learning. This possibility was also very radical because it made it difficult to accept the assumption that all stimuli and responses were inherently equal and equally associable. Flavor and illness are special things to a rat. It became more difficult to think of them as examples of abstract classes of events—CS and US.

The idea quickly emerged that learning mechanisms have evolved to deal with specific problems that animals face in the wild. With taste aversion learning, laboratory science had finally stumbled upon evolution's solution to the rat's problem of learning to avoid foods that contain slow-acting poisons. This was mentioned in an earlier chapter; however, what wasn't mentioned was the implication that created a shock wave through the community of scientific psychologists. If evolution can generate such uniqueness in a learning mechanism, why should there ever be any generality? Have all learning mechanisms evolved independently to solve every one of an animal's functional problems? Why should the principles of learning uncovered in rats that are run in Skinner boxes with arbitrary stimuli and responses ever generalize to other situations? I hope you can appreciate the importance of the idea. The methods used in learning theory were *based* on their actual arbitrariness. Studying rats in Skinner boxes with the thought that it was relevant to the human condition is based on the idea that learning is a general process. But once there was this strange new thing called taste aversion learning, why should we expect generality at all?

Before we go any further with this, it is important to remember that taste aversion learning does occur in humans (e.g., Bernstein, 1978). The question is not really whether learning principles generalize from species to species (many animals show taste aversion learning), but whether the principles generalize from one example of learning, or learning preparation, to another. Are the laws that describe taste aversion learning the same or different from the laws that work to explain fear conditioning, eyeblink conditioning, or autoshaping?

One illustration of the challenge was Martin Seligman's 1970 paper "On the generality of the laws of learning." In it, Seligman surveyed some of the research coming out of this period, which suggested that certain forms of learning were special and that not all Ss and S*s, or Rs and S*s, were equally associable. Seligman proposed that some examples of learning are evolutionarily "prepared," some are "unprepared," and others are "contraprepared." For example, rats are prepared by evolution to associate tastes with illness, but they are contraprepared to associate taste with an electric footshock. One of the most important things that distinguishes these types of learning was supposed to be how quickly they are learned—prepared things take one or two trials, while contraprepared things require a very large number of trials. But the main argument was that, although the laws of learning might generalize between examples from within each category (from prepared to prepared, unprepared to unprepared, and contraprepared to contraprepared), there is no reason to expect them to generalize between the categories. The laws of learning might not be as general as the founders of the field had supposed. Everything you know is wrong.

Martin Seligman

To some researchers, Seligman's vision of evolution's effect on the learning mechanism had a ring of implausibility to it. Why should there be any generality even among different examples of "prepared" learning? If prepared learning mechanisms have evolved to handle specific problems—which was implicit in the argument—why should there be any generality between types of learning that merely appear to be learned at comparable rates? Another version of the specialization idea was provided by Rozin and Kalat (1971), who argued that learning mechanisms might be specifically adapted to solving particular problems. Taste aversion learning is just one illustration of this. We might find that many—even all—mechanisms of learning are the result of specific adaptations designed to handle specific problems. This is the version of the challenge that has been passed down to us today.

Thus, at the beginning of the 1970s, there were disturbing questions about the very foundation of the scientific study of animal learning. Notice, however, that although articles like Seligman's and Rozin and Kalat's raised a very fundamental issue, they could not claim to have settled the problem. Instead, they really raised an empirical question: How general *are* the laws we have discussed in the previous chapters? This chapter addresses that question. We will first take a harder look at taste aversion learning, and ask how special the apparently unique features of taste aversion learning really are. We will see that there is some generality, and we will have occasion to wonder why that is. Then we will consider learning in organisms with brains that have evolved independently of the mammalian brain, honeybees, and finally, examine associative learning in humans. Throughout this chapter, the point is that there is actually a considerable amount of generality to the principles of learning and that the investigation of each new possible exception has mainly served to improve and expand the general laws (e.g., Domjan, 1983).

Special Characteristics of Flavor Aversion Learning

Several things about taste aversion learning have been considered special. The question is whether the unique characteristics really indicate that taste aversion learning is qualitatively different from other forms of conditioning.

One-trial learning

It is a remarkable fact that a potent flavor aversion can be learned in one conditioning trial. If you are one of the many people who have a flavor aversion, you know what I mean; tequila aversions can be learned after a single bad experience. Figure 6.1 shows the results of a fairly typical experiment using rats in which a novel saccharin drink was associated with an immediate injection of lithium chloride (Rosas & Bouton, 1996). The two groups tested averaged nearly zero consumption of the saccharin after just one saccharin-lithium pairing. But notice that consumption increased reasonably quickly when the saccharin was offered again without lithium. This

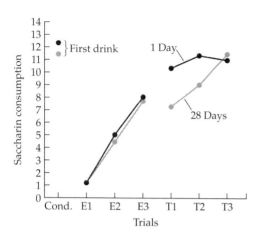

Figure 6.1 One-trial flavor aversion learning. The figure shows consumption of a saccharin solution over several trials. The rats' first drink of saccharin was followed by an injection of lithium chloride. This caused a strong aversion that was detected when the saccharin was offered on the next trial (E1). But over three daily trials without lithium (E1–E3), the aversion weakened through extinction. After a wait of 28 days, there was a modest spontaneous recovery (gray circles) as compared with a control group that received testing (T) one day—rather than 28 days—after the third extinction trial. (After Rosas & Bouton, 1996.)

is an example of extinction. Notice also that, when one of the groups was given a delay of 28 days between the third extinction trial and a test, there was a modest spontaneous recovery of the aversion. These results may help put flavor aversion learning into some perspective for you; conditioning is fast, but extinction and spontaneous recovery occur in a way that is not altogether different from more "typical" forms of classical conditioning.

Impressive as it is, can we say that one-trial learning is really unique to flavor aversion learning? Strong conditioned fear can be created after just a single conditioning trial (e.g., Mahoney & Ayres, 1976). And of course some learning probably occurs in all conditioning preparations as a result of the first CS-US pairing. According to theories of conditioning, the size of the increase depends on factors like the salience of the CS, the salience of the US, and so forth. One could easily argue that these parameters are high in flavor aversion learning. Although taste aversions are definitely impressive and can definitely be quick—especially under laboratory conditions—few people consider this strong grounds for arguing that taste aversions are an example of a qualitatively different form of learning.

Long-delay learning

The story is more interesting when one considers the delay between the flavor and the US that allows flavor-aversion conditioning. There is no doubt that this is unusual, but we need to consider why this might be so.

The methods used in a taste aversion learning experiment are a little special. Sam Revusky (1971) was among the first to note this, and he came up with a rather interesting psychological explanation of why they might allow learning over such long delays. A rat that learns an aversion to saccharin over a 1-hour delay in the typical lab experiment has little to do during the delay interval. That is, the animal might taste saccharin at 10:00 and then sit in the cage until 11:00, at which point it is made ill. Typically, the animal doesn't eat or taste anything during that period; often, it probably falls asleep. If we imagine it waking up and thinking "It must have been something I ate" when it is poisoned, then there is little besides saccharin to blame the illness on.

Revusky captured this very loose idea by emphasizing two things that are generally important in conditioning: **stimulus relevance** and **interference**. We have considered stimulus relevance before: For a given US, only some kinds of CSs are good ("relevant") predictors. When illness is the US, the most relevant CS is a flavor, and the rat therefore learns about flavors when it receives an illness US. Revusky's interference idea, in turn, is that relevant stimuli tend to compete with one another for conditioning. This idea should sound familiar—it is built into most of the theories of conditioning, which have emphasized effects like blocking. When our rat spends an hour in the cage between ingestion of saccharin and inducement of illness, the important thing is that *there is no relevant flavor present to compete with the conditioning of saccharin*. Revusky (1971) showed that if a relevant extra CS (i.e., taste of a second flavor) is introduced during the delay interval, there is considerably less conditioning to the saccharin. The result of one of Revusky's experiments is shown in Figure 6.2. In it, rats received a taste of saccharin (a small, 2-ml drink) before receiving lithium chloride about 75 minutes later. Fifteen minutes into the delay, the rats received 5 mls of either vinegar or water. As the subsequent tests of saccharin show, the vinegar taste interfered with the learned aversion to saccharin. (In other experiments, Revusky also showed that flavors occurring *before* the to-be-conditioned flavor likewise interfered with conditioning.) Thus, one thing that makes long-delay learning possible in flavor aversion learning experiments is the fact that there are no relevant interfering cues.

The story is different for other kinds of learning. If we ran a comparable experiment with a tone at 10:00 and a food pellet delivered at 11:15, many relevant noises and sights (and perhaps the rat's own behavior) would probably intervene. Therefore, learning over long delays will be more difficult when relevant competing cues are more likely to occur during the delay interval.

The Revusky hypothesis led to other experiments. Bow Lett Revusky (Sam's wife) ran some new experiments in the T-maze (e.g., Lett, 1973, 1977). Rats were trained to turn right or left in the maze, and then after a long delay the response was rewarded with sucrose. The trick, though, was to remove the rat from the maze immediately after a response and then return it to the home cage. When the delay interval was over, the rat was returned to

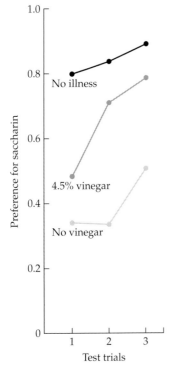

Figure 6.2 Interference reduces long-delay learning. One group (No vinegar) showed a strong aversion after a single trial in which saccharin was followed by lithium chloride after a delay. But when the rats also had a taste of 4.5% vinegar during the delay, the aversion was markedly weakened. These are extinction test trials. (After Revusky, 1971.)

the start box and given a reward (or not) as appropriate. With this procedure, the rats learned to make the correct response with intervals of at least
60 minutes between response and reward. Lett's idea was that removal from
the maze immediately after the response limited exposure to interfering cues
that were "situationally relevant." When control rats spent part of the delay
interval in the maze, the learning was not as good. Other researchers have
also produced evidence of surprisingly good learning with delayed reward
in mazes (e.g., Lieberman, McIntosh, & Thomas, 1979). Thus, long-delay
learning is not necessarily restricted to taste aversion learning. And
Revusky's approach suggests that long-delay learning involving flavor aversion can be predicted from *general* principles of conditioning: interference
and stimulus relevance.

Learned safety

Flavor aversion learning is presumably only one part of a whole system that
might have evolved so that omnivores can learn to discriminate foods containing poison from foods that are safe to eat. It is possible to think of the
rat actively sorting foods as either dangerous or safe; thus, when the rat
encounters any new food, it might detect and register its consequences. If
illness occurs, an aversion will be learned. But if nothing happens, the rat
might learn that the new flavor is safe.

It is conceivable that this kind of process happens with many types of
stimuli; for example, wary rats might also judge noises and lights as safe or
dangerous vis-a-vis attack from a predator, but this kind of idea has enjoyed
special status when people think about flavor learning. Kalat and Rozin
(1973) suggested this phenomenon has a role in long-delay learning. They
noted that Revusky's theory implies that an aversion could form over an
infinite delay if there were no interfering relevant flavors. But such an aversion typically does not form—why not? Their answer: During the delay
interval, the rat is gradually learning that the flavor it tasted is safe, and over
time this increasingly gets in the way of learning an aversion if illness does
eventually happen. To illustrate the phenomenon, Kalat and Rozin showed
that, while a rat given a taste of sucrose at 4:00 and then made ill at 4:30
acquired a strong aversion to sucrose, the aversion wasn't so strong if the
rat had also had an earlier exposure to saccharin at about 12:00. They suggested that, as time elapsed after the 12:00 exposure, the rat was learning
that the substance was safe, and this interfered with the aversion learning
made possible when sucrose was again ingested at 4:00 and then illness
occurred at 4:30. This unusual perspective makes sense if one considers
the rat's problem of discriminating safe and dangerous foods.

We actually considered this phenomenon in Chapter 4. As we saw, there
is another way to explain the effect of preexposing the rat to sucrose. Preexposure to the flavor at 12:00 might cause latent inhibition, a very general
phenomenon that can be understood without supposing the rat is learning
safety (remember that one explanation of latent inhibition is that attention
to the CS just habituates). In fairness to Kalat and Rozin, the importance of

latent inhibition was not well understood at the time they published their experiments. But the late Michael Best (1975) saw the difference quickly. He reasoned that, in aversion learning, learned safety would actually be analogous to conditioned inhibition; that is, if the learned aversion is excitation, then safety would be analogous to inhibition. Accordingly, Best first showed that conditioned inhibition can be produced in flavor aversion learning. Rats received a saccharin flavor that was paired with illness; the pairing caused an aversion to saccharin. On another trial, a salty taste (a saline solution) was presented just after the rats received a short taste of saccharin. On this trial, the rat was not made ill. The saline was thus presented on an occasion when saccharin was not paired with poison. This is Pavlov's conditioned inhibition paradigm (or the feature-negative procedure); as you know, in most conditioning methods, this would make the saline a conditioned inhibitor.

Best showed that this arrangement did indeed cause conditioned inhibition. In fact, it led the rats to prefer the saline taste to water when both were offered at the same time in separate drinking bottles—a "two-bottle test." Thus, inhibition led to an increased preference for the salty taste, the opposite of an excitatory aversion. This preference is shown by the group at left in Figure 6.3; they preferred the saline much more than a control group (adjacent in the figure) that received the same previous training, with the exception that saccharin had not been paired with illness. Speaking casually, the rats in the first group learned to like the saline when it signaled safety. Now, here is the kicker: If preexposure to salt without any illness were alone enough to allow the rat to learn safety, as Kalat and Rozin supposed, preex-

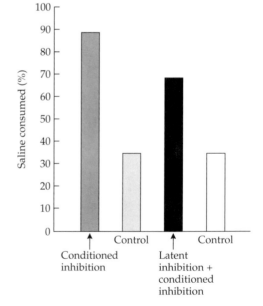

Figure 6.3 Preference for saline after conditioned inhibition training and after conditioned inhibition training that was preceded by exposure to saline. When saline received a treatment that made it a conditioned inhibitor, rats preferred to drink saline over water (first bar). Preexposure to the saline without illness caused latent inhibition, which reduced the preference caused by conditioned inhibition (third bar). (After Best, 1975.)

posure to salt before this inhibition conditioning procedure should *facilitate* the learning of inhibition. On the other hand, if salt acquires some latent inhibition, learning of inhibition should not be facilitated—it should be made more difficult as experiments with more traditional conditioning preparations have shown (e.g., Reiss & Wagner, 1972; Rescorla, 1971). As the group indicated by the third bar in Figure 6.3 shows, the latter result was obtained. Preexposure to the saline did not facilitate the learning of safety; rather, the group's preference for saline was reduced. (The final bar corresponds to a control group that received the same treatment without illness.) Simple exposure to a flavor does not yield learned safety in this sense. Instead, it causes latent inhibition, just as it does in other conditioning preparations.

You may recall that Best, Gemberling, and Johnson (1979) went on to view the Kalat and Rozin phenomenon from the perspective of Wagner's short-term memory model: The first exposure primed saccharin into short-term memory, rendering it less surprising when it was presented again later, which reduced the extent to which learning with it could occur. (Consistent with this approach, sticking a second flavor in between the prime at 12:00 and the exposure at 4:00 improved the learning about it again, presumably by knocking the prime out of short-term memory and making it surprising again; see Figure 4.11.) The interpretation assumes that short-term memory with flavors might last quite a bit longer than short-term memory with other kinds of stimuli. (This could also contribute to why taste aversions can be learned with long trace intervals.) But general processes do seem to apply. Indeed, as the Best et al. (1979) study illustrates, taste aversion learning has become a method that is now used to test implications of general theories of conditioning and learning.

Hedonic shift

If you have a conditioned taste aversion, you know there is something rather visceral and non-cognitive about it. Tequila doesn't seem like a signal for illness; instead, you just can't stand the stuff. Garcia, Hankins, and Rusiniak (1974) suggested that the main result of aversion learning is a shift in the hedonic (pleasant or unpleasant) properties of the flavor. The flavor isn't a cue for a US in the way that a tone is a cue for a food pellet. The main effect of aversion learning is to change the palatability of the flavor from pleasant to noxious. This is the so-called **hedonic shift**.

Subsequent research has borne this idea out. For example, several investigators have used an interesting method called the **taste-reactivity test** (Grill & Norgren, 1977; Parker, 1982). The test is based on the fact that rats react differently to flavors that differ in palatability. When exposed to a tasty sucrose solution, they show a set of "yum" behaviors, such as protruding their tongues and licking their paws. In contrast, when they are exposed to bitter flavors, like quinine, they react differently; they rub their chins on the floor and walls, they gape, and they shake their paws, all of which are essentially "yuck" responses. The discovery is that, if we give a rat a tasty sucrose flavor and pair it with illness, the rat first reacts to the sucrose with positive

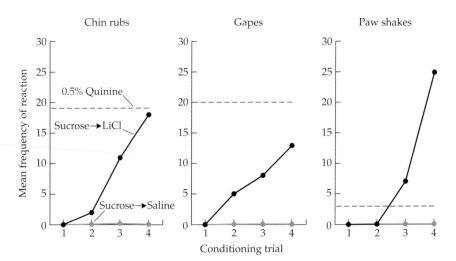

Figure 6.4 Results from a taste-reactivity test. When tasty sucrose is paired with illness, the rat begins to respond to it as if it were bitter. Closed circles indicate responding to sucrose over trials on which it was paired with lithium chloride. The dashed line indicates unconditional responding to the taste of a bitter quinine solution. (After Parker, 1998.)

"yum" responses. But on testing after conditioning, it shows the "yuck" pattern of responding, just as it does to a bitter taste (Figure 6.4). It is as if aversion learning has turned the tasty sucrose flavor into a bitter one. Interestingly, Linda Parker has shown that this sort of effect occurs with some USs (like injections of lithium chloride), which make a rat sick. But this effect doesn't occur with other USs (such as injections of amphetamine or cocaine), which do not make a rat sick, even though these USs will also condition suppressed consumption of the flavor (e.g., Parker, 1982, 1988, 1995, 1998). Thus, learning can suppress flavor consumption through at least two mechanisms, one of which involves a hedonic shift and another that does not. But when we are dealing with agents that cause sickness, the taste aversion is associated with a shift in the flavor's hedonic properties. The rat reacts as if the flavor is now bitter. Interestingly, flavors associated with calories, a positive US, likewise show an increase in positive palatability reactions, as if a neutral—or even aversive—flavor has become sweet (Forestell & LoLordo, 2003; Myers & Sclafani, 2001).

The question is whether hedonic shift makes flavor learning unique. You will remember from the last chapter that the nature of the CR in all conditioning preparations depends on the nature of both the CS and the US. In a broad sense, the same is also true in taste aversion learning. That is, the combination of a flavor CS and an illness US seems to support a particular pattern of behavior—suppressed consumption and a negative palatibility reaction—just as other CS-US combinations cause their own characteristic patterns. All CRs are unique; thus, it is easy to accept the idea that flavor

Linda Parker

aversions cause a hedonic shift without claiming a radical new law of learning and behavior.

The question can also be approached from another angle, however. The idea is that taste aversions involve only a hedonic shift—the flavor is not supposed to be treated as a signal for the US. Other forms of conditioning clearly can involve the subject learning that the CS is a signal for the US. For example, when humans receive pairings of a CS and an uncomfortable (but not painful) electric shock to the finger, the CS will elicit palm sweating (an "electrodermal" CR), and the participant will report an expectancy of shock (e.g., Lovibond, 2003). The person's ability to report the expectancy indicates some awareness that the CS signals shock. Some writers have argued that such awareness is actually necessary to get a CR in humans (e.g., Lovibond & Shanks, 2002), although the idea is not accepted universally (see Clark & Squire, 1998; Manns, Clark, & Squire, 2002; Öhman & Mineka, 2001; Wiens & Öhman, 2002). Interestingly, verbal instructions can have a powerful effect on the electrodermal CR. For example, after conditioning, if humans are told about changes in the CS-US contingencies, the verbal input can substantially modify the CR (Lovibond, 2003; see also Dawson & Schell, 1985). But I know of no similar experiment showing that verbal input can likewise influence a conditioned taste aversion. Indeed, the idea seems implausible—for example, despite repeated conversations throughout my childhood, I don't think my mother ever talked me out of my taste aversion to broccoli. The point is that taste aversions do not seem easy to penetrate with verbal input; they seem to be a more visceral form of learning than electrodermal conditioning.

There are findings with animals that also suggest that a taste aversion is rather visceral and noncognitive. After animal conditioning occurs, we can "revalue" the US in a number of different ways—we can habituate the US or reduce the original magnitude of the US in some other fashion (a "deflation" treatment, e.g., Rescorla, 1973; Holland and Rescorla, 1975b; Holland and Straub, 1979; see Chapter 3). Alternatively, we can expose the subject to a series of larger USs (an "inflation" treatment, Rescorla, 1974; Bouton, 1984). In fear conditioning and appetitive conditioning, these treatments influence the strength of the CR. That is, exposure to weakened USs after conditioning decreases the strength of the CR, and exposure to larger USs increases the strength of the CR. If we change the representation of the US after conditioning, responding to the CS changes accordingly. These results thus suggest that in fear conditioning and appetitive conditioning, the CS does indeed act as a signal for a representation of the US.

Little work has been done on these paradigms in taste aversion learning, but at least some of it suggests that taste aversions are *not* revalued in the same way. Perhaps the flavor *is* treated as something different from a signal for the US. Jacobs, Zellner, LoLordo, and Riley (1981) ran a deflation experiment in which rats first received a pairing of saccharin with an injection of morphine that made them sick. The conditioning trial created an aversion to the saccharin. In the next phase, the rats received repeated injections of morphine. As you know by now, repeated morphine injections make the body tolerant to the drug; because of this, the drug becomes less aversive than before. In fact, in Jacob et al.'s experiment, there was evidence that the animals became dependent on the morphine. To risk being a little anthropomorphic, at the end of the tolerance phase there was a sense in which the rats probably liked the morphine; in fact, they probably would have sought it out. Interestingly, even though the treatment revalued the rats' reaction to the morphine US, a final test showed that the saccharin aversion was not affected. In this sense, the rats did not behave as if they treated the saccharin as a signal for the US.

I ran some related unpublished experiments with Leigh Stockton many years ago. Instead of deflating the US, we inflated it. Rats received pairings of saccharin with a weak dose of lithium chloride and then several injections (spaced over many days) of a larger, stiffer dose. This had no impact on the strength of the aversion when we tested it again. (DeCola and Fanselow [1995] suggested that inflation effects can occur in taste aversion learning, but not if there is a delay between the CS and US on the conditioning trial.) Our results, in a tentative way, are again consistent with the idea that flavor-illness pairings might not always make the flavor a "signal" in the same sense that it is a signal in fear or appetitive conditioning.

An important point is in order here, though. The fact is, we do not know how "general" the US revaluation effect is. It has not been studied much outside of fear conditioning and appetitive conditioning. For example, one would be hard-pressed to find an experiment involving US revaluation in eyeblink conditioning. And even in the fear and appetitive conditioning preparations, there are some differences. For example, in fear conditioning, US deflation works with first-order conditioning (Rescorla, 1973), but not with second-order conditioning (Rizley & Rescorla, 1972). In appetitive conditioning with rats, the same pattern appears to hold (e.g., Holland & Rescorla, 1975b); but in autoshaping with pigeons, deflation effects have been observed (Rescorla, 1979). There is a possibility that conditioning can take the form of S-S or S-R learning in different conditioning systems and preparations; however, this question has not really been explored. For the time being, we may note that taste aversion learning might be represented differently than first-order fear conditioning or first-order appetitive conditioning.

Compound potentiation

John Garcia's laboratory dropped another bombshell in the late 1970s. In several new experiments (Rusiniak, Hankins, Garcia, & Brett, 1979), rats were given a dilute solution of almond extract mixed in water (Figure 6.5A). Although the rats took the solution into their mouths, the almond extract produced an odor; it was detected retronasally through the nasal holes rats (and humans) have in the back of the mouth. When presented alone before illness, the odor acquired only a weak conditioned aversion. But when it was combined with a saccharin taste, so that the rat drank a compound almond-saccharin mixture that combined the almond odor with sweet

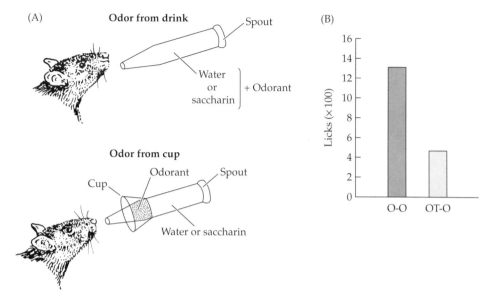

Figure 6.5 Potentiation of odor conditioning by taste. (A) A rat is given a taste in drinking water that also contains an odor. (In many experiments, the odor comes from a cup near the spout instead of being mixed in the drink.) (B) When odor is paired with illness on its own and then tested (O-O), it does not suppress consumption much. But if it has been combined with a taste on the conditioning trial (OT-O), strong odor conditioning is obtained. (A, after Inui, Shimura, & Yamamoto, 2006; B, after Palmerino et al., 1980.)

(roughly the flavor of marzipan), a remarkable new thing occurred. The saccharin taste, known to be a salient CS for illness, actually *increased* the conditioning acquired to the almond odor (Figure 6.5B). This result, called **compound potentiation**, is important because it is precisely the opposite of what most conditioning theories predict. For example, you may remember that the Rescorla-Wagner model assumes that CSs presented in a compound compete with one another for conditioning—they must share the overall amount of conditioning that is supported by the US. In fact, all the models considered in Chapter 4 predict that when a salient CS is compounded with a weaker CS, it should cause **overshadowing**—the stronger CS should reduce the associative strength acquired by the weaker element. All the models we have considered predict competition and overshadowing, rather than potentiation, of odor conditioning by the taste.

Other research has established that the effect also occurs when the odor is presented on a cup behind the drinking spout, rather than being mixed directly in the water (see Figure 6.5A). Garcia and his colleagues provided several explanations that all emphasized the different functional roles that odors and tastes have. One early view (Rusiniak et al., 1979) held that odor is a distal cue that controls the rat's approach to foods, while taste is a proximal cue that guides consumption. Because there was no redundancy in function, perhaps there was no competition. Another view (e.g., Garcia, 1989; Palmerino, Rusiniak, & Garcia, 1980) emphasized the fact that tastes are important in defending the gut from poison—the "gut defense" system. Odor, on the other hand, is connected with many things besides foods; odors mark the presence of other rats, potential predators, potential mates, etc. In fact, odors are sometimes described as part of the "skin defense" system. The effect of the taste was to make the odor a food cue, allowing it access to the gut defense system. That is what made it more connectable with poisoning, particularly over long delays. The approach emphasizes the special functional roles played by odor and taste.

The potentiation effect generated some intense research and debate. It was soon shown that tastes could also potentiate conditioning to contextual cues (e.g., Best, Brown, & Sowell, 1984; Best, Batson, Meachum, Brown, & Ringer, 1985; Best, Batson, & Bowman, 1990). In these experiments, either saccharin or water was presented in a particular box, and then the rat was made ill. When rats later received a different, palatable solution (e.g., saline) to drink in that same box, consumption was more suppressed in the group that had received the saccharin there during conditioning. The saccharin had potentiated conditioning of the box. Presumably, context cues differ from taste cues in the same way that odors differ from tastes, in that context cues are exteroceptive—distal cues that are not ordinarily used in "gut defense." More recent research has also discovered other interactions between odors and tastes that suggest that they do not merely compete with one another when they are conditioned in compound (e.g., Batsell & Batson, 1999; Batsell, Paschall, Gleason, & Batson, 2001; Batson & Batsell, 2000; see Batsell & Blankenship, 2002, for a review).

Durlach and Rescorla (1980), however, pointed out that potentiation could be understood in terms of general conditioning laws. When taste and odor (or taste and context) are combined, the animal has an opportunity to associate them. The animal might form a **within-compound association**—that is, an association between the two elements in the compound, which can happen widely in compound conditioning experiments (e.g., Rescorla & Durlach, 1981). Therefore, any conditioning that might accrue to the taste is readily transferred to the odor—a kind of guilt by association. Consistent with this idea, Durlach and Rescorla (1980) found that extinction of the taste after odor-taste conditioning reduced aversion to the odor (but see Lett, 1984). Similar effects of extinguishing the taste have been observed in taste-context potentiation (e.g., Best et al., 1985). Recent experiments have also shown that further *conditioning* of the taste also further strengthens aversion to the odor (Batsell, Trost, Cochran, Blankenship, & Batson, 2003). All of these results are consistent with a within-compound association explanation of potentiation, but there are still problems. Perhaps most important, animals appear to form within-compound associations whether potentiation or overshadowing is observed (e.g., Rescorla & Durlach, 1981). Therefore, although within-compound associations may sometimes be involved in potentiation, they are not sufficient to produce it.

There was other trouble as well. A number of reports emerged that failed to produce odor potentiation by taste (e.g., Bouton & Whiting, 1982; Mikulka, Pitts, & Philput, 1982). These results were not just failures to replicate the original phenomenon; in fact, in a series of studies, taste consistently overshadowed the conditioning of odor (e.g., Bouton & Whiting, 1982). Eventually, experiments showed that the odor had to be extremely non-salient—very weakly conditionable on its own—for potentiation to occur. When the odor in the drink was made very weakly conditionable by presenting it in an even more dilute solution (so dilute that it was 1/400 the concentration originally used by Rusiniak et al.), odor potentiation by taste occurred (Bouton, Jones, McPhillips, & Swartzentruber, 1986). It turns out that the potentiated cue's weak conditionability is far more important than its status as an odor or a taste. When a saline solution was similarly diluted so that it was a very weak cue for illness, this *taste* was potentiated by saccharin in further experiments (Bouton, Dunlap, & Swartzentruber, 1987). More recently, even odors have potentiated tastes (and tastes have potentiated odors), provided that a strongly conditionable cue is combined with a more weakly conditionable target (Slotnick, Westbrook, & Darling, 1997). The upshot of all this is that odors can often be readily associated with illness on their own, and that potentiation, though perhaps somewhat restricted in its generality, occurs under a wider range of conditions than Garcia would have originally predicted.

Where does this leave us? The main point is that both overshadowing and potentiation can occur in compound conditioning. This is an important conclusion, because it suggests that our understanding of conditioning is still incomplete. On the other hand, potentiation is not a freak result that is connected with certain combinations of odor and taste (or context and taste). It appears to happen when a very weakly conditionable cue is combined with a more salient cue. Other studies now suggest that a salient stimulus can also enhance conditioning of a weaker CS in autoshaping (Thomas, Robertson, & Lieberman, 1987), learning about locations in a maze (e.g., Graham, Good, McGregor, & Pearce, 2006), and even fear conditioning (Urushihara, Stout, & Miller, 2004). Instead of indicating that aversion learning obeys special laws, compound potentiation challenges us to come up with better general laws.

Summary

By the late 1970s and early 1980s, taste aversion learning had been absorbed into mainstream learning theory. It is now viewed as another example of associative learning along with other examples of classical conditioning. There will probably always be differences in the conditions that lead to better eyeblink conditioning, fear conditioning, and taste aversion learning—all of which are potentially illuminating. For example, we may discover that the preparations vary in whether they are examples of S-R or S-S learning. But the differences are not necessarily threats to a general understanding of learning. Chicken Little (Seligman, 1970) was wrong; the sky never fell.

Taste aversion learning did bring some very significant changes to the field, however. Students of learning theory now recognize that evolution does influence learning; stimulus relevance in particular is now a generally accepted aspect of conditioning and associative learning. And there is a new interest in the function of conditioning, as exemplified by the perspective of learning as an adaptation process (discussed in Chapter 2), and by the current thinking about the processes that influence the form of the CR (see Chapter 5). Taste aversion learning added a fresh biological and functional perspective to how we view conditioning. It didn't lead to reinvention of the wheel—it led to a better wheel.

Some Reasons Why Learning Laws May Be General

There is thus some generality to the laws of learning after all. Yet, if we accept the fundamental idea that learning processes evolved because the ability to learn is functional (see Chapter 2), why should this be? An animal's ability to sense and receive stimulus input from the external world is also functional, in a general way. Yet animals are not equipped with a general sensory system; instead, evolution has given them separate vision, auditory, and other sensory systems. Why shouldn't analogous divisions occur in learning systems? Why should there be a general learning process?

Evolution produces both generality and specificity

The answers to these questions are complex and far from resolved. But it is important to understand that an evolutionary approach to learning can accept general learning laws as well as adaptive specializations. When most of us try to see things from an evolutionary perspective, we tend to see traits as adaptations—things that were selected directly for the function they now perform. But evolution doesn't work in only this way. Sometimes a functional trait is an **exaptation**, a characteristic or feature that was not selected directly for the job it currently performs (e.g., Gould, 1991; Gould & Vrba, 1982; see also Buss, Haselton, Shackelford, Bleske, & Wakefield, 1998). The basic idea is that a trait adapted for solving one particular problem is sometimes good enough at solving another problem, too. In this case, the trait would solve two problems, but have been adapted for only one. One example of an exaptation is bird feathers. Nowadays, feathers function to help birds fly, but they were probably selected for a very different function—to keep animals warm. Once early feathers were in place, though, they probably helped the animals move around, too. The feathers were thus co-opted for flight. Thus, the flight function of feathers started as an exaptation, not an adaptation.

Sherry and Schacter (1987) noted that the exaptation concept may help explain why general-purpose learning and memory processes have evolved. A learning mechanism that was adapted to solving one problem might work reasonably well for solving another, and simply be co-opted. Sherry and Schacter observed that, for true adaptive specializations in learning and memory to evolve, it is probably necessary that a mechanism for solving one problem be functionally incompatible with solving others. For example, a learning mechanism that allows habits to build up incrementally over trials might be incompatible with a learning mechanism that responds to the need to remember a once-experienced place or episode. The point is that functional incompatibility between the two problems might be required to force the evolution of separate mechanisms. The solution to the food selection problem that taste aversion learning provides is probably not functionally incompatible with other problems that classical conditioning mechanisms solve. As Sherry and Schacter note, "[A]n evolutionary analysis indicates that both generality and specificity must be expected to occur as characteristics of memory and learning" (Sherry & Schacter, 1987, p. 449.)

There is another reason why learning principles can be general. It is possible for two learning mechanisms to evolve separately but converge on similar principles because the problems they solve are inherently similar. The bird's wing and the bee's wing have many common properties, even though these appendages evolved independently. In this case, the traits are said to be **analogous** rather than **homologous** (they are similar but have separate evolutionary origins). Learning principles may thus be rather similar (analogous) from situation to situation because the problems they deal with are similar. It is generally true that things that occur together in time or space generally go together, and so forth. Learning has evolved to help animals understand the causal structure, or causal links, between things in their world (Dickinson, 1980); there may be generality to that structure. Of course, a number of other general functions of operant and classical conditioning were considered in Chapter 2.

Still, Sherry and Schacter (1987) noted at least one place where there might be a functional incompatibility: incremental habit learning versus memory for episodes that happen just once. Perhaps there are more incompatible systems than just these. Human memory researchers have often divided memory into several different systems, including those that handle knowledge about facts, short-term information, habits, autobiographical episodes, and more (e.g., Squire, 1989; Tulving, 1972; see Klein, Cosmides, Tooby, & Chance, 2002, for recent discussions). It is currently popular to think that the "mind is like a Swiss army knife, a general purpose tool made of many specialized parts" (Shettleworth, 1998, p. 567). The specialized parts are sometimes called **modules**—that is, cognitive mechanisms that are designed to handle specific types of input (e.g., see Shettleworth, 2002). Modules are thought to be relatively "encapsulated"; that is, they are unaffected by other modules.

Öhman and Mineka (2001) have recently argued that fear learning in humans is controlled by a "fear module" that is selective to its own "prepared" type of environmental input (we seem prepared to associate snakes and spiders—but not flowers or mushrooms—with fear-arousing USs). It is also thought to be encapsulated in the sense that it is not affected by conscious influences. Nonetheless, the module operates according to familiar classical conditioning laws, with "preparedness" being one of them. Thus, it might not be the case that different modules that have been hypothesized are truly functionally incompatible in the Sherry and Schacter sense. Perhaps because of the way the world is generally organized, the associative learning rules that are represented in classical conditioning may generalize across many domains.

The generality of relative validity

It does appear that the laws of conditioning can sometimes have astonishing generality. One surprising example is the relative validity effect described in Chapter 3 (Wagner et al., 1968), which illustrates the point that conditioning occurs to the extent that the CS provides information about the US. In the basic experiment, one group (Group Correlated) received a mix of AX+ and BX– trials. During later testing, the animals showed strong learning to A, and relatively little to X, the latter of which was less informative about the US. The other group (Group Uncorrelated) received very similar trials, except that AX and BX were both paired with the US half the time (the animals received AX+, AX–, BX+, and BX– trials). This group showed better learning to X, even though it was paired equally often with the US, because A and B were not more informative. Wagner et al. reported the relative validity effect in experiments on fear conditioning in rats, operant learning in rats, and eyeblink conditioning in rabbits. It was also later shown in pigeon autoshaping (Wasserman, 1974). The results of one of the original experiments, which we already saw in Chapter 3, are summarized again in the left part of Figure 6.6.

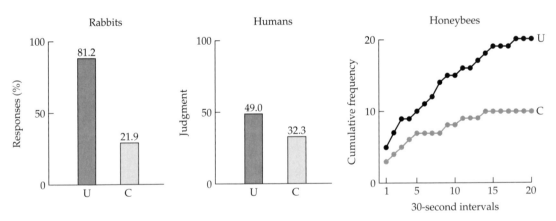

Figure 6.6 Results of relative validity experiments in rabbits, humans, and honeybees. C is the Correlated condition and U is the Uncorrelated condition. In all species and tasks, a cue acquires less associative strength when it is combined with more valid predictors of the US during learning (the Correlated condition). (After Wagner et al., 1968, Shanks, 1991, and Couvillon et al., 1983, respectively.)

What is remarkable about this result is that the relative validity effect has been demonstrated in an even wider range of species using a variety of conditioning preparations. For example, it has been shown in several experiments with human participants (Baker, Mercier, Vallee-Tourangeau, Frank, & Pan, 1993; Shanks, 1991; Wasserman, 1990). David Shanks brought human participants into the lab and asked them to pretend they were doctors diagnosing diseases. The participants saw a series of medical cases presented on a computer screen. In each case, a fictitious person was described as having one or several symptoms—such as puffy eyes, swollen glands, or sore arms. They might also have a fictitious disease, such as Dempes Disorder or Phipp's Syndrome. The participants were first given the symptoms, and required to guess which disease each patient had. Over trials, they learned that certain symptoms were associated with certain diseases. In this situation, each medical case is analogous to a conditioning trial—each symptom is a CS and each disease a US.

Several classic conditioning effects have been demonstrated with this method. In one experiment, Shanks (1991) repeated the relative validity conditions used by Wagner et al. (1968). In the Correlated condition, Dempes Disorder occurred with symptoms A and X (AX+), but not with symptoms B and X (BX–). In the Uncorrelated condition, the disease occurred half the time with A and X (AX+, AX–) and half the time with B and X (BX+, BX–). Once again, a potential predictor (X) was paired with a "US" half the time in both conditions. At the end of the experiment, Shanks asked the participants, "If you were to see 100 patients, each of which had puffy eyes, how many would you estimate would have Dempes Disorder?" The middle part of Figure 6.6 shows the data for the symptom that corresponded to CS X. The results were like the ones seen previously in rats, rabbits, and pigeons: People underestimated the symptom that was connected with more informative predictors in the Correlated condition.

The results have also been shown in another remarkable animal—the honeybee (Couvillon, Klosterhalfen, & Bitterman, 1983). Late in their lives, honeybees leave the hive and forage among flowers for nectar (which provides energy) and pollen (which provides protein). To do this efficiently, the honeybee learns to associate the color and odor of each type of flower with the reward contained within it. Consequently, on a given foraging trip away from the hive, a honeybee tends to visit only similar flowers. Associative learning is undoubtedly very important in the behavior of these insects.

Jeff Bitterman, Pat Couvillon, and their associates at the University of Hawaii have run many fascinating conditioning experiments with honeybees; they conduct their experiments in a laboratory that is open to the outdoors (Figure 6.7). Couvillon et al. (1983) caught individual honeybees near a hive the investigators maintained. (The bees were attracted to a feeding station where a sucrose solution could be obtained.) After capture, each bee was marked with a little nail polish for identification, and then transported a short distance to a windowsill of the laboratory where the experiment was run. A bee given a drop of sucrose at the windowsill would fly back to the

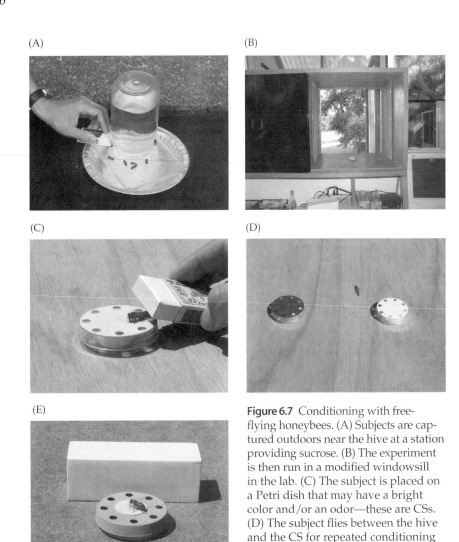

(A)

(B)

(C)

(D)

(E)

Figure 6.7 Conditioning with free-flying honeybees. (A) Subjects are captured outdoors near the hive at a station providing sucrose. (B) The experiment is then run in a modified windowsill in the lab. (C) The subject is placed on a Petri dish that may have a bright color and/or an odor—these are CSs. (D) The subject flies between the hive and the CS for repeated conditioning trials. (E) A rewarded trial—the subject feeds on sucrose in the middle of a Petri dish. (Photographs courtesy of Pat Couvillon.)

hive and then repeatedly return to the windowsill for more. Each visit allowed a new conditioning trial. On each visit, a drop of sucrose was presented on the lid of a petri dish that might be colored and/or have a scent. Different colors and odors thus provided CSs; the honeybees readily approached the petri dish lids once the bees had associated the colors and odors with the sucrose US.

Couvillon et al. gave two different groups of honeybees the Correlated and Uncorrelated treatments. On every trial, bees in both groups saw an orange disk in the center of the petri dish; the orange-colored disk played the role of X. On some trials, it was combined with a jasmine odor (A), and on other trials it was combined with a violet odor (B). As above, half the trials were paired with the US (sucrose), and half were not (water, instead of sucrose, was present in the dish). The Correlated group received the AX+ BX– treatment, while the Uncorrelated group received AX and BX with and without sucrose half the time (as usual). In a final test, the orange disk (X) was presented alone, without either of the odors, for 10 minutes. Couvillon et al. measured the number of times the honeybees contacted the orange disk (stronger conditioning leads to more contacts). As the right part of Figure 6.6 shows, the relative validity result was obtained: Bees in the Correlated condition were less likely to treat Orange (X) as a strong CS for sucrose.

The honeybee result is especially interesting because the bee's brain has evolved separately from the brains of the vertebrate animals we have usually considered in this book (i.e., rats, rabbits, and humans). As Bitterman has said, the common ancestor of humans and honeybees might have had one synapse—"hardly any brain at all" (Bitterman, 2000, p. 71). Thus, it seems truly remarkable that the honeybee reacts to the contingencies of the relative validity experiment in such a comparable way. Despite such different brains, the behavioral principles describing learning seem similar; indeed, there is an almost amazing generality to the relative validity effect. The similarity of results across species and methods makes it credible to think that, whatever the function the laws of conditioning were originally adapted to, they may occur rather widely in the animal kingdom. Let us therefore look a little deeper at associative learning in honeybees and humans, and ask whether the same rules of learning really do apply.

Associative Learning in Honeybees and Humans

Conditioning in bees

The learning and behavior of foraging honeybees has also been studied by ethologists—those who study the evolution of animal behavior in the natural environment (e.g., Gould, 1991; Menzel, Greggers, & Hammer, 1993). Ethologists might not be so surprised if learning processes differed across species, although they do see important commonalities in learning (e.g., Gould & Marler, 1987). A better way to characterize the ethologists' approach is to say that they tend to emphasize the fact that learning fine-tunes an animal's natural behavior and built-in predelictions. For example, we might find the honeybee naturally approaching and ready to learn about color and odor stimuli (which mark flowers) because such cues have reliably predicted the location of nectar over many generations of bees. In effect, learning might allow bees to know which colors and which odors are relevant in their search for food. Although this is sometimes seen as fundamentally different from the view taken by psychological learning theory (Gould, 1991), I hope you recognize that it is not. This book has accepted both phylogenetic selection of certain CSs over others (through preparedness or stimulus relevance) as well as ontogenetic selection (created by an individual's experience over time).

Jeff Bitterman

Pat Couvillon

The question is whether the principles that describe the foraging bee's learning about flowers are qualitatively similar to what we have been talking about here. To a large extent, the research suggests the answer is "yes." Honeybees clearly do learn about flowers, and the results of a large number of experiments suggest that their learning shows striking parallels with the principles discussed in this book (see Bitterman, 1988, 1996, for reviews). For example, honeybees have shown many classic compound conditioning effects—including summation, overshadowing, sensory preconditioning, and compound potentiation—in addition to the relative validity effect described above (see Figure 6.6). It does not seem unreasonable to think of the honeybee foraging in a world of compound flower CSs that guide its approach behavior following the rules described in the preceding chapters.

The generality also goes beyond effects we have discussed so far. For example, bees appear to have short-term memory: Using methods similar to ones used to study short-term memory in pigeons (see Chapter 8), Couvillon, Ferreira, and Bitterman (2003) showed that bees can use their memory of what color was encountered a few seconds before to determine which of two colors to approach to find a reward (cf. Brown, McKeon, Curley, Weston, Lambert, & Lebowitz, 1998). Honeybees also demonstrate some classic "paradoxical reward effects" that will be covered in Chapter 9 when we consider interactions between learning and motivation. In rats and other mammals (Bitterman, 1988), the presentation of a big reward can paradoxically decrease the positive value of a smaller reward when it is presented later (see Flaherty, 1996, for a review). To put it anthropomorphically, getting a small reward after a big one can be disappointing. For example, when rats have had experience drinking a tasty 32% sucrose solution, they drink less of a 4% sucrose solution (still sweet, but not as sweet) than animals that have had 4% all along (e.g., Flaherty, Becker, & Checke, 1983). It is as if animals become frustrated (Amsel, 1992) when a reward is smaller than expected. A similar **successive negative contrast** effect, and other related effects, has been observed in honeybees (e.g., Couvillon & Bitterman, 1984; Couvillon, Nagrampa, & Bitterman, 1994; Loo & Bitterman, 1992). Interestingly, however, the goldfish, a vertebrate that is more closely related to mammals than is the honeybee, does not show these effects (e.g., Couvillon & Bitterman, 1985). The contrast effect has probably evolved quite independently in bees and mammals.

Still, it would be a great mistake to think of the honeybee as a simple little rat or human. Not everything works in bees the way you might expect it to. For example, conditioned inhibition produced in the classic conditioned inhibition or feature-negative (A+/AX−) procedure has been difficult to show in honeybees despite several attempts to find it (Couvillon, Ablan, & Bitterman, 1999; Couvillon, Ablan, Ferreira, & Bitterman, 2001; see also Couvillon, Hsiung, Cooke, & Bitterman, 2005), although an unusual variation of the procedure produced some positive results (Couvillon, Bumanglag, & Bitterman, 2003). Inhibition is so important to theories of conditioning that failure to find it could turn out to be fundamental. However, it is also possible that we haven't run the right experiment yet. For example, the blocking effect, also central to our understanding of learning in vertebrates, was once thought to be absent in bees. Blocking did not seem to occur in bees when the compound involved both a color and an odor (Funayama, Couvillon, & Bitterman, 1995), although it did occur if the compound was made up of two CSs from the same modality—for example, odor–odor or color–color (Couvillon, Arakaki, & Bitterman, 1997; Smith & Cobey, 1994). More recent results suggest that blocking can be obtained with CSs from different modalities so long as the blocking CS is relatively salient (Couvillon, Campos, Bass, & Bitterman, 2001). All of this detail is mainly a reminder that research on honeybee conditioning is still in progress. Despite the occasional difference between bee learning and vertebrate learning, "the differences are far outweighed by the similarities" (Bitterman, 2000, p. 71).

In the end, although it is best to acknowledge that both similarities and differences are present in what we know about learning in different non-human animals, there is impressive generality to known conditioning principles. On the other hand, we must also acknowledge that any one behavioral effect (e.g., overshadowing, blocking, relative validity) can result from several processes. This idea is not new; we saw in earlier chapters that the blocking effect, even in one species, might be controlled by more than one psychological process. Perhaps some of these processes play a larger role in some species or in some conditioning preparations than in others. This question will stimulate more research that will continue to broaden our perspective on learning. Nonetheless, it seems clear that models of conditioning are an excellent place to start if one wants to study and understand learning in other species and in other preparations.

Category and causal learning in humans

Conditioning principles have also been important in recent work on associative learning in humans (e.g., Shanks, 1995). There are two situations where conditioning theories have been seen as especially relevant. First, in **category learning**, humans (or animals—see Chapter 8) learn to classify items as belonging to one category or another. For example, does this patient have Dempes Disorder or the dreaded Phipp's Syndrome? Is this thing in front of me a cat, a dog, or a bagel? As we saw in Chapter 1, one approach is to think that all items are made up of many features, and that categorization depends on learning to associate the right features with the right categories. The learning of feature-category associations in humans is similar to the learning of CS-US associations in animals.

Second, in **causal learning**, people learn about the causes of certain effects. Here again, the idea is that certain cues (causes) become associated with certain outcomes (effects). For example, some important early experiments involved human participants playing a video game (Dickinson, Shanks, & Evenden, 1984). In this game, military tanks occasionally rolled across the screen. Pressing the spacebar at the computer terminal caused shells to be fired at these tanks, which might then explode (Figure 6.8) either because of the shell that was fired (a kind of causal CS) or because of mines that were

(A)

(B)

(C)

(D)

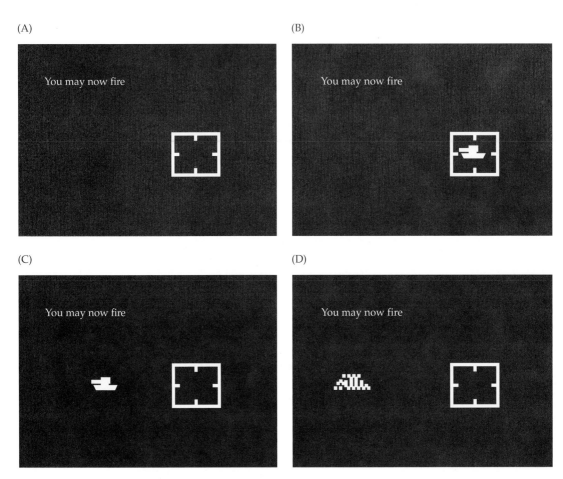

Figure 6.8 Shell or mine? Computer display used in experiments on conditioning and causal learning by Dickinson, Shanks, and Evenden (1984). Trials started with just a gunsight on the screen (A). A tank then appeared on the right-hand edge and began moving leftward. If a shot was fired while the tank was in the sight (B), a "hit" was registered and the tank would explode as it passed through an invisible minefield on the left (C,D). The question: What caused the tank to explode? (Courtesy of Anthony Dickinson.)

hidden in a mine field (another, competitive, causal CS). At the end of many trials, the participant was asked how effective the shells were in making the tank explode. The method can be expanded in different ways; for example, there can be other causes of explosions, such as planes flying overhead (e.g., Baker et al., 1993). In causal learning tasks, like categorization tasks, the human participant must sort out the connections between cues and outcomes, much as animals do in classical conditioning experiments.

Remarkably, experiments with these tasks have uncovered further correspondences between how humans and animals learn besides the relative validity example discussed above (e.g., see Shanks, Holyoak, & Medin, 1996, for a series of papers on the subject; and DeHouwer & Beckers, 2002, for a recent review). For example, humans show blocking effects. The subject might first be shown a series of trials in which the on-screen military tank explodes because of mines; in a second phase, the subject might now be able to blow up the tank with the shell. The earlier phase reduces the subject's belief in the effectiveness of the shell. Humans also show conditioned inhibition. Here, the subject might be shown trials with the mines exploding tanks, and when the shell is shot, no explosion occurs. Subjects given such treatments tend to rate the shell's effectiveness (e.g., as inhibitory or protecting against explosions) exactly as you would expect from your knowledge of conditioning. The research has generated considerable interest in whether models of conditioning—especially the Rescorla-Wagner model—can handle categorization and causal learning problems. One reason the Rescorla-Wagner model has attracted particular attention is that the equation is essentially the same as one of the equations that cognitive psychologists use to change the strength of the connections between units (or nodes) in connectionist networks (often called the "delta rule," see Gluck & Bower, 1988; Sutton & Barto, 1981). As shown in Chapter 1, connectionist models can describe categorization. Although the Rescorla-Wagner model does the job reasonably well, if people learn to associate causes and effects (or features and categories) in the ways animals associate CSs and USs, then the other models of classical conditioning that we have examined probably also apply.

To illustrate, let's consider how Shanks (1991) proposed to handle his relative-validity result in the symptom-disease situation. He proposed a simple connectionist network model (illustrated in Figure 6.9) that is quite similar to the connectionist model we considered in Chapter 1 (McClelland & Rumelhart, 1985). Here the nodes or units on the left correspond to features (i.e., symptoms like puffy eyes, swollen glands, and sore arms), while the nodes on the right correspond to categories (i.e., Dempes Disorder, Phipp's

David Shanks

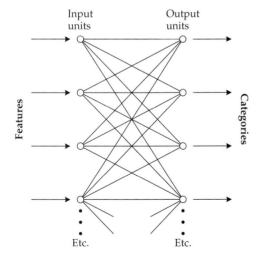

Figure 6.9 A connectionist model in which input units (or nodes) are associated with output units. In conditioning experiments, inputs and outputs are CSs and USs, respectively. In category learning (as shown), they are features and categories. In causal learning, they might be causes and effects. (After Shanks, 1991.)

Syndrome, etc.). Essentially, all the network does is learn to associate the features with the categories following the Rescorla-Wagner rule. On each trial, the nodes corresponding to the features that are present are activated, as are the nodes corresponding to the categories that are present. When features and categories occur together on a trial, the links between them are increased a bit, according to the Rescorla-Wagner equation. When a predicted category does not occur, the connection between the feature and the category is weakened, according to the same rule (this is an extinction trial). After learning has occurred, when the feature units are activated by themselves, the corresponding category units are also activated via the new connections, and in this way, the network "predicts" that, say, puffy eyes and swollen glands mean Dempes Disorder. The similarity to modern conditioning models should be obvious to the reader.

Because this kind of network is essentially a new presentation of the Rescorla-Wagner model, it predicts the same things the Rescorla-Wagner model predicts. Two features will compete with one another to gain connection with a category; the network will produce blocking effects, overexpectation, overshadowing, and so forth. And the network will learn inhibition, too. If we intermix A+ and AB– trials, the connection between B and the US takes on a negative value (e.g., Chapman & Robbins, 1990; Chapman, 1991; see also Williams, 1995). Of course, the Rescorla-Wagner model's weaknesses are also built into the network. For example, extinction will destroy or weaken the connection between a feature and a category. This characteristic of many network models is known as "catastrophic interference"—that is, training the network something new in Phase 2 catastrophically destroys what was learned in Phase 1. In the last chapter, we discussed various solutions to this problem that have been proposed for extinction in classical conditioning; perhaps they will also be brought to bear here someday.

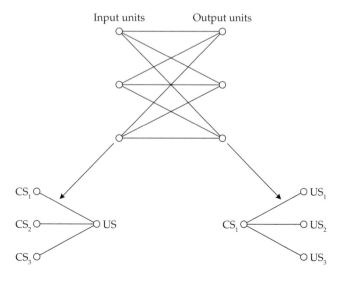

Figure 6.10 The model in Figure 6.9 actually contains even simpler networks in which several inputs are associated with a common output, and a common input is associated with several outputs.

This way of thinking about category learning in humans allows us to see research on animal learning in a new light. Conditioning experiments are designed to strip complex situations down to their essential details. For a conditioning theorist, even the simple model proposed by Shanks might be broken down into two simpler kinds of nets, which are superimposed (Figure 6.10). In one, multiple cues are connected with a single outcome. As you might recognize, this kind of network, in which several different cues can come to predict a US, is the kind of network we have routinely talked about. In a second kind of network, a single cue can be connected with more than one output. In this case, we are concerned with a CS that may be paired with more than one kind of US. As you probably recognize, this sort of network has not been studied nearly as extensively. Thinking about network models of categorization this way might reveal a gap in our understanding.

It should be noted that the models shown in Figures 6.9 and 6.10 barely scratch the surface of ideas about connectionist modeling (e.g., Rumelhart, Hinton, & Williams, 1986). Many other sorts of models have been proposed. For example, networks are sometimes expanded to include a layer of **hidden units**—that is, additional units that come between input and output (e.g., Rumelhart, et al., 1986) (Figure 6.11). Connections between these new units and the inputs and outputs can be learned by using a modification of the delta rule (the Rescorla-Wagner equation) known as the "generalized delta rule" (Rumelhart et al., 1986). Models with hidden units have some advantages, the main one being that they can learn problems in which the combinations of inputs are informative, rather than single inputs alone. We talked about configural conditioning in previous chapters; for example, recall that animals and humans can learn negative patterning , in which A+, B+, and AB– trials are intermixed. Basically, we can learn that either A or B alone sig-

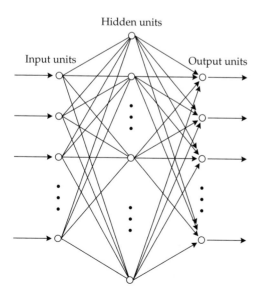

Figure 6.11 A connectionist model with hidden units between the inputs and outputs. (After Rumelhart, Hinton, & McClelland, 1986.)

nals the US or category while A and B together in a compound signals nothing. Negative patterning cannot be solved by the Figure 6.9 network, because A and B's separate connections with the US would always summate and activate the US node (because this is an elemental model). Conceptually, the network with hidden units solves the problem in the following way. A and B would both separately be associated with the US, but a combination of the two would activate a hidden unit that would acquire an inhibitory connection with the US. This inhibition would cancel the activation provided by A and B. The main alternative for fixing the simpler Figure 6.9 network would be to provide a novel "configural" input for when A and B are combined (see Figure 4.17 and the surrounding discussion in Chapter 4). This approach would need to supply a unique configural unit for every one of the billions of CS combinations that are out there in the world—a very large potential number of input units that strikes many theorists as awkward and implausible. An advantage of a network with hidden units is that it spontaneously finds an existing hidden unit to do the job; in principle, the same unit can do the same job for many other CS combinations. It is not necessary to invent a new stimulus for every new combination of stimuli.

Connectionist models like the one just described have largely been developed in the area of human cognition. However, their similarity to the animal conditioning models we have already discussed suggests that the basic associative learning principles uncovered in experiments on conditioning may have interesting applicability and generality. Connectionist modeling principles have also given conditioning theorists some interesting new tools to work with as they attempt to understand basic conditioning and learning phenomena (e.g., Gluck & Myers, 1993; Kehoe, 1988; McLaren, Kaye, & Mackintosh, 1989; McLaren & Mackintosh, 2000, 2002; O'Reilly & Rudy, 2001; Schmajuk, Lamoureux, & Holland, 1998).

Some disconnections between conditioning and human category and causal learning

Although there are many correspondences between conditioning and human learning, we haven't quite covered the whole story. Indeed, there are findings in human category and causal learning that seem inconsistent with classical conditioning in animals. For example, when humans are exposed to a series of learning trials, they may sometimes extract a rule that describes the trial outcomes instead of merely learning simple associations. Shanks and Darby (1998) gave humans a task in which different hypothetical foods were associated with an allergic reaction. Over a mixed series of trials, the participants received both positive patterning and negative patterning discriminations (e.g., A–, B–, AB+, C+, D+, CD–). To solve the discriminations, the participants could associate the foods (and their configurations) with the presence or absence of the allergic reaction, as associative learning models would assume, or they could simply learn the unstated rule that "a compound and its elements always predict opposite outcomes." To test this possibility, Shanks and Darby also gave the participants E+, F+, and GH– trials

	Phase 1	Phase 2	Test
Forward blocking	A+	AB+	B?
Backward blocking	AB+	A+	B?

Figure 6.12 In forward blocking, A+ precedes AB+. In backward blocking, A+ follows AB+. In either case, A+ training can reduce judgements of B's causal effectiveness.

intermixed with the ones just described. What would happen when they were then tested with EF and G and H for the first time? Although the participants had not been trained with these stimuli, many of them rated the combined EF as a weaker predictor than E or F, and G and H as stronger predictors than the combined GH—that is, they learned and applied the rule "compounds and elements are opposite." This sort of result is not predicted by an associative theory. Other results also suggest that humans may use inferential reasoning in associative learning tasks (e.g., Beckers, DeHouwer, Pineño, & Miller, 2005; Lovibond, Been, Mitchell, Bouton, & Frohardt, 2003; see also Beckers, Miller, DeHouwer, & Urushihara, 2006, for provocative preliminary evidence that rats might use similar processes). Thus, humans may do more than simply associate features with outcomes.

By far, the most well-studied effect that seems unique to humans is a phenomenon known as **backward blocking** (e.g., Chapman, 1991; Dickinson et al., 1984; Shanks, 1985; Williams, Sagness, & McPhee, 1994). The usual blocking procedure involves the sequence of A+ trials and then AB+ trials (Figure 6.12). As you must know by heart now, animals and humans don't learn much about B. The backward procedure reverses the order, so that AB+ occurs first, followed by A+. The Rescorla-Wagner model does not predict blocking here. When B is paired with the US on the first trials, A has no associative strength, and there is no way for it to block the conditioning of B. Nonetheless, backward blocking does occur in humans (Figure 6.13). Contrary to animal conditioning models, humans underrate the predictive value of B when A+ trials either precede or follow the AB+ trials.

Backward blocking is not usually obtained in rats and pigeons, although it does occur when no biologically significant USs are used in the two cru-

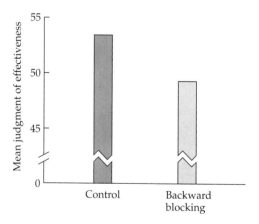

Figure 6.13 Backward blocking (see Figure 6.12) reduces the effectiveness rating of Cue B. In the control condition, the participant had no Phase-2 experience with Cue A. These data were collected with the tank and minefield method illustrated in Figure 6.8. (After Shanks, 1985.)

cial phases (Miller & Matute, 1996). (Human experiments differ from the typical animal experiment in that they do not involve biologically significant USs.) But when backward blocking does occur, how are we to explain it? There are two general approaches. One way is to expand existing conditioning models so they can handle the phenomenon. The other approach is to assume that humans learn about cues and outcomes in a fundamentally different way. Of course, this fundamentally different way might also then apply to nonhuman animals as well as it does to humans. Maybe everything we know is wrong.

Here is how the new story might go. In any blocking experiment, we might learn everything about A and B and then perform some mental computation at the time of the test that allows us to know that B is a less probable cause of the outcome than A. One influential approach is the **probabilistic contrast model** developed by Patricia Cheng (e.g., Cheng & Novick, 1992; Cheng & Holyoak, 1995; see also Cheng, 1997). The basic idea is that we can learn and remember something like the probability of an outcome given various cues. We might then judge the contingency between a cue and its outcome by comparing (or contrasting) the probability of the outcome when the cue is present with its probability when the cue is absent. If the outcome is more probable when the cue is present than when the cue is absent, there is a positive contingency; when the outcome is less probable when the cue is present, there is a negative contingency. Animals and humans are clearly sensitive to such contingencies (e.g., Rescorla, 1967b; Wasserman, Elek, Chatlosh, & Baker, 1993). The language might sound familiar, because it is exactly how CS/US contingency was presented when I discussed it in Chapter 3. The probabilistic contrast theory accepts this description of contingency as the way the organism actually computes and understands it. In contrast, conditioning models like the Rescorla-Wagner model work at a different level. Participants are not expected to store the probabilities and calculate a contrast at the test. Instead, there are increments and decrements to associations with all the cues present as experience accumulates over trials.

To explain effects like blocking, probabilistic contrast theory needs to take a further step. This is because in either forward or backward blocking, there is a contingency between B and the outcome; the outcome is more probable in the presence of B than in its absence! So, why does blocking to B occur? The answer is that the contingency between a cue and an outcome is actually further calculated within certain **focal sets**. If you look at the experimental designs in Figure 6.12, you recognize immediately that B is a poor predictor of the outcome because, *given the presence of A already*, it predicts no further change in the probability of the outcome. The presence of A is the focal set; within it, the contingency between B and the outcome is zero. Thus, by emphasizing the role of focal sets, the approach explains both forward and backward blocking, and it can be extended to handle many other effects as well. In every case, the model assumes at the time of testing that we choose the appropriate focal sets, contrast the appropriate probabilities within them, and then make judgments based on the various contrasts that we perform. (There can be many different focal sets and many different contrasts in more complex experiments.) One problem has been to predict exactly what focal sets will be used in each new situation that comes along. Newer versions of the theory have attempted to make this less ambiguous (e.g., Cheng, 1997).

One interesting feature of probabilistic contrast theory is that it ignores the possible effects of trial order. The model predicts that blocking should be equally strong in the backward and forward cases—either way, the contingency between B and the outcome given A is zero. Unfortunately, this isn't quite right. Backward blocking is not as potent as forward blocking (Chapman, 1991; see also Dickinson & Burke, 1996). Other trial order effects also clearly occur in human associative learning (e.g., Chapman, 1991; Shanks, Lopez, Darby, & Dickinson, 1996). Probabilistic contrast theory ignores trial sequence, which often matters, as conditioning models usually expect.

What, then, should we do? Conditioning models can also handle backward blocking if they are expanded a bit. Van Hamme and Wasserman (1994) suggested that one way to think of backward blocking is that the subject is actually learning about the absent cue (B) when the other cue is being treated alone in the second phase (A+). They showed that people do change their ratings of the predictive values of cues that are absent. This may occur because A and B were associated in the first compound stage (Dickinson & Burke, 1996). Thus, every time A occurs, it retrieves a representation of B, thus allowing the trial outcome to influence B.

The trick is then to figure out why the associative strength of the absent cue (B) is decremented every time the present cue (A) is paired with an outcome and incremented. Van Hamme and Wasserman (1994) and Dickinson and Burke (1996) suggested different ways this might be achieved. Dickinson and Burke (1996) suggested an extension of Wagner's SOP theory. Recall that, when a CS retrieves an associated stimulus, it puts the stimulus into a secondarily active state ("A2"). Therefore, when A occurs in Phase 2 of the backward blocking experiment, the associated cue (B) is being put into A2. In contrast, when the outcome is actually presented on these trials, its own node is being put into the focally active A1 state. Dickinson and Burke suggested that when two nodes are in different states at the same time, an inhibitory link may be established between them; when they are in the same state (either A1 or A2), an excitatory link may be established. (This is consistent with the spirit of SOP, although the original model only considered cases in which the CS was in A1.) The idea works: Backward blocking will occur because B is in A2 at the same time the US is in A1. The resulting inhibition will weaken any connection learned between B and the US during the preceding compound-conditioning trials.

If your head is spinning a little now, that's okay, because the heads of many experts are spinning too. But these ideas about how conditioning models can be expanded to explain backward blocking are leading to new discoveries. Dwyer, Mackintosh, and Boakes (1998) reasoned that the expanded models

Anthony Dickinson

imply that two completely absent cues can become associated if their associates are paired together. That is, if a CS and a US were both retrieved into A2 at the same time, we should expect a new association to form between them. In an experiment to test this prediction, rats received a peppermint flavor in one context (Context 1), and almond-sucrose pairings in another. The rats presumably learned a Context 1-peppermint association as well as an almond-sucrose association. In the next phase, Context 1 and almond were paired. Remarkably, this treatment caused the rats to associate the two absent cues (peppermint and sucrose), as indicated by an increase in the rat's preference for the peppermint flavor alone. (Remember that rats like flavors associated with sucrose.) This finding seems plausible and reasonable enough, and in a way it is surprising that it wasn't discovered until 1998. But its discovery was a direct result of the new theoretical ideas that were developed to account for phenomena like backward blocking.

Causes, effects, and causal power

Although conditioning theories have surprising scope, there may be limitations to what they can do. When humans learn about causes and effects, they appreciate the causal relation in a way that seems to go beyond a simple connection. When you observe an elephant crashing into a fence, you understand that the elephant caused the fence to collapse. The elephant and the collapsed fence are not merely associated; there is an understood "causal power" that is transmitted from the cause to the effect. The notion of causal power cannot be represented very easily in associative networks (e.g., Waldmann, 1996; Cheng, 1997).

The idea has testable implications. Waldmann and Holyoak (1992) argued that our understanding of how causes operate can influence causal judgments. For example, humans enter experiments already knowing that two potential causes of an effect can compete with one another. For example, if you notice that your grass is greener today, you may wonder whether it is because it rained yesterday or because someone ran the sprinkler. These two causes provide conflicting explanations of the effect. They can compete—as cues do in blocking, overshadowing, and relative validity. On the other hand, two effects may not compete for their connections with a cause. Rain may cause your grass to be both greener and wetter. Being green and being wet do not compete for an association with rain. (In fact, they tend to support one another—if the grass is green, you might reasonably infer that it is also moist.)

Waldmann and Holyoak (1992; see also Waldmann, 2000) ran several experiments in which people received associative learning trials with different cover stories. For example, different groups were asked to learn about a set of buttons that could be illuminated to turn on an alarm (e.g., cause an alarm to go on) or merely indicate that the alarm was on (i.e., were instead caused by the alarm). Both groups then received the same series of trials in a blocking design: An initial set of trials established one button-alarm association, and then a redundant button came on along with the first and was

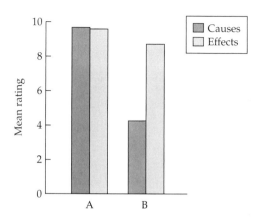

Figure 6.14 Ratings of stimuli A and B when they were in a forward blocking design (A+ trials followed by AB+ trials). When participants understood that A and B were causes of another event (+), blocking occurred—there was competition between causes. In contrast, when participants understood that A and B were effects of another event (+), blocking did not occur—there was no competition between effects. (After Waldmann & Holyoak, 1992.)

also paired with the alarm. When the participants thought the buttons activated the alarm, there was competition between buttons, and blocking occurred. But when the participants thought the buttons merely indicated the alarm was on, there was no blocking (Figure 6.14). Thus, given identical learning trials, whether blocking occurred or not depended on whether the lights were viewed as causes or effects. Causes compete, but effects do not.

Waldmann and Holyoak's interpretation has not gone unchallenged (e.g., see Matute, Arcediano, & Miller, 1996), and several recent experiments have produced competition (blocking or overshadowing) between "effects" as well as "causes" (e.g., Arcediano, Matute, Escobar, & Miller, 2005; Baker, Murphy, Mehta, & Baetu, 2005; Cobos, López, Caño, Almaraz, & Shanks, 2002; Tangen & Allan, 2003). This kind of result favors associative models. Yet, we all understand the difference between events that predict events versus events that cause other events. Smoke can predict fire—but does smoke cause fire? The analysis of causal power is sophisticated, and it can go some distance in explaining conditioning-like effects in humans (e.g., Cheng, 1997; but see, e.g., Baker et al., 2005). Does it handle the data better than conditioning models? It is probably fair to say that the jury is still out. Associative models have the upper hand in accounting for trial order effects; they also sometimes provide a better fit of the data (e.g., Wasserman et al., 1993). On the other hand, it is difficult to see how a conditioning model explains how a human can show blocking by just looking at a table printed on a page (such as the one in Figure 6.12), and then predicting which cue produced the outcome (cf. Wasserman, 1990). Psychologists have a tendency to assume that only one approach can be correct, and that the best model will win and destroy all the other ones. In fact, as Baker, Murphy, and Vallee-Tourangeau (1996) have argued, many mechanisms may easily contribute. This is really the same conclusion we reached with honeybees. Many processes contribute to one effect—whether in humans, rats, or insects. Nonetheless, it can definitely be said that associative learning models based on conditioning principles appear to apply surprisingly widely and that the attempt to apply them to different problems has strengthened and expanded their scope.

Conclusion

This chapter has covered many trees, although the forest has been consistent throughout. There have been good reasons to ask whether the learning principles discovered in the animal learning lab really generalize to the world outside. At this point, the answer is yes, they do apply. Conditioning principles have helped us understand a wide variety of phenomena. In addition to the ones considered in this chapter, I hope you haven't forgotten the many useful applications of conditioning principles to drug abuse, anxiety disorders, etc., that have been in the background of our discussion all along. Another point is that raising and investigating the question of generality has strengthened the theories by spurring experimenters to do research that has expanded and improved them. We saw this in taste aversion learning; more recently, we have seen it in the application of conditioning models to human associative learning. There is a kind of ratcheting effect of studying the basics—and then seeing how far they can go—that is good for everyone. There will probably always be some limits or differences. But even different classical conditioning preparations, like eyeblink conditioning, fear conditioning, and taste aversion learning, have things that make them different from one another. My preference is to see the differences as things that "fine-tune" a general associative process to their different functions. Appreciation of causal power may be a new example.

Where does this issue go from here? Perhaps it will always be in the background. Research investigating correspondences between conditioning and associative learning in humans is particularly active right now. In Chapter 8, we will see the principles in action again as we try to work out how organisms learn the spatial layout of the environment. There are signs that space may be the next (though, undoubtedly, not the final) frontier.

This chapter has actually focused on an issue that was raised in Chapter 1, where we saw a fundamental difference between how philosophers think knowledge and the mind are supposed to work. David Hume and the associationists argued that associations were everything; that we never know causality directly, but that we infer it from sense impressions; that the mind is a blank slate—a tabula rasa—at first. Immanuel Kant, in contrast, argued that the mind has a priori assumptions with which it molds experience. This chapter has considered several Kantian themes. The animal's apparent inborn tendency to associate certain kinds of events in taste aversion experiments is one of them; the cue-to-consequence effect is a major argument against the classic tabula rasa. Causal power (whether we know it directly or infer it from association) is another Kantian idea. The tension between empiricistic and rationalistic views will undoubtedly motivate research in the psychology of learning for many years to come.

Summary

1. By the early 1970s, research had uncovered several surprising properties of taste aversion learning. Writers began to question the generality of the laws of learning that had been discovered up to that point.

2. Many of the unusual properties of aversion learning were eventually also found in other examples of classical conditioning. These began to be explained by an expanding set of general learning principles.

3. Research on taste aversion learning produced many insights into the general aspects of learning. We now understand that learning serves a biological function, and that not all cues are equally associated with various consequences. Function and evolution have a powerful influence on learning.

4. General learning processes may evolve because of exaptation: the concept that a learning mechanism adapted for solving one particular problem may work well enough at handling other problems. True adaptive specialization may require that a mechanism adapted to handle one problem be functionally incompatible with the solution of another problem.

5. At a descriptive level, conditioning principles often seem surprisingly general across species and conditioning preparations. For example, the relative validity effect—originally demonstrated in rats, rabbits, and pigeons—has now been demonstrated in human categorization and causal judgment. It has also been shown in classical conditioning in honeybees. The honeybee result is interesting because the bee's brain evolved independently of the brains of rats, rabbits, pigeons, and humans.

6. There are many correspondences between conditioning in honeybees and vertebrates; however, there are also possible differences. Behavioral outcomes that look similar at a descriptive level may sometimes result from different processes.

7. There are also many correspondences between classical conditioning in animals and categorization and causal learning in humans. Categorization and causal learning may obey conditioning principles like the ones in the Rescorla-Wagner model. Another idea is that they involve other processes, such as probabilistic contrast and the perception of causal power.

8. Research on associative learning in humans has uncovered new effects. One is backward blocking. Although backward blocking was not predicted by models of classical conditioning, those models are being extended to account for it.

9. In the long run, research that has examined the scope and generality of learning laws developed in the animal learning laboratory has helped us to develop better general laws.

Key Terms

long-delay learning

stimulus relevance

interference

hedonic shift

taste-reactivity test

compound potentiation

overshadowing

within-compound association

exaptation

analogous

homologous

modules

successive negative contrast

category learning

causal learning

hidden units

backward blocking

probabilistic contrast model

focal sets

Chapter Seven Outline

Chapter

7

Behavior and Its Consequences

THIS CHAPTER TURNS AN IMPORTANT CORNER in our book. We have just concluded a rather extended discussion of Pavlovian conditioning (S-S* learning), which is important both as a phenomenon in its own right and as a powerful method for investigating how we learn about stimuli in our environment. We now begin a discussion of what I called "response learning" in the earliest chapters: how we learn about behaviors and their consequences (R-S* learning). This type of learning is widely known as instrumental learning or operant conditioning, and the classic example (of course) is the rat lever-pressing in the Skinner box. To the uninitiated, the rat in the Skinner box seems as trivial as Pavlov's original drooling dog. But once again we are dealing with something that is important both as a general phenomenon and as a method. Without response learning, we would be pitifully poor at adapting our behavior to the environment. And what the Skinner box really provides is a method for studying how this kind of learning operates. As we saw in Chapter 1, operant behavior is lawfully related to its consequences, and understanding the relationship between behavior and its consequences is a big part of what the study of response learning is all about.

Operant conditioning is usually discussed as if it were completely independent of classical conditioning, and we will stick with that tradition in this chapter. But there is something important from Chapters 1 and 2 that you should remember right from the start—that response learning and stimulus learning almost always go hand in hand. That is, whenever a behavior and a reinforcer are paired, there are always cues in the background that are also associated with the reinforcer. (Similarly, whenever a CS leads to a US, there are also behaviors that may be associated with the US.) This chapter will consider operant learning on its own, but the interconnectedness of S-S* and R-S* learning will become an issue in the chapters that follow. Chapter 8 will expand on the idea that operant behavior always occurs in the presence of stimuli that guide and set the occasion for it. Some of these stimuli (like categories and time and space) introduce a rather interesting cognitive dimension to the discussion. Chapter 9 will then consider the idea that reinforcers motivate operant behavior, instead of merely stamping it in. S-S* learning turns out to be critically involved in how reinforcers motivate. Finally, in Chapter 10, we will describe the modern "synthetic view" of response learning that combines behavioral and cognitive approaches, S-S* and R-S* learning, and also ethological ideas and themes. This discussion will provide an opportunity to summarize and integrate some of the book's main ideas.

In the meantime, the best place to start a discussion of response learning is by considering some of the early attempts to understand it. The early thinkers identified many of the basic issues, and they also developed many of the major methods and conceptual tools. What is most fascinating about the early thinkers, though, is how remarkably different their ideas were. From the very start, there were many ways to think about response learning; to be honest, there still are.

Basic Tools and Issues

Reinforcement versus contiguity theory

We discussed Edward Thorndike in Chapter 1. Thorndike's ideas had a huge effect on all of the thinking that followed afterwards. He emphasized the importance of reinforcement in instrumental learning. You remember that Thorndike's early experiments were concerned with cats learning to manipulate latches in order to get out of puzzle boxes and get food. Thorndike ran the experiments because he was interested in understanding the cat's intelligence, and he came away with the idea that the cat merely associated the stimulus and response in a gradual way. All that seemed to be required to explain the cat's learning was the idea that the reward strengthened an S-R association between the situation and the correct response. Thorndike eventually saw this as a very general principle of learning.

Thorndike's theory of learning was a **reinforcement theory**. By this we mean he emphasized the reinforcing consequences of behavior, which he thought were necessary for learning to occur. He thought that reinforcers created a satisfying state of affairs that "stamped in" the S-R association. He gave us the law of effect—the idea that positive consequences of behavior strengthen the behavior, while negative consequences weaken it. Thanks in part to theorists who built on Thorndike's ideas (most notably Clark Hull and B. F. Skinner), the law of effect is so widely known and influential today that most psychology students assume that no other emphasis is possible.

In fact, however, there were other views. Edwin R. Guthrie (1935), another early theorist, had a radically different idea. Guthrie did not believe that reinforcement was necessary for learning. Instead, learning occurred whenever an S and an R merely occurred together in time. Simple temporal contiguity was all that was required to learn an S-R association. Because of the centrality of this idea, Guthrie's theory is known as a **contiguity theory** (as opposed to a reinforcement theory). Another unusual aspect of Guthrie's theory was that he assumed learning took only one trial.

Edwin Guthrie

Today, Guthrie's contiguity approach strikes many people as rather strange. How could he possibly ignore the obvious importance of reinforcement? It would be very easy to show that a rat that is rewarded for running in a runway would run faster than a rat that receives no reward. And how could he deny the obvious gradualness of most learning curves? Guthrie did not deny these facts; instead, he offered a different way of explaining them. Consider the gradualness of the typical learning curve. Although he assumed that an S-R association was learned with just one trial, he defined the stimulus differently. He argued that any "stimulus," like a runway or a puzzle box, is actually made up of a very large number of **stimulus elements**. It is stimulus elements that get connected with the response on any trial. But note that the rat cannot possibly notice all of the elements on a single trial; therefore, on Trial 1 he only connects the response to the elements he has actually noticed or "sampled" (to use a more modern term). On Trial 2, the rat notices some of those elements, but not all, and he also notices some new (yet-to-be-connected) elements. The response is only a little bit bigger than the Trial 1 response. But after Trial 2, the new elements are connected, and so on. After many trials, the rat is more likely to notice a large number of elements that have been connected. The general idea, illustrated in Figure 7.1, explains why the learning curve is so gradual.

Guthrie's idea of stimulus elements is still around in psychological theory. In the 1950s and 1960s, William K. Estes developed a sophisticated mathematical theory (**stimulus sampling theory**) that extended the idea (e.g., Estes, 1950, 1955, 1959). The idea is now widely incorporated in models of human

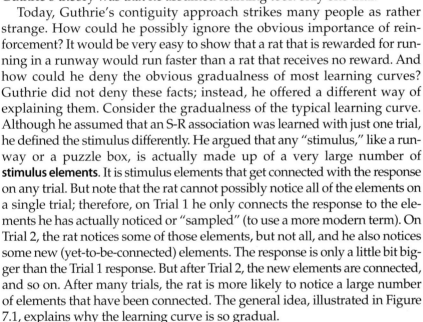

Figure 7.1 Learning as Guthrie saw it. On each trial, a small set of stimulus elements (in the circle) are connected with the response. As trials continue, more and more elements are associated with the response. These same elements are more and more likely to be sampled on subsequent conditioning trials.

Trial 1   Trial 2

Goal area

Without reward

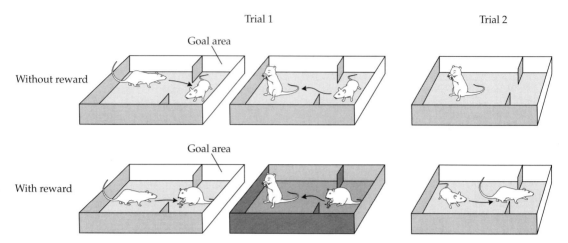

Goal area

With reward

Figure 7.2 The effect of reward as Guthrie saw it. Without a reward (top row), the rat runs down the alley, and once in the goal area eventually performs another response that may be associated with the alley stimuli. This competing response is therefore the one elicited by the alley stimuli at the start of the next trial. In contrast, if a reward is delivered (bottom row), the reward changes the situation (represented by the darkened alley in the figure) so much that the competing behavior is associated with the changed situation. The running response remains associated with the original alley stimuli (without reward), and that is what is elicited at the start of the next trial.

memory (e.g., Healy, Kosslyn, & Shiffrin, 1992; Mensink & Raijmakers, 1988), and in recent accounts of discrimination learning (see the next chapter). Connectionist views like the ones we considered in previous chapters, with their emphasis on the stimuli composed of many to-be-associated features, also accept a stimulus-elemental approach.

But what about the other problem? How did Guthrie explain the obvious impact of reinforcers on behavior? Here, his thinking was again subtle and sophisticated. Guthrie said that a reinforcer did not stamp in the S-R connection. Instead, it is merely a very salient stimulus—its presentation completely changes the situation. Consider an unrewarded rat in a runway (Figure 7.2). On Trial 1, the rat might wander into the goal area at one end of the runway. But then, having nothing else to do, the rat might wander in another direction and groom awhile before the experimenter removes it from the runway. The result is that grooming will become the last response to be connected with the situation. On Trial 2, when the rat is put back into the runway, it will therefore tend to groom again. This sort of connection of the situation with competing responses could go on indefinitely from trial to trial. In contrast, a rewarded rat will wander down the runway and encounter food, which it will eat, but the important thing is that the food now changes the situation. The rat might now groom before the experimenter removes it—but this time the grooming response is connected with the different situation. So, on Trial 2, when put in the start portion of the runway, the rewarded rat will run and not groom. By Guthrie's account, rewarded rats do better because competing responses get associated with a changed situation.

Guthrie's account of the effects of reward did not stimulate a large amount of research. However, Guthrie and Horton (1946) did publish some interesting results that followed directly on Thorndike's cat experiments. The results showed the plausibility of the contiguity approach even in Thorndike's puzzle box situation. Cats in Guthrie and Horton's experiment had to learn to move a vertical pole to get out of a puzzle box. They did so in a manner that was very stereotyped from trial to trial. Many cats learned to move the pole by rubbing up against it with their head, arched back, and then tail. This flank-rubbing response occurred repeatedly on trial after trial, and if it ever changed, it changed suddenly (and not gradually) to a different behavior. The fixity of the response from trial to trial was consistent with Guthrie's theory. Unfortunately, though, the rubbing response turns out to be a natural response any cat performs in courtship or "greeting" rituals. Guthrie and Horton (along with as many as eight other people) watched their cats while sitting in plain sight of the cat in the experimental room. It turns out the cats were merely rubbing the pole as a way of greeting the observers. Moore and Stuttard (1979) repeated the experiment and found that the flank-rubbing occurred when an experimenter was in the room but not when the experimenter was absent. Thus, the stereotyped response was not really produced by one-trial S-R learning but was a natural behavior elicited by stimuli present in the situation. We will return to this sort of theme when we examine instrumental learning from an ethological perspective in Chapter 10.

Some of Guthrie's ideas seem quaint by modern standards. On the other hand, many of his ideas—in particular, stimulus elements—have endured. The point here is not necessarily to convince you to accept Guthrie's theory but to point out that there have always been alternate ways of viewing even the simplest reinforcement situation. In effect, there is more than one way to skin Thorndike's cat.

Flexibility, purpose, and motivation

Yet another view of instrumental learning was promoted by Edward Tolman, the theorist whose innovation of intervening variables (and "operational behaviorism") was discussed in Chapter 1. Like Guthrie, Tolman was a little bit out of the mainstream. (In retrospect, this mainly means that his work did not descend directly from Thorndike's.) But his ideas were highly influential, and are perhaps more influential than ever today.

Tolman's main point was that it was not necessary to be mechanistic about behavior in order to be scientific about it. Instead of believing that animals learn rigid associations between a stimulus and a response, he argued that behavior is inherently flexible. It is a means to an end—a variable way to get to a goal. Tolman was skilled at demonstrating his ideas with simple experiments run in collaboration with his students. For example, in a classic study by Macfarlane (1930), rats learned to swim in a maze to receive a reward. After they learned the problem of which way to swim in order to reach the reward, MacFarlane drained the water from the maze, and then returned the rats to the start location. What did the rats do? They ran, rather than swam, to the goal location. Behavior is fundamentally goal-oriented; it is a flexible means of achieving a goal.

If behavior is so flexible, then what exactly is learned? Tolman (1948) suggested that the rats learned something like a map (a "cognitive map") of the environment. This idea will be considered further in Chapter 8. For now, the main point is that learning may not be primarily about behavior. Tolman thought that animals learn about stimuli (something like S-S associations) rather than connect a stimulus with a response.

Once again, Tolman managed to illustrate his points with clever experiments; one of the most famous was run by Tolman, Ritchie, and Kalish (1946a). They ran rats on an "elevated" maze (Figure 7.3A), meaning it was off the floor with an open view of the surrounding room. The rats began at the start location, ran across a table top, and then, after several turns, ran down a straightaway to find food at the goal. After the rats learned this, Tolman et al. removed the goal and replaced the maze with a fan of arms (Figure 7.3B). When tested in this setup, the rats mostly ran down arm number 6—that is, directly to where the goal had been during training. Thus, behavior was again flexible and goal-oriented. But whether the rats had truly learned a mental map of the original maze is not at all clear. A light bulb

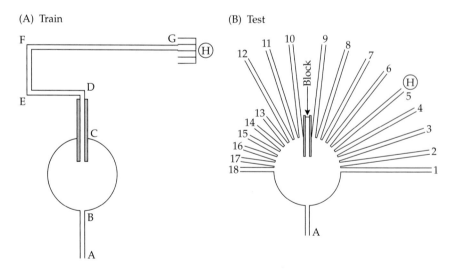

Figure 7.3 Bird's eye view of the apparatus used by Tolman, Ritchie, & Kalisch (1946a). (A) Training. The rat had to cross a table (the circle), then make a left and two right turns to get to the food that was located at the goal location (G). "H" shows the position of a light. (B) Testing with the goal and original runways removed. Most rats chose the arm that led to the original goal location. (After Tolman, 1948.)

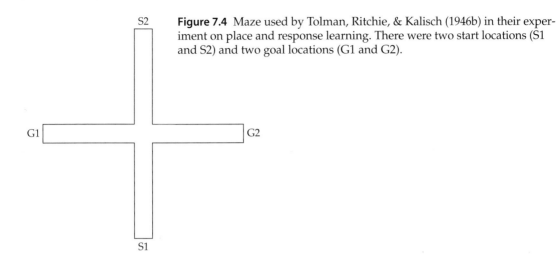

Figure 7.4 Maze used by Tolman, Ritchie, & Kalisch (1946b) in their experiment on place and response learning. There were two start locations (S1 and S2) and two goal locations (G1 and G2).

happened to be hanging near the goal location; during training, the rats could have associated the food with a particular location near the light, and mainly gone in that direction during the test.

The same authors published another experiment during the same year (Tolman, Ritchie, & Kalish, 1946b). In this one, they ran two groups of rats on the elevated "plus maze" illustrated in Figure 7.4. There were two start locations (S1 and S2), two goal locations (G1 and G2), and two groups of rats. Both groups started from S1 on half the trials and from S2 on the other half. One group was reinforced for performing a consistent response: Regardless of where they started from, turning right (for example) led to food. Notice that this meant going to a different place from trial to trial. The second group was reinforced for going to a consistent place: Regardless of the start point, G1 (for example) contained food. Notice that this group had to use a different response (turning left sometimes and turning right other times) to get to the goal. Which group learned better? The answer was clear: The rats that ran to a consistent place learned better. This result suggests that it is easier for rats to learn about places than about responses.

A final experiment by Tolman and Honzik (1930) summarizes Tolman's perspective very well. They used a complicated T-maze with 14 choice points (Figure 7.5A); a turn at one choice point led to another choice point, and so forth. One group of rats (R) was rewarded consistently when they reached the final goal location. As the figure shows, the number of errors these rats made (the blind alleys they entered) decreased slowly over trials. Another group (NR) was never rewarded. The experimental group (NR-R) received the same exposures to the maze, but they were not rewarded on the first 10 trials. (On nonrewarded trials, the experimenter simply removed the rat from the maze when it reached the goal location.) However, on trial 11 and on each trial thereafter, these rats received the same reward as the first group. As Figure 7.5B shows, these rats switched and got through the

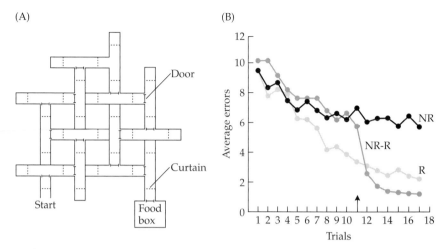

Figure 7.5 The latent learning experiment (Tolman & Honzik, 1930). (A) The 14-unit T-maze. (B) The results, which suggested that reinforcement isn't necessary for learning—although it was necessary to motivate the animal to translate what it had learned into performance. The arrow indicates the trial when the NR-R rats began to be rewarded. (After Tolman & Honzik, 1930.)

maze rather accurately after the first reward. Their change in performance over trials was much quicker than the group that had been rewarded all along. Loosely speaking, they had been learning about the maze all along, and rewarding them beginning on Trial 11 gave them a reason to get through the maze more efficiently.

The experiment suggests several potentially important conclusions about instrumental learning, which summarize Tolman's perspective very nicely. First, to switch so abruptly after the first reward, the animals must have been learning about the maze on the early nonreinforced trials; therefore, learning had been occurring without reinforcement. Second, whatever learning was occurring was not manifest in behavior until after a reward was provided. Learning is not the same as performance; the experiment demonstrates the so-called **learning/performance distinction**. (In fact, the learning was said to be "latent," and this experiment is often known as the **latent learning experiment**.) Third, although the reinforcer was not necessary for learning, it clearly had a powerful effect on behavior. But instead of stamping in the response, it motivated the rat by giving it a reason to get through the maze. Rewards are essential for translating learning—or knowledge—into performance. This very important idea was quickly adopted by other theorists and experimenters including Clark Hull and Kenneth Spence. That part of Tolman's story will be told in Chapter 9, which focuses on the motivational aspects of learning.

It is instructive to see that so many different perspectives on instrumental learning are possible, and it is worth pausing to summarize the views of this set of early theorists. Thorndike and Guthrie viewed learning as the acquisition of S-R associations, whereas Tolman viewed learning as something more like the acquisition of S-S associations. Thorndike assumed that reinforcement was necessary for learning, whereas Guthrie and Tolman did not. Nonetheless, both Guthrie and Tolman gave rewards a role: For Guthrie, rewards changed the situation; for Tolman rewards provided a crucial source of motivation. Rewards can thus have at least three possible functions: They might reinforce (Thorndike), they might function more or less as just another stimulus (Guthrie), and they might motivate performance (Tolman). It is worth keeping this in mind as we continue our discussion.

Operant psychology

Another person with an early perspective on instrumental learning was B. F. Skinner. Skinner's early writings were published around the same time as Guthrie's and Tolman's (in the 1930s), and that is why Skinner can be considered an early theorist. But he was a younger man, and he lived longer, and so his influence actually became strongest in the 1950s, 1960s, and beyond. As we saw in Chapter 1, Skinner's approach was different in that it was deliberately "atheoretical"; he actually never set out to explain instrumental learning in the same way that Thorndike, Guthrie, and Tolman did. Nonetheless, his methods and style of analysis have been extremely influential, and they help identify several crucial concepts and tools for understanding response learning. Most of the research reviewed in the rest of this chapter was stimulated by Skinner's approach.

In Skinner's original operant experiment (see Chapter 1), the rat was allowed to press a lever repeatedly in a Skinner box to earn food pellets. Beginning in the 1940s, pigeons were similarly allowed to peck illuminated discs or "keys" on the wall to earn grain. You will remember that, in either case, the response is considered an operant because it is a behavior that is controlled by its consequences (the reinforcer). Conversely, the food pellet is a reinforcer because it is a consequence that controls an increase in the operant behavior that produces it. One of the great insights of Skinner's method and analysis is the recurrent nature of the operant response. The animal is able to make the response as often as it wants to; in this sense, it is different from responding in the puzzle box or the maze. The behavior thus appears voluntary, and the method allows us to investigate how so-called voluntary behavior is related to payoff.

Operants are often learned through shaping, a process we considered in Chapter 2. In shaping, experimenters reinforce closer and closer approximations of the desired response. Skinner actually thought that the effects of reinforcers are so powerful they can be quite accidental and automatic. In a classic experiment (Skinner, 1948), he put pigeons in Skinner boxes and gave them food at brief and regular intervals, regardless of what they were doing. Even though there was no causal relation between the birds' behavior and getting food, each bird came to behave as if a causal relation was involved. One bird learned to turn counter-clockwise repeatedly, another bird learned to thrust its head into a corner of the box, and other birds learned to rock their heads back and forth. Skinner called these behaviors **superstitious behaviors**. Each presumably developed because of accidental pairings with a reward. For example, at one point in time, a bird might happen to rock a little just before a reinforcer occurred. The response would be repeated, making it more likely that it would happen before the next reinforcer, and so on. Superstitious behavior is fairly common in human experience. Many bowlers twist and contort their bodies after they let go of the ball, as if they can steer the rolling ball toward making a strike. Baseball batters knock their helmets, cross their hearts, bang the bat on their cleats, etc., as they get ready before every pitch. Presumably, these behaviors were also accidentally associated with a reinforcer, like getting a strike or spare (in bowling), making a hit, or getting a home run. Superstitious behavior suggests that reinforcers can have surprisingly arbitrary power. We will consider the topic again in Chapter 10.

In truth, operant behavior is even more interesting and complex than this. For one thing, Skinner was aware that operants are not emitted in a vacuum; they occur in the presence of stimuli that set the occasion for them. He illustrated this in some of his earliest work with rats pressing levers (e.g., Skinner, 1938). For example, Skinner arranged things so that a rat was reinforced for lever-pressing whenever a light was turned on. During periods when the light was turned off, however, lever-presses were not reinforced. Not surprisingly, the rat detected these different contingencies and began to confine his lever-pressing to periods when the light was on (Figure 7.6). This is a simple example of discrimination learning. In Skinner's terms, the operant response was brought under **stimulus control**: Its occurrence now depended on a stimulus that set the occasion for it.

Stimulus control is an extremely fundamental concept, one we will consider a number of interesting forms of in the next chapter. For now, just note that stimulus control is operating almost everywhere. For example, the behaviors reinforced at a fraternity party are very different from the ones reinforced in a classroom, and most of us learn to behave accordingly. Children probably also learn to name things in a similar way. Saying "apple"

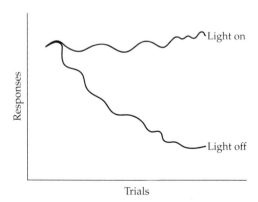

Figure 7.6 Simple demonstration of stimulus control. If a lever-press response yields a reinforcer when a light is on but not when the light is off, the organism learns to respond in the presence of the light. The light is a discriminative stimulus (or S^D) that sets the occasion for the response.

is reinforced in the presence an apple, but "banana" is reinforced in the presence of a banana. Naming an object can thus be seen as an operant behavior that is under stimulus control. Stimulus control is truly happening all the time.

With hard-to-discriminate stimuli, the acquisition of stimulus control can be facilitated by a procedure known as **fading**. The idea is to gradually transfer stimulus control from easy stimuli to harder stimuli by presenting both together and then fading the easy stimuli out. For example, pigeons have trouble learning to discriminate vertical and horizontal lines projected on the key, but it is easy for them to learn to discriminate between the colors red and green. To train a horizontal-vertical discrimination, pigeons can first be taught to peck at the color red but not green. Then, vertical and horizontal lines can be superimposed on the red and green colors, which can then be removed gradually (e.g., Terrace, 1963), leaving only the horizontal and vertical lines visible. There are many real-world examples of this concept. For example, the director of a play can encourage an actor to speak his or her lines at appropriate times by first prompting the actor and then gradually fading out the prompts. In this case, other aspects of the situation (e.g., another actor's lines) begin to set the occasion for the first actor's response.

Ultimately, stimulus control illustrates another way in which operant behavior is nicely adjusted to its environment. According to Skinner, the stimuli that initiate the response are not thought to elicit it; otherwise, this would make them respondents. Instead, the stimuli "set the occasion" for the response, and at a theoretical level, this occasion-setting role is similar to the Pavlovian occasion-setting function we discussed in Chapter 5. For now, the important point is that the operant is controlled by both the stimulus that sets the occasion for it and by the reinforcer that reinforces it. A stimulus that works in this fashion—by setting the occasion for, rather than eliciting a response—is known as a **discriminative stimulus**, or S^D. The stimulus that sets the occasion for not responding (the light-off in the rat experiment) is called an S^Δ, or "S delta."

Conditioned reinforcement

We can take the simple stimulus control experiment a step further. Suppose we have a rat that is responding at a good rate in S^D but very little in S^Δ. We can now introduce a new contingency: If the rat responds during S^Δ, we can turn S^D on and let the animal respond for reinforcers again. This new contingency (if lever-press, then turn the light back on) does something rather interesting. The rat begins responding more during S^Δ—that is, the rate of responding increases when we make the light a consequence of the response. In this sense, the S^D satisfies Skinner's definition of a reinforcer. Unlike the food, which has intrinsic reinforcing properties, S^D's reinforcing properties are conditional on being in our experiment. It is therefore called a **conditioned reinforcer** (or **secondary reinforcer**). Stimuli or events that reinforce because of their intrinsic properties—like food, water, or sex—are considered **primary reinforcers**.

Conditioned reinforcers acquire their value from their Pavlovian relationship with the primary reinforcer (e.g., Williams, 1994a; see also Fantino, 1969, 1977). The concept of conditioned reinforcement is a very important one in learning theory. For one thing, it is often considered crucial for generalizing principles developed in laboratory research with food rewards to the real world of human behavior. Only a small part of human behavior is directly reinforced by primary reinforcers like food, water, or sex. Instead, it is often controlled by conditioned reinforcers that operate because of their association with a primary reward. Money is the most famous example. People will do many things (emit many behaviors) to get money, but it has no value except that it signals or enables other things. Therefore, money is a classic example of a conditioned reinforcer.

Conditioned reinforcement is useful in understanding behavior in many settings. It is often involved even when we are studying primary rewards. When students shape a rat to press a lever in a Skinner box, they first give the rat some experience with the delivery of food pellets. While the rat is wandering around the box, the students deliver food pellets from time to time. Typically, the food pellets are delivered by an electrical gadget (a "feeder") that makes an audible "click" when it operates. Not surprisingly, the rat quickly learns to approach the food cup at the sound of the "click," to retrieve the food. That is, the "click" becomes an S^D—it sets the occasion for approaching the food cup. It also becomes a Pavlovian CS for food (these functions are probably learned together). The student next reinforces the rat for successive approximations of lever-pressing. As the animal is reinforced for moving near the lever, say, the most immediate consequence of the response is not the food pellet itself, but the click. In this manner, the student winds up exploiting the click's power as a conditioned reinforcer. Recall that a delayed reinforcer is typically not as effective as an immediate one (see Chapter 2). One important role of conditioned reinforcers is to facilitate learning when there is a delay between the response and the primary reinforcer.

The conditioned reinforcement concept also helps us understand behavior at a more fine-grained level of analysis. For example, the rat in the Skinner box is doing more than merely pressing the lever. After some training, it reliably performs a whole sequence of behaviors, or a **behavior chain**. The rat might approach the lever, press it, move to the food cup, consume the pellet, and then approach the lever and repeat the sequence again. The behaviors in the chain are glued together by discriminative stimuli, which are present at each step (Figure 7.7). These discriminative stimuli both reinforce the preceding behavior as well as set the occasion for the behavior that follows. Pressing the lever brings the "click," which reinforces it and then sets the occasion for approaching the food cup. Similarly, approaching the lever is reinforced by contact with the lever, which then sets the occasion for pressing it, and so on. The dual function of the S^D—to set the occasion for the next response and reinforce the preceding one—is the factor that binds complex sequences of behavior together.

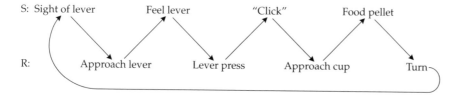

Figure 7.7 A behavior chain. Each response in the chain produces a stimulus that serves as a discriminative stimulus that (1) reinforces the previous response, and (2) sets the occasion for the next response.

   Although conditioned reinforcement seems crucial in a detailed understanding of behavior, it is interesting to note that the concept has been somewhat controversial (e.g., Bolles, 1967; Rachlin, 1976; Staddon, 1983). One reason is that there is very little evidence that conditioned reinforcers cause the learning of brand new behaviors when these reinforcers are presented without any primary reinforcement. Instead, researchers have usually emphasized that conditioned reinforcers boost performance that is otherwise maintained at a low level by primary reinforcement. For example, I already mentioned that conditioned reinforcers help boost responding when primary reinforcement is delayed (e.g., Spence, 1947, Williams, 1994a). In another type of experiment, Kelleher (1966) had pigeons peck a key in order to obtain food that was available only once every 60 minutes. Food was accompanied by a brief stimulus (a 0.7-sec presentation of a white key). Not surprisingly, the rather sparse delivery of food did not cause the pigeons to respond very much. But when the pigeons also received the brief white key stimulus (without food) for the first peck emitted at two-minute intervals, they started responding more. Thus, presenting the stimulus associated with food enhanced the low level of responding that was otherwise observed. After reviewing a large number of related studies, Williams (1994a) concluded that stimuli associated with primary reinforcers can in fact strengthen behavior because these stimuli acquire their own reinforcing value.

The Relationship between Behavior and Payoff

Different ways to schedule payoff

The concept of conditioned reinforcement comes up in part when one considers behavior outside the laboratory. The fact is, most operant responses in the real world are not reinforced every time they occur, and yet the behavior keeps on going anyway. This fact was amply appreciated by Skinner and the behavior analysts who followed him, who have therefore investigated the effects of scheduling rewards intermittently. Research on **schedules of reinforcement** has led to several fundamental insights about how operant behavior relates to its payoff.

   When a behavior is reinforced every time it occurs, we say it is reinforced on a **continuous reinforcement (CRF) schedule**. Not surprisingly, this method

(A) Cumulative recorder

(B) Cumulative record

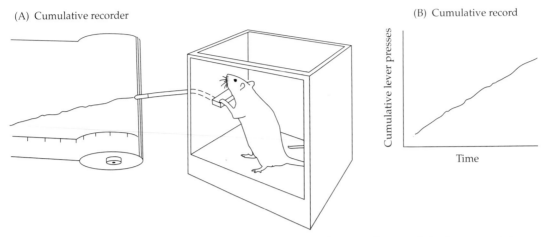

Figure 7.8 (A) Cumulative recorder. As the animal responds in the operant chamber, each response deflects a pen slightly upward on a piece of paper mounted to a drum that is moving at a constant slow rate. (B) The result is a graph that plots the cumulative number of responses over time—an elegant way to visualize the rate of an individual's operant behavior.

of scheduling reinforcers generates a steady rate of responding. Skinner developed a simple and elegant way to study the effects of reinforcers on operant behavior. He seemed to love gadgets, and in early work, he developed a clever way of portraying the rate of responding in a graphic manner (see Skinner, 1956, for the interesting story of how his love of gadgets led him to many of his methods). He mounted a piece of paper on a rotating drum so that it moved at a slow and steady rate (Figure 7.8A). A pen sat on the paper, tracing a line as the paper moved. Every time the rat pressed the lever, the pen was deflected upward a bit. At the end of 30 minutes or so, what could be seen on the paper was a trace of what the rat had done, in which the cumulative number of lever presses was shown on the y-axis over time (x-axis). The graph in Figure 7.8B is called a **cumulative record**; and the drum recorder is called a **cumulative recorder**.

Figure 7.8B shows the cumulative record of a rat that performed for several minutes. One of the virtues of the cumulative record is that the rate of behavior is readily appreciated by the slope of the line. It is immediately apparent that the rat pressed the lever at a steady rate.

A little thought reveals that reinforcers can be scheduled intermittently in at least two fundamental ways. First, a reinforcer can be delivered after a certain number of responses. Because this sort of schedule ensures a ratio between work (responding) and reward (reinforcement), it is called a **ratio schedule**. In a **fixed ratio (FR)** schedule, reward is scheduled after every Xth response. On an FR 2 schedule, an animal is reinforced every second response, while on an FR 150 schedule, it is reinforced after every 150th response. As reinforcers become fewer and farther between (the schedule is said to become "leaner"), animals begin pausing after each reinforcer. These

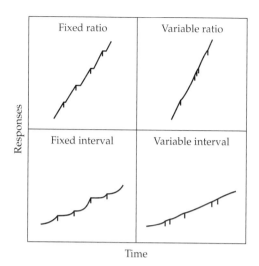

Figure 7.9 Cumulative records showing typical responding on different schedules of reinforcement. (After Williams, 1988.)

"post-reinforcer pauses" are evident in the cumulative record shown in the upper left cell of Figure 7.9. (The downward diagonal deflections of the pen in the graph indicate reinforcer deliveries.) Interestingly, it is not difficult to get a fair amount of behavior out of animals on these schedules. For example, under conditions that will be described in Chapter 9, rats learn to respond on an FR 5120 schedule fairly easily (Collier, Hirsch, & Hamlin, 1972).

Another variation on the ratio idea is the **variable ratio** (**VR**) schedule. In this case, as before, there is always a certain relationship between the number of responses and the number of reinforcers, but now the number of responses required to earn each individual reinforcer varies. On a VR 4 schedule, the average number of responses required to earn a reinforcer is 4, but the first pellet might be delivered after 2 responses, the second after 6, and so forth. Variable ratio schedules can generate very high and steady rates of behavior. (Overall, there is less post-reinforcement pausing.) The world's greatest example of a VR schedule is the slot machine. These devices deliver coins on a VR schedule, and the consequences are obvious: a steady stream of lever-pulling and income for the casino. A cumulative record from a VR schedule is illustrated in the upper right cell in Figure 7.9.

The second, and perhaps less obvious, way of scheduling intermittent rewards is with **interval schedules**. In this case, reinforcers are delivered for the first response made after a certain interval of time has elapsed. On a **fixed interval** (**FI**) schedule, that interval remains constant from one reinforcer to the next. For example, on an FI 1-minute schedule, the first response emitted after a minute has elapsed is reinforced; the timer is reset, and the first response emitted after the next minute is reinforced, and so on. One thing that makes these schedules interesting is that behavior begins to reflect the timing of the reinforcers. As shown in the lower left cell of Figure 7.9, the animal tends to respond only a little after each reward, but the rate of responding picks up as the next scheduled reinforcer becomes imminent. This characteristic pattern of behavior on FI schedules is known as "scalloping." In effect, the animal learns to time the interval, and elapsed time becomes a sort of S^D for responding. This feature of behavior on FI schedules has been used to investigate timing processes in animals, as we will see in Chapter 8.

As you have probably guessed, interval schedules can also be variable. In **variable interval (VI)** schedules, there is an average interval after which the first response is reinforced, but each reinforcer is set up after different intervals of time. On a VI 1-minute schedule, the first pellet may be earned after 30 seconds has elapsed, and the second pellet may be earned after 90 seconds, and so forth. Since time becomes less relevant in predicting reinforcer availability, VI schedules do not produce as much scalloping as FI schedules; instead, they tend to generate very steady rates of behavior (see Figure 7.9, lower right cell). One example of behavior on a VI schedule is my checking of my mailbox in the Psychology Department where I work. Mail, flyers, and university memos appear in that box at irregular intervals, and I find myself checking my mail at a low but fairly steady rate throughout the day. I do the same with e-mail.

Interval schedules have an interesting property that is not obvious until you think about it: The rate of responding can vary widely without affecting reinforcement rate. In ratio schedules, there is always a relationship between behavior rate and reinforcer rate. The faster the organism responds, the more rewards he or she will obtain. But this relationship is not true in interval schedules. For example, a fixed-interval 1-minute schedule will produce a maximum reinforcement rate of 60 reinforcers per hour. Once the organism hits this maximum, say, with 20 responses per minute, there will be no further increase in reinforcer rate with further increases in response rate. The "molar feedback functions" of interval and ratio schedules—which are the possible relationships between the rate of responding and the resulting rate of reinforcement—are very different. Perhaps because of this, response rates on ratio schedules tend to be faster than response rates on interval schedules when reinforcer rates are equated (Catania, Matthews, Silverman, & Yohalem, 1977). Alternatively, because interval schedules depend on the crucial interval timing out for reinforcement to be delivered, interval schedules are more likely than ratio schedules to reinforce waits between responses. Ratio schedules might also tend to reinforce rapid response bursts (e.g., Skinner, 1938).

The four basic types of reinforcement schedules just described only scratch the surface of the types of schedules that are possible. In so-called **compound schedules**, two or more schedules operate. One example is a **multiple schedule** in which two or more schedules alternate, with each individual schedule being signaled by its own S^D. (When there are no corresponding S^Ds, alternating schedules create a "mixed" schedule.) In a **chained schedule**, completion of the response requirement for one schedule leads to the S^D of the next component. (In this case, when there are no corresponding S^Ds, we have a "tandem" schedule.) For additional types of reinforcement schedules, see Catania (1998) or even *Schedules of Reinforcement* by Ferster and Skinner (1957), a book that is remarkable in the sense that it is almost nothing but cumulative records produced by rats and pigeons reinforced on almost every conceivable schedule.

Choice

Another fundamental kind of schedule is a **concurrent schedule**. In such a schedule, animals are given the opportunity to engage in two or more responses that are each reinforced according to separate schedules that are running at the same time. For example, on a concurrent VI VI schedule, a pigeon may peck either of two lighted keys, each of which pays off according to its own variable interval schedule, which operate independently. The bird may switch between keys whenever it wants to, but a reinforcer that happens to be waiting to be delivered for the first peck on the new key is usually not presented for several seconds after the changeover has occurred. Concurrent schedules of reinforcement are especially interesting because they involve choice. In the real world, we are always choosing among any number of alternative behaviors that each has its own separate payoff. By manipulating the reinforcement schedule on two alternatives, we can begin to discover the laws that govern how we choose what to do.

Richard Herrnstein (1961) showed that behavior on concurrent schedules is remarkably lawful. In his experiment, pigeons were allowed to respond on several pairs of VI schedules. A given pair of VI schedules remained in effect for many days (about a month); Herrnstein was interested in performance generated by the schedules after the performance had stabilized. In the final sessions on each pair of VI schedules, he counted the number of pecks at each key and also the number of reinforcers earned for pecks at each key. Overall, a very regular relationship was obtained. As Figure 7.10 shows, the percentage of pecks at any one key always equaled the percentage of reinforcers that were earned there. We can express this relationship in very simple terms. Let's call the number of pecks to the two alternatives B_1 and B_2 (for Behaviors 1 and 2), and the number of reinforcers earned on each alternative R_1 and R_2. If the proportion of pecks on B_1 equals the proportion of reinforcers that were earned there, then:

$$B_1 / (B_1 + B_2) = R_1 / (R_1 + R_2) \tag{7.1}$$

which merely says (again) that the two proportions are equal.

Equation (7.1) is known as the **matching law**, a fundamental rule that describes choice in concurrent schedules of reinforcement (Herrnstein, 1970). It is important to recognize that Herrnstein's results, and the matching law that describes them, are far from trivial. With two VI schedules, the birds could have earned a given number of reinforcers (R_1 or R_2) with any of a very large number of possible numbers of pecks (B_1 and B_2). Thus, the relationship described in Equation (7.1) is not inevitable; instead, it is rather subtle and interesting. With a little algebra, the equation can be written another way:

$$B_1 / B_2 = R_1 / R_2 \tag{7.2}$$

and this equality necessarily also holds true.

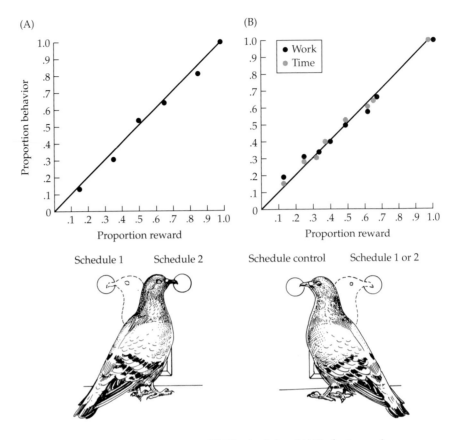

Figure 7.10 Matching on concurrent VI VI schedules. (A) Pecks to one key are reinforced on one VI schedule, and pecks to another key are reinforced on another VI schedule. When the proportion of responses on one alternative is plotted as a function of the proportion of rewards earned there, one observes a diagonal line— the two proportions are equal (i.e., they match). (B) The same results are obtained when the subject can switch between schedules presented on one key by pecking another key. (After Herrnstein, 1971.)

The relationship seems to hold up under a surprisingly wide range of species and methods; for example, the law also works in humans. Conger and Killeen (1974) had college students converse on the subject of drug abuse with two experimenters, who were seated at opposite ends of a long table. By saying things like "that's a good point," etc., the experimenters reinforced comments made by the participants. Unbeknownst to the subjects, the experimenters delivered these verbal reinforcers according to different VI schedules. After 15 minutes, the participants were directing their conversation in accordance with the reinforcers. In fact, as Figure 7.11 shows, the proportion of time the students spent talking to each of the experimenters matched the proportion of verbal reinforcers delivered by the exper-

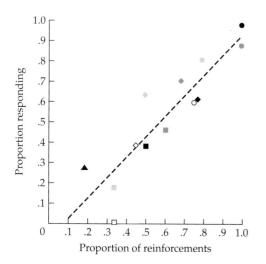

Figure 7.11 Matching in humans. Different symbols are results with different participants. (After Conger & Killeen, 1974.)

imenters. Verbal exchanges follow rules of operant conditioning, and in this case, they conformed nicely to the matching law.

The law has been studied in animals using other procedures. One slightly different procedure was invented by Findley (1958; see Figure 7.10B). In this case, pigeons choose to peck on one of two VI schedules that are available on a single key. One schedule is signaled by the key being one color, and the other schedule is signaled by the key being another color. The bird can switch between schedules by pecking a second key, the switching key. In this sort of method, very similar results are obtained, but in this case, experimenters typically measure the time the bird spends in the two schedules (T_1 and T_2). Here, the same relationship obtains:

$$T_1 / T_2 = R_1 / R_2 \qquad (7.3)$$

Still another indication of the law's generality is that the relationship still applies when experimenters have manipulated the magnitudes of the rewards and totaled the amount of the two reinforcers earned (Catania, 1963), or varied the delay in delivery of the reward after the response (Chung & Herrnstein, 1967). (Delay effects can be seen as immediacy, or the reciprocal of delay.) According to Williams (1988, 1994b), all of these parameters of reward can be put together (see also Davison & McCarthy, 1988; Grace, 1994) in a way that relates to a single variable—the reinforcer's "value." Thus, the most general statement of matching would be:

$$B_1 / B_2 = V_1 / V_2 \qquad (7.4)$$

where V_1 and V_2 mean the value of each reward as determined by its number, size, and immediacy. It is a remarkably general law.

Although a great deal of research attests to the matching law's generality (see Davison & McCarthy, 1988; Nevin, 1998; Williams, 1988, 1994b, for reviews), deviations from perfect matching are common. Sometimes animals "overmatch," so that B_1 / B_2 is consistently a little greater than R_1 / R_2. Other times, animals "undermatch," and B_1 / B_2 is a little less than R_1 / R_2. Baum (1974) proposed a more generalized form of the matching equation, which includes additional bias and sensitivity terms; this form has the power to describe cases of overmatching and undermatching (see McDowell, 2005, for further extensions).

Although the matching law describes the relationship between payoff and choice rather well, it says nothing about the psychological processes that lead the animal to behave in such a manner. In this sense, it is beautifully true to Skinner's interest in a purely empirical description of how operant behavior relates to its consequences. However, several explanations of matching have been proposed anyway. Animals might choose to respond on one alternative or the other on a moment-to-moment basis so as to maximize the momentary rate of reinforcement (e.g., Shimp, 1966). Or, perhaps the animals choose in a way that somehow maximizes the overall rate of reinforcement in the whole session (e.g., Rachlin, Green, Kagel, & Battalio, 1976). Still another possibility is that animals might keep shifting between the alternatives so as to always improve the local rate of reinforcement. In this case, they would stop shifting between the alternatives (and behavior would stabilize) when the two local rates of reinforcement are equal (e.g., Herrnstein & Vaughan, 1980). This process, called **melioration**, can produce matching, and has other interesting implications for behavior (e.g., Herrnstein & Prelec, 1992). At this point in time, there are results which are difficult for each of these explanations of matching to handle (Williams, 1994b). The matching law itself appears to work, however, and it provides additional insights that we will consider in the next section.

Although the matching law tells us a lot about what determines the relative rate of operant behavior, it would be a mistake to think that a behavior's rate is the same as its strength. Tony Nevin (e.g., 1998; Nevin & Grace, 2000) has argued that operant behavior also has a property that is analogous to "momentum"—just as a moving car is difficult to stop, a behavior can be resistant to change. Momentum is not just a function of an object's speed; it also depends on its mass. In a similar sense, a behavior's resistance to change is not necessarily predicted by behavior rate, or (hence) the matching equation (e.g., Nevin, Tota, Torquato, & Shull, 1990). Resistance to change also depends on other factors, such as the extent to which reward is associated with stimuli in the background.

Choice is everywhere

Although choice is an obvious aspect of concurrent schedules, it is also involved in even the simplest operant experiment. That is, even when the rat in the Skinner box is given only a single lever to press, it chooses to leverpress over a host of other alternative behaviors—it could instead scratch an itch, sniff around in a corner, or curl up and fall asleep. The same is true of any single operant that you or anyone else might perform; there are always a large number of available alternatives. Thus, I am currently writing at my

Richard Herrnstein

computer instead of playing solitaire, getting some coffee, or taking a nap. You are similarly reading this book right now instead of doing any of a number of other things, each of these other behaviors presumably having its own payoff. Choice is actually everywhere. In real life, concurrent schedules are probably the rule.

Given this idea, we can state the matching law in its most general form. Even when we focus on a single operant behavior (e.g., B_1) with its own reinforcement rate (e.g., R_1), we are always given a choice of performing the behavior or of performing other behavior. Let's call the other behavior, "B_O"; it has its own reinforcement rate, "R_O." The idea is that the matching law still applies. Thus:

$$B_1 / (B_1 + B_O) = R_1 / (R_1 + R_O) \qquad (7.5)$$

However, the quantity $B_1 + B_O$ is all the behavior possible in a given situation, and the total cannot vary from time to time; therefore, we can consider it a constant, "K." So, substituting:

$$B_1 / K = R_1 / (R_1 + R_O)$$

And, with a little additional algebra (cross-multiplying by K), we can rewrite the equation as:

$$B_1 = K \times R_1 / (R_1 + R_O) \qquad (7.6)$$

This final equation, which describes the rate of behavior to one alternative in any given operant situation, is called the **quantitative law of effect** (Herrnstein, 1970).

There are several points to make about this simple equation. First, it describes how behavior rate (B_1) varies as a function of reward rate (R_1) in single-operant situations. Figure 7.12 shows some classic results reported by Catania and Reynolds (1968), wherein different pigeons were trained on a series of VI schedules. After behavior had stabilized on each schedule, the number of responses (B_1) and number of reinforcers (R_1) were counted, and another data point was added to each bird's graph. As the figure shows, behavior rate increased as a function of reward rate, which is not terribly surprising. In general, though, the shape of the function is highly consistent with Equation 7.6. Each bird's behavior differed a little from the other birds' behavior; however, in each case, the functions are nicely captured by Equation 7.6, with K and R_O varying among birds. In effect, the birds for whom increases in reinforcer rate had less effect on B_1 had higher rates of R_O. Casually speaking, the quantitative law of effect implies that these birds were more distracted by the high rate of alternative reinforcement they were idiosyncratically deriving from the environment.

Let us take a step back and consider the broader implications of the idea that B_1 is influenced by both its own reinforcement (R_1) and reinforcement for alternatives (R_O). We might want to weaken an undesirable behavior in a person—say, taking dangerous drugs. One obvious technique would be to reduce R_1, perhaps by reducing the availability of the drug. This is a famil-

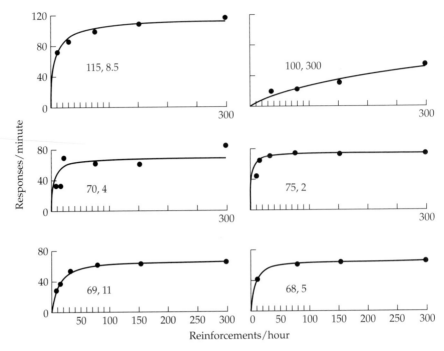

Figure 7.12 Response rates of six pigeons, each one tested with several different VI schedules (each of which paid off at different reinforcements/hour). The results of each bird are consistent with the quantitative law of effect. Numbers in each panel are the K and R_O values for each bird. (Data from Catania & Reynolds, 1968; after Herrnstein, 1971.)

iar idea: Any operant perspective predicts that reducing a behavior's rate of reinforcement will reduce the behavior. However, a less obvious alternative would be to increase R_O—increase the reinforcement delivered for other behaviors that are available. In the laboratory, this has been accomplished by presenting extra "free" reinforcers that were not contingent on the target response (e.g., Rachlin & Baum, 1972). The present interpretation is that by increasing R_O we are weakening B_1. According to the quantitative law of effect, operants can be weakened by increasing the reinforcement earned for alternative behaviors.

There is also a variation of this idea. Suppose you have a friend or an adolescent son or daughter who is beginning to experiment with drugs or alcohol. When is experimentation most likely to turn into a problem? Note again that drugs and alcohol are reinforcers; in fact, drug problems can be thought of as situations in which drug taking (an operant behavior, B_1) becomes very high. According to the quantitative law of effect, B_1 is most likely to become high for individuals who derive little other reinforcement from their environment (i.e., those for whom R_O is low). A drug will thus become especially addictive (generating a high rate of responding) when there is little other reinforcement around. We have already seen that B_1 can be weakened by increasing R_O. But now you can also see that problems in principle are *preventable* by building environments in which positive, pro-social behaviors are available and adequately reinforced. To me, this may be the most important implication of the quantitative law of effect.

Impulsiveness and self-control

While we are on such a righteous theme, there is another line of research that is also relevant. Choice has also been studied when animals and humans are allowed to choose between a large, delayed reward and a smaller reward that is more immediate. This seems analogous to many decisions we make in real life—we may decide to go to a movie (an immediate, but rather modest reward) instead of studying for the GREs (with its delayed, but potentially larger reward). Or, we may decide to sleep in a little later in the morning (immediate, small reward) instead of getting up and going to a class (delayed, possibly larger reward). If we delay our gratification, and choose the delayed (though larger) reward, we are said to have exercised "self-control." On the other hand, if we choose the more immediate (though smaller) reward, we are showing "impulsiveness." There is a large literature of research devoted to investigating the choices made by animals and humans in these kinds of situations (e.g., see Logue 1988, 1995, 1998, for reviews).

One of the key findings is that the behavior of animals and humans is often quite impulsive—they often choose immediate (though smaller) rewards over delayed (though larger) rewards, even though it seems rather maladaptive in the long run to do so. However, impulsive behavior is most likely if the smaller reward is really imminent—that is, if it is going to be presented soon after the choice response. For example, Green, Fisher, Perlow, and Sherman (1981) had pigeons choose between pecking a red key for a small reward and a green key for a larger reward. The larger reward was always delayed 4 seconds longer than the smaller reward. In one condition, the larger reward was presented after a delay of 6 seconds and the smaller reward was presented after only 2 seconds. The birds' behavior was impulsive—they consistently chose the smaller, more immediate reward. But, in another condition, both rewards were presented after longer and longer delays. As before, the smaller reward always occurred 4 seconds sooner than the bigger reward. But as the delays increased, the birds began demonstrating self-control—they began to choose the bigger, more delayed reward. The results are presented in Figure 7.13. When the average choice-to-reward delay was relatively short, the birds chose the smaller, more immediate reward; when the choice-to-reward delay was relatively long, they chose the larger, more delayed reward.

It is easy to account for this result by considering an approach suggested by George Ainslie (1975) and Howard Rachlin (1974). The idea is that choice is once again determined by the relative "value" of the two rewards, with the value of each of those rewards being determined by both their size and their delay. The idea is presented in Figure 7.14. As the figure illustrates,

Figure 7.13 Choice for a larger, delayed reward over a smaller, immediate reward. Self-control increases as the time between the choice and actual presentation of the reward increases. (After Green et al., 1981.)

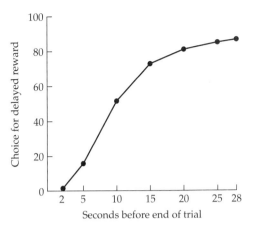

larger reinforcers have a higher value than smaller reinforcers. But more immediate reinforcers also have more value than reinforcers that are delayed: The figure shows that, as we move away from either reward in time (moving leftward on the x-axis increases the time before the reinforcer happens), its value falls off systematically (see Mazur, 1997, for a mathematical function). The value of a reward is "discounted" as a function of its delay. Now, here is the crucial thing. At any given time, the animal should choose the more valuable reward—that is, the reward whose value is currently higher. If we offer the animal the choice at Time 1, when both rewards will happen soon, the value of the more immediate reward is higher than the delayed reward. The animal therefore behaves impulsively and chooses the immediate reward. But if we offer the choice at Time 2, when the rewards are scheduled to happen more remotely in time, the relation between their values has flipped. Because of the way reward value decreases over the delay, the larger reward now has greater value than the smaller reward. The animal now demonstrates self-control and chooses the more-delayed reward. The different functions nicely describe how time-to-reward affects impulsive behavior and self-control.

Figure 7.14 The present value of a delayed reward depends on how far you are from the reward in time. At Time 1, a smaller, more immediate reward has more value than a larger reward that will occur after a longer delay. You therefore choose the smaller reward. In contrast, at Time 2, the larger reward has more value to you than the smaller reward—despite the same difference in delay. These hypothetical reward "discounting" functions explain the results in Figure 7.13.

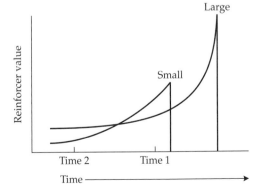

One of the nice things about this approach is that it immediately suggests a way to exercise "impulse control": If you can arrange to make the choice long before the rewards are actually due, you should be less tempted by the pesky little immediate reward. So-called **pre-commitment** strategies take advantage of this. The idea is to commit oneself early in such a way that an opportunity to make an impulsive choice later will be prevented. The classic example is using an alarm clock to get up in the morning and get to that early class. Early in the morning, just before the class, you have a choice of remaining in bed and getting a little extra sleep (a small, immediate reward) or getting up and going to class and getting intellectual stimulation or a better grade (a larger, delayed reward). Some of us might choose to snooze a little more and miss the class. But if you set your alarm clock the night before, you precommit to waking up and getting the larger reward by effectively precluding the response of continued sleep; it is much easier to make this choice earlier. Interestingly, pigeons given an analogous pre-commitment option (i.e., the choice to peck on a key that will produce an early commitment to a larger reward and preclude another choice later) will sometimes use it (Ainslie, 1975; Rachlin & Green, 1972), although not all pigeons do. Precommitment is a practical way to defeat impulsiveness and practice self-control.

Howard Rachlin

Other factors besides reinforcer size and reinforcer delay influence impulsiveness and self-control. Grosch and Neuringer (1981) studied choice in a situation in which pigeons received a less-preferred (but immediate) type of grain if they pecked a key, and a highly preferred (but delayed) type of grain if they did not peck the key. Grosch and Neuringer showed that "impulsive" choices for the immediate reward were more likely if the two rewards were visible throughout the trials. This effect was reduced if the birds could peck a key on a rear wall that moved their attention away from the visible grains. Interestingly, when Grosch and Neuringer presented Pavlovian CSs that predicted food, impulsive choices also increased. The results paralleled earlier findings with children reported by Walter Mischel and his associates (e.g., Mischel, Shoda, & Rodriguez, 1989). Mischel suggested that "hot thoughts"—ideas about how nice a reward will taste, etc.— can often defeat attempts at self-control, whereas distracting thoughts and behaviors (such as playing with a toy, or thinking "cool" thoughts) can often help efforts at self-control. Hot and cold thoughts are related to issues connected with the motivating effects of rewards (and their signals) that will be discussed in Chapter 9.

Do people show personality differences in their overall self-control or ability to delay gratification? Warren Bickel and his colleagues have studied drug abusers in situations analogous to the ones just described (see Bickel & Johnson, 2003; Bickel & Marsch, 2001). Drug users seem to choose an immediate "hit" of a drug over performing more positive, pro-social behaviors that might be more rewarding in the long-term. Several studies (e.g., Kirby, Petry, & Bickel, 1999; Madden, Bickel, & Jacobs, 1999) have confirmed that heroin abusers may be more likely than others to choose immediate over delayed rewards—even when the rewards are hypothetical and financial. Heroin abusers thus behave as if they are generally impulsive, with curves relating reward value to delay (see Figure 7.14) that are generally very steep—so that the value of a distant, large reward goes to zero very quickly. On the other hand, individuals who behave impulsively with hypothetical financial rewards do not necessarily do the same with hypothetical rewards related to health (Chapman, 1998). And especially interesting is the fact that, although cigarette smokers show steep curves relating reward value to delay (as do heroin users), ex-smokers do not. This difference suggests that the tendency for smokers to discount delayed reward so steeply is reversible, rather than a permanent personality trait (Bickel, Odum, & Madden, 1999).

You have probably noticed that the language in this section has become a little more anthropomorphic. However, although terms like "impulsiveness" and "self-control" may seem a little fuzzy, each is usually tied quite specifically to a particular behavioral result. Indeed, it is interesting to note that although most of us are used to thinking about "self-control" in terms of personal strength, willpower, etc., one of the messages of this research is really rather different. Instead of understanding these issues in terms of concepts like the self and will, the research shows how behavior that seems to reflect these virtues may come about quite directly and simply from what we know about the behavioral effects of rewards (e.g., Rachlin, 1974). The "control" is really still exerted by the reinforcers.

Behavioral economics: Are reinforcers all alike?

Perspectives on choice, like the quantitative law of effect and the Ainslie-Rachlin rule, accept a perspective that has been common in the psychology of learning: Different reinforcers are supposed to be all alike and can be scaled along a single dimension of value. In truth, this is an oversimplification. The world is full of things that reinforce but do not necessarily substitute for one another. A Pepsi might substitute perfectly for a Coke (for most of us, anyway), but neither one is quite the same as a good copulation or a good book.

The issue of reinforcer **substitutability** has been recognized by operant psychologists who have increasingly turned to principles of economics to help understand behavior (e.g., Allison, 1979, 1983; Hursh, 1980). The area within operant psychology in which behavior is analyzed using economic principles is called **behavioral economics** and is important and growing. In general, substitutability is recognized as a continuum that describes various ways in which reinforcers can actually interact with one another (Green & Freed, 1998).

A good way to discover the substitutability of two reinforcers is to vary the cost of obtaining one reinforcer and see how it affects consumption of the other. From an economic perspective, reinforcers are commodities that organisms consume. As every economics student knows, the consumption of a commodity depends upon its price: As the commodity becomes more expensive, we consume less of it; our "demand" for it decreases. The relationship between

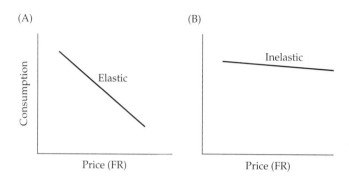

(A) (B)

Elastic

Inelastic

Consumption

Price (FR) Price (FR)

Figure 7.15 Demand curves describe the demand for a commodity as a function of its price (or fixed ratio requirement, FR). (A) Demand for an elastic commodity is very sensitive to price; therefore, demand typically decreases as prices increase. (B) Demand for an inelastic commodity is not so sensitive to price.

price and consumption is easy to study in the operant laboratory, where we can increase the price of a commodity by increasing the amount of work required to earn it—that is, by manipulating the schedule of reinforcement. Increasing the price of food by increasing the fixed-ratio schedule, for example, decreases the consumption of food (e.g., Foltin, 1991; Lea & Roper, 1977).

Figure 7.15 shows hypothetical data indicating how the consumption of a commodity or reinforcer might change as a function of its "price." This sort of function, showing demand for a commodity as a function of its price, is known as a **demand curve**. As described above, consumption tends to decrease as the price increases. This is especially true of commodities that are said to be "elastic"—consumption of them is very dependent on price (see Figure 7.15A). So-called "inelastic" commodities are ones whose consumption is fairly constant over price (see Figure 7.15B). Commodities whose demand functions are less elastic are necessities, while those commodities whose demand functions are very elastic are luxuries. Hursh and Natelson (1981) compared the rat's demand curves for food and for electrical stimulation of the brain. When price was increased with a leaner VI schedule, the demand for brain stimulation declined. As price for food increased, however, there was little decline in the demand for food.

Now let us consider what effect increasing the price of one reward might have on the consumption of a second reward that is also available. Three possibilities are shown in the panels of Figure 7.16. In panel A, as the price of one reinforcer, A, increases, its own consumption declines, and the consumption of the other reinforcer, B, goes up (e.g., Rachlin et al., 1976). These reinforcers are true **substitutes**: Subjects essentially exchange one commodity for the other. Real-world examples might be Coke and Pepsi or potato chips and pretzels. In panel B, the commodities are **independents**: As the price of one commodity, A, goes up and its consumption goes down, the consumption of the other commodity, B, does not change. Examples here might be compact discs and umbrellas, or Cokes and books. Panel C describes **complements**: As the price of one commodity, A, and its consumption decreases, so does consumption of the other commodity, B. Examples of this might be bagels and cream cheese, hot dogs and hot dog buns, chips and salsa, etc.

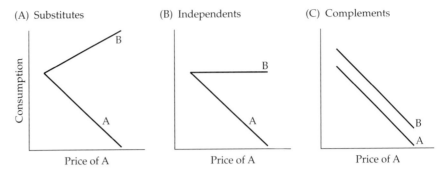

Figure 7.16 Demand for two commodities (A and B), as one of them (A) increases in price. Different panels illustrate commodities that are substitutes, independents, or complements of one another. Commodities are not always substitutes for one another—that is, reinforcers are not all alike.

The various relationships that are possible between rewards make it clear that different reinforcers are not necessarily equivalent. To understand the effects of one reinforcer, we must know what that reinforcer is and what its alternatives really are.

The substitutability concept is useful when we try to understand the interactions between reinforcers in the real world. For example, although drugs of abuse are reinforcers, they are not mere substitutes for one another. Bickel, DeGrandpre, and Higgins (1995) summarized 16 studies in which two or more drugs were available to humans or animals, and consumption was measured while the price of one drug was manipulated. They found evidence of substitutability, independence, and complementarity. For example, different ways of administering the same drug (e.g., orally or intravenously) were substitutes, showing the arrangement described in Figure 7.16A. Ethanol also appears to be a substitute for PCP: As the price of PCP increased, its consumption decreased, and that of ethanol increased. (Interestingly, the reverse did not hold true: Increasing the price of ethanol decreased ethanol consumption but did not change PCP consumption.) Other drugs were complements: When the price of alcohol increased, its consumption decreased, and so did the consumption of cigarettes. These relationships clearly demonstrate the utility of economic concepts when thinking about real-world reinforcers.

The general point is that reinforcers are not all alike. Although they have similar effects (each reinforcer increases the probability of a behavior that leads to it), they do not necessarily substitute for one another. Instead, reinforcers are real things that can interact in different ways. The quantitative law of effect and self-control theory are excellent tools for understanding the principles governing choice when the payoffs are substitutable. But when rewards have relationships of independence or complementarity, other principles will also be required.

Theories of Reinforcement

Skinner's definition of a reinforcer (something that leads to an increase in a response it is made a consequence of) is not a theory. It describes a relationship between a behavior and a consequence, but it does not explain how or why the reinforcer increases the behavior, or what kinds of things will be reinforcers and what kinds of things will not be. Notice that this is equally true of the matching law. When we use the matching equation, we count the responses made and the reinforcers earned, plug them into the equation, and find that the equation worked. But notice that we use the past tense. The matching equation describes what occurred, but it does not predict exactly how an individual organism will match. Nor, again, does it predict what events will be reinforcers. It is a perfect extension of Skinner's reinforcement principle.

For these reasons, Skinnerian definitions of reinforcers are sometimes called "circular" (e.g., Postman, 1947). The utterly empirical nature of these descriptions can be considered a strength, because each description automatically accommodates the potentially enormous range of factors that might reinforce different behaviors and different individuals. Got a kid who is acting out in school? Just find whatever it is that is a consequence of the behavior and manipulate it—that will usually work. But some people want more than this; they want some kind of explanation of how reinforcers work. And it would also be useful to know ahead of time what kinds of events will reinforce a behavior. One way to break the circularity is to note that reinforcers that work in one situation should also work in another (Meehl, 1950); thus, we might be able to predict a reinforcer's abilities by its effects in another situation. And, it might also lead to a theory.

Drive reduction

Thorndike had the beginnings of a theory. He thought that satisfaction stamped in the S-R connection. Reinforcers work because they strengthen a connection, and they do so only if they are satisfying. But what is "satisfaction"? Clark Hull, a theorist working from the Thorndike tradition, had a related view (Hull, 1943). He thought that reinforcers reduced drives. His theory of reinforcement was part of a much larger theory that was designed to understand all motivation and learning. Hull thought behavior was organized in a way that always helped the animal satisfy its needs. The theory can be summarized by imagining an animal who wakes up from a good sleep in the forest. He has slept long enough that his body now needs food— he is therefore hungry. Hunger, in turn, makes him restless and active, and the heightened general activity eventually leads him to perform, perhaps accidentally, an operant behavior that leads to food. The food then reduces the need, and the reduction in need reinforces behavior. So next time the animal needs food, the operant is performed again. In this way, motivation, learning, and behavior were organized to meet the organism's needs.

In Hull's theory, the need for food or water stimulated a theoretical construct called **Drive**, which motivated behavior, increasing the strength of general activity, and also the strength of behaviors that had been learned (reinforced) before. It also provided the basis for reinforcement. According to Hull, reinforcement occurs when the event that's made a consequence of behavior reduces Drive. Unlike Skinner's atheoretical approach, Hull's theory immediately indicated a class of events or stimuli that would reinforce—that is, things that would reduce Drive.

Hull's general theory shaped research in the field of learning and motivation for many years. However, many parts of the theory did not hold up to careful testing (see Bolles, 1967, 1975; see Chapter 9), and the drive reduction theory of reinforcement was one of the first elements to go. Contrary data were soon gathered by Fred Sheffield, a colleague of Hull's at Yale University, who showed that commodities that did not reduce need could still reinforce. Sheffield and Roby (1950) found that saccharin, a nonnutritive sweetener, served as a reinforcer. The body does not need saccharin. Sheffield, Wulff, and Backer (1951) also found that male rats would learn to run into an alley to copulate with a female—even if the copulation was terminated before the rat had ejaculated. Presumably, a "need" had not been reduced; one could even argue that a new one had been aroused.

Neal Miller (Miller, 1957) defended Hull's position against these findings. Miller pointed out that, although the body did not really "need" saccharin, there was something like a drive for it anyway. He showed that if a rat was fed a little saccharin, the rat would consume less of it when saccharin was offered again later; the animal also wouldn't work as hard for it. So feeding a rat saccharin did reduce some kind of motivation to get the saccharin. In this way, Miller reconceptualized Hull's concept of Drive. But Miller had broken the connection between Drive and biological need, and the theory found fewer and fewer adherents after that. This was partly because of other problems with the concept (see Chapter 9). It was also because another view of reinforcement came along and carried the day.

The Premack principle

In the late 1950s and early 1960s, David Premack presented a theory that more or less changed everything (see Premack, 1965, 1971a, for reviews). He offered a completely new way to think about how reinforcers work in operant learning. When most of us think about the classic experiment where a rat lever-presses for food, we usually see the crucial reinforcement contingency as one between a behavior (the lever-press) and a stimulus (the food pellet). Instead, Premack noted that the real contingency is between two behaviors. By giving the rat a food pellet after each lever-press, we are making the opportunity to eat contingent on lever-pressing. In any operant learning situation, there is an instrumental act that provides access to a "contingent" behavior. The reason lever-pressing increases in this arrangement is that it allows access to eating, a behavior that the rat would prefer to do.

Premack's idea is that reinforcement occurs *when the instrumental act allows access to a more preferred behavior.* The animal's preferences can be tested ahead of time, by giving the subject free access to both behaviors and then finding which behavior it spends the most time doing. In the lever-press-and-eat experiment, if we had allowed the rat to choose between lever-pressing and pellet-eating, we would have found the animal spending more time eating than pressing the lever. (Experimenters usually guarantee this preference by depriving the animal of food beforehand.) Eating can therefore reinforce lever-pressing because eating is preferred to lever-pressing. By pointing to the relevance of a preference test, Premack's theory allows one to predict what kinds of events will be reinforcing. Moreover, it has tremendous generality. Suppose we allowed a child to play with several toys and timed the number of seconds the child spent playing with each toy. We might discover that the child spends the most seconds playing with Toy A, the second-most seconds with Toy B, the third-most seconds with Toy C, and so forth. Other children might rank the toys very differently. But Premack would predict that, for this particular child, access to Toy A would reinforce playing with either Toy B or Toy C. And Toy B might reinforce playing with Toy C (but not Toy A). All we need to know is how the subject spends its time engaging in the various alternatives in an initial preference test.

David Premack

Premack showed the power of the principle in several clever experiments. In one of them (Premack, 1963b), he conducted an experiment much like the one just described, except that the subjects were cebus monkeys rather than children. He first observed several monkeys interacting freely with toys they could manipulate. In initial preference tests, when the items were freely available, one of the monkeys, Chicko, spent most of its time pulling on a hinged flap, then opening a door, and then pushing on a plunger. Premack predicted (and found) that access to the hinged flap would reinforce opening the door and pushing on the plunger. That is, door-opening and plunger-pushing increased when they allowed access to manipulating the flap. On the other hand, although opening the door reinforced plunger-pushing, it did not reinforce flap-flipping. A behavior was only reinforcing if it had been preferred to the operant behavior in the original tests. Monkeys with different preferences showed different results. All of this is consistent with Premack's principle that reinforcement occurs when the instrumental act allows access to a more preferred behavior.

In a similar experiment, Premack (1959) gave first-grade children a choice between eating candy and playing at a pinball machine. Some of the kids spent more time eating candy than playing pinball. Not surprisingly, for these children, when candy was made contingent on playing pinball, pinball-playing increased. Other children, though, preferred to spend more time playing pinball than eating candy in the initial preference test. For this latter group of kids, pinball-playing reinforced candy-eating—the reverse of the effect in the other group. The Premack principle predicts what things will reinforce other things, but it also accepts large individual differences. All that matters is the individual's initial preference ranking.

One of the interesting things about the pinball/candy experiment is that it demonstrates that there is nothing special about sweets (or foods) as reinforcers. Candy-eating served as either reinforcer or operant, depending on how the kids initially ranked it relative to pinball-playing. This point was made brilliantly in another experiment, this time using rats (Premack, 1962). Premack built a running wheel in which rats could either run or drink water from a spout; access by the rats to either the wheel or the water could be controlled. In one condition, rats were first deprived of water. In a preference test with both running and drinking available, they therefore spent more time drinking than running. Not surprisingly, but consistent with the principle, drinking reinforced running. However, in an interesting second condition, Premack gave rats all the water they needed but deprived them of running. In the preference test, the rats' preference was now reversed and they preferred running to drinking. And, consistent with the principle, in this case running reinforced drinking. This was a bit more surprising. There is nothing special about water as a reinforcer; in fact, the relation between instrumental act and reinforcing act was said to be reversible.

One of the interesting features of Premack's approach is that it uses no theoretical constructs whatsoever. It makes testable predictions, but it is as empirical as Skinner could ever have wanted. Premack was not interested in what actually caused an organism to prefer one activity over another; in fact, he was quite indifferent to this question. All that mattered were the subject's current preferences, regardless of what the actual behaviors were or how their levels came about. Like Hull, Premack would predict that food would be more reinforcing to hungry, rather than satiated, rats. However, while Hull would have explained this by noting that the hungry rats had greater Drive, Premack would merely note that the food-deprived rats would have a larger preference for eating. It is the strength of the preference, regardless of how it got there, that determines the reinforcement effect. Figure 7.17 shows the results of a rat experiment in which a variety of sucrose solutions (16%, 32%, or 64%), or the opportunity to run in a heavy wheel (HW) or a light wheel (LW), were each made contingent on lever-pressing (Premack, 1963a). Regardless of the type of reinforcer, its reinforcing effect on lever-pressing was clearly predicted by its initial baseline probability (*x*-axis).

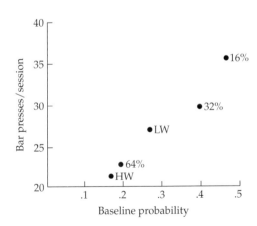

Figure 7.17 Reinforcing effect of different reinforcers as a function of the rat's preference for each reinforcer (baseline probability). (After Premack, 1965.)

Premack went on to run some famous, though unrelated, experiments on language learning in chimpanzees (e.g., Premack, 1971b). However, before he left the response learning question, he extended the principle to the case of punishment (Premack, 1971a). Punishment, of course, is the situation in which something made contingent upon an instrumental behavior weakens (rather than strengthens) the behavior. Premack's idea, based on the reinforcement rule, is that punishment will occur when the instrumental behavior leads to a less-preferred response. Thus, delivering a mild electric shock after a lever-press punishes lever-pressing, not because the shock is aversive or "annoying" (Thorndike), but because it elicits a behavior, like fear, that is less-preferred to lever-pressing. The idea was tested in at least one experiment (Weisman & Premack, as described in Premack, 1971a). Rats were put into a running wheel with the drinking spout again. This time, however, the wheel was motorized, so that the experimenter could flip a switch and force the rodent to run, when this behavior was needed. The rats were first drink-deprived, and in a preference test, they showed the usual preference for drinking over running. Then, running was made contingent on drinking; when the rat drank, the motor was switched on, and the rat was forced to run. Here, when drinking led to the less-preferred running, punishment was observed, and the rats stopped drinking. In a control condition, rats were tested while they weren't water-deprived. In the preference test, these subjects preferred running to drinking. And when drinks subsequently led to running initiated by turning on the motorized wheel, wheel-running reinforced drinking! There was nothing inherently aversive about running in the motorized wheel. When running was less preferred to drinking, it punished drinking, but when running was more preferred to drinking, it reinforced drinking.

Problems with the Premack principle

The Premack principle was an important landmark in the development of ideas about reinforcement. It began a fundamental shift toward thinking about relations between behaviors, rather than between behaviors and stimuli, and at the same time, it avoided Skinner's circularity problem. However, it had its points of weakness. One stemmed from the problem of how to arrange preference tests. Although the principle is very clear that reinforcement effects should be predictable from prior preferences, it is not always easy to know how to determine those preferences. For example, consider sex and coffee-drinking. It is quite possible that during the course of a 24-hour day you spend more time drinking coffee than having sex. (This is at least true of many professors I know.) This fact implies that you prefer coffee to sex, and that making coffee-drinking contingent on having sex will increase your amount of sexual activity. I'm not sure anyone has run this experiment, but you might agree that the principle seems to have things backward—it seems more likely that sex will reinforce coffee-drinking, not the reverse. In truth, an expert investigator would say that this more sensible prediction actually follows from the right kind of preference test. If we limited preference testing to, say, 30 minutes or so with both coffee and a boyfriend or girlfriend present, one might spend more time engaged in amorous activity than in coffee-drinking. Thus, based on an appropriate preference test, we might correctly predict that amorous activity would reinforce coffee-drinking. But what is appropriate is not always clear ahead of time, and this introduces an ad hoc aspect to Premack's principle.

Another problem is that many early experiments did not acknowledge the fact that, when you make a preferred behavior contingent on another behavior, you necessarily deny access to a preferred behavior that would ordinarily fill some time. For instance, when pinball-playing is made contingent on candy-eating, you don't allow pinball-playing until the kid eats some candy. So, what is the kid going to do now that he can't play pinball? The contingency leaves a void that must be filled by some activity, and maybe part of the increase observed in the instrumental activity occurs because something has to increase. Several investigations have included control conditions that help address this issue (see Dunham, 1977, for more discussion).

Nonetheless, there is an important idea here: Reinforcement contingencies always deprive an organism of the chance to engage in a behavior that it would ordinarily spend some time doing. Perhaps the crucial thing is that the instrumental behavior allows access to a behavior that has been deprived in this way. The importance of this idea became clear in experiments by Eisenberger, Karpman, and Trattner (1967) and Allison and Timberlake (1974). Both research groups showed that access even to a less-preferred behavior could reinforce a more-preferred behavior if the reinforcing behavior was denied below its initial baseline level. Eisenberger et al. (1967) let high school students manipulate a knob or a lever. Most subjects spent more time turning the knob, although they also pressed the lever at least a little bit. The experimenters then arranged things so that knob-turning allowed access to lever-pressing, which was otherwise completely denied. Premack would predict punishment here, because a preferred behavior is leading to a less-preferred response. Instead, lever-pressing reinforced knob-turning, and the probability of knob-turning actually increased. Allison and Timberlake (1974) observed a similar effect in rats drinking different concentrations of a saccharin solution. Drinking a less-preferred solution could reinforce drinking a more-preferred solution if the contingency deprived the rat of drinking the less-preferred solution below its baseline level.

The point of these results is that *access even to a less-preferred behavior can be reinforcing if its baseline level has been denied or deprived.* Behavior deprivation is inherent in the typical situation in which a more-preferred behavior is made contingent on a behavior that is less-preferred. It turns out that deprivation of the contingent response—rather than its higher probability—is the thing that makes reinforcement possible. The Premack principle is a good place to start, but it is not the final answer to the reinforcement story.

Behavioral regulation theory

Timberlake and Allison (1974) summarized the new idea in a view that is known as the **response deprivation hypothesis** (see also Timberlake, 1980, 1984; Timberlake & Farmer-Dougan, 1991). The idea of response deprivation is that every behavior has a preferred level, and once access to it is restricted, we will perform another behavior to get back to it. Thus, access to any behavior we perform at some level during a baseline test will become reinforcing if we are deprived of that behavior. It is as if we are motivated to defend and regulate a certain distribution of activities. When a reinforcement contingency denies an activity, we will do what we can to get it back. The general view is sometimes known as **behavioral regulation theory** (see Timberlake, 1980, 1984; Timberlake & Farmer-Dougan, 1991).

An explicit version of the theory makes some interesting further predictions (Staddon, 1979). Figure 7.18 shows two possible behaviors, A and B, on the *x*- and *y*-axes, respectively. The open circle represents a hypothetical animal's baseline preference between the two possible behaviors—that is, when the animal was given free access to both behaviors in a preference test, it performed behavior A 50 times, and behavior B 150 times. This relationship between A and B at baseline is called a "bliss point," because it is the amount of A and B that are chosen when everything is free. The idea of behavioral regulation theory is that, when deprived of either A or B, the animal will do its best to return to that point of bliss.

So let's consider a situation in which the animal must now perform behavior A in order to have access to behavior B. The line in Figure 7.18 represents one possible arrangement—a ratio schedule of reinforcement in which the animal must perform exactly one A response to earn one B response. Notice that the schedule constrains the animal's behavior; it sets up a limited number of possible pairs of A and B behaviors , and makes it impossible for the animal to return to the bliss point. What should the ani-

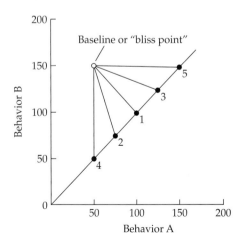

Figure 7.18 The minimum distance model. The open circle describes the baseline level or "bliss point," that is, the level of two behaviors (A and B) when they can be made freely in a preference test. When a certain number of A responses are required for every B response, the range of possibilities are indicated by a line. We perform the number of A responses that get us closest to the bliss point (point number 1 on the line). (After Allison, 1989.)

mal do now? According to the **minimum distance model** (e.g., Staddon, 1979), it will get as close as possible to the bliss point; the animal should make the number of A responses that gets it the "minimum distance" from the bliss point. The idea is easy to understand graphically. The closest point on a line will be the point that allows a perpendicular from the line to hit the bliss point. As Figure 7.18 illustrates, any other possible point on the line will be further away from the bliss point. The minimum distance model therefore predicts that the organism will perform the number of A responses that will get it closest to the bliss point. In this example, the animal will make about 100 A responses and then stop. Stopping shy of 100, or going beyond it, will merely take the animal further away from the bliss point.

Now, you can undoubtedly appreciate that the number of A responses required to get the minimum distance from bliss will depend on the reinforcement schedule. This idea is illustrated in Figure 7.19, which plots several more ratio schedules as new lines relating the number of A responses (in this case, lever-presses) required to get a B response (eating a food pellet). In some of the schedules (the steepest lines), the animal doesn't have to perform many A responses to get plenty of B responses; the ratio is low. In other schedules (the shallow ones) the animal must work considerably more; that is, the ratio is high. Using the perpendicular-line technique from above, it is easy to show that each schedule has its own number of A responses that gets as close as possible to the bliss point, and these are shown by the points on each of the lines. Something rather interesting emerges: As we increase the schedule ratio (going from very steep to very shallow lines), the rat will first perform more responses, and then fewer and fewer. This sort of function is consistent with the results of a number of experiments (see Staddon, 1979). Moreover, it makes interesting connections with economic analyses (Allison, 1989). First, notice that the reinforcement schedules that ought to produce the most lever-presses—the most work, if you want to think of it that way—are the intermediate ones. Neither leaner nor richer schedules produce as much behavior as the ones in between—future employers and

Figure 7.19 The number of responses that get us closest to the bliss point depends on the reinforcement schedule. Each line radiating out from 0 represents a different ratio schedule in which a different number of A responses (e.g., lever-presses) are required for each B response (e.g., eating of food pellets). The open circle is the bliss point; the solid circles are the points on each schedule line that are closest to the bliss point. (After Allison, 1989.)

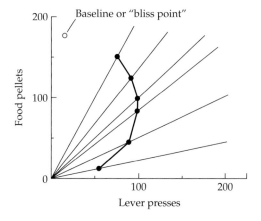

managers should take note. Note also that, as the price of food (or the amount of work required) increases (with shallower and shallower lines), the overall consumption of food declines—the familiar demand-curve described above. Once again, we discover connections between operant behavior and economics (e.g., Allison, 1983).

According to Staddon (1979), experiments with ratio schedules seem to follow the minimum-distance model. The model can also be applied to interval reinforcement schedules, although these are different because the schedule functions relating the number of behavior A to B responses are not simple, straight lines. Nonetheless, the minimum-distance model predicts a similar relationship between reinforcement rate and behavior rate: As we increase the potential reinforcement rate relative to the behavior rate, behavior rate should first increase and then decline. Interestingly, the matching law (or quantitative law of effect, see Equation 7.6) also makes predictions here; however, it does not predict that response rate will eventually decline. In fact, as shown in Figure 7.12, a decline does not occur with interval schedules in pigeons (e.g., Catania & Reynolds, 1968); that is, beyond a certain reinforcement rate, further increases in the reinforcement rate cause no further change in behavior rate. The matching law seems more accurate here. In general, the matching law seems to do a better job describing behavior on interval reinforcement schedules, while the minimum-distance model does a better job describing behavior on ratio schedules (Staddon, 1979). The minimum-distance model does, however, provide some insight into what actually makes a reinforcer reinforcing.

John Staddon

Selection by consequences

It would be a mistake to end this chapter without mentioning one last perspective on how reinforcers might operate. Several writers have noted the parallel between the effects of reinforcers and evolution by natural selection (e.g., Donahoe, 1998; Donahoe & Palmer, 1994; Skinner, 1981; Staddon & Simmelhag, 1971). According to this idea, reinforcers select behaviors by essentially weeding out the behaviors that are less useful. This is a bit different from the traditional Thorndikian view that reinforcers "stamp in" the behaviors that lead to them.

This idea was actually introduced in Chapter 2 during the discussion of shaping. Remember that natural selection operates through elimination. In Chapter 2, we saw how the color of pepper moths in England got darker and darker over generations during the Industrial Revolution. At the start of the Revolution, some moths were dark in color, many were light in color, and others were probably somewhere in-between. Over the years, as the trees darkened because of increasing factory smoke, birds began to detect light moths on the trees more readily, ate them, and thereby eliminated the light-colored moths (and their potential offspring) from the moth population. The moth population therefore gradually shifted from light-colored moths (less visible on light trees) to dark-colored moths (less visible on darkened trees). There are two important things to note here. First, there was some variation in the shading of the moths. Second, natural selection then acted on that variation by eliminating the less viable moths.

The idea that reinforcement works the same way was nicely described by Staddon and Simmelhag (1971). As in evolution, the organism starts with a variable set of behaviors from which reinforcers can then select. The initial behaviors are brought about by "principles of variation" that are analogous to those provided by genetics and heredity in evolution. That is, the animal initially does certain things in a new environment because of generalization from previous environments, innate tendencies in the environment, and so on. Reinforcers then select from these variations, just the way natural selection does. The behaviors that don't lead to reinforcement drop out—they extinguish, or (to use the word from evolution rather than learning theory) they become extinct. Reinforcers basically keep some behaviors from being eliminated this way. The noneliminated behaviors remain in the population, and new variations are then produced through processes like induction and generalization (see Chapter 2). Reinforcers then select again, and so on. The idea is that an understanding of how reinforcers work will require an understanding of (1) principles of behavior variation, and (2) selection by elimination just like evolution.

Toward the end of his long and distinguished career, Skinner himself emphasized the parallel between evolution and operant learning (Skinner, 1981). Both processes involve a principle he called "selection by consequences." He noted that the selection-by-consequences idea is relatively new in science, having been discovered around the time of Darwin in the middle of the nineteenth century. This concept was different from earlier scientific principles, which usually required mechanical forces, energies, and initiating causes to make things work. In contrast, selection-by-consequences just happens; no causal agent (like a creator in the case of evolution or a creative mind in the case of operant learning) is required.

Despite the simplicity of variation and selection, great complexity can emerge with their repeated application. This point is nicely illustrated in Richard Dawkins's book, *The Blind Watchmaker* (1986). The intricacy and complexity of living things suggests to many observers that they must have been designed by a great, creative mind—that is, a skilled and powerful watchmaker. But, in fact, no designer is required—the "watchmaker" might be blind. Great complexity can arise over the millions of generations in evolutionary time—or the millions of operant conditioning trials that presumably occur in an organism's lifetime. Dawkins, whose focus was evolution and not operant conditioning, created a computer program that generated simple "biomorphs" by variations in several "genes" that were built into the program. The program could start by generating a simple item (Figure 7.20), and then create a set of minor, random mutations of it. Dawkins himself would then select one of the mutations, and discard (eliminate) the others. The selected mutation would then be allowed to reproduce. That is, the computer created new mutations of it. And then Dawkins selected again from this new set of variations. After a number of such variation-and-elim-

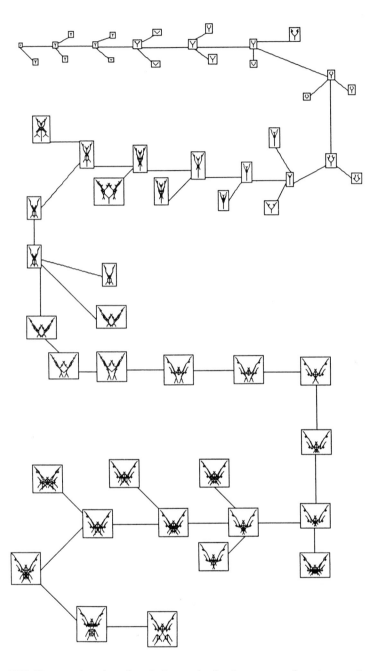

Figure 7.20 Repeated cycles of variation and selection can produce impressive beauty and complexity. Dawkins (1986) used the changes in this "biomorph" over variation/selection cycles to illustrate the process of evolution. The same case can be made for operant conditioning—complex behaviors might emerge from the extremely large number of variation and selection cycles that can occur in an organism's lifetime. (From Dawkins, 1986.)

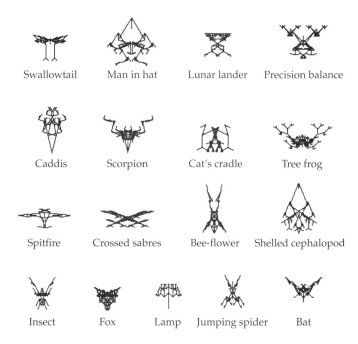

Swallowtail   Man in hat   Lunar lander   Precision balance

Caddis   Scorpion   Cat's cradle   Tree frog

Spitfire   Crossed sabres   Bee-flower   Shelled cephalopod

Insect   Fox   Lamp   Jumping spider   Bat

Figure 7.21 Different "biomorphs" that "evolved" in Dawkins' (1986) computer software program. (From Dawkins, 1986.)

ination cycles, some beautiful and complex "organisms" began to emerge. An example is shown in Figure 7.20. Repeated repetitions of a simple variation/selection process can produce end-products of impressive beauty and complexity (Figure 7.21). The same could be true of operant conditioning. Human behavior, which seems so miraculous and so complex, might similarly emerge from the very large number of variation/selection cycles that occur in a typical lifetime.

What impact has the variation/selection idea had on Learning Theory? Although the parallel between reinforcement and selection is fascinating, it has not stimulated much new research. There has been progress in understanding some of the principles of variation (see Balsam, Deich, Ohyama, & Stokes, 1998; Neuringer, 1993, 2004), and investigators now recognize that reinforcers function to select—as well as to strengthen—operant behavior (e.g., Williams, 1988). But there has been little research pursuing the idea that reinforcers work mainly by weeding out instead of stamping in. Advocates of the selection-by-consequences view (e.g., Donahoe, 1998; Donahoe & Burgos, 2000; Donahoe, Burgos, & Palmer, 1993; McDowell, 2004) sometimes tacitly endorse a stamping-in type of reinforcement mechanism. Although the selection-by-consequences view provides an interesting perspective on response learning, it is somewhat unique among the perspectives reviewed in this chapter in that it has yet to generate a new line of research that has led to new insights.

Summary

1. Early thinkers had different ideas about what was going on in instrumental learning. Thorndike emphasized reinforcement: Satisfaction was supposed to stamp in an S-R association. Guthrie claimed that reinforcement wasn't necessary for learning; S and R were associated if they merely occurred together in time. Tolman argued that learning was mostly about stimuli (S-S), and that reinforcers were important for motivating performance even though they were not necessary for learning. The early theorists identified at least three possible functions of reinforcers: They might stamp in behavior (Thorndike), they might provide another stimulus (Guthrie), and they might motivate (Tolman).

2. Skinner's "atheoretical" approach emphasized the strengthening effects of both primary and conditioned reinforcers and also emphasized stimulus control, the concept that operant behaviors occur in the presence of stimuli that set the occasion for them. Skinner invented the operant experiment, which is a method that examines how "voluntary" behavior relates to its payoff—the animal is free to repeat the operant response as often as it chooses.

3. Schedules of reinforcement provide a way to study how behavior relates to payoff. Ratio schedules require a certain number of responses for each reinforcer, and there is a direct relationship between behavior rate and payoff rate. Interval schedules reinforce the first response after a specified interval of time has elapsed. In this case, there is a less-direct relationship between behavior rate and payoff rate. Different schedules generate their own patterns of responding.

4. Choice is studied in concurrent schedules, where two behaviors are available and are reinforced according to their own schedules of reinforcement. Choice conforms to the matching law, which states that the percentage of behavior allocated to one alternative will match the percentage of reinforcers earned there. Even the simplest operant experiment involves this kind of choice, because the organism must choose between lever-pressing and all other available behaviors, which are reinforced according to their own schedules. According to the quantitative law of effect—an extension of the matching law—the rate of a behavior always depends on both its own reinforcement rate and on the reinforcement rate of other behaviors.

5. We often have to choose between behaviors that produce large, delayed rewards versus behaviors that yield smaller, but more immediate rewards. We are said to exercise self-control when we choose the large, delayed reward, but we are seen as impulsive when we go for the smaller, immediate reward. Choice here is a lawful function of how a reinforcer's value depends on both its size and its imminence in time.

6. Reinforcers are not all the same. According to economic principles, two reinforcers may substitute for one another (e.g., Coke for Pepsi, and vice versa), they may be independent of one another (Pepsi and books), or they may complement one another (chips and salsa). A complete understanding of choice will need to take into account the relationship between the different reinforcers.

7. The Premack reinforcement principle states that access to one behavior will reinforce another behavior if the first behavior is preferred in a baseline preference test. The principle has very wide applicability, and it rescues the Skinnerian definition of a reinforcer ("any consequence of a behavior that increases the probability of that behavior") from its circularity. Premack's punishment principle states that access to a behavior will punish another behavior if the first behavior is less preferred.

8. According to behavior regulation theory, animals have a preferred level of every behavior they engage in. When a behavior is blocked or prevented so that it is deprived below its preferred baseline level, access to it becomes reinforcing. Behavior regulation theory replaces the Premack principle as a way of identifying potential reinforcers.

9. Reinforcers may operate like natural selection. According to this idea, they may select certain behaviors largely by preventing them from elimination (extinction). As is true in evolution, great subtlety and complexity can emerge over time from repeated application of principles of variation and selection.

Key Terms

reinforcement theory
contiguity theory
stimulus elements
stimulus sampling theory
learning/performance distinction
latent learning experiment
superstitious behaviors
stimulus control
fading
discriminative stimulus (S^D)
S^Δ
conditioned reinforcer
secondary reinforcer
primary reinforcer
behavior chain
schedules of reinforcement
continuous reinforcement (CRF)
   schedule
cumulative record
cumulative recorder
ratio schedule
fixed ratio (FR)
variable ratio (VR)

interval schedules
fixed interval (FI)
variable interval (VI)
compound schedules
multiple schedule
chained schedule
concurrent schedule
matching law
melioration
quantitative law of effect
pre-commitment
substitutability
behavioral economics
demand curve
substitutes
independents
complements
Drive
Premack principle
response deprivation hypothesis
behavioral regulation theory
minimum distance model

Chapter Eight Outline

Chapter

8

How Stimuli Guide Instrumental Action

THE LAST CHAPTER MENTIONED that a behavior almost always has a bigger payoff in some situations than in others. There is thus a clear value in being able to learn to discriminate between different situations. That is what the mechanisms of **stimulus control** are all about; they allow us to learn to discriminate situations where behaviors are rewarded from situations where they are not. The classic demonstration of stimulus control was Skinner's rat pressing the lever in the presence of a light (when the response was reinforced) and not pressing the lever in the absence of the light (when the response was not reinforced). The presence of the light, a discriminative stimulus (S^D), allowed the rat to behave very efficiently.

It won't surprise you to learn that modern research on stimulus control uses stimuli that are a bit more interesting than light-on and light-off. For example, Bond and Kamil (1998, 2002) studied the behavior of blue jays in a Skinner box equipped with a computer screen on one wall (Figure 8.1A). They used the screen to project digital images of artificial moths resting on a granular-looking background (Figure 8.1B). When the display contained a moth, pecks at it were reinforced with a piece of mealworm, but if a moth was not displayed, pecks were not reinforced. (The bird had to peck the circle in the center to go on to the next trial.) The birds learned to peck accordingly, which shouldn't surprise you given what

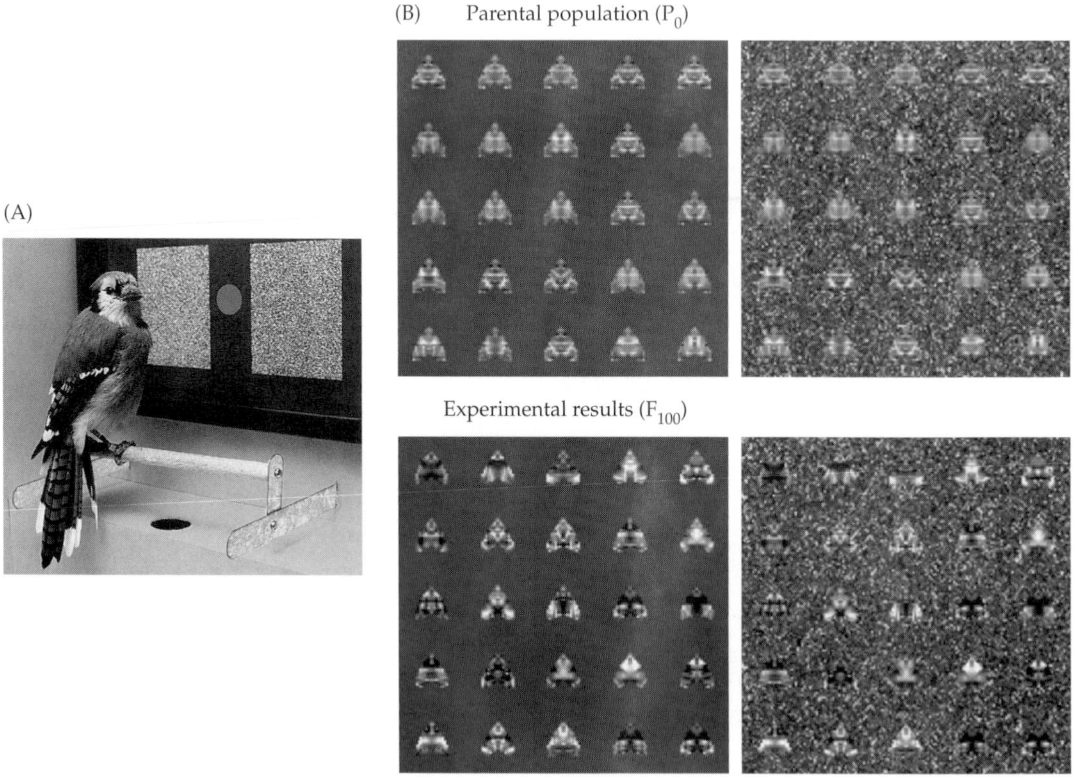

(B)   Parental population (P$_0$)

(A)

Experimental results (F$_{100}$)

Figure 8.1 Digital "moths" were shown to blue jays in experiments by Bond and Kamil (2002). (A) Experimental setup. On any trial, a single moth or no moth at all was embedded in one of the two granular backgrounds. (B) Top: A sample of moths from the population presented at the start of the experiment (shown on a solid background to make them visible to the reader, as well as on the granular background actually used). Bottom: A sample of moths from the end of the experiment—these are virtual offspring of moths that had evolved over many sessions in which the blue jays could detect and eliminate moths from the population. Over sessions, moths from the parent population became more cryptic and more variable in appearance. (A, courtesy of Alan Bond; B, from Bond and Kamil, 2002.)

you know about stimulus control and the fact that blue jays probably eat many moths sitting on trees in the wild. To state the obvious: The contingencies of reinforcement allowed the image of a moth to become an S^D for approaching and pecking. The psychological processes behind stimulus control helped the blue jays forage efficiently for food.

Bond and Kamil actually demonstrated that stimulus control processes can affect *both* a predator and its prey. When some of the moths were more conspicuous than others, the blue jays tended to detect and peck at the conspicuous ones and miss the more hidden (or "cryptic") moths. If the birds had actually been eating the moths, the conspicuous moths would not have survived. In evolutionary terms, there is thus a payoff for moths to be cryptic—cryptic moths that escape detection are more likely to have offspring in the next generation. Bond and Kamil recognized this, and their experiments were actually designed to study a kind of virtual evolution. Moths that the blue jays detected and pecked in one session were eliminated from the population that was presented in the next session. In contrast, moths that were not pecked (i.e., escaped detection) survived and were represented in the next session by "offspring" that differed only a little from the parents. The blue jays' behavior thus introduced a bit of natural selection, and, consequently, the moth population changed in interesting ways (see Figure 8.1B, bottom). For one thing, the moths did evolve to become a bit more cryptic. And, perhaps more noticeably, the moths gradually came to look different from one another. (Differences between individuals of a species, or "polymorphisms," are actually very common in real moths.) The differences resulted from the fact that the blue jays could learn about a particular moth over several trials and then search for a similar one on the next trial (a phenomenon called "search image" that will be considered later in this chapter). Therefore, moths that were different from their neighbors were more likely to survive. The psychology of stimulus control thus affected both the behavior of a predator and the evolution of its prey.

It is hard to overstate the importance of stimulus control. My goal in this chapter is therefore to reach a better understanding of it. We will begin by looking at how animals discriminate and respond to complex sets of stimuli in a way that suggests they can learn categories or "concepts." This will lead us to consider a number of basic processes behind the psychology of stimulus control. We will then see how the familiar information processing system (the so-called standard model of cognition) contributes to it all. And, in the final parts of this chapter, we will ask how organisms use time and spatial cues to optimize their interactions with the world. Throughout, we will see that it has become common to invoke cognitive processes (psychological processes that are not directly observed in behavior) to explain behavior under stimulus control. At the same time, researchers have also recognized that methods for studying stimulus control provide a powerful way to study those processes. Modern research on stimulus control is thus part of a research area that is sometimes known as **animal cognition**, or the study of cognitive processes in animals (e.g., Pearce, 1997; Roberts, 1998; Roitblat, 1987). We have learned a lot about cognition and behavior from experiments on the control of operant behavior by complex discriminative stimuli (e.g., Fetterman, 1996).

Categorization and Discrimination

Let's return to the pigeon—the favorite participant in experiments on operant behavior since Skinner first used them in the 1940s and 1950s. One reason the pigeon is a popular subject is that its eyesight is very good. Pigeons have color vision, for example, and they can discriminate between complex and colorful stimuli. Nowadays, a typical pigeon box (like the blue jay box, just described) is outfitted with a computer screen. This allows enormous flexibility in the type of image that can be presented as a potential S^D.

Trees, water, and Margaret

Herrnstein, Loveland, and Cable (1976) had a pigeon box with a screen that allowed them to show the birds a long series of color slides. The birds viewed each slide for about 30 seconds. In the presence of half the slides, pecking the key was reinforced. In the presence of the other slides, pecking was not reinforced. The logic of the experiment is again like Skinner's rats. In this case, the bird should have learned to peck only when a positive slide (the S^D) was showing on the screen.

The birds did exactly that, but what made the experiment interesting was the pictures that actually made up the slide show. Each bird was trained and tested with about 1700 slides (Figure 8.2). For some birds, the slides that signaled that pecking would be reinforced contained an image of a tree; slides that signaled no food did not contain a tree. The slides were taken during all four seasons in New England. Thus, a "positive" tree picture was sometimes a shot of a tree in the summer, sometimes in the winter, or sometimes in the fall. The tree could be the focus of a scene, or it could be an extra item in the background. Many slides contained only parts of trees, and the trees were photographed from many angles and vantage points. Despite the fact that the tree images were so variable, the birds learned to discriminate tree slides from other slides (pecking more during tree slides than "non-tree" slides) over many sessions of training. And, just as important, when the birds were tested with new slides they had never seen before, they also responded mainly if the new slide contained a tree. The pigeons hadn't just memorized particular pictures—they generalized to new examples, too. The birds had learned to categorize the pictures as those that contained trees and those that did not.

Other pigeons in the Herrnstein et al. (1976) experiment were trained and tested with other categories. Some pigeons learned to peck in the presence of pictures that contained images of water. These birds also saw hundreds of slides, some of which contained images of water (indoors as well as outdoors, during any season), and some of which did not. Only pictures with water signaled that pecking would be reinforced. The birds learned to categorize accurately, and they also responded accurately to new pictures. A final group of birds learned about a specific human female. Here again there were hundreds of pictures, half of which contained Margaret (inside, outside, dressed for any season, and with or without other people), and half of which did not. The birds learned to peck only in the presence of slides containing Margaret, and not slides containing other humans, or no human. And, once again, the pigeons accurately responded to new pictures they had never seen before.

The pigeons' feat is impressive because whatever defined the tree, water, and Margaret categories was fuzzy and hard to describe. They were "polymorphous" categories in the sense that no single feature was necessary or

Negative   Positive

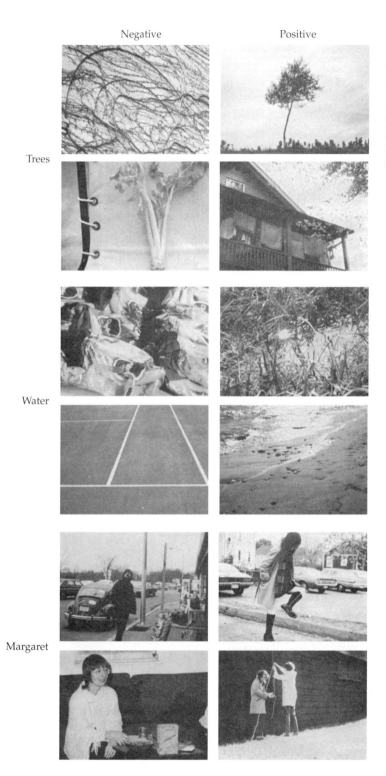

Trees

Water

Margaret

Figure 8.2 Examples of test slides from the tree, water, and Margaret categories in the study by Herrnstein et al. (1976). Pigeons correctly responded in the presence of the positive slides and did not respond in the presence of the negative slides. (From Herrnstein et al., 1976.)

sufficient to identify them. Trees can be green, orange, brown, or full of flowers; they can have trunks that are brown, grey, white, and so forth. New trees will have some, but not all, of these different features. And many non-tree slides, such as a stalk of celery, will have some of the same features, too. The categories are complex and open-ended. This makes them very different from "light on versus light off." But when you think about it, polymorphous stimulus sets are probably very common in the natural world, because the stimuli we respond to are inherently variable from trial to trial or over time. Many animals presumably learn to identify many stimuli in their natural environments from different vantage points. It shouldn't surprise us that learning and perception processes can make sense of variable input.

Other categories

Pigeons have been taught to categorize an astounding range of stimuli in experiments using similar methods. In the first paper ever published on **categorization** in pigeons (to my knowledge), Herrnstein and Loveland (1964) showed that pigeons could discriminate pictures containing people from pictures that did not. Later experiments (Herrnstein & de Villiers, 1980) used underwater pictures shot on coral reefs that either contained images of fish or did not. The birds had no trouble learning to discriminate between these types of slides, which seemed unnatural in the sense that no living pigeon— or ancestor of one—had ever needed to learn about tropical fish! Other experiments have shown that pigeons can discriminate between animals versus nonanimals and kingfishers versus other birds (Roberts & Mazmanian, 1988), and also letters of the alphabet (e.g., Lea & Ryan, 1990). You may remember another classic experiment that was described at the beginning of Chapter 1, where pigeons learned to discriminate between color images of paintings by Monet and Picasso (Watanabe et al., 1995). In that case, Monet-trained birds generalized to new images by Cezanne and Renoir, whereas Picasso-trained birds generalized to Braque and Matisse.

Ed Wasserman and his collaborators at the University of Iowa have run many experiments in which pigeons learn to discriminate between four categories at the same time (e.g., Bhatt, Wasserman, Reynolds, & Knauss, 1988; Wasserman & Bhatt, 1992; Wasserman, Kiedinger, & Bhatt, 1988). In a typical experiment, pigeons are shown images on a small computer screen and then they are required to peck one of four keys located near the corners of the screen (Figure 8.3). The picture might contain one of several examples of cars, chairs, flowers, or cats (or sometimes people, as in Figure 8.3). To receive a reinforcer, the pigeon must peck one of the keys depending on whether the image on the screen is a cat, car, flower, or chair. The birds thus essentially report the "name" of the image by pecking a particular key. The birds learn this task rapidly and accurately (Figure 8.4A). They also seem to do equally well with categories of human-made things (e.g., cars and chairs) or natural things (e.g., cats and flowers). It is not that pigeons can't tell the difference between different category members: If they are required to peck one key for some cats and another key for others, the birds can learn this

Ed Wasserman

(A)

(B)

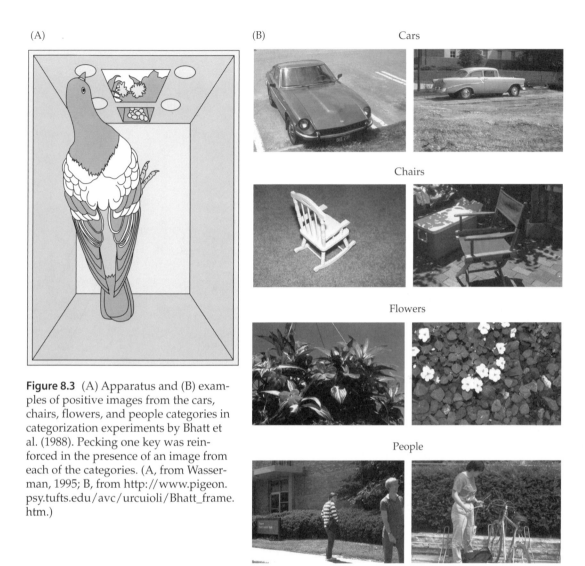

Figure 8.3 (A) Apparatus and (B) examples of positive images from the cars, chairs, flowers, and people categories in categorization experiments by Bhatt et al. (1988). Pecking one key was reinforced in the presence of an image from each of the categories. (A, from Wasserman, 1995; B, from http://www.pigeon.psy.tufts.edu/avc/urcuioli/Bhatt_frame.htm.)

too. Thus, the pictures that make up each category appear to be similar but still discriminably different to the birds.

When pigeons are tested with new images they have never seen before—new exemplars of the cat, car, flower, and chair categories—they respond well above chance, although performance is a bit worse than with images the birds have specifically been trained with (see Figure 8.4B). Transfer to new stimuli can be impressive. In one of my favorite experiments of this series, the birds were trained with a very large set of pictures that were never repeated. From the beginning, every time a picture of, say, a car appeared, it was a picture the birds had never seen before. (To be properly cautious, the experimenters used pictures of people instead of cats on the grounds

Figure 8.4 Results of an experiment in which pigeons learned four categories (cars, chairs, flowers, and cats). (A) Acquisition. (B) "Transfer" tests in which the birds were shown new slides (as well as old slides they had previously been trained with). Although accuracy declined a little with the new slides, it was still well above chance (25%). (After Bhatt et al., 1988.)

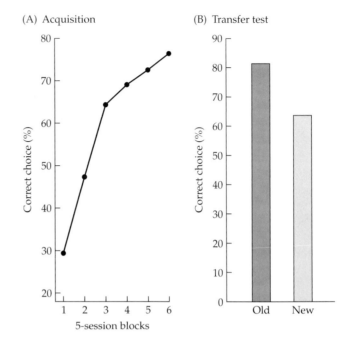

(A) Acquisition

(B) Transfer test

that cats, but not people, tend to look too much alike—although they were being a bit anthropocentric in hindsight.) Even when exemplars were never repeated, the pigeons rapidly learned to discriminate between cars, chairs, flowers, and people.

The ability to respond correctly to new stimuli is a crucial part of categorization. One reason it is important to test the animals with novel images (called **transfer tests**) after training is that pigeons have excellent memories for specific photographs. Based on experiments by Vaughan and Green (1984), investigators have long suspected that pigeons can remember 320 different photographs, and a more recent experiment suggests they have a capacity to remember over 800 (Cook, Levison, Gillett, & Blaisdell, 2005). Therefore, if experimenters do not test transfer to new images, it is possible that the birds have merely learned to respond to each specific training slide. Interestingly, to make the categorization of new stimuli more accurate, it is best if the bird has experience with many different examples during training. For example, during training, Bhatt (1988; described in Wasserman & Bhatt, 1992) gave different groups of pigeons either one example of each category (a single cat, car, flower, or chair set the occasion for pecks to the different keys), four examples of each category, or twelve examples of each category. Not surprisingly, the task involving only one example of each category was the easiest for the pigeons to learn. But as Figure 8.5 shows, transfer to new pictures, after training with only one example of each type, was rather bad (25% is no better than chance, because one-fourth of the guesses would have been right). The more examples used in training, the

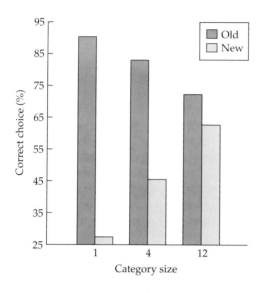

Figure 8.5 Categorization after training with categories of different sizes (1, 4, or 12 different pictures in each category). Although larger categories were more difficult to learn (see responding to "old" slides), they led to more accurate categorization when tested with new slides. (After Wasserman & Bhatt, 1992; data from Bhatt, 1988.)

better was the transfer to new images (see Figure 8.5). This result illustrates an important point: If your goal is to increase performance in new situations, then the more examples in training the better, even though the learning may be a little difficult.

How do they do it?

The experiments just described provide nice demonstrations of categorization in pigeons, but they do not tell us much about how the pigeons accomplish this feat. You might be surprised to know that theories we have considered in previous chapters do extremely well here.

For example, one approach to categorization is called **feature theory**. This approach accepts the idea that all pictures contain many different features, and the bird must essentially learn which features signal reinforcement and which features do not. This is a kind of analysis we saw as early as Chapter 1, and the Rescorla-Wagner model (as well as other theories described in Chapters 4, 5, and 6) readily applies. For example, consider a pigeon learning to discriminate images of cats from non-cats. One picture of a cat might contain several features, such as whiskers, ears, white paws, and a tail. The picture is therefore a compound stimulus, made up of a large number of elements that might not be that different from simpler compound stimuli that are made up of tones and lights. When the compound is paired with a reinforcer, each feature might be associated with it a little; the associative strength of each increasing a bit with each trial. On a second trial, the slide might contain such features as whiskers, a tabby face, and gray paws. The associative strength of these cues would likewise increase. On the next trial—a negative trial—the slide might show a dog rather than a cat. Here, we might have another set of features, say, whiskers, floppy ears, brown color, and a tail. Each of these cues would receive a decrement in associative

Figure 8.6 Faces used in the categorization experiment by Huber and Lenz (1993). (After Huber & Lenz, 1993.)

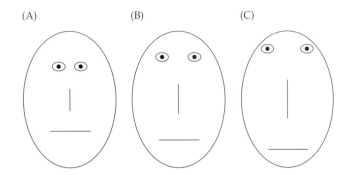

strength, and possibly some inhibition. In the long run, after a number of trials like these, several features would have associative strength. Some might be negative (inhibitory), some might be positive (excitatory), and many redundant or irrelevant features might have little associative strength. If a brand new cat or dog image were then presented, the system would detect its features, add their associative strengths, and then respond as a function of the sum of their strengths. In this way, a feature theory like the Rescorla-Wagner model could explain the bird's categorization performance. Given what you already know about the Rescorla-Wagner model, and the related connectionist theories described in Chapters 1 and 6 (e.g., McClelland & Rumelhart, 1985), you can see how this can all come together. Theories of conditioning are relevant here.

To test this kind of process, it has been necessary to present stimuli with features that the experimenter can manipulate easily. Photographs of cats, cars, trees, and Margaret contain features that are just too difficult to analyze. Huber and Lenz (1993) showed pigeons images of faces like the ones shown in Figure 8.6. The faces actually varied in four ways: the size of the forehead, the space between the eyes, the length of the nose, and the size of the chin below the mouth. As the pictures in the figure illustrate, each of these dimensions could have one of three different values (i.e., there were three forehead sizes, three widths of gaps between the eyes, three chin sizes, and so on). Moving from left to right in Figure 8.6, each feature shown was given an arbitrary value of -1, 0, and $+1$. On many trials, Huber and Lenz then showed the birds pictures of a number of faces made up of different combinations of these features. Pecking was reinforced if the face contained features with values that summed to more than zero. (Of the three faces shown in Figure 8.6, only [C] would have been reinforced.) The birds learned the discrimination. And, more important, their rate of pecking was a simple function of the sum of the features' values. Jitsumori and Yoshihara (1997) reached a similar conclusion in an experiment with photographs of 25 real people showing happy or angry expressions. Happy faces were reinforced. Before testing, the pictures were then doctored electronically so that happy and sad eyes (and eyebrows) and/or mouths were removed from the photographs or switched. The rate of pecking to the test faces was a function of the weighted sum of the happy features. The pigeons appeared to learn about the relevant mouth and eye features, and then respond according to their values. The feature-learning perspective is consistent with many findings in the categorization literature (see Loidolt, Aust, Meran, & Huber, 2003, for another example).

However, with some sets of stimuli, pigeons appear to respond as if they have learned a sort of **prototype** of the stimuli in the category (Jitsumori, 1996; Huber & Lenz, 1996; von Fersen & Lea, 1990). In this case, the birds responded to stimuli to the extent that the stimuli were similar to a kind of average cat or chair, rather than the sums of features. According to **prototype theory**, exposure to the different types of trials results in the formation of just such a prototype (e.g., Posner & Keele, 1968). To put it simply, Wasserman's pigeons might have formed a representation of the average cat, average car, average chair, and average flower, and then responded to new examples depending on how similar they were to one of the prototypes. One problem with this kind of approach is that results suggesting the learning of a prototype can often be explained by a feature theory (see Pearce, 1994). For example, in Chapter 1 we saw that a connectionist network (using the Rescorla-Wagner equation) can learn what looks like the prototype of a "dog" or "cat," even though the subject is merely associating different features. The idea is that the most predictive features become associated in a kind of net, analogous to a prototype and, with enough common features, one gets responding as if the animal was generalizing from a prototype (see also Mackintosh, 1995).

A third possible way animals might learn to categorize is the simplest way of all. According to **exemplar theory**, a bird might learn and remember each picture or image presented to them in the training phase. When novel stimuli are tested, the bird might then generalize from all of these exemplars and respond to the extent the new picture is similar to a picture that was reinforced before. The approach assumes that animals can remember a very large number of pictures. This is not impossible; as mentioned before, pigeons can remember a very large number of individual slides (Cook et al., 2005; Vaughan & Green, 1984). Furthermore, the exemplar approach has been very successful in understanding categorization in humans (e.g., Kruschke, 1992; Medin & Schaffer, 1978; Nosofsky, 1987). The idea that animals learn about whole configurations of stimuli and then respond to new stimuli, according to how well they generalize to them, is also consistent with the Pearce (1987, 1994) configural theory we encountered in Chapters 4 and 5.

At this point in time, it is probably safe to say that there is no one theory that explains all categorization in pigeons (Huber, 2001), but it should be clear that this fascinating example of animal learning is not miraculous. It almost certainly involves learning processes that are similar to the ones studied in experiments on classical conditioning. This is not really accidental. We have always studied classical conditioning in part because we think its principles will apply to other, more complex-looking examples of learning—like categorization.

Basic Processes of Generalization and Discrimination

Research on categorization is part of a long tradition in learning theory bent on figuring out how we generalize and discriminate between stimuli. That tradition has uncovered a number of basic facts and tools that will almost certainly help us understand more complex forms of learning and behavior.

The generalization gradient

First, as implied above (and also mentioned in previous chapters), behavior that has been reinforced in the presence of one stimulus generalizes quite lawfully to similar stimuli. In a classic pigeon experiment, Guttman and Kalish (1956) reinforced pecking at a simple key that was illuminated with a pure color (e.g., a yellowish-orange color with a wavelength of 580 nm). After training for several days, the birds were tested with trials in which the color of the keylight was varied in many steps between green (520 nm), yellow, orange, and finally into red (640 nm). The tests were conducted in extinction, which means that none of these new test colors were ever reinforced, and there was thus no payoff to respond to any of them. Nonetheless, the birds pecked at the new key colors if their wavelength was similar enough to the original 580 nm value. The results are shown in Figure 8.7. This is a well-known example of a **stimulus generalization gradient**—responding to a new stimulus depends on its similarity to a stimulus that has already been reinforced. Generalization gradients have been shown for a wide range of stimuli. For example, more recent experiments have shown similar gradients when pigeons are first trained to peck in the presence of computer images of three-dimensional objects, and the objects are then rotated in virtual space (e.g., Cook & Katz, 1999; Peissig, Young, Wasserman, & Biederman, 2000; Spetch & Friedman, 2003).

Notice that, if the birds had not learned about the color of the key, they might have responded to any keylight—regardless of its color. Thus, the steepness of the generalization gradient—the rate at which responding declines as the stimulus is changed—indicates how much the responding

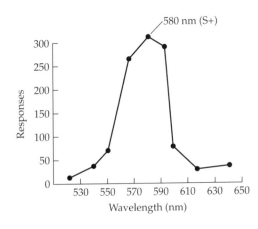

Figure 8.7 A stimulus generalization gradient. Responding by pigeons to a key illuminated by different colors (wavelengths in nm) after being reinforced for pecking a key of 580 nm. (After Guttman & Kalish, 1956.)

actually depends on a particular stimulus dimension. One of the major points of research on stimulus control is that the shape of the gradient is not automatically controlled by cues that are present when an operant is reinforced. *Instead, the shape of the gradient can be affected by learning.* Often, another stimulus has to be nonreinforced; that is, the S^D must be discriminated from an S^Δ (see Chapter 7). For example, Jenkins and Harrison (1960, 1962) reinforced pigeons for pecking a key that was white when the key was illuminated on each trial. The experiments manipulated the presence of a 1000-Hz tone that could be sounded in the background. In one condition, pecking the key was reinforced if the tone was on, but not reinforced if the tone was off. As you can imagine, the birds eventually responded mainly when the tone was on. In another condition, the birds learned to discriminate between two tones: Pecking was reinforced when the 1000-Hz tone was on, but pecking was not reinforced when a slightly lower tone (950 Hz) was on. Here again, you can imagine that the birds eventually confined their responding to when the 1000-Hz tone was on. In a final condition, the birds received no discrimination training. The 1000-Hz tone was always on, and the birds were reinforced whenever they pecked the illuminated key.

The crucial results are from a final generalization test in which the birds were tested for pecking in the presence of tones of other frequencies; test results are summarized in Figure 8.8. The steepness of the gradient depended on the previous training. When the birds had not received explicit discrimination training, the generalization gradient was flat, indicating equal responding to all of the tested tones—that is, there was no evidence of stimulus control by the tone in this situation (see Rudolph & van Houten, 1977, for an extension). In contrast, when the birds had been reinforced while the 1000-Hz tone was on but not reinforced when the tone was off, there was a lovely stimulus generalization gradient. And the sharpest gradient of all was produced by the group that had learned to discriminate 1000 Hz from

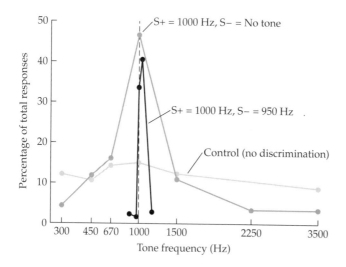

Figure 8.8 The sharpness of the generalization gradient depends on the type of training. When pigeons had to discriminate between a 1000-Hz tone S+ and a 950-Hz tone S−, the gradient was much sharper than when the pigeons discriminated between the 1000-Hz tone (S+) and silence (S−). The control group received no discrimination training with the tone before the test, and they showed little stimulus control by the tone. (After Jenkins & Harrison, 1960, 1962.)

950 Hz. These birds showed a maximum of responding at 1000 Hz, and virtually nothing to other stimuli. Thus, stimulus control is powerfully influenced by discrimination training.

Why should this be true? You can probably imagine that the birds had learned to pay attention to the tone when they had to discriminate it from silence or a tone of another frequency. We discussed the role of attention in learning about signals for reinforcement in Chapter 4, when we considered models of classical conditioning (Mackintosh, 1975; Pearce & Hall, 1980). Notice that the context was always present when the birds were reinforced in the tone's presence but not in its absence. We can therefore think of this situation as one in which the tone—plus context—was reinforced, but the context alone was not (TC+, C– training, where T is the tone and C is the context). Mackintosh's theory predicts that attention will be paid to the relevant predictor, or the birds might learn that the tone is the main predictor of the reinforcer, as is implied by models like the Rescorla-Wagner model.

Another process that can affect the steepness of the generalization gradient is **inhibition**, which might have developed when Jenkins and Harrison nonreinforced the 950-Hz S–. Honig, Boneau, Burstein, and Pennypacker (1963) ran an experiment that demonstrated the importance of inhibition in this sort of situation. The experiment included two groups of pigeons that were taught to discriminate a plain white key from a white key with a vertical black bar presented on it (Figure 8.9). For one of the groups, pecking was reinforced when the vertical black bar was present on the white key, but pecking was not reinforced when the bar was absent. The other group received the opposite treatment: Pecking was reinforced when the key was merely white, and not reinforced when the vertical black bar was present. Not surprisingly, both groups learned to peck when appropriate. But what

Figure 8.9 Excitatory and inhibitory generalization gradients with line-tilt stimuli. For one group of pigeons, a vertical black bar on a white key was S+, and the white key without the bar was S–. This group showed the familiar gradient when lines of different tilts were tested. For another group of pigeons, the white key without the vertical black bar was S+ and the white key with the bar was S–. For this group, the vertical black bar suppressed responding; this inhibitory effect decreased as the tilt was changed. (After Honig et al., 1963.)

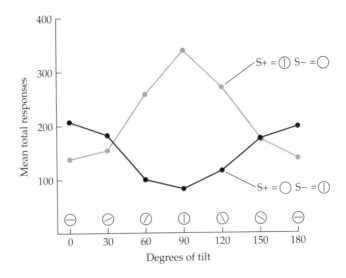

was interesting, again, was the responding that emerged during a final generalization test. Both groups were now presented with the usual vertical black bar on the key, but on different trials it was presented at different angles—deviating from vertical to horizontal. The results are summarized in Figure 8.9. Notice that the group that had been trained to peck in the presence of the vertical black bar showed another gradient like the ones we've seen in previous figures. There was a clear peak with vertical, and then responding declined lawfully as the angle of the bar changed.

The new result was the one with the group for which the vertical black bar had signaled no reinforcement. In this case, the birds responded little to the vertical black bar, but pecking increased systematically as the angle of the bar differed. In this group, the vertical black bar was actively suppressing the pecking response. This result implies that inhibition develops to a stimulus that signals nonreinforcement of an operant response. Again, this is not necessarily surprising based on what you already know. Notice that this group received reinforcement with the white key (W+) and nonreinforcement when the vertical black bar was added to the white key (BW–). This is another case of feature-negative discrimination learning (see Chapters 5 and 6).

One point worth making is that this line of research came out of the Skinnerian tradition, where inferring unobserved processes is somewhat frowned upon. In the end, investigators came to see the value of inferring processes like inhibition and attention—processes that were only indirectly observable.

Interactions between gradients

A role for inhibition in discrimination learning had been anticipated in earlier papers by Kenneth Spence (e.g., Spence, 1936). He suggested that an S+ will receive some excitatory conditioning when it is reinforced, and that the excitation will generalize from it to other similar stimuli. In a similar way, S– will receive some inhibitory conditioning when it is nonreinforced, and this inhibitory conditioning will also be ready to generalize. The gradients shown in Figure 8.9 seem nicely consistent with Spence's theory—as well as the many conditioning theories that we studied in Chapters 4 and 5, which trace their origins to Spence's approach.

Spence's theory generates some other interesting predictions, though, and these are worth considering. Figure 8.10 shows the theoretical result of training a discrimination between two very similar stimuli. Reinforcement of a 550-nm keylight will condition excitation to 550 nm, and this generalizes to similar stimuli. Nonreinforcement of a similar keylight color, 570 nm, conditions inhibition to it, and this likewise generalizes. Not surprising, right? But another implication is interesting. Suppose we were to test responding to all the stimuli surrounding S+ and S–. Spence assumed that responding to the new stimuli would depend on how much inhibition and excitation generalize to the new stimuli from S+ and S–. Inhibition (with its negative value) would subtract from excitation. Figure 8.10 shows the net generalization that would lead to predicted responding. Notice something rather subtle and interesting. Because of the inhibition generalizing

Kenneth Spence

Figure 8.10 Hypothetical excitatory and inhibitory gradients after discrimination training with a 550-nm key light as S+ and a 570-nm key light as S–. During generalization tests with keylights of other colors, the predicted level of responding (dark gray circles) is simply the difference between the amount of excitation and inhibition that generalizes there. Notice that generalization of inhibition causes the peak of responding to move away from S–; in this example, it would be at 540 nm rather than 550 nm, a peak shift. (After Rilling, 1977.)

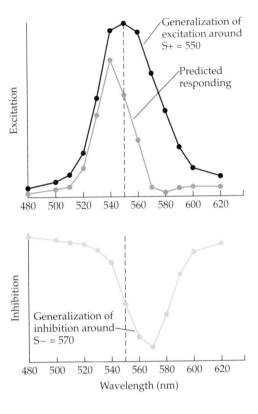

from S–, the theory does not predict the most responding at the trained S+. Instead, it predicts even more responding with stimuli that are further away from S–! That is, the peak of the generalization gradient should shift away from S–, to a stimulus (540 nm) that was never actually reinforced.

This prediction was nicely confirmed in several experiments that were conducted many years after Spence's theory was published. The most famous is one reported by Hanson (1959), who was working in Guttman and Kalish's lab. One of Hanson's groups of pigeons received a treatment very similar to the one just described. These pigeons were reinforced for pecking a 550-nm keylight, and not reinforced for pecking an extremely similar 555-nm keylight. A second group also received discrimination training, except that the nonreinforced S– was a distant 590 nm. A third group—a control—simply received reinforcement with 550 nm. Generalization was then tested by giving the birds the chance to respond to keylights of different wavelengths. The results are shown in Figure 8.11. These results are justly famous—it is clear that the groups given the discrimination training showed more responding to 540 nm than to 550 nm. This was especially true of pigeons given the 555-nm S–, which should have generalized most strongly to 550 nm. This phenomenon, in which the peak of the generalization gradient moves away from S–, is called **peak shift**. It has been shown in both operant and classical conditioning (Weiss & Weissman, 1992) and with a variety of stimuli, includ-

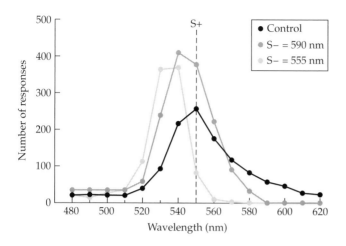

Figure 8.11 Peak shift. Three groups of pigeons were reinforced for responding in the presence of a 550-nm keylight. One group was nonreinforced when presented with 555 nm and another group was nonreinforced when presented with 590 nm. A control group received reinforcement with 550 nm, without any nonreinforced trials. The peak of responding for the two experimental groups shifted away from S–. (After Hanson, 1959.)

ing intensity of the stimulus (e.g., Ernst, Engberg, & Thomas, 1971), its spatial position on the computer screen (Cheng, Spetch, & Johnston, 1997), and even the tilt of the Skinner box floor (Riccio, Urda, & Thomas, 1966). It has even been shown in a categorization task (Mackintosh, 1995).

Peak shift is an important phenomenon for several reasons. It suggests that the highest level of responding can somewhat paradoxically occur to stimuli that have never been directly reinforced. It suggests the possible role of inhibition. And like other aspects of the psychology of stimulus control, it might have implications for evolution. For instance, in a discussion of beak color preferences in female zebra finches, Weary, Guilford, and Weisman (1992) suggested that peak shift might play a role in explaining why elaborate characteristics and extreme coloration might evolve in members of one sex. Female zebra finches tend to have orange beaks, but they prefer to mate with males that have bright red beaks. This preference is at least partly learned; it depends on the female's early experience with males with red beaks (e.g., Weisman, Schackleton, Ratcliffe, Weary, & Boag, 1994). During that experience, if a male's red beak is associated with reinforcement (perhaps sexual in nature), but an orange female's is not, then females might prefer to mate with males possessing extremely red beaks that differ even more from the female's orange S–. If this speculation is true, males with more extreme-colored beaks would have more offspring in the future. Peak shift in the female's mating preference would yield something like "beak shift" in the evolution of the male's beak coloration.

Spence's ideas about the interactions of gradients around S+ and S– have at least one other implication. Suppose we train an animal so that a relatively bright stimulus is reinforced (S+) and a relatively dark stimulus is not (S–). This could lead to gradients of excitation and inhibition around S+ and S–, as illustrated in Figure 8.12. As before, the strength of responding to a given stimulus will depend on the difference in the amount of excitation and inhibition that generalize to it. If given a choice between S+ and S–, the animal will therefore prefer S+. But now, suppose the animal is given a choice between

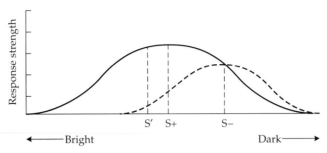

Figure 8.12 Transposition. Hypothetical excitatory (solid line) and inhibitory (dashed line) generalization gradients after discrimination training with a relatively bright S+ and a darker S–. If given a choice between a bright (S+) and an even brighter stimulus (S′), the animal might choose the brighter S′. This might occur because of the larger difference between the excitation and inhibition generalizing there, and not because the animal has learned a relationship between the stimuli ("always choose the brighter stimulus").

S+ and an even brighter stimulus, S′. The gradients in Figure 8.12 suggest that, in this case, the animal should prefer S′ over S+; that is, it should choose the even brighter stimulus. Such a result has been shown in a number of experiments (e.g., Honig, 1962; Lazareva, Wasserman, & Young, 2005), and is called **transposition**. Transposition seems to suggest that the animal responds to the relationship between two stimuli (i.e., their relative brightness) rather than their absolute properties. Yet, the power of Spence's analysis is that it explains transposition without supposing the animal learns about stimulus relationships. One problem for Spence is that transposition can still occur under conditions that can only be explained by relational learning. For example, Gonzalez, Gentry, and Bitterman (1954) trained chimps to respond to the middle stimulus of three stimuli that differed in size. When they tested the chimps with three altogether new stimuli (also varying in size), the chimps again chose the middle stimulus, even though Spence would predict a choice of the extreme stimulus closest to the original S+. One conclusion is that animals do sometimes learn about the relationships between stimuli (see also Lazareva et al., 2005). A similar interpretation has been provided for the peak shift effect in humans (e.g., Thomas, Mood, Morrison, & Wiertelak, 1991), although the role of relational learning here may be more consistent with the behavior of humans than that of other animals (e.g., Thomas & Barker, 1964).

   To summarize, organisms generalize lawfully from one stimulus to other stimuli that are similar. This process interacts with discrimination learning, though. The peak shift phenomenon suggests that generalization gradients can influence the results of explicit discrimination training. At the same time, discrimination learning can influence the extent to which animals generalize from stimulus to stimulus. One point is that discrimination and generalization processes are always interacting. Another is that theories of associative learning that emphasize inhibition, excitation, and generalization go a surprising distance in explaining stimulus control phenomena.

Perceptual learning

Discriminations can often be learned between impressively similar stimuli. For example, wine connoisseurs eventually make fine discriminations between different wines and vineyards, bird watchers make subtle discriminations between different birds (Figure 8.13), and musicians become exquisitely expert at discriminating different musical intervals and chords. It is possible, of course, that such fine discriminations can result from dif-

Figure 8.13 Experts can make astonishingly subtle discriminations between similar stimuli. You may recognize these birds as wrens, but only a seasoned bird watcher can discriminate the Bewick's Wren, the Carolina Wren, and the Marsh Wren among them. (Plate from *A Field Guide to the Birds of Eastern and Central North America*, 5th Edition by Roger Tory Peterson. Illustrations © 2002 by Marital Trust B u/a Roger Tory Peterson. Reprinted by permission of Houghton Mifflin Company.)

ferential reinforcement of the different stimuli (following the principles we have been discussing). But there is also evidence that discriminations can be further facilitated by mere exposure to the similar stimuli—without any differential reinforcement.

In a classic experiment, Gibson and Walk (1956) hung both a large metal rectangle and a triangle on the wall of the home cage of a group of rats for several weeks. Compared to rats that had no exposure to the rectangle and triangle during this period, the rats exposed to these cues were quicker to discriminate between them when one shape was eventually used as an S+ and the other shape as an S– in a discrimination experiment. Simple exposure somehow made the two different shapes easier to discriminate, a phenomenon known as **perceptual learning**. Because neither stimulus was reinforced in the initial phase, the rules for discrimination learning we have been considering don't easily apply; there would need to be some differential reinforcement of one stimulus over the other to achieve differences in excitation or inhibition. One idea was that exposure somehow led the animals to differentiate the stimuli (Gibson & Gibson, 1955), but the mechanisms surrounding the idea were vague (but see Saksida, 1999).

Theories of conditioning seem even further challenged by perceptual learning because they usually predict that nonreinforced exposure to a stimulus should reduce its conditionability—that is, it should cause latent inhibition. However, notice that Gibson and Walk were not interested in rate of conditioning, per se. They were looking at the rate at which two stimuli were discriminated, and not the rate of conditioning to the stimuli individually. In principle, the rate of learning could be quite slow, but the *difference* in responding to S+ and S– might develop relatively quickly.

All of this was recognized in an interesting approach suggested by Ian McLaren and Nicholas Mackintosh (McLaren & Mackintosh, 2000; McLaren, Kaye, & Mackintosh, 1989; see also Hall, 1991, 1996). McLaren and Mackintosh begin with the familiar assumption that any stimulus is made up of many features or elements. Organisms will generalize between two stimuli, and thus have trouble discriminating between them, to the extent that they share common features. For example, the circles in Figure 8.14 represent the sets of elements that are contained in each of two stimuli, A and B. Each stimulus has some unique elements (a and b) and some common, overlapping, elements—x. If one presents Stimulus A, one actually presents a combination of unique and shared elements (a and x together); if one presents Stimulus B, one similarly presents b and x. If Stimulus A is paired with a reinforcer, a and x would both acquire associative strength. The organism would respond to Stimulus B (bx), and therefore show generalization, because the common element (x) had received some conditioning.

When combined with what we already know about learning, this way of conceptualizing Stimuli A and B actually leads to at

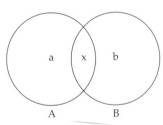

Figure 8.14 Two similar stimuli (A and B, represented by circles) are theoretically composed of unique elements (regions a and b) and also common, overlapping elements (region x). This has interesting implications for perceptual learning in which simple exposure to stimuli A and B may facilitate the learning of a discrimination between the two.

least three mechanisms that can contribute to perceptual learning. First, notice that preexposure to Stimuli A and B (as in the Gibson and Walk experiment) would really involve exposure to the two compounds, ax and bx. Since neither Stimulus A or B is reinforced in the preexposure phase, the consequence is that ax and bx would become latently inhibited—they would therefore be more difficult to condition in the next phase. But notice what actually happens to the separate elements. If there are four preexposures to Stimulus A and four preexposures to Stimulus B, there would be four preexposures to element a, four preexposures to element b, and eight preexposures to element x. That is, *the common elements receive more latent inhibition than the unique elements*. This means that the common elements should be especially difficult to condition. And, since generalization depends upon the conditioning of common elements, there will be less generalization (and easier discrimination) between Stimulus A and Stimulus B. We have just uncovered one explanation of perceptual learning.

Some nifty experiments by Mackintosh, Kaye, and Bennett (1991) support this approach. These experimenters used a taste aversion procedure in which rats drank saline and sucrose solutions that could be mixed with a third flavor, lemon. Let's call saline, sucrose, and lemon, stimuli a, b, and x (respectively), just to keep them consistent with Figure 8.14. The idea behind the experiments is sketched in Table 8.1. Mackintosh et al. (1991) knew that if rats simply received a pairing of saline (a) with illness, and were then tested with sucrose (b), there would be no generalization of the taste aversion from a to b. But things were different in the experiment, because the rats received conditioning with the saline-lemon compound (ax) and then testing with the sucrose-lemon compound (bx). As demonstrated by Group 1, there was a lot of generalization of the aversion from ax to bx, which is not surprising given the common lemon flavor (x). But if the rats had first received preexposures to ax and bx (Group 2), there was much less generalization between them. This is perceptual learning; preexposures to the compound stimuli made them easier to discriminate. The interesting group was Group 3. This group received the same preexposures to x—but alone, without a and b. After conditioning with the ax compound, this group also showed little generalization from ax to bx. This tells us that preexposure to the common element (x) is alone sufficient to make it easier to discrimi-

TABLE 8.1 Design and results of a perceptual learning experiment

		Phase		Result
Group	Pre-exposure	Conditioning	Test	Was there generalization between ax and bx?
1	—	ax+	bx?	Yes
2	6 ax–, 6 bx–	ax+	bx?	No
3	12 x–	ax+	bx?	No

Source: From Mackintosh, Kaye, & Bennet, 1991.

nate the compounds. Perceptual learning can thus result, at least in part, from latent inhibition to common elements.

But there is apparently even more than this going on (as other experiments reported by Mackintosh et al. [1991] suggested). McLaren et al. (1989) noted that, during exposures to complex cues, animals will learn to associate the various elements (e.g., Rescorla & Durlach, 1981). During ax, they might learn to associate a with x; and during bx, they might learn to associate b with x. (This is simply sensory preconditioning, a phenomenon we discussed in Chapter 3.) But think about an interesting consequence of this. Because x is associated with b, x will retrieve b when the rat is being exposed to ax. Casually speaking, the rat will "expect" b during ax, but it isn't there. Based on what we know about inhibition in classical conditioning, the rat will adjust its expectations accordingly: It will learn to expect "no b" in the presence of a. And, for exactly the same reason, the rat will learn to expect "no a" in the presence of b. McLaren et al. (1989) thus noted that the familiar rules of associative learning predict that mixed exposures to ax and bx will create inhibitory associations between a and b. This is a second reason why preexposure to ax and bx might reduce generalization between them. Consistent with the idea, Dwyer, Bennett, and Mackintosh (2001) have demonstrated inhibitory associations between saline and sucrose when rats receive intermixed exposures to saline-lemon and sucrose-lemon drinks. Inhibition between unique elements is thus a second mechanism behind perceptual learning.

There is a third mechanism as well. If the stimuli are especially complex (i.e., composed of a large number of different features), then an organism might be able to sample only a small portion of the elements on any given trial. If we associate those elements on each trial, and then sample and associate some new elements on each successive trial, a whole network of interconnected elements can be built up over trials. In effect, associations between the different elements will create a "unitized" representation of the stimulus (McLaren & Mackintosh, 2000) in the same way different features might call up a unitized category. Such a representation would allow a subset of the features sampled on any given trial to activate the entire representation (this process is sometimes called "pattern completion," and is a property of many connectionist models, e.g., McClelland & Rumelhart, 1985). There is evidence that unitization does operate. If a rat is put into a box and immediately given an electric shock, it will not learn to associate the box with the shock (e.g., Fanselow, 1990). But if the shock is delayed for a minute or two (so the rat has more time to learn about the box), or if the rat is exposed to the box for a minute or two the day before being placed in the box and immediately given a shock, then the rat will readily learn about the box (Fanselow, 1990; Kiernan & Westbrook, 1993). Without the extra exposure, there is no unitized representation of the box. Rudy and O'Reilly (1999) have further shown that different features must be experienced at the same time (rather than presented separately) if exposure to the different features is to facilitate conditioning. Animals do seem to form representations of complex stimuli when they are simply exposed to them. Unitization is thus a third possible mechanism that can lead to perceptual learning.

There are several points to remember from all of this. First, two stimuli can become more discriminable if we are merely exposed to them without differential reinforcement. Second, this might occur if stimuli are composed of many different elements that can be latently inhibited or interassociated. Third, by taking this sort of position, we find that the laws of learning we have discussed in previous chapters are once again really happening everywhere. The basic learning principles we have already studied seem to apply here, although there is probably room for additional processes (e.g., Symonds, Hall, & Bailey, 2002).

Mediated generalization and acquired equivalence

Other learning processes can actually lead us to *generalize* more between two different stimuli as a function of experience. The idea is that if two stimuli are each associated with a common third stimulus, then we will begin to generalize between the stimuli. The idea is simple but powerful: If you associate both Dave and Bill with motorcycles, you may start treating Dave and Bill as being more alike.

In a simple demonstration of this phenomenon (Table 8.2), Honey and Hall (1989) paired two auditory cues (A and N) with food. The common association with food was expected to increase the generalization between A and N. To test this hypothesis, N was subsequently paired with an electric shock on several trials, so that N aroused fear. Honey and Hall then tested fear to A and also to a new auditory cue, B. Fear generalized from N to A in this group, but not to B, and there was no generalization in a control group that did not have A and N paired with food. Honey and Hall (1991) reported a similar effect when stimuli like A and N were paired with a neutral stimulus (rather than paired with food). The point is that, when two stimuli are associated with something in common, we tend to treat them as if they are more equal. This effect is known as **acquired equivalence**, or **mediated generalization**. Generalization between A and B is "mediated" by their association with a common element; A and B are thought to retrieve a common representation.

There are many illustrations of this sort of effect. For example, pigeons can be run in experiments using variations on the **matching-to-sample** procedure illustrated in Figure 8.15. On each trial, after an initial "start" cue (that gets the subject ready for what is to follow), a "sample" stimulus is presented on a central key. For example, the key might be illuminated Red.

TABLE 8.2 Design of a mediated generalization experiment

Group	Phase 1	Phase 2	Test
1	A — Food, N — Food	N — Shock	A? B?
2	A — Food, N — No food	N — Shock	A? B?

Source: From Honey & Hall, 1989.

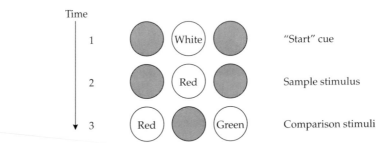

Figure 8.15 Example of a sequence of stimuli used in a matching-to-sample experiment. The circles are a row of response keys at the front of a pigeon chamber. (Gray circles indicate keys that are not illuminated.) The trial begins with a "start" cue, which the pigeon typically pecks in order to receive the sample stimulus. The sample stimulus stays on for a short period of time, and then two comparison keys are turned on. Pecks to one of these keys are reinforced. In matching to sample, pecks to the comparison stimulus that matches the sample, is reinforced. In delayed matching-to-sample ("DMTS"), a delay can be inserted between presentation of the sample and then the comparison stimuli.

Immediately after this stimulus, the bird is shown two "comparison" stimuli on the side keys: for example, a Red key and a Green key. In a matching-to-sample experiment, the bird is reinforced for pecking the comparison key that matches the sample—after a Red sample, the Red comparison (not the Green one) is reinforced. On trials when the sample stimulus is Green, the Green comparison (not the Red one) is reinforced. Many variations on this procedure are possible (as we will see shortly) and always involve a **conditional discrimination**, because either comparison stimulus is reinforced on half of the trials, but the one that will be reinforced on any particular trial depends on (i.e., is conditional on) the sample cue that came before it. Thomas Zentall (1998) has reviewed a large number of experiments, which all suggest that, when different samples signal that the same comparison stimulus is correct, the different samples are treated as equivalent (Kaiser, Sherburne, Steirn, & Zentall, 1997; Urcuioli, Zentall, Jackson-Smith, & Steirn, 1989; Zentall, Steirn, Sherburne, & Urcuioli, 1991). For example, birds will generalize between Red and Vertical Line samples if they both signal that a Dot comparison stimulus will be reinforced. Zentall and Peter Urcuioli have argued that this implies that samples with common comparisons become coded similarly in the bird's memory. The Red and Vertical Line samples will acquire a so-called "common code," which is much like saying they have acquired equivalence.

   Acquired equivalence and mediated generalization may play an interesting role in categorization, where they may allow the creation of ever-larger categories. For instance, Wasserman, DeVolder, & Coppage (1992) provided an intriguing extension of acquired equivalence to the categorization work described earlier (see also Astley & Wasserman, 1999; Ast-

TABLE 8.3 Mediated generalization in a categorization experiment

Phase 1	Phase 2	Test	
Original training	New responses	Old categories	Result
People: Key 1+	People: Key 3+	—	
Cars: Key 1+	—	Cars: Key 3? Key 4?	Cars: Peck Key 3
Flowers: Key 2+	Flowers: Key 4+	—	
Chairs: Key 2+	—	Chairs: Key 3? Key 4?	Chairs: Peck Key 4

Source: From Wasserman et al., 1992.

ley, Peissig, & Wasserman, 2001). The scheme of the experiment is summarized in Table 8.3. In the first phase, birds learned to categorize pictures of people, cars, flowers, and chairs. Unlike the experiments we discussed earlier in this chapter, in this experiment the birds responded in the presence of two types of pictures by making the same response (e.g., for some birds, pictures of people and cars required a peck to Key 1 for a reinforcer, whereas pictures of flowers and chairs required a peck to Key 2). Once the birds were responding well, one category from each of the pairs was associated with a *new* response in a second phase. For example, people pictures now required a peck to Key 3 for a reinforcer, and flower pictures now required a peck to Key 4. The birds learned this, too. But the best part was the final test, when the birds were given a chance to peck Keys 3 or 4 in the presence of cars and chairs—pictures that had never been associated with these two keys. Remarkably, the birds responded to the new key that the associated category had been linked with. That is, the birds behaved as if they had combined two different subcategories (people + cars vs. flowers + chairs) into superordinate categories. I hope that you can see the similarity to the simpler Honey and Hall experiment (see Table 8.2); in either case, animals generalize between physically different stimuli if these stimuli have been associated with a common stimulus or response.

Since people and cars (and flowers and chairs) do not look much alike, the birds were not merely responding to the pictures' physical similarities. Instead, they were responding to the *psychological* similarities created by their associations with a response to a common key. Lea (1984) has suggested that an ability to categorize stimuli on a basis that transcends mere physical appearance is an important step toward demonstrating true "conceptualization" in animals. Urcuioli (2001) has called this "categorization by association." Superordinate categories like these are not unusual in everyday experience. You know that shoes, belts, and jackets (or lamps, chairs, and beds) are similar, despite the fact that they are physically different. Each of these subcategories is associated with a common response ("clothing" or "furniture") that helps put the subcategories together into a larger one.

What this research tells us is that generalization can occur between cues that have little in the way of physical similarity. Common associations provide a kind of glue that gives different cues a psychological similarity or equivalence. Research thus indicates that learning processes can make physically similar stimuli different—as in perceptual learning or physically different stimuli similar—as in acquired equivalence and mediated generalization.

Summary

Organisms generalize lawfully and respond in the presence of stimuli that are similar to stimuli that have been associated with reinforcers or set the occasion for operant responses. Generalization is at least partly due to the physical properties of the stimuli; we generalize between stimuli that share common features or elements. However, a major theme of this section is that generalization is also influenced by psychological processes: It is powerfully influenced by learning. Discrimination training can sharpen the shape of generalization gradients and create surprising new peaks in responding. It does this by introducing inhibition. Mere exposure to stimuli can also help make these stimuli more discriminable by allowing various processes that create perceptual learning. And associating stimuli with common events can also increase generalization between them. These basic facts of stimulus control provide tools that can be used to understand complicated examples of stimulus control, including (of course) categorization.

Another Look at the Information Processing System

If stimuli are going to guide instrumental action, then modern thinking suggests they will also need to be processed in the familiar information-processing system—or standard model of cognition—that we have seen before (see Figure 1.14 and Figure 4.10). As you will recall, stimuli in the environment are thought to be processed in a predictable sequence. Their perceptual properties are first analyzed and put into a sensory memory store. If these stimuli are further attended to, the information is then transferred to a hypothetical short-term (or working) memory store, where it can be rehearsed, further processed, and eventually put into long-term (or reference) memory. Not surprisingly, each of these processes plays a role in allowing stimuli to guide instrumental action.

Visual perception in pigeons

Thanks in part to computer graphics technology, a great deal of interesting research has investigated visual perception processes in the pigeon (e.g., Cook, 2001a). Much of this research has been inspired by earlier research on perception in humans. For example, pigeons and humans may recognize visual objects based on their perception of primitive components called **geons** (for "geometric ions"). According to "recognition by components" theory (Biederman, 1987), humans must first perceive these simple components before they can recognize an object's overall structure. In a line drawing, most geons occur at line intersections. Using familiar techniques, Van Hamme, Wasserman, and Biederman (1992) first trained pigeons to peck a different key in the presence of each of the four drawings shown in the left

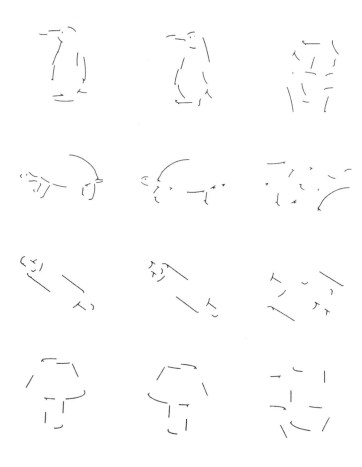

Figure 8.16 Stimuli used in the experiment by Van Hamme et al. (1992). Pigeons first learned to peck a unique key in the presence of each of the four stimuli shown in the left column. When tested with the new drawings shown in the middle column, the birds continued to respond reasonably accurately. But when tested with the new drawings shown in the right column, performance fell apart. Stimuli in the right column have the same line segments as stimuli in the middle column, but the geons are not preserved. (From Van Hamme et al., 1992.)

column of Figure 8.16. After the birds were responding well, the experimenters presented test trials with the stimuli shown in the middle and right-hand columns. Stimuli in the middle column are made up of brand new line segments, but geons are still detectable at their intersections, and the human eye perceives them as very similar to the stimuli at left. The birds responded the same way: Although they did not generalize perfectly to these new stimuli, their responding was very far above chance. In contrast, there was virtually no generalization to the images shown in the right-hand column, which contains the same line segments as the middle column, but scrambled. No geons are available in these stimuli. The results thus suggest that the birds did not perceive the original stimuli as haphazard sets of squiggles and lines. They recognized coherent patterns and generalized when the test stimuli preserved the basic geons.

A line of research by Robert Cook (see Cook, 2001b) suggests that pigeons may also be like humans in how they perceive stimuli embedded in a background of other stimuli. It is easy for you to see the Ts among the circles and the squares in the top of Figure 8.17, or the light circles among the darker squares and circles in the middle of the same figure. The unique regions

Figure 8.17 Examples of computer stimuli presented to pigeons by Cook (1992). Unique regions in the upper two displays "pop out" from the background. In contrast, the unique region in the bottom display requires more attention and effort to find—it is made up of a combination (or conjunction) of two dimensions that are varied in the background. (From Cook, 1992.)

Feature: shape

Feature: color

Feature: conjunctive

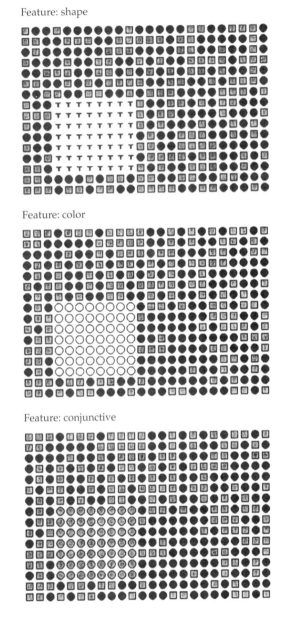

"pop out" from the background; they are processed automatically, without requiring attention and additional processing (Treisman, 1988). In contrast, the unique region in the bottom display is not as easy to find. It does not have a single unique feature, but is instead created by the combination of two of the features varied in the background—a light circle among dark circles and light squares. Here, the unique region does not pop out, and it takes more focus and attention to find it. Cook (1992) presented full-color versions of arrays like these on a computer screen that was viewed by pigeons. Responding was reinforced when the birds pecked at the unique regions on the screen. (Peck location was detected by a **touchscreen**—perpendicular sets of photobeams were projected along the computer screen's surface so that a location could be identified.) The birds were more accurate at identifying regions that differed from the surrounding area by only one feature (as in the top and middle displays). The birds were not as good at finding regions made up of combinations of more than one dimension (the "conjunctive" display at the bottom). Humans given the same stimuli were also slower to point at the conjunctive displays, suggesting that the two species might process the arrays similarly.

Robert Cook

Other experiments have examined the pigeon's ability to discriminate between displays that differ in their variability (see Wasserman, Young, & Cook, 2004, for one review). For example, Wasserman, Hugart, and Kirkpatrick-Steger (1995) showed pigeons displays of icons like those within each square in Figure 8.18. Pecks to a separate key were reinforced when all the items were the same; conversely, pecks to another key were reinforced when all the items were different. (Note that this is merely yet another example of establishing stimulus control by discrimination training.) After extensive training on 16 displays of each type, the birds were doing well, pecking the correct key over 80% of the time. They were then tested with new "same" and "different" displays made up of novel items. Their performance was not bad here either. Although generalization to the new stimuli was not perfect, it was well above chance (see also Cook, Cavoto, & Cavoto,

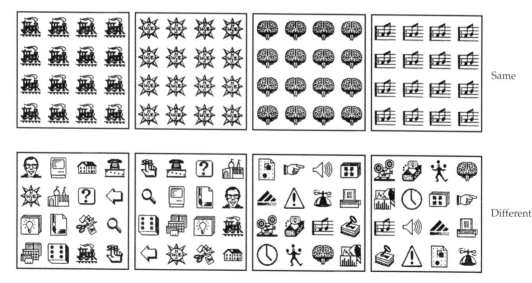

Same

Different

Figure 8.18 "Same" (top) and "different" (bottom) displays used in the experiment by Wasserman et al. (1995). (From Wasserman et al., 1995.)

1995; Young & Wasserman, 1997). More recent experiments have shown that same and different judgments are not affected much by small displacements of the icons, so the displays were not in perfectly straight rows and columns (Wasserman, Frank, & Young, 2002). And importantly, whereas birds identify "same" displays accurately regardless of the number of icons contained in them (from 2 to 16), "different" displays are not identified as "different" until roughly 8 or more icons appear in the displays (Young, Wasserman, & Garner, 1997). The best predictor of the birds' same and different judgments turns out to be "entropy," a mathematical measure of the variability contained in the display. Roughly speaking, the entropy value of a display increases as the number of different items in it increases; a "same" display has an entropy of 0. Thus, birds peck "same" when entropy is low and "different" when entropy is high. Pecks at the "same" key gradually shift to pecks at the "different" key as a test display's entropy is gradually increased.

There is some controversy about how entropy should be interpreted. On one view, entropy mainly captures the visual texture in the display. Same displays (with low entropy) have a smoother visual texture than different displays (with high entropy), which look rough. The birds thus respond to the smoothness of the display. Another possibility, though, is that the birds compare the individual icons and respond according to whether they are truly same or different. On this view, the decision to respond is made at a more advanced level of information processing than perception (e.g., Wasserman et al., 2002).The idea that the pigeons are making a same/different judgment would be more convincing if they performed better with small displays—when the displays contain only 2 items instead of 16 or so. Unfortunately, as already mentioned, pigeons do not correctly identify different displays as "different" until the arrays contain roughly 8 items (see Young et al., 1997; but see Katz & Wright, 2006). (The value of entropy is low when different displays have a small number of items.) Some have argued that true same/different judgments may require language (Premack, 1983). It is worth noting, though, that not all discriminations between same and different displays in pigeons are a simple function of entropy (e.g., Cook, Katz, & Cavoto, 1997; see also Katz & Wright, 2006). For the time being, it may be safest to conclude that animals are somehow good at discriminating variability—an important dimension of stimulus displays in the natural world (see Wasserman et al., 2004).

Attention

Many of the basic perceptual processes sketched above are thought to operate automatically, without requiring either attention or mental effort. Nonetheless, we already know that attention can be important in Pavlovian learning (see Chapter 4), and it is similarly important in stimulus control. For example, Donald Blough (1969) reinforced pigeons to peck a key when a yellow-orange dot (582 nm) was projected onto the key at the same time a high-pitched tone (3990 Hz) was audible. On other trials, other combinations of color and tone frequency were not reinforced. This training led the birds to respond to both sound and color, as if they were paying attention to both stimuli: In generalization tests, when the dot color was changed, responding declined, and when the tone frequency was decreased, responding also declined. Over the next series of sessions, Blough then continued to reinforce the 3990-Hz tone and nonreinforce all others, but made color irrelevant by presenting the same yellow-orange (582 nm) dot on every trial. In generalization tests that followed, the birds' responding was strongly affected by variation in the tone but not much by variation in the color—as if they had stopped paying attention to color. The same thing happened when the tone was next made irrelevant (by keeping it constant on every trial) and only colors were differentially reinforced. This caused the birds to tune out the tone—that is, they responded mainly to the color rather than to the tone. As we saw in Chapters 3 and 4, whether or not we pay attention to a dimension depends upon whether the dimension is informative.

Attention processes also come into play when we search for items in our environment. I recently found a lost checkbook that was hidden among the many papers cluttering my desk—but it took a fair amount of focus and concentration (not to mention patience). Consider animals analogously searching on the ground for food items. When prey items are abundant but cryptic (hard to detect because they blend into the background), there is a payoff for searching for (attending to) features that might help detect them. The animal is said to form a **search image** (Tinbergen, 1960). To investigate the process, experimenters presented birds with a series of displays that contained cryptic moths or pieces of grain, either of which needed to be pecked for reinforcement (e.g., Bond, 1983; Langley, 1996; Pietrewicz & Kamil, 1981; Reid & Shettleworth, 1992). (We saw an example of this type of method in the blue jay experiment described at the start of this chapter.) When cryptic items are presented in "runs" (i.e., repeated many times over a series of trials), birds detect them more quickly and/or more accurately than when the cryptic items are intermixed with trials having other items. Detection of the item on a trial may boost attention to its features, aiding its detection on the next trials (see Plaisted, 1997, for another interpretation). The idea that prey detection is affected by attention is also consistent with experiments on "divided attention." Your attention is limited, as you no doubt know from when two or more people have tried to talk to you at the same time. (Typically, you must switch your attention between the two speakers.) Dukas and Kamil (2001) had blue jays finding cryptic prey items on a computer screen. On some trials, a picture of the cryptic item was presented just before presentation of a display in which it was hidden. On other trials, *two* different prey items were presented before a screen in which one of the items was hidden. Detection rate was slower on the two-item trials, perhaps because the blue jay was dividing its attention between two images.

Patricia Blough (e.g., 1989, 1991) has noted that search image effects are similar to **attentional priming** effects that are easy to observe in visual search tasks in humans (e.g., Posner & Snyder, 1975). For example, in a pigeon version of such a task, Blough (1989) had pigeons find and peck at small-sized

Figure 8.19 Attentional priming. Pigeons performed in a visual search task in which they were reinforced for finding and pecking at target letters (e.g., A or L) presented among other letters and numbers on a video screen. (A) Pigeons took less time to find the target letter when the target was repeatedly presented on "runs" of trials. (B) Pigeons also found the target letter faster when it was cued by another stimulus ahead of time. (After Blough, 1989; Blough & Blough, 1997.)

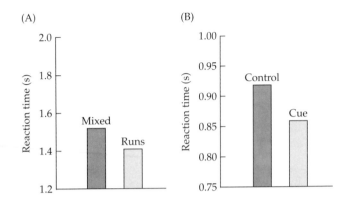

letters (e.g., an A or an L) that could be presented on a computer screen among many distractors (other letters and numbers). As shown in Figure 8.19A, the birds took less time to find and peck a letter if it occurred in runs of several trials, as above. The birds also found and pecked a particular letter more quickly if it was "cued" ahead of time by a signal that was associated with it (e.g., bars presented on the sides of the screen; Figure 8.19B; see also Blough, 2002). Both the previous run and the signal are thought to focus attention on features of the primed item. Interestingly, priming effects seem to disappear if pigeons are given extensive practice with the task (Vreven & Blough, 1998), as if the birds shift from a controlled or effortful style of processing to a more rapid, automatic one (see Chapters 4 and 10). Other research also suggests that repetition of distractor items in the background increases accuracy—that is, in addition to learning to attend to the target, the birds can learn to ignore distractors in the background (Katz & Cook, 2000).

Working memory

In a changing environment, stimuli are often present for only a short period of time. However, the fact that information can be held for a while in working memory allows even brief stimuli or events to guide instrumental behavior after the stimuli are gone. Working memory has been extensively studied using the methods of stimulus control. For example, the matching-to-sample procedure described earlier (see Figure 8.15) is easily adapted for this purpose. Recall that the pigeon is shown a "sample" stimulus (e.g., a Red key) and required to peck the same color key when given a choice between a Red and a Green key (the "comparison" stimuli) to receive a reward. In **delayed matching-to-sample**, or **DMTS**, the pigeon is first trained to respond this way, and then a delay is inserted between presentation of the sample and the comparison stimuli on test trials. The pigeon must now remember the sample (or perhaps remember what it should do next) over the delay in order to peck the correct comparison stimulus. As shown in Figure 8.20, performance declines as the interval between sample offset and comparison onset increases. In the study shown, a classic by William Roberts

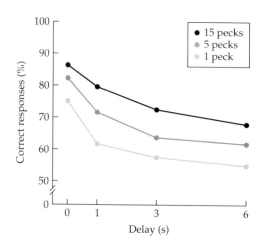

Figure 8.20 Pigeon working memory in the delayed matching-to-sample (DMTS) task. Different curves illustrate retention over different delay intervals when the bird had to peck the sample stimulus 1, 5, or 15 times. (After Roberts, 1972.)

(Roberts, 1972), the pigeon's performance is getting close to chance (50%) when the delay between the sample and comparison is a mere six seconds. The pigeon's short-term memory seems very short indeed.

Working memory in this task is influenced by several factors. In the experiment shown in Figure 8.20, the bird was required to peck the sample stimulus either one, five, or fifteen times before the sample went off and the delay began. As the curves show, performance was better with the larger peck requirement. Since the sample stayed on longer when the birds had more pecks to make, this kind of result is usually interpreted to mean that increasing exposure to the sample increases working memory. A second factor that improves performance is practice. For example, Doug Grant (1976) found that pigeons that were tested over thousands of trials with several delays eventually had retention functions that stretched out to approximately 60 seconds (rather than only 6 seconds). Sargisson and White (2001) found that training with the 6-second interval essentially eliminated all forgetting, over the intervals shown in Figure 8.20. One implication is that at least some of the "forgetting" implied in results like Figure 8.20 is caused by generalization decrement. That is, the birds fail to generalize from training with no delay to tests with longer delays (see Zentall, 1997, for an interesting discussion of this kind of possibility in several settings).

A third factor that influences memory in pigeon DMTS is our old friend *interference* (see Chapter 5). Retroactive interference—where information after an event can hurt memory of the event—is thought to be created by turning on an overhead light during the interval between the sample and the comparison stimuli (e.g., Roberts & Grant, 1978). The brighter the light, the more it hurts performance. Proactive interference, where information from before a trial hurts performance on the trial, seems to play an especially important role in DMTS. It can be created by making the sample key one color (say, green) for some seconds before the true sample color (say, red) occurs. This makes performance worse in the DMTS task (e.g., Grant & Roberts, 1973). Memory on one trial can also be hurt by conflicting information from previous trials. For example, performance on a trial in which the sample is red is worse if the sample on the previous trial was green (e.g., Edhouse & White, 1988; Grant 1975; Roberts, 1980; White, Parkinson, Brown, & Wixted, 2004). Notice that, when the sample was different on the previous trial, the bird probably made a different response, too; it turns out that both the incompatible sample and the incompatible response create interference on the next trial. Interference appears to weaken with longer intertrial intervals (e.g., Roberts, 1980), although explaining this effect turns out to be complex (e.g., Edhouse & White, 1988). There is no question, though, that interference has powerful effects on working memory as studied in DMTS.

Another method that is used to study working memory involves rats rather than pigeons. Figure 8.21 illustrates a **radial maze** developed by the late David Olton (Olton & Samuelson, 1976). The maze is elevated above the floor, and the different arms radiating from the center have no walls. As the rat moves around the maze, it can see different things in the room beyond the maze ("extra-maze cues"). On each trial in a typical experiment, the rat is allowed to explore the maze freely and retrieve all the bits of food (often Froot Loops®) that have been left at the end of each of the eight arms. Once a bit of food is retrieved, that arm is left empty until the next trial. The rat becomes very efficient at this task—if the experimenter allows the rat to leave the center part of the maze only eight times, it will enter an average of 7.5 arms without repeating itself (Olton, 1978). On a similar maze with 17 arms, the rat enters more than 14 different arms on the first 17 choices (Olton, Collison, & Werz, 1977). Performance is well above chance.

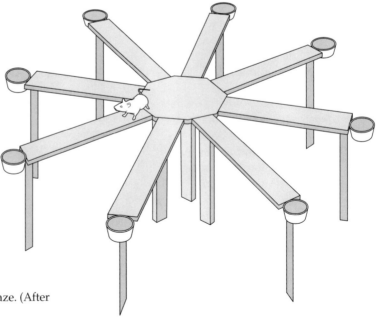

Figure 8.21 An 8-arm radial maze. (After Roitblat, 1987.)

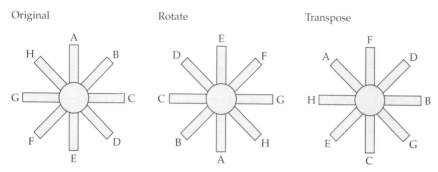

Figure 8.22 Extra-maze cues positioned at the end of each arm of a radial maze could be rotated or transposed. When the cues were rotated after the rat made some initial choices, the next choices rotated, as well. In contrast, when the cues were transposed, the next choices dropped to chance. (After Suzuki et al., 1980.)

It turns out that the rats are not systematically making their way through the maze by visiting adjacent arms. And they do not merely avoid odors that they leave behind on the visited arms (a possible sign that "I've been here already"). Instead, they remember places they have visited as defined by cues outside the maze. For example, Suzuki, Augerinos, and Black (1980) surrounded the maze with a black curtain, which eliminated all extra-maze cues. (Looking out from a maze surrounded by a black curtain is a little like looking out into deep space.) They then pinned odd items (things like a toy bird, a yellow card, Christmas tree lights, etc.) to the black curtain near the end of each arm. After the rat had learned to perform on the maze, on a test trial it made a few choices and was then confined to the center of the maze. At this time the experimenters rotated the curtain 180 degrees (Figure 8.22). When released, the rat likewise rotated its next choices so that it approached the items it hadn't approached before. This meant that the rat walked down many arms it had recently traveled. The rats were thus remembering the places as defined by extra maze cues, rather than individual arms themselves or odors they had left on the arms. And, interestingly, if the items were interchanged or "transposed" rather than merely rotated (see Figure 8.22), the rat's choices were severely disrupted. This result suggests that the rats had been using a configuration of several landmarks to define each location in the maze.

To perform accurately on a given trial, the rat must be remembering locations in working memory as it makes choices on the maze. With the right training, the rat can remember its first four choices for at least four hours, after which its working memory (as measured by its next four choices) begins to decline (Beatty & Shavalia, 1980). The rat also needs to use long-term or **reference memory** to perform. That is, the rat also needs to remember that food is present on the arms at the start of a trial. Working memory and reference memory can both be studied (and distinguished) on the radial maze. For example, Olton and Papas (1979) always baited some of the arms but never baited several others. The rats learned to avoid the arms that were never baited, and work their way (without repeating themselves) through the arms that were baited. Surgical damage to the neurons coming out of the hippocampus, a part of the brain known to influence learning and memory, hurt the ability of the rats to visit the baited arms without repeating themselves. But it did not affect their ability to avoid the never-baited arms. The results thus suggest that the hippocampus plays a role in working memory rather than reference memory.

We can be even more specific about how working memory operates in this task. If you think about it, the rat could be using its memory in two ways. First, as it makes its choices throughout a trial, the rat might simply remember the places it has recently visited—a **retrospective code** of places from the past. Memory would be especially taxed on later choices—when there are more visited locations to remember. On the other hand, the rat might remember places on the maze it has yet to visit, a so-called **prospective code**. (Prospective coding looks forward, rather than backward, in time.) In this case, the memory load would be highest on the early choices, not the later choices, because that is when the number of sites yet to be visited is high. Robert Cook, Michael Brown, and Donald Riley (1985) found evidence that the rat uses both types of codes. The experimenters first trained rats on a 12-arm version of the maze. Then, on different test trials, they removed the rats from the maze for 15 minutes following the second, fourth, sixth, eighth, or tenth choice on the trial. The rats were then returned to make the remaining choices. If the rat was solely using a retrospective code, inserting the retention interval after the tenth choice should have been especially disruptive—this was when the rat was holding a lot of information in memory. But after the second choice, things were relatively easy, and a retention interval shouldn't have as much effect. In contrast, if the rat was solely using a prospective code, a retention interval after the second choice would have been most difficult to handle, and one after the tenth choice should have been a piece of cake. Amazingly, the results (Figure 8.23A) suggested that there was little disruption when the interval was inserted after *either*

Figure 8.23 Retrospective and prospective coding in working memory. (A) Error scores of rats in a 12-arm radial maze when a retention interval was inserted after choices 2, 4, 6, 8, or 10. Rats behaved as if they remembered the places they had been for the first several choices, and then they switched to remembering places they still needed to visit. (B) Similar results with pigeons required to peck 5 different keys without repeat; delays were inserted after choices 1, 2, 3, or 4. (A, after Cook et al., 1985; B, after Zentall et al., 1990.)

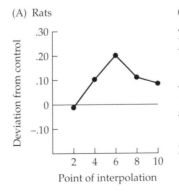

(A) Rats

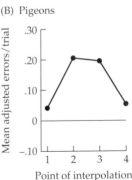

(B) Pigeons

early or late choices; the biggest disruption occurred in the middle—after the sixth choice (see also Kesner & DeSpain, 1988)! Apparently, the first few choices were guided by remembering places past, and later choices were guided by remembering places yet to go. This flexibility is remarkable. But it might also be efficient. By switching from retrospective to prospective coding in the middle of the trial, the rat only needed to remember 5 or 6 locations at one time instead of 11 or 12.

Pigeons may likewise use either retrospective or prospective coding in the DMTS task. That is, during the delay between sample and comparison stimuli they might remember either the sample (a retrospective code) or the comparison stimulus they need to peck (a prospective code). The distinction is especially clear in "symbolic" delayed matching-to-sample, where a red sample (for instance) might signal that pecking a horizontal line will be reinforced, and a green sample might signal that pecking a vertical line will be reinforced. Is the bird remembering the red or green sample during the delay, or is it remembering to peck the upcoming vertical or horizontal line? There is evidence that pigeons can use either type of code (e.g., Roitblat, 1980; Urcuioli & Zentall, 1986). And, as we just saw for rats in the radial maze, the pigeons switch between the two types of codes with impressive flexibility. Zentall, Steirn, and Jackson-Smith (1990) arranged an experiment with pigeons that was similar to the rat experiment by Cook et al. (1985). At the start of a trial, five different keys were illuminated. The pigeon's job was to peck at each of the keys, without a repeat, to receive reinforcement for every response. Once each correct key was pecked, reinforcement was delivered, and all five keys were turned off for 2.5 seconds before they came back on again. After the birds had learned the task, the experimenters inserted longer delays between the different choices (first, second, third, etc.) on different trials. Once again, as we saw in the radial maze, delays after the early and later choices were not as disruptive as delays after the middle choices (see Figure 8.23B). The birds were apparently using a retrospective code for the first few choices and then a prospective code for the final choices. Studies of working memory thus suggest that animals can learn to use their memories actively and efficiently.

Thomas Zentall

Reference memory

We have already discussed long-term (or reference) memory earlier in this book (especially in Chapter 4). To briefly review, this sort of memory is more permanent than working memory, and it has a much larger capacity. Information from long-term memory is thought to be activated by retrieval cues. And forgetting is generally held to be a result of interference (either proactive or retroactive) or retrieval failure caused by a mismatch between contextual cues in the background at the time of learning and retrieval.

Researchers studying human long-term memory have often distinguished between several types. For example, Squire (1987) has distinguished between **procedural memory** and **declarative memory**. Procedural memory is one's memory for behavioral procedures, or how to do things (e.g., ride a bike, swim, or play a guitar). Declarative memory, in contrast, is essentially everything else. For instance, **semantic memory** is one's memory for things like words, facts, and so forth (e.g., Tulving, 1972); this is the kind of information that is remembered when you have a good night playing Trivial Pursuit®. **Episodic memory**, on the other hand, is memory for specific personal experiences, such as what happened when you visited your aunt and uncle yesterday or when you last traveled to Washington, DC. This type of memory involves information about what, where, and when an event happened. The distinctions between these forms of long-term memory have been tricky to study in animals, because animals cannot verbalize, and it is often not clear how to conceptualize the reference memory involved in many laboratory tasks. For example, is memory in a Pavlovian conditioning experiment procedural (knowing what to do when the CS comes on) or declarative (knowing what the CS means)? Since conditioning may involve both S-R associations (procedural memory?) and S-S associations (declarative memory?), there is probably an element of both involved.

It would seem especially hard to find evidence of episodic memory in animals. Nonetheless, Nicky Clayton and Anthony Dickinson have provided interesting evidence in some wonderful experiments with scrub jays. These birds naturally hide (or cache) bits of food in their environment and then recover the food bits later (see Clayton, Griffiths, & Dickinson, 2000, for one review). Clayton and Dickinson's experiments took advantage of the fact that captive birds will take food items from a bowl and cache them in nearby ice cube trays filled with sand. (The birds recover the items later.) Consider the following experimental arrangement (Clayton & Dickinson, 1999). In an initial training phase, the birds were given a series of trials designed to teach them something about peanuts and mealworms. On each trial, the birds were given a bowl of either peanuts or mealworms and allowed to cache them in a unique ice cube tray that was decorated with unique plastic legos. They could then recover the cached items either 4 hours or 124 hours later. At the 4-hour interval, the peanuts and mealworms were always fine. But at the 124-hour interval, two groups of birds had different experiences. In the control group, the peanuts and mealworms were once again intact and fine. But in the "Spoiled" group, the experimenters had replaced the cached mealworms with mealworms that had been dried and then soaked in disgusting dishwashing detergent. The worms had essentially gone bad (or, spoiled) over the 124-hour period. The training procedure thus allowed the birds in the Spoiled group to learn that mealworms, but not peanuts, are bad if they are recovered after several days.

In subsequent test trials, the birds first cached the peanuts and mealworms as usual, and during recovery tests 4 and 124 hours later, the birds were given the trays in which they had cached the food items. But on these trials, the food had been removed from the trays and the sand had been replaced, so the bird's searching behavior could only be guided by the memory of what they had cached and where. The idea of the experiment and the results are summarized in Figures 8.24 and 8.25. In the control group, the

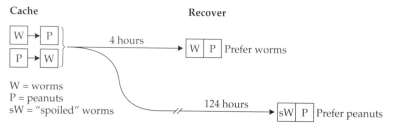

Figure 8.24 Training procedure and predictions of what the "Spoiled" group should do in the experiment testing episodic-like memory in scrub jays (Clayton & Dickinson, 1999). During training, mealworms were "spoiled" when the birds recovered them 124 hours—but not 4 hours—after caching (storing) them.

birds searched more for mealworms than peanuts at both the long- and short-retention intervals. They preferred the mealworms, and evidently remembered what they had cached and where. The Spoiled group did essentially the same at the 4-hour interval, but did something quite remarkable at the 124-hour interval. At this time, their preference switched almost exclusively to peanut sites over mealworm sites. The birds had learned that mealworms are bad if caching occurred a long time ago, and they were using this information to avoid the "spoiled" mealworms. To perform this way, the birds must have remembered what they had cached, where they had cached it, and *when* they had cached it, too. Clayton and Dickinson have therefore argued that this and related results indicate episodic-like memory in this interesting bird.

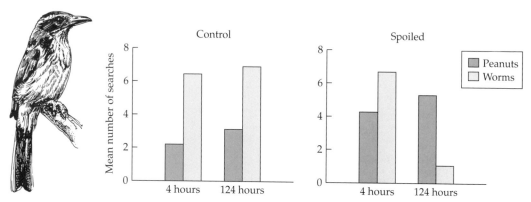

Figure 8.25 Number of searches by scrub jays at peanut or mealworm sites when testing occurred 4 hours or 124 hours after caching. The control group always preferred to search for mealworms over peanuts. The same was true for the "Spoiled" group when tested 4 hours after caching; but after 124 hours, these birds searched for peanuts instead of mealworms—they had previously learned that mealworms spoil after this interval of time (see Figure 8.24). To perform this way, the Spoiled group must have remembered what they had cached as well as where and when they had cached it. (After Clayton & Dickinson, 1999.)

The Cognition of Time

One remarkable aspect of behavior is that it is very sensitive to time. For example, if you are sitting in your car waiting for a red light to change, but the timer gets stuck, you will eventually realize something is wrong. You also become impatient when a waiter is slow to serve you dinner at a restaurant, or when a website is unusually slow to load. And when you buy a new and faster computer, you might feel like familiar programs are running very quickly. Time, and the perception of time, is often in the background guiding actions and behavior throughout the day. Accordingly, there has been a great deal of interest in how organisms learn about and organize their behavior in time.

Time of day cues

Animals have an internal source of temporal information that corresponds to the time of day. For example, Robert Bolles and Sam Moot (1973) isolated rats in a room with constant dim light and fed them every day at 10:00 a.m. and 4:00 p.m. The rats had access to a running wheel throughout the day. They used their sense of time of day to anticipate each of the meals—that is, they became active in the wheel an hour or two before each meal. Similarly, birds—including pigeons (e.g., Carr & Wilkie, 1998; Saksida & Wilkie, 1994) and garden warblers (e.g., Biebach, Gordijn, & Krebs, 1989)—have been trained to peck different keys or visit different locations at different times of the day to obtain food (Figure 8.26). All of the results suggest that animals can use time of day cues as CSs or occasion setters to predict or locate food.

Most animals, including humans, have a so-called **circadian rhythm** that responds to the 24-hour period. These rhythms are easily observed in rodents

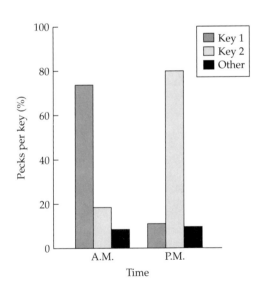

Figure 8.26 Pigeons can use time of day cues to set the occasion for which of two keys will be reinforced. Before the tests shown, pecks to Key 1 had been reinforced during morning sessions and pecks to Key 2 had been reinforced during afternoon sessions. (After Saksida & Wilkie, 1994.)

with continuous access to running wheels. Rodents become active at night, and this tendency persists even when experimenters keep the animals under constant light—thus eliminating the usual day and night cues. The animals appear to respond according to an internal clock that has a period of approximately one day (circadian roughly means "about a day"). Actually, under these "free-running" conditions, the rodent's activity tends to begin a little later each day, as if the average clock has a period that is a bit longer than a day. Under normal conditions, the animal's circadian clock is "entrained," or brought into phase with the actual day, by stimuli like natural light. These entraining stimuli are called "zeitgebers" ("timegivers" in German). You experience your own circadian clock when you become jet-lagged after flying to a distant time zone. Your clock is out of phase with the new conditions, although exposure to local zeitgeibers gradually entrains and shifts your clock to local time. The fact that an animal's circadian clock can be shifted gradually is often used to study its role in timing behavior. For example, in the research mentioned above (e.g., see Figure 8.26), Saksida and Wilkie (1994) trained pigeons to peck different keys in a Skinner box at two different times (about 9:00 a.m. and 3:30 p.m.) each day. Then they shifted the lighting schedule in the birds' home room so that the artificial day began at midnight instead of 6:00 a.m. This did not change the birds' performance on the first day; thus, the birds were not merely timing the interval between lights on and the test to set the occasion for the correct key peck. But when the birds were tested again six days later, after enough time for the clock to be entrained to the new photoperiod, performance changed. The results suggested that the birds had learned to use the circadian clock to peck the correct key.

As mentioned above, rats appear to use the circadian clock to anticipate a daily meal when it is scheduled at the same time each day. Interestingly, other intervals are more difficult to use. Bolles and de Lorge (1962) and Bolles and Stokes (1965) found that rats anticipated meals spaced 24 hours apart, but never learned to anticipate meals spaced by 19 or 29 hours apart. Notice that meals spaced 19 or 29 hours apart would be delivered at a different time each day. One interpretation is that "preparedness" once again operates here (see Chapter 2): The rats use a 24-hour circadian signal as a CS for food, but not a cue that is incompatible with its natural clock (e.g., Boakes, 1997).

Interval timing

Animals are also good at timing intervals in the range of seconds and minutes. We have already seen some examples of this. In Chapter 3, we considered inhibition of delay, where responding in a CS starts slowly and then peaks toward the end of the CS, when the US is usually delivered. The animal times the duration of the signal and performs its behavior appropriately. In Chapter 7, we also saw that the rate of operant behavior on a fixed-interval schedule of reinforcement "scallops"—or anticipates—the point at which the next reinforcer will be delivered. Unlike the circadian clock, which runs on its own once it is entrained, these demonstrations suggest a flexible timing process that can be turned on and off, almost like a stopwatch. Because of this kind of observation, investigators have become extremely interested in how animals perceive and utilize information about temporal intervals.

To study interval timing, experimenters have developed several methods that are clever extensions of the simple stimulus control experiment. For example, in a **temporal generalization** procedure, an animal in a Skinner box is reinforced if it responds after presentation of a signal of one duration, but not after signals of other durations (e.g., Church & Gibbon, 1982). When the subject is exposed to signals of various durations, there is a nice generalization gradient in which the highest responding is observed after the reinforced duration. Another important method is the **peak procedure** (e.g., Catania, 1970; S. Roberts, 1981). In this method, animals receive many trials in which a signal is presented and the first response after some fixed-interval (say, 20 seconds) is reinforced. As you might expect, the animal begins to delay its responding until the reinforcer is expected in time. To study the accuracy of the animal's timing, the experimenter occasionally introduces blank or "empty" trials in which the signal stays on for a much longer period, and the animal receives no reinforcement. The animal shows a "peak" of responding at the point in time when the reinforcer was other-

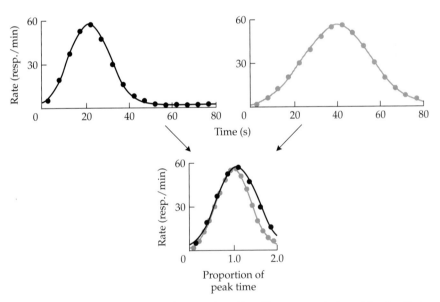

Figure 8.27 Results from the peak procedure. Top: Rats were reinforced for the first response 20 or 40 seconds after the start of a signal. In the "empty" trials shown, the reinforcer was not delivered and the signal stayed on longer. Notice that response rate peaked around the time when responding had been reinforced, but that timing was more accurate with the shorter 20-second interval (there was less spread around the peak). Bottom: The same data with the x-axis now showing time as the proportion of the timed interval. Notice that the two curves almost lie on top of one another—they "superpose." (Data from Roberts, 1981; after Shettleworth, 1998.)

wise expected, and then responding declines. The top parts of Figure 8.27 illustrate responding on empty trials for different groups of rats that had been reinforced 20 seconds or 40 seconds into the signal (Roberts, 1981). Clearly, the animals have learned to expect reinforcers at roughly 20 seconds or 40 seconds into the signal.

It is interesting that the shapes of the response curves are similar for the 20-second and 40-second intervals. Timing is reasonably accurate in both cases, but not perfect. Notice, though, that the spread of responding around the peak at the 40-second interval is quite a bit broader than the spread around the 20-second interval. This illustrates an important fact about timing: Longer intervals are timed less accurately than shorter intervals. One of the fascinating facts about timing is that the spread of responding around the peak is lawfully related to the interval that is being timed. This property of timing is illustrated by the lower graph in Figure 8.27. Here, response rate is plotted as a function of the proportion of the timed interval, rather than absolute time, on the *x*-axis. Thus, for animals that were timing the 20-second interval, "1.0" is 20 seconds, whereas "0.5" is 10 seconds and "2.0" is 40 seconds. For the 40-second interval, in contrast, 1.0 is 40 seconds, whereas 0.5 is 20 seconds and 2.0 is 80 seconds. What happens here is that the two response curves look alike; they are said to **superpose**. (The result is sometimes called **superposition**.) Regardless of the interval that is being timed, on a given task the probability of responding is related to the proportion of the time into the interval. This property of timing is sometimes called the **scalar property** (e.g., Gibbon & Church, 1984). It is an example of Weber's law, a law in psychophysics which holds that perceived differences are a constant proportion of the value being judged.

The scalar property of interval timing pops up wherever investigators have looked for it. It showed up in the temporal generalization procedure mentioned earlier (Church & Gibbon, 1982). It also shows up in inhibition of delay (Figure 8.28A; Rosas & Alonso, 1996) and in behavior on FI schedules of reinforcement (Figure 8.28B; Dews, 1970). Regardless of the method used to investigate timing, longer intervals are timed less accurately, and the amount of error is proportional to the length of the timed interval. One way to think of this is that, on a given trial, the animal is comparing elapsed time with its memory for the interval that has previously been reinforced. If its decision to respond is based on the ratio of the current time and the memory for time (which is the current proportion of the reinforced interval shown in Figures 8.27 and 8.28), then everything falls into place; you will get the kind of pattern shown in Figures 8.27 and 8.28.

The idea that animals compare the ratio of the current and remembered time is also supported by research using a **temporal bisection** procedure. Church and Deluty (1977) presented rats in a Skinner box with a cue that was either 2 seconds or 8 seconds long. Immediately after the cue was presented, two levers were inserted into the chamber. If the cue had been 2 seconds long, pressing the left lever was reinforced; if the cue had been 8 seconds long, pressing the right lever was reinforced. The rats learned this discrimina-

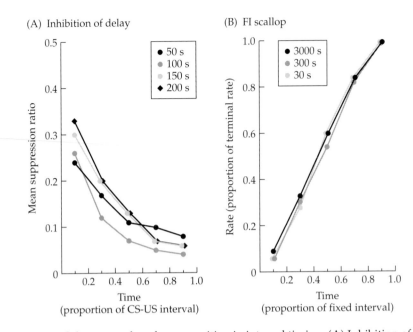

Figure 8.28 Other examples of superposition in interval timing. (A) Inhibition of delay in conditioned suppression in rats. Rats received an electric shock US at the end of a tone CS that was either 50, 100, 150, or 200 seconds long. Suppression increased during later parts of the CS—as a function of relative time in the CS. (B) Responding of pigeons on different fixed-interval (FI) schedules of reinforcement. Different groups received FI 30 second, FI 300 second, and FI 3000 second reinforcement schedules. Remember that in such schedules, the first response after a given interval since the last reinforcer is reinforced. FI schedules cause "scallops" in responding—the increase in response rate over the fixed interval shown here. Once again, response rate is a consistent function of relative time in the interval. (A, after Rosas & Alonso, 1996; B, data from Dews, 1970, after Gibbon, 1991.)

tion. What was interesting, though, were the results of test trials in which the experimenters presented cues that were between 2 and 8 seconds in duration. Generally speaking, responding changed gradually as a function of the duration of the test signal. The test signals less than 4 seconds were judged to be short—the rat tended to press the left lever after each signal. And cues longer than 4 seconds were judged to be long (the rat tended to press the right lever after each signal). But the 4-second cue was the psychological middle; the rats judged it to be long or short (pressing left or right) with about equal probability. One way to think of it is that there was equal generalization to 4 seconds from the 2-second ("press left") and 8-second ("press right") cues. For this to occur, the animal was once again comparing the ratio of time in the test to remembered time (4:2 is the same as 8:4). And, basically, the same results were obtained when the experiment was repeated with 4 and 16-second cues (the middle point being 8), 1- and 4-second cues (the middle point being 2), and 3- and 12-second cues (the middle point being 6). The animal always behaved as if it was comparing ratios. Similar results have been obtained with humans (Allan & Gibbon, 1991). In timing tasks, organisms seem to respond to the *ratio* of current time and remembered time.

How do they do it?

Theorists have often assumed that humans and other animals use a kind of **internal clock** to estimate time. The most influential approach to timing is the information-processing approach developed by the late John Gibbon and Russell Church (e.g., Gibbon, Church, & Meck, 1984). They proposed a system that fits nicely with the standard cognitive model that we have discussed throughout this book. The model is illustrated in Figure 8.29. It supposes that timing involves a clock, working and reference memory, and a decision process. The clock has several interesting parts. First, there is a "pacemaker"—a hypothetical device that emits pulses at a lawful rate. When an event occurs that starts the clock (like the onset of a to-be-timed signal), a "switch" is closed that allows pulses from the pacemaker to collect in an "accumulator"—the animal's working memory for elapsed time. Elapsed time is represented as the number of pulses that have accumulated, or n. When the animal is reinforced after some duration, the system stores an approximation of the current value of n in reference memory; the reinforced duration in reference memory—or, essentially the expected time to a reinforcer—is n^*. In any timing task, the animal continuously compares its working memory for the amount of time that has elapsed in the current trial (n,

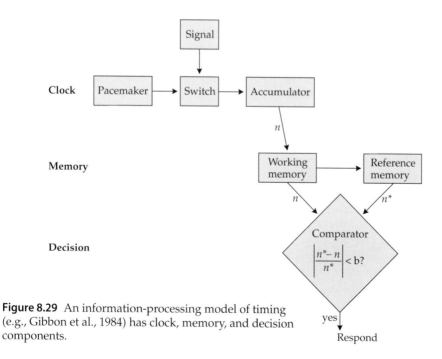

Figure 8.29 An information-processing model of timing (e.g., Gibbon et al., 1984) has clock, memory, and decision components.

Russell Church

John Gibbon

in the accumulator) with a reference memory for the expected time to the reinforcer (n^*). In the model, the comparison is made by a "comparator" that generates a response when the difference between n and n^* gets smaller than a certain value (b, see Figure 8.29). (Notice that the difference between n and n^* becomes smaller as n approaches n^*.) Error in the accuracy of timing can be introduced in a number of ways, most notably because the pacemaker varies in rate slightly from trial to trial (Gibbon & Church, 1984). But because the crucial difference between time in working and reference memory is expressed as a proportion of the expected interval to reinforcement (n^*, see Figure 8.29), the scalar property is obtained.

The information processing model of timing has had a large influence on timing research. It is intuitively plausible, and it seems to fit how psychologists think perception and memory relate to one another. What's more, investigators have used a number of experimental manipulations to separate the clock and memory systems in a way that is consistent with Figure 8.29 (e.g., Church, 1989; Meck, 1996; Roberts, 1981). For example, giving rats methamphetamine ("speed") seems to speed up the pacemaker (e.g., Meck, 1983). This is suggested by several intriguing results. If rats have already been trained on a timing task, introducing the drug initially makes the rats judge timed intervals as longer than they really are—as if the pacemaker is revved up and pulsing quickly. But if extensive training is then conducted while the animal is drugged, the system stores an abnormally large number of pulses (n) as the expected interval to reinforcement (n^*). Timing becomes accurate under the influence of the drug. If the rat is now tested without the drug, it behaves as if its clock is running slow—pulses now accumulate at the normal rate, but it takes more of them to accumulate before the animal reaches the remembered interval! These results are consistent with the clock and memory functions built into the information-processing model.

Russell Church and Hilary Broadbent later suggested another way to conceptualize the internal clock (Church & Broadbent, 1990). They got rid of the pacemaker and accumulator, and instead suggested that the clock might consist of a group of "oscillators"—that is, units that switch between two different states at a regular rate over time (see Gallistel, 1990). The idea behind their **multiple oscillator model** is sketched in Figure 8.30. Each of the curves represents the status of an oscillator that varies between values of +1 and –1, with a fixed period. Each oscillator changes at a different rate. Any point in time can be represented by listing the status of each of the different oscillators. For example, at Time 3, the oscillators from top to bottom have values of – – + – +. Notice that their values are different at Time 1 and Time 2. Each readout can thus label a different point in time. In this model, the start of a trial starts the oscillators going; the current readout of the oscillators is what's in working memory, and a remembered readout is in reference memory. A model with a multiple oscillator can do a good job of simulating the findings of the timing literature (e.g., see Church & Broadbent, 1990; Wearden & Doherty, 1995). It also has a number of advantages, one

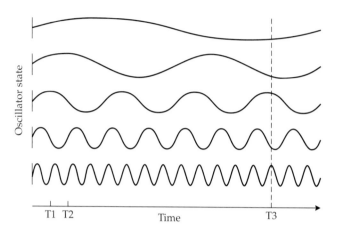

Figure 8.30 How multiple oscillators can tell time. Each of several oscillators cycles through values of +1 and −1 at a different rate. Any given point in time can be represented by reading the current status of all the oscillators. (After Shettleworth, 1998.)

of which is that it seems more plausible from a biological perspective. Oscillators like the ones supposed here are thought to be in control of repetitive activities like licking, breathing, and circadian rhythms. In contrast, it is hard to find a biological event that corresponds to a switch or an accumulator. More important, unlike the pacemaker–accumulator, a clock made up of oscillators is likely to time certain intervals with greater precision than other intervals. This is because the readout from the oscillators does not change in a perfectly linear way over time—sometimes a small change in time will correlate with a relatively big change in readout from the oscillators, and vice versa. Consistent with this possibility, Jonathon Crystal and others have found that rats can time certain intervals especially accurately (Crystal, 1999, 2003; Crystal, Church, & Broadbent, 1997).

It is also possible to explain timing behavior without appealing to an internal clock at all. Staddon and Higa (1999) have proposed that the start of the trial is recorded in short-term memory, and that the strength of this memory then fades systematically over time. Animals can learn to time a reinforcer by merely associating the reinforcer with the current strength of the memory from the start of the trial. (For reasons that there isn't space to explain, Staddon and Higa's model is called the **multiple-time-scale model**.) Alternatively, in the **behavioral theory of timing** (Killeen & Fetterman, 1988; see also Machado, 1997), animals are assumed to go through a fixed sequence of behaviors during any to-be-timed interval. Animals can time the reinforcer by learning what behavior they were doing when reinforcement was delivered. Neither of these views supposes an internal clock, but both can account for many features of timing, including the scalar property illustrated in Figures 8.27 and 8.28. Staddon and Higa explain it by assuming that the memory of the start of the trial fades according to a logarithmic function that causes its strength to decrease rapidly at first, and then slower and slower over time. Thus, short intervals can be timed more accurately than long intervals. Killeen and Fetterman assume that animals go through the sequence of different behaviors more rapidly when shorter intervals are being timed. It may be unnecessary to link timing so rigidly to overt behaviors, though; attempts to find the sequence required have not always been successful (Lejeune, Cornet, Ferreira, & Wearden, 1998). The behavioral theory of timing has also been challenged by other findings (e.g., see Bizo & White, 1995; Leak & Gibbon, 1995).

To summarize, research on interval timing illustrates that animals readily use the passage of time as a cue to predict the presentation of reinforcers, and experiments from many methods have produced compatible and lawful results. The results clearly suggest that animals can use some cognitive or behavioral variable that correlates with the passage of time to make judgments about it. There has been disagreement, though, about what the temporal variable is. A common assumption has been that animals represent time with an internal clock, although this idea has not been accepted by everyone. Although the pacemaker–accumulator mechanism used in scalar expectancy theory has been highly influential, a number of important questions have been raised about it (e.g., Crystal, 2003; Staddon & Higa, 1999), and other interesting ways to represent time are possible.

The Cognition of Space

Cues that guide spatial behavior

Most animals (including humans) need to find their way through space in order to reach goals like food, mates, shelter, and so forth. Thus, instrumental behavior occurs in the context of space as well as time. How animals use spatial information has interested psychologists at least since Tolman first proposed the role of "cognitive maps" (see Chapter 7). Although we already know from Tolman's experiments that rats are good place learners, whether they represent their environment as a kind of global map in memory is still controversial. The idea has its proponents (see pp. 316–325), but research has often pursued the more modest goal of figuring out what kinds of cues are utilized when we get around in space—and how we go about using those cues.

Sometimes navigation can occur without immediate reference to any cues in the environment at all. In **dead reckoning**, the animal uses an internal sense of direction and distance to get from one location to a goal in a straight line. For example, golden hamsters can be led in the dark to a location away from the nest by moving them a few feet in one direction, turning, and then moving in another. They return directly to the starting point by somehow integrating information about the outward paths (e.g., Etienne, 1992; Etienne, Berlie, Georgakopolous, & Maurer, 1998). Otherwise, animals do use available cues to navigate to a goal. Sometimes they can use **beacons**—that is, cues that are very close to the goal that the animal can see at a distance and simply approach. You are using a beacon when you reach a gas station or the exit of a building by spotting and approaching a sign. Learning about beacons is presumably another example of stimulus learning—the animal learns that the stimulus is associated with the goal and then approaches it, as in sign tracking (see Chapter 2).

Often, though, beacons are not positioned so conveniently next to the goal, and the animal must therefore use **landmarks**—that is, cues that have a fixed relationship with the goal but are not very close to it. The extra-maze cues that a rat uses to get around a radial maze are one example. You will remember that the rat uses configurations of these cues, rather than just a single cue, to identify locations on the maze (e.g., Suzuki et al., 1980). Other research has built upon this point. For example, Marcia Spetch, Ken Cheng, Suzanne Mac-Donald and others (1997) trained pigeons to find food that was buried in sawdust on the floor. The location of the food was consistently in the middle of four bottles that were arranged as four corners of an imaginary square (Figure 8.31). The birds readily learned to find the food using the landmarks.

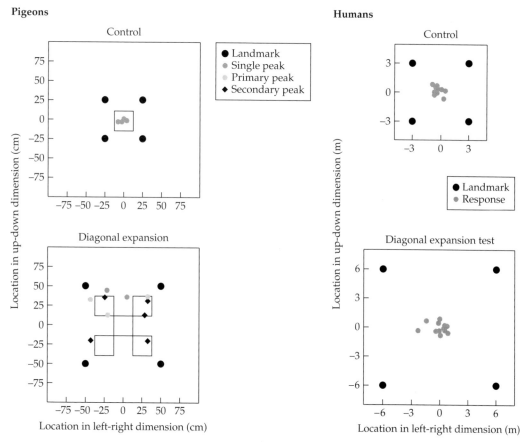

Figure 8.31 Performance of pigeons (left) and humans (right) taught to find rewards in the middle of four landmarks arranged in a square. Top: the configuration of landmarks in training and location of searches in the middle. Bottom: results of test trials, after the square created by the landmarks was expanded. Pigeons searched in the same position a fixed distance from an individual landmark, whereas humans continued to search in the center of the expanded square. (After Spetch et al., 1997.)

When Spetch et al. (1997) expanded the arrangement of the bottles during the test trials (see bottom left of Figure 8.31), instead of searching at the "middle" of the expanded square, the birds continued to search in the usual position, a fixed distance from one of the landmarks. This suggests that the birds were using the configuration of landmarks, but only for direction—rather than distance—information (see also Spetch, Cheng, & MacDonald, 1996).

Interestingly, Spetch et al. (1996, 1997) also tested humans in related experiments. For example, in an experiment conducted outdoors in a grassy field, people were asked to find a small object in the middle of four landmarks provided by upright pool noodles. When the 6 x 6 meter "square" was expanded, the people always searched in the "middle" of the shape, rather than a fixed distance from one landmark as the pigeons had. Pigeons and other birds can be trained to use "middle" if the absolute distance between two landmarks is made irrelevant by separating them by different distances on different trials (e.g., Jones, Antoniadis, Shettleworth, & Kamil, 2002; see also Kamil & Jones, 2000; Spetch, Rust, Kamil, & Jones, 2003). So, the system is flexible, but there is a natural tendency for some species to use a configuration of landmarks to indicate direction from an individual landmark (see also Collette, Cartwright, & Smith, 1986, for similar results with gerbils).

The idea that organisms might use actual shape or geometric information has been an important issue in spatial learning research. In some influential experiments, Ken Cheng (1986) had rats locate food (Cocoa Puffs®) in a small (120 × 60 cm) rectangular box with unique walls and corners (Figure 8.32). The apparatus was housed in a black environment so that extra-maze cues could not be seen and used to get around. In one set of experiments, the rats could always find food in a consistent corner of the box. They

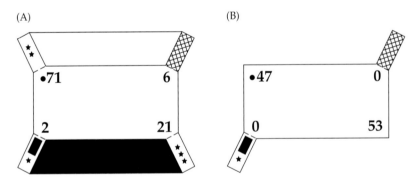

Figure 8.32 Apparatus and results of experiments reported by Cheng (1986). (A) Food was hidden in the location indicated by the dot. Rats were accurate in finding the food (numbers indicate percentage of responses there), but often made errors—"rotational errors"—by going to the diagonally opposite corner of the box. (B) When rats were tested after cues from nearby walls and corners were removed, they went exclusively to the two geometrically equivalent corners. Perhaps they were using global information about the shape of the environment to find the food (see also Figure 8.37). (After Cheng, 1986.)

were reasonably good at finding it, which is not terribly surprising. But Cheng found that the rats often made "rotational errors" by going to the diagonally opposite corner of the rectangle. For example, in the test summarized in Figure 8.32A, rats went to the correct place 71% of the time, but they also went to the opposite corner 21% of the time. When the rats were tested after the nearby corners and distinct walls were removed (replaced with black), the preference for the opposite corner was even more extreme; they now went to the correct corner 47% of the time and the diagonally opposite corner 53% of the time (see Figure 8.32B). The increase in errors that occurred when the local cues were removed suggests that the rats had been using these cues to some extent. But the persistent choice of the *opposite* corner was especially impressive and interesting.

Ken Cheng

Cheng noted that the diagonal corners are geometrically equivalent (e.g., both corners had a long wall on the right and a short wall on the left); therefore, the rats were using geometric information. He suggested that the rats were using a global representation of the shape of the box to the find the food, and that there might be a **geometric module** in their brains that is exclusively dedicated to encoding the shape of the environment (see also Gallistel, 1990). Shape was assumed to be stored and remembered separately from any landmarks. Whether shape is truly stored separately is debatable at the present time (see Cheng & Newcombe, 2005), but similar experiments in rectangular environments suggest that rotational errors often occur in a number of species, including pigeons (e.g., Kelly & Spetch, 2001), fish (e.g., Sovrano, Bisazza, & Vallortigara, 2003), and young children (Hermer & Spelke, 1994) among others (see Cheng & Newcombe, 2005, for a review). This suggests that a geometric module may be generally important. The possibility that animals learn about the global shape of an environment seems especially consistent with the idea that they learn a kind of map (but see pp. 323–325).

Spatial learning in the radial maze and water maze

Although experimenters have used a wide variety of methods for studying spatial learning in animals, two laboratory tasks have become especially common. The first is the good old radial maze. As you already know, rats clearly use cues at the end of the maze arms to get around efficiently in this environment. In addition, when experimenters use electrodes to measure activity in cells in the hippocampus, the cells appear to fire only when the rat is in a particular place on the maze (e.g., O'Keefe & Speakman, 1987). The discovery of such **place cells** encourages the view that the brain (the hippocampus, in particular) is wired and organized to detect an animal's place in space.

There are at least two ways to think about how the rat represents space in this task. One is that it might learn a mental map, and somehow "mark" each location on the map after it has been visited (e.g., Roberts, 1984). Another possibility is that locations might be stored as items in a list (e.g., Olton, 1978). As the rat moves around the center of the radial maze, it might look down an arm and make a decision about whether or not to visit that particular arm. The decision would be guided by memory, of course, but it would not necessarily be in the form of a map. There is evidence that the list-type of representation occurs. Michael Brown (1992) noticed that rats on the center of the maze would first orient toward an arm and often stop before deciding to enter or reject it. He called these orienting responses "microchoices," and discovered that they occurred at different arms more or less randomly—that is, the rats did not appear to be guided by a map. However, in subsequent experiments, Brown, Rish, Von Culin, and Edberg (1993) forced the rat to make a few choices before removing it from the maze. While the rat was away, they put an opaque cylinder around the center of the maze. When the rat was returned to the maze, it was put inside the cylinder, and now had to push a door open to look down any arm. Even though the rats couldn't see the arms or locations at the ends of the arms, they still preferred to open doors to those arms they had not previously visited on the first trial. Some sort of memory was thus guiding their "blind" choices within the cylinder, and Brown et al. (1993) suggested it might have been a map. In contrast, when extra maze cues are easier to view from the center, it might be easier to depend on the microchoice strategy.

Another laboratory maze is the **water maze**, first developed by Richard Morris (1981). The water maze is typically a circular pool of water, 1–2 meters in diameter that is situated in a room (Figure 8.33A). The water in the pool is made opaque with a substance that gives it a milky quality. The rat is required to swim in the pool to find a submerged platform that it can stand on to keep its head above the water. If the platform is marked by a beacon, such as a stick protruding from the water next to it, the rat readily learns to approach the beacon to reach the platform. But if there is no beacon, the rat is forced to use landmarks from the room outside the pool to locate the hidden platform efficiently.

In one of his original experiments, Morris (1981) gave rats training trials in which they always left from a start point at the west side of a tank to find a hidden platform in the northeast. (There was no beacon in this experiment.) On a test trial (summarized in Figure 8.33B), one group of rats (the Same-place group) were started from a point they had never started from before (i.e., north, east, or south), but the platform was in the same place as usual. As shown in the top row of Figure 8.33B, these rats had no trouble finding the location of the platform despite the change in starting point. A second group (the New-place group) was also started from new locations,

Figure 8.33 (A) A rat in a typical water maze. (B) Paths taken by individual rats ▶ on test trials in the water-maze experiment by Morris (1981). Rats in the Same-place group found the hidden platform (small circle) easily, even though they were started from a new location on the perimeter of the pool. Rats in the New-place group continued to search in the area where the platform had been located previously, before it was moved. In either condition, the rats had to use landmarks from the room outside the pool to locate the hidden platform. Control rats were started from their usual starting place. (A, after Morris et al., 1982; B, after Morris, 1981.)

(A)

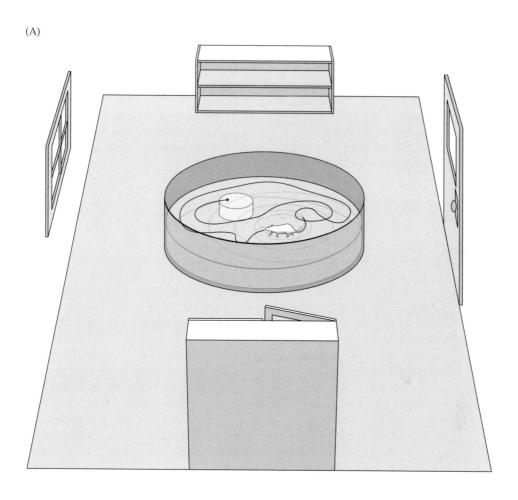

(B)

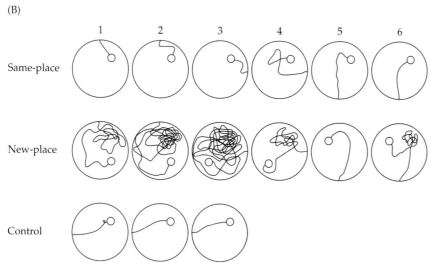

but their platform had been deviously moved. As shown in the figure, they eventually found the new platform location, but first searched a while in the original place. A control group had a test that was no different from what it had learned at the start; their performance held no surprises. Morris also soon showed that rats that had lesions of the hippocampus were very bad at learning this task (e.g., Morris, Garrud, Rawlins, & O'Keefe, 1982). Over the years since these early experiments, there have been so many other experiments that have shown that rats with lesions of the hippocampus do poorly in the water maze that poor performance has become a kind of litmus test of a good hippocampal lesion.

How do they do it?

Although the research just described tells us what kinds of cues animals use when they get around in space, it has not told us much about how they actually learn about those cues. Similarly, although Tolman talked about maps, and provided evidence that animals might learn about mazes without reinforcement (e.g., the latent learning experiment), he said relatively little about how maps were actually learned. It has been fairly common to assume that spatial learning follows unique learning principles. For example, Gallistel (1990, 1994) has noted a number of unique mental computations that would be required for an animal to construct a map. And, in an influential book, O'Keefe and Nadel (1978) distinguished between two memory systems: what they called the "locale system," which involved learning and using a cognitive map through exploration, and the "taxon system," which involved learning routes through space and S-R connections. Classical conditioning and most other types of learning we have considered were thought to be examples of the taxon system but not the locale system, which instead was devoted to spatial learning and mapping.

Exploration that allows the animal to connect different parts of the environment seems to be important in spatial learning. For example, Sutherland, Chew, Baker, and Linggard (1987) had rats learn to find a hidden platform in a water maze. Some rats were able to swim freely around the maze and observe the extra-maze cues from all vantage points. Other rats, however, could only see half the room at any one time because a black curtain was hung over the middle of the water maze so that it bisected the pool. When the rats were tested from a new starting point, the rats that had been allowed to view the room from all vantage points did better than those that had not. Similar results have been reported by Ellen, Soteres, and Wages (1984), who had rats learn about an elevated maze like the one shown in Figure 8.34. Three different tables were connected by open runways that joined in the center in a Y configuration. Wooden screens were positioned on the three tables so that observation from one table to the others was obstructed, except for a small entrance. On test trials, the rats were allowed to eat a little food on one of the tables, and then they had to find their way back to that table after being put on another table. Rats that had been allowed to explore the runways and connections between all three tables did better than those that

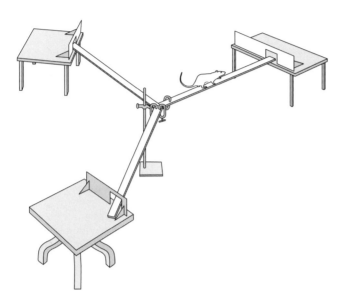

had been allowed to explore only one or two tables (and their runways) at a time. Unfortunately, this experiment did not control for the amount of exposure to the tables or practice walking on the narrow runways (the experimental groups had had more practice). But preliminary results do suggest that exploring the links between places is important for being able to move efficiently through a larger space.

There is also growing evidence that animals may learn about landmarks through familiar learning principles. For example, Roberts and Pearce (1999) demonstrated a blocking effect (see Chapters 3 and 4), suggesting that spatial learning might involve the kind of cue competition we know so well in other types of learning. The design of one experiment is shown in Figure 8.35A. In Phase 1, rats were trained to find a submerged platform located near a beacon in a water maze. A curtain around the maze eliminated external room cues. Control groups received none of this training, or only a single session (which was not expected to allow much learning about the beacon). In Phase 2, the curtains around the pool were opened so that the rats could now see cues from the surrounding room. At this point, the groups all received several sessions in which they swam to the hidden platform (marked by the beacon) in the presence of all the room cues. Notice that in Group Block, the room cues were redundant to the beacon in helping find the platform. The beacon might therefore have blocked learning about the room cues in this group.

To test this possibility, the experimenters finally allowed the rats to swim in the pool in the presence of the room cues with the beacon and platform removed. The results are shown in Figure 8.35B. Group Block showed more or less directionless behavior; the rats did not spend much time swimming in the quadrant of the pool where the platform had been. But the control groups searched near the former platform location—they had clearly learned

(A)

Group	Phase 1 (No room cues)	Phase 2	Test
Block	8 Beacon — Platform	4 Beacon + Room — Platform	Room?
1 session control	1 Beacon — Platform	4 Beacon + Room — Platform	Room?
No training control	—	4 Beacon + Room — Platform	Room?

(B)

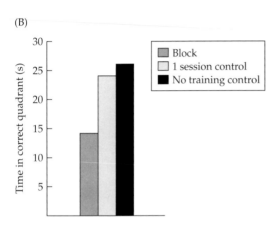

Figure 8.35 Design (A) and test results (B) of an experiment on blocking in the water maze. In Phase 1, the "Block" group was given eight sessions in which they learned to find a hidden platform near a beacon. Room cues were made unavailable by a curtain surrounding the maze. In Phase 2, the beacon was still present while the rats could learn the platform's position with respect to room cues (the curtain was removed). In the final test, the room cues were present while the beacon was not. Rats in the "Block" group spent little time searching for the platform in the correct quadrant of the pool. Learning about the beacon in Phase 1 thus blocked learning about the extra-maze room cues in Phase 2. (B, after Roberts & Pearce, 1999.)

more about the room cues. The beacon had thus blocked learning about the room cues in Group Block. In a similar experiment run in Richard Morris's lab (Biegler & Morris, 1999), blocking occurred on dry land when landmarks standing on the floor of a sawdust-covered arena signaled the location of food. In this case, when the to-be-blocked cue was added at the start of the compound phase (Phase 2), there was evidence that the rats noticed it—they went over and sniffed it and investigated. Thus, blocking in spatial learning is not simply due to a failure to notice the added cue. Competition between landmarks in spatial learning tasks has now been observed by several investigators using several methods (Redhead, Roberts, Good, & Pearce, 1997; Rodrigo, Chamizo, McLaren, & Mackintosh, 1997; Spetch, 1995; see also Chamizo, Sterio, & Mackintosh, 1985, for evidence in a radial maze).

These results suggest that the rules that govern learning about beacons and landmarks might not be entirely different from the rules that govern associative learning as it is represented in Pavlovian conditioning. For example, models like the Rescorla-Wagner model and others discussed in Chapter 4 may apply. On this view, landmarks may compete with one another for association with the goal the same way CSs compete for association with a US. Once again, there seems to be some generality to the laws of learning derived from studies of conditioning.

However, there are limits to this conclusion. Beacons do not seem to block learning about geometric cues, as opposed to landmarks and other beacons. In further experiments, Pearce, Ward-Robinson, Good, Fussell, and Aydin

(2001) first trained rats to swim to a hidden platform in a circular pool by using a beacon. (Extra-maze cues were again made unavailable by a curtain around the maze.) Then, the experimenters used the beacon to signal a platform near a corner of a "triangular" shape, which was created by suspending two plastic walls in the pool (Figure 8.36). Because extra-maze cues were again eliminated by putting a curtain around the pool, the training consisted of a compound of a previously trained beacon and a new geometric shape. When rats were then tested in the triangle without the beacon, they searched the location of the platform as much as the control had. That is, there was no evidence that the beacon had caused blocking! Additional experiments strongly suggested that the blocking failure was not because the beacon was too weak or not salient (Hayward, Good, & Pearce, 2004). Instead, it looked as if geometric cues were immune to blocking by beacons—as if the different kinds of spatial cues do not compete (see also Wall, Botly, Black, & Shettleworth, 2004). This kind of result is consistent with the possibility that animals learn about the shape of the environment in a "geometric module" that is not influenced by information from other cues (Cheng, 1986; Gallistel, 1990).

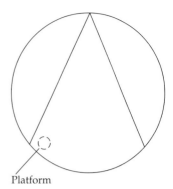

Figure 8.36 Walls (straight lines) inserted in the typical water maze introduce strong geometric cues. Learning about geometric information (e.g., the platform is near a corner) is difficult for a beacon to block.

But what exactly is the geometric cue? As described earlier, the idea has been that organisms that find goals in rectangular environments learn a global representation of the space (Cheng, 1986; Gallistel, 1990). The main evidence is that, in an environment like the one at the left in Figure 8.37A, many organisms make rotational errors—if the reward or goal is at Corner A, they often incorrectly go to Corner C. Pearce, Good, Jones, and McGregor (2004) recently thought about the explanation of this finding. They noted that, although the confusion between Corners A and C was consistent with the idea that the rat had a global geometric representation of the space, it was also possible that the mistakes were guided by purely local cues. For example, the rat might simply learn to approach a corner where a short wall is to the left of a long wall; or, the animal might merely learn to approach a long wall and then turn left. Either of these possibilities would get the animal to Corner A or Corner C equally often. But neither choice requires the rat to learn a global representation of the shape of the environment.

Pearce et al. (2004) ran an ingenious experiment that tested these ideas. They suspended large walls in a pool so that the walls created a rectangle that the rat could be confined in. There were no features or landmarks on the walls, and a featureless curtain surrounded the maze (so once again, extra-maze cues were not available). The rats had to learn to find a submerged platform near Point A. The rats showed the usual rotational errors: At the end of training, they swam to Corner A at the start of 44% of the trials, and Corner C on 45% of the trials. In a second phase, the walls were rearranged to make a kite shape (see Figure 8.37A, right). If the rats had learned to respond in the first phase according to the global representation

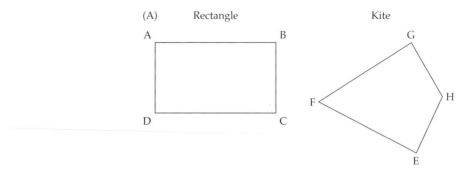

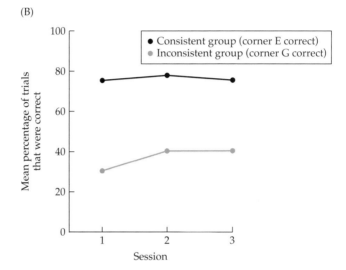

Figure 8.37 Environments (A) and results (B) of the experiment by Pearce et al. (2004). Rats were first trained to find the platform at Corner A in the Rectangle. Interestingly, the rats went to Corner C just as often as they went to Corner A (rotational errors, as in Figure 8.32), suggesting they were using a global representation of the rectangular environment. Such a representation would have been useless in the Kite, at right. But in the second phase, conducted in the Kite, the rats that could find a platform at Corner E did much better than the rats that could find the platform in Corner G. Corner E in the Kite was consistent with Corner A in the Rectangle because both were to the left of a long wall (for example). To get to Corners A or E, the rats might have merely found a long wall and turned left. They were using local cues, rather than a global representation of the environment. (After Pearce et al., 2004.)

of a rectangular environment, then initial training should have had little effect on responding in the kite configuration. But notice that Corner E was otherwise the same as Corners A and C—all were right angles, with a short wall to the left of a long wall. If the rat had learned to respond to local cues, there were grounds for thinking it might find a hidden platform in the kite configuration if the platform were positioned near Corner E.

In fact, there were two groups in the Pearce et al. (2004) experiment, and each group received different treatments in the kite phase. The Consistent group had to find the hidden platform in Corner E—the corner consistent with the corner that had been correct in the rectangle. The Inconsistent group instead had to find a platform at Corner G. The results are shown in Figure 8.37B, which shows the percentage of trials on which the rat first went to the correct corner in the kite phase. Both groups went to Corner E, the "correct" corner for Group Consistent but an incorrect corner for Group Inconsistent. They were thus responding to the local cues. And equally interesting, the rats went to Corner F (the apex of the kite) about as often as they went to Corner E—as if they really had learned to go to a long wall and turn left. The results clearly indicate that rats can behave as if they have learned a global geometric representation by responding to purely local cues.

These results, along with others (Esber, McGregor, Good, Hayward, & Pearce, 2005), raise new questions about evidence suggesting that animals learn a global geometric representation of the environment. We are once again left with the conclusion that simple learning rules, not unlike the ones we have discussed throughout this book, may account for behavior in a wide range of situations. You might be reminded of a theme we have seen many times before: Although many types of learning at first appear different from the types of learning we have seen in earlier chapters, there is surprising generality to the basic principles of learning.

Summary

1. Stimulus control techniques provide a powerful method for studying processes of animal cognition.

2. Animals can sort stimuli into polymorphous categories—that is, categories that are not defined by a single feature (e.g., people, cats, cars, flowers, and chairs). Such categorization probably depends on the basic learning mechanisms discussed in Chapters 4 and 5. The learning process may (a) find the most predictive features and associate them with each category, (b) construct a prototype of each category, or (c) allow the animal to remember each example and respond to new stimuli according to how similar they are. The Rescorla-Wagner model and its successors accomplish (a) and (b) and the Pearce configural learning model accomplishes (c).

3. Organisms generalize from one stimulus to another depending on their physical similarity. We generalize between two stimuli depending on the number of common features (elements) they share.

4. Generalization is also affected by learning:

   (a) Generalization gradients are sharpened by discrimination training, in part because the training introduces inhibition to S–. The presence of inhibition to S– can produce surprising peaks in responding to other stimuli. For example, in peak shift, the highest level of responding occurs in the presence of a stimulus that has never actually been reinforced.

(b) Generalization between two stimuli will increase if they are associated with a common event or stimulus. Such mediated generalization allows new, superordinate categories (e.g., furniture, clothing) to be built without physical similarity between the individual stimuli.

(c) Mere exposure to similar stimuli (like various birds or types of wine) can make them easier to discriminate. Such perceptual learning may occur because exposure to similar stimuli latently inhibits their common elements, creates inhibition between their unique elements, and/or creates a unitized representation of each stimulus.

5. For a stimulus to guide instrumental action, it must be perceived, attended to, and remembered.

6. Attention requires that the stimulus be informative. Attention can also be boosted by attentional priming.

7. Working memory allows stimuli or events to guide behavior after they are gone. It has been studied in the delayed matching-to-sample method and in the radial maze. Working memory is influenced by practice, and by retroactive and proactive interference. Animals appear to use it actively and efficiently, as when they switch between retrospective codes (remembering events that have come before) and prospective codes (remembering events that are coming in the future).

8. There are several different types of human long-term or reference memory. These can be difficult to study in animals, although there is evidence that scrub jays have an episodic-like memory that incorporates what, when, and where information about food items they have stored.

9. Time can be an important guide to instrumental action. Animals (and humans) are sensitive to time of day cues, which appear to depend on a circadian clock with a period of about a day. Organisms are also good at timing intervals on the order of minutes and seconds. Timing may be accomplished with an "internal clock" that may involve a pacemaker and an accumulator or the readout of a set of oscillators whose states change at different rates. Timing might also be accomplished with mechanisms that don't require a "clock."

10. Spatial cues also guide instrumental action, and organisms use beacons, landmarks, and dead reckoning to get around in space. Organisms might also form a geometric representation of the environment. Although spatial learning might be accomplished by specialized learning mechanisms, recent research suggests that it depends at least partly on familiar learning principles that allow animals to associate beacons and landmarks with goals.

Key Terms

stimulus control
animal cognition
categorization
transfer tests
feature theory
prototype
prototype theory
exemplar theory
stimulus generalization gradient
inhibition
peak shift
transposition
perceptual learning
acquired equivalence
mediated generalization
matching-to-sample
conditional discrimination
geons
touchscreen
search image
attentional priming
delayed matching-to-sample (DMTS)
radial maze
reference memory

retrospective code
prospective code
procedural memory
declarative memory
semantic memory
episodic memory
circadian rhythm
temporal generalization
peak procedure
superpose
superposition
scalar property
temporal bisection
internal clock
multiple oscillator model
multiple-time-scale model
behavioral theory of timing
dead reckoning
beacon
landmark
geometric module
place cells
water maze

Chapter

9

The Motivation of Instrumental Action

ONE DETAIL THAT HAS BEEN ALL BUT MISSING from the previous two chapters is the idea that instrumental behavior is motivated. To many people, the importance of motivation is self-evident. Emotions and motives are important parts of our lives, and the purpose of instrumental action is obviously to satisfy them. Behavior seems inherently goal-oriented or organized around achieving desired outcomes. That is what motivation is all about.

At least two formal properties of behavior suggest that it is motivated. For one thing, behavior is *variable*. In the presence of the same discriminative stimuli (see Chapter 8) and the same history of reinforcement (see Chapter 7), a rat might press the lever faster on Tuesday than on Monday. I might likewise ride my bike home a bit more quickly that day. What's the difference? Maybe the rat was hungrier on Tuesday. Maybe I was too; I usually go home thinking about dinner. Or maybe I wanted to get home quickly to watch my daughter's Tuesday soccer game. The point is that different levels of motivation can help explain variability in behavior that is not explained by knowing only the prior contingencies of reinforcement and the stimuli that set the occasion for the behavior.

Another property of behavior is its *persistence*. Often, behavior just keeps on going until it is satisfied. Variability and persistence are evident when the dog chases a rabbit—one whiff of the rabbit and the chase begins, taking the dog over hills, through bushes, and across streams until the rabbit is caught. While biking home, you might take a long detour to avoid a traffic jam or some dusty road construction, but you keep moving until you get home. Variability and persistence are common features of instrumental action, and they both suggest that behavior is motivated.

These ideas were well appreciated by Edward Tolman. You will remember (see Chapter 7) that he saw instrumental behavior as fundamentally goal-oriented—a variable means to a fixed end. Based on experiments like the latent learning experiment (Tolman & Honzik, 1930), Tolman argued that reinforcers were not really necessary for learning, but were instead essential for motivating behavior and giving it a purpose. He separated learning from performance. Rats that dawdle in the maze without reward may actually be learning about the maze. The rats merely have no reason to show what they know until a reward gives them a reason to perform efficiently. The distinction between learning and performance is another thing that motivation is all about. You can have knowledge on the one hand, and behavior on the other, but motivation is the thing that often translates knowledge into action.

This chapter continues our discussion of instrumental behavior by considering some of its motivational aspects. As we will see, motivational principles are indeed relevant for a complete understanding of instrumental action. And interestingly, what you already know about learning turns out to be quite crucial in understanding motivational processes themselves.

How Motivational States Affect Behavior

Motivation versus learning

Laboratory studies of motivation began in the 1920s and 1930s, when several kinds of experiments convinced everyone that motivation is important. For one thing, rats that were deprived of food appeared to be more active in mazes and running wheels than nondeprived rats (e.g., Richter, 1927). Other experiments indicated that rats that were deprived of food or water—or even sex— would walk across an electrified grid floor to get to the corresponding goal object (Warden, 1931). The number of floor-crossings the rats would tolerate was also a lawful function of the degree of deprivation—so motivation could be quantified. Still other experiments suggested that humans and other animals that were deprived of specific nutrients had **specific hungers** that motivated them to eat more of these missing nutrients. For example, Curt Richter told of a boy who was admitted to the Johns Hopkins hospital with an amazing appetite for salt—he would add salt to all of his food. The kid was probably born without adrenal glands, which are necessary for producing a hormone (aldosterone) that retains salt in the kidneys. He was therefore in a continual state of salt need. Sure enough, rats whose adrenal glands were surgically removed also demonstrated great persistence in working for salt (Richter, 1936). Other experiments seemed to suggest that rats (Richter, Holt, & Barelare, 1938), children (Davis, e.g., 1928), and other animals could select a healthy diet for themselves when offered a cafeteria of relatively purified foods. It was as if behavior was organized quite naturally and automatically to detect specific needs and then go about satisfying them.

Clark Hull

All of this work was consistent with the concept of **homeostasis**. The idea is that the body defends an equilibrium, and when there is some movement away from equilibrium, the body goes about correcting for it. Thus, when the body is depleted of something (such as food, or water, or salt), it goes about repleting itself. This turns out to be an important function of behavior—that is, it helps the body defend an equilibrium.

Homeostasis was one of the main ideas behind Clark Hull's influential theory of learning and motivation (Hull, 1943). We already talked a bit about Hull's theory in the context of theories of reinforcement; his idea was that reinforcers function to reduce Drive. In fact, Hull was extremely systematic and specific about what he meant by Drive, and how it was supposed to influence behavior. Drive was thought to be a very general motivational state that was activated whenever the body was in need. Hull described it in a very systematic and quantitative way. The core idea was that Drive (D), the major motivator, multiplies with Habit (H)—which was Hull's term for "learning"—to produce behavior strength:

$$\text{Behavior strength} = D \times H$$

Notice that Hull gave motivation and learning equal importance. If either Drive or Habit was equal to zero, there would be no behavior at all. The idea that D and H multiplied one another was consistent with the results of experiments in which rats, given different numbers of reinforcers for lever-pressing, were tested for lever-pressing at two levels of food deprivation (Figure 9.1; Perin, 1942; Williams, 1938). The number of reinforcers influenced Habit, and the amount of food deprivation determined Drive. Both clearly had a powerful impact on performance, and the two did not interact in the sense that the effect of Habit was the same regardless of the level of Drive. (In

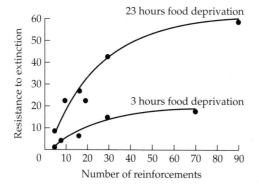

Figure 9.1 Resistance to extinction is independently affected by both the amount of food deprivation (which affects Drive, or D) and the number of prior reinforcements (which affects Habit, or H). (Data from Perin, 1942, and Williams, 1938; after Bolles, 1975.)

Figure 9.1, the two lines can be described by equations of the same form.) Habit and Drive were thus independent, and appeared to multiply.

Hull's theory was successful at describing the state of knowledge about motivation and behavior at the time. It was also beautifully specific and testable. For these reasons, it guided research in learning and motivation for many years, and in doing so it advanced our understanding appreciably. The theory is consistent with the rat-in-the-forest fable described in Chapter 7. Remember that the rat that wakes up hungry in the morning is motivated by its need for food, so it runs around blindly and restlessly, and therefore happens on an instrumental action that leads to food and is therefore reinforced by need reduction. Next time the rat is hungry, the drive will energize this new habit. The theory described an adaptive system in which behavior was organized to compensate and respond to need. There were several specific factors involved. First, Drive was caused by need. The rat was only motivated by Drive when it actually needed something in a biological kind of way. Second, Drive was thought to energize (1) consummatory behavior, like eating or drinking, (2) general activity, consistent with the rat's restless performance in the fable (and in Richter, 1927), and (3) instrumental behavior, like lever-pressing or runway-running, which are examples of goal-directed action. These are sensible ideas, and they seem consistent with most intuitions about how a motivational state like hunger motivates behavior. Let us see how accurate they are.

Does Drive merely energize?

Unfortunately, the theory really only worked up to a point. It is true that need increases the strength of consummatory activities. For example, the more food-deprived rats are, the quicker they begin eating (Bolles, 1962, 1965). But things got strange when investigators studied the effects of Drive on general activity. A lot of the increased activity shown by food-deprived rats was in response to changes in stimulation, including signals of food (Campbell & Sheffield, 1953; Sheffield & Campbell, 1954). And, food-deprivation itself caused many different patterns of activity. For example, Campbell (1964) and Campbell, Smith, Misanin, and Jaynes (1966) tested a number of species (rats, chicks, guinea pigs, hamsters, and rabbits) under food- or water-deprivation conditions. They also used two apparatuses as measures of activity, namely a running wheel and a stabilimeter, the latter of which is a cage that is mounted in such a way that switches detect movement. The effects of Drive on general activity were highly variable. For example, rats showed an increase in activity—especially in the running wheel—under either food or water deprivation. But hungry and thirsty rabbits showed *less* stabilimeter activity than satiated rabbits. Thirsty hamsters were less active in the running wheel than satiated hamsters, but about the same in the stabilimeter. The picture that emerged was very messy—there seemed to be nothing very general about general activity.

Part of the reason for the divergence between species and activity measurements was probably the fact that hunger and thirst tend to increase behav-

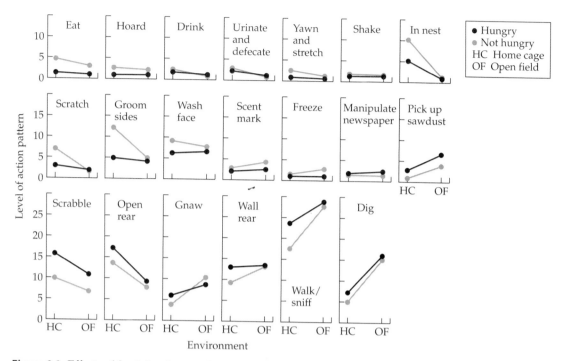

Figure 9.2 Effects of food deprivation (hunger) on various behaviors in the golden hamster. Hunger does not blindly energize activity, but selects behaviors from an organized behavior system. (After Shettleworth, 1975.)

iors that are naturally related to finding food or water in different species. Different apparatuses could differ in their sensitivity to different types of movement. Sara Shettleworth (1975) used careful observational methods to examine what hamsters do when they are food-deprived. She found that hungry hamsters showed higher levels of scrabbling (pawing the walls), open rearing, and digging—and lower levels of face washing, scratching and scent marking (Figure 9.2). A similar pattern emerged in anticipation of daily feedings, and you may remember that another similar pattern also emerged when Shettleworth reinforced these behaviors with food (see Chapter 2, Figure 2.18). The overall picture suggests that motivational states increase functional sets of behavior that are organized to deal with such states. This may sound familiar, because it is a premise of behavior systems theory (see Chapter 5); one example of a behavior system was shown in Figure 5.17 (Timberlake, 1994). The idea here is that motivational states select specific sets of behaviors rather than energizing everything blindly.

Other problems with Drive appeared when investigators started asking whether instrumental action is a simple function of deprivation level (see Bolles, 1975, for one review). To some extent it certainly is: When rats are food- or water-deprived, their operant lever-pressing increases while they work for the corresponding reinforcer (Collier & Levitsky, 1967; Collier, Lev-

Figure 9.3 Lever-pressing for food pellets as a function of the amount of body weight-loss caused by different amounts of food deprivation. (Data from Collier et al., 1967; after Collier & Johnson, 1997.)

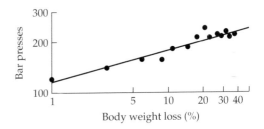

itsky, & Squibb, 1967). One of those experiments is illustrated in Figure 9.3. But things got less clear when the operant behavior became more difficult, as in complex discriminations (Bolles, 1975). And, even in simple operant situations in which an animal performs an instrumental act to get a reinforcer, the relationship between instrumental behavior and motivational state is now known to be much more interesting than Hull had initially thought.

Tony Dickinson and Bernard Balleine have argued that the effects of motivational state on instrumental behavior depend crucially on the animal's knowledge of how the reinforcer actually affects the motivational state (e.g., Balleine, 2001; Dickinson, 1989; Dickinson & Balleine, 1994). This type of knowledge depends on a process Dickinson and Balleine call **incentive learning**, which occurs when the animal ingests a reinforcer while it is in a particular motivational state. For example, when a hungry rat eats a new food, it may learn that the food is satisfying while it is hungry. Similarly, when a thirsty rat drinks a new fluid, it can learn that the stuff makes it feel good when it is thirsty. Once this sort of knowledge about an incentive is learned, it can be combined with knowledge about what instrumental actions lead to it. In this way, a motivational state like hunger will invigorate an instrumental act like lever-pressing if (and only if) the animal knows that lever-pressing produces an incentive that makes the rat feel better in the hunger state.

An experiment by Balleine (1992) illustrates this idea. Balleine first taught rats to lever-press for a food pellet reward while the rats were satiated (not hungry). The rats had never had these food pellets before. In a crucial test, some of the rats were returned to the Skinner box while they were now hungry and allowed to lever-press again. Unlike the experiment shown in Figure 9.4A, the reinforcer was not available during the test—that is, lever-pressing was tested in extinction. What happened was rather embarrassing for Hull: Rats tested for the first time while they were hungry showed no effect of hunger on performance (at left in Figure 9.4A). Hull got it wrong here; he would have predicted the new D would have automatically multiplied H to produce stronger responding in the tested-while-hungry group. (It is worth noting that moving a flap on the front of the food cup—a behavior that was more proximate to the reinforcer—did increase; see Balleine, Garner, Gonzalez, & Dickinson, 1995.)

Bernard Balleine

Balleine's experiment also included another pair of groups, and these are the ones that make the experiment really interesting. As before, the rats were taught to lever-press for food pellets while they were satiated, and then half were ultimately tested for lever-pressing in extinction while they were hungry. But these rats also had an opportunity for incentive learning at the start of the experiment. That is, before the instrumental-learning phase began, these rats were allowed to eat the pellets while they were actually food-deprived and hungry. The idea, again, is that this experience could allow the rats to learn that the pellets were "good" while they were in the hunger state. (The other pair of groups received a similar exposure to hunger, but there was no opportunity for incentive learning to occur.) This time, when the rats were made hungry and tested in extinction, hunger had a strong effect on lever-pressing (at right in Figure 9.4A). Thus, hunger does invigorate lever-pressing—but only if the rat knows that the outcome of responding is a good thing while in the hunger state. In other experiments, Balleine also found that downshifts in hunger decreased lever-pressing only if the rats had the opportunity to learn about the effects of food pellets while in the satiated state. The effects of either increases in hunger (Figure 9.4A) or decreases in hunger (Figure 9.4B)

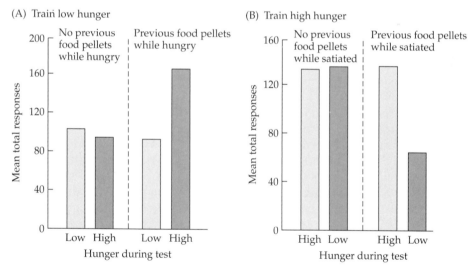

Figure 9.4 Incentive learning: The effect of hunger on instrumental behavior depends on what the organism has learned about the reinforcer while in the hunger state. (A) Rats were trained to lever-press for pellets while hunger was Low. They were then tested in extinction with either Low or High levels of hunger. High hunger motivated (increased) lever-pressing only if the rats had previously eaten the pellets while in the hungry state—and therefore learned about the pellets' effects on hunger. (B) Results of a similar experiment in which rats were trained while hunger was High and then tested in extinction with either High or Low levels of hunger. Here, the Low level of hunger during the test de-motivated behavior only if the rats had previously eaten pellets in the nonhungry state. (After Balleine, 1992.)

on instrumental behavior depended crucially on the rats' knowledge of the effect of the pellets while in the tested motivational state.

Similar results have been shown with thirst and liquid reinforcers (Dickinson & Dawson, 1989; Lopez, Balleine, & Dickinson, 1992). Interestingly, other evidence further suggests that baby rats do not instinctively drink water when they are dehydrated, or eat rat chow when they are food-deprived. Instead, they first need a chance to consume and learn about the effects of water and chow while they are either thirsty or hungry (Changizi, McGehee, & Hall, 2002; Hall, Arnold, & Myers, 2000; Myers & Hall, 2001). This natural incentive learning apparently happens when the growing pup first samples water and chow in the week or two that follows weaning from the mother's milk. There is also evidence that animals need to learn about the motivational effects of feeling warm. Hendersen and Graham (1979) first trained adult rats to avoid heat from a heat lamp, which was unpleasant in a warm (27°C) environment. Then they tested the rats in extinction when the room was either warm (27°C) or cold (7°C). The rats continued to avoid the heat regardless of the current room temperature. But before the test, some rats had a chance to experience the heat lamp while the environment was cold. This presumably allowed them to learn that the lamp felt good, not bad, when they were cold. Sure enough, when these rats were tested in the cold environment, they did not avoid the heat lamp anymore. In fact, they delayed responding longer, as if waiting for the heat to come on. Thus, incentive learning seems to be important in several motivational systems. For a motivational state to influence instrumental performance, we need to learn about the value of the reinforcer in that state.

Dickinson (1989) and Dickinson and Balleine (1994) have noted that their emphasis on incentive learning overlaps with some of Tolman's earlier thinking about instrumental action (Tolman, 1949). Tolman emphasized the importance of "cathexes" in motivated behavior, by which he meant the connection between a goal and its corresponding motivational state, which he thought was learned during consumption of the goal object. How this learning actually operates is still not completely understood. Garcia (1989) and others have emphasized how foods become connected with their effects on the digestive system; you may remember ideas like the "hedonic shift" from Chapter 6. Cabanac (1971) has demonstrated that people rate reinforcers (such as heat and sweet flavors) as especially pleasant when they experience these reinforcers in the motivational state they satisfy, and learning about one's own hedonic reaction to the outcome may be involved in incentive learning (see also Chapter 10). Consistent with this idea, foods and solutions consumed while animals are in a corresponding state of deprivation become preferred or more reinforcing later (Capaldi, Davidson, & Myers, 1981; Revusky, 1967, 1968). Terry Davidson (1993, 1998) has suggested that motivational states like hunger set the occasion for relations between stimuli, like the flavor of a food and its ingestional consequences. Through experience, we learn that hunger signals that a flavor in turn signals something good. Perhaps this mechanism is involved in learning about incentive value. An interesting discussion of some of these views, as well as Tolman's own view and its limitations, can be found in Dickinson and Balleine (1994; see also Balleine, 2001; Dickinson, 1989; Dickinson & Balleine, 2002).

To summarize, motivational states do affect instrumental behavior, but their effects are more subtle and interesting than Hull imagined 60 years ago. First, states like hunger do not blindly energize all behaviors, but instead seem to select specific sets of behaviors or behavior systems that evolution has organized to deal with the goal. Second, for a motivational state to energize an instrumental action, the organism must first learn that the action leads to a particular reinforcer, and that this reinforcer has a positive effect on the motivational state. The motivational state thus influences instrumental behavior by increasing the desirability of particular reinforcers, and the animal will then perform those behaviors that lead to these reinforcers. This sort of view is consistent with a more cognitive view of instrumental learning, and will be considered further in the next chapter. Hull was an S-R theorist, and as we will also see in later parts of the present chapter, his ideas about learning—like his ideas about Drive—are now a bit out of date.

Is motivated behavior a response to need?

One of the reasons the rat-in-the-forest fable is so relevant is that it also emphasizes another important assumption present in early thinking about motivation. The rat in the forest wakes up in a state of need, and everything that follows is basically a response to this need. In Hull's system, Drive was a *response to need*—the state of depletion motivates behaviors that cause repletion. Hull's thinking about motivation and Drive, often called a depletion-repletion theory (e.g., Collier & Johnson, 1997), seem to come naturally to people thinking about motivation and hunger.

Although it makes sense for animals to have a system that can respond to depletion, it is worth wondering whether evolution would design an animal to wait until it is in a state of need to begin seeking reinforcers, like food or water. If an animal always waits until it needs food before going about finding it, the animal could be in trouble if food suddenly becomes truly scarce. Instead of waiting to need food, a better system might have the animal acquiring food before there is really a need for it. In this sense, we might expect to see motivated behavior organized to anticipate needs rather than respond to them. Responses to depletion must be available, of course. But they may be designed to deal with emergencies, rather than the normal everyday state of affairs.

There is actually a great deal of evidence that motivated behavior is organized in anticipation of—rather than in response to—need. One of my favorite experiments illustrates the point beautifully. Fitzsimons and LeMagnen (1969) were studying drinking in rats. Half of the rats being studied were maintained on a high-protein diet, which requires a great deal of water for digestion; the other half were maintained on a lower-protein diet, which requires less water. Not surprisingly, rats in the lower-protein group drank less water every day. But in a second phase, the low-protein rats were switched to the high-protein diet. What they did was very revealing. At first they responded to the new demand for water after each meal. But then, within a few days, the extra drinking moved forward in time so that the rats began taking extra water with each meal. Thus, the extra drinking began to be done in anticipation of the need rather than in response to it. When rats on the high-protein diet were switched to the lower-protein diet, they continued to drink water with their meals, although the amount of water they drank gradually decreased. The study suggests that, although the rat can adjust its water intake so that it responds to need, drinking occurs to prevent need rather than to escape it.

Another ingenious experiment made a similar point about eating (LeMagnen, 1959, described in Seeley, Ramsay, & Woods, 1997). This time LeMagnen gave rats three one-hour opportunities to eat food (Meals 1, 2, and 3) each day. After the rats had become accustomed to this schedule, LeMagnen withdrew Meal 2. Initially, the rats compensated by increasing their consumption during Meal 3—that is, in response to the new need generated by missing Meal 2. But eventually, the rats began to eat the extra food during Meal 1, which LeMagnen attributed to learning. In effect, although eating initially responded to need, in the long run eating seems to be influenced by learning and organized to prevent—rather than respond to—depletion.

The idea that eating occurs in response to need suggests that animals might wait until the tank is empty before they fill it. In reality, if one stops and checks the fullness of the lab rat's stomach under ordinary free-feeding conditions, it is never empty (Collier, Hirsch, & Kanarek, 1977). When food is freely available, the typical rat eats 9–12 meals a day, mostly at night and around the time the lights switch on or off on the day-night light schedule. Various attempts have been made to predict the size of each meal based on the amount of time that has passed since the last meal. If the animal is repleting some depletion, then it should consume a bigger meal the longer the time since the last meal. Generally, there is little correlation between the intermeal interval and the size of the next meal (Collier et al., 1977), and the generality of the finding when it occurs is controversial (Collier & Johnson, 1997). Woods and Strubbe (1994) have emphasized the fact that a great deal of the rat's food is eaten when the lights in the colony room go on or off at the beginning and end of each day (presumably, regardless of the time since the last meal). Woods and Strubbe note that meals are actually disruptive events, because they put so many difficult metabolic demands on the animal's body (Woods, 1991). Pavlovian cues that predict meals can actually help the animal adapt because the cues elicit CRs that compensate for the upcoming meal (see Chapter 2). By eating food at the time of salient events, like lights-on and lights-off, the system takes advantage of Pavlovian CRs that can occur in response to these cues. Once again, learning factors—rather than merely need factors—may play a powerful role in controlling motivated behavior. Learning is now thought to be very important in the control of feeding and food regulation (e.g., Seeley et al., 1997).

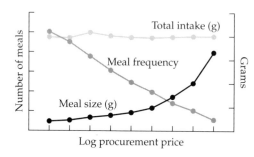

Figure 9.5 Meal frequency, meal size, and total (daily) intake as a function of the cost of procuring access to food. The data are hypothetical but represent results that have been obtained in studies of a number of different species. (After Collier & Johnson, 1997.)

For the last 30 years or so, George Collier has studied several species of animals using a method in which the animals live in Skinner boxes, where they earn all of their daily food (Collier, 1981; Collier & Johnson, 1997; Collier et al., 1977). In a typical experiment, Collier and his colleagues manipulate the cost of meals by requiring the animals to make a certain number of lever-presses to get the food. The animals determine the size of each meal, because once a meal is earned, the food bin stays available until they stop eating. In this way, the animals can control the number of meals—and the size of each meal—each day. Collier finds that, regardless of species, daily meal size and meal number are lawfully related to meal cost. As the cost increases, the animals take fewer—but bigger—meals in a way that keeps their total daily intake more or less constant (Figure 9.5). At any given meal cost, though, meal size, meal number, and intermeal intervals are still variable, and time since the last meal is a poor predictor of the size of the next meal—or the rate at which the animals consume it. In the long run, Collier and his colleagues have concluded that "meal patterns are tools in the service of the optimization of expenditures of time and effort to exploit resources. They do not reflect the cyclic processes of depletion and repletion…" (Collier & Johnson, 1997, p. 126). Something other than the momentary state of need explains feeding.

Leanne Birch and her colleagues have studied eating in young children, and they have come to a complementary conclusion (e.g., Birch & Fisher, 1996). Newborns start out as depletion-repletion feeders who cry when they need food, and then get fed. But not much later in development, other learning processes begin to take over. By about six months of age, babies learn that cues in the evening predict a period of fasting overnight, and they begin to take larger meals in anticipation of the fast. By preschool age, environmental and social cues begin to control the initiation of meals. For example, in one study (Birch, 1991) children played repeatedly in two rooms. In one room, food was freely available, and in another room, food was never available. In a final test, the kids were first given a large dish of ice cream, and then allowed to play in these rooms with snacks freely available. Despite being full, the children consumed more snack food—and they were quicker to begin eating it—in the room that had been associated with food (Figure 9.6). This finding is similar to a remarkable phenomenon known to occur in

Figure 9.6 Children who are otherwise "full" eat more snack food (left) and take less time to begin eating it (right) when they are tested in a room that has been previously associated with food (CS+). (After Birch, 1991.)

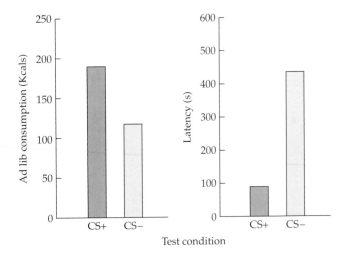

rats. On a number of trials, Harvey Weingarten (1983, 1984) gave rats a combination light and buzzer CS before delivery of evaporated milk in the rats' home cage. Later, when the light and buzzer were presented, even satiated rats got up within 5 seconds and ate about 20% of their ordinary daily intake! (See also Weingarten, 1990.) This phenomenon seems familiar to me. I tend to eat at noon, or around 7:00 pm, because temporal cues associated with previous meals basically tell me (motivate me?) to eat again.

Children's food intake is also strongly influenced by their food preferences, which are learned through their repeated experiences with foods and eating as they mature (Birch & Fisher, 1996). For example, in several experiments, children acquired preferences for flavors that had been mixed with maltodextrin (a starch; Birch, McPhee, Steinberg, & Sullivan, 1990) or high-fat concentrations of yogurt (Johnson, McPhee, & Birch, 1991; Kern, McPhee, Fisher, Johnson, & Birch, 1993). The results are reminiscent of other research in rats, discussed in Chapter 2, which indicate that animals learn to prefer flavors associated with a variety of nutrients (e.g., Sclafani, 1997). Interestingly, children can also be taught to pay attention to both internal and external cues. Four-year-olds who were taught to pay attention to their internal fullness (by filling the glass stomach of a doll, or talking with an adult about how you know when you are full, etc.) were less likely to eat additional snacks after eating yogurt than were others who had been taught to pay attention to external cues (e.g., eating at the sound of a bell, etc.) (Birch, McPhee, Shoba, Steinberg, & Krehbiel, 1987). Learning clearly plays an important role in eating and food selection.

A final comment is in order on specific hungers—one of the early phenomena that stimulated interest in the depletion-repletion model. One relatively recent review has raised doubt about the idea that animals can select healthy diets when given various foods in a cafeteria arrangement (Galef, 1991). Many of these "automatic" adaptations to specific needs are not auto-

(A) Old vs. new diet

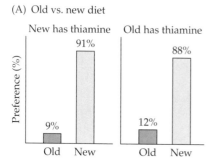

(B) Two new diets

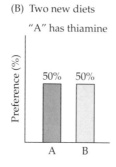

Figure 9.7 (A) Thiamine-deficient rats prefer a new diet over the old one regardless of whether new or old has been fortified with thiamine. (B) Deficient rats also initially choose indiscriminately between new diets—whether the diets contain thiamine or not. The explanation: The rats have learned an aversion to the old diet (because they got sick while eating it) and now avoid it. (Data from Rodgers, 1967; and Rozin & Rodgers, 1967.)

matic at all—that is, when specific hungers seem evident in behavior, they often depend on learning. For example, Rozin and Kalat (1971) reviewed a number of experiments from the late 1960s that had been conducted on specific hungers for nutrients like thiamine. Typically, rats are made deficient in thiamine by giving them a diet that is lacking this nutrient. As a consequence, after a few weeks the rats get scruffy and sick. If the rats are then offered a new diet that is rich in thiamine, they will choose it, but preference for the new diet is blind. For example, the rats choose the new diet regardless of whether the new diet or the old diet now has thiamine in it (Rozin & Rodgers, 1967; Figure 9.7A). And, when given a choice between two new diets—one that contains thiamine and one that does not—the rats go to either diet indiscriminately (Rodgers, 1967; Figure 9.7B). When Rozin (1967) watched the behavior of rats while they ate the original thiamine-deficient diet, they ate little of it, but also tended to paw it and spill it. In the end, the main explanation of the phenomenon was that the rats learned an aversion to the diet that made them sick, and they subsequently avoided it. Except perhaps for sodium deficiency—and possibly phosphorous deficiency—there is no behavioral response that automatically comes into play to satisfy a specific nutritional need. Instead, rats learn aversions to foods that make them sick, and they may ultimately also learn to prefer foods that make them well. Once again, the relation between need and motivation is not as tight as originally supposed, and once again we find an important role for learning.

To summarize, although animals in need of food or water will perform behaviors that correct their deficit, responding to depletion is probably something saved for emergencies. Instead, a great deal of motivated behavior seems to anticipate—rather than respond to—need. Learning thus plays another very powerful role. Given all this research, we might wonder what we mean when we say we are "hungry." We might describe ourselves this way *either* when we need food (for example, hours after our last meal or after a strenuous hike) or when we are exposed to cues that have been associated with food, such as meal times or restaurants emanating lovely food aromas. Hunger motivation seems to be aroused by either biological need or by signals for food (Weingarten, 1985). It is therefore worth thinking more about how signals actually motivate.

Anticipating Reward and Punishment

Bait and switch

The idea that signals and expectations motivate behavior was another one of Tolman's ideas. You might remember that, in the latent learning experiment (Tolman & Honzik, 1930), rats that explored a maze without reward quickly got through the maze efficiently once they were rewarded. The idea was that knowledge that there was a reward at the end of the tunnel, so to speak, gave the rats a reason to get through the maze efficiently. **Acquired motivation** is a name that is given to this kind of motivation, because it is acquired through experience—unlike the motivation thought to be provided by drives and needs.

Other experiments conducted in Tolman's lab supported the same kind of idea. For example, Tinklepaugh (1928) had monkeys learn to open a box in order to find a tasty piece of banana inside. On test trials, Tinklepaugh secretly replaced the banana with a piece of lettuce. Lettuce is a reasonable reward for a monkey, but it is not as good as banana, and the bait and switch trick had a major effect on the monkey once the lettuce was discovered. According to Tinklepaugh, the monkeys shrieked, looked angry and frustrated, and appeared to search for the missing banana. They behaved as if they had expected banana, and that the switch to lettuce made them mad. In a related experiment with rats, Elliott (1928) showed that rats ran quickly through a maze for a tasty wet food mash reward. When the reward was switched to sunflower seeds (which rats like a bit less), the previous behavior fell apart. The rats who were switched to sunflower seeds became even slower to run through the maze than a group of rats that had been rewarded with sunflower seeds all along. Once again, animals appeared to expect a certain outcome, and an emotional effect occurred when they discovered a less-preferred commodity.

These motivating effects of rewards were not mentioned in Hull's original theory (1943). In fact, the idea that rewards motivate seems to have been rather slow to take hold, presumably because the field was so enthralled with Thorndike's stamping-in reinforcement mechanism. However, everyone did finally notice some experiments by Crespi (1942). Crespi also examined the effects of incentive switches in rats. In one experiment, he trained rats to run down a 20-ft runway to get 1, 16, or 256 food pellets. As shown at left in Figure 9.8, running speed was faster the bigger the reward. In the next phase, all the rats received 16 pellets. The effect on performance was immediate. The rats that were switched from 256 pellets down to 16 showed a **negative contrast** effect: Their running speed abruptly went lower than that of the rats that had been receiving 16 pellets all along. (This is like being switched from banana to lettuce, or mash to sunflower seeds.) Rats switched from 1 to 16 pellets showed a **positive contrast** effect: Their running speed

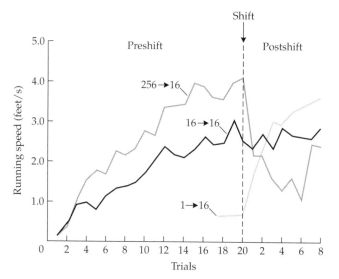

Figure 9.8 Running speeds of rats given rewards of different sizes. When shifted from 256 pellets to 16 pellets, running speed went below the speed of a group that received 16 pellets all along ("negative contrast"). When shifted from 1 to 16 pellets, running speed went above ("positive contrast"). (Data from Crespi, 1942; after Bolles, 1975.)

immediately increased and overshot the rats that had been receiving 16 pellets all along. It was as if the upshift in reward-size made the rats elated (Crespi called positive and negative contrast, "elation" and "depression" effects, respectively). The idea is that reward shifts can have emotional effects on behavior. The effects of the 16-pellet reward in the second phase clearly depended on prior experience—previous exposure to better made the middle value feel bad (negative contrast), whereas previous exposure to worse made the middle value feel pretty good (positive contrast).

More recent studies have confirmed and extended these effects. The late Charles Flaherty and his students ran a large number of related experiments, and Flaherty reviewed the literature in a book aptly entitled *Incentive Relativity* (Flaherty, 1996). Both positive and negative contrast have been widely demonstrated, although negative contrast effects are easier to obtain and are more widely studied. In one method, rats are given a daily 5-minute drink of a very tasty 32% sucrose solution, or a tasty (but less-so) 4% sucrose solution. The experimenters usually measure licking of the solutions; not surprisingly, the rats lick more of the 32% solution (Figure 9.9). Then, after several days of drinking the 32% solution, the rats are suddenly given a 4% solution for several days. As shown in Figure 9.9, there is once again an abrupt shift in performance, and the 4% solution elicits less licking in the rats that had been previously drinking the 32% solution. Flaherty asked whether this example of negative contrast is associated with an emotional effect by measuring the level of a stress hormone (corticosterone) in the blood after the 4% solution drinking sessions (Flaherty, Becker, & Pohorecky, 1985). He also tested the effects of several tranquilizing drugs, like chlordiazepoxide (librium), on negative contrast (Flaherty, Lombardi, Wrightson, & Deptula, 1980). An interesting pattern emerged: Remarkably, there was no emotional effect on the first day of exposure to the new 4% solution; neg-

Figure 9.9 Successive negative contrast. Rats were given brief daily drinks of either a 32% or a 4% sucrose-water solution. When switched from 32% to 4%, they licked less of the 4% solution than the group that was given 4% all along. (After Flaherty, 1991.)

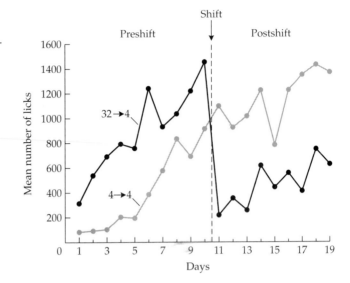

ative contrast was clearly evident in drinking behavior, but there was no elevation of corticosterone and no effect of tranquilizers. But emotions kicked in on the second day after the shift, when plasma corticosterone levels rose and tranquilizers abolished the contrast effect. On Day 1, the rats drank less because they detected the downshift and became busy exploring elsewhere in the environment, as if they were searching for the 32% solution (Flaherty, 1991; Pecoraro, Timberlake, & Tinsley, 1999). Then, on Day 2 with the less-palatable solution, the rats began to get frustrated. An initial exploratory response was followed by an emotional response. Interestingly, Tinklepaugh (1928) had also described both types of effects.

The Hullian response: Incentive motivation

Given experiments like Crespi's, by the 1950s it became clear that rewards and their anticipations had motivating effects. In addition to stamping in or reinforcing behavior, rewards also motivated. To capture the idea, Hull (1952)—and especially his student Kenneth Spence (1951, 1956), who we met in the preceding chapter when we considered discrimination learning—began to emphasize a new motivational construct, **incentive motivation**. Hull (1952) added another term in his equation for behavior strength. In addition to behavior being a function of learning ("Habit") and need ("Drive"), behavior was said to depend on the motivating effect of reward. This new theoretical construct was called "K" in Hull's equation, perhaps after Kenneth ("I" had already been taken by several inhibitory factors that I have not told you about). The bottom line, though, was that

$$\text{Behavior strength} = D \times H \times K$$

so that, if we want to predict the vigor of an instrumental action, we need to think about two motivational factors in addition to how well the action is

Figure 9.10 How a "fractional anticipatory goal reaction" (r_G) causes incentive motivation in the runway, according to Hull and Spence. When rewarded with food in the goal area, the reward elicits a large goal reaction (R_G). This response is associated with stimuli in the goal box, which generalize to the start box. The conditioned response elicited by the cues in the start box (r_G) now provides motivation for the rat to run rapidly on the next trial. Although the emphasis on S-R learning seems old-fashioned, the big idea is that Pavlovian conditioning motivates instrumental behavior.

learned. Notice that Incentive (K) was given a status equal to that of Drive (D) and Habit (H)—if any of three was equal to zero, there would be no behavior strength. Drive was not learned, but was internal and linked to need. In contrast, Incentive was learned, externally driven, and linked to reward. Incentive pulled behavior, whereas Drive was said to push behavior.

The reward effects that led to proposing incentive motivation all seemed to depend on the animal learning to expect a particular reward. This was clear in Tinklepaugh's banana-to-lettuce experiment, but it was also clear in Crespi's experiment, as well: It is the change from the *expected* value of the reward that causes positive and negative contrast effects. This kind of description was difficult to accept in the 1950s because it seemed mentalistic and nonscientific. Instead, Hull and his students—especially Spence (e.g., 1951, 1956)—developed a powerful way to understand incentive motivation in terms of S-R theory. The general idea is known as the **r_G-s_G mechanism**, and it is based on an earlier paper by Hull (1931).

The idea can be simplified with a picture (Figure 9.10). A rat runs down a runway and gets rewarded in a goal box. In Hullian theory, one effect of the reward is to reinforce the running response through drive reduction, but another thing happens, too. The food itself elicits a big response—called a goal reaction, or R_G. For example, the rat may salivate when it eats the food—exactly as in Pavlov's experiments. The crucial thing is that this goal reaction becomes associated with stimuli in the goal box through classical conditioning. As a consequence, the goal box itself will elicit a smaller version of the goal reaction. This was called a "fractional anticipatory goal reaction," or r_G. (The "r" is little because CRs are not quite as big as URs.) There are two important consequences of the conditioning of r_G. First, if the start box is similar to the goal box, there will be some generalization between them, and when the rat is put into the start box on the next trial, the start box will therefore elicit some r_G. This anticipatory reaction provides incentive motivation—it energizes the running response. A second consequence is that r_G has stimulus effects—that is, the rat detects the salivation, and this is a stimulus that responses can be attached to. The stimulus was called "s_G." The elicitation of r_G increases the vigor of responding, and the presence of s_G provides a stimulus that can persist and allow an integration of a series of responses. The ideas seem a little quaint these days, but in the hands of a brilliant theorist like Spence, they could be expanded to explain many complex and sophisticated experimental results. The bottom line, though, is that *the motivating effects of reward were attributed to a mechanism based on classical conditioning*. In this important sense, incentive motivation involves all the conditioning laws and processes we discussed in Chapters 3–5.

The incentive motivation concept is consistent with the results. For example, consider Crespi's group of rats that was shifted from 1 pellet to 16 pellets. Habit was learned in Phase 1. Then, on the first trial of Phase 2, there was a bigger R_G to the bigger reward; this was quickly conditioned, generalized to the start box, and the bigger r_G then energized the running response all the more. The same scenario was thought to be involved in the latent learning experiment (see Figure 7.5), where animals also received an upshift from zero to some larger reward. Here, the argument was that there was some unknown reinforcer that was allowing learning to occur in Phase 1— perhaps the rats found it reinforcing to be greeted by Honzik at the end of the maze. Then, as in Crespi's experiment, there was a big goal reaction that became conditioned to the maze and then invigorated the response on the next trial.

Frustration

In fact, there is more than this going on. r_G was just one of several anticipatory responses learned through classical conditioning that were thought to motivate instrumental action. While positive events like food or water were thought to condition positive goal reactions, aversive events like electric footshock or pain were thought to condition fear responses, or r_E (Mowrer, 1947). This kind of response was crucial for motivating avoidance learning, as we will see later and in the next chapter. And there was another "little r" that was developed by another important theorist, Abram Amsel (1958, 1962, 1992). When the animal expects a big reward (which is to say, it has a large conditioned r_G), but then receives a small reward, there is a primary **frustration** reaction, or R_F. The size of this frustration reaction is determined by the size of the discrepancy between the reward expected and the reward obtained. Frustration is also conditioned through classical conditioning, so that another little r, or r_F, becomes elicited by cues associated with decreases in reward. Frustration is unpleasant, evokes withdrawal, and the rat will learn to escape conditioned stimuli that elicit it (Daly, 1969). It is the emotional part of the negative contrast effect: Frustration connected with a decrease in the size of reward becomes conditioned, generalizes to the start box, demotivates, and elicits competing behavior.

Frustration is a powerful emotion. If you have ever been thwarted in reaching a goal, you know what it means. A good place to observe frustration reactions is near a coke machine that is temporarily out of order: Peo-

Abram Amsel

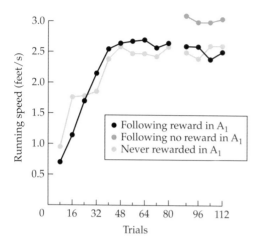

Figure 9.11 The effect of frustration in the double runway. In the test trials at the right, speed of running in the second alley is especially fast when an expected reward in Alley 1 (A_1) did not occur. Control rats that never received a reward in A_1—and therefore never expected it—did not run as fast. (After Wagner, 1959.)

Legend:
- Following reward in A_1
- Following no reward in A_1
- Never rewarded in A_1

Y-axis: Running speed (feet/s)
X-axis: Trials

ple put money in, expecting a cool and tasty drink, and when they get nothing in return they may rattle the coin return, look a little angry, gesticulate wildly, and bang on the machine. Amsel and Roussel (1952) reported an early experiment that convinced people of the importance of frustration. Rats were run in a double runway in which the goal box of the first runway was also the start box for a second runway. Amsel and Roussel sometimes provided a reward in the first goal box, and sometimes not. Running speed in the second runway was faster following nonreward than following reward; the second running response was motivated by frustration (see also Amsel & Ward, 1965). The thwarted expectation was what counted: Rats that never received a reward in the first runway—and therefore didn't expect it—did not run as fast in the second runway (Wagner, 1959, Figure 9.11). Getting no reward when one is expected causes a frustration response that energizes performance.

Frustration theory helps explain a host of interesting phenomena that are known as **paradoxical reward effects**. The word "paradoxical" refers to the fact that a reward can sometimes seem to weaken—and nonreward can sometimes seem to strengthen—instrumental action. One example is the successive negative contrast effect shown in Figures 9.8 and 9.9. Prior experience with a large reward can make a perfectly good smaller reward rather ineffective. Another example is the "magnitude of reinforcement extinction effect." In instrumental learning, reinforcement with a large reward can actually lead to faster extinction than reinforcement with a smaller reward (Hulse, 1958; Wagner, 1961). Still another example is the "overlearning extinction effect": Many rewarded trials can paradoxically increase the rate of extinction, relative to fewer rewarded trials (e.g., Ison, 1962; Siegel & Wagner, 1963). All of these effects are consistent with frustration theory, because large rewards and extensive training will cause a large amount of frustration when a reward is suddenly omitted at the start of extinction. Helen and John Daly (1982, 1994) presented a model that combined the principles of frustration theory with the Rescorla-Wagner model in order to explain a large number of these effects. The administration of reward and nonreward can have peculiar outcomes that are not predicted by the simple law of effect—or most theories of classical conditioning, for that matter.

Another paradoxical reward effect

A quite separate line of experiments with humans also suggests that rewards can have negative effects. Deci (1971) had college students play with puzzles in the lab. In a crucial phase, participants in an experimental group were given $1 for every puzzle they finished, while a control group was allowed to continue playing without reward. In a subsequent test without reward, the previously rewarded group tended to spend less time solving puzzles than the non-rewarded group. "Extrinsic reward" was said to hurt "intrinsic motivation" for playing with the puzzles. In another study, Lepper, Greene, and Nisbett (1973) studied preschool children who initially spent a great deal of time drawing with magic markers. The children were divided into three groups: One group received no reward for drawing, and two groups received a "Good Player Award" certificate with a gold seal and ribbon. The two rewarded groups were either told they would receive the award, or else they received it unexpectedly. In a subsequent test, the group that received the expected reward spent less time drawing than the other groups. The unexpected reward had no such effect. Once again, for the expected reward group at least, an extrinsic reward appeared to hurt performance.

The "punished-by-reward" phenomenon, and related phenomena that have been reported since (see Deci, Koestner, & Ryan, 1999), has suggested to some writers that the use of positive rewards can actually hurt human creativity, productivity, and potential (see discussion in Eisenberger & Cameron, 1996; Figure 9.12). In fact, though, the effect is easy to exaggerate. It would be a stretch to believe that the very high monetary rewards paid to stars like Shaquille O'Neill, Tiger Woods, or Bill Gates really hurt their extraordinary basketball, golf, or business games. Moreover, the finding is not necessarily inconsistent with what we already know about reinforcement. In Chapter 7, we saw that modern views of reinforcement allow rewards (contingent activities) to punish instrumental activities that are more preferred (Premack, 1971a). And, we have just considered other paradoxical reward effects. Large rewards can lead to quicker extinction, and the effect of a reward in the second phase of a contrast experiment clearly depends on what reward came before. The point is that we already know that reward effects are relative; whether a reward has a positive or negative effect can depend on many factors.

A necessary step in understanding the punished-by-reward phenomenon, then, is to figure out what contexts make the phenomenon happen. Cameron and Pierce (1994) and Eisenberger and Cameron (1996) divided the experiments that have been published on the phenomenon into several categories. A statistical analysis of the overall results (a "meta-analysis") then suggested that the harmful effects of extrinsic reward were restricted to situations in which people were given tangible rewards (e.g.,

"We lost!"

Figure 9.12 Trouble for the future of American sports? (Cartoon © The New Yorker Collection, 2006, Leo Cullum, from cartoonbank.com. All Rights Reserved.)

money) that were announced ahead of time but delivered in a way that was not dependent on the person's actual performance. Verbal rewards generally *improved* performance. A different meta-analysis by Deci et al. (1999) confirmed this result and also found that rewards mostly have harmful effects when they can be perceived as a means by which someone is trying to control you (presumably a less-preferred state of affairs in the Premackian sense). It is worth noting that a theory built on these effects (Deci & Ryan, 1985) predicts that many positive rewards (for example verbal, performance-contingent, and unexpected rewards) will improve performance. In the long run, there seems to be little question that the skilled use of rewards can therefore increase human performance in a very large number of instances (Eisenberger & Cameron, 1996). What matters are factors like expectations and perhaps the interpersonal context in which rewards occur.

Partial reinforcement and persistence

The most well-known paradoxical reward effect is one that hasn't been mentioned yet: the **partial reinforcement extinction effect**, or **PREE**. This effect, which may be the most extensively studied phenomenon in all of instrumental learning, goes something like this. One group of subjects is continuously reinforced—that is, the subjects are reinforced every time they run down a runway. Another group is reinforced only 50% of the time—that

Figure 9.13 The Partial Reinforcement Extinction Effect (PREE). During acquisition, a continuously reinforced group (CRF) receives reward on 100% of the trials. In contrast, a partially reinforced group (PRF) receives reward on only 50% of the trials (for example). When extinction occurs, and trials are no longer reinforced, the PRF group is more persistent—that is, it is slower to stop responding than the CRF group.

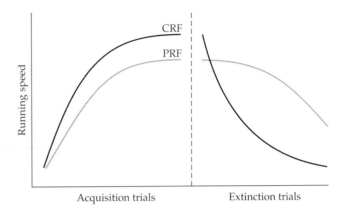

is, half of the trials lead to reinforcement (R), and half of the trials lead to nonreinforcement (N). As shown in Figure 9.13, the continuously reinforced group shows more performance during the acquisition phase. But when extinction occurs, the partially reinforced group is slower to stop responding. Nonrewarded trials in acquisition can make behavior more persistent. The effect is widely known in instrumental learning (e.g., Sheffield, 1949; Weinstock, 1954) and occurs in classical conditioning, too (e.g., Gibbs, Latham, & Gormezano, 1978; Rescorla, 1999b).

The partial reinforcement extinction effect is important for both theoretical and practical reasons. On the theoretical side, it suggests that there is more to learning than habit or associative strength, both of which are supposed to be some function of the number of reinforced trials. Associative strength would arguably be weaker in the partially reinforced group, because they receive half the reinforced trials, and yet behavior is more persistent. The practical implication is that the PREE provides a way to help make behavior more persistent. If you want to teach your children to persevere in the face of adversity, the idea would be to expose them to some partial reinforcement in their lives. In rats, a partially reinforced behavior is more resistant to punishment (it is less suppressed when it is later paired with something nasty, like an electric shock) in addition to being more resistant to extinction (Brown & Wagner, 1964). Partial reinforcement of one behavior can also produce generalized persistence with other behaviors in both animals (e.g., McCuller, Wong, & Amsel, 1976) and humans (e.g., see Nation, Cooney, & Gartrell, 1979). Thus, partial reinforcement may be a technique that increases general persistence (see Amsel, 1992). Robert Eisenberger has investigated similar issues in a number of experiments with humans and animals (e.g., Eisenberger, 1992). He argues that rewarding effort on one task can increase the persistence and effort that we spend on other tasks—something he calls "learned industriousness."

Frustration theory provides an interesting explanation of the PREE (e.g., Amsel, 1958, 1962). The idea is that a partially reinforced subject experiences some frustration (r_F) on the nonrewarded trials. Frustration, like r_G, also has a stimulus effect: s_F, which is present on the next reinforced trial, when the animal is reinforced again. In the long run, the animal is reinforced for responding in the presence of frustration. So, when extinction begins, frustration occurs, but the animal continues to respond (and thus persists) because that is what it has been reinforced to do.

Frustration theory's approach to the PREE is powerful and interesting, but a rival theory known as **sequential theory** was soon proposed by John Capaldi (e.g., Capaldi, 1967, 1994). Sequential theory is a sophisticated version of the idea that behavior will persist in extinction as long as the stimulus conditions are similar to those that were present during acquisition. Extinction is full of lots of nonrewarded (N) trials, and partially reinforced subjects have been reinforced for responding after they have received N trials; in contrast, continuously reinforced subjects have not. Capaldi argued that the crucial stimulus here is the animal's *memory* of previous trials. During acquisition, a partially reinforced subject is reinforced while it remembers recent N trials, whereas a continuously reinforced subject is always reinforced while remembering recent reinforcement (R). Once extinction begins, all subjects are asked to respond on each trial while remembering previous N trials; the partially reinforced subject responds more than does the continuously reinforced subject, because that is what it has been trained to do. The explanation sounds a little like that of frustration theory. But sequential theory emphasizes memory rather than frustration.

John Capaldi

The length of the preceding string of N trials ("N-length") is also important. In extinction, N-length keeps increasing as extinction trials continue. Eventually, even a partially reinforced subject will stop responding when the string of recent N trials gets noticeably longer than the one that was reinforced during training. For example, a rat that receives an RNRNRNR sequence during training is always reinforced for responding after a single N trial (an N-length of one). As extinction continues, the subject is asked to respond after a longer and longer string of N trials; the test conditions thus become increasingly different from the training conditions. But consider a partially reinforced subject that was reinforced for responding every fourth trial (RNNNRNNNRNNNR). You can think of the animal learning that a memory with an N-length of 3 is a signal for reward on the next trial (Capaldi, 1994). Hopefully, you will see that this subject will be even more persistent in extinction, because an N-length of 3 will generalize over a longer string of extinction trials. According to the theory, the number of different N-lengths that are reinforced will also increase resistance to extinction.

Sequential theory makes a number of unique predictions that have been confirmed in the laboratory (e.g., Capaldi & Birmingham, 1998). Several experiments have established that rather subtle variations in the sequence of rewarded and nonrewarded trials during training can be important. For example, Capaldi and Capaldi (1970) and Leonard (1969) compared groups that received different sequences of nonreinforced trials, trials with large rewards (R), and trials with small rewards (r). One group received repetitions of an rNR sequence during training, while a second group received

Figure 9.14 Response speed at the end of acquisition (left) and then on extinction trials after receiving acquisition with rNR or RNr sequences (right). Having the large reward (R) after the N trial caused more resistance to extinction than having it before the N trial. The results were predicted by sequential theory. (After Leonard, 1969.)

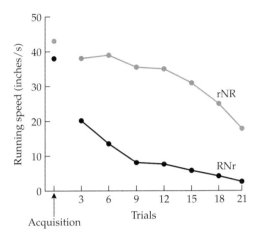

repetitions of RNr. The former group received a big reinforcer while remembering N, which should have produced stronger reinforcement of responding in the presence of the memory of N. The second group received less reinforcement while remembering N. For that reason, the theory predicted that rNR would lead to more persistence in extinction then RNr, which is exactly the result that was obtained (Figure 9.14).

Other experiments suggest that it is the memory of R and N that really counts. For example, in the middle of a string of N trials during aquisition, Capaldi (1964) and Capaldi and Spivey (1963) occasionally put the rats in the goal box and gave them food. These feedings were designed to insert a memory of R into a string of Ns, thereby shortening the N-length that was present when the rat actually ran on the next reinforced trial. The technique worked; running extinguished more quickly in the subjects that had received the inserted memories of R in their strings of N. Sequential theory thus made a number of specific and testable predictions that were confirmed and that frustration theory was not ready to handle.

What does all this mean? On the practical side, we now know quite a bit about how to slow down extinction—and thus, maintain persistence in behavior—with partial reinforcement techniques. On the theoretical side, we also know quite a bit about why behavioral persistence is not merely a function of the number of response-reinforcer pairings. Interestingly, although the PREE was intensively investigated through the mid- to late-1960s, experimental interest in it declined a bit after that, perhaps partly due to the fact that it seemed so well understood—existing theories, particularly sequential theory, did an amazingly good job explaining the PREE.

It is also worth noting that research on the PREE has further expanded our understanding of extinction. In our earlier discussion of extinction in Chapter 5, I emphasized the observation that extinction involves new learning that appears to be relatively dependent on its context. That is a good way to understand certain recovery-after-extinction phenomena, such as spontaneous recovery and the renewal effect. But research on the PREE suggests that two additional factors are also important. First, sequential theory emphasizes the fact that responding can stop in extinction when the animal stops generalizing from acquisition. Thus, extinction can result in part from simple generalization decrement. Second, frustration theory reminds us that there are emotional and motivational consequences of occasions when expected reinforcers do not occur. These motivating effects, along with generalization decrement, need to be acknowledged in any complete account of extinction (e.g., Bouton, 2004; Rescorla, 2001).

It is interesting to observe that sequential theory actually has nothing very motivational in it—subtle extinction effects can be explained in terms of memory and associative strength, without any appeal to motivational constructs, like frustration. So, what became of frustration theory? In the last analysis, frustration seems to be a very real emotion that comes into play when we are disappointed by a smaller-than-expected reinforcer. But, while frustration might play a role in the PREE—especially after a large number of acquisition trials (see Mackintosh, 1974)—it isn't always necessary to talk about frustration. By the late 1960s, an interest in the relationship between learning and motivation was making room for a new interest in the relationship between learning and memory and information processing. The cognitive "revolution" in psychology had begun.

Motivation by expectancies

Spence, Mowrer, and Amsel had built a system that emphasized the role of classically conditioned peripheral responses (r_G, r_E, and r_F) in motivating instrumental action. Although these little "r"s could be taken as hypothetical events, if classical conditioning does provide the motivational background for instrumental learning, then the strength of conditioning measured on a given trial should correlate with the strength of the instrumental behavior. That is, we should be able to predict the vigor of an instrumental action from the vigor of the Pavlovian motivational response.

The problem was that, by the mid-1960s, it was becoming clear that no such correlation was going to be found. Many **concurrent measurement studies** were run in which the little "r"s and instrumental behavior were both monitored at the same time. The correlation between them was not impressive. In appetitive experiments, where animals were performing for a food or water reward, there was little evidence that the vigor of instrumental responding was related to the vigor of a Pavlovian response like salivation (e.g., Ellison & Konorski, 1964; Williams, 1965). If anything, drooling tended to follow the instrumental response, rather than precede it—as a motivational role for it would predict. The picture was equally disheartening in avoidance learning, where rats and dogs were trained to perform instrumental actions to avoid receiving a mild electric shock. Fear (r_E) was supposed to motivate this behavior, and Richard Solomon's laboratories at Harvard (and subsequently, the University of Pennsylvania) were devoted to studying its role. There was no correlation between measures of r_E and the vigor of avoidance behavior—for example, heart rate was not consistently related to the avoidance response in either acquisition or extinction (e.g., Black, 1958, 1959). Although there is a gross relationship between Pavlovian responding and instrumental behavior (animals do salivate in appetitive experiments or show gross heart rate changes in avoidance experiments), Pavlovian responses are not tightly coupled with instrumental behavior in a way that suggests that Pavlovian responses instigate or motivate it.

Findings like these suggested to some that we should discard the idea that Pavlovian processes motivate instrumental behavior. But to trash would be a little rash. In an important paper, Rescorla and Solomon (1967) argued that the problem highlighted by these disappointing correlations was only a problem if you have an old-fashioned idea about what Pavlovian conditioning is all about. The motivation provided by the Pavlovian process is not necessarily provided by peripheral responses, which are just crude indices of a "central state"—like fear or appetitive excitement—that is learned during classical conditioning (see also Mowrer, 1960). It is the central state excited by a CS, not some peripheral heart rate or drooling response, which motivates instrumental action. Although they did not use the term, Rescorla and Solomon came close to saying that motivation was provided by an expectancy of the reinforcer that is aroused by cues that predict it (e.g., Bolles & Moot, 1972). In some respects, this idea is actually consistent with Tolman's original view.

The Rescorla and Solomon paper is one of the inputs—along with effects like blocking, contingency learning, and flavor aversion learning (Chapter 3)—that caused a major change in our thinking about Pavlovian conditioning in the late-1960s. As you know by now, conditioning theory is no longer merely the study of "spit and twitches." Moreover, the idea that a Pavlovian state or expectancy motivates instrumental action is consistent with the evidence. If such a state really motivates behavior, then we should be able to show that increasing or decreasing the intensity of the state will cause a corresponding increase or decrease in the vigor of instrumental action. This is exactly what **transfer-of-control experiments** are designed to test. In these experiments, an instrumental behavior is trained, and a Pavlovian CS is conditioned in a separate phase. In a final test, the CS is then presented while the animal is performing the instrumental behavior. Presenting the CS at this time should affect the animal's expectancy of the reinforcer. If it does, and if that expectancy motivates, we should see the vigor of the instrumental action change accordingly. Such effects are sometimes called **Pavlovian-instrumental transfer**.

The idea is illustrated by a classic experiment run in Solomon's lab by Rescorla and LoLordo (1965); other experiments with a similar logic had been run before (e.g., Solomon & Turner, 1962). In an initial phase, dogs were trained to avoid a brief electric shock by shuttling across a barrier in a shuttlebox. Once the dogs were avoiding shock by responding at a stable rate, they were confined to one side of the box and given Pavlovian conditioning. One CS was conditioned as an excitor (it was paired with shock), while another CS was conditioned as an inhibitor (several inhibitory conditioning methods—see Chapter 3—were used). In the final test, the dogs were

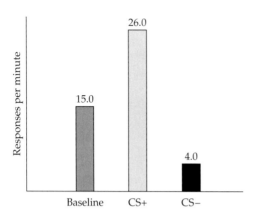

Figure 9.15 A transfer-of-control (or Pavlovian-instrumental transfer) experiment. Dogs that were responding to avoid an electric shock were presented with a fear excitor (CS+) or a fear inhibitor (CS–) while they exhibited avoidance behavior. (The CSs had been conditioned in a phase separated from avoidance training.) Presentation of the excitor enhanced avoidance rate, whereas presentation of the inhibitor reduced the avoidance rate. Results like this suggest that a conditioned motivational state ("fear") motivates the instrumental avoidance response. (After Rescorla & LoLordo, 1965.)

put back into the shuttlebox, where they began to shuttle again to avoid receiving shock. Then Rescorla and LoLordo merely presented the Pavlovian excitor and inhibitor and watched how they affected the dog's avoidance rate. As Figure 9.15 shows, avoidance responding increased in the presence of the excitor and decreased below the baseline in the presence of the inhibitor. A conditioned motivational state—excited by excitors and inhibited by inhibitors—thus appears to influence avoidance behavior.

Rescorla and Solomon saw this sort of finding as evidence suggesting that instrumental action was influenced by a Pavlovian motivational state. They also predicted great generality to the idea. That is, regardless of whether the instrumental action is motivated by appetitive reinforcers or aversive events like shock, it should be influenced by corresponding excitors and inhibitors. This idea is summarized in the two shaded boxes in Table 9.1, where instrumental actions are expected to increase or decrease in the presence of a Pavlovian CS+ or CS– conditioned with the same reinforcer or S*. By further assuming that fear and appetitive motivation inhibit one another (see also Dickinson & Dearing, 1979; Konorski, 1967), Rescorla and Solomon made the second set

TABLE 9.1 How Pavlovian states should influence instrumental action

	Pavlovian state			
	Appetitive US (excitement)		**Aversive US (fear)**	
Instrumental action	Excitor (CS+)	Inhibitor (CS–)	Excitor (CS+)	Inhibitor (CS–)
Appetitve (motivated by anticipation of food)	Increase	Decrease	Decrease	Increase
Avoidance (motivated by fear)	Decrease	Increase	Increase	Decrease

Source: After Rescorla and Solomon, 1967.

of predictions shown outside the shaded boxes. While a fear excitor was supposed to increase the motivation for avoidance behavior, it was predicted to inhibit the motivation for appetitive behavior. This result itself is rather interesting—Pavlovian CSs can't just elicit peripheral CRs, because whether they increase or decrease the rate of an instrumental response depends on whether the rats are responding to avoid shock or obtain food (e.g., Scobie, 1972).

A great number of experiments on Pavlovian-instrumental transfer have been run, and there are enough data that conform to the major Rescorla-and-Solomon predictions to believe that the framework is basically correct. For example, an appetitive instrumental action can analogously be influenced by a Pavlovian appetitive state (e.g., Lovibond, 1983). Thus, the motivating effects of excitatory Pavlovian expectancies seem reasonably clear. There are complications, though. The effects of inhibitors are not as well documented as the effects of excitors. More important, in addition to their motivational effects, Pavlovian CSs also evoke *behaviors* that can influence instrumental behavior in ways that have nothing to do with motivation. For example, auditory fear CSs evoke freezing in rats, and at least part of the suppression of appetitive performance that occurs when they are presented is undoubtedly due to this effect (e.g., Bouton & Bolles, 1980). Defensive behaviors evoked by a fear CS can also sometimes interfere with avoidance behavior (Hurwitz & Roberts, 1977). In appetitive experiments, localized CSs can evoke sign-tracking behaviors that can either facilitate or suppress instrumental responding depending on where the CS is located with respect to the operant response lever (Karpicke, Christoph, Peterson, & Hearst, 1977). The general point is that Pavlovian signals evoke specific behavioral CRs as well as motivational states, and this can make proof of true motivational interactions pretty tricky. Nonetheless, a number of elegant experiments by J. Bruce Overmier and his colleagues at the University of Minnesota have confirmed interactions like the ones predicted in Table 9.1 in a way that cannot be explained by simple mechanical response interactions (see Overmier & Lawry, 1979; Trapold & Overmier, 1972).

Another complication is that Pavlovian states may influence instrumental actions in more than one way. Rescorla and Solomon (1967) assumed that the motivational effects of the CS potentiate or invigorate the instrumental response. Konorski (1967) developed a compatible view that has been adopted and extended by others. In Chapters 4 and 5, we saw that a CS may actually be associated with nodes corresponding to both the sensory and emotional aspects of the US (this is at the heart of the "affective extension" of SOP, or AESOP, Wagner & Brandon, 1989). When the CS activates the sensory node, it evokes a sensory response (Konorski called this a "consummatory" response), and when the CS activates the emotive node, it evokes an emotional response (Konorski called this a "preparatory" response). In this sort of scheme, the preparatory or emotive CS activates an entire appetitive or aversive motivational system. Since the CS activates an entire system, a CS should invigorate instrumental responding that is reinforced by any reinforcer within the system. For example, Balleine (1994; see also Cor-

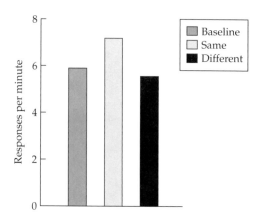

Figure 9.16 In Pavlovian-instrumental transfer, CSs sometimes have their strongest effect on instrumental responses associated with the same reinforcer. In this experiment, lever-pressing and chain-pulling were associated with different reinforcers (food pellets or liquid sucrose). Two CSs were also associated with either pellets or sucrose. When each CS was presented, it mainly increased the rate of the instrumental response that earned the same reinforcer. (After Delamater, 1996.)

bit & Balleine, 2005; Holland, 2004) showed that presenting a CS associated with liquid sucrose will enhance an operant response reinforced with food pellets in hungry rats. Evidently, the motivation provided by a Pavlovian CS can be fairly general over different reinforcers in the appetitive system.

On the other hand, under some conditions the effects of a CS can be more specific (Colwill & Motzkin, 1994; Colwill & Rescorla, 1988; Delamater, 1996; Kruse, Overmier, Konz, & Rokke, 1983). For example, Delamater (1996) trained rats to lever-press for a food pellet and chain-pull for a few drops of liquid sucrose (half the rats actually received the reverse pairings). In a separate Pavlovian phase, one CS was associated with a pellet, and another CS was associated with sucrose. When these different CSs were presented while the rats were free to lever-press or chain-pull in extinction, the rats mainly increased the instrumental action that led to the same outcome (Figure 9.16). Often, however, this reinforcer-specific effect takes the form of the CS associated with the different outcome suppressing the instrumental response (e.g., Colwill & Motzkin, 1994; Colwill & Rescorla, 1988, 1990). This sort of result has led some to think that the reinforcer-specific effect may depend on some process other than a truly motivational one (e.g., Dickinson & Balleine, 2002; Holland, 2004; Rescorla, 1994).

What might that nonmotivational process be? Trapold and Overmier (1972) suggested another way to think of Pavlovian-instrumental transfer. They suggested that an emotional state or expectancy may merely act as a discriminative stimulus (S^D). That is, an expectancy of a food pellet may set the occasion for a lever-press response, and an expectancy of shock may set the occasion for an avoidance response. When these states are excited or inhibited by excitors or inhibitors, you have more or less of the stimulus that sets the occasion for the action. This sort of account can go some distance in explaining the effects in Table 9.1, and even results like the ones shown in Figure 9.16, because specific reinforcer expectancies can set the occasion for specific behaviors (e.g., Overmier, Bull, & Trapold, 1971; Peterson & Trapold, 1980; Trapold, 1970). (Arousing the expectancy of a *different* reinforcer could decrease the strength of instrumental responding by causing generalization decrement.) There are, however, results that seem inconsistent with this view (e.g., Rescorla & Colwill, 1989). Yet another alternative is that a CS might activate a representation of the sensory properties of the reinforcer, and this representation might in turn activate a response that has been specifically associated with it (Mackintosh & Dickinson, 1979; see also Rescorla, 1994). Like the expectancy-as-an-S^D approach, this approach does not appeal to motivation. However, it emphasizes a direct association between a response and a reinforcer (the role of response-reinforcer associations will be discussed further in Chapter 10). Neither view seems ready to explain why CS effects can be general over different reinforcers in the same motivational system (e.g., Balleine, 1994); such effects are usually assumed to result from the actual motivational impact of the CS. At the present time, we are only beginning to understand the conditions that lead to general (motivational) and more specific forms of Pavlovian-instrumental transfer (see Balleine, 2005; Holland, 2004).

What does it all mean?

Our discussion has gotten awfully abstract and theoretical again, but the issues do have practical implications. Perhaps the main point of this section is that detailed study of how rewards and punishers motivate instrumental behavior has led to a conclusion you have been warned about all along: Pavlovian learning is always occurring whenever instrumental or operant conditioning is going on. Now we see that this second learning process can modulate instrumental action. This is an important point to remember when you go about understanding behavior that you encounter, say, in the clinic. For example, an obsessive-compulsive patient might be deathly afraid of leaving their apartment without repeatedly checking to make sure that all the electrical appliances are turned off. Checking behavior is an operant avoidance behavior that is thought to be reinforced by the reduction of anxiety. According to what we have been discussing, checking behavior will be exacerbated if CSs or cues in the environment make the individual more afraid. Checking behavior would likewise be reduced by CSs or cues in the environment that inhibit fear.

The same case can be made for drug dependence. Addictive drugs are appetitive reinforcers, and drug-taking is an instrumental act that drugs reinforce. The idea we have been discussing is that CSs or cues in the background that are associated with a drug may increase or decrease the motivation to perform the behavior (Stewart, de Wit, and Eikelboom, 1984). There is laboratory evidence of such Pavlovian-instrumental transfer effects. For example, in rat subjects, Chris Cunningham (1994) has shown that a CS associated with alcohol enhances the rate at which rats lever-press for alcohol, while an inhibitor suppresses the rate (see also Krank, 1989). Remarkably, in Cunningham's experiment, the increase in lever-pressing was also correlated with the size of a body-temperature CR that was concurrently elicited by the CS! Cues predicting an addictive substance thus increase the motivation to work for it. Panililio, Weiss, and Schindler (1996) have also shown that rats that

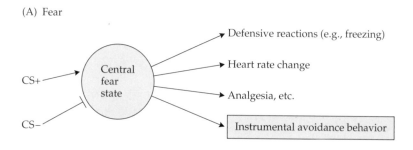

(A) Fear

CS+ → Central fear state

CS– →

Central fear state →
- Defensive reactions (e.g., freezing)
- Heart rate change
- Analgesia, etc.
- Instrumental avoidance behavior

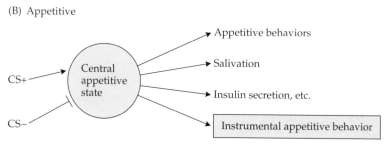

(B) Appetitive

CS+ → Central appetitive state

CS– →

Central appetitive state →
- Appetitive behaviors
- Salivation
- Insulin secretion, etc.
- Instrumental appetitive behavior

Figure 9.17 One important effect of a CS is to excite or inhibit a motivational state. That state can, in turn, evoke a constellation of behaviors connected with the state, and also—as emphasized in this chapter—modulate instrumental behavior.

have been trained to lever-press for cocaine delivered intravenously, increase their response rate when two separately trained S^Ds are combined. Because S^Ds involve implicit Pavlovian S-S* associations (see Chapter 10), this may be another transfer-of-control effect. The results are consistent with the idea that Pavlovian expectancies modulate instrumental drug-seeking.

Another implication is one that should be familiar by now: Classical conditioning does not merely involve the attachment of a specific response to a CS. Instead, the CS acquires the power to engage a whole set—or system—of responses (see Chapter 5), and we now see that the CS has the power to motivate or modulate instrumentally learned actions too. A kind of summary of how fear and food CSs might affect performance is presented in Figure 9.17. In addition to evoking natural behaviors, the CS modulates learned instrumental actions. The CS's modulation of instrumental actions can be seen as another way in which stimulus learning helps the animal get ready to deal with motivationally significant events (see Chapter 2).

Dynamic Effects of Motivating Stimuli

It is worth taking a closer look at how the emotional effects of rewards and punishers can further unfold and change over time. This is what Richard Solomon actually spent the last 20 years of his distinguished career think-

Richard Solomon

ing and writing about. His analysis revealed some very interesting general features of the effects of rewards and punishers, and how their effects might change quite fundamentally with repeated exposure.

Opponent-process theory

Solomon's **opponent-process theory** was originally worked out with John Corbit (Solomon & Corbit, 1974; see also Solomon, 1980). It takes its cue from "opponent processes" you are already aware of in color vision. Figure 9.18 is a loose rendering of what you might experience if you sat down in a dimly lit room and looked at a bright red stimulus for a minute or two. At the start of the stimulus, you would perceive a very saturated red color; but as the stimulus continued, the intensity of the perception might fade a bit. Then, if the stimulus were turned off and you were shown a simple neutral white background, you might see a green **after-image**. A similar peak, adaptation, and after-image would occur if you were shown a green stimulus (this time the after-image would be red). With a yellow stimulus, the after-image would be blue, and with a blue stimulus, the after-image would be yellow. You get the idea; color perception is organized so that an opposite after-image occurs when the stimulus is terminated after exposure.

Solomon and Corbit (1974) argued that the same pattern holds for emotional stimuli. That is, exposure to any emotional stimulus creates an initial emotional response, followed by an adaptation phase, and then an opposite **after-reaction** when the stimulus terminates. Consider something frightening like an encounter with a bear in the woods or a surprisingly difficult final exam. You have an initial fear reaction, which may peak and then adapt a bit as the encounter continues. Then, once the stimulus ends, you have an opposite emotional reaction—you feel relieved, and pretty darn good. An analogous pattern occurs with positive events, like a euphoric drug or an

Figure 9.18 The standard pattern of affective dynamics. When an emotion-arousing event or stimulus happens (turns "on"), there is an initial emotional reaction that peaks and then adapts. Then, once the stimulus has ended (turns "off"), there is often an after-reaction that is opposite in valence to the primary reaction. (After Solomon & Corbit, 1974.)

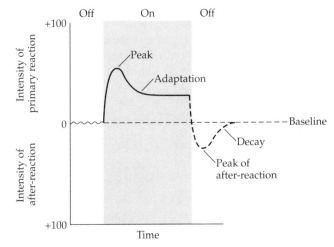

encounter with a boy- or girlfriend. Here, there is an initial thrill or "rush" that peaks and then adapts a bit. And, when the encounter terminates, you might also feel an opposite after-reaction—this time you may feel a little bad. This **standard pattern of affective dynamics** rings true of most emotional stimuli. The pattern fits some experiments in Solomon's laboratory on dogs' reactions to shock, which showed the initial peak, adaptation, and then after-reaction (Church, LoLordo, Overmier, Solomon, & Turner, 1966; Katcher, Solomon, Turner, LoLordo, Overmier, & Rescorla, 1969). It is also consistent with the emotional reactions of skydivers on their initial jump (Epstein, 1967), who feel terror, adaptation, and then relief when the whole thing is over.

The standard pattern changes, though, with repeated exposure to the emotional stimulus, and this is possibly the theory's most significant insight. Figure 9.19 (upper left) repeats the standard pattern of affective dynamics (see Figure 9.18), the pattern observed during the first exposures to an emotional stimulus. With repeated stimulations, though, the pattern changes to the one shown in the upper right of Figure 9.19. The primary affective reaction habituates: There is less terror connected with jumping out of an airplane, or less of a rush connected with taking the drug. Equally important, though, is that the opposite after-reaction has strengthened and deepened. Jumping out of an airplane now causes a longer and more positive relief state. And conversely, taking the positive drug now causes an intense and prolonged withdrawal state.

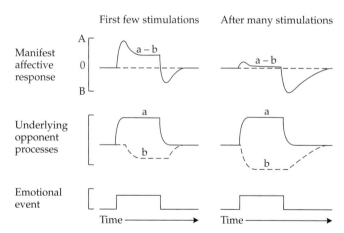

Figure 9.19 The standard pattern of affective dynamics changes with repeated exposure to the emotional stimulus. Top: Behaviorally, one observes habituation of the primary emotional reaction and intensification of the after-reaction. Middle: At a theoretical level, the emotion is controlled by the difference between two opposing processes. The "a-process" is closely linked in time to the emotional event. The opponent "b-process" is more sluggish than the "a-process"—this accounts for adaptation and the after-reaction. Unlike the a-process, the b-process also strengthens with repeated exposure. This causes habituation and intensification of the after-reaction. (After Solomon & Corbit, 1974.)

In the long run, repeated exposure to rewards or punishers can thus cause a profound change in their motivational consequences. A negative stimulus, like jumping out of a perfectly good airplane, can actually become positively reinforcing because the negative affect eventually habituates and the after-reaction comes to feel so good. Similarly, a positive stimulus may start out as a positive reinforcer, but after a great deal of exposure we may begin to seek it, not because it makes us feel good, but because it helps us escape from an aversive after-state. The change in motivational pattern is consistent with what opiate users report in the early and late stages of their addiction (O'Brien, Ehrman, & Ternes, 1986). At first, abusers may take the drug because it makes them feel good, but later the rush seems less important. "If [later-stage addicts] are asked why they use heroin, they often still say, 'to get high.' But if they are asked when was the last time they actually became high after an injection, it may have been months or years in the past" (O'Brien et al., 1986, p. 333). Repeated exposure to rewards and punishers can thus change their motivational effects on behavior.

The theory offers an explanation of how this comes about, and this is depicted in the middle part of Figure 9.19. The stimulus actually elicits two psychological processes, and behind the scenes these combine to create the emotional dynamics we see in behavior. The first process is the **a-process**, which has the affective quality and intensity of the stimulus itself. It is stable, quick, and synchronized with the onset and offset of the emotional stimulus. The other process, the **b-process** or **opponent-process**, is a homeostatic adjustment response. It has the opposite emotional quality and thus subtracts from the a-process. It is a "slave process" in the sense that it is aroused by the a-process. And importantly, the b-process is sluggish; it is slow to recruit and reach its maximum, and then it is also slow to decay. The emotion we feel (shown in the upper panels of Figure 9.19) is the algebraic combination of the two processes (a − b). Thus, the adaptation phase occurs as the b-process comes on slowly. And the after-reaction occurs because the a-process turns off quickly, leaving the slower b-process to decay on its own for a while.

The change in dynamics that occurs with repeated exposure comes about because *the b-process strengthens with repeated use*. As the middle right panel of Figure 9.19 illustrates, after repeated use, the b-process comes on quicker, reaches a deeper maximum, and is ultimately also slower to decay. This change yields the habituation and withdrawal effects described above. The a-process remains unchanged; the only thing that has changed is b. The theory assumes that this type of acquired motivation (which is acquired through experience) is an automatic consequence of use, and is not at all learned.

Emotions in social attachment

Some of the most intriguing tests of the theory were conducted by Howard Hoffman and his colleagues while they studied the emotional dynamics of **imprinting** in ducklings. Filial imprinting is the learning process by which young animals may become attached to their mothers. Konrad Lorenz, the ethologist, wrote widely about the phenomenon, and you may remember pictures of him being followed by a string of little goslings crossing a road. Within limits (Gottlieb, 1965), young birds may become attached to many types of moving stimuli that they experience at a young age. Although ethologists saw imprinting as a unique learning process (e.g., Lorenz, 1937), it is probably another example of the kind of associative learning we study in Pavlovian learning. Hoffman and Ratner (1973b) noted that very young ducklings (e.g., 17 hours old) are comforted by stimuli that move. Stimulus movement is thus a reinforcer and/or a positive US for a young duckling. Hoffman and Ratner exposed ducklings to either a moving electric train or a spinning light from a police car. When the stimuli were presented in motion, they suppressed distress calls that the ducklings made when they were first put into the apparatus. In contrast, if the stimuli were presented in a stationary manner, they had no such calming effect. Repeated exposure to a stimulus in motion, however, allowed the stimulus to suppress distress-calling even when presented in a stationary manner (Hoffman, Eiserer, & Singer, 1972). The birds associated the static features of the imprinting stimulus (CS) with its movement (US). These stimuli consequently become motivationally significant, calming the birds down; they may also have begun to elicit sign tracking—as in the goslings that followed Lorenz around.

The emotional dynamics of imprinting fit opponent-process theory. Hoffman and Ratner (1973b) measured 17-hour-old ducklings' distress-calling before, during, and after their first 10-minute exposure to a moving HO train. The results are shown in Figure 9.20. The group shown at the top was put into the apparatus for the first time just before the whole experience began. The ducklings were distressed at first, then calmed down when the moving train was presented, and then became distressed again when the train was turned off and withdrawn. The interesting group, however, is in the lower panel of Figure 9.20. These ducklings were actually hatched in the imprinting apparatus, where they were left undisturbed until testing began 17 hours later. This group showed no distress prior to presentation of the moving train—they were used to the test environment. But after 10 minutes of exposure to the moving train, turning it off caused major distress. Hoffman and Ratner had made calm ducklings miserable by giving them the "positive" imprinting experience. Here is real acquired motivation—the ducklings were doing just fine until the imprinting stimulus was presented and then withdrawn. In terms of the theory, the distress is the after-reaction caused by the b-process lingering after removal of the positive train stimulus.

Once the birds have imprinted, brief exposures to the train stimulus can reinforce operant responses, such as pecking at a pole. In other experiments, Eiserer and Hoffman (1973) tested pole-pecking after the birds were "primed" by free exposures to the train. These primes stimulated pole-pecking after the stimulus, presumably by motivating the bird to escape the aversive after-reaction discussed above. What is more, the amount of pecking increased as a function of the duration of the prime. In effect, the stronger

Figure 9.20 Distress-calling in ducklings before, during, and after exposure to a moving toy train. Upper panel: When 17-hour-old ducklings are brought into a novel environment, there is considerable distress-calling that is suppressed by presentation of the moving train (stimulus period). When the train is then removed from sight, the birds begin distress-calling again. Lower panel: When the duckling has spent most of its 17 hours of life in the test environment, the familiar environment evokes no distress-calling, and presentation of the moving train has no obvious effect. But when the train is then removed, distress-calling begins. Thus, although the train is soothing to a distressed animal (upper panel), its removal causes an aversive after-reaction that makes even a calm duckling distressed. (After Hoffman & Ratner, 1973b.)

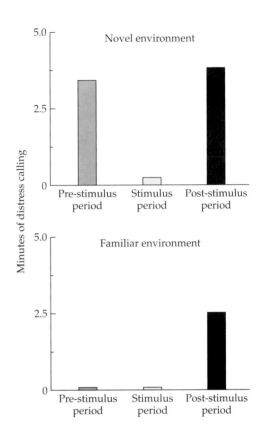

opponent process elicited by the longer primes (remember that the b-process is slow to recruit) motivated instrumental behavior especially well.

Working in Solomon's laboratory, Starr (1978) discovered something important about the growth of the b-process during imprinting. He took very young ducklings and gave them 30-second exposures to a moving, stuffed duck. Different groups of ducklings received their exposures separated by 1-minute, 2-minute, or 5-minute intervals. Distress-calling increased after each successive termination of the imprinting stimulus, but its growth was most impressive the shorter the inter-stimulus interval (Figure 9.21); at the longest interval, there was little growth. This sort of result suggests that the growth of the opponent process does not merely depend on "repeated use" (Solomon & Corbit, 1974), but actually depends on repeated exposure under massed conditions. Starr suggested that there is a "critical decay duration"—that is, a crucial interval between successive stimulus presentations beyond which the b-process will not grow. Seaman (1985) reported compatible results for the acquisition of morphine tolerance. The implication for addiction is that massed exposure to an S*, as might happen in a binge, may cause more immediate risk for addiction than the same number of exposures that are spaced more widely in time.

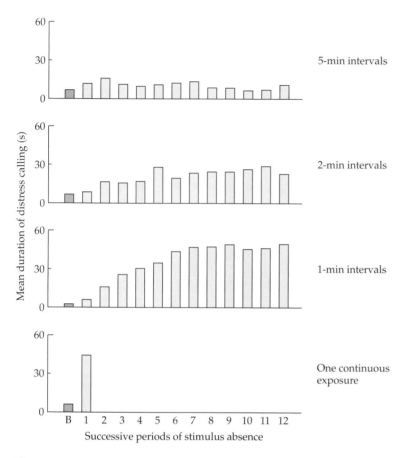

Figure 9.21 Distress-calling in ducklings after 30-second exposures to a moving, stuffed duck. The growth of distress-calling (the after-reaction) was most pronounced when exposures were massed in time (i.e., separated by 1 or 2 minutes). There was little growth when exposures were separated by 5 minutes. The bottom panel is a group that received one continuous 6-minute exposure. (After Starr, 1978.)

A further look at addiction

How does opponent-process theory hold up? The theory provides a significant insight into an aspect of motivation that had been ignored before—that the motivating effects of rewards and punishers can change in a big way with repeated exposure. A lot of a good thing can make the good thing bad, and a lot of a bad thing can make the bad thing better. Because of the growth of the opponent-process, an addiction syndrome can kick in; the organism may make the transition from casual to compulsive-looking instrumental behavior (see Robinson & Berridge, 2003). When opponent-process theory was first proposed in the 1970s, it added to a growing sense of excitement about the role of opponent or "compensatory responses" in drug tolerance and drug dependence (see Chapters 2 and 5). However, nowadays (thirty years later) there is less certainty that the growth of the b-process is automatic and unlearned, as the original theory proposed. Instead, most researchers are now convinced that the growth of the b-process is at least partly governed by Pavlovian conditioning.

You might remember Siegel's work (e.g., 1975) suggesting that repeated pairings of a CS with a drug allows the CS to elicit responses that compensate for unconditional effects of the drug (see Chapters 3 and 5). The compensatory CR is essentially an opponent process—it subtracts from the effect of an S*. Compensatory responses are also linked theoretically with withdrawal responses (e.g., Siegel et al., 2000), and they are not uncommon in conditioning (see Chapter 5). Notice further that conditioned compensatory responses will grow with repeated exposure to the US—in this case, though, their growth would be the result of learning, and the full-blown opponent-process would be seen specifically in the presence of the CS. There is now so much evidence suggesting a role of conditioning in the development of drug tolerance (and so comparatively little evidence that tolerance is merely automatic and not learned), that the "associative" (learned) mechanism seems to have won the day. The implication is that the opponent process will mainly be elicited by CSs associated with S*. CSs will motivate behavior, an idea we have clearly seen before. But the new twist is that CSs might motivate in part because they trigger the opponent b-process.

The idea that CSs might elicit a b-process had an impact on theories that followed the original opponent-process theory. Jonathan Schull (1979) combined Solomon's theory with a modern understanding of conditioning. Schull argued that, during conditioning, CSs come to elicit a b-process that cancels the impact of the upcoming US. Interestingly, Schull noted that blocking effects (L+, then LN+) can be explained if the CS doing the blocking cancels the effectiveness of the US by eliciting the opponent-process. The idea has implications that are similar to the more conventional view that the CS reduces the US's "surprisingness" (see Chapter 4), although it does not imply a cognitive information processing system. Wagner's SOP ("sometimes opponent process") theory has some of the same character. The amount of conditioning that a US creates will depend on the extent to which its elements go into the A1 state. A CS prevents this by putting the elements into the A2 state instead. And as we saw in Chapter 5, the response controlled by A2 sometimes looks like an opponent process (Paletta & Wagner, 1986). These models thus show how the growth of an opponent-process might be linked to classical conditioning.

One challenge for the idea that the growth of the opponent-process depends *exclusively* on conditioning is the finding that massed exposure is especially effective at increasing withdrawal reactions or tolerance (Starr, 1978; see Figure 9.21; Seaman, 1985). Conditioning is usually *worse* with massed trials, not better (see Chapter 3). So how can we put all the facts together? It seems possible that both learned and nonlearned mechanisms influence habituation and withdrawal. For example, research on the habituation of startle reactions suggests that there is a short-term habituation effect that develops best with massed trials, and a longer-term habituation effect that develops best with spaced trials (Davis, 1970). Such findings are consistent with Wagner's (1978, 1981) distinction between habituation resulting from self-generated and retrieval-generated priming (see Chapter 4). Baker and Tiffany (1985) have shown how this distinction can be applied to drug tolerance (see also, e.g., Tiffany, Drobes, & Cepeda-Benito, 1992). Thus, there are reasonable grounds for thinking that both learned and nonlearned factors might contribute to habituation and tolerance to S*.

So what does all this mean? The opponent process, or the strength of the opposite after-reaction, may grow for two reasons. First, massed exposures to a positive S* may cause some short-term, nonassociative growth, leaving the organism craving more after a series of quickly repeated stimulations. A weekend binge can thus generate a lot of motivation for more S*, although this might fade reasonably quickly after the last S* exposure. Second, classical conditioning may cause a longer-term growth of an opponent-process that will be elicited by the CSs associated with S* ("longer-term" because CSs can still elicit CRs even after very long retention intervals). This sort of growth may depend on more spaced exposures to S* and will follow the laws of conditioning we discussed in earlier chapters. Opponent processes that grow through either mechanism will presumably motivate instrumental actions reinforced by S*. The conditioning mechanism, though, will allow an enduring form of motivation that will always be potentially elicited by cues that have been associated with S*.

Conclusion

The opponent-process approach emphasizes withdrawal-like effects as the motivational basis for addictive behavior. After repeated exposure to a drug, the strong b-process causes a withdrawal state—an acquired need for the drug—that is aversive and motivates the user to escape. One implication is that the addict might not be motivated to take the drug until he or she goes into the withdrawal state. There is a similarity here to the depletion-repletion account of hunger, where motivation was likewise seen as a response to need.

This point brings our chapter full circle. At the start, we learned two important lessons about how need states like hunger and thirst actually motivate. First, need states do not automatically energize instrumental action; instead, the organism must first learn about the impact S* has on the need state (e.g., Balleine, 1992)—the process called "incentive learning." In a similar way, if a withdrawal state is going to motivate drug-seeking, the organism might first need to learn that the drug makes her feel better in the withdrawal state (see Hutcheson, Everitt, Robbins, & Dickinson, 2001). Second, other parts of the chapter raised doubts about whether animals wait until they need food or water in order to engage in motivated behavior: Much eating and drinking actually occurs in anticipation of—rather than in response to—need. The same may be true of drug-taking. Drug abusers may normally crave or seek drugs before they physically "need" them; incentive factors, rather than need factors, often predominate (Robinson & Berridge,

2003; Stewart et al., 1984). One recent view suggests that these incentive factors—like recent tastes of the drug, or exposure to drug-associated CSs—motivate instrumental behavior by creating a kind of "wanting" for the drug (Berridge & Robinson, 1995; Robinson & Berridge, 1993, 2003; Wyvell & Berridge, 2000). (Interestingly, "wanting" the drug can be distinguished from actually "liking" the drug, which involves separate incentive learning processes [Balleine, 1992; Dickinson & Balleine, 2002].) There is plenty of food for thought, and room for new research, about issues surrounding the motivation of instrumental action.

Summary

1. Early thinking about motivation and behavior linked motivation to biological need. Hull emphasized Drive, a form of motivation that was caused by need. Drive was supposed to energize consummatory behavior, random ("general") activity, and instrumental action.

2. The Drive concept ran into trouble. Drive does not energize activity in a random or general way; instead, hunger and thirst seem to select or potentiate behavior systems that are designed (by evolution) to deal with the motivational state. Drive does not blindly energize instrumental action either. Motivational states influence instrumental behavior only if the animal has had a chance to learn the reinforcer's value in the presence of the motivational state. The latter process is called "incentive learning."

3. Eating and drinking seem to anticipate—rather than be a response to—need. For example, animals drink or forage for food in ways that seem to prevent them from becoming depleted. This usually involves learning, and what we eat and when we eat it (for example) are strongly influenced by learning processes.

4. Instrumental behavior is motivated by the anticipation of reward. Upshifts and downshifts in the size of reward cause positive and negative "contrast effects." These involve emotion, and they suggest that the motivating effects of a reward depend on what we have learned to expect. The anticipation of reward causes "incentive motivation," which Hull added to his theory. The bottom line was that a classically conditioned anticipatory goal response, r_G, was thought to energize instrumental action.

5. There are other conditioned motivators besides r_G. Avoidance learning is motivated by fear, or r_E. When rewards are smaller than expected, frustration, r_E, becomes important. Frustration is especially useful in explaining many "paradoxical reward effects" in which reinforcers are less positive than our intuitions suggest they should be.

6. Extrinsic rewards (like prizes or money) can sometimes hurt human performance that is said to be "intrinsically" motivated. The effect is restricted to certain situations. Like other paradoxical reward effects, it is consistent with the idea that the effects of reinforcers can depend on expectations and psychological context.

7. The "partial reinforcement extinction effect" (PREE) is an especially important paradoxical reward effect. Behaviors that are reinforced only some of the

time are more resistant to extinction than those that are always reinforced. Behavior may be more persistent after partial reinforcement because we have learned to respond in the presence of frustration. Alternatively, partial reinforcement may make it more difficult to discriminate extinction from acquisition. The latter idea is refined in "sequential theory."

8. It was difficult to confirm a role for peripheral responses like r_G and r_E in motivating instrumental behavior. However, "transfer of control" or "Pavlovian-instrumental transfer" experiments demonstrate that presenting a Pavlovian CS while the animal is performing an instrumental action can influence instrumental performance. The motivating effects of rewards and punishers are mediated by classically conditioned expectancies or motivational states, and not peripheral responses. In any instrumental learning situation, cues in the background can become associated with S* and thereby motivate instrumental action.

9. The motivational effects of rewards and punishers can further change as a function of experience with them. Exposure to an emotional stimulus can cause an opposite after-reaction when the stimulus is withdrawn. With repeated exposure to the emotional stimulus, the after-reaction may also get stronger while the original emotional effect habituates. According to "opponent-process theory," this change occurs because an opponent-process elicited by the stimulus grows with repeated use. Ultimately, the change can cause a reversal of the motivation behind instrumental action. For example, although a positive stimulus is a positive reinforcer at first, we may eventually seek it in order to escape the strong aversive after-reaction. This may be a hallmark of addiction.

10. Opponent-process theory explains the emotional dynamics of imprinting. However, the growth of opponent processes may depend more on learning than the theory originally supposed. Conditioned compensatory responses, which are essentially conditioned opponent-processes, may play a role in tolerance and habituation, although a growth of the opponent-process like the one envisioned by opponent-process theory may still occur as a consequence of massed exposures to S*.

Key Terms

specific hungers
homeostasis
incentive learning
acquired motivation
negative contrast
positive contrast
incentive motivation
r_G-s_G mechanism
frustration
paradoxical reward effects
partial reinforcement extinction
    effect (PREE)
sequential theory

concurrent measurement studies
transfer-of-control experiments
Pavlovian-instrumental transfer
opponent-process theory
after-image
after-reaction
standard pattern of affective
    dynamics
a-process
b-process
opponent-process
imprinting

Chapter Ten Outline

Chapter

10

A Synthetic Perspective on Instrumental Action

IN THIS FINAL CHAPTER, we will conclude our discussion of instrumental learning by describing what I consider the contemporary, synthetic perspective on the problem. This perspective began to develop in the late 1970s and 1980s, and continues to develop today, although it seems somewhat underappreciated by many psychologists, who often assume that the study of operant behavior ended with the behavior analytic approach covered in Chapter 7. The synthetic approach draws on material covered in Chapter 7, but it also draws on Chapters 8 and 9 as well as material throughout the rest of this book. It can be seen as a "cognitive" approach to instrumental learning, because so much of what we now think is learned in even simple operant situations is not directly manifest in behavior. It is also biological, because we will be reminded that evolutionary factors that shape behavior are not exactly irrelevant either.

My version of the story behind the contemporary synthesis begins with a review of avoidance learning. It seems obvious that organisms must be able to learn to avoid dangerous, aversive, noxious events—especially events that can do them bodily harm. Although avoidance learning was mentioned when we first considered the law of effect many chapters ago (see Chapter 2), I have resisted ("avoided") talking about it in any depth because it touches on many themes that first needed to be developed in other chapters. It is also especially good for helping integrate what we have been talking about throughout this book. So, this chapter begins with a discussion of avoidance learning. Its overall goal, though, is to give you a perspective that I hope will help you summarize and reassemble some of the themes we have covered in different parts of the book. The whole may be more than the sum of its parts.

Avoidance Learning

The puzzle and solution: Two-factor theory

Avoidance learning has always been a puzzle to learning theorists for a simple reason. In other operant learning situations, it is easy to identify an event that reinforces the behavior: For the rat lever-pressing in the Skinner box, it is the pellets that are delivered as a consequence of the lever-press response. But the reinforcer in avoidance learning is much less obvious. For example, one way that avoidance learning is studied in animals is with the use of an apparatus called a shuttle box (Figure 10.1). In this situation, a rat is trained to avoid a brief electric shock by running from one side of a compartment to the other, on each trial. Once the animal has learned to shuttle in this manner, it will make the response repeatedly without getting shocked again. So, what keeps the shuttle behavior going? Saying something like "the fact that shock does not happen" is not very helpful, because a very large number of things do not happen whenever the rat shuttles. The animal isn't hit by a black SUV or a laser beam blast from an alien spacecraft either. The absence of these events cannot explain the behavior. How can the nonoccurrence of an event be a reinforcer?

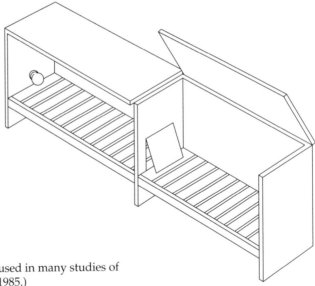

Figure 10.1 The shuttlebox—an apparatus used in many studies of avoidance learning in rats. (After Flaherty, 1985.)

A theoretical answer to this question was provided by O. H. Mowrer many years ago (Mowrer, 1939, 1942). Mowrer's **two-factor theory** is still very influential today, and it combines many of the pieces of instrumental behavior we have been discussing in the last few chapters. Put casually, Mowrer noted that, in any avoidance situation, there are usually cues or *warning signals* in the environment that tell the organism that an aversive event is about to happen. In the shuttle box experiment, each trial typically starts with the presentation of a stimulus like a buzzer. If the rat does not shuttle soon after the buzzer comes on, it will be shocked. But if it shuttles during the buzzer, shock is avoided, and the buzzer is usually turned off until the next trial.

O. H. Mowrer

There are really two kinds of trials that occur in avoidance learning experiments, and these are summarized in Figure 10.2. In one type of trial—which is typical early in training (before the animal has learned the avoidance response)—the warning signal comes on and is paired with shock. Mowrer noted that these are classical fear conditioning trials, and the result of several buzzer-shock pairings is that the buzzer becomes a CS that elicits fear. This is the first factor in two-factor theory: Pavlovian fear conditioning of warning stimuli. This process then enables something else to occur. If the rat now happens to make the shuttling response during the presentation of the buzzer, the buzzer is turned off. Because the response terminates the fear CS, it is associated with fear reduction. This is the second factor in the theory: reinforcement of the instrumental response through fear reduction. Notice that, although the shuttle box experiment is artificial, Mowrer's idea has broad implications. We perform avoidance behaviors because they reduce or escape anxiety and

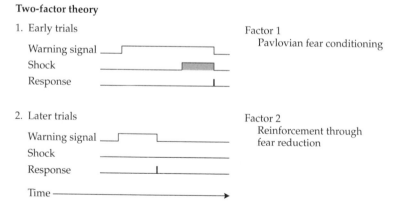

Figure 10.2 The two factors in the two-factor theory of avoidance learning. On early avoidance learning trials, before the organism knows how to avoid, there are trials in which stimuli in the environment are paired with the to-be-avoided event (an electric shock). Because of Pavlovian fear conditioning, those stimuli become warning signals and arouse fear. (The animal is usually able to terminate the shock by making a response—as shown.) On later trials, when the organism makes the response that avoids the shock, the response also terminates the warning signal. This allows reinforcement through fear reduction.

fear. And, to step back even further, Mowrer's resolution of the avoidance learning puzzle is that Pavlovian conditioning and instrumental learning are happening and interacting at the same time. The Pavlovian fear process is essential here because it allows the reinforcement of avoidance learning.

Mowrer's ideas were supported by several early experiments. In one experiment, Mowrer and Lamoureaux (1942) had two groups of rats learn to avoid in a shuttle box whenever a buzzer came on. For one of the groups, making the avoidance response turned the buzzer off—the avoidance response was therefore associated with immediate fear reduction. For the other group, the shuttling response avoided the shock, but the buzzer remained on for another 10 seconds after the response. Here, fear reduction eventually occurred, but it was considerably delayed, and there was theoretically less reinforcement. Consistent with the theory, rats in the first group (with the immediate buzz-off contingency) learned better than the second group. It appeared that turning the buzzer off immediately was necessary for good avoidance learning, presumably because it provided the reinforcement.

The idea was also supported by another experiment by Neal Miller (1948; see also Brown & Jacobs, 1949). Miller's is one of those rare experiments that is so famous, it has its own name—the "Acquired Drive Experiment." It separated the Pavlovian and instrumental processes into two phases. Rats were first put into the white side of a box (that had white and black sides), where they received shock a few times. This arguably conditioned fear to the white part of the box. Miller then allowed the rats to escape from the white compartment to the black compartment by performing a new instrumental response. Initially, he merely opened a door in the wall separating the two compartments and allowed the rats to run from the white compartment to the black compartment, which the rats learned to do readily. Then, Miller required them to turn a small wheel above the door to open the door between the compartments—most of the rats learned this response, too. Finally, the rats learned to press a lever to open the door instead of turning the wheel. At this point, turning the wheel extinguished and was replaced by lever-pressing. All of these instrumental responses were learned in the absence of any additional shocks. Apparently, simply escaping from the white cues was sufficient to reinforce new instrumental behaviors. Conditioned fear thus served as an acquired drive—that is, once acquired through conditioning, it reinforced new behavior through a kind of drive reduction (see also McAllister & McAllister, 1971, 1991).

The idea that people also learn behaviors that escape or reduce negative emotion is a pervasive one in clinical psychology. For example, many accounts of drug abuse propose that drug-taking is reinforced by escape from the negative affect that is generated by the drug (e.g., Baker, Piper, McCarthy, Majeskie, & Fiore, 2004). The connection is especially clear with anxiety disorders. For example, humans who acquire panic disorder with agoraphobia stay at home and avoid going to places (like the shopping mall) that might evoke fear or anxiety. Presumably, one reason they do this is that they have learned to escape learned anxiety or fear. Similarly, you might have encountered someone with an obsessive-compulsive disorder who (for example) obsessively washes their hands in the bathroom of the dorm. One account of such behavior (e.g., Mineka & Zinbarg, 2006) is that the person is washing his hands to reduce a learned fear of contamination. Finally, you might know someone with bulimia nervosa, the eating disorder in which a person eats excessively and then vomits afterwards. One explanation (e.g., Rosen & Leitenberg, 1982) is that food and eating have become associated with fear about getting fat. Vomiting is then reinforced by anxiety reduction—one eats and then purges the food to feel better. One implication is that these various disorders can be helped by extinguishing the anxiety that provides their motivational basis. For example, Leitenberg, Gross, Peterson, and Rosen (1984) had bulimics eat and then forced the extinction of anxiety by preventing the vomiting response (this technique is called "response prevention"). This reduced the anxiety, and also the bulimic symptoms.

Problems with two-factor theory

By the early 1950s, things were looking good for Mowrer's theory, and several more recent writers have continued to refine it (e.g., Levis & Brewer, 2001; McAllister & McAllister, 1991). However, the theory has encountered some challenges along the way. The theory has two main predictions, both of which have stimulated research. One prediction is that, if fear motivates avoidance behavior, then the strength of the avoidance response should correlate with the amount of fear the subject shows in the situation. Another prediction is the one pursued by the Mower and Lamoureaux (1942) and Miller (1948) experiments: Terminating the warning signal (and escaping fear) should play a major role in allowing avoidance learning.

We considered the first prediction—that fear correlates with the strength of the avoidance response—in Chapter 9. You will remember that many experiments failed to discover the kind of correlation Mowrer predicted between overt signs of fear and avoidance responding. Dogs avoiding in the shuttle box don't always look afraid, and their heart rates—a possible overt sign of fear—don't correlate very well with avoidance either. Other experiments removed the warning signal from the experimental chamber and tested it elsewhere for how much fear it evoked. For example, Kamin, Brimer, and Black (1963) tested the CS in a conditioned suppression situation (where it was probed on a lever-pressing baseline reinforced by food) and found that the CS evoked relatively little fear after the rats had received extensive avoidance training (see also Cook, Mineka, & Trumble, 1987; Mineka & Gino, 1980; Starr & Mineka, 1977; Figure 10.3). Thus there seemed to be relatively little fear of the CS when the avoidance response was very strong. These problems are not necessarily fatal to two-factor theory, though. For example, after extensive training, a large amount of fear reduction (and, thus, a large amount of fear) might not be necessary to maintain the behavior (the situation might be different when you are first learning the response). In addition, later in this chapter we will see that, after extensive training,

Figure 10.3 Fear of the warning signal declines after extensive avoidance training. In this experiment, rats received avoidance training in a shuttlebox until they made 1, 3, 9, or 27 avoidance responses in a row (the avoidance "criterion"). Then the warning signal was tested for its ability to evoke conditioned suppression: It was presented while the rats lever-pressed in a separate Skinner box. The "adjusted suppression ratio" is the difference between suppression during the test and during a test that preceded avoidance training; fear is represented by a lower score. (After Kamin et al., 1963.)

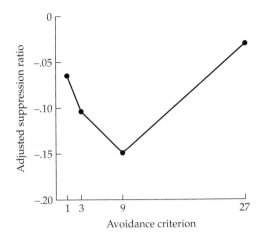

animals may perform instrumental behaviors simply out of habit. (In the presence of the shuttle box or the buzzer, they may reflexively perform the response.) Fear and fear reduction might not be as important once the response is a habit. Furthermore, in Chapter 9 we discussed the fact that the current view of Pavlovian-induced motivation is that CSs excite central states, rather than peripheral responses (e.g., Rescorla & Solomon, 1967). By and large, the idea that fear motivates avoidance behavior is consistent with transfer of control experiments indicating that the presentation of Pavlovian fear excitors and inhibitors can increase or decrease avoidance rate. Thus, the idea that fear motivates avoidance behavior is on reasonably firm ground.

On the other hand, there has also been controversy about the role of warning signal termination, the crucial event that is supposed to provide reinforcement through fear reduction. First consider an interesting series of experiments that came out of the behavior analytic (i.e., Skinnerian) tradition. Initially, many radical empiricists had trouble accepting the concept of "fear" but essentially adopted a two-factor theory in which "aversiveness" instead of fear was conditioned to the warning signal and provided reinforcement when the aversiveness was reduced (Schoenfield, 1950). Murray Sidman (1953) invented an avoidance learning procedure that had a huge influence. This procedure, called "Sidman avoidance" or "free-operant avoidance," was important because it eliminated the warning signal. Sidman set things up so that the rat received a brief electric shock at regular intervals unless it made a lever-press response. The procedure is illustrated in Figure 10.4. If the rat did not lever-press, it received shocks at a standard interval (the "shock-shock interval") of, say, one shock every 5 seconds; however, if the rat happened to lever-press, the response initiated a "response-shock" interval which could be, for example, 20 seconds. If the response-shock interval was longer than the shock-shock interval, so that the response produced a period of time that was free of shock, the rat would

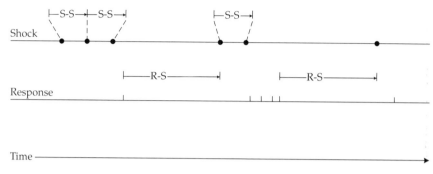

Figure 10.4 A Sidman, or "free-operant," avoidance procedure. Brief electric shocks occur at regular intervals (the S-S interval) unless a response is made—which initiates a longer interval (the R-S interval). Notice that each response resets the R-S interval. Animals can make the response whenever they "want" to and learn to avoid shock despite the fact that there is no explicit warning signal.

learn to lever-press. The response is a free operant because, like the typical lever-press for food, the rat can make the response whenever—and as often as—it wants to. The fact that a warning signal isn't necessary to make avoidance learning happen raised doubts about two-factor theory, because without a warning signal there would seem to be little opportunity for reinforcement by fear reduction.

Unfortunately, although Sidman's procedure eliminated all *explicit* signals for shock, it is not difficult to imagine the animal using time as a CS for shock. Anger (1963) pointed out that the animal needs only to sense the time that has passed since it made its last response. Timing processes were discussed in Chapter 8. In modern terms, we might suppose that the response starts a clock, and that the next shock becomes more and more likely as the clock ticks along. The passage of time would thus elicit increasing fear, and if the next response were to reset the clock, the response would be associated with fear reduction. Thus, a simple two-factor account of the Sidman avoidance procedure is possible.

At this point, Richard Herrnstein (1969) stepped in. Herrnstein suggested that it is unnecessary to infer unobservable entities like temporal cues or even aversiveness or fear. Instead, one can understand avoidance learning by merely recognizing that the response simply reduces the overall rate of shock. Consistent with this idea, Herrnstein and Hineline (1966) found that rats would lever-press if the response caused shocks to occur at a lower average rate. In their procedure, responding did not prevent the occurrence of shocks, but caused them to occur at quasi-random times at a lower frequency than they did when the rats did not respond. A reduction in shock rate is thus all that is necessary to maintain avoidance behavior; according to Herrnstein (1969), speculations about fear and Pavlovian learning were superfluous. This idea is still around (e.g., Baum, 2001; Hineline, 2001), although it has been challenged in many places (e.g., Ayres, 1998; Dinsmoor, 2001). One problem is that it just doesn't explain many of the results in the literature on avoidance learning, such as the acquired drive experiment—or, in fact, any of the phenomena to be mentioned in the next several pages. At least as important, it is not necessarily clear that claiming that an avoidance response is learned because it reduces the shock rate does much more than restate the original observation (that animals learn to avoid shock). Although Herrnstein was being true to his radical behaviorist roots, many investigators would like an understanding of the psychological processes behind the avoidance learning phenomenon. And, even in the Herrnstein-Hineline (1966) experiment, although the rats learned to perform responses that were occasionally followed soon by a shock, on average those shocks still occurred longer after the response than they did after any other event in the situation (e.g., Ayres, 1998). If a CS can signal a reduction in the average frequency of shock (e.g., as in negative contingency learning, see Chapter 3), why can't an avoidance response do the same thing? There are thus grounds for thinking the rats were still responding to reduce the level of fear.

Other research, however, began to show that the importance of warning signal termination was not universal. Several investigators began investigating the role of manipulating the contingencies in the avoidance experiment (e.g., Kamin, 1957). One especially interesting set of experiments was conducted in the laboratory of the late Robert C. Bolles (Bolles, Stokes, & Younger, 1966). The main results are summarized in Figure 10.5. In one experiment, groups of rats were run in a shuttle box. For some of these

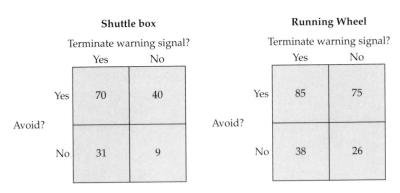

Figure 10.5 The effect of turning off the warning signal depends on the avoidance behavior being trained. Numbers in the cells indicate the percentage of trials on which rats responded during a warning signal before an electric shock occurred. Rats were trained in either a shuttlebox or a running wheel. When the response occurred, it terminated (turned off) the warning signal for some rats but not for others. It also prevented (avoided) presentation of the shock for some rats but not others. Two-factor theory did not predict that warning signal termination would be relatively unimportant in the running wheel—and does not explain why its importance depends so much on the response. (Data from Bolles et al., 1966; after Bolles, 1972a.)

groups, performing the response turned off the warning signal, but for the other groups, it did not. For yet another portion of the groups, performing the response avoided the shock, but for the other groups it did not. (These two variables were combined factorially, as shown in Figure 10.5.) The overall pattern seems clear. Turning off the warning signal made a difference; overall, rats that terminated it made a response about 50.5% of the time, whereas those that did not made a response about 24.5% of the time. Interestingly, just being able to avoid on its own also made a difference (overall, 55% to about 20%). The important thing, though, is that a different pattern of results emerged when rats were tested in a running wheel instead of the shuttle box. In this condition, the rat was inside the wheel and had to run in it to make it spin a quarter turn in order to register a response. As the figure shows, in this case being able to turn the warning signal off again made a difference, albeit a fairly small one. On the other hand, simply being able to avoid the shock—regardless of whether the warning signal went off—made a huge difference. The results suggested that warning signal termination might not have general reinforcing properties. Its role depends on what response the animal is asked to make. Of course, the comparison of running in the wheel and shuttling in the shuttle box confounded the two responses with the actual apparatus they were tested in—so the specific role of the response was not completely clear.

Bolles (1969) therefore pursued the role of the response further in another experiment. Here, all rats were tested in the same running wheel. In order to avoid an electric shock (and terminate the warning signal), the rats either needed to run, turn around, or stand on their hind paws when the warning signal sounded. As Figure 10.6 shows, although the probability of each of these responses was nearly equal at the start of training, running was the easiest behavior to learn. In contrast, standing never increased in strength; thus, the success of avoidance learning depended on the response requirement.

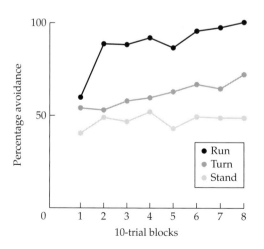

Figure 10.6 Avoidance behaviors are not equally learnable—another example of preparedness. Different rats were allowed to run, turn, or stand to avoid receiving an electric shock in the running wheel. Running is far easier to learn than turning or standing in the wheel. (After Bolles, 1969.)

Robert C. Bolles

Bolles (1972a) noted that this conclusion is actually consistent with the entire literature on avoidance learning, which suggests that some avoidance responses are almost trivially easy to learn, whereas others are exceedingly difficult. For example, if the rat is required to jump out of a box where it is shocked in order to avoid, learning happens in approximately one trial (the rat needs only one or two shocks to learn to jump out of the box on the next trial). "One-way" avoidance, in which the rat is always asked to run from one side of a two-compartment box to the other side—in the same direction—is also learned in one or two trials. The famous shuttle box is considerably more difficult. Here learning doesn't get much better than about 70% avoidance after 100 or so trials. And, the task that is truly difficult is lever-pressing. According to Bolles, after 100 trials, the average rat only responds 10% to 30% of the time. (Bolles once suggested that the best way to ensure one-trial avoidance learning in a Skinner box was to leave the lid off the box.) It does seem odd that lever-pressing—which is so easy to learn when it is reinforced by food—seems so difficult to learn as an avoidance response. On the other hand, this is a theme we have seen before. As demonstrated by flavor aversion learning (e.g., Chapters 2 and 6), animals seem "prepared" to learn some things and not others. The differences in how readily some avoidance responses are learned over others may be another example of preparedness (i.e., a biological "constraint" on learning).

Species-specific defense reactions

In a classic paper, Bolles (1970, see also Bolles, 1972a) put this argument in its evolutionary context. He suggested that animals have evolved certain innate behaviors that protect them from being preyed upon by other animals. He called these behaviors **species-specific defense reactions (SSDRs)**. As noted in Chapter 2, it now seems clear that some behaviors must be innate if the animal is to defend itself in the wild. For example, when a rat is attacked by a predator like an owl, there is usually no second trial. If the rat doesn't get away the first time, the owl irrevocably wins the contest. Thus, if the rat is lucky enough to detect the owl before it strikes, it pays for the rat to have a prepackaged defensive response ready in order to avoid being attacked. In addition to making this point, Bolles proposed that an avoidance response is easy to learn in the lab provided it is similar to a natural SSDR. He also proposed that two important SSDRs are flight (getting out of a dangerous situation) and freezing (a common behavior in which an animal stops dead in its tracks). As mentioned in Chapter 2, and as we will see in a moment, freezing does produce less predation (Hirsch & Bolles, 1980).

Bolles's idea was consistent with the general picture on avoidance learning mentioned above. Jump-out and one-way avoidance are readily learned because they are effective flight responses. Lever-pressing is not; it is not compatible with an SSDR, and it is therefore difficult to learn. Shuttling in a shuttle box is somewhere in the middle. It is a kind of flight response, but it is not truly flight because on the second trial the rat must return to the other side of the box, where it had received shock during the previous trial. Therefore, shuttling is not a true SSDR, and it requires a lot of feedback—or reinforcement—to learn. Consistent with this idea, warning signal termination is much more important in the shuttle box than in the one-way situation or the running wheel (Bolles & Grossen, 1969). SSDR theory initially had a rather ad hoc flavor to it, but additional research helped tighten it up. For example, Grossen and Kelley (1972) soon discovered another SSDR in the rat, and confirmed the prediction that it was easy to learn as an avoidance response. Specifically, they found that if a rat receives shock while it is in a large enclosure (about a meter square), it will immediately run to the wall. This wall-seeking behavior is called "thigmotaxis," and it is quite common in rodents; if you have ever noticed a mouse in your home or in a camp shelter or a barn, you will usually find it near a wall, where it is presumably protected on the wall side from attack. The bottom line, though, is that Grossen and Kelley reasoned that thigmotaxis would be learned very quickly as an avoidance response. If rats could avoid shock by jumping onto a ledge around the perimeter of their enclosure, they learned very rapidly. In contrast, if a platform of the same area was positioned in the center of the arena, the rats never learned to jump to it. And, if given a choice between a center platform and a ledge around the perimeter, they always chose the ledge. Thigmotaxis-like responding was indeed learned rapidly, confirming a prediction of SSDR theory.

The theory was also advanced by additional research on freezing, one of the rat's most common SSDRs (e.g., Fanselow & Lester, 1988). One thing we now know about freezing behavior is that it is truly innate and functional. This was beautifully shown in an experiment by Hirsch and Bolles (1980), who went about the state of Washington trapping deer mice and then breeding them in the lab. (Bolles was based at the University of Washington in Seattle.) The geography of Washington (Figure 10.7) is interesting because the state is bisected by the Cascade Mountains, which run north-south; these mountains create two distinct climates—one to the east and one to the west. Prevailing winds from the Pacific Ocean bring moisture to the western side of the mountains, but there is little moisture left for the eastern side. Because of this, Hirsch and Bolles realized that subspecies that have adapted to western and eastern Washington are preyed upon by different species of predators. In the arid east, a natural predator of the mouse is the gopher snake. In the lush west, there are no gopher snakes, but there is another natural predator—the weasel. Hirsch and Bolles therefore trapped mice in eastern and western Washington, and then allowed them to breed, in separate lines, for several generations in the lab. The subjects in their experiment were two generations removed from the live-trapped mice—they had never been outside the lab, and had never been exposed to a natural predator. In the experiment proper, mice from each line were put into a large, naturalistic arena with animals of different types. When a gopher snake was in the arena, the eastern Washington mice froze substantially and the western Washington mice did not. In fact, eastern

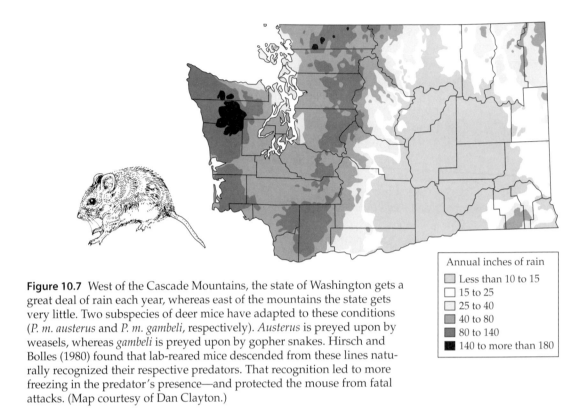

Figure 10.7 West of the Cascade Mountains, the state of Washington gets a great deal of rain each year, whereas east of the mountains the state gets very little. Two subspecies of deer mice have adapted to these conditions (*P. m. austerus* and *P. m. gambeli*, respectively). *Austerus* is preyed upon by weasels, whereas *gambeli* is preyed upon by gopher snakes. Hirsch and Bolles (1980) found that lab-reared mice descended from these lines naturally recognized their respective predators. That recognition led to more freezing in the predator's presence—and protected the mouse from fatal attacks. (Map courtesy of Dan Clayton.)

Annual inches of rain
- Less than 10 to 15
- 15 to 25
- 25 to 40
- 40 to 80
- 80 to 140
- 140 to more than 180

Washington mice died less frequently. In contrast, when a weasel was in the arena, the western Washington mice froze and the eastern Washington mice did not. Here, the western mice died less frequently. Mice did not freeze at all to a non-predatory garter snake or ground squirrel. The results made two important points. First, freezing has a clear pay-off. As SSDR theory assumes, it reduces predation. Second, there appears to be an innate recognition system that allows mice from different regions to recognize their natural predators.

Another important advance was made in an experiment in which Bolles and Riley (1973) simply required rats to freeze in order to avoid shock. The obvious prediction was that freezing would be learned very easily as an avoidance response. Bolles and Riley used a Sidman avoidance procedure like the one described above. Rats were placed inside a small box and given a brief electric shock at 5-second intervals (the "shock-shock interval"). If the rat froze, the next shock did not occur for 15 seconds (the "response-shock interval"). It is important to realize that, once a rat starts freezing, it can freeze continuously for several minutes. In the Bolles and Riley experiment, the next shock was continuously postponed until freezing stopped. The results are shown in Figure 10.8A. Consistent with the theory, the rats learned to freeze immediately.

(A)

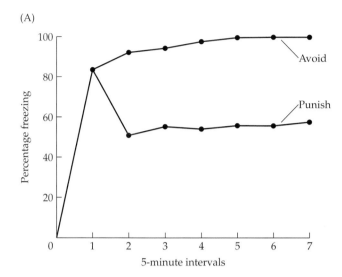

(B)

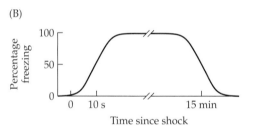

Figure 10.8 Freezing is rapidly learned as an avoidance response, but it turns out to be a respondent rather than an operant. (A) Rats quickly learned to freeze to avoid receiving shock. When shocks were then used to punish freezing, freezing decreased immediately, but never declined further. (B) Regardless of the group, freezing followed the same time-course after each shock. A shock elicits an initial burst of activity (making freezing zero), but the rat soon begins to freeze. If left undisturbed, the rat will freeze for 15 minutes or so and then eventually stop. This explains why rats learned to freeze so quickly after they were first shocked. However, when shock was used to punish freezing, each shock first elicited the activity burst (making freezing go to zero) and then freezing again. Once freezing resumed, another shock was delivered, and the same activity-then-freeze cycle began all over again, causing the rat to freeze about 60% of the time. (After Bolles, 1975; Bolles & Riley, 1973.)

The experiment actually included several other groups, one of which is included in Figure 10.8A. In this group, once the rats were freezing, the contingency between freezing and shocking was reversed so that now the shock was programmed to *punish* freezing. Specifically, the rats now received shocks at 5-second intervals once they froze for 15 seconds. Interestingly, as the figure shows, once the new punishment contingency began, freezing decreased abruptly, and the rats began freezing about 60% of the time. Despite delivery of the shock, freezing never went down to zero. The fact that it decreased so quickly, and then never decreased any further, made Bolles and Riley suspicious about what the rats were learning. They therefore took a closer look at the results and found that, no matter what, the rats always showed a characteristic pattern or cycle of responding after receiving each shock. This is shown in Figure 10.8B. When a shock occurred, it immediately elicited a burst of activity for a few seconds (Fanselow, 1982), and then the animal began to freeze; it then froze for a long period of time. Remarkably, this is all you need to know to understand the results shown in Figure 10.8A. For rats in the avoidance group, the first shock caused a brief burst of activity, and then freezing proceeded for several minutes— with nearly 100% freezing right away. On the other hand, when freezing was punished, the rats began cycling through the same pattern in another way. As usual, the first shock elicited a burst of activity for a few seconds, and then the rats froze again. But once it accumulated 15 more seconds of freezing, another shock was delivered, eliciting another activity burst and then more freezing. Each shock delivered after freezing broke up the freeze for a few seconds and then caused freezing to occur again. What this means is that all the freezing measured in the Bolles and Riley experiment was entirely elicited. It was controlled by its antecedents, and not by its consequences. If you remember Skinner's fundamental distinction between operants and respondents (see Chapter 1), freezing turns out to be a respondent (controlled by its antecedents) and not an operant (controlled by its consequences). This classic SSDR—one of the easiest of all responses to learn in order to avoid shock—does not seem to be an operant behavior at all.

This point needs a little further amplification. In the Bolles and Riley experiment, shocking the rat inside the box actually allowed rapid Pavlovian learning to occur. That is, the rat quickly associated the shock with the box. It turns out that the box CS, and not the shock itself, is what probably elicited all the freezing. (The shock itself mainly elicits the activity burst.) If a rat is given an electric shock and then removed and put into a different box, it does not freeze; the rat must be returned to the box in which it was just shocked (Blanchard & Blanchard, 1969; see also Fanselow, 1980). Freezing occurs in anticipation of shock; therefore, the rats froze in the Bolles and Riley experiment because of Pavlovian learning. The rats quickly learned that the box was associated with an electric shock and froze there until (a) another shock occurred and interrupted the freeze, or (b) some extinction occurred after an extended period of further exposure to the box, without another shock. This avoidance learning experiment was actually a Pavlovian learning experiment in disguise.

There are two points to remember from all of this. First, the animal's biology—or, its evolutionary history—matters. The success of avoidance learning depends at least partly on the degree to which the response required is a natural defensive response. Second, there is a lot of Pavlovian learning in avoidance learning. This point was originally made by the two-factor theory. But according to SSDR theory and the results of some of the research it stimulated, a great amount of behavior is controlled by learning about cues in the environment. In the freezing experiment, the rats mainly learned that the box was dangerous, and a natural behavior was addressed to the box. In a jump-out or one-way avoidance experiment, the situation is similar. According to SSDR theory in its later forms (e.g., Bolles, 1978), the rat simply learns through Pavlovian learning that one place is dangerous (a fear excitor) and the other place is safe (a fear inhibitor), and its natural flight behavior takes care of the rest. Natural defensive behaviors are supported by what the animal learns about cues in the environment. SSDR theory was one of the earliest "behavior systems" theories we discussed in Chapter 5.

Bolles went on to extend this idea even further with his student Michael Fanselow (e.g., Bolles & Fanselow, 1980). Working in Bolles's laboratory,

Fanselow had discovered that CSs associated with an electric shock come to elicit endorphins—natural substances that are released in the brain that deaden pain (e.g., Fanselow, 1979). Thus, in addition to eliciting an SSDR, a CS associated with shock also elicits a natural painkiller. The argument was that this analgesic response served to get the animal ready for—and thus adapt to—the upcoming shock. (Remember that Pavlovian signals evoke whole constellations of behavior that serve to optimize the animal's interactions with upcoming events, as discussed in Chapters 2 and 5.) According to Bolles and Fanselow (1980), one function of this analgesia is to suppress **recuperative behaviors**—that is, behaviors elicited by tissue damage (like licking a wound) that function to promote healing. Stopping to lick a wound while fending off a predator would not make sense—such an action would interfere with defense; thus, analgesia elicited by cues for attack suppresses recuperative behaviors. The model envisioned by Bolles and Fanselow is illustrated in Figure 10.9. Both danger signals (Pavlovian excitors for shock) and the sight, smell, or sound of an actual predator arouse the motivational state of fear, which in turn potentiates SSDRs. We have already seen that a natural predator evokes freezing in rodents; Lester and Fanselow (1985) likewise demonstrated that the presence of a potential predator will also evoke an endorphin response. Which SSDR actually emerges in the situation depends on support stimuli in the environment. If the situation supports flight, the rat will flee; if the situation doesn't support flight, the rat might freeze. If the rat is shocked when it touches a small prod, the rat will bury the prod if sawdust

Michael S. Fanselow

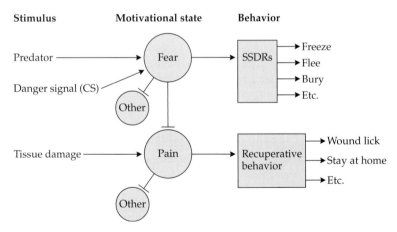

Figure 10.9 The perceptual-defensive-recuperative model of fear and pain. The presence of a predator or a "danger signal" (CS) arouses fear, which then potentiates SSDRs (which are further selected by support stimuli in the environment). Fear also inhibits other motivational states or systems, including pain. Pain itself is aroused by tissue damage and selects another class of behaviors—recuperative behaviors. Notice how the Fear and Pain systems are functionally organized to allow an animal to defend itself and recover from attack. (After Bolles & Fanselow, 1980.)

or some other material is available (e.g., Pinel & Mana, 1989). Fear also inhibits pain, a motivational state evoked by tissue damage. That state, like fear itself, otherwise potentiates recuperative behaviors designed, essentially, to now promote defense of the body after an attack.

Fanselow and Lester (1988; see also Fanselow, 1994) extended this model even further with the predatory imminence theory I introduced you to in Chapter 5. You may remember that different defensive behaviors are now thought to engage at "pre-encounter," "post-encounter," and "circa-strike" points along the imminence continuum. Each behavior is designed to prevent the animal from going to the next point further along the continuum, (i.e., moving closer to the predator). In effect, the recuperative behaviors illustrated in Figure 10.9 are behaviors that are then evoked in a kind of post-strike phase. In perhaps a further extension of this approach, we have also seen that long-duration cues that might signal trauma at a temporal distance are thought to evoke anxiety, while those temporally closer to trauma evoke fear and panic (Bouton, 2005; Bouton, Mineka, & Barlow, 2001). These functional analyses of fear, anxiety, and defense after trauma are the intellectual legacy of the SSDR theory of avoidance learning.

Cognitive factors in avoidance learning

One direction that theories of avoidance learning thus began to take was very ethological. There has been an emphasis on natural defensive behaviors rather than new behaviors learned through reinforcement. One might ask, though, what can all these innate behaviors in rats and mice really tell us about avoidance behavior in humans? Part of the answer is that the emphasis has shifted from operant reinforcement mechanisms to Pavlovian mechanisms; Pavlovian cues associated with pain or emotional trauma in humans will evoke behaviors that have evolved as natural defensive responses. Trauma will almost certainly engage Pavlovian processes, and these may go a long way in explaining anxiety disorders. For example, in panic disorder with agoraphobia, associating anxiety or panic with the local shopping mall might be sufficient to keep the patient away from the mall. In Chapter 2, we discussed *sign tracking*: We approach CSs for positive events and withdraw from CSs for negative events. This might explain quite a lot of avoidance behavior. And, if we want to treat avoidance behavior therapeutically, we will need to extinguish the Pavlovian fear.

Although there is an explicit biological emphasis, the approach is also cognitive in the sense that it emphasizes that organisms learn about danger and safety cues (e.g., Bolles, 1978). Instead of emphasizing S-R learning, though, the approach notes that the behavioral effects of fear (freezing, fleeing, burying, etc.) can vary and are supported by other stimuli in the environment. Loosely speaking, the rat recognizes the CS as a danger cue, but the response the CS evokes depends on other support stimuli (see Chapter 5). Furthermore, in order for organisms to learn about cues in the environment (that then engage the defensive behavior system), the facts and theories of classical conditioning that we have discussed in detail in earlier chapters now necessarily apply. Remember that the empirical facts of Pavlovian learning caused most theorists to invoke processes that are not immediately apparent in behavior (like short-term memory, attention, priming, and so forth) to explain them. Thus, modern avoidance theory now envisions an organism not only performing natural defensive behaviors but also learning about cues in its environment through the Pavlovian processes defined and evaluated in Chapter 4.

But we must also understand how organisms learn avoidance behaviors that are not, in fact, SSDRs. Although such learning takes more training, it is still possible for many rats to learn to shuttle in shuttle boxes, and (with more difficulty) they can even be taught to lever-press. The starting insight here is that, in these cases, unlike cases where the task requires an SSDR, the warning signal termination contingency is important. That is, turning the warning signal off once the response is made is necessary to achieve good learning (e.g., Bolles & Grossen, 1969; Bolles et al., 1966). One possibility, therefore, is that reinforcement through fear reduction—that is, escape from learned fear—is still important when the required behavior is not an SSDR. A somewhat different idea is that warning signal termination provides the animal in these situations with "feedback" for the correct response (Bolles, 1970).

The idea that CS termination provides feedback was consistent with experiments by Bolles and Grossen (1969), which showed that, in situations where warning signal termination is important, leaving the warning signal on and merely adding a brief cue at the moment the response was made was equally effective at improving learning. Subsequent research showed, however, that the feedback cue might have become a conditioned fear inhibitor. Notice that, if the buzzer is paired with an electric shock on its own, but not when it is accompanied by a response (and the feedback stimulus), the feedback stimulus and the response are essentially negative features in a feature-negative discrimination (see Chapters 4 and 5). Morris (1974) and Rescorla (1968a) showed that feedback stimuli used in avoidance training do, in fact, become conditioned inhibitors. Furthermore, when animals are first given Pavlovian training that establishes the feedback stimulus as a fear inhibitor, this training increases the strength of an avoidance response when it is presented as a consequence of the response (Rescorla, 1969a; Weisman & Litner, 1969). Thus, feedback stimuli may reinforce avoidance because they inhibit fear.

Given that any response probably produces some natural stimulus feedback, it is worth entertaining the possibility that the avoidance response *itself* becomes a conditioned inhibitor, acquiring a kind of negative association with the shock. The idea that behaviors can function as safety signals is consistent with observations made by clinical psychologists who have noticed that people with anxiety disorders often acquire certain "safety behaviors" (e.g., Salkovkis, Clark, & Gelder, 1996). Such behaviors, such as carrying an empty pill bottle around everywhere for comfort, are basically avoidance behaviors that reduce fear (e.g., Bouton et al., 2001). Safety behaviors are arguably problematic for therapy, because their presence may maintain fear of the warning signal. Carrying the pill bottle might make an agoraphobic feel safe leaving the house—but only as long as the pill bottle is present. As we saw in Chapter 4, the presence of an inhibitor in compound with the CS will "protect" the CS from extinction (e.g., Rescorla, 2003). So, thinking of the response and its consequences as the equivalent of a Pavlovian cue has further predictive and explanatory power.

In another cognitive approach to avoidance, Seligman and Johnston (1973) suggested that organisms learn that the avoidance response predicts no aversive US; in addition, not performing the response predicts the US. These expectancies lead the organism to avoid. The approach implies that avoidance behavior can become very persistent, because if shock is never actually associated with the response, there is never anything to disconfirm the expectancy of "response-no shock." There are at least three problems with this approach. One problem is that avoidance responding does not persist forever. That is, responses do eventually decline if they are allowed to occur over and over without shock (Mackintosh, 1974), despite the fact that each response would presumably further confirm the response-no shock expectancy. Another problem is that the theory does not make much contact with modern theories of learning—it merely states what seems rational or logical. And, third, the idea is inconsistent with a recent avoidance learning experiment conducted by DeHouwer, Crombez, and Baeyens (2005).

In DeHouwer et al.'s experiment, humans learned to avoid a mild electric shock by pressing different keys on a computer keyboard. One response (R_1) avoided shock in the presence of one warning signal (A, e.g., a square presented on the computer monitor), and another response (R_2) avoided an electric shock in the presence of a second signal (B, e.g., a triangle). After the responses were learned, a second phase began. The avoidance trials with R_1 and R_2 continued. However, on separate trials the participants were also instructed to make R_2 (without its warning signal); this time, each response made an electric shock occur. Although this caused the participants to report that they expected shock whenever they made the response, in a final phase they also reported that they expected "*no* shock" when the response was tested again in the presence of the original warning stimulus (Figure 10.10)! The result cannot be explained by the Seligman-Johnston theory, because the response-shock pairings should have changed the "response-no shock" expectancy to "response-shock." (If Seligman and Johnston merely assumed that the response-no shock expectancy is specific to the warning signal the response is trained with, then it would not transfer to a third warning stimulus, C; unfortunately for Seligman and Johnston, DeHouwer et al. [2005] found such a transfer, although for simplicity it is not shown in Figure 10.10.)

The overall pattern of DeHouwer et al.'s results is exactly what you would expect if the response had become a negative occasion-setter informing the subject that the shock would not follow the warning signal (see Chapter 5). During training, the warning signal was paired with an electric shock unless the response was made; the response then set the occasion for a signal-no shock relation. Remember that the power of an occasion-setter is not affected by its direct association with the US (see Chapter 5). Thus,

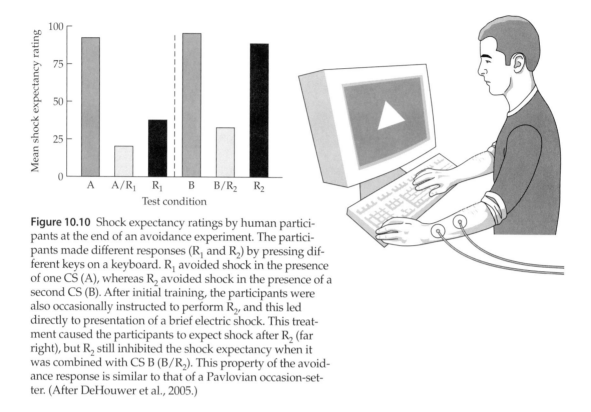

Figure 10.10 Shock expectancy ratings by human participants at the end of an avoidance experiment. The participants made different responses (R_1 and R_2) by pressing different keys on a keyboard. R_1 avoided shock in the presence of one CS (A), whereas R_2 avoided shock in the presence of a second CS (B). After initial training, the participants were also occasionally instructed to perform R_2, and this led directly to presentation of a brief electric shock. This treatment caused the participants to expect shock after R_2 (far right), but R_2 still inhibited the shock expectancy when it was combined with CS B (B/R_2). This property of the avoidance response is similar to that of a Pavlovian occasion-setter. (After DeHouwer et al., 2005.)

associating the response with shock in the second phase had no impact on its ability to set the occasion for the signal-no shock relationship.

The idea that an avoidance response may be a negative occasion-setter is a variation of the idea that the response is analogous to a conditioned inhibitor—negative occasion-setting is a form of inhibition. In the long run, the evidence currently favors the idea that we learn about avoidance responses in a way that's similar to how we learn about CSs in similar arrangements. Response learning seems to follow the rules of Pavlovian learning.

Learned helplessness

Another line of research also led to a cognitive perspective on avoidance behavior. Overmier and Seligman (1967) found that avoidance learning proceeded very slowly if their dog subjects were first given inescapable shocks before the avoidance training (see Overmier & Leaf, 1965, for earlier observations). Seligman and Maier (1967) then showed that it was the *uncontrollability* of the initial shocks that was crucial. Their experiment is summarized in Figure 10.11. They used three groups in what has become known as the "triadic design." In the first phase, one group was given a series of electric shocks that could be escaped (turned off once they had started) if the dog pressed a panel with its nose. A second group was "yoked" to the first; each animal received exactly

Group	Phase 1	Phase 2	Phase 2 % Shocks escaped
Escapable	Escapable shock	Escape training	74%
Inescapable	Yoked, inescapable shock	Escape training	28%
No shock	—	Escape training	78%

Figure 10.11 The learned helplessness effect. In Phase 1, different groups receive escapable electric shocks (shocks they can turn off with an instrumental response), inescapable shocks (the same shocks controlled by a member of the escapable group, the so-called "yoked" procedure), or no shock. In Phase 2, when allowed to escape and/or avoid shock in a different environment, the group exposed to inescapable shocks does poorly. (Data from Seligman & Maier, 1967.)

the same shocks at the same points in time as a partner animal in the first group, but the behavior of the second group of dogs did not influence when the shock went on or off. A third group of dogs received no shocks at all in the first phase. In the second phase, all groups could escape shock in a shuttle box by shuttling from one side to another. As shown in Figure 10.11, the groups differed in how well they performed in this phase. The groups given either no shock or escapable shock escaped most of the shocks. But the group first given inescapable shock was very poor at learning to escape. Six out of ten subjects never responded during the shock. Exposure to inescapable shock—but not escapable shock—caused a profound deficit in subsequent escape learning.

Seligman and Maier suggested that exposure to inescapable shock actually had several effects. Dogs exposed to inescapable shock did not initiate responding in the second phase; they had what appeared to be a "motivational deficit." They also failed to show as much learning in the second phase; they had what was termed a "cognitive deficit." And, they seemed to accept the shocks delivered in the second phase passively—that is, they also seemed to have an "affective" or "emotional deficit." In another experiment published in the same paper, Seligman and Maier (1967) also demonstrated that exposure to *escapable* shocks before exposure to inescapable shocks protected the animal from these deficits. This is called the **immunization effect** (see also Seligman, Rosellini, & Kozak, 1975; Williams & Maier, 1977). The idea that emerged was that organisms do more than merely learn to respond in instrumental learning experiments; they may acquire knowledge about the relationship between their behavior and its outcomes. When exposed to inescapable shock, the dogs behaved as if they had acquired the belief that their actions and shock termination were independent, and this belief seemed to generalize to a new action in a new situation in the second phase (Maier & Seligman, 1976; Maier, Seligman, & Solomon, 1969; Seligman, Maier, & Solomon, 1971). This view is often referred to as the **learned helplessness hypothesis**. The phenomenon itself—the finding that inescapable shock interferes with subsequent escape learning—is often called the **learned helplessness effect**.

Steven Maier

J. Bruce Overmier

Notice that, when a shock is inescapable, shock termination is equally probable whether the animal responds or not. In this sense, there is no contingency between the action and the outcome. There is a connection here with what we have previously seen in Pavlovian learning. Remember that Rescorla (e.g., 1967b, 1968a, see Chapter 3) discovered that the contingency between a CS and a US determines what the animal learns about the CS: When the probability of a US is greater in the CS than outside it, the CS becomes an excitor; when the probability of the US is less in the CS then outside it, the CS becomes an inhibitor; and when the probability of the US is the same regardless of whether the CS is on or off, the CS becomes neither. Rescorla never claimed that the animals learned about the contingency itself; the contingency between CS and US simply predicts whether the CS will be an excitor or an inhibitor. (This agnostic view was accepted by the theories of conditioning, covered in Chapter 4, that were developed later.) On the other hand, other theorists have come closer to claiming that animals do learn about the contingency. Mackintosh (e.g., 1973; see also Baker, 1974; Baker & Mackintosh, 1977) found that, when there is zero contingency between a CS and a US, it is harder to learn to associate the two events when they are later paired (but see Bonardi & Hall, 1996; Bonardi & Ong, 2003; Killcross & Dickinson, 1996). This effect is called **learned irrelevance**. Although Mackintosh argued that zero contingency between a tone and a shock might reduce attention to—or associability of—the tone, there is also evidence that a more "generalized learned irrelevance" can develop. That is, exposure to a zero contingency between a tone and a shock can also make it difficult to learn that a different CS, like a light, is associated with shock (Dess & Overmier, 1989; Linden, Savage, & Overmier, 1997). I hope you see the parallel with the learned helplessness effect. When exposed either to an uncorrelated CS and US or an uncorrelated action and outcome, organisms may learn a kind of "belief" that similar events will also be independent.

The learned helplessness hypothesis became generally well known to psychologists. Maier and Seligman (1976) wrote an influential paper that was read by many experimental psychologists. And Seligman (1975) wrote a book for a general audience that linked the phenomenon to depression in humans (the book was entitled *Helplessness: On depression, development, and death*). The idea was that uncontrollable events like the loss of a job or death of a loved one may lead a person to the kind of motivational, cognitive, and emotional deficits seen in the original animal experiments. Thus a depressed person may acquire a belief that nothing that he or she does makes a difference or matters, and this leads to a kind of giving up about life. The theory has moved forward since then (e.g., see Overmier & LoLordo, 1998, for one review). For example, Seligman and his colleagues (e.g., Abramson, Seligman, & Teasdale, 1978) went on to emphasize causal attributions people make about the events in their lives; helplessness and depression mainly develop when uncontrollability is attributed to the person's own failures (rather than an external cause), is assumed to be persistent, and is assumed to be a global characteristic of life. Seligman (e.g., 1990) went on to emphasize the positive impact of learning "optimism," which results from attributions that outcomes are globally and persistently affected by one's behavior.

Research in animal laboratories went in a somewhat different direction. Investigators quickly realized that several different factors can contribute to the escape deficit reported by Seligman and Maier (1967) (see LoLordo & Taylor, 2001, for a review). In the long run, none of these factors replaced the idea that animals can learn about the relation between behavior and outcome, but they need to be summarized here because they remind us that behavioral effects rarely have single causes. First, exposure to inescapable shock can simply make an animal less active (e.g., Anisman, deCatanzaro, & Remington, 1978; Glazer & Weiss, 1976). Although suppressed activity could make it difficult to learn an active escape response, this cannot be the whole story. Maier (1970) compared active escape learning in groups that first had inescapable shocks or escape training in which they had to stand *motionless* to escape. Even though standing still was especially incompatible with the active escape response, subjects in the escape group still learned the active response better than subjects that had been inescapably shocked! Inescapable shock can also interfere with escape in a maze where the animal must choose to go left or right (Jackson, Alexander, & Maier, 1980; Lee & Maier, 1988; Minor, Jackson, & Maier, 1984). Suppressed activity should make responding slow, but not make choices inaccurate. The results, therefore, further suggest that suppressed activity cannot completely explain the learned helplessness effect.

A second possibility is that inescapable shock numbs the animal and makes it feel less pain. Analgesia does result from inescapable shock exposure (e.g., Jackson, Maier, & Coon, 1979; Maier, Sherman, Lewis, Terman, & Liebeskind, 1983), but it is not necessary for helplessness. Certain physiological manipulations that eliminate analgesia do not eliminate the helplessness effect (MacLennan, Drugan, Hyson, Maier, Madden, & Barchas, 1982). Third, exposure to inescapable shock can reduce the brain level of certain neurotransmitters, such as norepinephrine and serotonin (e.g., Weiss, Goodman, Losito, Corrigan, Charry, & Bailey, 1981). But how these effects play out over time after the receipt of inescapable shock does not always match the time course of the helplessness effect—and, equally important, it is not clear whether they interfere directly with escape learning or merely reflect the animal's expectation of act-outcome independence (e.g., Overmier & LoLordo, 1998). A good deal of excellent research has further studied the brain events that accompany learned helplessness (e.g., Maier & Watkins, 2005), but it has not replaced the idea that learned controllability/uncontrollability is the major factor. The bottom line is that, although exposure to inescapable shock has a large number of effects, animals do learn something other than a competing response that interferes with escape learning in the second phase.

But what is the nature of the cognitive deficit? One possibility is that inescapable shock somehow causes the animal to pay less attention to its behavior, just as the animal may pay less attention to a CS that is not correlated with a US (Minor et al., 1984). Consistent with this idea, if one adds a feedback stimulus during escape training in the second phase so that the new response terminates shock and also causes an attention-grabbing termination of the lights, inescapably shocked rats begin to learn as well as unshocked rats (Maier, Jackson, & Tomie, 1987). Unfortunately, other evidence is not so clearly consistent with an attentional interpretation. After finally learning the response in a second phase, inescapably shocked rats will extinguish responding quickly (Testa, Juraska, & Maier, 1974) or they can be quick to learn that behavior and outcome are uncorrelated again (Rosellini, DeCola, Plonsky, Warren, & Stilman, 1984). Neither result seems consistent with the idea that "helpless" animals do not pay attention to their behavior (LoLordo & Taylor, 2001).

One of the most important take-home messages of the research that followed discovery of the learned helplessness effect is that controllability of a bad event has a powerful influence on the stress it produces (Minor, Dess, & Overmier, 1991). For example, exposure to uncontrollable (and unpredictable) shocks is stressful enough that it can cause rats to develop ulcers; the level of ulceration is reduced, though, if the same shocks are controllable (and predictable) (Seligman, 1968; Weiss, 1968). Uncontrollable shock also causes more fear conditioning than controllable shock when the two are compared as USs in fear conditioning (e.g., Mineka, Cook, & Miller, 1984; Rosellini, DeCola, & Warren, 1986). In the long run, the controllability of events turns out to be an important dimension that influences their psychological impact (see Mineka & Hendersen, 1985, and Mineka, Gunnar, & Champoux, 1986, for further evidence).

Why does being able to escape a shock reduce its stressfulness? It seems to boil down to the predictive value of the escape response. As illustrated in Figure 10.12, a response that turns a shock off might predict both shock

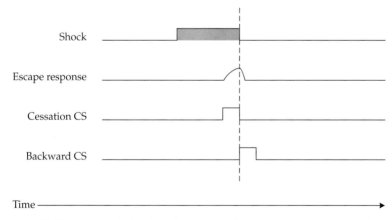

Figure 10.12 Temporal relationships between a shock, an escape response that turns it off, a cessation CS, and a backward CS. The escape response is initiated just before the electric shock ends and then persists a bit afterward. A cessation CS precedes the offset of shock, whereas a backward CS follows it. A cessation CS is especially good at reducing the effects of inescapable shock—it has effects like an escape response. (After Minor et al., 1990.)

offset and the upcoming intertrial interval that is free from shock. Investigators have therefore asked whether a CS presented either right before shock termination (a shock-cessation cue) or right after the shock (a "backward" cue, see Chapters 3 and 4) similarly softens the impact of inescapable shock. Adding a backward CS just after each inescapable shock does reduce the fear conditioning the shock causes (e.g., Mineka et al., 1984). However, a backward CS is less effective than an escape response at reducing the impact of the shock when there are short intertrial intervals between shocks (e.g., Minor, Trauner, Lee, & Dess, 1990; Rosellini et al., 1986; Rosellini, Warren, & DeCola, 1987). The backward CS—but not the escape response—seems to work only when it signals a fairly long minimum period free from shock (Moscovitch & LoLordo, 1968). A cessation cue has a bigger impact. It softens the impact of inescapable shock, regardless of whether the next intertrial interval is short or long (Minor et al., 1990). It also produces an immunization effect—that is, exposure to inescapable shocks with an added cessation cue protects the subject from helplessness caused by future inescapable shocks (Minor et al., 1990). A combination of cessation and backward signals seems especially effective. To conclude, escapable shocks might be less harmful than inescapable shocks because the escape response signals shock cessation. This might weaken the aversiveness of shock through a process like counterconditioning (see LoLordo & Taylor, 2001, for further discussion); association of the shock with the positive properties of the response might make the shock less aversive. Once again, we discover that an important feature of an instrumental action is its signaling properties.

Summary: What does it all mean?

In addition to its practical relevance in helping us to understand stress and depression, research on learned helplessness has had a broad influence on theories of learning. First, from its earliest days, the helplessness phenomenon suggested a parallel between how animals learn in instrumental and Pavlovian situations. That is, the apparent effects of action-outcome independence paralleled the effects of CS-US independence in Pavlovian learning. (Interestingly, Rescorla's work on contingencies and Overmier, Maier, and Seligman's work on helplessness were all initially conducted while these investigators were graduate students in Richard Solomon's laboratory.) Second, research on helplessness began to reinforce the idea that the response has signaling attributes—escapable shock is less detrimental than inescapable shock because the response works like a Pavlovian cessation cue. Finally, the phenomenon led to a more cognitive perspective on instrumental learning. Animals may learn more than merely performing a certain response in a certain situation. Their knowledge about the relationship between their actions and outcomes also seems to count.

More generally, research on avoidance learning has highlighted the influence of Pavlovian learning on instrumental performance ever since Mowrer's two-factor theory was first proposed. Nowadays, in addition to motivating and providing a possible basis for reinforcement, Pavlovian fear is thought to arouse a system of natural behaviors that gets the system ready for the aversive S* (see also Chapters 2 and 5). Furthermore, the increasing emphasis on feedback stimuli and inhibition in explaining avoidance behavior suggests that behavior is like a safety signal or negative occasion-setter. Avoidance behavior is strongly influenced by S-S* learning, and the response has properties analogous to those of a CS.

Parallels in Appetitive Learning

Of course, another implication of research on avoidance learning was that not all behaviors are equally learnable—that is, biology and evolution also have an influence. A surprising amount of the learning is about stimuli in the environment; animals learn about cues that predict danger and safety, and organisms then direct their natural behavior toward these CSs. One of the interesting things about this aspect of avoidance learning is that it has an almost perfect parallel in learning about appetitive goals and S*s, such as food.

The misbehavior of organisms

In a classic paper that was mentioned briefly in Chapter 2, Breland and Breland (1961) described many attempts to train animals to perform different behaviors by applying the principles of reinforcement. (You may remember that the Brelands had a business in which they trained animals to perform, for example, on TV commercials.) Unfortunately, reinforcement didn't always work; the paper was titled "The Misbehavior of Organisms," a clever play on the title of Skinner's famous book, *The Behavior of Organisms* (1938). You may remember that the Brelands tried to reinforce a pig for putting wooden coins into a piggy bank. As the Brelands patiently shaped the pig to take the coins and deposit them, the pig began dropping them and rooting them around the pen with its snout as if the coins were bits of food. The behavior persisted despite never being reinforced. The Brelands also tried to train a raccoon to do the same thing—to put a coin into a piggy bank. This animal learned to drop a coin into a container when reinforced to do so, but when the Brelands pressed their luck and tried to shape the raccoon to deposit *two* coins rather than one, things began to fall apart. At this point, the raccoon took the coins, and instead of depositing them in the container, it rubbed them together and dipped them in and out. Again, this behavior persisted despite no reinforcement. Other reinforcement failures involved chickens. At one point, the Brelands tried to train one or two chickens to stand on a platform for 15 seconds in order to receive food. The chickens wouldn't quite do this; instead of standing still during the interval, they scratched the floor persistently with their feet. (The Brelands took advantage of this and instead taught the chickens to dance for 15 seconds to the sound of a juke box.) Other chickens were taught to play baseball in a miniature baseball park. Pulling a loop made a small bat swing and hit a ball that went rolling out into the outfield. If the bird then ran to first base, it was reinforced. Things were fine as long as the bird was confined to a cage along the first-base line. But if the bird was let loose and had access to the ball park, it would chase the ball and peck it all around the outfield.

Other examples of misbehavior have been reported (e.g., Timberlake, Wahl, & King, 1982). The Brelands emphasized that each case represented a failure of reinforcement, and noted that each involved the intrusion of an instinctive behavior that got in the way (they called this "instinctive drift"). Notice, however, that although the operant part of the experiment failed, the animals were, in fact, learning something. Each was associating a salient cue (or CS) with food. During shaping, the pig and raccoon presumably had many coin-food pairings, and the chicken had several opportunities to learn that the 15-second interval—or the miniature baseball—signaled food. Each of these CSs then evoked a natural food-getting behavior. As Bolles had discovered in avoidance learning, a lot of learning in operant situations is about Pavlovian signals, and these can sometimes exert control by eliciting natural behaviors.

Superstition revisited

The idea that reinforcement can fail seems inconsistent with the view that reinforcers are so powerful they can even increase the strength of a behavior they are accidentally paired with. This is the theoretical basis for "superstitious behavior" we discussed in Chapter 7. You may recall that in the "superstition experiment," Skinner (1948) delivered food to pigeons at regular intervals—regardless of what the pigeons happened to be doing. When Skinner looked in on the birds a few hours later, some of them were thrusting their heads in the corner, some were rocking back and forth, and so on, as if these responses had been required to obtain food. Skinner suggested that somewhere along the line each bird had emitted a chance behavior at the instant food was presented. The effect of this accidental pairing of behavior and reinforcer was to make the bird respond enough so that the behavior was (accidentally) rewarded again when the next reinforcer was presented. The implication: Even arbitrary, accidental pairings seem to cause change. How can this idea be reconciled with the kinds of failures suggested by Breland and Breland?

Staddon and Simmelhag (1971) repeated Skinner's experiment and carefully watched the birds' behavior develop over time. What emerged was a pattern of behaviors between successive presentations of food like the one illustrated in Figure 10.13A. As time went by after a presentation of food, a behavior began to emerge and fill up all the time until the next reinforcer was delivered. Because this behavior occurred at the end of the food-food interval, Staddon and Simmelhag called it **terminal behavior**. In every bird, terminal behavior involved pecking movements, usually oriented toward the front of the chamber or near the food hopper. Though the pecking tended to occur when food was about to be presented, careful analysis suggested that it was not the behavior that was paired with food early in training. For example, early in training, the typical behavior that was actually paired with the next reinforcer was the bird having its head in the hopper, rather than pecking near the front wall. Such observations suggest that, if reinforcement

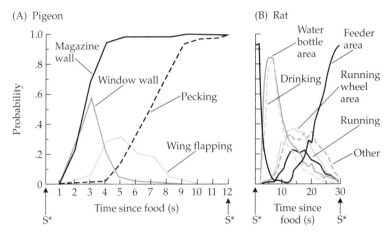

(A) Pigeon

(B) Rat

Figure 10.13 Behavior of a pigeon (A) and rat (B) given food S*s at regular intervals. The pigeon was given food every 12 seconds. Soon after S*, there was behavior directed toward the window of the Skinner box (window wall) and also some wing-flapping, but these behaviors then declined over time as the next food presentation became imminent. These are interim behaviors (or adjunctive behaviors). Other behaviors (being near the magazine wall and pecking) increased and then peaked toward the end of the interval, when food was expected—these are terminal behaviors. The rat (B) was given a food pellet every 30 seconds. Here again, some behaviors, namely drinking, running in a wheel, and being in the drinking and running areas, peaked early and then declined (they are interim behaviors). Being near the feeder, in contrast, peaked toward the end of the interval when food was expected (a terminal behavior). (A, after Staddon & Simmelhag, 1971; B, after Staddon & Ayres, 1975; figure inspired by Staddon, 1977.)

was operating here, head-in-hopper should have been learned as the bird's terminal behavior.

Earlier in the food-food interval, other kinds of behaviors were more probable. These behaviors varied between birds, although an individual bird would be fairly persistent at demonstrating the same behaviors from interval to interval (e.g., some birds turned in three-quarters of a circle, some birds flapped their wings, etc.). These behaviors were called **interim behaviors**. It is not entirely clear what Skinner (1948) had originally observed. But many of his superstitious behaviors were probably interim behaviors. The important thing, though, is that according to Staddon and Simmelhag's observations, the interim behaviors were never occurring at the moment a reinforcer was delivered. They were behaviors the pigeons seemed to do to pass the time before the next reinforcer was going to happen. There was very little operant learning in their superstition experiment. Instead, the birds learned about the time between food deliveries and began predicting food based on a temporal CS. When time predicted feeding, terminal behaviors were evoked. When time didn't predict food for awhile, the bird engaged in behavior that seemed to kill or pass the time between bouts of terminal behavior.

Interim behavior is related to many **adjunctive behaviors** that experimenters have observed in operant situations (Falk, 1961, 1977). Perhaps the most remarkable of these is a phenomenon called **schedule-induced polydipsia** (Falk, 1961). In the typical experiment, rats are reinforced for lever-pressing in a Skinner box with a food pellet delivered on an interval schedule (see Chapter 7). A water bottle is attached to the side of the chamber. The animal lever-presses as expected, but remarkably, soon after earning each reinforcer, the rat goes over to the water bottle and consumes an excessive amount of liquid before returning to the lever-pressing task (see Figure 10.13B). Falk (1961) reported that, in a 3-hour session, a rat on a VI 1-minute schedule drank about half its body weight in water. (Note that there is relatively little cost to excessive drinking like this, since the rat has a bladder.) Interestingly, if an ethanol solution is available, rats will drink so much of it over sessions that they eventually show signs of becoming alcohol-dependent (e.g., Falk, Samson, & Winger, 1972; Samson & Pfeffer, 1987; see Doyle & Samson, 1988, for one application to humans). Animals will perform a variety of behaviors as adjuncts to schedules of reinforcement. For example, pigeons may attack another pigeon (e.g., Cohen, Looney, Campagnoni, & Lawler, 1985) and rats may run in wheels (Levitsky & Collier, 1968; Staddon & Ayres, 1975). One explanation is that schedules of reinforcement engage approach behavior when they are rich and a tendency to escape when they are lean. Adjunctive behavior tends to emerge at intermediate reinforcement rates, when there may be conflict between the tendencies to approach and escape (Falk & Kupfer, 1998). The phenomenon may be analogous to certain "displacement activities" noted by ethologists in conflict situations (e.g., Falk, 1977). For example, a gull in a dispute with another gull over a territorial boundary may often stop its aggressive posturing and grab and pull a wad of grass in its beak. Adjunctive behaviors might also be part of the natural behavior system evoked by the reinforcer (e.g., Lucas, Timberlake, & Gawley, 1988; Timberlake, 2001; Timberlake & Lucas, 1985, 1991). For example, interim (adjunctive) and terminal behaviors may be seen as focal search and consummatory behaviors that occur at different temporal distances from the next reward (see Chapter 5). Timberlake (2001) has also noted that excessive drinking may occur because drinking is part of the rat's natural post-meal repertoire—a drink after a meal is functional because it aids digestion. Thus it is a post-food (rather than pre-food) part of the behavior system that might come to the fore when the animal learns to expect food at regular intervals.

You may have seen examples of adjunctive behaviors in computer rooms where students can be found drumming with their pencils, biting their nails, scratching their heads, or fiddling with candy wrappers or water bottles between bursts of actual work. These behaviors can become habitual, and they basically fill the gaps between reinforcers. Many writers have argued that this process controls many repetitive and sometimes harmful behaviors in humans (e.g., Cantor & Wilson, 1985; Falk & Kupfer, 1998). For the present, though, it is worth emphasizing that some rather surprising behaviors can emerge and dominate when reinforcers are scheduled intermittently. And, importantly, they seem to have little to do with reinforcement in the traditional law-of-effect sense: No direct response-reinforcer pairing has "stamped" them in. As the name implies, adjuncts are adjuncts to operant behaviors, and they appear to occur at precisely the time when periodically scheduled and predictable reinforcers are not about to occur.

A general role for stimulus learning in response learning situations

One intriguing feature of the revisited pigeon superstition experiment (Staddon & Simmelhag, 1971) is the pecking behavior itself. Although other replications of the superstition experiment have found far less pecking (e.g., Timberlake & Lucas, 1985), there is no doubt that pecking can be powerfully controlled by Pavlovian—as opposed to operant—contingencies. "Autoshaping" was introduced in Chapter 3. That phenomenon was discovered by Brown and Jenkins (1968), who put pigeons into a standard Skinner box in which birds can direct key pecks at the usual key. All Brown and Jenkins did was illuminate the key for 8 seconds and then present the food. Within about 50 trials like this, the typical bird went up to the key when it was illuminated and pecked at it. The key peck behavior was automatically shaped, and the rest is history. Pecking appears to result automatically from Pavlovian pairings of the keylight and food, and autoshaping has become a standard method for studying Pavlovian learning.

In an experiment that followed closely on the original, Williams and Williams (1969) repeated the study with a devious twist. As in the Brown and Jenkins experiment, the keylight was turned on and paired with food. But, in this case, the food only occurred if the bird did not peck. If the bird pecked, the light was turned off and the presentation of food was prevented. There was therefore a negative contingency between pecking and reinforcement, a so-called "omission" contingency (Sheffield, 1965). If the pecking response was controlled by its consequences, the bird should not have pecked. On the other hand, if the bird did not peck on every trial, at least some keylight pairings will have still occurred, and the keylight may have remained a positive predictor of food. What happened in this experiment was famous. The birds continued to peck on most of the trials when the keylight came on. Despite the negative peck-reinforcer contingency, the behavior was maintained. This phenomenon is therefore known as **negative automaintenance**. The pecking response was elicited by the light coming on, but it was not strongly controlled by its consequences. Both autoshaping and negative automaintenance suggest that pecking is largely a respondent behavior rather than an operant. The pigeon behaves as if it can't help pecking at a keylight signaling food.

It is interesting to note that negative automaintenance is really very similar to the misbehavior noted by Breland and Breland (1961). In either case, a signal for food elicited food behavior that, in the long run, resulted in the omission of reward. The results generally tell us that Pavlovian contingencies embedded in experiments can produce surprisingly strong control over behavior. Autoshaping and negative automaintenance also began to establish the phenomenon of sign-tracking—that is, animals tend to approach CSs for positive events (see Chapter 2). In fact, according to Jenkins and Moore (1973), CSs also do something more specific. When pigeons receive pairings of one colored keylight with food and another color keylight with water, the birds use an eating movement to peck the food key and a drinking movement to peck the water key—as if they are eating and drinking the CSs. Moore (1973; see also Bindra, 1972) noted that Pavlovian contingencies may subtly control the behavior observed in almost any operant situation. When a laboratory operant is shaped by successive approximations, for example, the animal is first reinforced in one location (typically near the food cup), and is then required to move away from that site and more toward the lever or key. At each step, the animal may notice new stimuli, and these new CSs may now become associated with the reinforcer and evoke consummatory or approach responses. Even operant response chains (see Chapter 7) can follow from Pavlovian rules. Although the outcome of one response in a chain is thought to reinforce the previous response and set the occasion for the next, it is conceivable that each behavior brings the subject into contact with a new stimulus that evokes the next behavior. Although the case is not necessarily proven, sign-tracking can go some distance in explaining behavior in complex situations.

What does this mean for human behavior? Arthur Tomie (e.g., 1996, 2001) has noted that many addictive disorders involve the handling of small implements that can become CSs directly associated with reward. The opiate user handles a needle and syringe, a crack smoker handles a pipe, an alcoholic might handle beer or whiskey bottles that are associated with alcohol over many trials. When an activity involves handling a salient CS that is associated with reward, the kinds of Pavlovian sign-tracking processes under discussion might combine with purer operant learning to make behavior especially strong and seemingly compulsive. (There is something compulsive-like in the behavior of the pigeon in the negative automaintenance experiment who keeps pecking as if it can't be helped.) The more general point, though, is that S-S* contingencies and R-S* contingencies almost always go hand-in-hand in any learning situation. If we want to understand a particular behavior—even a nominally voluntary or operant behavior—we will do well to consider both the operant and embedded Pavlovian contingencies.

Punishment

We are thus suggesting that either S-S* or R-S* learning can often lead to the same behavioral outcome. Now, let's consider their role in punishment, where organisms stop performing behaviors that have unpleasant consequences. Punishment is not uncommon in life. For example, to stop a child from stealing cookies from a cookie jar in the kitchen, a parent might punish the behavior with a mild scolding ("Stop it!"). But notice that punishment might work (the child might stop stealing cookies) for at least two reasons. First, the child might quit because he learns that the response (stealing cookies) is connected with the punisher (R-S* learning). Alternatively, the child might learn that certain stimuli in the environment predict that punishment can occur (S-S*), and he might merely stay away from those cues. For example, he might learn that the cookie jar is associated with punishment, or that the combination of cookie jar and parent in the kitchen is associated with punishment. Obviously, such learning might not prevent the theft of cookies if the parent leaves the house for a while. A similar scenario is present when a state government tries to keep drivers from speeding on the freeway. The police might give out more speeding tickets—but will drivers slow down, or will they merely learn to spot police cars in the distance (and perhaps buy radar detectors) to avoid detection? The fact that punishment contingencies can support either stimulus learning or response learning is one reason why punishment is not always effective at suppressing behavior.

Exactly this point was made in some experiments by Bolles, Holz, Dunn, and Hill (1980). In one experiment, a special lever with handle bars was installed in a Skinner box. The rats could either push the lever down or pull it out from the wall; both of these responses were initially reinforced on variable interval schedules of reinforcement. After the rats were performing each response at an equal rate, Bolles et al. (1980) began punishing one of the responses (e.g., the action of pushing the lever down) by presenting a mild electric footshock every tenth time pushing occurred. If the rat was associating the response with the shock, pushing (but not pulling) should have specifically declined. But notice that, when shocks were presented, the rat also must have been touching the lever. Does this allow the lever to be associated with shock as well? To the extent this is true, the rat might merely stay away from the lever, and *both* pushing and pulling might decline.

The results of the two sessions in which one of the responses was punished are presented in Figure 10.14. (In actuality, half the rats were punished for pushing and half were punished for pulling.) Notice that, for the first 20 minutes or so, both behaviors declined together. This might have been the result of stimulus learning; the rats were either staying away from the lever generally, or perhaps they had associated the box with shock. Eventually, though, the unpunished behavior returned to its original strength while the punished behavior stayed low. The final difference between the two responses suggests that the rats ultimately learned the R-S* contingency. They learned to discriminate between two responses (Rs) that were directed at the same manipulandum (S).

Other experiments in this series used a Skinner box with two levers (Ss) that could each be either pressed or lifted for a food reward. Again, all responses were reinforced on VI schedules, and at the end of a training phase, the rats were performing all of the desired actions about equally. (Interestingly, the rats pressed both levers with their paws but spontaneously learned to lift the levers with their noses.) In one experiment, Bolles et al. (1980) punished one of the four responses (e.g., left lift) by presenting a foot-

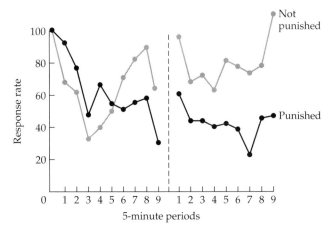

Figure 10.14 The rate of two behaviors (pushing and pulling) directed at the same lever over two sessions while one of the behaviors was occasionally punished with a mild electric shock. Both behaviors first declined, and then eventually the unpunished response recovered. The initial decline might have occurred because the lever was being associated with the shock (S-S* learning), and the rats withdrew from the lever. But the eventual discrimination between responses presumably resulted from a more specific association of the punished response with shock (R-S* learning). (After Bolles et al., 1980.)

shock every tenth time this response occurred. The results of this experiment are shown in Figure 10.15. As in the previous experiment, all responses initially declined, perhaps because the rats were associating the context with shock and this was generally suppressing performance. As time went on, the rats stopped performing both of the responses directed at the punished lever—and only gradually learned to discriminate the two responses on that lever. A subsequent experiment punished either both responses at one lever (e.g., left lift and left press) or both of the same responses regardless of the lever (e.g., both left and right lifts). Rats in the group that could avoid shock by avoiding a single lever learned much better than rats that needed to stop emitting one response directed at both levers, although this was also learned. The results suggest that both S-S* and R-S* learning can contribute to punishment, but the results also show that the S-S* piece is quickly evident in behavior and the R-S* piece becomes evident only later. Both types of learning can suppress behavior, but the Pavlovian piece seems easier and dominates. You might remember an experiment by Tolman, Ritchie, and Kalish (1946b) in Chapter 7 that had much the same message regarding place learning and response learning (see Figure 7.4). Rats that ran in a plus maze from two different start locations found it easier to go to a consistent place than to make a consistent response on the maze. Although it is possible that Tolman's places and Bolles et al.'s levers were unusually salient, the results suggest that stimulus learning may often be easier than response learning.

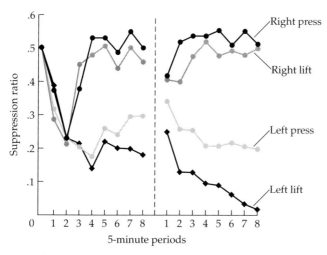

Figure 10.15 The suppression of pressing and lifting each of two levers (left and right) when a left lift (as an example) was punished with a mild electric shock. All responses initially declined, perhaps because the rats associated the environment with shock (S-S* learning). With continued training, the rats suppressed both responses directed toward the left lever (S-S* learning), but also eventually began to discriminate pressing from lifting (R-S* learning). As in Figure 10.14, S-S* and R-S* learning both occur during punishment, although S-S* learning may happen first. (After Bolles et al., 1980.)

Summary: What does it all mean?

As we saw in avoidance learning, animals can often direct natural species-specific behaviors to cues in the experiment that are associated with S*. In many ways, this kind of learning can dominate behavior, and in the case of misbehavior and negative automaintenance, can actually interfere with getting rewards that are otherwise available. The message here, again, is that biology matters. And, second, that every operant situation also allows stimulus learning. Moreover, because of the rules of sign tracking (we tend to approach signals for good things and move away from signals for bad things), stimulus learning can often provide a fairly complete explanation of behavior in an operant situation. The contribution of Pavlovian learning in instrumental learning situations cannot be ignored.

A Cognitive Analysis of Instrumental Action

The research summarized above forces us to acknowledge that any instrumental learning situation is made up of S-S* and R-S* components. Figure 10.16 therefore returns us to a description of behavior that was introduced way back in Chapter 1. We can think of any instrumental learning situation as one in which we perform an action (R) that leads to a biologically important event (S*) in the presence of some set of stimuli (S). This is the framework

Figure 10.16 The various types of learning that can occur in any instrumental learning situation. The description is the same as the one introduced in Chapter 1 (see Figure 1.18), except that terms often associated with learning each of the links are also indicated.

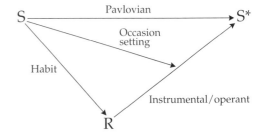

that Learning Theory provides for understanding all behavior. As was illustrated in Chapter 1, a very large number of behaviors can be summarized this way. If you are trying to understand a behavior in the real world, identifying an S, an R, and an S* is a very solid place to start. In many ways, this general perspective was one of B. F. Skinner's most important contributions.

What we have been doing in this book is filling in the details. In many classic instrumental learning theories, for example Thorndike's and Hull's, an S* was an event that mainly "stamped in" an association between S and R. Similarly, although Skinner was not inclined to talk about associations or unobserved processes like "stamping-in," he assumed that the occurrence of S* had a fairly direct effect of making R more probable. Subsequent theories, like Mowrer's two-factor theory or the more "cognitive" style of two-process theory proposed by Rescorla and Solomon (1967), brought in the additional role of S and its association with S*: In these views, conditioning of S is supposed to occur in parallel with S-R learning and motivate R. But what has emerged in the last two decades is a somewhat different view recognizing that animals associate all the items in Figure 10.16; behavior comes about as a product of this knowledge (e.g., Balleine, 2001, 2005; Bolles, 1972a; Colwill, 1994; Colwill & Rescorla, 1986; Dickinson, 1989, 1994; Dickinson & Balleine, 1994; Mackintosh & Dickinson, 1979; Rescorla, 1987). The approach can be considered "cognitive," because much of what is learned is not directly manifest in behavior. The organism develops what seems to be a relatively rich representation of the world, and uses it to direct behavior. Let's see what this perspective is all about.

Knowledge of the R-S* relation

I have been arguing all along that organisms behave as if they associate R and S*. This may be a reasonable short-hand description of operant learning, but the classic theorists did not find it necessary to explain things this way, and so it is worth asking, what exactly is the evidence? The most important finding supporting the idea is the **reinforcer devaluation effect** (e.g., Adams & Dickinson, 1981; Colwill & Rescorla, 1985a). The design of a representative experiment is shown in Figure 10.17A (Colwill & Rescorla, 1985a). In the first phase, rats were shaped to perform two operant responses, pressing a lever and pulling a chain dangling from the ceiling of the Skinner box. Each of these behaviors was reinforced by a different

(A) Design

Phase 1	**Phase 2**	**Test**
$R_1 - O_1, R_2 - O_2$	$O_1 -$ Illness	R_1? R_2?

(B) Test results

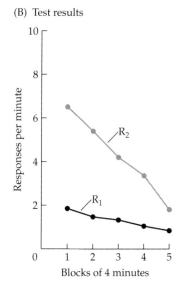

Figure 10.17 The reinforcer devaluation effect. (A) Experimental design. In the first phase, one response (R) was reinforced with one reinforcer ("outcome," or O) and another response was reinforced with another outcome. In a second, separate phase, one of the reinforcers was now paired with illness, which resulted in a conditioned taste aversion to it. When the rats were then allowed to perform either response, they stayed away from the response that produced the reinforcer that had since been paired with illness. Because the test was conducted in extinction, the rat had never received a pairing of the response and the reinforcer after the reinforcer acquired its taste aversion. (B) The test results therefore indicate that the rat remembered what action led to what outcome, and chose to make the response that would lead to the outcome it currently liked or valued. (After Colwill & Rescorla, 1985a.)

reinforcer—either a food pellet or a little taste of 32% sucrose solution. Thus, for some of the rats, lever-pressing produced a pellet, while chain-pulling produced sucrose. (Half the rats received the reverse.) In a second phase, one of the reinforcers (e.g., the pellet) was paired with a lithium chloride injection over a series of several trials. This is the classic treatment that conditions a taste aversion, and as a result of it, the rats rejected all pellets that were offered at the end of the second phase. The reinforcer had been "devalued" in the sense that it was now something the rat rejected. In the final test, the rats were returned to the Skinner box and allowed to lever-press or chain-pull. *This test was conducted in extinction, so that neither response was paired with a reinforcer again after the devaluation treatment.* Nonetheless, the rat's behavior during testing reflected that treatment. As shown in Figure 10.17B, the response whose reinforcer had been devalued was suppressed; the rats preferred to perform the other behavior. The result is rather subtle, but it has two clear implications. First, the rats must have learned which behavior led to which reinforcer—that is, they specifically stopped performing the response that delivered the pellet. Second, whether the rats made a response was determined by how much they valued its reinforcer— because they no longer liked the pellet, they stopped performing the behavior that led to it. The classic view that reinforcers merely stamp in an S-R association or increase the probability of R has no way of explaining this result. Instead, the rat learned which action led to which reinforcer, and then engaged in that action depending on how much he "liked" its reinforcer during the test.

There is another way to devalue a reinforcer without conditioning an aversion to it. Just before the test, the animal can be allowed to feed freely on the reinforcer. This temporarily satiates the animal on that foodstuff— that is, it causes the animal to reject any more of it, as if he is tired of the substance or flavor, a phenomenon known as "sensory-specific satiety" (e.g., Hetherington & Rolls, 1996). Experiments using this method again initially train the rat that one response produces one outcome and another response yields another. Then, one reinforcer is devalued by allowing the rat to consume it freely before the test. If the rat is then put into the Skinner box and tested on the two responses in extinction, the animal will tend not to perform the behavior that leads to the reinforcer he has just filled up on (e.g., Balleine & Dickinson, 1998; Colwill & Rescorla, 1985a). Once again, behavior is determined by (1) the animal's knowledge of what action leads to which outcome, and (2) how much the outcomes are currently valued.

We actually saw another type of experiment in which the reinforcer was revalued after instrumental learning when we discussed the importance of *incentive learning* in Chapter 9. Organisms need to learn about the effects different reinforcers have on their motivational states; that is how they assign value to the reinforcers. For example, remember that Balleine (1992) had rats learn to lever-press for pellets while they were completely satiated. During an extinction test, when the rats could lever-press without pellets, Balleine made them hungry. Surprisingly, hunger had no impact on the rate of lever-pressing unless the rat had been given an opportunity to eat the pellets while hungry. This allowed the rat to learn that the pellet made him feel good when he needed food. Thus, the rat had knowledge that pellets are good when hungry, so when he was made hungry during the test, he valued the pellet even more—and responded more frequently accordingly. Remarkably, an analogous incentive learning process seems to be involved in the devaluation experiment shown in Figure 10.17. Over trials, when the pellets were being paired with illness, the rats had several opportunities to learn that the taste of the pellets was awful. That is, after the first pellet-sickness pairing, the rats tasted the pellets and could associate them with a negative emotional "yuck!" reaction. This is how they learned that they didn't like the stuff so much.

We know this incentive learning step is necessary because, if rats don't have a chance to taste the pellets after a single aversion conditioning trial, they do not show the reinforcer devaluation effect (Balleine & Dickinson, 1991). A single flavor-illness pairing isn't enough to allow the rats to know that they don't like the pellet. Instead, the animal has to taste the flavor again—and experience a negative reaction to it. This point is further illustrated in a fascinating experiment summarized in Figure 10.18 (Balleine, Garner, & Dickinson, 1995). The experiment used a drug, ondansetron, which is an anti-emetic that makes humans feel less nauseated. Rats received

(A) Design

	Phase 1	Phase 2	Test
	$(R_1 - O_1, R_2 - O_2)$ — Illness	Ondansetron: O_1, Vehicle: O_2	R_1? R_2?

(B) Test results

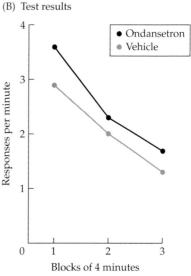

Figure 10.18 Incentive learning plays a role in the reinforcer devaluation effect. (A) In this experiment, two responses were first paired with two different reinforcers (i.e., outcomes) in a single session that preceded illness. Although the illness would condition taste aversions to both outcomes, the rat could not learn that he didn't like an outcome until he experienced his reaction to the outcome when he tried it again. To test this, rats were allowed to taste both of the outcomes in Phase 2. O_1 was tasted after the rats were injected with ondansetron, a drug that reduces nausea. O_2 was tasted without ondansetron (but after a control injection of the "vehicle" it was mixed with). During re-tasting, the rat could experience the "yuck!" reaction to O_2, but ondansetron suppressed the "yuck!" reaction to O_1. (B) When the rats were finally tested with the two operant responses, the rats tended to stay away from the behavior that had produced the outcome associated with the "yuck!" reaction. (After Balleine et al., 1995.)

a single session in which lever-pressing led to sucrose, and chain-pulling led to a saline solution (as usual, these relations were reversed in half the animals). They then received an immediate injection of lithium chloride, which could create a taste aversion to both the sucrose and the saline. In two separate sessions, the rats then received re-exposures to each reinforcer; these would ordinarily allow the rat to associate each flavor with the "yuck!" reaction. However, before re-exposure to one reinforcer (e.g., saline), the rats were injected with ondansetron; before re-exposure to the other reinforcer (e.g., sucrose), they were injected with a placebo. The ondansetron would reduce any nausea the rat might feel upon re-tasting the averted flavor. When the rats were subsequently allowed to lever-press or chain-pull in extinction, they mainly performed the behavior associated with the reinforcer that had been re-exposed under ondansetron (Figure 10.18B). They avoided the behavior connected with the reinforcer that was re-tasted under the placebo. The rats thus assigned value to each reinforcer according to how it made them feel during the re-exposure. Interestingly, in another experiment, injecting ondansetron during the final extinction test had no affect on the choice of lever-pressing or chain-pulling (Balleine et al., 1995; see also Balleine & Dickinson, 1994, for related results). Thus, the rats didn't need to feel bad when they remembered sucrose or saline during the test. As a result of incentive learning, they apparently remembered something simple like "saline is good" and "sucrose is bad." During the extinction test, the rats used that information—along with knowledge of specific R-S* relations—in deciding how to respond.

These results suggest that operant learning involves some very subtle learning processes. There are three things to remember. First, the organism associates its operant behavior with the outcome that the operant behavior leads to. Second, the organism decides what to do based on how it currently values the reinforcer associated with each action. Third, value is assigned through incentive learning. For this process to take place, the animal must experience the reinforcer—potentially, in the appropriate motivational state—to know how much the animal likes it in that state. All three processes come into play in operant/instrumental learning.

Once we accept that organisms associate R and S*, the next question is how do they actually learn the connection? The answer is at least partly that the laws governing R-S* learning are similar to those that govern S-S* (Pavlovian) learning. In fact, I have encouraged you to accept this idea all along. For example, the parallels between R-S* and S-S* learning were discussed way back in Chapter 2, when you were shown that they are sensitive to the same kinds of factors (e.g., extinction, timing of S*, size of S*, and preparedness). It is also worth noting that R-S* learning may be sensitive to the "informational variables" that seem so important in Pavlovian learning. Chapter 3 described contingency learning, blocking, and relative validity; these effects were the ones that led to the conditioning theories reviewed in Chapter 4. Analogous informational effects have been demonstrated in operant learning. For example, we can reduce the contingency between R and S* by merely presenting S* while the animal is not performing R. This reduces the rate of operant responding (e.g., Colwill & Rescorla, 1986; Dickinson & Mulatero, 1989; Hammond, 1980; Williams, 1989). As we saw above, learned helplessness is another parallel with contingency learning. Others have reported blocking and relative validity effects in operant learning (e.g., Mackintosh & Dickinson, 1979). For example, St. Claire-Smith (1979) had lever-pressing rats receive a mild electric shock a few milliseconds after an occasional lever-press. The shocks caused punishment, and lever-pressing declined once the shocks were introduced. But, if a brief CS was paired with shock prior to the punishment test, and the CS was inserted between the response and the punishing shock, there was less punishment—as if the CS "blocked" learning of the R-shock association. This kind of result suggests that factors we think are so important in S-S* learning—that is, surprisingness of S*, the extent to which it is rehearsed or processed, etc.—may be important in operant learning too.

Nonetheless, there is probably still something more than a simple Pavlovian association between R and S*. As we saw in Chapter 7, we can allow R to produce S* according to either a ratio schedule (S* is delivered after every *nth* response) or an interval schedule (S* is delivered on occasion of the first response after some temporal interval since the last S*). These schedules can have quite different effects. For example, response rate is higher on ratio than interval schedules when the rate of reinforcement is equated between them (e.g., Catania, Matthews, Silverman, & Yohalem, 1977). There is a paradox here: If response rate is higher on the ratio schedule than on the interval schedule when reinforcement rate is otherwise the same, then the percentage of responses actually paired with S* must be lower. By most rules of associative learning, the strength of the R-S* association (associative strength) should consequently be lower. But how could lower associative strength lead to stronger responding? Perhaps even more relevant to the present discussion, the reinforcer devaluation effect is stronger if R has been trained with a ratio schedule rather than with an interval schedule (Dickinson, Nicholas, & Adams, 1983); that is, a powerful aversion to the S* has less influence on the interval-trained response, as if knowledge of the R-S* relation is less important.

The difference between ratio and interval schedules may be fundamental. As we saw in Chapter 7, ratio and interval schedules differ in terms of their "molar feedback functions." In the ratio schedule, response rate directly affects reinforcement rate. If the rat makes more Rs, it always earns more S*s; if it makes fewer Rs, it earns fewer S*s. Thus, over time, reward rate is highly correlated with response rate (e.g., Baum, 1973). This is not as true in an interval schedule: Once the animal is responding enough to receive the maximal rate of S* (say, one per minute in an FI 1-minute schedule), increasing response rate has no further effect on reward rate. Reward rate is not as strongly correlated with response rate. Perhaps knowledge of the connection between action and outcome (R-S*) depends on the strength of the action-outcome correlation (e.g., Dickinson, 1989, 1994). Some writers (e.g., Balleine, 2005; Dickinson, 1994) have claimed that, because of the stronger correlation between R and S*, ratio schedules engender true action-outcome learning, whereas interval schedules might generate habit, which will be discussed further below.

Knowledge of the S-S relation*

We have already seen that it is useful to acknowledge the role of stimulus learning whenever operant learning occurs; as emphasized in Chapter 9, such learning is minimally thought to motivate instrumental responding. To further push the general parallel with R-S* learning, Pavlovian CSs also signal specific S*s. This is very clear in simple Pavlovian experiments. For example, in Chapter 2 we saw that, after conditioning has occurred, one can modify the animal's representation of the US (e.g., by habituating the response to it), and behavior changes accordingly (e.g., Rescorla, 1973a, 1974). And there have been experiments more directly analogous to those in the reinforcer devaluation effect. For example, Holland and Rescorla (1975b) and Holland and Straub (1979) paired a CS with food pellets and then conditioned an aversion to the pellets. This reduced the strength of the conditioned response to the CS when it was tested again, suggesting that the rat associated the CS with a particular US (see also Colwill & Motzkin, 1994). Peter Holland (1990b; see also 2005) has run many very sophisticated experiments suggesting that rats encode a very rich representation of the US during Pavlovian learning.

There is also evidence that a stimulus trained as an S^D in an operant setting conveys specific information about the reinforcer. For example, in an

(A) Design

Phase 1	Phase 2	Test
L: R_P — O_1, N: R_P — O_2	R_1 — O_1, R_2 — O_2	L: R_1?, R_2? N: R_1?, R_2?

Figure 10.19 Discriminative stimuli are associated with specific S*s. (A) In this experiment, rats first learned to poke their noses into a hole (R_p) in the presence of Light (L) and Noise (N) S^Ds. In the Light, the nose-poke was reinforced with one outcome, and in the Noise, it was reinforced with another. (Poking was not reinforced at all in the absence of the Light or the Noise.) In the next phase, different responses were then reinforced with the two outcomes. (B) In a final test (conducted in extinction), the Light and Noise both increased the rate of the new response that had been associated with the Same outcome, but not the Different outcome. (After Colwill & Rescorla, 1988.)

(B) Test results

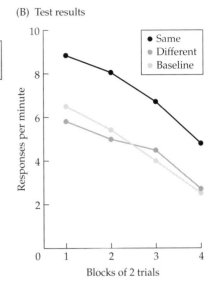

experiment by Colwill and Rescorla (1988) described in Figure 10.19A (see also Colwill & Triola, 2002), rats learned to poke their noses into a hole in the wall of a Skinner box during both Light and Noise S^Ds. In the presence of the Light, nose-poking produced one reinforcer (e.g., a pellet), whereas in the presence of the Noise it produced another (e.g., sucrose). Because of the training, the rats did most of their nose-poking when the Light or the Noise was turned on. But the question was, were Light and Noise also specifically associated with pellet and sucrose, respectively? To test this, our old friends lever-press and chain-pull were each associated with one of the reinforcers in a second phase. The Light and Noise were never presented at this time. But in a final test, the Light and Noise were presented while the rats could lever-press or chain-pull. As Figure 10.19B shows, the S^D mainly affected the new response that had been associated with the same reinforcer. Thus, the S^D was indeed associated with a particular reinforcer. "Transfer tests" like this suggest that both R and S are associated with specific S*s.

In Chapter 9 we discussed the effects of similar transfer tests in which Pavlovian CSs, rather than operant S^Ds, have been presented while the animal is performing an operant response (these are called "transfer of control" or "Pavlovian-instrumental transfer" tests). We saw that the effects of Pavlovian CSs are actually multiple and complex. First, like the S^D in Figure 10.19, a simple CS can also enhance operant responses associated with the same reinforcer (e.g., Delamater, 1996; see Figure 9.16). Perhaps, as noted earlier, one effect of a CS is to evoke an expectancy of a particular reinforcer—itself providing an S^D for the instrumental response (e.g., Overmier & Lawry, 1979; Trapold & Overmier, 1972). But remember, there is a second, more general effect: A CS can also have a more general motivating or arous-

ing effect on responses that are not necessarily associated with the same S*
(e.g., Balleine, 1994; Corbit & Balleine, 2005). This effect is more like the
process envisioned by two-process theory (Rescorla & Solomon, 1967; see
also Konorski, 1967). The third possible effect of a CS, of course, is one that
was emphasized in earlier parts of the present chapter: CSs associated with
S*s can also evoke natural behaviors of their own. S-S* learning thus has
several effects on behavior in instrumental situations: It can evoke a representation of a specific S* that strengthens behaviors associated with the same
S*; it can cause a general arousing effect; and it can evoke CRs (e.g., fear or
sign tracking) on its own.

The learning process behind S-S* learning was thoroughly examined in
previous chapters (e.g., Chapters 3–6). A complete review of all that material is, of course, beyond the scope of the current chapter. But, given the role
of S-S* learning in operant behavior, it is worth at least noting the relevance
of this material. Thus (for example), we know that the learning process tends
to find the most valid or reliable predictor of S*, as is suggested in effects
like blocking and relative validity. And we know that attention and memory processes may play a role as well. It should also be added that we specifically discussed how the stimulus guides operant behavior in Chapter 8,
where we encountered additional stimulus-learning processes (such as perceptual learning and mediated generalization) and explicitly considered the
effects of complex stimuli like categories, space, and time. Instrumental
behavior occurs in the presence of many kinds of stimuli, and a synthetic
view of instrumental action must acknowledge all of them. Interestingly,
one theme in the Chapter 8 discussion was that the learning and memory
processes involved when complex stimuli guide instrumental action may
not be that different from those in "simpler" forms of Pavlovian learning.

One rather interesting issue comes up as we consider interactions
between S-S* and R-S* learning. In the operant situation, an R must always
occur in order for the S* to appear—that is the very definition of an instrumental action. Because of this, if we are to consider informational variables,
we must acknowledge that the R is actually more informative than S about
the next presentation of S*. Shouldn't R therefore compete with the S for
association with S*? The answer is "yes." Ultimately, we also need to
acknowledge another important point: The S^D is more than just a Pavlovian CS. It also provides information about the R-S* relationship. That is, the
S^D truly sets the occasion for the R-S* relationship, another relationship represented in Figure 10.16.

S-(R-S*) learning (occasion setting)

Skinner (1938), of course, had always claimed that the stimulus in operant
conditioning set the occasion for the response-reinforcer relationship. But
as we have previously seen in this chapter, often this "three-termed" role
reduces to simple S-S* learning; the key peck is often merely elicited by excitation conditioned to the keylight CS. On the other hand, there is good evidence of true occasion-setting, and interestingly, some of it even comes from

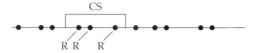

Figure 10.20 If reinforcers are presented with the same probability in the presence and absence of a CS, the CS will not be treated as a signal for S* (e.g., Chapter 3). However, if the CS nonetheless signals that a response is now required to earn the reinforcer that is otherwise presented for free, the animal will learn to respond during the CS. Since the CS cannot be a Pavlovian excitor, responding cannot result from simple S-S* learning—it must result from true S-(R-S*) learning in which the animal learns that R is associated with S* during S.

research using the pecking response. In a very thoughtful experiment, Jenkins (1977) (of the Brown and Jenkins autoshaping experiment) set things up as illustrated in Figure 10.20. Reinforcers were scheduled by a computer so that they were equally probable whether a keylight was on or off. Since the keylight therefore predicted no change in the probability of the US, it could not be an excitor or an inhibitor. But Jenkins also arranged a clever twist. When the keylight was off, reinforcers were presented regardless of what the pigeon was doing, but when the keylight was on, the bird had to peck the key to produce them. Thus, although the keylight could not have been a simple Pavlovian CS, it did convey some important information: It said, "Pigeon, you must now peck to get those reinforcers you otherwise get for free." Under these conditions, pigeons *did* learn to peck when the keylight was turned on (and not when it was off). Not only was the pecking response controlled by its consequences (and, therefore, at least partly an operant after all!), but the keylight served as a stimulus that truly signaled the relationship between R and S*.

There is other good evidence that an S^D can control behavior in a way that does not reduce to its simple association with S*. Consider the experiment sketched in Figure 10.21A (Colwill & Rescorla, 1990b). Rats were put through an experiment involving two behaviors (lever-pressing and chain-pulling—what else?), two S*s (pellets and sucrose), and two S^Ds (Light and Noise). In the first phase, when the Light came on, R_1 was associated with pellets and R_2 was associated with sucrose. But when the Noise came on, the reverse was true: R_1 was now associated with sucrose and R_2 was now associated with pellets. Both Noise and Light were equally associated with both S*s and both Rs. In the second phase, one of the reinforcers was now paired several times with lithium chloride to create reinforcer devaluation. In a final test conducted in extinction, the rats were allowed to lever-press and chain-pull when the Light and the Noise were presented. As Figure 10.21B indicates, the rats demonstrated that they knew that the averted reinforcer followed R_2 when the Light was on, but that it followed R_1 when the Noise was on. Thus, the Light and Noise signaled specific relationships between the Rs and S*s. The results of this experiment require that we accept

(A) Design

Phase 1	Phase 2	Test
L: $R_1 — O_1, R_2 — O_2$ N: $R_1 — O_2, R_2 — O_1$	O_2 — Illness	L: $R_1?, R_2?$ N: $R_1?, R_2?$

(B) Test results

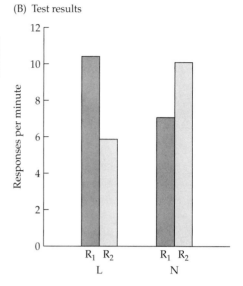

Figure 10.21 A clear demonstration of S-(R-S*) learning. (A) In Phase 1, different responses were paired with different outcomes, but the specific outcome depended on whether a Light (L) or a Noise (N) S^D was present. In the second phase, a taste aversion was conditioned with O_2. (B) During the final extinction tests, the rats stayed away from the specific response that led to the devalued outcome in each of the S^Ds. To perform this way, the rats must have learned that R_2 led to O_2 in the Light and that R_1 led to O_2 in the Noise—S-(R-S*) learning. (After Colwill & Rescorla, 1990b; data from Rescorla, 1991.)

the fact that the rats had a fairly sophisticated knowledge of the various contingencies. There can be no question that there is more going on in operant learning than S* merely stamping in a response.

You may recognize that this occasion-setting effect is directly analogous to one we considered in Pavlovian learning (see Chapter 5). In the Pavlovian case, a stimulus signals a particular S-S* relationship: S-(S-S*). The parallel is further reinforced by the fact that a Pavlovian occasion-setter can apparently substitute for an operant S^D (e.g., Davidson, Aparicio, & Rescorla, 1988). As in other forms of learning, S-(R-S*) learning requires that S be informative, rather than redundant. In this case, S must be informative about the occurrence of a particular R-S* relationship (e.g., Rescorla, 1991).

S-R and "habit" learning

It is interesting to note that, despite all the evidence of R-S*, S-S*, and S-(R-S*) knowledge, there is still a place in the synthetic view for good old S-R learning. The basic argument (e.g., Colwill, 1994; Colwill & Rescorla, 1985a; Dickinson, 1989) is that even after a reinforcer devaluation manipulation is thorough and complete, so that the rat completely rejects the S* when it is offered, the animal will still go over and perform the action a little during the extinction test. If you look closely at the level at which the rat performs the response associated with the devalued reinforcer in Figure 10.17, for example, you will see that it is still performing that action a little bit—the rat is simply doing it out of habit. If put into the box, the rat will run over to the lever and press it a few times without much regard to the action's actual consequences.

There is a fair amount of interest in the idea that the S-R association begins to take over as an action is performed repeatedly. This seems consistent with our everyday intuitions about the difference between true goal-oriented behavior and simple habits. Although I presumably used to make coffee when I got out of bed because I liked its effects, I have by now made coffee so many times that I can practically do it in my sleep, and certainly with little thought about the process. In fact, a surprising amount of everyday human behavior occurs automatically, without much awareness (e.g., Bargh & Chartrand, 1999). From a functional perspective, the conversion of actions into habits makes sense; our working memories are thus liberated to devote space to other mental problems. According to the philosopher Alfred North Whitehead (1911), "Civilization advances by extending the number of operations which we can perform without thinking about them."

In fact, there is evidence consistent with the idea that habit takes over with repeated practice. For example, an operant behavior that is given extensive training can be quite insensitive to the reinforcer devaluation effect. Holland (2004) gave different groups of rats 2, 5, or 20 sessions of instrumental training in which lever-pressing produced food pellets. Different groups then had the pellets paired (or not paired) with injection of lithium chloride. Although this appeared to produce equivalent aversions to the food pellets in the paired groups, when the rats were returned to the Skinner box and tested for lever-pressing in extinction, only the groups given 2 or 5 sessions of instrumental training suppressed their lever-pressing (Figure 10.22). Thus, the rats behaved as if a highly practiced operant was less dependent on their knowledge of the R-S* association (see also Adams, 1982; Adams & Dickinson, 1981; Dickinson, Balleine, Watt, Gonzalez, & Boakes, 1995; Killcross & Coutureau, 2003). One explanation is that, with extensive practice, the animal's rate of behavior becomes relatively constant over time. Because of this, it no longer experiences variation in both response rate and reward rate—which would be necessary to perceive their correlation and thus the relation between R and S* (e.g., Dickinson, 1989).

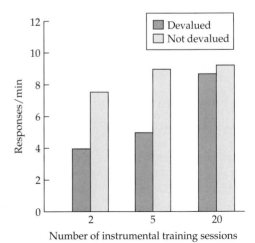

Figure 10.22 The reinforcer devaluation effect weakens with extensive instrumental training. Rats received either 2, 5, or 20 sessions of operant lever-press training and then the pellet reinforcer was paired with illness in some rats (Devalued) or presented separate from illness in others (Not Devalued). In the extinction tests shown, reinforcer devaluation suppressed lever-press responding in the groups that had received only 2 or 5 sessions of instrumental training, but not 20. With extensive training, instrumental responding may depend less on knowledge of the R-S* association and more on the S-R habit. (After Holland, 2004.)

It is worth noting, though, that extensive training does not always make an action immune to reinforcer devaluation (Colwill & Rescorla, 1985b, 1988; Colwill & Triola, 2002). That is, under some conditions, operant lever-pressing and chain-pulling are still determined by the rat's knowledge of what leads to what, even after extended training. Those conditions appear to be ones in which rats are trained with multiple operants and multiple reinforcers (see Holland, 2004). Exposure to more than one R-S* relationship in the same situation may encourage the animal to maintain attention to its different behaviors, or, since it requires not performing one R (and not earning its S*) while engaging in the other R, it maintains variation in response rate and reward rate—and thus a correlation between each action and outcome over time (e.g., Dickinson, 1989). Perhaps repetition eventually turns your actions into habits unless there is some reason to pay attention to what you are doing.

The distinction between S-R habits and more cognitively-mediated behavior is not really new. You may remember that Edward Tolman was interested in the distinction as far back as the 1940s. He and his students ran many ingenious experiments in mazes suggesting that rats may be more ready to learn about places than simple S-R responses (see Chapter 7). Some relatively modern research has returned to some of Tolman's methods and made some interesting new discoveries. For example, Packard and McGaugh (1996) ran rats in the simple plus maze illustrated in Figure 10.23A. The rats were first rewarded for going from a consistent start place (the south) to a consistent goal location (the west) for four trials a day over a period of several days. During a test trial on Day 8, they were started from a new location—namely, the north. Most of the rats went west—that is, they returned to the rewarded place, rather than making the rewarded response (a left turn; see Figure 10.22B, top left). They then received additional training for several more days; that is, they were rewarded again for going west from the start location in the south. When the rats were finally tested from the north again on Day 16, they now turned left rather than heading west (see Figure 10.22B, top right). Extended training thus converted the rat's behavior from a goal- or place-directed activity into a kind of S-R habit (see also Hicks, 1964; Ritchie, Aeschliman, & Pierce, 1950).

Packard and McGaugh's study was especially interesting because they also temporarily inactivated different areas in the rats' brains with lidocaine during testing. One area they inactivated was the hippocampus, which we have already seen is important in spatial learning (see Chapter 8). As shown in the middle of Figure 10.23B, during the first test, on Day 8, when control animals were choosing the correct place, inactivation of the hippocampus abolished the place preference. However, after extended training, when control rats had shifted to an S-R habit, inactivating the hippocampus had no effect (Day 16). Packard and McGaugh also inactivated another brain area—the caudate nucleus—in another group of rats. As shown at the bottom in Figure 10.23B, inactivating the caudate after initial training (when place-learning was evident) produced no change in behavior (Day 8). But

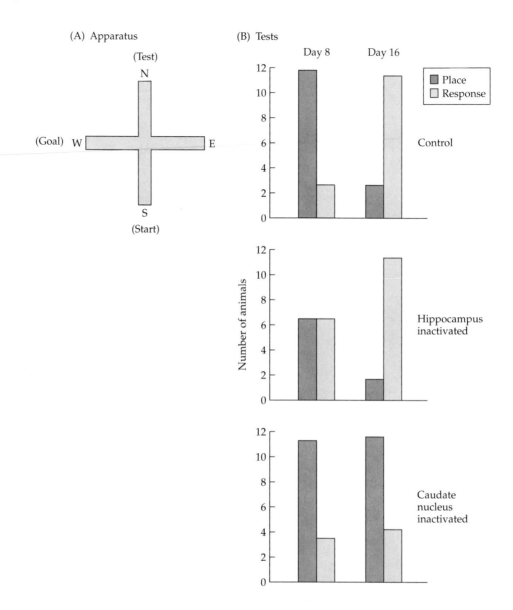

(A) Apparatus

(B) Tests

after extended training (when S-R learning was evident in controls) inactivation of the caudate had a big effect (Day 16). At this point, caudate inactivation abolished the S-R response preference, and the rats chose the correct place again! As habit takes over with extended training, it appears to engage the caudate, but it does not abolish place knowledge. Other evidence suggests that place and response learning can also go hand-in-hand, although they may compete with one another to some extent (Gibson & Shettleworth, 2005).

◀ **Figure 10.23** More evidence that extensive training may turn cognitively mediated behavior into habit. (A) A plus maze. Rats were started from the south and rewarded for going to the western goal location. During test trials, they were started from the north. If they went west, they returned to the rewarded Place; if they went east, they performed the rewarded Response (turning left). (B) Number of animals that went to the rewarded Place or performed the rewarded Response during test trials conducted after 8 days or 16 days of training. Top: Control rats went to the correct Place after 8 days of training, but chose the rewarded Response after 16 days—as if the behavior switched from place learning to an S-R habit. Middle: Rats whose hippocampus was inactivated during the test did not show place learning at Day 8, but showed normal S-R learning at Day 16. Bottom: Rats whose caudate nucleus was inactivated during the tests showed normal place learning at Day 8 and continued to show place responding at Day 16. Apparently, the caudate nucleus is necessary for an S-R habit to be expressed, and when habit takes over it does not destroy knowledge about the rewarded place. (After Packard & McGaugh, 1996.)

There is now quite a bit of research that seems to separate place and habit learning as well as the brain areas that underlie them (see Packard, 2001; White & McDonald, 2002, for reviews). This work also complements research correlating different brain areas with other forms of actions and habits assessed by reinforcer devaluation methods (e.g., Balleine, 2005). Research in behavioral neuroscience is consistent with the purely behavioral research reviewed in this chapter in supporting the roles of S-S*, R-S*, S-(R-S*), S-R, and incentive learning processes in instrumental learning.

Summary

1. Two-factor theory addressed the question of "what reinforces an avoidance response?" In modern terms, the theory proposes that (1) organisms associate stimuli in the environment with an aversive S*, and this allows those stimuli to evoke fear; (2) the avoidance response is reinforced when it eliminates or escapes those warning stimuli, and therefore causes fear reduction. The theory emphasizes the interaction between stimulus learning (Pavlovian fear-conditioning) and response learning (operant/instrumental reinforcement through fear reduction).

2. Two-factor theory was challenged by the fact that avoidance learning can occur if the response simply reduces the rate of aversive stimulation, without any explicit warning stimuli, and by the fact that the strength of avoidance behavior is not correlated with overt levels of fear. However, these challenges were addressed by noting that temporal cues that predict S* can become conditioned fear stimuli and that "fear" is best defined as a central state or expectancy rather than a peripheral response (see Chapter 9).

3. Two-factor theory's emphasis on reinforcement by fear-reduction ran into difficulty when it was discovered that escaping the warning signal is not important when the animal can avoid by performing a natural behavior that has

presumably evolved to avoid predation—a so-called species-specific defense reaction (SSDR).

4. SSDR theory emphasized the organism's evolutionary history. Avoidance learning was thought to occur rapidly if the required response resembled a natural defensive behavior. If not, learning depends more on feedback (or perhaps reinforcement provided by the inhibition of fear, which is provided by feedback cues).

5. The field's approach to avoidance behavior has become more ethological (it considers the function of natural defensive behavior), more Pavlovian (natural SSDRs appear to be respondents guided by learning about environmental cues rather than operants reinforced by their consequences), and more cognitive in the sense that what is learned now appears to be separate from what is shown in behavior.

6. Exposure to uncontrollable aversive events can interfere with subsequent escape or avoidance learning (the "learned helplessness effect"). Although exposure to uncontrollable aversive events has many effects, one is that organisms may learn that their behavior is independent of S*. If an aversive S* is uncontrollable, it also has especially pernicious effects (e.g., it can cause more fear conditioning and may lead to stomach ulceration).

7. In appetitive learning (where organisms learn to respond to earn positive S*s like food), different behaviors are also learned at unequal rates, and natural behaviors that are elicited by Ss that predict S*s can intrude. Pavlovian learning is always occurring in operant learning situations, and its impact is difficult to ignore.

8. S-S* and R-S* learning often work in concert. For example, when an operant behavior is punished, the organism may stop responding either because it associates the response with the aversive consequence (R-S*) or because it associates nearby stimuli with that consequence (S-S*) and withdraws from them (negative sign tracking). Conversely, in reward learning, the organism may respond either because it associates the response with reward or because it associates nearby stimuli with reward and approaches them (positive sign-tracking).

9. Animals learn several things in instrumental/operant situations: They associate their behavior with its consequences (R-S*); they associate stimuli in the environment with those consequences (S-S*); they may learn that stimuli in the environment signal the current relationship between the behavior and its consequences (occasion setting or S-[R-S*]); and they may learn a simple association between the environmental cues and the response (S-R).

10. The reinforcer devaluation effect provides clear evidence of R-S* learning: If a rat is taught to lever-press for sucrose, and then sucrose is then separately associated with illness, it will lever-press less—even though the response has never been paired with sucrose after its association with illness. Thus, the rat learns that lever-pressing leads to sucrose, and then responds according to how much sucrose is liked or valued. Incentive learning plays a crucial role in the assignment of value.

11. Organisms can also learn what specific S* follows an S. S-S* learning influences instrumental action by motivating the response (see Chapter 9) and by allowing S to evoke behavior directly (including positive or negative sign tracking). The laws of S-S* learning were discussed in Chapters 3–5. Learning about more "complex" stimuli, such as polymorphous categories and temporal and spatial cues, was reviewed in Chapter 8; it appears to follow similar rules.

12. S can also "set the occasion" for an R-S* relationship (S-[R-S*] learning) in a way that is distinct from simple S-S* learning. For example, organisms can learn that S signals that the animal must now perform R in order to obtain an S* that is otherwise freely available.

13. Organisms may also learn to perform an R reflexively, without regard to its consequences—out of habit (S-R learning). S-R learning may become especially important after many repetitions of the instrumental action, and may function to keep working memory free and available for other activities.

Key terms

two-factor theory
species-specific defense reactions (SSDRs)
recuperative behavior
immunization effect
learned helplessness hypothesis
learned helplessness effect
learned irrelevance
terminal behavior
interim behaviors
adjunctive behaviors
schedule-induced polydipsia
negative automaintenance
reinforcer devaluation effect

Glossary

A1 In SOP theory, the maximal state to which elements in a memory node can be activated when the corresponding conditional stimulus or unconditional stimulus is presented.

A2 In SOP theory, a secondary, or lower state of activation to which elements decay after they have been in *A1*. A retrieval cue also activates elements in an associated node to the level of A2.

Acquired equivalence See *mediated generalization.*

Acquired motivation Motivation that originates from experience with reinforcers or punishers in instrumental learning tasks. For example, see *incentive motivation.*

Acquisition The phase in a learning experiment in which the subject is first learning a behavior or contingency.

Adjunctive behaviors Stereotyped behaviors, such as excessive drinking (*schedule-induced polydipsia*), which may emerge when animals receive positive reinforcers at regular intervals.

Affect Emotion.

After-image The visual image seen after a stimulus is removed; typically, it is an opposite color than the stimulus.

After-reaction The reaction after a stimulus is removed; according to opponent-process theory, it is typically the opposite of the initial reaction to the stimulus.

Agoraphobia An abnormal fear and avoidance of open or public places that often accompanies panic disorder.

Analogous Two or more traits that are similar in function but not in structure or evolutionary origin.

Animal cognition A subfield of learning theory that examines the cognitive (mental) processes and abilities of animals, often by using stimulus control techniques. Sometimes involves comparisons across species.

Antecedent An event that precedes another one. Respondent behaviors are responses to antecedent events.

a-process In opponent-process theory, the process underlying the initial emotional response to a stimulus. Compare to *b-process*.

Artificial selection When humans intervene in animal or plant reproduction to ensure that desirable traits are represented in successive generations. Individuals with less desirable traits are not allowed to reproduce.

Association A connection or relation between two things, such as sense impressions, ideas, stimuli, or stimuli and responses.

Atomistic Consisting or made up of many separate elements. The British empiricists were said to have an atomistic view of the mind because they believed that complex thoughts resulted from the accumulation of many different associations.

Attentional priming The finding that recent exposures to a stimulus or to cues associated with that stimulus can decrease the time it takes to find the stimulus when it is presented among distractors.

Autoshaping A form of *sign tracking* in which a key-light that is paired with food elicits pecking in the pigeon. It has become a popular method for studying classical conditioning.

Avoidance An instrumental learning situation in which performing an action or response prevents a noxious or aversive stimulus from occurring. Involves *negative reinforcement.*

B. F. Skinner (1904–1990) Influential 20th-century American psychologist who first promoted *radical behaviorism* and pioneered the operant experiment and the study of operant conditioning.

Backward blocking The finding (primarily in humans) that little or no conditioning occurs to a conditional stimulus if it is combined, during conditioning trials, with another conditional stimulus that is later paired with the unconditional stimulus. Backward blocking differs from ordinary *blocking* (i.e., "forward blocking") in that conditioning with the other stimulus occurs after (rather than before) the compound conditioning.

Backward conditioning A classical conditioning procedure in which the conditioned stimulus is presented after the unconditioned stimulus has occurred. Can lead to either no conditioning, conditioned excitation, or conditioned inhibition depending on the timing of the two stimuli.

Beacon A cue that is close to a goal that can be detected from a distance and approached.

Behavior chain A sequence of behaviors that is theoretically put together with the help of discriminative stimuli that reinforce the preceding behavior and set the occasion for the next behavior.

Behavior systems theory A type of theory that proposes that the behaviors that emerge in classical and instrumental conditioning situations originate in systems of behaviors that have evolved to optimize interactions with the unconditional stimulus (or reinforcer) in the natural environment.

Behavioral economics An approach that incorporates economic principles in understanding operant behavior.

Behavioral regulation theory The view that an organism will work to maintain a preferred distribution of behavior. See *response deprivation hypothesis; bliss point.*

Behavioral theory of timing A theory of interval timing that proposes that animals use changes in their own behaviors to measure the passage of time.

Bidirectional response system An experimental setup where it is possible to measure both excitation and inhibition because response levels can go either above or below a starting baseline.

Bliss point An organism's preferred distribution of behavior.

Blocking In classical conditioning, the finding that little or no conditioning occurs to a new stimulus if it is combined with a previously conditioned stimulus during conditioning trials. Suggests that information or surprise value is important in conditioning.

b-process In opponent-process theory, the process underlying an emotional response that is opposite the one controlled by the *a-process*. The b-process functions to compensate for the a-process, and starts and then decays relatively slowly.

British Empiricists (also British Associationists) British philosophers (including John Locke and David Hume) who proposed that the mind is built up from of a person's experiences.

Categorization Arranging items into classes or categories. See *category learning.*

Category learning Learning to identify specific items as members, or not, of a larger group or set of items.

Causal learning Learning about the causes of an event.

Chained schedule A set of two or more reinforcement schedules, each signaled by its own discriminative stimulus, that must be completed in sequence before the primary reinforcer occurs.

Charles Darwin (1809–1882) British biologist who proposed the theory of evolution in his 1859 book, *On the Origin of Species.*

Circadian rhythm A daily activity cycle, based roughly on 24-hour intervals.

Clark L. Hull (1884–1952) An influential American learning theorist who presented an ambitious theory of learning and motivation that emphasized *Drive* and *Habit.*

Classical conditioning The procedure in which an initially neutral stimulus (the conditional stimulus, or CS) is repeatedly paired with an unconditional stimulus (or US). The result is that the conditional stimulus begins to elicit a conditional response (CR). Nowadays, classical conditioning is important as both a behavioral phenomenon and as a method used to study simple associative learning.

Comparator theory A theory of classical conditioning which proposes that the strength of the response to a conditional stimulus depends on a comparison of the strength of that stimulus's association with the unconditioned stimulus and that of another stimulus.

Complements Two or more commodities or reinforcers that "go together" in the sense that increasing the price of one will decrease the demand for both of them. For example, chips and salsa; bagels and cream cheese.

Compound potentiation In classical conditioning, the finding that there is more conditioning to a weak conditional stimulus if it is combined with a more salient conditional stimulus during conditioning. Mainly known in flavor aversion learning, where conditioning of a weak odor may be especially strong if it is combined with a salient taste during conditioning. The opposite of *overshadowing*.

Compound schedules A procedure in which two or more schedules operate, such as a *multiple schedule* or a *chained schedule*.

Compound In classical conditioning, the presentation of two or more conditional stimuli at about the same time. In a "simultaneous" compound, the conditional stimuli are presented at the same time; in a "serial" compound, the stimuli are presented in a sequence. Also called compound CS.

Concurrent measurement studies Experiments in which Pavlovian responses and instrumental (or operant) responses are measured at the same time in order to investigate their relationship.

Concurrent schedule A situation in which the organism can choose between two or more different operant behaviors; each behavior pays off according to its own schedule of reinforcement.

Conditional discrimination A discrimination in which two stimuli are presented, and the correct stimulus is determined based on which of the two stimuli is present or was presented recently.

Conditional response (CR) The response that is elicited by the conditional stimulus after classical conditioning has taken place. The response is "conditional" in the sense that it depends on the conditioning experience.

Conditional stimulus (CS) An initially neutral stimulus (like a bell, light, or tone) that begins to elicit a conditional response after it has been paired with an unconditional stimulus.

Conditioned compensatory response In classical conditioning, a conditional response that opposes, rather than being the same as, the unconditional response. It functions to reduce the strength of the unconditional response, as in *drug tolerance*.

Conditioned emotional response (CER) A method for studying classical conditioning in which the conditional stimulus is associated with a mild electric shock and the CS comes to suppress an ongoing behavior, such as lever-pressing reinforced by food. Also called *conditioned suppression*.

Conditioned inhibition *Inhibition* that is learned through classical conditioning. The term also refers to a specific inhibitory conditioning procedure in which one conditional stimulus is always paired with an unconditional stimulus, except when the CS is combined with a second conditional stimulus. The second stimulus acquires inhibition. The procedure is also known as the *feature-negative discrimination*.

Conditioned inhibitor (CS–) A conditional stimulus that evokes inhibition; e.g., one that suppresses or reduces the size of the conditioned response that would otherwise be elicited by a second conditional stimulus. See *retardation-of-acquisition test* and *summation test*.

Conditioned reflex Another name for a conditional response, i.e., the response that is elicited by a conditional stimulus after classical conditioning has taken place. The term "reflex" is used here to connect the concept with the tradition of studying reflexes in physiology.

Conditioned reinforcer or secondary reinforcer A stimulus that has acquired the capacity to reinforce behavior through its association with a primary reinforcer.

Conditioned suppression See *conditioned emotional response*.

Conditioning preparation Any of several methods for studying classical conditioning.

Configural cue The unique new stimulus that is present when two or more conditional stimuli are combined.

Configural theory A theory that assumes that, when organisms receive classical conditioning with a compound conditional stimulus, they associate the entire compound with the unconditional stimulus rather than forming separate associations between each of its elements and the unconditional stimulus.

Connectionism An approach in cognitive psychology and artificial intelligence in which knowledge is represented by a large number of connections between nodes or units in a network that bears a metaphorical resemblance to connections in the brain. Also called *parallel distributed processing* or *neural networks*.

Connections Associations.

Consequence Something that follows from an action. Operant behaviors are actions that are controlled by their consequences (such as the reinforcers or punishers they might produce).

Context or contextual stimuli External or internal stimuli that are in the background whenever learning or remembering occurs.

Contiguity theory Guthrie's idea that learning depends on a stimulus and response occurring together in time rather than depending on reinforcement.

Contingency The "if-then" relationship between two events. See *positive contigency* and *negative contingency*.

Continuous reinforcement schedule A schedule of reinforcement in which a reinforcer is delivered after each response.

Counterconditioning A conditioning procedure that reverses the organism's response to a stimulus. For example, by pairing the stimulus with a positive event, an organism may be conditioned to respond positively to a stimulus that would otherwise conditionally or unconditionally elicit fear.

Cumulative record A graph in which the cumulative number of operant responses is plotted as a function of time. The slope of the line gives the rate of responding. Usually created by a *cumulative recorder*.

Cumulative recorder A device used to analyze operant behavior in which a pen that rides on a slowly-moving piece of paper is deflected upward with each response (press of a lever, for example). This creates a graph or *cumulative record* which shows the cumulative number of responses as a function of time.

David Hume (1711–1776) One of the *British Empiricists*.

Dead reckoning A method of navigation in which an animal travels to its goal by using an internal sense of direction and distance.

Declarative memory Memory for things other than actual behavioral procedures.

Delay conditioning A classical conditioning procedure in which the conditional stimulus commences on its own and then terminates with presentation of the unconditional stimulus.

Delayed matching-to-sample (DMTS) A procedure used to study working memory in which the organism is reinforced for responding to a test stimulus if it is the same as a "sample" stimulus presented earlier.

Demand curve A graph showing the demand for a product at different prices. In behavioral economics, the amount of a commodity (or reinforcer) that is taken when the experimenter varies the amount of work that is required to earn it.

Differential inhibition or discriminative inhibition A procedure in classical conditioning in which a conditional stimulus is paired with the unconditional stimulus on some trials and another conditional stimulus is presented without the unconditional stimulus on other trials. The second CS may acquire inhibition.

Discriminative stimulus In operant conditioning, a stimulus that signals whether or not the response will be reinforced. It is said to "set the occasion" for the operant response.

Drive A theoretical construct which corresponds to motivation arising from biological needs, such as the need for food or water.

Drug tolerance A reduction in the effectiveness of a drug that can occur with repeated exposure to the drug.

Early comparative psychologists A group of primarily British biologists (e.g., C. Lloyd Morgan and George Romanes) who were active in the late 1800s and who sought to study the evolution of the mind by inferring the mental activities of animals from their behavior.

Edward L. Thorndike (1874–1949) American psychologist whose experiments with cats learning to get out of puzzle boxes profoundly influenced our thinking about the importance of *instrumental conditioning* and the central place of animal learning experiments in psychology.

Edward Tolman (1886–1959) American psychologist whose ideas about the value and scientific validity of using *intervening variables* to explain behavior had a profound impact on all of scientific psychology. Tolman also ran many important experiments that emphasized cognitive and motivational factors in behavior and learning.

Elemental theory A theory that assumes that, when organisms receive conditioning with a compound conditional stimulus, they associate each element of the compound separately with the unconditional stimulus.

Elicited Brought on by something that comes before. Respondent behaviors are elicited by an antecedent event.

Emitted Literally, "to send forth." Organisms are said to emit operant behaviors in the sense that such behaviors are not elicited by an antecedent event; they appear spontaneous (but are really controlled by their consequences).

Episodic memory Memory for personal, often autobiographical, experiences and events that typically involve what, where, and when information.

Escape An instrumental learning situation in which performing an action or response terminates a noxious or aversive stimulus that is already present. Involves *negative reinforcement*.

Ethology The study of how animals behave in their natural environments, typically with an emphasis on the evolution of the behavior.

Exaptation A trait that has adaptive value but was not originally selected for its current function.

Excitation In classical conditioning, the potential of a conditional stimulus to signal an unconditional stimulus or elicit a conditional response.

Excitor or CS+ A conditional stimulus that is associated with an unconditional stimulus, and has the potential to elicit a conditional response.

Exemplar theory An approach to categorization which assumes that organisms store representations of a large number of individual members of a category and then respond to new items depending on how similar they are to the items that were presented before.

Explicitly unpaired In classical conditioning, a procedure in which a conditional stimulus is presented alone and the unconditional stimulus is presented at another time.

Exposure therapy A form of cognitive behavior therapy in which a patient is exposed, without consequence, to stimuli that elicit undesirable cognitions, emotions, or behaviors in order to weaken their strength. A form of either *extinction* (if the undesirable responses were learned) or *habituation* (if the undesirable responses were not learned).

External inhibition Weakening of a conditional response elicited by a conditional stimulus when a neutral stimulus is added. Usually thought to occur through *generalization decrement*; that is, the organism does not generalize well between the conditional stimulus alone and its combination with the second stimulus.

Extinction Reduction in the strength or probability of a learned behavior that occurs when the conditional stimulus is presented without the unconditional stimulus (in classical conditioning) or when the behavior is no longer reinforced (in operant or instrumental conditioning). The term describes both the procedure and the result of the procedure. Behaviors that have been reduced in strength through extinction are said to be "extinguished."

Fading A procedure in which a prompt or discriminative stimulus for a desired behavior is gradually withdrawn so that the organism is able to emit the behavior without the prompt.

Fear potentiated startle An exaggerated startle reaction to a sudden stimulus that occurs when the stimulus is presented while the organism is afraid, e.g., in the presence of a fear excitor.

Feature stimulus In *feature-positive* and *feature-negative discriminations*, the second conditional stimulus that is added to the other (*target stimulus*) conditional stimulus to signal trials on which the unconditional stimulus will or will not occur.

Feature theory An approach to categorization which assumes that organisms associate the many features

of category exemplars with reinforcers (or category labels) and then respond to new items according to the combined associative strengths of their features. Learning rules like the Rescorla-Wagner model would tend to isolate the most predictive features.

Feature-negative discrimination A conditioning procedure in which a conditional stimulus is presented with the unconditional stimulus on some trials and without the unconditional stimulus on other trials. A second conditional stimulus is added to signal when the unconditional stimulus will *not* occur. See also *conditioned inhibition*.

Feature-positive discrimination A conditioning procedure in which a conditional stimulus is presented with the unconditional stimulus on some trials and without the unconditional stimulus on other trials. A second conditional stimulus is added to signal when the unconditional stimulus will occur.

Fitness An individual's ability to survive and reproduce in a particular environment—and to have offspring that will survive and reproduce.

Fixed action pattern An innate sequence of behaviors that is triggered by a specific stimulus and continues to its end without regard to immediate consequences or feedback.

Fixed interval schedule A schedule of reinforcement in which the first response after a fixed amount of time has elapsed (since the last reinforcer) is reinforced.

Fixed ratio schedule A schedule of reinforcement in which a fixed number of responses is required for the delivery of each reinforcer.

Focal sets In probabilistic contrast theory, the idea that the contingency between two events is calculated over a relevant subset of the trials.

Frustration Motivational response that occurs when a reward is smaller than expected.

Generalization The transfer of a learned response from one stimulus to a similar stimulus.

Generalization decrement A decrease in the transfer of a learned response from one stimulus to another (i.e., *generalization*) if the two stimuli are made to be different.

Generalize To respond to a new stimulus to the extent that it is similar to another stimulus that has been reinforced or trained.

Geometric module A representation of the global shape of the environment that is thought to be separate from the representations of individual landmarks.

Geons Short for geometric ions; primitive components of visual perception according to recognition by components theory.

Habituation A decrease in the strength of a naturally elicited behavior that occurs through repeated presentations of the eliciting stimulus.

Hall-Pearce negative transfer Interference with conditioning that is produced by pairing a conditional stimulus with a weak unconditional stimulus before pairing it with a stronger unconditional stimulus.

Hedonic shift The observation that in taste aversion learning, the flavor conditional stimulus actually becomes unpleasant.

Hedonism The pursuit of pleasure and the avoidance of pain.

Hidden units Nodes or units in a connectionist network that come between the input and output units and usually have no other connections outside the network (and are thus are not "visible" to outside systems).

Homeostasis The tendency of an organism to maintain an internal equilibrium.

Homologous Two or more traits that are similar in structure and evolutionary origin.

Immanuel Kant (1724–1804) German philosopher who thought that the mind comes into the world with certain inborn assumptions or predilections with which it molds experience.

Immunization effect The finding that exposure to escapable shocks before exposure to inescapable shocks can protect an animal from the *learned helplessness effect*.

Imprinting Learning in very young organisms that establishes attachment to a parent (or an object identified as a parent; sometimes called "filial imprinting"). In "sexual imprinting," a similar process may influence later sexual behavior.

Inactive Resting state of a memory representation or node. In SOP theory, it is the final state to which elements in a node decay after they have been in *A1* and then *A2*.

Incentive learning A process in which organisms learn about the value of a specific reinforcer while they are in a particular motivational state.

Incentive motivation Motivation for instrumental behavior created by anticipation of a positive reinforcer. See also r_G-s_G *mechanism*.

Independents Two or more commodities or reinforcers that do *not* "go together" in the sense that increasing the price of one causes its consumption to decrease without changing consumption of the other. Umbrellas and compact disks, for example.

Information processing A model of cognition, based on a computer metaphor, in which the organism receives sensory input from the environment and then proceeds to operate on that information through a sequence of activities in sensory memory, short-term memory (*working memory*), and long-term memory (*reference memory*).

Inhibition of delay In classical conditioning, inhibition that develops to the early portion of a conditional stimulus in a *delay conditioning* procedure. The early part of a conditional stimulus signals a period without the unconditional stimulus.

Inhibition In classical conditioning, the capacity of a conditional stimulus to signal a decrease in the probability of the unconditional stimulus. More generally, an active process that suppresses excitation or reduces the strength of a response.

Inhibitor (CS–) A conditional stimulus that signals a decrease in the probability or intensity of the unconditional stimulus and therefore evokes inhibition.

Instrumental conditioning or instrumental learning Any situation based on Thorndike's method in which animals can learn about the relationship between their actions and consequences. Essentially the same as *operant conditioning*, except that in instrumental learning experiments the experimenter must set up each and every opportunity the organism has to respond.

Interference Memory impairment caused by conflicting information that was learned at some other time.

Interim behaviors Stereotyped behaviors that occur early in the interval between regularly delivered reinforcers.

Internal clock A hypothetical cognitive device that codes or represents the passage of time.

Intertrial interval The period of time between two successive trials.

Interval schedule A schedule of reinforcement in which a response is reinforced only if it occurs after a set amount of time has elapsed since the last reinforcer.

Intervening variable A theoretical concept that cannot be observed directly, but is used in science to understand the relationship between independent and dependent variables. To be scientific, intervening variables must be carefully defined in terms of the events that lead to them and the behavioral outputs they lead to. Also known as *theoretical constructs*.

Ivan Pavlov (1849–1936) Russian physiologist who published the first systematic observations of *classical conditioning* (also known as Pavlovian learning) and introduced many of the terms that are still used to describe such conditioning today.

John Locke (1632–1704) One of the *British Empiricists*.

Julien de la Mettrie (1709–1751) French writer who believed that the body affects the mind.

Landmark A cue that has a fixed relationship with a goal, but is not close to it, which organisms learn about and use to get around in space.

Latent inhibition or CS-preexposure effect Interference with conditioning that is produced by repeated exposures to the conditional stimulus before conditioning begins.

Latent learning experiment An experiment by Tolman and Honzik (1930) in which animals were not rewarded during initial trials, and then were rewarded for correct responding in a second phase. After the first rewarded trial, the rats began responding efficiently, as if they had previously been learning without reward. Although the reward was not necessary for learning, it did appear necessary to motivate performance.

Law of effect Originally, Thorndike's idea that responses that are followed by pleasure will be strengthened and those that are followed by discomfort will be weakened. Nowadays, the term refers to the idea that operant or instrumental behaviors are lawfully controlled by their consequences.

Learned helplessness effect Interference with learning a new instrumental action, typically an escape response, that is produced by exposure to uncontrollable (inescapable) electric shock.

Learned helplessness hypothesis The theoretical idea that organisms exposed to inescapable and unavoidable shocks learn that their actions do not control environmental outcomes.

Learned irrelevance In classical conditioning, the finding that when there is no contingency between a CS and a US in an initial phase, animals have difficulty learning an association between the two events when the events are later paired.

Learning theory The modern field in which principles of learning, cognition, and behavior are investigated by studying animals learning under controlled laboratory conditions.

Learning/performance distinction The idea that learning is not the same as performance, and that behavior may not always be an accurate indicator of knowledge.

Long-delay learning Conditioning that occurs when there is a long period of time between the conditional stimulus and the unconditional stimulus.

Long-term memory A theoretical part of memory that has a very large capacity and can retain information over long periods or retention intervals. Also used to characterize situations in which an experience has a long-lasting effect on behavior.

Massed trials Conditioning trials separated by a short *intertrial interval*.

Matching law A principle of choice behavior which states that the proportion of responses directed toward one alternative will equal (match) the percentage of reinforcers that are earned by performing that alternative.

Matching-to-sample A procedure in which the organism is reinforced for responding to a test stimulus if it is the same as a "sample" stimulus.

McCollough effect In color perception, the evocation of an opposite-color after-image by black-and-white stimuli that have been associated with a color.

Mediated generalization Treating two stimuli as alike not because they are physically similar but because they are associated with a common stimulus.

Melioration An explanation of *matching* which claims that the organism will always respond so as to improve the local rate of reinforcement. This ultimately leads to a steady state of behavior that matches the rates of reinforcement on the two alternatives.

Memory reactivation Restoration of forgotten information after reexposure to part of the learning situation.

Minimum distance model A model of operant behavior which states that when given any reinforcement schedule, the organism will respond in a way that gets it as close as possible to the *bliss point*.

Modulation When a stimulus influences behavior by increasing or decreasing the response evoked by another stimulus, rather than by eliciting a response itself.

Modules Hypothetical specialized cognitive mechanisms that have evolved to deal with information in a restricted domain.

Morgan's Canon A law proposed by C. Lloyd Morgan which states that a behavior should always be explained by the simplest mental process possible (also known as the law of parsimony).

Multiple oscillator model A model of interval timing that represents time in terms of the status of a set of hypothetical units that cycle between different values, each with a different fixed period over time.

Multiple schedule A procedure in which two or more reinforcement schedules, each signaled by its own discriminative stimulus, are presented one at a time and alternated.

Multiple-time-scale model A model of interval timing which assumes that the start of a trial is recorded in short-term memory and then gradually fades over time. Animals time events by associating them with the strength of this memory at a given point in time.

Natural selection A process that allows individuals with certain features to leave more offspring in the next generation; typically, individuals without those features are less successful.

Negative automaintenance The finding that pecking at a keylight conditional stimulus in pigeons may persist even when the peck prevents the reinforcer from occurring.

Negative contingency A situation where the probability of one event is lower if another event has occurred. In classical conditioning, if the unconditional stimulus is less probable when the conditional stimulus has occurred, the conditional stimulus becomes a *conditioned inhibitor*. In instrumental conditioning, a biologically significant event may likewise be less probable if a behavior occurs. If the significant event is negative or aversive, then *escape* or *avoidance learning* occurs; if the significant event is positive, it is called omission. Also called *negative correlation*.

Negative contrast effect When "expectation" of a large positive reward decreases the positive reaction to a smaller positive reward.

Negative correlation See *negative contingency*.

Negative occasion setter In classical conditioning, a type of modulator that decreases the response evoked by another conditional stimulus in a way that does not depend on the modulator's direct inhibitory relation with the unconditional stimulus.

Negative patterning In classical conditioning, a procedure in which two conditional stimuli are paired with an unconditional stimulus when they are presented alone, but occur without the unconditional stimulus when they are combined. It is difficult for an *elemental theory* to explain why an organism can respond accordingly.

Negative reinforcement A situation in which an operant behavior is strengthened ("reinforced") because it removes or prevents a negative (aversive) stimulus.

Negative sign tracking Movement away from a stimulus that signals either an aversive event or the reduced probability of a positive event.

Negative transfer When learning one task interferes with learning or performance of a second task.

Network A set of interconnected memory nodes.

Neural networks See *connectionism*.

Nodes Memory representations of items in the world.

Occasion setter In classical conditioning, a stimulus that may not itself elicit a response, but modulates behavior to another stimulus.

Omission An instrumental or operant conditioning procedure in which the behavior prevents the delivery of a positive (reinforcing) stimulus. The behavior typically decreases in strength.

Operant conditioning Any situation based on Skinner's setup in which an organism can learn about its actions and consequences. The same as *instrumental conditioning* except that in an operant conditioning experiment the organism is "free" to make the operant response (e.g., lever-pressing) as often as it "wants" to.

Operant experiment An experimental arrangement in which a reinforcer (such as a food pellet) is made contingent upon a certain behavior (such as lever-pressing).

Operant A behavior that is controlled by its consequences. The canonical example is the rat's lever-pressing, which is controlled by the food-pellet reinforcer.

Operant-respondent distinction Skinner's distinction between operant behavior, which is said to be *emitted* and controlled by its consequences, and respondent behavior, which is said to be *elicited* and controlled by its antecedents.

Operational behaviorism An approach, started by Edward Tolman, which departs from radical behaviorism by using unobservable *intervening variables* (*theoretical constructs*) in the explanation of behavior. The approach is scientific as long as the theoretical constructs are carefully defined and falsifiable. It is the approach generally accepted by most modern scientific psychologists.

Opponent process A more general term for the type of compensatory process exemplified by the *b-process* in *opponent-process theory*.

Opponent-process theory A theory that emphasizes the fact that emotional stimuli often evoke an initial emotional reaction followed by an after-reaction of the opposite valence. With repeated exposure to the emotional stimulus, the after-reaction grows and the initial reaction weakens, which may fundamentally change the motivation behind instrumental behavior controlled by positive and negative stimuli.

Ordinal prediction A hypothesis that specifies a greater-than or less-than relationship between two conditions or two groups.

Overexpectation effect In classical conditioning, the finding that two conditional stimuli that have been separately paired with an unconditional stimulus may actually lose some of their potential to elicit conditional responding if they are combined and the compound is paired with the same unconditional stimulus.

Overshadowing In classical conditioning, the finding that there is less conditioning to a weak conditional stimulus if it is combined with a more salient conditional stimulus during conditioning trials.

Panic disorder A psychological disorder characterized by recurrent panic attacks and the fear of having additional ones.

Paradoxical reward effects Any of several behavioral effects in which exposure to nonreinforcement appears to increase the strength of instrumental behavior (as in the *partial reinforcement extinction* *effect*), or exposure to larger reinforcers appears to decrease the strength of instrumental behavior (as in the "magnitude of reinforcement extinction effect"). Often involves *frustration*.

Parallel distributed processing See *connectionism*.

Partial reinforcement extinction effect (PREE) The finding that behaviors that are intermittently reinforced are more persistent (take longer to extinguish) than behaviors that are reinforced every time they occur.

Pavlovian-instrumental transfer An effect in which a Pavlovian conditional stimulus is shown to influence the rate of an ongoing instrumental behavior if the conditional stimulus is presented while the organism is engaged in that behavior.

Peak procedure A method for studying timing processes in which the first response after a fixed interval after the start of a signal is reinforced. Response rate as a function of time in the signal is used to assess the accuracy of timing.

Peak shift In discrimination learning, a change in the generalization gradient surrounding S+ such that the highest level of responding moves away from S+ in a direction away from the S–.

Perceptual learning An increase in the discriminability of two stimuli that results from simple exposure to the two stimuli.

Place cells Cells in the rat hippocampus that become active when the animal is in a particular location.

Positive contingency A situation where the probability of one event is higher if another event has occurred. In classical conditioning, if the unconditional stimulus is more probable when the conditional stimulus has occurred, the conditional stimulus becomes a *conditioned* excitor. In instrumental conditioning, a biologically significant event may likewise be more probable if a behavior occurs. If the significant event is negative or aversive, then *punishment* occurs; if the significant event is positive, then *reward learning* occurs.

Positive contrast effect "Expectation" of a small positive reward can increase the positive reaction to a larger positive reward.

Positive occasion setter In classical conditioning, a type of modulator that increases the response evoked by another conditional stimulus in a way that does not depend on the modulator's direct association with the unconditional stimulus.

Positive patterning In classical conditioning, a procedure in which two conditional stimuli are presented with the unconditional stimulus when they are presented together, but without the unconditional stimulus when they are presented alone.

Positive reinforcement An instrumental or operant conditioning procedure in which the behavior is followed by a positive stimulus or reinforcer. The behavior typically increases in strength.

Pre-commitment strategies A method for decreasing impulsiveness and increasing self-control in which the individual makes choices well in advance.

Predatory imminence An organism's perceived spatial or temporal proximity to a predator, which can determine the form of its anti-predator response (or *species-specific defense reaction*).

Premack principle The idea that reinforcement is possible when a less-preferred behavior will allow access to a more-preferred behavior.

Preparedness The extent to which an organism's evolutionary history makes it easy for the organism to learn a particular association or response. If evolution has made something easy to learn, it is said to be "prepared."

Primary reinforcer An event that unconditionally reinforces operant behavior without any particular training.

Primed When a node or representation has been activated in short-term memory.

Proactive interference Memory impairment caused by information learned or presented before the item that is to be remembered.

Probabilistic contrast model A model developed to explain associative learning in humans that computes contingencies between events by defining and comparing the probability of an event in the presence and absence of selected cues.

Procedural memory Memory for how to automatically execute or perform a particular behavioral or cognitive task.

Prospective code Memory held in working memory about what to do (or what will come) next. Compare to *retrospective code*.

Protection from extinction In classical conditioning, the finding that extinction trials with a conditioned excitor may be ineffective at reducing conditional responding if the excitor is combined with a conditioned inhibitor during extinction.

Prototype theory An approach to categorization which assumes that organisms learn what is typical or average for a category and then respond to new exemplars according to how similar they are to the average.

Prototype Representation of what is typical or average for a particular category.

Pseudoconditioning A process whereby a conditional stimulus can evoke responding because the organism has merely been exposed to the unconditional stimulus, rather than true associative learning.

Punisher An aversive stimulus that decreases the strength or probability of an operant behavior when it is made a consequence of the response.

Punishment An instrumental or operant conditioning procedure in which the behavior is followed by a negative or aversive stimulus. The behavior typically decreases in strength.

Quantitative law of effect A more general, but still quantitative, statement of the matching law in which an operant response is viewed as being chosen over all other potential responses.

Radial maze An elevated maze that has a central area from which arms extend in all directions.

Radical behaviorism The type of behaviorism identified with B. F. Skinner which emphasizes the exclusive study of external events, such as observable stimuli and responses, and avoids any inferences about processes inside the organism.

Rapid reacquisition In classical conditioning, the quick return of an extinguished conditional response when the conditional stimulus and unconditional stimulus are paired again. In instrumental conditioning, the quick return of extinguished behavior once the response and reinforcer are paired again.

Ratio schedule A schedule of reinforcement in which the delivery of each reinforcer depends on the number of responses the organism has performed since the last reinforcer.

Rationalism Term used to refer to Kant's school of thought, in which the mind was thought to act on experience with a set of inborn predilections and assumptions.

Recuperative behaviors Behaviors, such as licking a wound, which are elicited by tissue damage and function to promote healing.

Reference memory Another name for long-term memory.

Reflex action A mechanism through which a specific environmental event or stimulus elicits a specific response. Originated from Rene Descartes.

Reinforcement theory A phrase used to describe learning theories, like Thorndike's, which assume that reinforcement is necessary for learning.

Reinforcement An instrumental or operant conditioning procedure in which the behavior's consequence strengthens or increases the probability of the response. See *positive reinforcement* and *negative reinforcement*.

Reinforcer devaluation effect The finding that an organism will stop performing an instrumental action that previously led to a reinforcer if the reinforcer is separately made undesirable through association with illness or satiation.

Reinforcer substitutability See *substitutability*.

Reinforcer Any consequence of a behavior that strengthens the behavior or increases the probability that the organism will perform it again.

Reinstatement Recovery of the learned response in either classical or instrumental conditioning when the unconditional stimulus or reinforcer is presented alone after extinction.

Relapse The return of undesirable cognitions, emotions, or behaviors after apparent improvement.

Relative validity In classical conditioning, an experimental design and result that supports the view that conditioning is poor when the conditional stimulus is combined with a better predictor of the unconditional stimulus.

Releaser or releasing stimulus A specific stimulus that elicits a *fixed action pattern*. Also called *sign stimulus*.

René Descartes (1596–1650) French philosopher and mathematician who distinguished between mind and body, and also discussed *reflex action* as a mechanical principle that controls the activity of the body.

Renewal effect Recovery of responding that occurs when the context is changed after extinction. Especially strong when the context is changed back to the original context of conditioning.

Respondent A behavior that is elicited by an antecedent stimulus.

Response deprivation hypothesis The idea that restricting access to a behavior below its baseline or preferred level will make access to that behavior a positive reinforcer.

Response form The qualitative nature of the conditional response. Determined by both the unconditional stimulus and by the nature of the conditional stimulus.

Response learning See *R-S* learning*.

Retardation-of-acquisition test A test procedure that identifies a stimulus as a conditioned inhibitor if it is slower than a comparison stimulus to acquire excitation when it is paired with an unconditional stimulus.

Retrieval failure Inability to recover information that is stored in long-term memory. A common cause of forgetting.

Retrieval-generated priming Activation of an item, node, or representation in short-term memory that occurs when a cue that is associated with that item is presented.

Retroactive interference Memory impairment caused by information learned or presented after the item that is to be remembered.

Retrospective code A memory held in working memory about what stimuli have occurred previously. Compare to *prospective code*.

Reward learning An instrumental or operant conditioning procedure in which the behavior is followed by a positive event. The behavior typically increases in strength.

r_G-s_G mechanism A theoretical process that allowed Hull, Spence, and others to explain in S-R terms how "expectations" of reward motivate instrumental responding.

R-S* learning Another term used to describe instrumental and operant conditioning that emphasizes the theoretical content of that learning (an association between a behavior, R, and a biologically significant event, S*).

Scalar property A property of interval timing in which the probability of responding is a similar function of the proportion of time in the interval being timed, regardless of the actual duration of that interval.

Schedule of reinforcement A relationship between an operant behavior and its consequences or payoff. See *ratio*, *interval*, and *concurrent schedules*.

Schedule-induced polydipsia Excessive drinking that is observed if animals are given food reinforcers at regular intervals.

Search image An attentional or memory mechanism that helps predators search for specific cryptic prey.

Secondary reinforcer See *conditioned reinforcer*.

Second-order or higher-order conditioning A classical conditioning procedure in which a conditional response is acquired by a neutral stimulus when the latter is paired with a stimulus that has previously been conditioned.

Self-generated priming Activation of an item, node, or representation in short-term memory that occurs when the item is presented.

Semantic memory A subset of declarative memory that corresponds to memory for various invariant facts about the world.

Sensitization An increase in the strength of an elicited behavior that results merely from repeated presentations of the eliciting stimulus.

Sensory preconditioning A classical conditioning procedure in which two neutral stimuli are first paired with each other, and then one of them is paired with an unconditional stimulus. When the other neutral stimulus is tested, it evokes a conditional response, even though it was never paired with the unconditional stimulus itself.

Sequential theory A theory of the partial reinforcement extinction effect that suggests that extinction is slow after partial reinforcement because the behavior has been reinforced while the organism remembers recent nonrewarded trials.

Shaping or shaping by successive approximations A procedure for training a new operant behavior by reinforcing behaviors that are closer and closer to the final behavior that is desired.

Short-term memory A theoretical part of memory that has a small capacity and can retain information only briefly. Also used to characterize situations in which an experience has only a short-lasting effect on behavior.

Sign stimulus See *releaser*.

Sign tracking Movement toward a stimulus that signals a positive event or the reduced probability of a negative event.

Simultaneous conditioning In classical conditioning, a procedure in which the conditional stimulus and unconditional stimulus are presented at the same time.

Skinner box An experimental chamber that provides the subject something it can repeatedly manipulate, such as a lever (for a rat) or a pecking key (for a pigeon). The chamber is also equipped with mechanisms that can deliver a reinforcer (such as food) and other stimuli (such as lights, noises, or tones).

Sometimes opponent process (SOP) In SOP theory, the idea that a memory node that is in *A2* can sometimes evoke a response that is opposite to the response that is evoked when the node is in *A1*.

SOP theory A theory of classical conditioning that emphasizes activation levels of elements in memory nodes corresponding to conditional stimuli and unconditional stimuli, especially as the activation levels change over time.

Spaced trials Conditioning trials separated by a long *intertrial interval*.

Species-specific defense reactions (SSDRs) Innate reactions that occur when an animal encounters a predator or a conditional stimulus that arouses fear. They have probably evolved to reduce predation. Examples are freezing and fleeing.

Specific hungers The tendency for animals to seek and prefer certain foods that might contain specific nutrients they are currently deprived of.

Spontaneous recovery The reappearance, after the passage of time, of a response that had previously undergone extinction. Can occur after extinction in either classical or instrumental conditioning.

S-R learning The learning of an association between a stimulus and a response.

S-S learning The learning of an association between two stimuli.

S-S* learning Another term used to describe classical or Pavlovian conditioning that emphasizes the theoretical content of that learning (an association between a stimulus, S, and a biologically significant event, S*).

Standard operating procedures (SOP) An established procedure to be followed in carrying out a given operation or in a given situation. In SOP theory of classical conditioning, the standard dynamics of memory.

Standard pattern of affective dynamics According to opponent process theory, the characteristic sequence of responses elicited by a novel emotional stimulus.

Stimulus compound See *compound*.

Stimulus control When operant behaviors are controlled by the stimuli that precede them.

Stimulus elements Theoretical stimuli or features that make up more complex stimuli.

Stimulus generalization gradient A characteristic change in responding that is observed when organisms are tested with stimuli that differ in increasing and/or decreasing steps from the stimulus that was used during training.

Stimulus generalization See *generalization*.

Stimulus learning See *S-S* learning*.

Stimulus relevance The observation that learning occurs more rapidly with certain combinations of conditional and unconditional stimuli (such as a taste and illness) than with other stimulus combinations (such as taste and shock).

Stimulus sampling theory A mathematical theory proposed by Estes which extended Guthrie's idea of stimulus elements.

Stimulus substitution In classical conditioning, the idea that the conditional stimulus is associated with the unconditional stimulus and becomes a substitute for it (eliciting the same response).

Structuralism A school of psychology, especially active in the late 1800s and early 1900s, which relied on introspection as a method for investigating the human mind.

Substitutability A way of conceptualizing the relationships between different reinforcers or commodities as *substitutes*, *complements*, and *independents*.

Substitutes Two or more commodities or reinforcers that can replace or be exchanged for one another, as demonstrated when increasing the price of one of them will decrease the consumption of it and increase demand for the other. For example, Coke and Pepsi.

Successive negative contrast A negative contrast effect in which exposure to a large positive reward decreases the subsequent positive reaction to a smaller positive reward than would ordinarily be observed.

Summation test A test procedure in which conditional stimuli that are conditioned separately are then combined in a compound. The procedure can identify a stimulus as a *conditioned inhibitor* if it suppresses responding evoked by the other stimulus (and does so more than a comparison stimulus that might reduce responding through *generalization decrement*).

Superposition The common finding in research on interval timing that responding as a function of the proportion of the interval being timed is the same regardless of the duration of the actual interval being timed—the curves appear identical when they are plotted on the same graph. Demonstrates the *scalar property*.

Superstitious behavior A behavior that increases in strength or frequency because of accidental pairings with a reinforcer.

Suppression ratio The measure of conditioning used in the *conditioned emotional response* or *conditioned suppression method*. It is the value obtained by dividing the number of responses made during the conditional stimulus by the sum of the responses made during the conditional stimulus and during an equal period of time before the stimulus. If the value is .50, no conditioned suppression has occurred. If the value is 0, a maximum amount of conditioned suppression has occurred.

Surprisingness of the CS The difference between the actual properties of a conditional stimulus and those already predicted or represented (*primed*) in short-term memory.

Surprisingness of the US The difference between the actual magnitude of the unconditional stimulus and that which is predicted by conditional stimuli present on a conditioning trial. In the Rescorla-Wagner model, learning only occurs if there is a discrepancy between the unconditional stimulus that is predicted and the one that actually occurs.

S$^\Delta$ (S–) A discriminative stimulus that suppresses operant responding because it signals a decrease in the availability of reinforcement or sets the occasion for not responding.

Tabula rasa The view, endorsed by the *British Empiricists*, that the mind is a "blank slate" before it is written upon by experience.

Target stimulus In *feature-positive* and *feature-negative discriminations*, the conditional stimulus that is present on every trial.

Taste aversion learning The phenomenon in which a taste is paired with sickness, and this causes the organism to reject that taste in the future.

Taste-reactivity test A method in which experimenters examine the rat's behavioral reactions to tastes delivered directly to the tongue.

Temporal bisection A procedure used to study interval timing in which one response is reinforced after a signal of one duration, and another response is reinforced after a signal of another duration. When responding to stimuli with intermediate durations is tested, the middle point (the duration at which the animal makes either response with equal probability) occurs at the geometric mean of the two reinforced durations (e.g., 4 seconds if 2 and 8 second cues have been reinforced).

Temporal context *Contextual stimuli* that change with the passage of time.

Temporal generalization A procedure for studying interval timing in which an animal is first reinforced if it responds after stimuli of a specific duration and then stimuli of increasing and/or decreasing durations are tested.

Terminal behavior Stereotyped behaviors that occur toward the end of the interval between regularly delivered reinforcers.

Theoretical construct See *intervening variable*.

Thomas Hobbes (1588–1679) A philosopher who suggested that human thoughts and actions follow the principle of *hedonism*.

Touchscreen A device used for detecting the location of responses directed at a screen. Usually consists of perpendicular sets of photobeams across the surface of the screen.

Trace conditioning A classical conditioning procedure in which the unconditional stimulus is presented after the conditional stimulus has been terminated.

Trace decay The theoretical idea that forgetting is due to the actual loss or destruction of information that is stored in memory.

Transfer tests A procedure in which an organism is tested with new stimuli or with old stimuli in a new situation. In categorization experiments, this is the method of testing the animal's ability to categorize stimuli it has not categorized before.

Transfer-of-control experiments Experiments that test for *Pavlovian-instrumental transfer*, and thus demonstrate the effects of presenting a Pavlovian conditional stimulus on the rate of an ongoing instrumental behavior.

Transposition Differential responding to two stimuli, apparently according to their relation rather than their absolute properties or individual features. For example, after discrimination training with two stimuli that differ along a dimension (e.g., size), the organism might choose a more extreme stimulus along the dimension rather than the stimulus that was previously reinforced.

Two-factor theory (two-process theory) A theory of avoidance learning that states that (1) Pavlovian fear learning allows warning stimuli to evoke conditioned fear that motivates avoidance behavior and provides the opportunity for (2) reinforcement of the instrumental avoidance response through fear reduction. More generally, the theoretical idea that Pavlovian learning is always a second process at work in instrumental learning situations.

Unconditional response (UR) In classical conditioning, an innate response that is elicited by a stimulus in the absence of conditioning.

Unconditional stimulus (US) In classical conditioning, the stimulus that elicits the response before conditioning occurs.

US preexposure effect Interference with conditioning that is produced by repeated exposures to the unconditional stimulus before conditioning begins.

Variable interval schedule A schedule of reinforcement in which the behavior is reinforced the first time it occurs after a variable amount of time since the last reinforcer.

Variable ratio schedule A schedule of reinforcement in which a variable number of responses are required for delivery of each reinforcer.

Warning signals Environmental stimuli in avoidance learning situations that are associated with the aversive stimulus through Pavlovian conditioning.

Water maze An apparatus used to investigate spatial learning in which the rat or mouse subject swims in a circular pool of milky water to find a submerged platform on which to stand.

Within-compound association A learned association that may be formed between two conditional stimuli when they are presented together in a compound.

Working memory A system for temporarily holding and manipulating information; another name for short-term memory.

References

Abramson, L. Y., Seligman, M. E. P., & Teasdale, J. (1978). Learned helplessness in humans: Critique and reformulation. *Journal of Abnormal Psychology, 87*, 49–74.

Adams, C. D. (1982). Variations in the sensitivity of instrumental responding to reinforcer devaluation. *Quarterly Journal of Experimental Psychology, 34B*, 77–98.

Adams, C. D., & Dickinson, A. (1981). Instrumental responding following reinforcer devaluation. *Quarterly Journal of Experimental Psychology, 33B*, 109–121.

Adams, C. D., & Dickinson, A. (1982). Variations in the sensitivity of instrumental responding to reinforcer devaluation. *Quarterly Journal of Experimental Psychology, 34B*, 77–98.

Aguado, L., Symonds, M., & Hall, G. (1994). Interval between preexposure and test determines the magnitude of latent inhibition: Implications for an interference account. *Animal Learning & Behavior, 22*, 188–194.

Ainslie, G. (1975). Specious reward: A behavioral theory of impulsiveness and impulse control. *Psychological Bulletin, 82*, 463–496.

Akins, C. K. (2000). Effects of species-specific cues and the CS-US interval on the topography of the sexually conditioned response. *Learning and Motivation, 31*, 211–235.

Akins, C. K., Domjan, M., & Gutierrez, G. (1994). Topography of sexually conditioned behavior in male Japanese quail (*Coturnix japonica*) depends on the CS-US interval. *Journal of Experimental Psychology: Animal Behavior Processes, 20*, 199–209.

Alcock, J. (2005). *Animal behavior: An evolutionary approach* (8th ed.). Sunderland, MA: Sinauer Associates, Inc.

Allan, L. G., & Gibbon, J. (1991). Human bisection at the geometric mean. *Learning and Motivation, 22*, 39–58.

Allison, J. (1979). Demand economics and experimental psychology. *Behavioral Science, 24*, 403–415.

Allison, J. (1983). Behavioral substitutes and complements. In R. L. Malgren (Ed.), *Animal cognition and behavior*. Amsterdam: North-Holland.

Allison, J. (1989). The nature of reinforcement. In S. B. Klein & R. R. Mowrer (Eds.), *Contemporary learning theories: Instrumental conditioning theory and the impact of biological constraints on learning* (pp. 13–39). Hillsdale, NJ: Lawrence Erlbaum Associates, Inc.

Allison, J., & Timberlake, W. (1974). Instrumental and contingent saccharin licking in rats: Response deprivation and reinforcement. *Learning and Motivation, 5*, 231–247.

Amsel, A. (1958). The role of frustrative nonreward in noncontinuous reward situations. *Psychological Bulletin, 55*, 102–119.

Amsel, A. (1962). Frustrative nonreward in partial reinforcement and discrimination learning: Some recent history and a theoretical extension. *Psychological Review, 69*, 306–328.

Amsel, A. (1992). *Frustration theory: An analysis of dispositional learning and memory*. Cambridge, England: Cambridge University Press.

Amsel, A., & Roussel, J. (1952). Motivational properties of frustration: I. Effect on a running response of the addition of frustration to the motivational complex. *Journal of Experimental Psychology, 43*, 363–368.

Amsel, A., & Ward, J. S. (1965). Frustration and persistence: Resistance to discrimination following prior experience with the discriminanda. *Psychological Monographs (General and Applied), 79*, 41.

Anderson, J. R. (1995). *Learning and memory: An integrated approach*. New York: John Wiley.

Anger, D. (1963). The role of temporal discrimination in the reinforcement of Sidman avoidance behavior. *Journal of the Experimental Analysis of Behavior, 6*, 477–506.

Anisman, H., DeCatanzaro, D., & Remington, G. (1978). Escape performance following exposure to inescapable shock: Deficits in motor response maintenance. *Journal of Experimental Psychology: Animal Behavior Processes, 4*, 197–218.

Annau, Z., & Kamin, L. J. (1961). The conditioned emotional response as a function of intensity of the US. *Journal of Comparative and Physiological Psychology, 54*, 428–432.

Arcediano, F., Matutue, H., Escobar, M., & Miller, R. R. (2005). Competition between antecedent and between subsequent stimuli in causal judgments. *Journal of Experimental Psychology: Learning, Memory, and Cognition, 31*, 228–237.

Astley, S. L., & Wasserman, E. A. (1992). Categorical discrimination and generalization in pigeons: All negative stimuli are not created equal. *Journal of Experimental Psychology: Animal Behavior Processes, 18*, 193–207.

Astley, S. L., & Wasserman, E. A. (1999). Superordinate category formation in pigeons: Association with a common delay or probability of food reinforcement makes perceptually dissimilar stimuli functionally equivalent. *Journal of Experimental Psychology: Animal Behavior Processes, 25*, 415–432.

Astley, S. L., Peissig, J. J., & Wasserman, E. A. (2001). Superordinate categorization via learned stimulus equivalence: Quantity of reinforcement, hedonic value, and the nature of the mediator. *Journal of Experimental Psychology: Animal Behavior Processes, 27*, 252–268.

Atkinson, R. C., & Shiffrin, R. M. (1971). The control of short-term memory. *Scientific American, 225*, 82–90.

Ayres, J. J. B. (1998). Fear conditioning and avoidance. In W. O'Donohue (Ed.), *Learning and behavior therapy* (pp. 122–145). Needham Heights, MA: Allyn & Bacon.

Ayres, J. J., Haddad, C., & Albert, M. (1987). One-trial excitatory backward conditioning as assessed by conditioned suppression of licking in rats: Concurrent observations of lick suppression and defensive behaviors. *Animal Learning & Behavior, 15*, 212–217.

Azrin, N. H. (1960). Effects of punishment intensity during variable-interval reinforcement. *Journal of the Experimental Analysis of Behavior, 3*, 123–142.

Baerends, G. P. (1950). Specializations in organs and movements with a releasing function, *Society for Experimental Biology. Physiological mechanisms in animal behavior (Society's Symposium IV)* (pp. 337–360).

Baerends, G. P. (1976). The functional organization of behaviour. *Animal Behaviour, 24*, 726–738.

Baker, A. G. (1974). Conditioned inhibition is not the symmetrical opposite of conditioned excitation: A test of the Rescorla-Wagner model. *Learning and Motivation, 5*, 369–379.

Baker, A. G. (1977). Conditioned inhibition arising from a between-sessions negative correlation. *Journal of Experimental Psychology: Animal Behavior Processes, 3*, 144–155.

Baker, A. G., & Mackintosh, N. J. (1977). Excitatory and inhibitory conditioning following uncorrelated presentations of CS and UCS. *Animal Learning & Behavior, 5*, 315–319.

Baker, A. G., & Mercier, P. (1982). Extinction of the context and latent inhibition. *Learning and Motivation, 13*, 391–416.

Baker, A. G., Mercier, P., Vallee-Tourangeau, F., Frank, R., & Pans, M. (1993). Selective associations and causality judgments: Presence of a strong causal factor may reduce judgments of a weaker one. *Journal of Experimental Psychology: Learning, Memory, and Cognition, 19*, 414–432.

Baker, A. G., Murphy, R. A., & Vallee-Tourangeau, F. (1996). Associative and normative models of causal induction: Reacting to versus understanding cause. In D. R. Shanks, K. Holyoak, & D. L. Medin (Ed.), *Causal Learning* (pp. 1–45). San Diego: Academic Press.

Baker, A. G., Murphy, R., Mehta, R., & Baetu, I. (2005). Mental models of causation: A comparative view. In A. J. Wills (Ed.), *New directions in human associative learning*. Mahwah, NJ: Erlbaum.

Baker, T. B., & Tiffany, S. T. (1985). Morphine tolerance as habituation. *Psychological Review, 92*, 78–108.

Baker, T. B., Piper, M. E., McCarthy, D. E., Majeskie, M. R., & Fiore, M. C. (2004). Addiction motivation reformulated: An affective processing model of negative reinforcement. *Psychological Review, 111*, 33–51.

Balaz, M. A., Kasprow, W. J., & Miller, R. R. (1982). Blocking with a single compound trial. *Animal Learning & Behavior, 10*, 271–276.

Balleine, B. W. (1992). Instrumental performance following a shift in primary motivation depends on incentive learning. *Journal of Experimental Psychology: Animal Behavior Processes, 18*, 236–250.

Balleine, B. W. (1994). Asymmetrical interactions between thirst and hunger in Pavlovian-instrumental transfer. *The Quarterly Journal of Experimental Psychology, 47B*, 211–231.

Balleine, B. W. (2001). Incentive processes in instrumental conditioning. In R. R. Mowrer, & S. B. Klein (Ed.), *Handbook of contemporary learning theories* (pp. 307–366). Hillsdale, NJ: Erlbaum.

Balleine, B. W. (2005). Neural bases of food-seeking: Affect, arousal and reward in corticostriatolimbic circuits. *Physiology and Behavior, 86*, 717–730.

Balleine, B. W., & Dickinson A. (1991). Instrumental performance following reinforcer devaluation depends upon incentive learning. *Quarterly Journal of Experimental Psychology, 43B*, 279–296.

Balleine, B. W., & Dickinson A. (1998). Consciousness: The interface between affect and cognition. In J. Cornwell (Ed.), *Consciousness and human identity* (pp. 57–85). Oxford: Oxford University Press.

Balleine, B. W., & Dickinson, A. (1994). Role of cholecystokinin in the motivational control of instrumental action in rats. *Behavioral Neuroscience, 108*, 590–605.

Balleine, B. W., Garner, C., & Dickinson, A. (1995). Instrumental outcome devaluation is attenuated by the antiemetic ondansetron. *Quarterly Journal of Experimental Psychology, 48*, 235–251.

Balleine, B. W., Garner, C., Gonzalez, F., & Dickinson, A. (1995). Motivational control of heterogeneous instrumental chains. *Journal of Experimental Psychology: Animal Behavior Processes, 21*, 203–217.

Balsam, P. (1984). Relative time in trace conditioning. *Annals of the New York Academy of Sciences, 423*, 211–227.

Balsam, P. D., & Payne, D. (1979). Intertrial interval and unconditioned stimulus durations in autoshaping. *Animal Learning & Behavior, 7*, 477–482.

Balsam, P. D., & Tomie, A. (Eds.). (1985). *Context and learning.* Hillsdale, NJ: Lawrence Erlbaum Associates, Inc.

Balsam, P. D., Deich, J. D., Ohyama, T., & Stokes, P. D. (1998). Origins of new behavior. In W. T. O'Donohue (Ed.), *Learning and behavior therapy* (pp. 403–420). Boston, MA: Allyn and Bacon.

Barash, D. (1982). *Sociobiology and behavior* (2nd ed.). New York: Elsevier.

Bargh, J. A., & Chartrand, T. L. (1999). The unbearable automaticity of being. *American Psychologist, 54*, 462–479.

Barlow, D. H. (1988). *Anxiety and its disorders: The nature and treatment of anxiety and panic*. New York: Guilford Press.

Barlow, D. H. (2002). *Anxiety and its disorders: The nature and treatment of anxiety and panic* (2nd ed.). New York: Guilford Press.

Barnes, J. M., & Underwood, B. J. (1959). "Fate" of first-list associations in transfer theory. *Journal of Experimental Psychology, 58*, 97–105.

Basoglu, M., Marks, I. M., & Sengun, S. (1992). A prospective study of panic and anxiety in agoraphobia with panic disorder. *British Journal of Psychiatry, 160*, 57–64.

Batsell, W. R., & Blankenship, A. G. (2002). Beyond potentiation: Synergistic conditioning in flavor-aversion learning. *Brain and Mind, 3*, 383–408.

Batsell, W. R., Jr., & Batson, J. D. (1999). Augmentation of taste conditioning by a preconditioned odor. *Journal of Experimental Psychology: Animal Behavior Processes, 25*, 374–388.

Batsell, W. R., Paschall, G. Y., Gleason, D. I., & Batson, J. D. (2001). Taste preconditioning augments odor-aversion learning. *Journal of Experimental Psychology: Animal Behavior Processes, 28*, 30–47.

Batsell, W. R., Trost, C. A., Cochran, S. R., Blankenship, A. G., & Batson, J. D. (2003). Effects of postconditioning inflation on odor + taste compound conditioning. *Learning & Behavior, 31*, 173–184.

Batson, J. D., & Batsell, W. R. (2000). Augmentation, not blocking, in an A+/AX+ flavor-conditionaing procedure. *Psychonomic Bulletin & Review, 7*, 466–471.

Baum, W. M. (1973). The correlation-based law of effect. *Journal of the Experimental Analysis of Behavior, 20*, 137–153.

Baum, W. M. (1974). On two types of deviation from the matching law: Bias and undermatching. *Journal of the Experimental Analysis of Behavior, 22*, 231–242.

Baum, W. M. (2001). Molar versus molecular as a paradigm clash. *Journal of the Experimental Analysis of Behavior, 75*, 338–341.

Beatty, W. W., & Shavalia, D. A. (1980). Rat spatial memory: Resistance to retroactive interference at long retention intervals. *Animal Learning & Behavior, 8*, 550–552.

Beatty, W. W., & Shavalia, D. A. (1980). Spatial memory in rats: Time course of working memory and effect of anesthetics. *Behavioral and Neural Biology, 28*, 454–462.

Beckers, T., De Houwer, J., Pineno, O., & Miller, R. R. (2005). Outcome additivity and outcome maximality influence cue competition in human causal learning. *Journal of Experimental Psychology: Learning, Memory, and Cognition, 31*, 238–249.

Beckers, T., Miller, R. R., De Houwer, J., & Urushihara, K. (2006). Reasoning rats: Forward blocking in Pavlovian animal conditioning is sensitive to constraints of causal inference. *Journal of Experimental Psychology: General, 135*, 92–102.

Belli, R. F., & Loftus, E. F. (1996). The pliability of autobiographical memory: Misinformation and the false memory problem. In D. C. Rubin (Ed.), *Remembering our past: Studies in autobiographical memory* (pp. 157–179). Cambridge, England: Cambridge University Press.

Bernstein, I. L. (1978). Learned taste aversions in children receiving chemotherapy. *Science, 200*, 1302–1303.

Bernstein, I. L., & Webster, M. M. (1980). Learned taste aversions in humans. *Physiology and Behavior, 25*, 363–366.

Berridge, K. C., & Robinson, T. E. (1995). The mind of an addicted brain: Neural sensitization of wanting versus liking. *Current Directions in Psychological Science, 4*, 71–76.

Best, M. R. (1975). Conditioned and latent inhibition in taste-aversion learning: Clarifying the role of learned safety. *Journal of Experimental Psychology: Animal Behavior Processes, 1*, 97–113.

Best, M. R., Batson, J. B., Meachum, C. L., Brown, E. R., & Ringer, M. R. (1985). Characteristics of taste-mediated environmental potentiation in rats. *Learning and Motivation, 16*, 190–209.

Best, M. R., Batson, J. D., & Bowman, M. T. (1990). The role of ingestional delay in taste-mediated environmental potentiation. *Bulletin of the Psychonomic Society, 28*, 215–218.

Best, M. R., Batson, J. D., Meachum, C. L., Brown, E. R., & Ringer, M. (1985). Characteristics of taste-mediated environmental potentiation in rats. *Learning and Motivation, 16*, 190–209.

Best, M. R., Brown, E. R., & Sowell, M. K. (1984). Taste-mediated potentiation of noningestional stimuli in rats. *Learning and Motivation, 15*, 244–258.

Best, M. R., Gemberling, G. A., & Johnson, P. E. (1979). Disrupting the conditioned stimulus preexposure effect in flavor-aversion learning: Effects of interoceptive distractor manipulations. *Journal of Experimental Psychology: Animal Behavior Processes, 5*, 321–334.

Betts, S. L., Brandon, S. E., & Wagner, A. R. (1996). Dissociation of the blocking of conditioned eyeblink and conditioned fear following a shift in US locus. *Animal Learning & Behavior, 24*, 459–470.

Bevins, R. A., & Bardo, M. T. (Ed.). (2004). *Motivational factors in the etiology of drug abuse* (Vol. 50). Lincoln, NE: University of Nebraska Press.

Bhatt, R. S. (1989). Categorization in pigeons: Effects of category size, congruity with human categories, selective attention, and secondary generalization. *Dissertation Abstracts International, 50*, 1668.

Bhatt, R. S., Wasserman, E. A., Reynolds, W. F., & Knauss, K. S. (1988). Conceptual behavior in pigeons: Categorization of both familiar and novel examples from four classes of natural and artificial stimuli. *Journal of Experimental Psychology: Animal Behavior Processes, 14*, 219–234.

Bickel, W. K., & Johnson, M. W. (2003). Delay discounting: A fundamental behavioral process of drug dependence. In G. Loewenstein, D. Read, & R. Baumeister (Ed.), *Time and decision: Economic and psychological perspectives on intertemporal choice* (pp. 419–440). New York: Russell Sage Foundation.

Bickel, W. K., & Marsch, L. A. (2001). Toward a behavioral economic understanding of drug dependence: Delay discounting processes. *Addiction, 96*, 73–86.

Bickel, W. K., DeGrandpre, R. J., & Higgins, S. T. (1995). The behavioral economics of concurrent drug reinforcers: A review and reanalysis of drug self-administration research. *Psychopharmacology, 118*, 250–259.

Bickel, W. K., Odum, A. L., & Madden, G. J. (1999). Impulsivity and cigarette smoking: Delay discounting in current, never, and ex-smokers. *Psychopharmacology, 146*, 447–454.

Biebach, H., Gordijn, M., & Krebs, J. R. (1989). Time-and-place learning by garden warblers, *Sylvia borin*. *Animal Behaviour, 37*, 353–360.

Biederman, I. (1987). Recognition-by-components: A theory of human image understanding. *Psychological Review, 94*, 115–147.

Biegler, R., & Morris, R. G. M. (1999). Blocking in the spatial domain with arrays of discrete landmarks. *Journal of Experimental Psychology: Animal Behavior Processes, 25*, 334–351.

Bindra, D. (1972). A unified account of Pavlovian conditioning and operant training. In H. A. Black, & W. F. Prokasy (Ed.), *Classical conditioning II: Current research and theory*. New York: Appleton-Century-Crofts.

Birch, L. L. (1991). Obesity and eating disorders: A developmental perspective. *Bulletin of the Psychonomic Society, 29*, 265–272.

Birch, L. L., & Fisher, J. A. (1996). The role of experience in the development of children's eating behavior. In E. D. Capaldi (Ed.), *Why we eat what we eat: The psychology of eating* (pp. 113–141). Washington, DC: American Psychological Association.

Birch, L. L., McPhee, L., Shoba, B. C., Steinberg, L., & Krehbiel, R. (1987). "Clean up your plate": Effects of child feeding practices on the conditioning of meal size. *Learning and Motivation, 18*, 301–317.

Birch, L. L., McPhee, L., Steinberg, L., & Sullivan, S. (1990). Conditioned flavor preferences in young children. *Physiology and Behavior, 47*, 501–505.

Bitterman, M. E. (1988). Vertebrate-invertebrate comparisons. In H. J. Jerison & I. Jerison (Eds.), *Intelligence and evolutionary biology* (pp. 251–276). Berlin: Springer.

Bitterman, M. E. (1996). Comparative analysis of learning in honeybees. *Animal Learning & Behavior, 24*, 123–141.

Bitterman, M. E. (2000). Cognitive evolution: A psychological perspective. In C. Heyes, & L. Huber (Ed.), *The evolution of cognition* (pp. 61–79). Cambridge, MA: The MIT Press.

Bizo, L. A., & White, K. G. (1995). Reinforcement context and pacemaker rate in the behavioral theory of timing. *Animal Learning & Behavior, 23*, 376–382.

Black, A. H. (1958). The extinction of avoidance responses under curare. *Journal of Comparative and Physiological Psychology, 51*, 519–524.

Black, A. H. (1959). Heart rate changes during avoidance learning in dogs. *Canadian Journal of Psychology, 13*, 229–242.

Blaisdell, A. P., Bristol, A. S., Gunther, L. M., & Miller, R. R. (1998). Overshadowing and latent inhibition counteract each other: Support for the comparator hypothesis. *Journal of Experimental Psychology: Animal Behavior Processes, 24*, 335–351

Blanchard, R. J., & Blanchard, D. C. (1969). Crouching as an index of fear. *Journal of Comparative and Physiological Psychology, 67*, 370–375.

Blough, D. S. (1969). Attention shifts in a maintained discrimination. *Science, 166*, 125–126.

Blough, D. S. (2002). Measuring the search image: Expectation, detection and recognition in pigeon visual search. *Journal of Experimental Psychology: Animal Behavior Processes, 28*, 397–405.

Blough, D. S., & Blough, P. M. (1997). Form perception and attention in pigeons. *Animal Learning & Behavior, 25*, 1–20.

Blough, P. M. (1989). Attention priming and visual search in pigeons. *Journal of Experimental Psychology: Animal Behavior Processes, 15*, 358–365.

Blough, P. M. (1991). Selective attention and search images in pigeons. *Journal of Experimental Psychology: Animal Behavior Processes, 17*, 292–298.

Blough, P. M., & Lacourse, D. M. (1994). Sequential priming in visual search: Contributions of stimulus-driven facilitation and learned expectancies. *Animal Learning & Behavior, 22*, 275–281.

Boakes, R. (1984). *From Darwin to behaviourism: Psychology and the minds of animals*. Cambridge, England: Cambridge University Press.

Boakes, R. A. (1997). Wheels, clocks, and anorexia in the rat. In M. E. Bouton & M. S. Fanselow (Eds.), *Learning, motivation, and cognition* (pp. 163–176). Washington DC: American Psychological Association.

Bolles, R. C. (1962). The readiness to eat and drink: The effect of deprivation conditions. *Journal of Comparative and Physiological Psychology, 55*, 230–234.

Bolles, R. C. (1965). Readiness to eat: Effects of age, sex, and weight loss. *Journal of Comparative and Physiological Psychology, 60*, 88–92.

Bolles, R. C. (1967). *Theory of motivation*. New York: Harper and Row.

Bolles, R. C. (1969). Avoidance and escape learning: Simultaneous acquisition of different responses. *Journal of Comparative and Physiological Psychology, 68*, 355–358.

Bolles, R. C. (1970). Species-specific defense reactions and avoidance learning. *Psychological Review, 77*, 32–48.

Bolles, R. C. (1972a). Reinforcement, expectancy, and learning. *Psychological Review, 79*, 394–409.

Bolles, R. C. (1972b). The avoidance learning problem. In G. H. Bower (Ed.), *The psychology of learning and motivation*. New York: Academic Press.

Bolles, R. C. (1975). *Theory of motivation* (2nd ed.). New York: Harper and Row.

Bolles, R. C. (1978). The role of stimulus learning in defensive behavior. In S. H. Hulse, H. Fowler, & W. K. Honig (Ed.), *Cognitive processes in animal behavior* (pp. 89–107). Hillsdale, NJ: Erlbaum.

Bolles, R. C. (1979). *Learning theory*. New York: Holt, Rinhart and Winston.

Bolles, R. C. (1993). *The story of psychology: A thematic history*. Belmont, CA: Brooks-Cole.

Bolles, R. C., & de Lorge, J. (1962). The rat's adjustment to a-diurnal feeding cycles. *Journal of Comparative and Physiological Psychology, 55*, 760–762.

Bolles, R. C., & Fanselow, M. S. (1980). A perceptual defensive-recuperative model of fear and pain. *Behavioral and Brain Sciences, 3*, 291–323.

Bolles, R. C., & Grossen, N. E. (1969). Effects of an informational stimulus on the acquisition of avoidance behavior in rats. *Journal of Comparative and Physiological Psychology, 68*, 90–99.

Bolles, R. C., & Moot, S. A. (1972). Derived motives. *Annual Review of Psychology, 23*, 51–72.

Bolles, R. C., & Moot, S. A. (1973). The rat's anticipation of two meals a day. *Journal of Comparative and Physiological Psychology, 83*, 510–514.

Bolles, R. C., & Riley, A. L. (1973). Freezing as an avoidance response: Another look at the operant-respondent distinction. *Learning and Motivation, 4*, 268–275.

Bolles, R. C., & Stokes, L. W. (1965). Rat's anticipation of diurnal and a-diurnal feeding. *Journal of Comparative and Physiological Psychology, 60*, 290–294.

Bolles, R. C., Collier, A. C., Bouton, M. E., & Marlin, N. A. (1978). Some tricks for ameliorating the trace-conditioning deficit. *Bulletin of the Psychonomic Society, 11*, 403–406.

Bolles, R. C., Hayward, L., & Crandall, C. (1981). Conditioned taste preferences based on caloric density. *Journal of Experimental Psychology: Animal Behavior Processes, 7*, 59–69.

Bolles, R. C., Holtz, R., Dunn, T., & Hill, W. (1980). Comparison of stimulus learning and response learning in a punishment situation. *Learning and Motivation, 11*, 78–96.

Bolles, R. C., Stokes, L. W., & Younger, M. S. (1966). Does CS termination reinforce avoidance behavior? *Journal of Comparative and Physiological Psychology, 62*, 201–207.

Bonardi, C., & Hall, G. (1996). Learned irrelevance: No more than the sum of CS and US preexposure effects? *Journal of Experimental Psychology: Animal Behavior Processes, 22*, 183–191.

Bonardi, C., & Ong, S. Y. (2003). Learned irrelevance: A contemporary overview. *Quarterly Journal of Experimental Psychology B: Comparative and Physiological Psychology, 56B*, 80–89.

Bond, A. B. (1983). Visual search and selection of natural stimuli in the pigeon: The attention threshold hypothesis. *Journal of Experimental Psychology: Animal Behavior Processes, 9*, 292–306.

Bond, A. B., & Kamil, A. C. (1998). Apostatic selection by blue jays produces balanced polymorphism in virtual prey. *Nature, 395*, 594–596.

Bond, A. B., & Kamil, A. C. (1999). Searching image in blue jays: Facilitation and interference in sequential priming. *Animal Learning & Behavior, 27*, 461–471.

Bond, A. B., & Kamil, A. C. (2002). Visual predators select for crypticity and polymorphism in virtual prey. *Nature, 415*, 609–613.

Bouton, M. E. (1984). Differential control by context in the inflation and reinstatement paradigms. *Journal of Experimental Psychology: Animal Behavior Processes, 10*, 56–74.

Bouton, M. E. (1986). Slow reacquisition following the extinction of conditioned suppression. *Learning and Motivation, 17*, 1–15.

Bouton, M. E. (1988). Context and ambiguity in the extinction of emotional learning: Implications for exposure therapy. *Behaviour Research & Therapy, 26*, 137–149.

Bouton, M. E. (1991). Context and retrieval in extinction and in other examples of interference in simple associative learning. In L. Dachowski & C. F. Flaherty (Eds.), *Current topics in animal learning: Brain, emotion, and cognition.* (pp. 25–53). Hillsdale, NJ: Lawrence Erlbaum Associates, Inc.

Bouton, M. E. (1993). Context, time, and memory retrieval in the interference paradigms of Pavlovian learning. *Psychological Bulletin, 114*, 80–99.

Bouton, M. E. (1994a). Conditioning, remembering, and forgetting. *Journal of Experimental Psychology: Animal Behavior Processes, 20*, 219–231.

Bouton, M. E. (1994b). Context, ambiguity, and classical conditioning. *Current Directions in Psychological Science, 3*, 49–53.

Bouton, M. E. (1997). Signals for whether versus when an event will occur. In M. E. Bouton & M. S. Fanselow (Eds.), *Learning, motivation, and cognition: The functional behaviorism of Robert C. Bolles.* (pp. 385–409). Washington, DC: American Psychological Association.

Bouton, M. E. (2000). A learning theory perspective on lapse, relapse, and the maintenance of behavior change. *Health Psychology, 19*(Suppl.), 57–63.

Bouton, M. E. (2002). Context, ambiguity, and unlearning: Sources of relapse after behavioral extinction. *Biological Psychiatry, 52*, 976–986.

Bouton, M. E. (2004). Context and behavioral processes in extinction. *Learning and Memory, 11*, 485–494.

Bouton, M. E. (2005). Behavior systems and the contextual control of anxiety, fear, and panic. In L. F. Barrett, P. Niedenthal, & P. Winkielman (Eds.), *Emotion: Conscious and unconcscious* (Vol. 205–227). New York: Guilford Press.

Bouton, M. E., & Bolles, R. C. (1979a). Contextual control of the extinction of conditioned fear. *Learning and Motivation, 10*, 445–466.

Bouton, M. E., & Bolles, R. C. (1979b). Role of conditioned contextual stimuli in reinstatement of extinguished fear. *Journal of Experimental Psychology: Animal Behavior Processes, 5*, 368–378.

Bouton, M. E., & Bolles, R. C. (1980). Conditioned fear assessed by freezing and by the suppression of three different baselines. *Animal Learning & Behavior, 8*, 429–434.

Bouton, M. E., & King, D. A. (1983). Contextual control of the extinction of conditioned fear: Tests for the associative value of the context. *Journal of Experimental Psychology: Animal Behavior Processes, 9*, 248–265.

Bouton, M. E., & Nelson, J. B. (1994). Context-specificity of target versus feature inhibition in a feature-negative discrimination. *Journal of Experimental Psychology: Animal Behavior Processes, 20*, 51–65.

Bouton, M. E., & Nelson, J. B. (1998a). Mechanisms of feature-positive and feature-negative discrimination learning in an appetitive conditioning paradigm. In N. A. Schmajuk & P. C. Holland (Eds.), *Occasion setting: Associative learning and cognition in animals* (pp. 69–112). Washington, DC: American Psychological Association.

Bouton, M. E., & Nelson, J. B. (1998b). The role of context in classical conditioning: Some implications for cognitive behavior therapy. In W. T. O'Donohue (Ed.), *Learning and behavior therapy* (pp. 59–84). Needham Heights, MA: Allyn & Bacon.

Bouton, M. E., & Peck, C. A. (1989). Context effects on conditioning, extinction, and reinstatement in an appetitive conditioning preparation. *Animal Learning & Behavior, 17*, 188–198.

Bouton, M. E., & Peck, C. A. (1992). Spontaneous recovery in cross-motivational transfer (counterconditioning). *Animal Learning & Behavior, 20*, 313–321.

Bouton, M. E., & Ricker, S. T. (1994). Renewal of extinguished responding in a second context. *Animal Learning & Behavior, 22*, 317–324.

Bouton, M. E., & Swartzentruber, D. (1986). Analysis of the associative and occasion-setting properties of contexts participating in a Pavlovian discrimination. *Journal of Experimental Psychology: Animal Behavior Processes, 12*, 333–350.

Bouton, M. E., & Swartzentruber, D. (1991). Sources of relapse after extinction in Pavlovian and instrumental learning. *Clinical Psychology Review, 11*, 123–140.

Bouton, M. E., & Whiting, M. R. (1982). Simultaneous odor-taste and taste-taste compounds in poison-avoidance learning. *Learning and Motivation, 13*, 472–494.

Bouton, M. E., Dunlap, C. M., & Swartzentruber, D. (1987). Potentiation of taste by another taste during compound aversion learning. *Animal Learning & Behavior, 15*, 433–438.

Bouton, M. E., Jones, D. L., McPhillips, S. A., & Swartzentruber, D. (1986). Potentiation and overshadowing in odor-aversion learning: Role of method of odor presentation, the distal-proximal cue distinction, and the conditionability of odor. *Learning and Motivation, 17*, 115–138.

Bouton, M. E., Kenney, F. A., & Rosengard, C. (1990). State-dependent fear extinction with two benzodiazepine tranquilizers. *Behavioral Neuroscience, 104*, 44–55.

Bouton, M. E., Mineka, S., & Barlow, D. H. (2001). A modern learning theory perspective on the etiology of panic disorder. *Psychological Review, 108*, 4–32.

Bouton, M. E., Nelson, J. B., & Rosas, J. M. (1999). Stimulus generalization, context change, and forgetting. *Psychological Bulletin, 125*, 171–186.

Bouton, M. E., Woods, A. M., & Pineno, O. (2004). Occasional reinforced trials during extinction can slow the rate of rapid reacquisition. *Learning and Motivation, 35*, 371–390.

Bower, G. H. (1961). A contrast effect in differential conditioning. *Journal of Experimental Psychology, 62*, 196–199.

Bower, G. H., & Hilgard, E. R. (1981). *Theories of learning* (5th ed.). Englewood Cliffs, NJ: Prentice and Hall.

Brandon, S. E., & Wagner, A. R. (1991). Modulation of a discrete Pavlovian conditioned reflex by a putative emotive Pavlovian conditioned stimulus. *Journal of Experimental Psychology: Animal Behavior Processes, 17*, 299–311.

Brandon, S. E., Bombace, J. C., Falls, W. A., & Wagner, A. R. (1991). Modulation of unconditioned defensive reflexes by a putative emotive Pavlovian conditioned stimulus. *Journal of Experimental Psychology: Animal Behavior Processes, 17*, 312–322.

Brandon, S. E., Vogel, E. H., & Wagner, A. R. (2000). A componential view of configural cues in generalization and discrimination in Pavlovian conditioning. *Behavioural Brain Research, 110*, 67–72.

Breland, K., & Breland, M. (1961). The misbehavior of organisms. *American Psychologist, 16*, 681–684.

Briggs, G. E. (1954). Acquisition, extinction, and recovery functions in retroactive inhibition. *Journal of Experimental Psychology, 47*, 285–293.

Broadbent, D. E. (1958). *Perception and communication*. New York: Pergamon Press.

Brooks, D. C., & Bouton, M. E. (1993). A retrieval cue for extinction attenuates spontaneous recovery. *Journal of Experimental Psychology: Animal Behavior Processes, 19*, 77–89.

Brooks, D. C., & Bouton, M. E. (1994). A retrieval cue for extinction attenuates response recovery (renewal) caused by a return to the conditioning context. *Journal of Experimental Psychology: Animal Behavior Processes, 20*, 366–379.

Brown, J. S., & Jacobs, A. (1949). The role of fear in the motivation and acquisition of responses. *Journal of Experimental Psychology, 39*, 747–759.

Brown, J. S., Kalish, H. I., & Farber, I. E. (1951). Conditioned fear as revealed by magnitude of startle response to an auditory stimulus. *Journal of Experimental Psychology, 41*, 317–327.

Brown, M. F. (1992). Does a cognitive map guide choices in the radial-arm maze? *Journal of Experimental Psychology: Animal Behavior Processes, 18*, 56–66.

Brown, M. F., McKeon, D., Curley, T., Weston, B., Lambert, C., & Lebowitz, B. (1998). Working memory for color in honeybees. *Animal Learning & Behavior, 26*, 264–271.

Brown, M. F., Rish, P. A., Culin, J. E. V., & Edberg, J. A. (1993). Spatial guidance of choice behavior in the radial-arm maze. *Journal of Experimental Psychology: Animal Behavior Processes, 19*, 195–214.

Brown, P. L., & Jenkins, H. M. (1968). Auto-shaping of the pigeon's key-peck. *Journal of the Experimental Analysis of Behavior, 11*, 1–8.

Brown, R. T., & Wagner, A. R. (1964). Resistance to punishment and extinction following training with shock or non-reinforcement. *Journal of Experimental Psychology, 68*, 503–507.

Burish, T. G., Levy, S. M., & Meyerowitz, B. E. (Eds.). (1985). *Cancer, nutrition and eating behavior: A biobehavioral perspective*. Hillsdale, NJ: Lawrence Erlbaum Associates, Inc.

Burkhardt, P. E., & Ayres, J. J. (1978). CS and US duration effects in one-trial simultaneous fear conditioning as assessed by conditioned suppression of licking in rats. *Animal Learning & Behavior, 6*, 225–230.

Bush, R. R., & Mosteller, F. (1955). *Stochastic models for learning*. New York: John Wiley and Sons, Inc.

Buss, D. M., Haselton, M. G., Shackelford, T. K., Bleske, A. L., & Wakefield, J. C. (1998). Adaptations, exaptations, and spandrels. *American Psychologist, 53*, 533–548.

Cabanac, M. (1971). Physiological role of pleasure. *Science, 173*, 1103–1107.

Cade, W. H. (1981). Alternative male strategies: Genetic differences in crickets. *Science, 212*, 563–564.

Cameron, J., & Pierce, W. D. (1994). Reinforcement, reward, and intrinsic motivation: A meta-analysis. *Review of Educational Research, 64*, 363–423.

Camp, D. S., Raymond, G. A., & Church, R. M. (1967). Temporal relationship between response and punishment. *Journal of Experimental Psychology, 74*, 114–123.

Campbell, B. A. (1964). Theory and research on the effects of water deprivation on random activity in the rat. In M. J. Wayner (Ed.), *Thirst*. Oxford: Pergamon.

Campbell, B. A., & Jaynes, J. (1966). Reinstatement. *Psychological Review, 73*, 478–480.

Campbell, B. A., & Sheffield, F. D. (1953). Relation of random activity to food deprivation. *Journal of Comparative and Physiological Psychology, 46*, 320–322.

Campbell, B. A., Smith, N. F., Misanin, J. R., & Jaynes, J. (1966). Species differences in activity during hunger and thirst. *Journal of Comparative and Physiological Psychology, 61*, 123–127.

Cantor, M. B., & Wilson, J. F. (1985). Feeding the face: New directions in adjunctive behavior research. In F. R. Brush, & J. B. Overmier (Eds.), *Affect, conditioning, and cognition: Essays on the determinants of behavior* (Vol. 299–314). Hillsdale, NJ: Erlbaum.

Capaldi, E. D., Campbell, D. H., Sheffer, J. D., & Bradford, J. P. (1987). Conditioned flavor preferences based on delayed caloric consequences. *Journal of Experimental Psychology: Animal Behavior Processes, 13*, 150–155.

Capaldi, E. J. (1964). Effect of N-length, number of different N-lengths, and number of reinforcements on resistance to extinction. *Journal of Experimental Psychology, 68*, 230–239.

Capaldi, E. J. (1967). A sequential hypothesis of instrumental learning. In K. W. Spence & J. T. Spence (Eds.), *The psychology of learning and motivation: I* (pp. 1–65). New York: Academic Press.

Capaldi, E. J. (1978). Effects of schedule and delay of reinforcement on acquisition speed. *Animal Learning & Behavior, 6,* 330–334.

Capaldi, E. J. (1994). The sequential view: From rapidly fading stimulus traces to the organization of memory and the abstract concept of number. *Psychonomic Bulletin & Review, 1,* 156–181.

Capaldi, E. J., & Birmingham, K. M. (1998). Reward produced memories regulate memory-discrimination learning, extinction, and other forms of discrimination learning. *Journal of Experimental Psychology: Animal Behavior Processes, 24,* 254–264.

Capaldi, E. J., & Capaldi, E. D. (1970). A discrepancy between anticipated reward and obtained reward with no increase in resistance to extinction. *Psychonomic Science, 18,* 19–21.

Capaldi, E. J., & Spivey, J. E. (1963). Effect of goal box similarity on the after-effect of nonreinforcement and resistance to extinction. *Journal of Experimental Psychology, 66,* 461–465.

Capaldi, E. J., Davidson, T. L., & Myers, D. E. (1981). Resistance to satiation: Reinforcing effects of food and eating under satiation. *Learning and Motivation, 12,* 171–195.

Carr, J. A. R., & Wilkie, D. M. (1998). Characterization of the strategy used by rats in an interval time-place learning task. *Journal of Experimental Psychology: Animal Behavior Processes, 24,* 151–162.

Catania, A. C. (1963). Concurrent performances: A baseline for the study of reinforcement magnitude. *Journal of Experimental Analysis of Behavior, 6,* 253–253.

Catania, A. C. (1970). Reinforcement schedules and psychophysical judgments: A study of some temporal properties of behavior. In W. N. Schoenfeld (Ed.), *The theory of reinforcement schedules* (pp. 1–42). New York: Appleton-Century-Crofts.

Catania, A. C. (1998). *Learning* (4th ed.). Upper Saddle River, NJ: Prentice Hall.

Catania, A. C., & Reynolds, G. S. (1968). A quantitative analysis of the responding maintained by interval schedules of reinforcement. *Journal of the Experimental Analysis of Behavior, 11,* 327–383.

Catania, A. C., Matthews, T. J., Silverman, P. J., & Yohalem, R. (1977). Yoked variable-ration and variable-interval responding in pigeons. *Journal of the Experimental Analysis of Behavior, 28,* 155–161.

Cavoto, K. K., & Cook, R. G. (2001). Cognitive precedence for local information in hierarchical stimulus processing by pigeons. *Journal of Experimental Psychology: Animal Behavior Processes, 27,* 3–16.

Changizi, M. A., McGehee, R. M. F., & Hall, W. G. (2002). Evidence that appetitive responses for dehydration and food-deprivation are learned. *Physiology and Behavior, 75,* 295–304.

Chapman, G. B. (1991). Trial order affects cue interaction in contingency judgment. *Journal of Experimental Psychology: Learning, Memory, and Cognition, 17,* 837–854.

Chapman, G. B. (1998). Sooner or later: The psychology of intertemporal choice. In D. L. Medin (Ed.), *The psychology of learning and motivation: Advances in research and theory.* New York: Academic Press.

Chapman, G. B., & Robbins, S. J. (1990). Cue interaction in human contingency judgment. *Memory and Cognition, 18,* 537–545.

Cheng, K. (1986). A purely geometric module in the rat's spatial representation. *Cognition, 23,* 149–178.

Cheng, K., & Newcombe, N. S. (2005). Is there a geometric module for spatial orientation? Squaring theory and evidence. *Psychonomic Bulletin & Review, 12,* 1–23.

Cheng, K., & Spetch, M. L. (1998). Mechanisms of landmark use in mammals and birds. In S. Healy (Ed.), *Spatial representation in animals* (pp. 1–17). New York: Oxford University Press.

Cheng, K., Spetch, M. L., & Johnston, M. (1997). Spatial peak shift and generalization in pigeons. *Journal of Experimental Psychology: Animal Behavior Processes, 23,* 469–481.

Cheng, P. W. (1997). From covariation to causation: A causal power theory. *Psychological Review, 104,* 368–405.

Cheng, P. W., & Holyoak, K. J. (1995). Complex adaptive systems as intuitive statisticians: Causality, contingency, and prediction. In H. L. Roitblat & J.-A. Meyer (Eds.), *Comparative approaches to cognitive science. Complex adaptive systems* (pp. 271–302). Cambridge, MA: MIT Press.

Cheng, P. W., & Novick, L. R. (1992). Covariation in natural causal induction. *Psychological Review, 99,* 365–382.

Christian, K. M., & Thompson, R. F. (2003). Neural substrates of eyeblink conditioning: Acquisition and retention. *Learning and Memory, 10,* 427–455.

Chung, S.-H., & Herrnstein, R. J. (1967). Choice and delay of reinforcement. *Journal of the Experimental Analysis of Behavior, 10,* 67–74.

Church, R. M. (1969). Response suppression. In B. A. Campbell & R. M. Church (Eds.), *Punishment and aversive behavior* (pp. 111–156). New York: Appleton-Century-Crofts.

Church, R. M. (1989). Theories of timing behavior. In R. R. Mowrer & S. B. Klein (Eds.), *Contemporary learning theories: Instrumental conditioning theory and impact of biological constraints on learning* (pp. 41–71). Hillsdale, NJ: Erlbaum.

Church, R. M., & Broadbent, H. A. (1990). Alternative representations of time, number, and rate. *Cognition, 37,* 55–81.

Church, R. M., & Deluty, M. Z. (1977). Bisection of temporal intervals. *Journal of Experimental Psychology: Animal Behavior Processes, 3,* 216–228.

Church, R. M., & Gibbon, J. (1982). Temporal generalization. *Journal of Experimental Psychology: Animal Behavior Processes, 8,* 165–186.

Church, R. M., Lolordo, V. M., Overmier, J. B., Solomon, R. L., & Turner, L. H. (1966). Cardiac responses to shock in curarized dogs: Effects of shock intensity and duration, warning signal, and prior experience with shock. *Journal of Comparative and Physiological Psychology, 62,* 1–7.

Churchill, M., Remington, B., & Siddle, D. A. (1987). The effects of context change on long-term habituation of the orienting response in humans. *Quarterly Journal of Experimental Psychology B, 39,* 315–338.

Clark, R. E., & Squire, L. R. (1998). Classical conditioning and brain systems: The role of awareness. *Science, 280,* 77–81.

Clayton, N. S., & Dickinson, A. (1999). Scrub jays (*Aphelocoma coerulescens*) remember the relative time of caching as well as the location and content of their caches. *Journal of Comparative Psychology, 113,* 403–416.

Clayton, N. S., Griffiths, D. P., & Dickinson, A. (2000). Declarative and episodic-like memory in animals: Personal musings of a Scrub Jay. In C. Heyes, & L. Huber (Eds.), *The evo-*

lution of cognition (pp. 273–288). Cambridge, MA: MIT Press.

Clayton, N. S., Yu, K. S., & Dickinson, A. (2001). Scrub jays (*Aphelocoma coerulescens*) form integrated memories of the multiple features of caching episodes. *Journal of Experimental Psychology: Animal Behavior Processes, 27*, 17–29.

Clayton, N. S., Yu, K. S., & Dickinson, A. (2003). Interacting cache memories: Evidence for flexible memory use by western scrub jays (*Aphelocoma californica*). *Journal of Experimental Psychology: Animal Behavior Processes, 29*, 14–22.

Cobos, P. L., Lopez, F. J., Cano, A., Almaraz, J., & Shanks, D. R. (2002). Mechanisms of predictive and diagnostic causal induction. *Journal of Experimental Psychology: Animal Behavior Processes, 28*, 331–346.

Cohen, P. S., Looney, T. A., Campagnoni, F. R., & Lawler, C. P. (1985). A two-state model of reinforcer-induced motivation. In F. R. Brush & J. B. Overmier (Eds.), *Affect, conditioning, and cognition: Essays on the determinants of behavior* (pp. 281–297). Hillsdale, N.J.: Erlbaum.

Collett, T. S., Cartwright, B. A., & Smith, B. A. (1986). Landmark learning and visuospatial memories in gerbils. *Journal of Comparative Physiology A, 170*, 435–442.

Collier, G. H. (1981). Determinants of choice. *Nebraska Symposium on Motivation, 29*, 69–127.

Collier, G., & Johnson, D. (1997). Motivation as a function of animal versus experimenter control. In M. E. Bouton & M. S. Fanselow (Eds.), *Learning, motivation, and cognition: The functional behaviorism of Robert C. Bolles* (pp. 117–129). Washington, DC: American Psychological Association.

Collier, G., & Levitsky, D. (1967). Defense of water balance in rats: Behavioral and physiological responses to depletion. *Journal of Comparative and Physiological Psychology, 64*, 59–67.

Collier, G., Hirsch, E., & Hamlin, P. H. (1972). The ecological determinants of reinforcement in the rat. *Physiology and Behavior, 9*, 705–716.

Collier, G., Hirsch, E., & Kanarek, R. B. (1977). The operant revisited. In W. K. Honig & J. E. R. Staddon (Eds.), *Handbook of operant behavior*. Englewood Cliffs, NJ: Prentice-Hall.

Collier, G., Levitsky, D., & Squibb, R. L. (1967). Instrumental performance as a function of the energy content of the diet. *Journal of Comparative and Physiological Psychology, 64*, 68–72.

Collins, B. N., & Brandon, T. H. (2002). Effects of extinction context and retrieval cues on alcohol cue reactivity among nonalcoholic drinkers. *Journal of Consulting and Clinical Psychology, 70*, 390–397.

Colwill, R. M. (1994). Associative representations of instrumental contingencies. In G. Bower (Ed.), *The psychology of learning and motivation* (Vol. 31, pp. 1–72). San Diego, CA: Academic Press.

Colwill, R. M., & Motzkin, D. K. (1994). Encoding of the unconditioned stimulus in Pavlovian conditioning. *Animal Learning & Behavior, 22*, 384–394.

Colwill, R. M., & Rescorla R. A. (1985a). Post-conditioning devaluation of a reinforcer affects instrumental responding. *Journal of Experimental Psychology: Animal Behavior Processes, 11*, 120–132.

Colwill, R. M., & Rescorla R. A. (1985b). Instrumental responding remains sensitive to reinforcer devaluation after extensive training. *Journal of Experimental Psychology: Animal Behavior Processes, 11*, 520–536.

Colwill, R. M., & Rescorla R. A. (1990a). Effect of reinforcer devaluation on discriminative control of instrumental behavior. *Journal of Experimental Psychology: Animal Behavior Processes, 16*, 40–47.

Colwill, R. M., & Rescorla R. A. (1990b). Evidence for the hierarchical structure of instrumental learning. *Animal Learning and Behavior, 18*, 71–82.

Colwill, R. M., & Rescorla, R. A. (1986). Associative structures in instrumental learning. In G. H. Bower (Ed.), *The psychology of learning and motivation* (Vol. 20, pp. 55–104). Orlando, FL: Academic Press.

Colwill, R. M., & Rescorla, R. A. (1988). Associations between the discriminative stimulus and the reinforcer in instrumental learning. *Journal of Experimental Psychology: Animal Behavior Processes, 14*, 155–164.

Colwill, R. M., & Triola, S. M. (2002). Instrumental responding remains under the control of the consequent outcome after extended training. *Behavioural Processes, 57*, 51–64.

Conger, R., & Killeen, P. (1974). Use of concurrent operants in small group research. *Pacific Sociological Review, 17*, 399–416.

Conway, M. A. (2005). Memory and the self. *Journal of Memory and Language, 53*, 594–628.

Cook, M., & Mineka, S. (1989). Observational conditioning of fear to fear-relevant versus fear-irrelevant stimuli in rhesus monkeys. *Journal of Abnormal Psychology, 98*, 448–459.

Cook, M., & Mineka, S. (1990). Selective associations in the observational conditioning of fear in rhesus monkeys. *Journal of Experimental Psychology: Animal Behavior Processes, 16*, 372–389.

Cook, M., Mineka, S., & Trumble, D. (1987). The role of response-produced and exteroceptive feedback in the attenuation of fear over the course of avoidance learning. *Journal of Experimental Psychology: Animal Behavior Processes, 13*, 239–249.

Cook, R. G. (1992). Dimensional organization and texture discrimination in pigeons. *Journal of Experimental Psychology: Animal Behavior Processes, 18*, 354–363.

Cook, R. G. (2001b). Hierarchical stimulus processing in pigeons. In R. G. Cook (Ed.), *Avian visual cognition* [Online]. Available: www.pigeon.psy.tufts.edu/avc/cook/

Cook, R. G. (Ed.) (2001a). *Avian visual cognition* [On-line]. Available: www.pigeon.psy.tufts.edu/avc/

Cook, R. G., & Katz, J. S. (1999). Dynamic object perception by pigeons. *Journal of Experimental Psychology: Animal Behavior Processes, 25*, 194–210.

Cook, R. G., Brown, M. F., & Riley, D. A. (1985). Flexible memory processing by rats: Use of prospective and retrospective information in the radial maze. *Journal of Experimental Psychology: Animal Behavior Processes, 11*, 453–469.

Cook, R. G., Cavoto, K. K., & Cavoto, B. R. (1995). Same–different texture discrimination and concept learning by pigeons. *Journal of Experimental Psychology: Animal Behavior Processes, 21*, 253–260.

Cook, R. G., Katz, J. S., & Cavoto, B. R. (1997). Pigeon same–different concept learning with multiple stimulus classes. *Journal of Experimental Psychology: Animal Behavior Processes, 23*, 417–433.

Cook, R. G., Levison, D. G., Gillet, S. R., & Blaisdell, A. P. (2005). Capacity and limits of associative memory in pigeons. *Psychonomic Bulletin & Review, 12*, 350–358.

Cooper, R. M., & Zubek, J. P. (1958). Effects of enriched and restricted early environments on the learning ability of bright and dull rats. *Canadian Journal of Psychology, 12,* 159–164.

Corbit, L. H., & Balleine B. W. (2005). Double dissociation of basolateral and central amygdala lesions on the general and outcome-specific forms of Pavlovian-instrumental transfer. *Journal of Neuroscience, 25,* 962–970.

Couvillon, P. A., & Bitterman, M. E. (1980). Some phenomena of associative learning in honeybees. *Journal of Comparative and Physiological Psychology, 94,* 878–885.

Couvillon, P. A., & Bitterman, M. E. (1984). The overlearning-extinction effect and successive negative contrast in honeybees (*Apis mellifera*). *Journal of Comparative Psychology, 98,* 100–109.

Couvillon, P. A., & Bitterman, M. E. (1985). Effect of experience with a preferred food on consummatory responding for a less preferred food in goldfish. *Animal Learning & Behavior, 13,* 433–438.

Couvillon, P. A., Ablan, C. D., & Bitterman, M. E. (1999). Exploratory studies of inhibitory conditioning in honeybees (*Apis mellifera*). *Journal of Experimental Psychology: Animal Behavior Processes, 25,* 103–112.

Couvillon, P. A., Ablan, C. D., Ferreira, T. P., & Bitterman, M. E. (2001). The rold of nonreinforcement in the learning of honeybees. *The Quarterly Journal of Experimental Psychology B: Comparative and Physiological Psychology, 54B,* 127–144.

Couvillon, P. A., Arakaki, L., & Bitterman, M. E. (1997). Intramodal blocking in honeybees. *Animal Learning & Behavior, 25,* 277–282.

Couvillon, P. A., Bumanglag, A. V., & Bitterman, M. E. (2003). Inhibitory conditioning in honeybees. *Quarterly Journal of Experimental Psychology B: Comparative and Physiological Psychology, 56B,* 359–370.

Couvillon, P. A., Campos, A. C., Bass, T. D., & Bitterman, M. E. (2001). Intermodal blocking in honeybees. *Quarterly Journal of Experimental Psychology B, 4,* 369–381.

Couvillon, P. A., Ferreira, T. P., & Bitterman, M. E. (2003). Delayed alternation in honeybees (*Apis mellifera*). *Journal of Comparative Psychology, 117,* 31–35.

Couvillon, P. A., Hsiung, R., Cooke, A. M., & Bitterman, M. E. (2005). The role of context in the inhibitory conditioning of honeybees. *Quarterly Journal of Experimental Psychology B: Comparative and Physiological Psychology, 48B,* 59–67.

Couvillon, P. A., Klosterhalfen, S., & Bitterman, M. E. (1983). Analysis of overshadowing in honeybees. *Journal of Comparative Psychology, 97,* 154–166.

Couvillon, P. A., Nagrampa, J. A., & Bitterman, M. E. (1994). Learning in honeybees (*Apis mellifera*) as a function of sucrose concentration: Analysis of the retrospective effect. *Journal of Comparative Psychology, 108,* 274–281.

Crawford, L. L., & Domjan, M. (1993). Sexual approach conditioning: Omission contingency tests. *Animal Learning & Behavior, 21,* 42–50.

Crespi, L. P. (1942). Quantitative variation of incentive and performance in the white rat. *American Journal of Psychology, 55,* 467–517.

Crombag, H. S., & Shaham, Y. (2002). Renewal of drug seeking by contextual cues after prolonged extinction in rats. *Behavioral Neuroscience, 116,* 169–173.

Crowell, C. R., Hinson, R. E., & Siegel, S. (1981). The role of conditional drug responses in tolerance to the hypothermic effects of ethanol. *Psychopharmacologia, 73,* 51–54.

Crystal, J. D. (1999). Systematic nonlinearities in the perception of temporal intervals. *Journal of Experimental Psychology: Animal Behavior Processes, 25,* 3–17.

Crystal, J. D. (2001). Circadian time perception. *Journal of Experimental Psychology: Animal Behavior Processes, 27,* 68–78.

Crystal, J. D. (2003). Nonlinearities in sensitivity to time: Implications for oscillator-based representations of interval and circadian clocks. In W. H. Meck (Ed.), *Functional and neural mechanisms of interval timing* (pp. 61–75). Boca Raton, FL: CRC Press.

Crystal, J. D., Church, R. M., & Broadbent, H. A. (1997). Systematic nonlinearities in the memory representation of time. *Journal of Experimental Psychology: Animal Behavior Processes, 23,* 267–282.

Cullen, E. (1957). Adaptations in the kittiwake to cliff-nesting. *Ibis, 99,* 275–302.

Cunningham, C. L. (1979). Alcohol as a cue for extinction: State dependency produced by conditioned inhibition. *Animal Learning & Behavior, 7,* 45–52.

Cunningham, C. L. (1994). Modulation of ethanol reinforcement by conditioned hyperthermia. *Psychopharmacology, 115,* 79–85.

Daly, H. B. (1969). Learning of a hurdle-jump response to escape cues paired with reduced reward or frustrative nonreward. *Journal of Experimental Psychology, 79,* 146–157.

Daly, H. B., & Daly, J. T. (1982). A mathematical model of reward and aversive nonreward: Its application in over 30 appetitive learning situations. *Journal of Experimental Psychology: General, 111,* 441–480.

Daly, H. B., & Daly, J. T. (1994). Persistence and the importance of nonreward: Some applications of frustration theory and DMOD. *Psychonomic Bulletin & Review, 1,* 311–317.

Darwin, C. (1859). *On the origin of species by means of natural selection.* London: John Murray.

Darwin, C. (1871). *The descent of man and selection in relation to sex.* London: John Murray.

Davey, G. C. (1992). Classical conditioning and the acquisition of human fears and phobias: A review and synthesis of the literature. *Advances in Behaviour Research and Therapy, 14,* 29–66.

Davidson, T. L. (1993). The nature and function of interoceptive signals to feed: Toward integration of physiological and learning perspectives. *Psychological Review, 100,* 640–657.

Davidson, T. L. (1998). Hunger cues as modulatory stimuli. In N. A. Schmajuk & P. C. Holland (Eds.), *Occasion setting: Associative learning and cognition in animals* (pp. 223–248). Washington, DC: American Psychological Association.

Davidson, T. L., Aparicio, J., & Rescorla, R. A. (1988). Transfer between Pavlovian facilitators and instrumental discriminative stimuli. *Animal Learning and Behavior, 16,* 285–291.

Davis, C. M. (1928). Self-selection of diet by newly weaned infants: An experimental study. *American Journal of Diseases in Children, 36,* 651–679.

Davis, M. (1970). Effects of interstimulus interval length and variability on startle-response habituation in the rat. *Journal of Comparative and Physiological Psychology, 72,* 177–192.

Davis, M. (1992). The role of the amygdala in conditioned fear. In J. P. Aggleton (Ed.), *The amygdala: Neurobiological aspects of emotion, memory, and mental dysfunction* (pp. 255–306). New York: Wiley-Liss.

Davison, M., & McCarthy, D. (1988). *The matching law: A research review*. Hillsdale, NJ: Lawrence Erlbaum Associates, Inc.

Dawkins, R. (1986). *The blind watchmaker*. New York: Norton.

Dawkins, R. (1989). *The selfish gene*. Oxford: Oxford University Press.

Dawson, M. E., & Schell, A. M. (1985). Information processing and human autonomic classical conditioning. In P. K. Ackles, J. R. Jennings, & M. G. H. Coles (Eds.), *Advances in psychophysiology* (Vol. 1, pp. 89–165). Greenwich, CT: JAI Press.

De Houwer, J., & Beckers, T. (2002). A review of recent developments in research and theories on human contingency learning. *Quarterly Journal of Experimental Psychology B, 4,* 289–310.

De Houwer, J., Crombez, G., & Baeyens, F. (2005). Avoidance behavior can function as a negative occasion setter. *Journal of Experimental Psychology: Animal Behavior Processes, 31,* 101–106.

de la Mettrie, J. (1912). *Man a machine*. (French original, 1748 ed.). La Salle, IL: Open Court.

Deci, E. L. (1971). Effects of externally mediated rewards on intrinsic motivation. *Journal of Personality and Social Psychology, 18,* 105–115.

Deci, E. L., & Ryan, R. M. (1985). *Intrinsic motivation and self-determination in human behavior*. New York: Plenum Press.

Deci, E. L., Koestner, R., & Ryan, R. M. (1999). A meta-analytic review of experiments examining the effects of extrinsic rewards on intrinsic motivation. *Psychological Bulletin, 125,* 627–668.

DeCola, J. P., & Fanselow, M. S. (1995). Differential inflation with short and long CS-US intervals: Evidence of a nonassociative process in long-delay taste avoidance. *Animal Learning & Behavior, 23,* 154–163.

Delamater, A. R. (1996). Effects of several extinction treatments upon the integrity of Pavlovian stimulus-outcome associations. *Animal Learning & Behavior, 24,* 437–449.

Delamater, A. R. (1997). Selective reinstatement of stimulus-outcome associations. *Animal Learning & Behavior, 25,* 400–412.

Denniston, J. C., Savastano, H. I., & Miller, R. R. (2001). The extended comparator hypothesis: Learning by contiguity, responding by relative strength. In R. R. Mowrer & S. B. Klein (Eds.), *Handbook of contemporary learning theories* (pp. 65–117). Mahwah, NJ: Erlbaum.

Descartes, R. (1912). *A discourse on method* (French original, 1637 ed.). London: Dent.

Dess, N. K., & Overmier, J. B. (1989). General learned irrelevance: Proactive effects on Pavlovian conditioning in dogs. *Learning and Motivation, 20,* 1–14.

DeVito, P. L., & Fowler, H. (1986). Effects of contingency violations on the extinction of a conditioned fear inhibitor and a conditioned fear excitor. *Journal of Experimental Psychology: Animal Behavior Processes, 12,* 99–115.

Dews, P. B. (1970). The theory of fixed-interval responding. In W. N. Schoenfeld (Ed.), *The theory of reinforcement schedules*. New York: Appleton-Century-Crofts.

Dickinson, A. (1980). *Contemporary animal learning theory*. Cambridge, England: Cambridge University Press.

Dickinson, A. (1989). Expectancy theory in animal conditioning. In S. B. Klein & R. R. Mowrer (Eds.), *Contemporary learning theories: Pavlovian conditioning and the status of traditional learning theory* (pp. 279–308). Hillsdale, N.J.: L. Erlbaum Associates.

Dickinson, A. (1994). Instrumental conditioning. In N. J. Mackintosh (Ed.), *Animal cognition and learning* (pp. 4–79). London: Academic Press.

Dickinson, A., & Balleine, B. W. (1994). Motivational control of goal directed action. *Animal Learning and Behavior, 22,* 1–18.

Dickinson, A., & Balleine, B. W. (2002). The role of learning in the operation of motivational systems. In H. Pashler & R. Gallistel (Eds.), *Steven's handbook of experimental psychology* (Vol. 3: Learning, motivation, and emotion). Hoboken, NJ: John Wiley & Sons.

Dickinson, A., & Burke, J. (1996). Within-compound associations mediate the retrospective revaluation of causality judgments. *Quarterly Journal of Experimental Psychology B, 1,* 60–80.

Dickinson, A., & Dawson, G. R. (1989). Incentive learning and the motivational control of instrumental performance. *Quarterly Journal of Experimental Psychology B, 1,* 99–112.

Dickinson, A., & Dearing, M. F. (1979). Appetitive-aversive interactions and inhibitory processes. In A. Dickinson & R. A. Boakes (Eds.), *Mechanisms of learning and motivation* (pp. 203–231). Hillsdale, NJ: Lawrence Erlbaum Associates, Inc.

Dickinson, A., & Mulatero, C. W. (1989). Reinforcer specificity of the suppression of instrumental performance on a non-contingent schedule. *Behavioural Processes, 19,* 167–180.

Dickinson, A., Balleine, B., Watt, A., Gonzalez, F., & Boakes, R. A. (1995). Motivational control after extended instrumental learning. *Animal Learning & Behavior, 23,* 197–206.

Dickinson, A., Nicholas, D. J., & Adams, C. D. (1983). The effect of the instrumental training contingency on susceptibility to reinforcer devaluation. *Quarterly Journal of Experimental Psychology, 35B,* 35–51.

Dickinson, A., Shanks, D., & Evenden, J. (1984). Judgment of act-outcome contingency: The role of selective attribution. *Quarterly Journal of Experimental Psychology A, 36,* 29–50.

Dimberg, U., & Öhman, A. (1983). The effects of directional facial cues on electrodermal conditioning to facial stimuli. *Psychophysiology, 20,* 160–167.

Dinsmoor, J. A. (2001). Stimuli inevitably generated by behavior that avoids electric shock are inherently reinforcing. *Journal of the Experimental Analysis of Behavior, 75,* 311–333.

Dodwell, P. C., & Humphrey, G. K. (1990). A functional theory of the McCollough effect. *Psychological Review, 97,* 78–89.

Domjan, M. (1983). Biological constraints on instrumental and classical conditioning: Implications for general process theory. In G. H. Bower (Ed.), *The psychology of learning and motivation, Vol. 17* (pp. 215–277). New York: Academic Press.

Domjan, M. (1994). Formulation of a behavior system for sexual conditioning. *Psychonomic Bulletin & Review, 1,* 421–428.

Domjan, M. (1997). Behavior systems and the demise of equipotentiality: Historical antecedents and evidence from sexual conditioning. In M. E. Bouton & M. S. Fanselow (Eds.), *Learning, motivation, and cognition: The functional behaviorism of Robert C. Bolles.* (pp. 31–51). Washington, D.C.: American Psychological Association.

Domjan, M. (1998). Going wild in the laboratory: Learning about species typical cues. In D. L. Medin (Ed.), *The psy-*

chology of learning and motivation: Advances in research and theory, Vol. 38 (pp. 155–186). New York: Academic Press, Inc.

Domjan, M. (2005). Pavlovian conditioning: A functional perspective. *Annual Review of Psychology, 56,* 179–206.

Domjan, M., & Galef, B. G. (1983). Biological constraints on instrumental and classical conditioning: Retrospect and prospect. *Animal Learning & Behavior, 11,* 151–161.

Domjan, M., & Hall, S. (1986). Sexual dimorphism in the social proximity behavior of Japanese quail (*Coturnix coturnix japonica*). *Journal of Comparative Psychology, 100,* 68–71.

Domjan, M., & Hollis, K. L. (1988). Reproductive behavior: A potential model system for adaptive specializations in learning. In R. C. Bolles & M. D. Beecher (Eds.), *Evolution and learning.* (pp. 213–237). Hillsdale, NJ: Lawrence Erlbaum Associates, Inc.

Domjan, M., & Purdy, J. E. (1985). Animal research in psychology: More than meets the eye of the general psychology student. *American Psychologist, 50,* 496–503.

Domjan, M., & Wilson, N. E. (1972). Specificity of cue to consequence in aversion learning in the rat. *Psychonomic Science, 26,* 143–145.

Domjan, M., Akins, C., & Vandergriff, D. H. (1992). Increased responding to female stimuli as a result of sexual experience: Tests of mechanisms of learning. *Quarterly Journal of Experimental Psychology B, 2,* 139–157.

Domjan, M., Blesbois, E., & Williams, J. (1998). The adaptive significance of sexual conditioning: Pavlovian control of sperm release. *Psychological Science, 9,* 411–415.

Domjan, M., Greene, P., & North, N. C. (1989). Contextual conditioning and the control of copulatory behavior by species-specific sign stimuli in male Japanese quail. *Journal of Experimental Psychology: Animal Behavior Processes, 15,* 147–153.

Domjan, M., Huber-McDonald, M., & Holloway, K. S. (1992). Conditioning copulatory behavior to an artificial object: Efficacy of stimulus fading. *Animal Learning & Behavior, 20,* 350–362.

Domjan, M., Lyons, R., North, N. C., & Bruell, J. (1986). Sexual Pavlovian conditioned approach behavior in male Japanese quail (*Coturnix coturnix japonica*). *Journal of Comparative Psychology, 100,* 413–421.

Donahoe, J. W. (1998). Positive reinforcement: The selection of behavior. In W. T. O'Donohue (Ed.), *Learning and behavior therapy* (pp. 169–187). Boston, MA: Allyn & Bacon.

Donahoe, J. W., & Burgos, J. E. (2000). Behavior analysis and revaluation. *Journal of the Experimental Analysis of Behavior, 74,* 331–346.

Donahoe, J. W., & Palmer, D. C. (1994). *Learning and complex behavior.* Boston, MA: Allyn and Bacon.

Donahoe, J. W., Burgos, J. E., & Palmer, D. C. (1993). A selectionist approach to reinforcement. *Journal of the Experimental Analysis of Behavior, 60,* 17–40.

Doyle, T. A., & Samson, H. H. (1988). Adjunctive alcohol drinking in humans. *Physiology and Behavior, 27,* 419–431.

Duda, J. J., & Bolles, R. C. (1963). Effects of prior deprivation, current deprivation, and weight loss on the activity of the hungry rat. *Journal of Comparative and Physiological Psychology, 56,* 569–571.

Dukas, R., & Kamil, A. C. (2001). Limited attention: The constraint underlying search image. *Behavioral Ecology, 12,* 192–199.

Dunham, P. (1977). The nature of the reinforcing stimulus. In W. K. Honig & J. E. Staddon (Eds.), *Handbook of operant behavior* (pp. 98–124). Englewood Cliffs, NJ: Prentice-Hall.

Durlach, P. J. (1989). Learning and performance in Pavlovian conditioning: Are failures of contiguity failures of learning or performance? In S. B. Klein & R. R. Mowrer (Eds.), *Contemporary learning theories: Pavlovian conditioning and the status of traditional learning theory* (pp. 19–59). Hillsdale, NJ: Lawrence Erlbaum Associates, Inc.

Durlach, P. J., & Rescorla, R. A. (1980). Potentiation rather than overshadowing in flavor-aversion learning: An analysis in terms of within-compound associations. *Journal of Experimental Psychology: Animal Behavior Processes, 6,* 175–187.

Dweck, C. S., & Wagner, A. R. (1970). Situational cues and correlation between CS and US as determinants of the conditioned emotional response. *Psychonomic Science, 18,* 145–147.

Dworkin, B. R. (1993). *Learning and physiological regulation.* Chicago, IL: University of Chicago Press.

Dwyer, D. M., Bennett, C. H., & Mackintosh, N. J. (2001). Evidence for inhibitory associations between the unique elements of two compound flavours. *Quarterly Journal of Experimental Psychology, 54B,* 97–108.

Dwyer, D. M., Mackintosh, N. J., & Boakes, R. A. (1998). Simultaneous activation of the representations of absent cues results in the formation of an excitatory association between them. *Journal of Experimental Psychology: Animal Behavior Processes, 24,* 163–171.

Edhouse, W. V., & White, K. G. (1988). Sources of proactive interference in animal memory. *Journal of Experimental Psychology: Animal Behavior Processes, 14,* 56–70.

Edmunds, M. (1974). *Defense in animals.* Harlow, Essex: Longman.

Ehlers, A., Hackmann, A., & Michael, T. (2004). Intrusive re-experiencing in post-traumatic stress disorder: Phenomenology, theory, and therapy. *Memory, 12,* 403–415.

Eibl-Ebesfeldt, I. (1989). *Human ethology.* New York: Aldine de Gruyter.

Eibl-Eibesfeldt, I. (1970). *Ethology: The biology of behavior.* New York: Holt Rinehard and Winston.

Eibl-Eibesfeldt, I. (1979). Human ethology: Concepts and implications for the sciences of man. *Behavioral and Brain Sciences, 2,* 1–57.

Eikelboom, R., & Stewart, J. (1982). Conditioning of drug-induced physiological responses. *Psychological Review, 89,* 507–528.

Eisenberger, R. (1992). Learned industriousness. *Psychological Review, 99,* 248–267.

Eisenberger, R., & Cameron, J. (1996). Detrimental effects of reward: Reality or myth? *American Psychologist, 51,* 1153–1166.

Eisenberger, R., Karpman, M., & Trattner, J. (1967). What is the necessary and sufficient condition for reinforcement in the contingency situation? *Journal of Experimental Psychology, 74,* 342–350.

Eiserer, L. A., & Hoffman, H. S. (1973). Priming of ducklings' responses by presenting an imprinted stimulus. *Journal of Comparative and Physiological Psychology, 82,* 345–359.

Ellen, P., Soteres, B. J., & Wages, C. (1984). Problem solving in the rat: Piecemeal acquisition of cognitive maps. *Animal Learning & Behavior, 12,* 232–237.

Elliott, M. H. (1928). The effect of change of reward on the maze performance of rats. *University of California Publications in Psychology, 4,* 19–30.

Ellison, G. D., & Konorski, J. (1964). Separation of the salivary and motor responses in instrumental conditioning. *Science, 146,* 1071–1073.

Epstein, S. (1967). Toward a unified theory of anxiety. In B. Maher (Ed.), *Progress in experimental personality research* (pp. 1–89). New York: Academic Press.

Ernst, A. J., Engberg, L., & Thomas, D. R. (1971). On the form of stimulus generalization curves for visual intensity. *Journal of the Experimental Analysis of Behavior, 16,* 177–180.

Esber, G. R., McGregor, A., Good, M. A., Hayward, A., & Pearce, J. M. (2005). Transfer of spatial behaviour controlled by a landmark array with a distinctive shape. *Quarterly Journal of Experimental Psychology, 58,* 69–91.

Estes, W. K. (1950). Toward a statistical theory of learning. *Psychological Review, 57,* 94–107.

Estes, W. K. (1955). Statistical theory of distributional phenomena in learning. *Psychological Review, 62,* 369–377.

Estes, W. K. (1959). Component and pattern models with Markovian interpretation. In R. R. Bush & W. K. Estes (Eds.), *Studies in mathematical learning theory* (pp. 239–263). Stanford, CA: Stanford University Press.

Estes, W. K., & Skinner, B. F. (1941). Some quantitative properties of anxiety. *Journal of Experimental Psychology, 29,* 390–400.

Etienne, A. S. (1992). Navigation of a small mammal by dead reckoning and local cues. *Current Directions in Psychological Science, 1,* 48–52.

Etienne, A. S., Berlie, J., Georgakopoulos, J., & Maurer, R. (1998). Role of dead reckoning in navigation. In S. Healy (Ed.), *Spatial representation in animals* (pp. 54–68). New York: Oxford University Press.

Eysenck, H. J. (1979). The conditioning model of neurosis. *Behavioral and Brain Sciences, 2,* 155–199.

Falk, J. L. (1961). Production of polydipsia in normal rats by an intermittent food schedule. *Science, 133,* 195.

Falk, J. L. (1977). The origin and functions of adjunctive behavior. *Animal Learning and Behavior, 5,* 325–335.

Falk, J. L., & Kupfer, A. S. (1998). Adjunctive behavior: Application to the analysis and treatment of behavior problems. In W. O'Donohue (Ed.), *Learning and behavior therapy* (pp. 334–351). Needham Heights, MA: Allyn & Bacon.

Falk, J. L., Samson, H. H., & Winger, G. (1972). Behavioral maintenance of high concentrations of blood ethanol and physical dependence in the rat. *Science, 177,* 811–813.

Fanselow, M. S. (1979). Naloxone attenuates rat's preference for signaled shock. *Physiological Psychology, 7,* 70–74.

Fanselow, M. S. (1980). Conditional and unconditional components of post-shock freezing. *Pavlovian Journal of Biological Sciences, 15,* 177–182.

Fanselow, M. S. (1982). The post-shock activity burst. *Animal Learning and Behavior, 190,* 448–454.

Fanselow, M. S. (1985). Odors released by stressed rats produce opioid analgesia in unstressed rats. *Behavioral Neuroscience, 99,* 589–592.

Fanselow, M. S. (1989). The adaptive function of conditioned defensive behavior: An ecological approach to Pavlovian stimulus-substitution theory. In R. J. Blanchard, P. F. Brain., D. C. Blanchard, & S. Parmigiani (Eds.), *Ethoexperimental approaches to thte study of behavior* (pp. 151–166). New York: Kluwer Academic/Plenum Publishers.

Fanselow, M. S. (1990). Factors governing one-trial contextual conditioning. *Animal Learning & Behavior, 18,* 264–270.

Fanselow, M. S. (1994). Neural organization of the defensive behavior system responsible for fear. *Psychonomic Bulletin and Review, 1,* 429–438.

Fanselow, M. S., & Baackes, M. P. (1982). Conditioned fear-induced opiate analgesia on the formalin test: Evidence for two aversive motivational systems. *Learning and Motivation, 13,* 200–221.

Fanselow, M. S., & Birk, J. (1982). Flavor-flavor associations induce hedonic shifts in taste preference. *Animal Learning & Behavior, 10,* 223–228.

Fanselow, M. S., & Lester, L. S. (1988). A functional behavioristic approach to aversively motivated behavior: Predatory imminence as a determinant of the topography of defensive behavior. In R. C. Bolles & M. D. Beecher (Eds.), *Evolution and learning* (pp. 185–212). Hillsdale, NJ: Lawrence Erlbaum Associates.

Fanselow, M. S., & Poulos, A. M. (2005). The neuroscience of mammalian associative learning. *Annual Review of Psychology, 56,* 207–234.

Fantino, E. (1969). Choice and rate of reinforcement. *Journal of the Experimental Analysis of Behavior, 12,* 723–730.

Fantino, E. (1977). Conditioned reinforcement: Choice and information. In W. K. Honig & J. E. Staddon (Eds.), *Handbook of operant behavior* (pp. 313–339). Englewood Cliffs, NJ: Prentice Hall.

Fedorchak, P. M., & Bolles, R. C. (1987). Hunger enhances the expression of calorie- but not taste-mediated conditioned flavor preferences. *Journal of Experimental Psychology: Animal Behavior Processes, 13,* 73–79.

Fedorchak, P. M., & Bolles, R. C. (1988). Nutritive expectancies mediate cholecystokinin's suppression-of-intake effect. *Behavioral Neuroscience, 102,* 451–455.

Ferster, C. B., & Skinner, B. F. (1957). *Schedules of reinforcement.* East Norwalk, CT: Appleton-Century-Crofts.

Fetterman, J. G. (1996). Dimensions of stimulus complexity. *Journal of Experimental Psychology: Animal Behavior Processes, 22,* 3–18.

Findley, J. D. (1958). Preference and switching under concurrent scheduling. *Journal of the Experimental Analysis of Behavior, 1,* 123–144.

Fitzsimons, T. J., & Le Magnen, J. (1969). Eating as a regulatory control of drinking in the rat. *Journal of Comparative and Physiological Psychology, 67,* 273–283.

Flaherty, C. F. (1985). *Animal learning and cognition.* New York: Alfred A. Knopf.

Flaherty, C. F. (1991). Incentive contrast and selected animal models of anxiety. In L. Dachowski & C. F. Flaherty (Eds.), *Current topics in animal learning: Brain, emotion and cognition* (pp. 207–243). Hillsdale, NJ: Lawrence Erlbaum Associates, Inc.

Flaherty, C. F. (1996). *Incentive relativity.* New York: Cambridge University Press.

Flaherty, C. F., Becker, H. C., & Checke, S. (1983). Repeated successive contrast in consummatory behavior with repeated shifts in sucrose concentration. *Animal Learning & Behavior, 11,* 407–414.

Flaherty, C. F., Becker, H. C., & Pohorecky, L. (1985). Correlation of corticosterone elevation and negative contrast varies as a function of postshift day. *Animal Learning & Behavior, 13*, 309–314.

Flaherty, C. F., Lombardi, B. R., Wrightson, J., & Deptula, D. (1980). Conditions under which chlordiazepoxide influences gustatory contrast. *Psychopharmacologia, 67*, 269–277.

Foltin, R. W. (1991). An economic analysis of "demand" for food in baboons. *Journal of the Experimental Analysis of Behavior, 56*, 445–454.

Forestell, C. A., & LoLordo, V. M. (2003). Palatability shifts in taste and flavor preference conditioning. *Quarterly Journal of Experimental Psychology B, 1*, 140–160.

Friedman, B. X., Blaisdell, A. P., Escobar, M., & Miller, R. R. (1998). Comparator mechanisms and conditioned inhibition: Conditioned stimulus preexposure disrupts Pavlovian conditioned inhibition but not explicitly unpaired inhibition. *Journal of Experimental Psychology: Animal Behavior Processes, 24*, 453–466.

Funayama, E. S., Couvillon, P. A., & Bitterman, M. E. (1995). Compound conditioning in honeybees: Blocking tests of the independence assumption. *Animal Learning & Behavior, 23*, 429–437.

Gale, G. D., Anagnostaras, S. G., Godsil, B. P., Mitchell, S., Nozawa, T., Sage, J. R., Wiltgen, B., & Fanselow, M. S. (2004). Role of the basolateral amygdala in the storage of fear memories across the adult lifetime of rats. *Journal of Neuroscience, 24*, 3810–3815.

Galef, B. G. (1991). A contrarian view of the wisdom of the body as it relates to dietary self-selection. *Psychological Review, 98*, 218–223.

Gallistel, C. R. (1990). *The organization of learning.* Cambridge, MA: MIT Press.

Gallistel, C. R. (1994). Space and time. In N. J. Mackintosh (Ed.), *Animal learning and cognition* (pp. 221–253). San Diego: Academic Press.

Gallistel, C. R., & Gibbon, J. (2000). Time, rate, and conditioning. *Psychological Review, 107*, 289–344.

Garb, J. L., & Stunkard, A. J. (1974). Taste aversions in man. *American Journal of Psychiatry, 131*, 1204–1207.

Garcia, J. (1989). Food for Tolman: Cognition and cathexis in concert. In T. Archer & L.-G. Nilsson (Eds.), *Aversion, avoidance, and anxiety: Perspectives on aversively motivated behavior* (pp. 45–85). Hillsdale, NJ: Lawrence Erlbaum Associates, Inc.

Garcia, J., & Koelling, R. A. (1966). Relation of cue to consequence in avoidance learning. *Psychonomic Science, 4*, 123–124.

Garcia, J., Ervin, F. R., & Koelling, R. A. (1966). Learning with prolonged delay of reinforcement. *Psychonomic Science, 5*, 121–122.

Garcia, J., Hankins, W. G., & Rusiniak, K. W. (1974). Behavioral regulation of the milieu interne in man and rat. *Science, 185*, 824–831.

Garcia, J., Kimeldorf, D. J., & Koelling, R. A. (1955). Conditioned aversion to saccharin resulting from exposure to gamma radiation. *Science, 122*, 157–158.

Gemberling, G. A., & Domjan, M. (1982). Selective associations in one-day-old rats: Taste-toxicosis and texture-shock aversion learning. *Journal of Comparative and Physiological Psychology, 96*, 105–113.

George, D. N., & Pearce, J. M. (1999). Acquired distinctiveness is controlled by stimulus relevance not correlation

with reward. *Journal of Experimental Psychology: Animal Behavior Processes, 25*, 363–373.

George, D. N., & Pearce, J. M. (2003). Visual search asymmetry in pigeons. *Journal of Experimental Psychology: Animal Behavior Processes, 29*, 118–129.

Gibbon, J. (1991). Origins of scalar timing. *Learning and Motivation, 22*, 3–38.

Gibbon, J., & Balsam, P. (1981). Spreading association in time. In C. Locurto, H. S. Terrace, & J. Gibbon (Eds.), *Autoshaping and conditioning theory* (pp. 219–235). New York: Academic Press.

Gibbon, J., & Church, R. M. (1984). Sources of variance in an information processing theory of timing. In H. L. Roitblat, T. G. Bever, & H. S. Terrace (Eds.), *Animal Cognition* (pp. 465–488). Hillsdale, NJ: Erlbaum.

Gibbon, J., Baldock, M. D., Locurto, C., Gold, L., & Terrace, H. S. (1977). Trial and intertrial durations in autoshaping. *Journal of Experimental Psychology: Animal Behavior Processes, 3*, 264–284.

Gibbon, J., Church, R. M., & Meck, W. H. (1984). Scalar timing in memory. *Annals of the New York Academy of Sciences, 423*, 52–77.

Gibbs, C. M., Latham, S. B., & Gormezano, I. (1978). Classical conditioning of the rabbit nictitating membrane response: Effects of reinforcement schedule on response maintenance and resistance to extinction. *Animal Learning & Behavior, 6*, 209–215.

Gibson, B. M., & Shettleworth, S. J. (2003). Competition among spatial cues in a naturalistic food-carrying task. *Learning & Behavior, 31*, 143–159.

Gibson, B. M., & Shettleworth, S. J. (2005). Place versus response learning revisited: Tests of blocking on the radial maze. *Behavioral Neuroscience, 119*, 567–586.

Gibson, E. J., & Wilson, R. D. (1956). The effect of prolonged exposure to visually presented patterns on learning to discriminate them. *Journal of Comparative and Physiological Psychology, 49*, 239–242.

Gibson, J. J., & Gibson, E. J. (1955). Perceptual learning: Differentiation or enrichment? *Psychological Review, 62*, 32–41.

Glazer, H. I., & Weiss, J. M. (1976). Long-term interference effect: An alternative to "learned helplessness." *Journal of Experimental Psychology: Animal Behavior Processes, 2*, 202–213.

Gleitman, H. (1971). Forgetting of long-term memories in animals. In W. K. Honig & H. James (Eds.), *Animal Memory.* New York, NY: Academic Press.

Gluck, M. A., & Bower, G. H. (1988). From conditioning to category learning: An adaptive network model. *Journal of Experimental Psychology: General, 117*, 227–247.

Gluck, M. A., & Myers, C. E. (1993). Hippocampal mediation of stimulus representation: A computational theory. *Hippocampus, 3*, 491–516.

Goddard, M. J. (1999). The role of US signal value in contingency, drug conditioning, and learned helplessness. *Psychonomic Bulletin & Review, 6*, 412–423.

Godden, D. R., & Baddeley, A. D. (1975). Context-dependent memory in two natural environments: On land and underwater. *British Journal of Psychology, 66*, 325–331.

Godden, D., & Baddeley, A. (1980). When does context influence recognition memory? *British Journal of Psychology, 71*, 99–104.

Gonzalez, F., Quinn, J. J., & Fanselow, M. S. (2003). Differential effects of adding and removing components of a context on the generalization of conditional freezing. *Journal of Experimental Psychology: Animal Behavior Processes, 29,* 78–83.

Gonzalez, R. C., Gentry, G. V., & Bitterman, M. E. (1954). Relational discrimination of intermediate size in the chimpanzee. *Journal of Comparative and Physiological Psychology, 47,* 385–388.

Goodyear, A. J., & Kamil, A. C. (2004). Clark's nutcrackers (*Nucifraga columbiana*) and the effects of goal-landmark distance on overshadowing. *Journal of Comparative Psychology, 118,* 258–264.

Gordon, W. C., & Weaver, M. S. (1989). Cue-induced transfer of CS preexposure effects across contexts. *Animal Learning & Behavior, 17,* 409–417.

Gordon, W. C., McCracken, K. M., Dess-Beech, N., & Mowrer, R. R. (1981). Mechanisms for the Cueing Phenomenon: The Addition of the Cueing Context to the Training Memory. *Learning and Motivation, 12,* 196–211.

Gordon, W. C., Smith, G. J., & Katz, D. S. (1979). Dual effects of response blocking following avoidance learning. *Behaviour Research and Therapy, 17,* 479–487.

Gordon, W. C., Taylor, J. R., & Mowrer, R. R. (1981). Enhancement of short-term retention in rats with pretest cues: Effects of the training-cueing interval and the specific cueing treatment. *American Journal of Psychology, 94,* 309–322.

Gormezano, I., Kehoe, E. J., & Marshall, B. S. (1983). Twenty years of classical conditioning research with the rabbit. *Progress in Psychobiology and Physiological Psychology, 10,* 197–275.

Gormezano, I., Prokasy, W. F., & Thompson, R. F. (Eds.). (1987). *Classical conditioning* (3rd ed.). Hillsdale, NJ: Lawrence Erlbaum Associates, Inc.

Gottlieb, G. (1965). Imprinting in relation to parental and species identification by avian neonates. *Journal of Comparative and Physiological Psychology, 59,* 345–356.

Gould, J. L. (1984). Natural history of honeybee learning. In P. Marler & H. S. Terrace (Eds.), *The biology of learning* (pp. 150–180). Berlin: Springer.

Gould, J. L. (1996). Specializations in honeybee learning. In C. F. Moss & S. J. Shettleworth (Eds.), *Neuroethological studies of cognitive and perceptual processes* (pp. 11–30). Princeton, NJ: Princeton University Press.

Gould, J. L., & Marler, P. (1987). Learning by instinct. *Scientific American, 256,* 74–85

Gould, S. J. (1991). Exaptation: A crucial tool for an evolutionary psychology. *Journal of Social Issues, 47,* 43–65.

Gould, S. J., & Vrba, E. S. (1982). Exaptation: A missing term in the science of form. *Paleobiology, 8,* 4–15.

Grace, R. C. (1994). A contextual model of concurrent-chains choice. *Journal of the Experimental Analysis of Behavior, 61,* 113–129.

Graham, M., Good, M. A., McGregor, A., & Pearce, J. M. (2006). Spatial learning based on the shape of the environment is influenced by properties of the objects forming the shape. *Journal of Experimental Psychology: Animal Behavior Processes, 32,* 44–59.

Grant, D. S. (1975). Proactive interference in pigeon short-term memory. *Journal of Experimental Psychology: Animal Behavior Processes, 1,* 207–220.

Grant, D. S. (1976). Effect of sampling presentation time in long-delay matching in the pigeon. *Learning and Motivation, 7,* 580–590.

Grant, D. S., & Roberts, W. A. (1973). Trace interaction in pigeon short-term memory. *Journal of Experimental Psychology, 101,* 21–29.

Grant, P. R., & Grant, B. R. (2002). Unpredictable evolution in a 30-year study of Darwin's finches. *Science, 296,* 707–711

Green, L., & Freed, D. E. (1998). Behavioral economics. In W. T. O'Donohue (Ed.), *Learning and behavior therapy* (pp. 274–300). Needham Heights, MA: Allyn and Bacon.

Green, L., Fisher, E. B., Perlow, S., & Sherman, L. (1981). Preference reversal and self control: Choice as a function of reward amount and delay. *Behaviour Analysis Letters, 1,* 43–51.

Grice, G. R. (1948). The relation of secondary reinforcement to delayed reward in visual discrimination learning. *Journal of Experimental Psychology, 38,* 1–16.

Grill, H. J., & Norgren, R. (1978). The taste reactivity test: I. Mimetic responses to gustatory stimuli in neurologically normal rats. *Brain Research, 143,* 263–279.

Grosch, J., & Neuringer, A. (1981). Self-control in pigeons under the Mischel paradigm. *Journal of the Experimental Analysis of Behavior, 35,* 3–21.

Grossen, N. E., & Kelley, M. J. (1972). Species-specific behavior and acquisition of avoidance in rats. *Journal of Comparative and Physiological Psychology, 81,* 307–310.

Groves, P. M., & Thompson, R. F. (1970). Habituation: A dual-process theory. *Psychological Review, 77,* 419–450.

Guthrie, E. R. (1935). *The psychology of learning.* New York: Harper.

Guthrie, E. R., & Horton, G. P. (1946). *Cats in a puzzle box.* New York: Rinehart.

Guttman, N., & Kalish, H. I. (1956). Discriminability and stimulus generalization. *Journal of Experimental Psychology, 51,* 79–88.

Hailman, J. P. (1967). The ontogeny of an instinct. *Behaviour Supplement, 15,* 1–159.

Hall, G. (1991). *Perceptual and associative learning.* Oxford: Clarendon Press.

Hall, G. (1996). Learning about associatively activated stimulus representations: Implications for acquired equivalence and perceptual learning. *Animal Learning and Behavior, 24,* 233–255.

Hall, G., & Channell, S. (1985). Differential effects of contextual change on latent inhibition and on the habituation of an orienting response. *Journal of Experimental Psychology: Animal Behavior Processes, 11,* 470–481.

Hall, G., & Pearce, J. M. (1979). Latent inhibition of a CS during CS-US pairings. *Journal of Experimental Psychology: Animal Behavior Processes, 5,* 31–42.

Hall, G., & Pearce, J. M. (1982). Restoring the associability of a pre-exposed CS by a surprising event. *Quarterly Journal of Experimental Psychology B, 3,* 127–140.

Hall, G., & Schachtman, T. R. (1987). Differential effects of a retention interval on latent inhibition and the habituation of an orienting response. *Animal Learning and Behavior, 15,* 76–82.

Hall, G., Channell, S., & Schachtman, T. R. (1987). The instrumental overshadowing effect in pigeons: The role of response bursts. *Quarterly Journal of Experimental Psychology B, 39,* 173–188.

Hall, G., Prados, J., & Sansa, J. (2005). Modulation of the effective salience of a stimulus by direct and associative activation of its representation. *Journal of Experimental Psychology: Animal Behavior Processes, 31,* 267–276.

Hall, W. G., Arnold, H. M., & Myers, K. P. (2000). The acquisition of an appetite. *Psychological Science, 11,* 101–105.

Hamilton, W. D. (1964). The genetical theory of social behavior: I and II. *Journal of Theoretical Biology, 7,* 1–52.

Hamm, J., Matheson, W. R., & Honig, W. K. (1997). Mental rotation in pigeons (*Columbia livia*). *Journal of Comparative Psychology, 111,* 76–81.

Hammond, L. J. (1980). The effect of contingency upon the appetitive conditioning of free-operant behavior. *Journal of the Experimental Analysis of Behavior, 34,* 297–304.

Hanson, H. M. (1959). Effects of discrimination training on stimulus generalization. *Journal of Experimental Psychology, 58,* 321–334.

Hayward, A., Good, M. A., & Pearce, J. M. (2004). Failure of a landmark to restrict spatial learning based on the shape of the environment. *Quarterly Journal of Experimental Psychology, 57,* 289–314.

Healy, A. F., Kosslyn, S. M., & Shiffrin, R. M. (1992). *Essays in honor of William K. Estes, Vol. 1: From learning theory to connectionist theory; Vol. 2: From learning processes to cognitive processes.* Hillsdale, NJ: Lawrence Erlbaum Associates, Inc.

Hearst, E., & Franklin, S. R. (1977). Positive and negative relations between a signal and food: Approach-withdrawal behavior to the signal. *Journal of Experimental Psychology: Animal Behavior Processes, 3,* 37–52.

Hearst, E., & Jenkins, H. M. (1974). *Sign-tracking: The stimulus-reinforcer relation and directed action.* Austin, TX: The Psychonomic Society.

Hendersen, R. W. (1978). Forgetting of conditioned fear inhibition. *Learning and Motivation, 9,* 16–30.

Hendersen, R. W. (1985). Fearful memories: The motivational significance of forgetting. In F. R. Brush & J. B. Overmier (Eds.), *Affect, conditioning and cognition: Essays on the determinants of behavior.* Hillsdale, NJ: Lawrence Erlbaum Associates, Inc.

Hendersen, R. W., & Graham, J. (1979). Avoidance of heat by rats: Effects of thermal context on rapidity of extinction. *Learning and Motivation, 10,* 351–363.

Hendersen, R. W., Patterson, J. M., & Jackson, R. L. (1980). Acquisition and retention of control of instrumental behavior by a cue-signaling airblast: How specific are conditioned anticipations? *Learning and Motivation, 11,* 407–426.

Herbranson, W. T., Fremouw, T., & Shimp, C. P. (1999). The randomization procedure in the study of categorization of multidimensional stimuli by pigeons. *Journal of Experimental Psychology: Animal Behavior Processes, 25,* 113–125.

Hermer, L., & Spelke, E. S. (1994). A geometric process for spatial reorientation in young children. *Nature, 370,* 57–59.

Herrnstein, R. J. (1961). Relative and absolute strength of response as a function of frequency of reinforcement. *Journal of the Experimental Analysis of Behavior, 4,* 267–272.

Herrnstein, R. J. (1969). Method and theory in the study of avoidance. *Psychological Review, 76,* 49–69.

Herrnstein, R. J. (1970). On the law of effect. *Journal of the Experimental Analysis of Behavior, 13,* 243–266.

Herrnstein, R. J. (1971). Quantitative hedonism. *Journal of Psychiatric Research, 8,* 399–412.

Herrnstein, R. J., & deVilliers, P. A. (1980). Fish as a natural category for people and pigeons. In G. H. Bower (Ed.), *The psychology of learning and motivation* (Vol. 14, pp. 59–95). New York: Academic Press.

Herrnstein, R. J., & Hineline, P. N. (1966). Negative reinforcement as shock frequency reduction. *Journal of the Experimental Analysis of Behavior, 9,* 421–430.

Herrnstein, R. J., & Loveland, D. H. (1964). Complex visual concept in the pigeon. *Science, 146,* 549–551.

Herrnstein, R. J., & Prelec, D. (1992). Melioration. In G. Loewenstein & J. Elster (Eds.), *Choice over time* (pp. 235–263). New York: Russell Sage.

Herrnstein, R. J., & Vaughan, W. (1980). Melioration and behavioral allocation. In J. E. Staddon (Ed.), *Limits to action: The allocation of individual behavior* (pp. 143–176). New York: Academic Press.

Herrnstein, R. J., Loveland, D. H., & Cable, C. (1976). Natural concepts in pigeons. *Journal of Experimental Psychology: Animal Behavior Processes, 2,* 285–302.

Heth, C. D. (1976). Simultaneous and backward fear conditioning as a function of number of CS-UCS pairings. *Journal of Experimental Psychology: Animal Behavior Processes, 2,* 117–129.

Hetherington, M. M., & Rolls, B. J. (1996). Sensory-specific satiety: Theoretical frameworks and central characteristics. In E. D. Capaldi (Ed.), *Why we eat what we eat: The psychology of eating* (pp. 267–290). Washington, DC: American Psychological Association.

Hicks, L. H. (1964). Effects of overtraining on acquisition and reversal of place and response learning. *Psychological Reports, 15,* 459–462.

Hinde, R. A. (1966). *Animal behavior: A synthesis of ethology and comparative psychology.* London: Academic Press.

Hinde, R. A. (1970). *Animal behavior* (2nd ed.). New York: McGraw-Hill.

Hinde, R. A., & Stevenson-Hinde, J. (1973). *Constraints on learning: Limitations and predispositions.* London: Academic Press.

Hineline, P. N. (2001). Beyond the molar-molecular distinction: We need multiscaled analyses. *Journal of the Experimental Analysis of Behavior, 75,* 342–347.

Hinson, R. E., Poulos, C. X., & Cappell, H. (1982). Effects of pentobarbital and cocaine in rats expecting pentobarbital. *Pharmacology, Biochemistry & Behavior, 16,* 661–666.

Hirsch, J. (1963). Behavior genetics and individuality understood. *Science, 142,* 1436–1442.

Hirsch, S. M., & Bolles, R. C. (1980). On the ability of prey to recognize predators. *Zeitschrift fur Tierpsychologie, 54,* 71–84.

Hobbes, T. (1650). *Human nature.* London.

Hoffman, H. S., & Ratner, A. M. (1973a). A reinforcement model of imprinting: Implications for socialization in monkeys and men. *Psychological Review, 80,* 527–544.

Hoffman, H. S., & Ratner, A. M. (1973b). Effects of stimulus and environmental familiarity on visual imprinting in newly hatched ducklings. *Journal of Comparative & Physiological Psychology, 85,* 11–19.

Hoffman, H. S., Eiserer, L. A., & Singer, D. (1972). Acquisition of behavioral control by a stationary imprinting stimulus. *Psychonomic Science, 26,* 146–148.

Hoffman, H. S., Ratner, A. M., & Eiserer, L. A. (1972). Role of visual imprinting in the emergence of specific filial attachments in ducklings. *Journal of Comparative & Physiological Psychology, 81,* 399–409.

Hoffman, H. S., Selekman, W., & Fleshler, M. (1966). Stimulus aspects of aversive controls: Long term effects of suppression procedures. *Journal of the Experimental Analysis of Behavior, 9*, 659–662.

Holland, P. C. (1977). Conditioned stimulus as a determinant of the form of the Pavlovian conditioned response. *Journal of Experimental Psychology: Animal Behavior Processes, 3*, 77–104.

Holland, P. C. (1979). The effects of qualitative and quantitative variation in the US on individual components of Pavlovian appetitive conditioned behavior in rats. *Animal Learning & Behavior, 7*, 424–432.

Holland, P. C. (1984). Differential effects of reinforcement of an inhibitory feature after serial and simultaneous feature negative discrimination training. *Journal of Experimental Psychology: Animal Behavior Processes, 10*, 461–475.

Holland, P. C. (1985). The nature of conditioned inhibition in serial and simultaneous feature negative discrimination. In R. R. Miller & N. E. Spear (Eds.), *Information processing in animals: Conditioned inhibition* (pp. 267–298). Hillsdale, NJ: Lawrence Erlbaum Associates, Inc.

Holland, P. C. (1986). Transfer after serial feature positive discrimination training. *Learning and Motivation, 17*, 243–268.

Holland, P. C. (1989a). Occasion setting with simultaneous compounds in rats. *Journal of Experimental Psychology: Animal Behavior Processes, 15*, 183–193.

Holland, P. C. (1989b). Transfer of negative occasion setting and conditioned inhibition across conditioned and unconditioned stimuli. *Journal of Experimental Psychology: Animal Behavior Processes, 15*, 311–328.

Holland, P. C. (1990a). Event representation in Pavlovian conditioning: Image and action. *Cognition, 37*, 105–131.

Holland, P. C. (1990b). Forms of memory in Pavlovian conditioning. In N. M. Weinberger, & G. Lynch (Eds.), *Brain organization and memory: Cells, systems, and circuits* (pp. 78–104). New York: Oxford University Press.

Holland, P. C. (1992). Occasion setting in Pavlovian conditioning. In G. Bower (Ed.), *The psychology of learning and motivation* (Vol. 28, pp. 69–125). Orlando, FL: Academic Press.

Holland, P. C. (1999). Overshadowing and blocking as acquisition deficits: No recovery after extinction of overshadowing or blocking cues. *Quarterly Journal of Experimental Psychology B: Comparative and Physiological Psychology, 52b*, 307–333.

Holland, P. C. (2000). Trial and intertrial durations in appetitive conditioning in rats. *Animal Learning & Behavior, 28*, 121–135.

Holland, P. C. (2004). Relations between Pavlovian-instrumental transfer and reinforcer devaluation. *Journal of Experimental Psychology: Animal Behavior Processes, 30*, 104–117.

Holland, P. C. (2005). Amount of training effects in representation-mediated food aversion learning: No evidence of a role for associability changes. *Learning & Behavior, 33*, 464–478.

Holland, P. C., & Rescorla, R. A. (1975a). Second-order conditioning with food unconditioned stimulus. *Journal of Comparative and Physiological Psychology, 88*, 459–467.

Holland, P. C., & Rescorla, R. A. (1975b). The effect of two ways of devaluing the unconditioned stimulus after first- and second-order appetitive conditioning. *Journal of Experimental Psychology: Animal Behavior Processes, 1*, 355–363.

Holland, P. C., & Straub, J. J. (1979). Differential effects of two ways of devaluing the unconditioned stimulus after Pavlovian appetitive conditioning. *Journal of Experimental Psychology: Animal Behavior Processes, 5*, 65–78.

Hollis, K. L. (1982). Pavlovian conditioning of signal-centered action patterns and autonomic behavior: A biological analysis of function. In R. A. Rosenblatt, R. A. Hinde, C. Beer, & M. C. Busnel (Eds.), *Advances in the study of behavior, Vol. 12* (pp. 1–64). New York: Academic Press.

Hollis, K. L. (1984). The biological function of Pavlovian conditioning: The best defense is a good offense. *Journal of Experimental Psychology: Animal Behavior Processes, 10*, 413–425.

Hollis, K. L. (1990). The role of Pavlovian conditioning in territorial aggression and reproduction. In D. A. Dewsbury (Ed.), *Contemporary issues in comparative psychology* (pp. 197–219). Sunderland, MA: Sinauer Associates, Inc.

Hollis, K. L. (1997). Contemporary research on Pavlovian conditioning: A "new" functional analysis. *American Psychologist, 52*, 956–965.

Hollis, K. L., Cadieux, E. L., & Colbert, M. M. (1989). The biological function of Pavlovian conditioning: A mechanism for mating success in the blue gourami (*Trichogaster trichopterus*). *Journal of Comparative Psychology, 103*, 115–121.

Hollis, K. L., Pharr, V. L., Dumas, M. J., Britton, G. B., & et al. (1997). Classical conditioning provides paternity advantage for territorial male blue gouramis (*Trichogaster trichopterus*). *Journal of Comparative Psychology, 111*, 219–225.

Honey, R. C., & Hall, G. (1989). Acquired equivalence and distinctiveness of cues. *Journal of Experimental Psychology: Animal Behavior Processes, 15*, 338–346.

Honey, R. C., & Hall, G. (1991). Acquired equivalence and distinctiveness of cues using a sensory-preconditioning procedure. *Quarterly Journal of Experimental Psychology, 43B*, 121–135.

Honey, R. C., & Watt, A. (1998). Acquired relational equivalence: Implications for the nature of associative structures. *Journal of Experimental Psychology: Animal Behavior Processes, 24*, 325–334.

Honig, W. K. (1962). Prediction of preference, transposition, and transposition-reversal from the generalization gradient. *Journal of Experimental Psychology, 64*, 239–248.

Honig, W. K., Boneau, C. A., Burstein, K. R., & Pennypacker, H. S. (1963). Positive and negative generalization gradients obtained under equivalent training conditions. *Journal of Comparative and Physiological Psychology, 56*, 111–116.

Howlett, R. J., & Majerus, M. E. N. (1987) The understanding of industrial melanism in the peppered moth (*Biston betularia*) (Lepidoptera: Geometridae). *Biological Journal of the Linnean Society, 30*, 31-44.

Huber, L. (2001). Visual categorization in pigeons. In R. G. Cook (Ed.), *Avian visual cognition* [Online]. Available: www.pigeon.psy.tufts.edu/avc/huber/

Huber, L., & Lenz, R. (1993). A test of the linear feature model of polymorphous concept discrimination with pigeons. *Quarterly Journal of Experimental Psychology, 46B*, 1–18.

Huber, L., & Lenz, R. (1996). Categorization of prototype stimulus classes by pigeons. *Quarterly Journal of Experimental Psychology, 49B*, 111–133.

Hull, C. L. (1931). Goal attraction and directing ideas conceived as habit phenomena. *Psychological Review, 38*, 487–506.

Hull, C. L. (1943). *Principles of behavior: An introduction to behavior theory.* New York: Appleton-Century-Crofts.

Hull, C. L. (1952). *A behavior system: An introduction to behavior theory concerning the individual organism.* New Haven, CT: Yale University Press.

Hulse, S. H., Fowler, H., & Honig, W. K. (Eds.). (1978). *Cognitive processes in animal behavior.* Hillsdale, NJ: Lawrence Erlbaum Associates.

Hulse, S. H., Jr. (1958). Amount and percentage of reinforcement and duration of goal confinement in conditioning and extinction. *Journal of Experimental Psychology, 56,* 48–57.

Hume, D. (1739). *A treatise of human nature.*

Hursh, S. R. (1980). Economic concepts for the analysis of behavior. *Journal of the Experimental Analysis of Behavior, 34,* 219–238.

Hursh, S. R., & Natelson, B. H. (1981). Electrical brain stimulation and food reinforcement dissociated by demand elasticity. *Physiology and Behavior, 26,* 509–515.

Hurwitz, H. M., & Roberts, A. E. (1977). Aversively controlled behavior and the analysis of conditioned suppression. In H. Davis & H. M. Hurwitz (Eds.), *Operant-Pavlovian interactions* (pp. 189–224). Hillsdale, NJ: Lawrence Erlbaum Associates, Inc.

Hutcheson, D. M., Everitt, B. J., Robbins, T. W., & Dickinson, A. (2001). The role of withdrawal in heroin addiction: Enhances reward or promotes avoidance? *Nature Neuroscience, 4,* 943–947.

Inui, T., Shimura, T., & Yamamoto, T. (2006). Effect of brain lesions on taste-potentiated odor aversion in rats. *Behavioral Neuroscience, 120,* 590–599.

Ison, J. R. (1962). Experimental extinction as a function of number of reinforcements. *Journal of Experimental Psychology, 64,* 314–317.

Jackson, R. L., Alexander, J. H., & Maier, S. F. (1980). Learned helplessness, inactivity, and associative deficits: Effects of inescapable shock on response choice escape learning. *Journal of Experimental Psychology: Animal Behavior Processes, 6,* 1–20.

Jackson, R. L., Maier, S. F., & Coon, D. J. (1979). Long-term analgesic effects of inescapable shock and learned helplessness. *Science, 206,* 91–94.

Jacobs, W. J., Zellner, D. A., LoLordo, V. M., & Riley, A. C. (1981). The effect of post-conditioning exposure to morphine on the retention of a morphine-induced conditional taste aversion. *Pharmacology, Biochemistry and Behavior, 14,* 779–785.

Jenkins, H. M. (1977). Sensitivity of different response systems to stimulus-reinforcer and response-reinforcer relations. In H. Davis & H. M. B. Hurwitz (Eds.), *Operant-Pavlovian interactions* (pp. 47–62). Hillsdale, NJ: Erlbaum.

Jenkins, H. M. (1985). Conditioned inhibition of key pecking in the pigeon. In R. R. Miller & N. E. Spear (Eds.), *Information processing in animals: Conditioned inhibition* (pp. 327–354). Hillsdale, NJ: Lawrence Erlbaum Associates, Inc.

Jenkins, H. M., & Harrison, R. H. (1960). Effects of discrimination training on auditory generalization. *Journal of Experimental Psychology, 59,* 246–253.

Jenkins, H. M., & Harrison, R. H. (1962). Generalization gradients of inhibition following auditory discrimination learning. *Journal of the Experimental Analysis of Behavior, 5,* 435–441.

Jenkins, H. M., & Moore, B. R. (1973). The form of the auto-shaped response with food or water reinforcers. *Journal of the Experimental Analysis of Behavior, 20,* 163–181.

Jenkins, H. M., Barnes, R. A., & Barrera, F. J. (1981). Why autoshaping depends on trial spacing. In C. Locurto, H. S. Terrace, & J. Gibbon (Eds.), *Autoshaping and conditioning theory* (pp. 255–284). New York: Academic Press.

Jitsumori, M. (1996). A prototype effect and categorization of artificial polymorphous stimuli in pigeons. *Journal of Experimental Psychology: Animal Behavior Processes, 22,* 405–419.

Jitsumori, M., & Yoshihara, M. (1997). Categorical discrimination of human facial expressions by pigeons: A test of the linear feature model. *Quarterly Journal of Experimental Psychology, 50B,* 253–268.

Johnson, S. L., McPhee, L., & Birch, L. L. (1991). Conditioned preferences: Young children prefer flavors associated with high dietary fat. *Physiology and Behavior, 50,* 1245–1251.

Jones, J. E., Antoniadis, E., Shettleworth, S. J., & Kamil, A. C. (2002). A comparative study of geometric rule learning by nutcrackers (*Nucifraga columbiana*), pigeons (*Columba livia*), and jackdaws (*Corvus moedula*). *Journal of Comparative Psychology, 116,* 350–356.

Jordan, W. P., Strasser, H. C., & McHale, L. (2000). Contextual control of long-term habituation in rats. *Journal of Experimental Psychology: Animal Behavior Processes, 26,* 323–339.

Kaiser, D. H., Sherburne, L. M., Steirn, J. N., & Zentall, T. R. (1997). Perceptual learning in pigeons: Decreased ability to discriminate samples mapped onto the same comparison in many-to-one matching. *Psychonomic Bulletin & Review, 4,* 378–381.

Kalat, J. W., & Rozin, P. (1973). "Learned safety" as a mechanism in long-delay taste-aversion learning in rats. *Journal of Comparative and Physiological Psychology, 83,* 198–207.

Kamil, A. C., & Jones, J. E. (2000). Geometric rule learning by Clark's nutcrackers (*Nucifraga columbiana*). *Journal of Experimental Psychology: Animal Behavior Processes, 26,* 439–453.

Kamin, L. J. (1957). The gradient of delay of secondary reward in avoidance learning tested on avoidance trials only. *Journal of Comparative and Physiological Psychology, 50,* 450–456.

Kamin, L. J. (1965). Temporal and intensity characteristics of the conditioned stimulus. In W. F. Prokasy (Ed.), *Classical conditioning* (pp. 118–147). New York: Appleton-Century Crofts.

Kamin, L. J. (1968). "Attention-like" processes in classical conditioning. In M. R. Jones (Ed.), *Miami symposium on the prediction of behavior: Aversive stimulation* (pp. 9–33). Miami, FL: University of Miami Press.

Kamin, L. J. (1969). Predictability, surprise, attention and conditioning. In B. A. Campbell & R. M. Church (Eds.), *Punishment and aversive behavior* (pp. 279–296). New York: Appleton-Century-Crofts.

Kamin, L. J., Brimer, C. J., & Black, A. H. (1963). Conditioned suppression as a monitor of fear of the CS in the course of avoidance training. *Journal of Comparative and Physiological Psychology, 56,* 497–501.

Kant, I. (1781). *Critique of pure reason.*

Kaplan, P. S. (1984). Importance of relative temporal parameters in trace autoshaping: From excitation to inhibition. *Journal of Experimental Psychology: Animal Behavior Processes, 10,* 113–126.

Kaplan, P. S., & Hearst, E. (1982). Bridging temporal gaps between CS and US in autoshaping: Insertion of other stimuli before, during, and after CS. *Journal of Experimental Psychology: Animal Behavior Processes, 8*, 187–203.

Karpicke, J., Christoph, G., Peterson, G., & Hearst, E. (1977). Signal location and positive versus negative conditioned suppression in the rat. *Journal of Experimental Psychology: Animal Behavior Processes, 3*, 105–118.

Kasprow, W. J., Schachtman, T. R., & Miller, R. R. (1987). The comparator hypothesis of conditioned response generation: Manifest conditioned excitation and inhibition as a function of relative excitatory strengths of CS and conditioning context at the time of testing. *Journal of Experimental Psychology: Animal Behavior Processes, 13*, 395–406.

Katcher, A. H., Solomon, R. L., Turner, L. H., Lolordo, V. M., Overmier, J. B., & Rescorla, R. A. (1969). Heart rate and blood pressure responses to signaled and unsignaled shocks: Effects of cardiac sympathectomy. *Journal of Comparative and Physiological Psychology, 68*, 163–174.

Katz, J. S., & Cook, R. G. (2000). Stimulus repetition effects on texture-based visual search by pigeons. *Journal of Experimental Psychology: Animal Behavior Processes, 26*, 220–236.

Katz, J. S., & Wright, A. A. (2006). Same/different abstract-concept learning by pigeons. *Journal of Experimental Psychology: Animal Behavior Processes, 32*, 80–86.

Kaye, H., & Pearce, J. M. (1984). The strength of the orienting response during Pavlovian conditioning. *Journal of Experimental Psychology: Animal Behavior Processes, 10*, 90–109.

Kehoe, E. J. (1988). A layered network model of associative learning: Learning to learn and configuration. *Psychological Review, 95*, 411–433.

Kehoe, E. J., & Gormezano, I. (1980). Configuration and combination laws in conditioning with compound stimuli. *Psychological Bulletin, 87*, 351–378.

Kelleher, R. T. (1966). Conditioned reinforcement in second-order schedules. *Journal of the Experimental Analysis of Behavior, 9*, 475–485.

Kelly, D. M., & Spetch, M. L. (2001). Pigeons encode relative geometry. *Journal of Experimental Psychology: Animal Behavior Processes, 27*, 417–422.

Kern, D. L., McPhee, L., Fisher, J., Johnson, S., & et al. (1993). The postingestive consequences of fat condition preferences for flavors associated with high dietary fat. *Physiology and Behavior, 54*, 71–76.

Kesner, R. P., & Despain, M. J. (1988). Correspondence between rats and humans in the utilization of retrospective and prospective codes. *Animal Learning & Behavior, 16*, 299–302.

Kessel, E. L. (1955). The mating activities of balloon flies. *Systematic Zoology, 4*, 97–104.

Kettlewell, H. B. D. (1956). Further selection experiments on industrial melanism in the Lepidoptera. *Heredity, 10*, 287–301.

Kiernan, M. J., & Westbrook, R. F. (1993). Effects of exposure to a to-be-shocked environment upon the rat's freezing response: Evidence for facilitation, latent inhibition, and perceptual learning. *Quarterly Journal of Experimental Psychology, 46B*, 271–288.

Killcross, S., & Balleine, B. (1996). Role of primary motivation in stimulus preexposure effects. *Journal of Experimental Psychology: Animal Behavior Processes, 22*, 32–42.

Killcross, S., & Coutureau, E. (2003). Coordination of actions and habits in the medial prefrontal cortex of rats. *Cerebral Cortex, 13*, 400–408.

Killcross, S., & Dickinson, A. (1996). Contextual control of latent inhibition by the reinforcer. *Quarterly Journal of Experimental Psychology, 49B*, 45–59.

Killeen, P. R., & Fetterman, J. G. (1988). A behavioral theory of timing. *Psychological Review, 95*.

Kim, J. A., Siegel, S., & Patenall, V. R. A. (1999). Drug-onset cues as signals: Intraadministration associations and tolerance. *Journal of Experimental Psychology: Animal Behavior Processes, 25*, 491–504.

Kim, J. J., & Fanselow, M. S. (1992). Modality-specific retrograde amnesia of fear. *Science, 256*, 675–677.

King, D. A., Bouton, M. E., & Musty, R. E. (1987). Associative control of tolerance to the sedative effects of a short-acting benzodiazepine. *Behavioral Neuroscience, 101*, 104–114.

Kirby, K. N., Petry, N. M., & Bickel, W. K. (1999). Heroin addicts have higher discount rates for delayed rewards than non-drug-using controls. *Journal of Experimental Psychology: General, 128*, 78–87.

Kissinger, S. C., & Riccio, D. C. (1995). Stimulus conditions influencing the development of tolerance to repeated cold exposure in rats. *Animal Learning & Behavior, 23*, 9–16.

Klein, S. B., Cosmides, L., Tooby, J., & Chance, S. (2002). Decisions and the evolution of memory: Multiple systems, multiple functions. *Psychological Review, 109*, 306–329.

Konorski, J. (1967). *Integrative activity of the brain: An interdisciplinary approach.* Chicago, IL: University of Chicago Press.

Korol, B., Sletten, I. W., & Brown, M. L. (1966). Conditioned physiological adaptation to anticholinergic drugs. *American Journal of Physiology, 211*, 911–914.

Kraemer, P. J., & Roberts, W. A. (1984). The influence of flavor preexposure and test interval on conditioned taste aversions in the rat. *Learning and Motivation, 15*, 259–278.

Krank, M. D. (1989). Environmental signals for ethanol enhance free-choice ethanol consumption. *Behavioral Neuroscience, 103*, 365–372.

Kremer, E. F. (1978). The Rescorla-Wagner model: Losses in associative strength in compound conditioned stimuli. *Journal of Experimental Psychology: Animal Behavior Processes, 4*, 22–36.

Kruschke, J. K. (1992). ALCOVE: A connectionist model of human category learning. In R. P. Lippman, J. E. Moody, & D. S. Touretzky (Eds.), *Advances in neural information processing systems* (Vol. 3, pp. 649–655). San Mateo, CA: Morgan Kaufmann.

Kruse, J. M., Overmier, J. B., Konz, W. A., & Rokke, E. (1983). Pavlovian conditioned stimulus effects upon instrumental choice behavior are reinforcer specific. *Learning and Motivation, 14*, 165–181.

Kuhn, T. (1962). *The structure of scientific revolutions.* Chicago, IL: University of Chicago Press.

Lamarre, J., & Holland, P. C. (1987). Transfer of inhibition after serial feature negative discrimination training. *Learning and Motivation, 18*, 319–342.

Lamon, S., Wilson, G. T., & Leaf, R. C. (1977). Human classical aversion conditioning: Nausea versus electric shock in the reduction of target beverage consumption. *Behaviour Research and Therapy, 15*, 313–320.

Lamoureux, J. A., Buhusi, C. V., & Schmajuk, N. A. (1998). A real-time theory of Pavlovian conditioning: Simple stimuli and occasion setters. In N. A. Schmajuk & P. C. Holland (Eds.), *Occasion setting: Associative learning and cognition in animals* (pp. 383–424). Washington, DC: American Psychological Association.

Lang, P. J. (1995). The emotion probe: Studies of motivation and attention. *American Psychologist, 50*, 372–385.

Langley, C. M. (1996). Search images: Selective attention to specific visual features of prey. *Journal of Experimental Psychology: Animal Behavior Processes, 22*, 152–163.

Lattal, K. M. (1999). Trial and intertrial durations in Pavlovian conditioning: Issues of learning and performance. *Journal of Experimental Psychology: Animal Behavior Processes, 25*, 433–450.

Lattal, K. M., & Nakajima, S. (1998). Overexpectation in appetitive Pavlovian and instrumental conditioning. *Animal Learning & Behavior, 26*, 351–360.

Lazareva, O. F., Wasserman, E. A., & Young, M. E. (2005). Transposition in pigeons: Reassessing Spence (1937) with multiple discrimination training. *Learning & Behavior, 33*, 22–46.

Le Magnen, J. (1959). Etude d'un phenomene d'appetit provisionnel [Study of the phenomenon of provisional appetite]. *Comptes Rendus de l'Academie des Sciences (Paris), 249*, 2400–2402.

Le Pelley, M. E. (2004). The role of associative history in models of associative learning: A selective review and a hybrid model. *The Quarterly Journal of Experimental Psychology, 57B*, 193–243.

Lea, S. E. G. (1984). In what sense do pigeons learn concepts? In H. L. Roitblat, T. G. Bever, & H. S. Terrace (Eds.), *Animal cognition* (pp. 263–276). Hillsdale, NJ: Erlbaum.

Lea, S. E. G., & Ryan, C. M. E. (1990). Unnatural concepts and the theory of concept discrimination in birds. In M. L. Commons, R. J. Herrnstein, S. M. Kosslyn, & D. B. Mumford (Eds.), *Quantitative analyses of behavior (Vol. 8): Behavioral approaches to pattern recognition and concept formation* (pp. 165–185). Hillsdale, NJ: Erlbaum.

Lea, S. E., & Roper, T. J. (1977). Demand for food on fixed-ratio schedules as a function of the quality of concurrently available reinforcement. *Journal of the Experimental Analysis of Behavior, 27*, 371–380.

Leak, T. M., & Gibbon, J. (1995). Simultaneous timing of multiple intervals: Implications of the scalar property. *Journal of Experimental Psychology: Animal Behavior Processes, 21*, 3–19.

Leaton, R. N. (1974). Long-term retention of the habituation of lick suppression in rats. *Journal of Comparative and Physiological Psychology, 87*, 1157–1164.

Leclerc, R., & Reberg, D. (1980). Sign-tracking in aversive conditioning. *Learning and Motivation, 11*, 302–317.

Lee, R. K. K., Maier, S. F. (1988). Inescapable shock and attention to internal versus external cues in a water escape discrimination task. *Journal of Experimental Psychology: Animal Behavior Processes, 14*, 302–311.

Leitenberg, H., Gross, J., Peterson, J., & Rosen, J. C. (1984). Analysis of an anxiety model and the process of change during exposure plus response prevention treatment of bulimia nervosa. *Behavior Therapy, 15*, 3–20.

Lejeune, H., Cornet, S., Ferreira, M. A., & Wearden, J. H. (1998). How do Mongolian gerbils (*Meriones unguiculatus*) pass the time? Adjunctive behavior during temporal differentiation in gerbils. *Journal of Experimental Psychology: Animal Behavior Processes, 24*, 352–368.

Leonard, D. W. (1969). Amount and sequence of reward in partial and continuous reinforcement. *Journal of Comparative and Physiological Psychology, 67*, 204–211.

Lepper, M. R., Greene, D., & Nisbett, R. E. (1973). Undermining children's intrinsic interest with extrinsic reward: A test of the "overjustification" hypothesis. *Journal of Personality and Social Psychology, 28*, 129–137.

Lester, L. S., & Fanselow, M. S. (1985). Exposure to a cat produces opioid analgesia in rats. *Behavioral Neuroscience, 99*, 756–759.

Lett, B. T. (1973). Delayed reward learning: Disproof of the traditional theory. *Learning and Motivation, 4*, 237–246.

Lett, B. T. (1977). Long delay learning in the T-maze: Effect of reward given in the home cage. *Bulletin of the Psychonomic Society, 10*, 211–214.

Lett, B. T. (1984). Extinction of taste aversion does not eliminate taste potentiated odor aversion in rats or color aversion in pigeons. *Animal Learning & Behavior, 12*, 414–420.

Levis, D. J., & Brewer, K. E. (2001). The neurotic paradox: Attempts by two-factor fear theory and alternative avoidance models to resolve the issues associated with sustained avoidance responding in extinction. In R. R. Mowrer & S. B. Klein (Eds.), *Handbook of comtemporary learning theories* (pp. 561–597). Mahwah, NJ: Erlbaum.

Levitsky, D., & Collier, G. (1968). Schedule-induced wheel running. *Physiology and Behavior, 3*, 571–573.

Lieberman, D. A., McIntosh, D. C., & Thomas, G. V. (1979). Learning when reward is delayed: A marking hypothesis. *Journal of Experimental Psychology: Animal Behavior Processes, 5*, 224–242.

Linden, D. R., Savage, L. M., & Overmier, J. B. (1997). General learned irrelevance: A Pavlovian analog to learned helplessness. *Learning and Motivation, 28*, 230–247.

Lipsitt, L. P. (1990). Learning and memory in infants. *Merrill Palmer Quarterly, 36*, 53–66.

Locke, J. (1690). *An essay concerning human understanding.*

Locurto, C., Terrace, H. S., & Gibbon, J. (Eds.). (1981). *Autoshaping and conditioning theory.* New York: Academic Press.

Loftus, E. F. (1979). The malleability of human memory. *American Scientist, 67*, 312–320.

Logue, A. W. (1985). Conditioned food aversion learning in humans. *Annals of the New York Academy of Sciences, 443*, 316–329.

Logue, A. W. (1988). Research on self-control: An integrating framework. *Behavioral and Brain Sciences, 11*, 665–709.

Logue, A. W. (1995). *Self-control.* Englewood Cliffs, NJ: Prentice Hall.

Logue, A. W. (1998). Self-control. In W. T. O'Donohue (Ed.), *Learning and behavior therapy* (pp. 252–273). Needham Heights, MA: Allyn and Bacon.

Loidolt, M., Aust, U., Meran, I., & Huber, L. (2003). Pigeons use item-specific and category-level information in the identification and categorization of human faces. *Journal of Experimental Psychology: Animal Behavior Processes, 29*, 261–276.

LoLordo, V. M., & Fairless, J. L. (1985). Pavlovian conditioned inhibition: The literature since 1969. In R. R. Miller & N. E. Spear (Eds.), *Information processing in animals: Con-*

ditioned inhibition. Hillsdale, NJ: Lawrence Erlbaum Associates, Inc.

LoLordo, V. M., & Taylor, T. L. (2001). Effects of uncontrollable aversive events: Some unsolved puzzles. In R. R. Mowrer & S. B. Klein (Eds.), *Handbook of contemporary learning theories* (pp. 469–504). Mahwah, NJ: Erlbaum.

Loo, S. K., & Bitterman, M. E. (1992). Learning in honeybees (*Apis mellifera*) as a function of sucrose concentration. *Journal of Comparative Psychology, 106*, 29–36.

Lopez, M., Balleine, B., & Dickinson, A. (1992). Incentive learning and the motivational control of instrumental performance by thirst. *Animal Learning & Behavior, 20*, 322–328.

Lorenz, K. (1937). The companion in the bird's world. *Auk, 54*, 245–273.

Lovaas, O. I. (1967). A behavior therapy approach to the treatment of childhood schizophrenia. In J. P. Hill (Ed.), *Minnesota symposium on child psychology*. Minneapolis: University of Minnesota Press.

Lovibond, P. F. (1983). Facilitation of instrumental behavior by a Pavlovian appetitive conditioned stimulus. *Journal of Experimental Psychology: Animal Behavior Processes, 9*, 225–247.

Lovibond, P. F. (2003). Causal beliefs and conditioned responses: Retrospective revaluation induced by experience and by instruction. *Journal of Experimental Psychology: Learning, Memory, and Cognition, 29*, 97–106.

Lovibond, P. F., & Shanks, D. R. (2002). The role of awareness in Pavlovian conditioning: Empirical evidence and theoretical implications. *Journal of Experimental Psychology: Animal Behavior Processes, 28*, 3–26.

Lovibond, P. F., Been, S., Mitchell, C. J., Bouton, M. E., & Frohardt, R. (2003). Forward and backward blocking of causal judgment is enhanced by additivity of effect magnitude. *Memory and Cognition, 31*, 133–142.

Lovibond, P. F., Preston, G. C., & Mackintosh, N. J. (1984). Context specificity of conditioning, extinction, and latent inhibition. *Journal of Experimental Psychology: Animal Behavior Processes, 10*, 360–375.

Lubow, R. E. (1973). Latent inhibition. *Psychological Bulletin, 79*, 398–407.

Lucas, G. A., Deich, J. D., & Wasserman, E. A. (1981). Trace autoshaping: Acquisition, maintenance, and path dependence at long trace intervals. *Journal of the Experimental Analysis of Behavior, 36*, 61–74.

Lucas, G. A., Timberlake, W., & Gawley, D. J. (1988). Adjunctive behavior in the rat under periodic food delivery in a 24-hr environment. *Animal Learning & Behavior, 16*, 19–30.

Macfarlane, D. A. (1930). The role of kinesthesis in maze learning. *University of California Publications in Psychology, 4*, 277–305.

Machado, A. (1997). Learning the temporal dynamics of behavior. *Psychological Review, 104*, 241–265.

Mackintosh, N. J. (1973). Stimulus selection: Learning to ignore stimuli that predict no change in reinforcement. In R. A. Hinde & J. S. Hinde (Eds.), *Constraints on learning* (pp. 75–96). London: Academic Press.

Mackintosh, N. J. (1974). *The psychology of animal learning.* London: Academic Press.

Mackintosh, N. J. (1975a). A theory of attention: Variations in the associability of stimuli with reinforcement. *Psychological Review, 82*, 276–298.

Mackintosh, N. J. (1975b). Blocking of conditioned suppression: Role of the first compound trial. *Journal of Experimental Psychology: Animal Behavior Processes, 1*, 335–345.

Mackintosh, N. J. (1978). Cognitive or associative theories of conditioning: Implications of an analysis of blocking. In S. Hulse & H. Fowler, & W. K. Honig (Eds.), *Cognitive processes in animal behavior* (pp. 155–176). Hillsdale, NJ: Lawrence Erlbaum Associates, Inc.

Mackintosh, N. J. (1983). *Conditioning and associative learning.* New York: Clarendon Press.

Mackintosh, N. J. (1995). Categorization by people and pigeons: The twenty-second Bartlett Memorial lecture. *Quarterly Journal of Experimental Psychology, 48*, 193–214.

Mackintosh, N. J., & Dickinson, A. (1979). Instrumental (Type II) conditioning. In A. Dickinson & R. A. Boakes (Eds.), *Mechanisms of learning and motivation: A memorial volume to Jerzy Konorski* (pp. 143–169). Hillsdale, NJ: Erlbaum.

Mackintosh, N. J., & Turner, C. (1971). Blocking as a function of novelty of CS and predictability of UCS. *Quarterly Journal of Experimental Psychology A, 23*, 359–366.

Mackintosh, N. J., Kaye, H., & Bennett, C. H. (1991). Perceptual learning in flavor aversion conditioning. *Quarterly Journal of Experimental Psychology, 43B*, 297–322.

MacLennan, A. J., Drugan, R. C., Hyson, R. L., Maier, S. F., Madden, J., IV, & Barchas, J. D. (1982). Dissociation of long-term analgesia and the shuttlebox escape deficit caused by inescapable shock. *Journal of Comparative and Physiological Psychology, 96*, 904–913.

Madden, G. J., Bickel, W. K., & Jacobs, E. A. (1999). Discounting of delayed rewards in opioid-dependent outpatients: Exponential or hyperbolic discounting functions? *Experimental and Clinical Psychopharmacology, 7*, 284–293.

Mahoney, W. J., & Ayres, J. J. (1976). One-trial simultaneous and backward fear conditioning as reflected in conditioned suppression of licking in rats. *Animal Learning & Behavior, 4*, 357–362.

Maier, S. F. (1970). Failure to escape traumatic electric shock: Incompatible skeletal motor response or learned helplessness? *Learning and Motivation, 1*, 157–169.

Maier, S. F., & Seligman. M. E. P. (1976). Learned helplessness: Theory and evidence. *Journal of Experimental Psychology: General, 103*, 3–46.

Maier, S. F., & Watkins, L. R. (1998). Stressor controllability, anxiety, and serotonin. *Cognitive Therapy and Research, 22*, 595–613.

Maier, S. F., & Watkins, L. R. (2005). Stressor controllability and learned helplessness: The roles of the dorsal raphe nucleus, serotonin, and corticotropin-releasing factor. *Neuroscience and Biobehavioral Reviews, 29*, 829–841.

Maier, S. F., Jackson, R. L., & Tomie, A. (1987). Potentiation, overshadowing, and prior exposure to inescapable shock. *Journal of Experimental Psychology: Animal Behavior Processes, 13*, 226–238.

Maier, S. F., Rapaport, P., & Wheatly, K. L. (1976). Conditioned inhibition and the CS-US interval. *Animal Learning & Behavior, 4*, 217–220.

Maier, S. F., Seligman, M. E. P., & Solomon, R. L. (1969). Pavlovian fear conditioning and learned helplessness. In B. A. Campbell & R. M. Church (Eds.), *Punishment* (pp. 299–342). New York: Appleton.

Maier, S. F., Sherman, J. E., Lewis, J. W., Terman, G. W., & Liebeskind, J. C. (1983). The opioid/nonopioid nature of stress-induced analgesia and learned helplessness. *Journal of Experimental Psychology: Animal Behavior Processes, 9,* 80–90.

Manns, J. R., Clark, R. E., & Squire, L. R. (2002). Standard delay eyeblink classical conditioning is independent of awareness. *Journal of Experimental Psychology: Animal Behavior Processes, 28,* 32–37.

Mansfield, J. G., & Cunningham, C. L. (1980). Conditioning and extinction of tolerance to the hypothermic effect of ethanol in rats. *Journal of Comparative and Physiological Psychology, 94,* 962–969.

Maren, S., & Fanselow, M. S. (1998). Appetitive motivational states differ in their ability to augment aversive fear conditioning in rats (*Rattus norvegicus*). *Journal of Experimental Psychology: Animal Behavior Processes, 24,* 369–373.

Marks, I. M. (1978). *Living with fear: Understanding and coping with anxiety.* New York: McGraw-Hill.

Marlin, N. A. (1981). Contextual associations in trace conditioning. *Animal Learning & Behavior, 9,* 519–523.

Marlin, N. A., & Miller, R. R. (1981). Associations to contextual stimuli as a determinant of long-term habituation. *Journal of Experimental Psychology: Animal Behavior Processes, 7,* 313–333.

Matute, H., Arcediano, F., & Miller, R. R. (1996). Test question modulates cue competition between causes and between effects. *Journal of Experimental Psychology: Learning, Memory, and Cognition, 22,* 182–196.

Matzel, L. D., Brown, A. M., & Miller, R. R. (1987). Associative effects of US preexposure: Modulation of conditioned responding by an excitatory training context. *Journal of Experimental Psychology: Animal Behavior Processes, 13,* 65–72.

Matzel, L. D., Held, F. P., & Miller, R. R. (1988). Information and expression of simultaneous and backward associations: Implications for contiguity theory. *Learning and Motivation, 19,* 317–344.

Mazur, J. E. (1993). Predicting the strength of a conditioned reinforcer: Effects of delay and uncertainty. *Current Directions in Psychological Science, 2,* 70–74.

Mazur, J. E. (1997). Choice, delay, probability, and conditioned reinforcement. *Animal Learning & Behavior, 25,* 131–147.

Mazur, J. E., & Wagner, A. R. (1982). An episodic model of associative learning. In M. Commons, R. Herrnstein, & A. R. Wagner (Eds.), *Quantitative analyses of behavior: Acquisition* (Vol. 3, pp. 3–39). Cambridge, MA: Ballinger.

McAllister, W. R., & McAllister, D. E. (1971). Behavioral measurement of conditioned fear. In F. R. Brush (Ed.), *Aversive conditioning and learning.* New York: Academic Press.

McAllister, W. R., & McAllister, D. E. (1991). Fear theory and aversively motivated behavior: Some controversial issues. In M. R. Denny (Ed.), *Fear, avoidance, and phobias: A fundamental analysis* (pp. 135–163). Hillsdale, NK: Erlbaum.

McClelland, J. L., & Rumelhard, D. E. (1985). Distributed memory and the representation of general and specific information. *Journal of Experimental Psychology: General, 114,* 159–188.

McCollough, C. (1965). Color adaptation of edge-detectors in the human visual system. *Science, 149,* 1115–1116.

McCuller, T., Wong, P. T., & Amsel, A. (1976). Transfer of persistence from fixed-ratio barpress training to runway extinction. *Animal Learning & Behavior, 4,* 53–57.

McDowell, J. J. (2004). A computational model of selection by consequences. *Journal of the Experimental Analysis of Behavior, 81,* 297–317.

McDowell, J. J. (2005). On the classic and modern theories of matching. *Journal of the Experimental Analysis of Behavior, 84,* 111–127.

McFarland, D. (1993). *Animal behaviour: Psychobiology, ethology, and evolution* (2nd ed.). Menlo Park, CA: Benjamin Cummings.

McGeoch, J. A. (1932). Forgetting and the law of disuse. *Psychological Review, 39,* 352–370.

McLaren, I. P. L., & Mackintosh, N. J. (2000). An elemental model of associative learning: I. Latent inhibition and perceptual learning. *Animal Learning & Behavior, 28,* 211–246.

McLaren, I. P. L., & Mackintosh, N. J. (2002). Associative learning and elemental representation: II. Generalization and discrimination. *Animal Learning & Behavior, 30,* 177–200.

McLaren, I. P. L., Kaye, H., & Mackintosh, N. J. (1989). An associative theory of the representation of stimuli: Applications to perceptual learning and latent inhibition. In R. G. M. Morris (Ed.), *Parallel distributed processing: Implications for psychology and neurobiology* (pp. 102–130). New York: Oxford University Press.

McLaren, I. P. L., Kaye, H., & Mackintosh, N. J. (1989). An associative theory of the representation of stimuli: Applications to perceptual learning and latent inhibition. In R. G. M. Morris (Ed.), *Parallel distributed processing* (pp. 102–130). Oxford: Clarendon Press.

McNally, R. J. (1990). Psychological approaches to panic disorder: A review. *Psychological Bulletin, 108,* 403–419.

McNally, R. J. (1994). *Panic disorder: A critical analysis.* New York: The Guilford Press.

McNish, K. A., Betts, S. L., Brandon, S. E., & Wagner, A. R. (1997). Divergence of conditioned eyeblink and conditioned fear in backward Pavlovian training. *Animal Learning & Behavior, 25,* 43–52.

Meck, W. H. (1983). Selective adjustment of the speed of internal clock and memory processes. *Journal of Experimental Psychology: Animal Behavior Processes, 9,* 320–334.

Meck, W. H. (1996). Neuropharmacology of timing and time perception. *Cognitive Brain Research, 3,* 227–242.

Medin, D. L., & Schaffer, M. M. (1978). A context theory of classification learning. *Psychological Review, 85,* 217–238.

Meehl, P. E. (1950). On the circularity of the law of effect. *Psychological Bulletin, 47,* 52–75.

Mehiel, R., & Bolles, R. C. (1984). Learned flavor preferences based on caloric outcome. *Animal Learning & Behavior, 12,* 421–427.

Melchior, C. L. (1990). Conditioned tolerance provides protection against ethanol lethality. *Pharmacology, Biochemistry, and Behavior, 37,* 205–206.

Mensink, G.-J. M., & Raaijmakers, J. G. (1988). A model for interference and forgetting. *Psychological Review, 95,* 434–455.

Mensink, G.-J. M., & Raaijmakers, J. G. (1989). A model for contextual fluctuation. *Journal of Mathematical Psychology, 33,* 172–186.

Menzel, R., Greggers, U., & Hammer, M. (1993). Functional organization of appetitive learning and memory in a generalist pollinator, the Honey Bee. In D. Papaj & A. C. Lewis (Eds.), *Insect learning: Ecological and evolutionary perspectives* (pp. 79–125). New York: Chapman & Hall.

Mikulka, P. J., Pitts, E., & Philput, C. (1982). Overshadowing not potentiation in taste aversion conditioning. *Bulletin of the Psychonomic Society, 20*, 101–104.

Miller, N. E. (1948). Studies of fear as an acquirable drive: I. Fear as motivation and fear-reduction as reinforcement in the learning of new responses. *Journal of Experimental Psychology, 38*, 89–101.

Miller, N. E. (1957). Experiments on motivation. *Science, 126*, 1271–1278.

Miller, N. E. (1959). Liberalization of basic S-R concepts: Extensions to conflict behavior, motivation and social learning. In S. Koch (Ed.), *Psychology: A study of science, Vol. 2* (pp. 196–292). New York: McGraw-Hill.

Miller, N. E. (1985). The value of behavioral research on animals. *American Psychologist, 40*, 423–440

Miller, R. M., Kasprow, W. J., & Schachtman, T. R. (1986). Retrieval variability: Sources and consequences. *American Journal of Psychology, 99*, 145–218.

Miller, R. R., & Matute, H. (1996). Biological significance in forward and backward blocking: Resolution of a discrepancy between animal conditioning and human causal judgment. *Journal of Experimental Psychology: General, 125*, 370–386.

Miller, R. R., & Schachtman, T. R. (1985). The several roles of context at the time of retrieval. In P. D. Balsam & A. Tomie (Eds.), *Context and learning*. Hillsdale, NJ: Cognitive or associative theories of conditioning.

Miller, R. R., Barnet, R. C., & Grahame, N. J. (1995). Assessment of the Rescorla-Wagner model. *Psychological Bulletin, 117*, 363–386.

Miller, R. R., Hallam, S. C., & Grahame, N. J. (1990). Inflation of comparator stimuli following CS training. *Animal Learning & Behavior, 18*, 434–443.

Mineka, S. (1985). Animal models of anxiety-based disorders: Their usefulness and limitations. In A. H. Tuma & J. D. Maser (Eds.), *Anxiety and the anxiety disorders* (pp. 199–244). Hillsdale, NJ: Lawrence Erlbaum Associates, Inc.

Mineka, S. (1992). Evolutionary memories, emotional processing, and the emotional disorders. In D. Medin (Ed.), *The psychology of learning and motivation. Vol. 28* (pp. 161–206). New York: Academic Press.

Mineka, S., & Gino, A. (1980). Dissociation between conditioned emotional response and extended avoidance performance. *Learning and Motivation, 11*, 476–502.

Mineka, S., & Henderson, R. W. (1985). Controllability and predictability in acquired motivation. *Annual Review of Psychology, 36*, 495–529.

Mineka, S., & Zinbarg, R. (2006). A contemporary learning theory perspective on the etiology of anxiety disorders: It's not what you thought it was. *American Psychologist, 61*, 10–26.

Mineka, S., Cook, M., & Miller, S. (1984). Fear conditioned with escapable and inescapable shock: Effects of a feedback stimulus. *Journal of Experimental Psychology: Animal Behavior Processes, 10*, 307–323.

Mineka, S., Gunnar, M., & Champoux, M. (1986). Control and early socioemotional development: Infant rhesus monkeys reared in controllable versus uncontrollable environments. *Child Development, 57*, 1241–1256.

Minor, T. R., Dess, N. K., & Overmier, J. B. (1991). Inverting the traditional view of "learned helplessness." In M. R. Denny (Ed.), *Fear, avoidance, and phobias: A fundamental*

analysis (pp. 87–134). Hillsdale, NJ: Lawrence Erlbaum Associates.

Minor, T. R., Jackson, R. L., & Maier, S. F. (1984). Effects of task irrelevant cues and reinforcement delay on choice escape learning following inescapable shock: Evidence for a deficit. *Journal of Experimental Psychology: Animal Behavior Processes, 10*, 543–556.

Minor, T. R., Trauner, M. A., Lee, C., & Dess, N. K. (1990). Modeling signal features of escape response: Effects of cessation conditioning in the "learned helplessness" paradigm. *Journal of Experimental Psychology: Animal Behavior Processes, 16*, 123–136.

Mischel, W., Shoda, Y., & Rodriguez, M. (1989). Delay of gratification in children. *Science, 244*, 933–938.

Moore, B. R. (1973). The role of directed Pavlovian reactions in simple instrumental learning in the pigeon. In R. A. Hinde & J. Stevenson-Hinde (Eds.), *Constraints on learning* (pp. 159–188). New York: Academic Press.

Moore, B. R., & Stuttard, S. (1979). Dr. Guthrie and *Felis domesticus*: Or, tripping over the cat. *Science, 205*, 1031–1033.

Moore, J. W., Newman, F. L., & Glasgow, B. (1969). Intertrial cues as discriminative stimuli in human eyelid conditioning. *Journal of Experimental Psychology, 79*, 319–326.

Morgan, C. L. (1890). *Animal life and intelligence*. London: Edward Arnold.

Morgan, C. L. (1894). *An introduction to comparative psychology*. London: Walter Scott.

Morris, R. G. M. (1974). Pavlovian conditioned inhibition of fear during shuttlebox avoidance behavior. *Learning and Motivation, 5*, 424–447.

Morris, R. G. M. (1981). Spatial localization does not require the presence of local cues. *Learning and Motivation, 12*, 239–260.

Morris, R. G., Garrud, P, Rawlins, J. N., & J. O'Keefe. (1982). Place navigation impaired in rats with hippocampal lesions. *Nature, 297*, 681–683.

Morris, R. W., & Bouton, M. E. (2006). Effect of unconditioned stimulus magnitude on the emergence of conditioned responding. *Journal of Experimental Psychology: Animal Behavior Processes*, in press.

Morrison, S. D. (1976). Control of food intake in cancer cachexia: A challenge and a tool. *Physiology and Behavior, 17*, 705–714.

Moscovitch, A., & LoLordo, V. M. (1968). Role of safety in the Pavlovian backward fear conditioning procedure. *Journal of Comparative and Physiological Psychology, 66*, 673–678.

Mowrer, O. H. (1939). A stimulus-response analysis of anxiety and its role as a reinforcing agent. *Psychological Review, 46*, 553–565.

Mowrer, O. H. (1947). On the dual nature of learning: A reinterpretation of "conditioning" and "problem-solving." *Harvard Educational Review, 17*, 102–150.

Mowrer, O. H. (1960). *Learning theory and behavior*. New York: Wiley.

Mowrer, O. H., & Lamoreaux, R. R. (1942). Avoidance conditioning and signal duration—a study of secondary motivation and reward. *Psychological Monographs, 54* (Whole No. 247).

Myers, K. P., & Hall, W. G. (2001). Effects of prior experience with dehydration and water on the time course of dehydration-induced drinking in weanling rats. *Developmental Psychobiology, 38*, 145–153.

Myers, K. P., & Sclafani, A. (2001). Conditioned enhancement of flavor evaluation reinforced by intragastric glucose: I. Intake acceptance and preference analysis. *Physiology and Behavior, 74,* 481–493.

Myers, K. P., & Sclafani, A. (2001). Conditioned enhancement of flavor evaluation reinforced by intragastric glucose: II. Taste reactivity analysis. *Physiology and Behavior, 74,* 495–505.

Mystkowski, J. L., Craske, M. G., & Echiverri, A. M. (2002). Treatment context and return of fear in spider phobia. *Behavior Therapy, 33,* 399–416.

Mystkowski, J. L., Craske, M. G., Echiverri, A. M., & Labus, J. S. (2006). Mental reinstatement of context and return of fear in spider-fearful participants. *Behavior Therapy, 37,* 49–60.

Nakajima, S., Tanaka, S., Urushihara, K., & Imada, H. (2000). Renewal of extinguished lever-press responses upon return to the training context. *Learning and Motivation, 31,* 416–431.

Napier, R. M., Macrae, M., & Kehoe, E. J. (1992). Rapid reacquisition in conditioning of the rabbit's nictitating membrane response. *Journal of Experimental Psychology: Animal Behavior Processes, 18,* 182–192.

Nash, S., & Domjan, M. (1991). Learning to discriminate the sex of conspecifics in male Japanese quail *(Coturnix coturnix japonica)*: Tests of "biological constraints." *Journal of Experimental Psychology: Animal Behavior Processes, 17,* 342–353.

Nation, J. R., Cooney, J. B., & Gartrell, K. E. (1979). Durability and generalizability of persistence training. *Journal of Abnormal Psychology, 88,* 121–136.

Nelson, J. B. (2002). Context specificity of excitation and inhibition in ambiguous stimuli. *Learning and Motivation, 33,* 284–310.

Neuringer, A. (1993). Reinforced variation and selection. *Animal Learning & Behavior, 21,* 83–91.

Neuringer, A. (2004). Reinforced variability in animals and people: Implications for adaptive action. *American Psychologist, 59,* 891–906.

Nevin, J. A. (1998). Choice and behavior momentum. In W. T. O'Donohue (Ed.), *Learning and behavior therapy* (pp. 230–251). Needham Heights, MA: Allyn and Bacon.

Nevin, J. A., & Grace, R. C. (2000). Behavioral momentum and the Law of Effect. *Behavioral and Brain Sciences, 23,* 73–130.

Nevin, J. A., Tota, M. E., Torquato, R. D., & Shull, R. L. (1990). Alternative reinforcement increases resistance to change: Pavlovian or operant contingencies? *Journal of the Experimental Analysis of Behavior, 53,* 359–379.

Newell, A., & Simon, H. A. (1961). Computer simulation of human thinking. *Science, 134,* 2011–2017.

Nosofsky, R. M. (1987). Attention and learning processes in the identification and categorization of integral stimuli. *Journal of Experimental Psychology: Learning, Memory, and Cognition, 13,* 87–108.

O'Keefe, J., & Speakman, A. (1987). Single unit activity in the rat hippocampus during a spatial memory task. *Experimental Brain Research, 68,* 1–27.

O'Brien, C. P., Ehrman, R., & Ternes, J. W. (1986). Classical conditioning in human opioid dependence. In S. R. Goldberg & I. P. Stolerman (Eds.), *Behavioral analysis of drug dependence* (pp. 329–356). New York: Academic Press.

Odling-Smee, F. J. (1975). The role of background stimuli during Pavlovian conditioning. *Quarterly Journal of Experimental Psychology A, 27,* 201–209.

O'Donohue, W. T. (Ed.). (1998). *Learning and behavior therapy.* Boston, MA: Allyn & Bacon, Inc.

Öhman, A., & Mineka, S. (2001). Fears, phobias, and preparedness: Toward an evolved module of fear and fear learning. *Psychological Review, 108,* 483–522.

Öhman, A., Dimberg, U., & Ost, L.-G. (1985). Animal and social phobias: Biological constraints on learned fear responses. In S. Reiss & R. R. Bootzin (Eds.), *Theoretical issues in behavior therapy* (pp. 123–178). San Diego, CA: Academic Press.

O'Keefe, J., & Nadel, L. (1978). *The hippocampus as a cognitive map.* Oxford: Oxford University Press.

Olton, D. S. (1978). Characteristics of spatial memory. In S. H. Hulse, H. Fowler, & W. K. Honig (Eds.), *Cognitive processes in animal behavior* (pp. 341–373). Hillsdale, NJ: Erlbaum.

Olton, D. S., & Papas, B. C. (1979). Spatial memory and hippocampal function. *Neuropsychologia, 17,* 669–682.

Olton, D. S., & Samuelson, R. J. (1976). Remembrance of places passed: Spatial memory in rats. *Journal of Experimental Psychology: Animal Behavior Processes, 2,* 97–116.

Olton, D. S., Collison, C., & Werz, M. A. (1977). Spatial memory and radial arm maze performance of rats. *Learning and Motivation, 8,* 289–314.

O'Reilly, R. C., & Rudy, J. W. (2001). Conjunctive representations in learning and memory: Principles of cortical and hippocampal function. *Psychological Review, 108,* 311–345.

Overmier, J. B., & Lawry, J. A. (1979). Pavlovian conditioning and the mediation of behavior. In G. H. Bower (Ed.), *The psychology of learning and motivation* (Vol. 13, pp. 1–55). New York: Academic Press.

Overmier, J. B., & Leaf, R. C. (1965). Effects of discriminative Pavlovian fear conditioning upon previously or subsequently acquired avoidance responding. *Journal of Comparative and Physiological Psychology, 60,* 213–217.

Overmier, J. B., & LoLordo, V. M. (1998). Learned helplessness. In W. O'Donohue (Ed.), *Learning and behavior therapy* (pp. 352–373). Needham Heights, MA: Allyn & Bacon.

Overmier, J. B., & Seligman, M. E. P. (1967). Effects of inescapable shock upon subsequent escape and avoidance behavior. *Journal of Comparative and Physiological Psychology, 63,* 23–33.

Overmier, J. B., Bull, J. A., & Trapold, M. A. (1971). Discriminative cue properties of different fears and their role in response selection in dogs. *Journal of Comparative and Physiological Psychology, 76,* 478–482.

Packard, M. G. (2001). On the neurobiology of multiple memory systems: Tolman versus Hull, system interactions, and the emotion-memory bank. *Cognitive Processing, 2,* 3–24.

Packard, M. G., & McGaugh, J. L. (1996). Inactivation of hippocampus or caudate nucleus with lidocaine differentially affects expression of place and response learning. *Neurobiology of Learning and Memory, 65,* 65–72.

Paletta, M. S., & Wagner, A. R. (1986). Development of context-specific tolerance to morphine: Support for a dual-process interpretation. *Behavioral Neuroscience, 100,* 611–623.

Palmerino, C. C., Rusiniak, K. W., & Garcia, J. (1980). Flavor-illness aversions: The peculiar roles of odor and taste in memory for poison. *Science, 208,* 753–755.

Panililio, L. V., Weiss, S. J., & Schnidler, C. W. (1996). Cocaine self-administration increased by compounding discriminative stimuli. *Psychopharmacology, 125,* 202–208.

Papini, M. R., & Bitterman, M. E. (1990). The role of contingency in classical conditioning. *Psychological Review, 97,* 396–403.

Parker, L. (1982). Nonconsummatory and consummatory behavioral CRs elicited by lithium- and amphetamine-paired flavors. *Learning and Motivation, 13,* 281–303.

Parker, L. A. (1988). Positively reinforcing drugs may produce a different kind of CTA than drugs which are not positively reinforcing. *Learning and Motivation, 19,* 207–220.

Parker, L. A. (1995). Rewarding drugs produce taste avoidance, but not taste aversion. *Neuroscience and Biobehavioral Reviews, 19,* 143–151.

Parker, L. A. (1998). Emetic drugs produce conditioned rejection reactions in the taste reactivity test. *Journal of Psychophysiology, 12*(Supp 1), 3–13.

Pavlov, I. P. (1927). *Conditioned reflexes* (G. V. Anrep, translation). London: Oxford University Press.

Pearce, J. M. (1987). A model for stimulus generalization in Pavlovian conditioning. *Psychological Review, 94,* 61–73.

Pearce, J. M. (1994). Discrimination and categorization. In N. J. Mackintosh (Ed.), *Animal learning and cognition* (pp. 109–134). San Diego: Academic Press.

Pearce, J. M. (1994). Similarity and discrimination: A selective review and a connectionist model. *Psychological Review, 101,* 587–607.

Pearce, J. M. (1997). *Animal learning and cognition* (2nd ed.). East Sussex, UK: Psychology Press Ltd.

Pearce, J. M. (2002). Evaluation and development of a connectionist theory of configural learning. *Animal Learning & Behavior, 30,* 73–95.

Pearce, J. M., & Bouton, M. E. (2001). Theories of associative learning in animals. *Annual Review of Psychology, 52,* 111–139.

Pearce, J. M., & Hall, G. (1980). A model for Pavlovian learning: Variations in the effectiveness of conditioned but not of unconditioned stimuli. *Psychological Review, 87,* 532–552.

Pearce, J. M., & Redhead, E. S. (1993). The influence of an irrelevant stimulus on two discriminations. *Journal of Experimental Psychology: Animal Behavior Processes, 19,* 180–190.

Pearce, J. M., Good, M. A., Jones, P. M., & McGregor, A. (2004). Transfer of spatial behavior between different environments: Implications for theories of spatial learning and for the role of the hippocampus in spatial learning. *Journal of Experimental Psychology: Animal Behavior Processes, 30,* 135–147.

Pearce, J. M., Ward-Robinson, J., Good, M., Fussell, C., & Aydin, A. (2001). Influence of a beacon on spatial learning based on the shape of the test environment. *Journal of Experimental Psychology: Animal Behavior Processes, 27,* 329–344.

Peck, C. A., & Bouton, M. E. (1990). Context and performance in aversive-to-appetitive and appetitive-to-aversive transfer. *Learning and Motivation, 21,* 1–31.

Pecoraro, N. C., Timberlake, W. D., & Tinsley, M. (1999). Incentive downshifts evoke search repertoires in rats. *Journal of Experimental Psychology: Animal Behavior Processes, 25,* 153–167.

Peissig, J. J., Young, M. E., Wasserman, E. A., & Biederman, I. (2000). Seeing things from a different angle: The pigeon's recognition of single geons rotated in depth. *Journal of Experimental Psychology: Animal Behavior Processes, 26,* 115–132.

Perin, C. T. (1942). Behavior potentiality as a joint function of the amount of training and the degree of hunger at the time of extinction. *Journal of Experimental Psychology, 30,* 93–113.

Perkins, C. C., Jr., & Weyant, R. G. (1958). The interval between training and test trials as a determiner of the slope of generalization gradients. *Journal of Comparative and Physiological Psychology, 51,* 596–600.

Peterson, G. B., & Trapold, M. A. (1980). Effects of altering outcome expectancies on pigeons' delayed conditional discrimination performance. *Learning and Motivation, 11,* 267–288.

Pietrewicz, A. T., & Kamil, A. C. (1981). Search images and the detection of cryptic prey: An operant approach. In A. C. Kamil & T. D. Sargent (Eds.), *Foraging behavior: Ecological, ethological, and psychological approaches* (pp. 311–331). New York: Garland STPM Press.

Pinel, J. P. J., & Mana, M. J. (1989). Adaptive interactions of rats with dangerous inanimate objects: Support for a cognitive theory of defensive behavior. In R. J. Blanchard, P. F. Brain, D. C. Blanchard, & S. Parmigiani (Eds.), *Ethoexperimental approaches to the study of behavior* (Vol. 48, pp. 137–150). New York: Springer-Verlag.

Plaisted, K. (1997). The effect of interstimulus interval on the discrimination of cryptic targets. *Journal of Experimental Psychology: Animal Behavior Processes, 23,* 248–259.

Poling, A., Nickel, M., & Alling, K. (1990). Free birds aren't fat: Weight gain in captured wild pigeons maintained under laboratory conditions. *Journal of the Experimental Analysis of Behavior, 53,* 423–424.

Posner, M. I., & Keele, S. W. (1968). On the genesis of abstract ideas. *Journal of Experimental Psychology, 77,* 353–363.

Posner, M. I., & Snyder, C. R. R. (1975). Facilitation and inhibition in the processing of signals. In P. M. Rabbitt & S. Dornic (Eds.), *Attention and performance* (Vol. 5, pp. 669–682). San Diego, CA: Academic Press.

Postman, L. (1947). The history and present status of the law of effect. *Psychological Bulletin, 44,* 489–563.

Postman, L., & Underwood, B. J. (1973). Critical issues in interference theory. *Memory and Cognition, 1,* 19–40.

Postman, L., Stark, K., & Fraser, J. (1968). Temporal changes in interference. *Journal of Verbal Learning and Verbal Behavior, 7,* 672–694.

Poulos, C. X., Wilkinson, D. A., & Cappell, H. (1981). Homeostatic regulation and Pavlovian conditioning in tolerance to amphetamine-induced anorexia. *Journal of Comparative and Physiological Psychology, 95,* 735–746.

Powley, T. L. (1977). The ventromedial hypothalamic syndrome, satiety, and a cephalic phase hypothesis. *Psychological Review, 84,* 89–126.

Premack, D. (1959). Toward empirical behavior laws: I. Positive reinforcement. *Psychological Review, 66,* 219–233.

Premack, D. (1962). Reversibility of the reinforcement relation. *Science, 136,* 255–257.

Premack, D. (1963a). Prediction of the comparative reinforcement values of running and drinking. *Science, 139,* 1062–1063.

Premack, D. (1963b). Rate differential reinforcement in monkey manipulation. *Journal of the Experimental Analysis of Behavior, 6,* 81–89.

Premack, D. (1965). Reinforcement theory. In D. Levine (Ed.), *Nebraska symposium on motivation* (Vol. 13, pp. 123–188). Lincoln, NE: University of Nebraska Press.

Premack, D. (1971a). Catching up with common sense or two sides of a generalization: Reinforcement and punishment. In R. Glaser (Ed.), *The nature of reinforcement* (pp. 121–150). New York: Academic Press.

Premack, D. (1971b). Language in chimpanzee? *Science, 172*, 808–822.

Premack, D. (1983). Animal cognition. *Annual Review of Psychology, 34*, 351–362.

Rachlin, H. (1974). Self-control. *Behaviorism, 3*, 94–107.

Rachlin, H. (1976). *Behavior and learning*. San Francisco: W.H. Freeman.

Rachlin, H., & Baum, W. M. (1972). Effects of alternative reinforcement: Does the source matter? *Journal of the Experimental Analysis of Behavior, 18*, 231–241.

Rachlin, H., & Green, L. (1972). Commitment, choice and self-control. *Journal of the Experimental Analysis of Behavior, 17*, 15–22.

Rachlin, H., Green, L., Kagel, J. H., & Battalio, R. C. (1976). Economic demand theory and psychological studies of choice. In G. Bower (Ed.), *The psychology of learning and motivation. Vol. 10* (pp. 129–154). New York: Academic Press.

Ramsay, D. S., & Woods, S. C. (1997). Biological consequences of drug administration: Implications for acute and chronic tolerance. *Psychological Review, 104*, 170–193.

Randich, A., & LoLordo, V. M. (1979). Associative and nonassociative theories of the CS preexposure phenomenon: Implications for Pavlovian conditioning. *Psychological Bulletin, 86*, 523–548.

Reberg, D. (1972). Compound tests for excitation in early acquisition and after prolonged extinction of conditioned suppression. *Learning and Motivation, 3*, 246–258.

Redhead, E. S., & Pearce, J. M. (1995). Similarity and discrimination learning. *Quarterly Journal of Experimental Psychology B: Comparative and Physiological Psychology, 48B*, 46–66.

Redhead, E. S., Roberts, A., Good, M., & Pearce, J. M. (1997). Interaction between piloting and beacon homing by rats in a swimming pool. *Journal of Experimental Psychology: Animal Behavior Processes, 23*, 340–350.

Reid, P. J., & Shettleworth, S. J. (1992). Detection of cryptic prey: Search image or search rate? *Journal of Experimental Psychology: Animal Behavior Processes, 18*, 273–286.

Reilly, S., & Schachtman, T. R. (1987). The effects of ITI fillers in autoshaping. *Learning and Motivation, 18*, 202–219.

Reiss, S., & Wagner, A. R. (1972). CS habituation produces a "latent inhibition effect" but no active "conditioned inhibition." *Learning and Motivation, 3*, 237–245.

Renner, K. E. (1964). Delay of reinforcement: A historical review. *Psychological Bulletin, 61*, 341–361.

Rescorla, R. A. (1966). Predictability and number of pairings in Pavlovian fear conditioning. *Psychonomic Science, 4*, 383–384.

Rescorla, R. A. (1967a). Inhibition of delay in Pavlovian fear conditioning. *Journal of Comparative and Physiological Psychology, 64*, 114–120.

Rescorla, R. A. (1967b). Pavlovian conditioning and its proper control procedures. *Psychological Review, 74*, 71–80.

Rescorla, R. A. (1968a). Pavlovian conditioned fear in Sidman avoidance learning. *Journal of Comparative and Physiological Psychology, 65*, 55–60.

Rescorla, R. A. (1968b). Probability of shock in the presence and absence of CS in fear conditioning. *Journal of Comparative and Physiological Psychology, 66*, 1–5.

Rescorla, R. A. (1969a). Establishment of a positive reinforcer through contrast with shock. *Journal of Comparative and Physiological Psychology, 67*, 504–509.

Rescorla, R. A. (1969b). Pavlovian conditioned inhibition. *Psychological Bulletin, 72*, 77–94.

Rescorla, R. A. (1970). Reduction in the effectiveness of reinforcement after prior excitatory conditioning. *Learning and Motivation, 1*, 372–381.

Rescorla, R. A. (1971). Summation and retardation tests of latent inhibition. *Journal of Comparative and Physiological Psychology, 75*, 77–81.

Rescorla, R. A. (1972). Informational variables in Pavlovian conditioning. In G. H. Bower (Ed.), *The psychology of learning and motivation.* (Vol. 6, pp. 1–46). New York: Academic Press.

Rescorla, R. A. (1973). Effects of US habituation following conditioning. *Journal of Comparative and Physiological Psychology, 82*, 137–143.

Rescorla, R. A. (1974). Effect of inflation of the unconditioned stimulus value following conditioning. *Journal of Comparative and Physiological Psychology, 86*, 101–106.

Rescorla, R. A. (1978). Some implications of a cognitive perspective on Pavlovian conditioning. In S. S. Hulse, H. Fowler, & K. Honig (Eds.), *Cognitive processes in animal behavior*. Hillsdale, NJ: Lawrence Erlbaum Associates, Inc.

Rescorla, R. A. (1979). Aspects of the reinforcer learned in second-order Pavlovian conditioning. *Journal of Experimental Psychology: Animal Behavior Processes, 5*, 79–95.

Rescorla, R. A. (1980). *Pavlovian second order conditioning: Studies in associative learning*. Hillsdale, NJ: Lawrence Erlbaum Associates, Inc.

Rescorla, R. A. (1985). Conditioned inhibition and facilitation. In R. R. Miller & N. E. Spear (Eds.), *Information processing in animals: Conditioned inhibition* (pp. 299–326). Hillsdale, NJ: Lawrence Erlbaum Associates, Inc.

Rescorla, R. A. (1986). Extinction of facilitation. *Journal of Experimental Psychology: Animal Behavior Processes, 12*, 16–24.

Rescorla, R. A. (1987). A Pavlovian analysis of goal-directed behavior. *American Psychologist, 42*, 119–129.

Rescorla, R. A. (1988a). Facilitation based on inhibition. *Animal Learning & Behavior, 16*, 169–176.

Rescorla, R. A. (1988b). Pavlovian conditioning: It's not what you think it is. *American Psychologist, 43*, 151–160.

Rescorla, R. A. (1991). Associative relations in instrumental learning: The eighteenth Bartlett Memorial Lecture. *Quarterly Journal of Experimental Psychology, 43B*, 1–23.

Rescorla, R. A. (1994). Transfer of instrumental control mediated by a devalued outcome. *Animal Learning & Behavior, 22*, 27–33.

Rescorla, R. A. (1999a). Associative changes in elements and compounds when the other is reinforced. *Journal of Experimental Psychology: Animal Behavior Processes, 25*, 247–255.

Rescorla, R. A. (1999b). Partial reinforcement reduces the associative change produced by nonreinforcement. *Journal of Experimental Psychology: Animal Behavior Processes, 25,* 403–414.

Rescorla, R. A. (2000). Extinction can be enhanced by a concurrent excitor. *Journal of Experimental Psychology: Animal Behavior Processes, 26,* 251–260.

Rescorla, R. A. (2001). Experimental extinction. In R. R. Mowrer & S. B. Klein (Eds.), *Handbook of contemporary learning theories* (pp. 119–154). Mahwah, NJ: Erlbaum.

Rescorla, R. A. (2003). Protection from extinction. *Learning & Behavior, 31,* 124–132.

Rescorla, R. A., & Colwill, R. M. (1989). Associations with anticipated and obtained outcomes in instrumental learning. *Animal Learning & Behavior, 17,* 291–303.

Rescorla, R. A., & Durlach, P. J. (1981). Within-event learning in Pavlovian conditioning. In N. E. Spear & R. R. Miller (Eds.), *Information processing in animals: Memory mechanisms* (pp. 81–112). Hillsdale, NJ: Lawrence Erlbaum Associates, Inc.

Rescorla, R. A., & Heth, C. D. (1975). Reinstatement of fear to an extinguished conditioned stimulus. *Journal of Experimental Psychology: Animal Behavior Processes, 1,* 88–96.

Rescorla, R. A., & Holland, P. C. (1977). Associations in Pavlovian conditioned inhibition. *Learning and Motivation, 8,* 429–447.

Rescorla, R. A., & Lolordo, V. M. (1965). Inhibition of avoidance behavior. *Journal of Comparative and Physiological Psychology, 59,* 406–412.

Rescorla, R. A., & Solomon, R. L. (1967). Two-process learning theory: Relationships between Pavlovian conditioning and instrumental learning. *Psychological Review, 74,* 151–182.

Rescorla, R. A., & Wagner, A. R. (1972). A theory of Pavlovian conditioning: Variations in the effectiveness of reinforcement and nonreinforcement. In A. H. Black & W. F. Prokasy (Eds.), *Classical conditioning II.* New York: Appleton-Century-Crofts.

Revusky, S. H. (1967). Hunger level during food consumption: Effects on subsequent preference. *Psychonomic Science, 7,* 109–110.

Revusky, S. H. (1968). Effects of thirst level during consumption of flavored water on subsequent preference. *Journal of Comparative and Physiological Psychology, 66,* 777–779.

Revusky, S. H. (1971). The role of interference in association over a delay. In W. K. Honig & P. H. R. James (Eds.), *Animal memory.* New York: Academic Press.

Riccio, D. C., Rabinowitz, V. C., & Axelrod, S. (1994). Memory: When less is more. *American Psychologist, 49,* 917–926.

Riccio, D. C., Richardson, R., & Ebner, D. L. (1984). Memory retrieval deficits based upon altered contextual cues: A paradox. *Psychological Bulletin, 96,* 152–165.

Riccio, D. C., Urda, M., & Thomas, D. R. (1966). Stimulus control in pigeons based on proprioceptive stimuli from floor inclination. *Science, 153,* 434–436.

Richter, C. P. (1927). Animal behavior and internal drives. *Quarterly Review of Biology, 2,* 307–343.

Richter, C. P. (1936). Increased salt appetite in adrenalectomized rats. *American Journal of Physiology, 115,* 155–161.

Richter, C. P., Holt, L. E., Jr., & Barelare, B., Jr. (1938). Nutritional requirements for normal growth and reproduction in rats studied by the self-selection method. *American Journal of Physiology, 122,* 734–744.

Ricker, S. T., & Bouton, M. E. (1996). Reacquisition following extinction in appetitive conditioning. *Animal Learning & Behavior, 24,* 423–436.

Rilling, M. (1977). Stimulus control and inhibitory processes. In W. K. Honig & J. E. R. Staddon (Eds.), *Handbook of operant behavior* (pp. 432–480). Englewood Cliffs, NJ: Prentice-Hall.

Ritchie, B. F., Aeschliman, B., & Peirce, P. (1950). Studies in spatial learning: VIII. Place performance and acquisition of place dispositions. *Journal of Comparative and Physiological Psychology, 43,* 73–85.

Rizley, R. C., & Rescorla, R. A. (1972). Associations in second-order conditioning and sensory preconditioning. *Journal of Comparative and Physiological Psychology, 81,* 1–11.

Roberts, A. D. L., & Pearce, J. M. (1999). Blocking in the Morris swimming pool. *Journal of Experimental Psychology: Animal Behavior Processes, 25,* 225–235.

Roberts, S. (1981). Isolation of an internal clock. *Journal of Experimental Psychology: Animal Behavior Processes, 7,* 242–268.

Roberts, W. A. (1972). Short-term memory in the pigeon: Effects of repetition and spacing. *Journal of Experimental Psychology, 94,* 74–83.

Roberts, W. A. (1980). Distribution of trials and intertrial retention in delayed matching to sample with pigeons. *Journal of Experimental Psychology: Animal Behavior Processes, 6,* 217–237.

Roberts, W. A. (1984). Some issues in animal spatial memory. In H. L. Roitblat, T. G. Bever, & H. S. Terrace (Eds.), *Animal cognition.* Hillsdale, NJ: Lawrence Erlbaum Associates, Inc.

Roberts, W. A. (1998). *Principles of animal cognition.* Boston: McGraw Hill.

Roberts, W. A., & Grant, D. S. (1978). An analysis of light-induced retroactive inhibition in pigeon short-term memory. *Journal of Experimental Psychology: Animal Behavior Processes, 4,* 219–236.

Roberts, W. A., & Mazmanian, D. S. (1988). Concept learning at different levels of abstraction by pigeons, monkeys, and people. *Journal of Experimental Psychology: Animal Behavior Processes, 14,* 247–260.

Robinson, T. E., & Berridge, K. C. (1993). The neural basis of drug craving: An incentive-sensitization theory of addiction. *Brain Research Reviews, 18,* 247–291.

Robinson, T. E., & Berridge, K. C. (2003). Addiction. *Annual Review of Psychology, 54,* 25–53.

Rodgers, W. L. (1967). Specificity of specific hungers. *Journal of Comparative and Physiological Psychology, 64,* 49–58.

Rodrigo, T., Chamizo, V. D., McLaren, I. P., & Mackintosh, N. J. (1997). Blocking in the spatial domain. *Journal of Experimental Psychology: Animal Behavior Processes, 23,* 110–118.

Roitblat, H. L. (1980). Codes and coding processes in pigeon short-term memory. *Animal Learning & Behavior, 8,* 341–351.

Roitblat, H. L. (1987). *Introduction to comparative cognition.* New York: W. H. Freeman.

Romanes, G. J. (1882). *Animal intelligence.* London: Kegan, Paul, Trench and Co.

Rosas, J. M., & Alonso, G. (1996). Temporal discrimination and forgetting of CS duration in conditioned suppression. *Learning and Motivation, 27,* 43–57.

Rosas, J. M., & Alonso, G. (1997). Forgetting of the CS duration in rats: The role of retention interval and training level. *Learning and Motivation, 28,* 404–423.

Rosas, J. M., & Bouton, M. E. (1996). Spontaneous recovery after extinction of a conditioned taste aversion. *Animal Learning & Behavior, 24,* 341–348.

Rosellini, R. A., DeCola, J. P., & Warren, D. A. (1986). The effect of feedback stimuli on contextual fear depends upon the length of the intertrial interval. *Learning and Motivation, 17,* 229–242.

Rosellini, R. A., DeCola, J. P., Plonsky, M., Warren, D. A., & Stilman, A. J. (1984). Uncontrollable shock proactively increases sensitivity to response-reinforcer independence in rats. *Journal of Experimental Psychology: Animal Behavior Processes, 10,* 346–359.

Rosellini, R. A., Warren, D. A., & DeCola, J. P. (1987). Predictability and controllability: Differential effects upon contextual fear. *Learning and Motivation, 18,* 392–420.

Rosen, J. C., & Leitenberg, H. (1982). Bulimia nervosa: Treatment with exposure and response prevention. *Behavior Therapy, 13,* 117–124.

Ross, R. T., & Holland, P. C. (1981). Conditioning of simultaneous and serial feature-positive discriminations. *Animal Learning & Behavior, 9,* 293–303.

Rovee-Collier, C. (1987). Learning and memory in infancy. In J. D. Osofsky (Ed.), *Handbook of infant development.* (pp. 98–148). New York: Wiley.

Rovee-Collier, C. (1999). The development of infant memory. *Current Directions in Psychological Science, 8,* 80–85.

Rozin, P. (1967). Specific aversions as a component of specific hungers. *Journal of Comparative and Physiological Psychology, 64,* 237–242.

Rozin, P., & Kalat, J. W. (1971). Specific hungers and poison avoidance as adaptive specializations of learning. *Psychological Review, 78,* 459–486.

Rozin, P., & Rodgers, W. (1967). Novel-diet preferences in vitamin deficient rats and rats recovered from vitamin deficiency. *Journal of Comparative and Physiological Psychology, 63,* 421–428.

Rudolph, R. L., & Van Houten, R. (1977). Auditory stimulus control in pigeons: Jenkins and Harrison (1960) revisited. *Journal of the Experimental Analysis of Behavior, 27,* 327–330.

Rudy, J. W., & O'Reilly, R. C. (1999). Contextual fear conditioning, conjunctive representations, pattern completion, and the hippocampus. *Behavioral Neuroscience, 113,* 867–880.

Rumelhart, D. E. (1989). The architecture of mind: A connectionist approach. In M. I. Posner (Ed.), *Foundations of cognitive science.* (pp. 133–159). Cambridge, MA: MIT Press.

Rumelhart, D. E., & McClelland, J. L. (Eds.). (1986a). *Parallel distributed processing. Explorations in the microstructure of cognition. Vol. 1: Foundations.* Cambridge, MA: MIT Press.

Rumelhart, D. E., & McClelland, J. L. (Eds.). (1986b). *Parallel distributed processing. Explorations in the microstructure of cognition. Vol. 2: Psychological and biological models.* Cambridge, MA: MIT Press.

Rumelhart, D. E., Hinton, G. E., & Williams, R. J. (1986). Learning representations by back-propagating errors. *Nature, 323,* 533–536.

Rusiniak, K. W., Hankins, W. G., Garcia, J., & Brett, L. P. (1979). Flavor-illness aversions: Potentiation of odor by taste in rats. *Behavioral and Neural Biology, 25,* 1–17.

Saksida, L. M. (1999). Effects of similarity and experience on discrimination learning: A nonassociative connectionist model of perceptual learning. *Journal of Experimental Psychology: Animal Behavior Processes, 25,* 308–323.

Saksida, L. M., & Wilkie, D. M. (1994). Time-of-day discrimination by pigeons. *Animal Learning & Behavior, 22,* 143–154.

Salkovskis, P. M., Clark, D. M., & Gelder, M. G. (1996). Cognition-behaviour links in the persistence of panic. *Behaviour Research and Therapy, 34,* 453–458.

Samson, H. H., & Pfeffer, A. O. (1987). Initiation of ethanol-maintained responding using a schedule-induction procedure in free feeding rats. *Alcohol and Drug Research, 7,* 461–469.

Sargisson, R. J., & White, K. G. (2001). Generalization of delayed matching to sample following training at different delays. *Journal of the Experimental Analysis of Behavior, 75,* 1–14.

Save, E., Poucet, B., & Thinus-Blanc, C. (1998). Landmark use in the cognitive map in the rat. In S. Healy (Ed.), *Spatial representation in animals* (pp. 119–132). New York: Oxford University Press.

Schachtman, T. R., Brown, A. M., Gordon, E. L., Catterson, D. A., & Miller, R. R. (1987). Mechanisms underlying retarded emergence of conditioned responding following inhibitory training: Evidence for the comparator hypothesis. *Journal of Experimental Psychology: Animal Behavior Processes, 13,* 310–322.

Schleidt, W. M. (1961). Reaction of turkeys to flying predators and experiment to analyse their AAM's. *Zeitschrift fur Tierpsychologie, 18,* 543–560.

Schmajuk, N. A., & Holland, P. C. (Eds.). (1998). *Occasion setting: Associative learning and cognition in animals.* Washington, DC: American Psychological Association.

Schmajuk, N. A., Lamoureux, J. A., & Holland, P. C. (1998). Occasion setting: A neural network approach. *Psychological Review, 105,* 3–32.

Schneider, W., & Shiffrin, R. M. (1977). Controlled and automatic human information processing: I. Detection, search, and attention. *Psychological Review, 84,* 1–66.

Schoenfeld, W. N. (1950). An experimental approach to anxiety, escape, and avoidance behavior. In J. Z. P. H. Hock (Ed.), *Anxiety.* New York: Grune & Stratton.

Schull, J. (1979). A conditioned opponent theory of Pavlovian conditioning and habituation. In G. H. Bower (Ed.), *The psychology of learning and motivation* (pp. 57–90). New York: Academic Press.

Schultz, W. (2006). Behavior theories and the neurophysiology of reward. *Annual Review of Psychology, 57,* 87–115.

Sclafani, A. (1995). How food preferences are learned: Laboratory animal models. *Proceedings of the Nutrition Society, 54,* 419–427.

Sclafani, A. (1997). Learned controls of ingestive behavior. *Appetite, 29,* 153–158.

Scobie, S. R. (1972). Interaction of an aversive Pavlovian conditional stimulus with aversively and appetitively motivated operants in rats. *Journal of Comparative and Physiological Psychology, 79,* 171–188.

Seaman, S. F. (1985). Growth of morphine tolerance: The effect of dose and interval between doses. In F. R. Brush & J. B. Overmier (Eds.), *Affect, conditioning and cognition: Essays on the determinants of behavior* (pp. 249–262). Hillsdale, NJ: Lawrence Erlbaum Associates, Inc.

Sechenov, I. M. (1965). *Reflexes of the brain* (Originally published, 1863 ed.). Cambridge, MA: MIT Press.

Seeley, R. J., Ramsay, D. S., & Woods, S. C. (1997). Regulation of food intake: Interactions between learning and physiology. In M. E. Bouton & M. S. Fanselow (Eds.), *Learning, motivation, and cognition: The functional behaviorism of Robert C. Bolles* (pp. 99–115). Washington, DC: American Psychological Association.

Seligman, M. E. (1970). On the generality of the laws of learning. *Psychological Review, 77*, 406–418.

Seligman, M. E. (1971). Phobias and preparedness. *Behavior Therapy, 2*, 307–320.

Seligman, M. E. P. (1968). Chronic fear produced by unpredictable shock. *Journal of Comparative and Physiological Psychology, 66*, 402–411.

Seligman, M. E. P. (1975). *Helplessness: On depression, development, and death*. San Francisco: Freeman.

Seligman, M. E. P. (1990). *Learned optimism*. New York: A. A. Knopf.

Seligman, M. E. P., & Johnston, J. C. (1973). A cognitive theory of avoidance learning. In F. J. McGuigan, & D. B. Lumsden (Eds.), *Contemporary approaches to conditioning and learning*. Washington, DC: Winston.

Seligman, M. E. P., & Maier, S. F. (1967). Failure to escape traumatic shock. *Journal of Experimental Psychology, 74*, 1–9.

Seligman, M. E. P., Maier, S. F., & Solomon, R. L. (1971). Unpredictable and uncontrollable aversive events. In F. R. Brush (Ed.), *Aversive conditioning and learning* (pp. 347–401). New York: Academic Press.

Seligman, M. E. P., Rosellini, R. A., & Kozak, M. J. (1975). Learned helplessness in the rat: Time course, immunization, and reversibility. *Journal of Comparative and Physiological Psychology, 88*, 542–547.

Shanks, D. R. (1985). Forward and backward blocking in human contingency judgment. *Quarterly Journal of Experimental Psychology B, 37B*, 1–21.

Shanks, D. R. (1991). Categorization by a connectionist network. *Journal of Experimental Psychology: Learning, Memory, and Cognition, 17*, 433–443.

Shanks, D. R. (1995). *The psychology of associative learning*. Cambridge, England: Cambridge University Press.

Shanks, D. R., & Darby, R. J. (1998). Feature- and rule-based generalization in human associative learning. *Journal of Experimental Psychology: Animal Behavior Processes, 24*, 405–415.

Shanks, D. R., Holyoak, K. J., & Medin, D. L. (Eds.). (1996). *The Psychology of Learning and Motivation (Vol. 34): Causal Learning*. San Diego, CA: Academic Press.

Shanks, D. R., Lopez, F. J., Darby, R. J., & Dickinson, A. (1996). Distinguishing associative and probabilistic contrast theories of human contingency judgments. In D. R. Shanks, K. J. Holyoak, & D. E. Medin (Eds.), *The psychology of learning and motivation: Vol. 34. Causal learning* (pp. 265–312). San Diego, CA: Academic Press.

Sheffield, F. D. (1965). Relation between classical conditioning and instrumental learning. In W. F. Prokasy (Ed.), *Classical conditioning* (pp. 302–322). New York: Appleton-Century-Crofts.

Sheffield, F. D., & Campbell, B. A. (1954). The role of experience in the "spontaneous" activity of hungry rats. *Journal of Comparative and Physiological Psychology, 47*, 97–100.

Sheffield, F. D., & Roby, T. B. (1950). Reward value of a nonnutritive sweet taste. *Journal of Comparative and Physiological Psychology, 43*, 471–481.

Sheffield, F. D., Wulff, J. J., & Barker, R. (1951). Reward value of copulation without sex drive reduction. *Journal of Comparative and Physiological Psychology, 44*, 3–8.

Sheffield, V. F. (1949). Extinction as a function of partial reinforcement and distribution of practice. *Journal of Experimental Psychology, 39*, 511–526.

Sherry, D. F., & Schacter, D. L. (1987). The evolution of multiple memory systems. *Psychological Review, 94*, 439–454.

Shettleworth, S. J. (1975). Reinforcement and the organization of behavior in golden hamsters: Hunger, environment, and food reinforcement. *Journal of Experimental Psychology: Animal Behavior Processes, 1*, 56–87.

Shettleworth, S. J. (1978). Reinforcement and the organization of behavior in golden hamsters: Pavlovian conditioning with food and shock unconditioned stimuli. *Journal of Experimental Psychology: Animal Behavior Processes, 4*, 152–169.

Shettleworth, S. J. (1998). *Cognition, evolution, and behavior*. New York: Oxford University Press.

Shettleworth, S. J. (2002). Spatial behavior, food storing, and the modular mind. In M. Bekoff, C. Allen, & G. M. Burghardt (Ed.), *The cognitive animal: Empirical and theoretical perspectives on animal cognition* (pp. 123–128). Cambridge, MA: MIT Press.

Shettleworth, S. J., & Juergensen, M. R. (1980). Reinforcement and the organization of behavior in golden hamsters: Brain stimulation reinforcement for seven action patterns. *Journal of Experimental Psychology: Animal Behavior Processes, 6*, 352–375.

Shimp, C. P. (1966). Probabilistically reinforced choice behavior in pigeons. *Journal of the Experimental Analysis of Behavior, 9*, 443–455.

Shors, T. J., & Mathew, P. R. (1998). NMDA receptor antagonism in the lateral/basolateral but not central nucleus of the amygdala prevents the induction of facilitated learning in response to stress. *Learning and Memory, 5*, 220–230.

Sidman, M. (1953). Avoidance conditioning with brief shock and no exteroceptive warning signal. *Science, 118*, 157–158.

Sidman, M. (1990). Equivalence relations: Where do they come from? In D. E. Blackman & H. Lejeune (Eds.), *Behavioral analysis in theory and practice: Contributions and controversies* (pp. 93–114). Hillsdale, NJ: Lawrence Erlbaum Associates, Inc.

Sidman, M. (2000). Equivalence relations and the reinforcement contingency. *Journal of the Experimental Analysis of Behavior, 74*, 127–146.

Siegel, S. (1969). Generalization of latent inhibition. *Journal of Comparative and Physiological Psychology, 69*, 157–159.

Siegel, S. (1972). Conditioning of insulin-induced glycemia. *Journal of Comparative and Physiological Psychology, 78*, 233–241.

Siegel, S. (1975). Evidence from rats that morphine tolerance is a learned response. *Journal of Comparative and Physiological Psychology, 89*, 498–506.

Siegel, S. (1984). Pavlovian conditioning and heroin overdose: Reports by overdose victims. *Bulletin of the Psychonomic Society, 22*, 428–430.

Siegel, S. (1989). Pharmacological conditioning and drug effects. In A. J. Goudie & M. W. Emmett-Oglesby (Eds.), *Psychoactive drugs: Tolerance and sensitization. Contemporary neuroscience.* (pp. 115–180). Clifton, NJ: Humana Press.

Siegel, S., & Allan, L. G. (1998). Learning and homeostasis: Drug addiction and the McCollough effect. *Psychological Bulletin, 124*, 230–239.

Siegel, S., & Ellsworth, D. W. (1986). Pavlovian conditioning and death from apparent overdose of medically prescribed morphine: A case report. *Bulletin of the Psychonomic Society, 24,* 278–280.

Siegel, S., & Ramos, B. M. C. (2002). Applying laboratory research: Drug anticipation and the treatment of drug addiction. *Experimental and Clinical Psychopharmacology, 10,* 162–183.

Siegel, S., & Wagner, A. R. (1963). Extended acquisition training and resistance to extinction. *Journal of Experimental Psychology, 66,* 308–310.

Siegel, S., Allan, L. G., & Eissenberg, T. (1994). Scanning and form-contingent color aftereffects. *Journal of Experimental Psychology: General, 123,* 91–94.

Siegel, S., Baptista, M. A. S., Kim, J. A., McDonald, R. V., & Weise-Kelly, L. (2000). Pavlovian psychopharmacology: The associative basis of tolerance. *Experimental and Clinical Psychopharmacology, 8,* 276–293.

Siegel, S., Hinson, R. E., Krank, M. D., & McCully, J. (1982). Heroin "overdose" death: Contribution of drug-associated environmental cues. *Science, 216,* 436–437.

Simon, H. A., & Kaplan, C. A. (1989). Foundations of cognitive science. In M. I. Posner (Ed.), *Foundations of cognitive science.* (pp. 1–47). Cambridge, MA: MIT Press.

Skinner, B. F. (1931). The concept of the reflex in the description of behavior. *Journal of General Psychology, 5,* 427–458.

Skinner, B. F. (1935). Two types of conditioned reflex and a pseudo-type. *Journal of General Psychology, 12,* 66–77.

Skinner, B. F. (1938). *The behavior of organisms: An experimental analysis.* New York: D. Appleton-Century Company, Inc.

Skinner, B. F. (1948). "Superstition" in the pigeon. *Journal of Experimental Psychology, 38,* 168–172.

Skinner, B. F. (1956). A case history in scientific method. *American Psychologist, 11,* 221–233.

Skinner, B. F. (1981). Selection by consequences. *Science, 213,* 501–504.

Slotnick, B. M., Westbrook, F., & Darling, F. M. C. (1997). What the rat's nose tells the rat's mouth: Long delay aversion conditioning with aqueous odors and potentiation of taste by odors. *Animal Learning & Behavior, 25,* 357–369.

Smith, B. H., & Cobey, S. C. (1994). The olfactory memory of the honeybee *Apis mellifera* II. Blocking between odorants and binary mixtures. *Journal of Experimental Biology, 195,* 91–108.

Smith, J. C., & Roll, D. L. (1967). Trace conditioning with x-rays as an aversive stimulus. *Psychonomic Science, 9,* 11–12.

Smith, M. C. (1968). CS-US interval and US intensity in classical conditioning of the rabbit's nictitating membrane response. *Journal of Comparative and Physiological Psychology, 66,* 679–687.

Smith, M. C., Coleman, S. R., & Gormezano, I. (1969). Classical conditioning of the rabbit's nictitating membrane response at backward, simultaneous, and forward CS-US intervals. *Journal of Comparative and Physiological Psychology, 69,* 226–231.

Smith, S. M. (1979). Remembering in and out of context. *Journal of Experimental Psychology: Human Learning and Memory, 5,* 460–471.

Smith, S. M. (1988). Environmental context-dependent memory. In G. M. Davies & D. M. Thomson (Eds.), *Memory in context: Context in memory* (pp. 13–34). Chilchester, UK: J. Wiley.

Smith, S. M., & Vela, E. (2001). Environmental context-dependent memory: A review and meta-analysis. *Psychonomic Bulletin & Review, 8,* 203–220.

Solomon, R. L. (1980). The opponent-process theory of acquired motivation: The costs of pleasure and the benefits of pain. *American Psychologist, 35,* 691–712.

Solomon, R. L., & Corbit, J. D. (1974). An opponent-process theory of motivation: I. Temporal dynamics of affect. *Psychological Review, 81,* 119–145.

Solomon, R. L., & Turner, L. H. (1962). Discriminative classical conditioning in dogs paralyzed by curare can later control discriminative avoidance responses in the normal state. *Psychological Review, 69,* 202–218.

Soltysik, S. S., Wolfe, G. E., Nicholas, T., Wilson, W. J., & Garcia-Sanchez, J. L. (1983). Blocking of inhibitory conditioning within a serial conditioned stimulus-conditioned inhibitor compound: Maintenance of acquired behavior without an unconditioned stimulus. *Learning and Motivation, 14,* 1–29.

Sovrano, V. A., Bisazza, A., & Vallortigara, G. (2003). Modularity as a fish (*Xenotoca eiseni*) views it: Conjoining geometric and nongeometric information for spatial reorientation. *Journal of Experimental Psychology: Animal Behavior Processes, 29,* 199–210.

Spear, N. E. (1978). *The processing of memories: Forgetting and retention.* Hillsdale, NJ: Lawrence Erlbaum Associates, Inc.

Spear, N. E., & Parsons, P. J. (1976). Analysis of a reactivation treatment: Ontogenetic determinants of alleviated forgetting. In D. C. Medin, W. A. Roberts, & R. T. Davis (Eds.), *Processes of animal memory* (pp. 135–166). Hillsdale, NJ: Lawrence Erlbaum Associates, Inc.

Spence, K. W. (1936). The nature of discrimination learning in animals. *Psychological Review, 43,* 427–449.

Spence, K. W. (1947). The role of secondary reinforcement in delayed reward learning. *Psychological Review, 54,* 1–8.

Spence, K. W. (1951). Theoretical interpretations of learning. In S. S. Stevens (Ed.), *Handbook of experimental psychology* (pp. 690–729). New York: Wiley.

Spence, K. W. (1956). *Behavior theory and conditioning.* New Haven, CT: Yale University Press.

Spetch, M. L. (1995). Overshadowing in landmark learning: Touch-screen studies with pigeons and humans. *Journal of Experimental Psychology: Animal Behavior Processes, 21,* 166–181.

Spetch, M. L., & Friedman, A. (2003). Recognizing rotated views of objects: Interpolation versus generalization by humans and pigeons. *Psychonomic Bulletin & Review, 10,* 135–140.

Spetch, M. L., Cheng, K., & MacDonald, S. E. (1996). Learning the configuration of a landmark array: I. Touch-screen studies with pigeons and humans. *Journal of Comparative Psychology, 110,* 55–68.

Spetch, M. L., Cheng, K., MacDonald, S. E., Linkenhoker, B. A., Kelly, D. M., & Doerkson, S. R. (1997). Use of landmark configuration in pigeons and humans: II. Generality across search tasks. *Journal of Comparative Psychology, 111,* 14–24.

Spetch, M. L., Rust, T. B., Kamil, A. C., & Jones, J. E. (2003). Search by rules: Pigeons' (*Columbia livia*) landmark-based search according to constant bearing or constant distance. *Journal of Comparative Psychology, 117,* 123–132.

Spreat, S., & Spreat, S. R. (1982). Learning principles. In V. Voith & P. L. Borchelt (Eds.), *Veterinary clinics of North*

America: Small animal practice (pp. 593–606). Philadelphia, PA: W. B. Saunders.

Squire, L. R. (1987). *Memory and brain.* New York: Oxford University Press.

St. Claire-Smith, R. (1979). The overshadowing and blocking of punishment. *Quarterly Journal of Experimental Psychology, 31B,* 51–61.

Staddon, J. E. (1979). Operant behavior as adaptation to constraint. *Journal of Experimental Psychology: General, 108,* 48–67.

Staddon, J. E. (1983). *Adaptive behavior and learning.* New York: Cambridge University Press.

Staddon, J. E. R. (1977). Schedule-induced behavior. In W. K. Honig & J. E. R. Staddon (Eds.), *Handbook of operant behavior* (pp. 125–152). Englewood Cliffs, NJ: Prentice-Hall.

Staddon, J. E. R., & Ayres, S. L. (1975). Sequential and temporal properties of behavior induced by a schedule of periodic food delivery. *Behaviour, 54,* 26–49.

Staddon, J. E. R., & Higa, J. J. (1999). Time and memory: Towards a pacemaker-free theory of interval timing. *Journal of the Experimental Analysis of Behavior, 72,* 225–252.

Staddon, J. E. R., & Simmelhag, V. L. (1971). The "superstition" experiment: A reexamination of its implications for the principle of adaptive behavior. *Psychological Review, 78,* 3–43.

Stampfl, T. G., & Levis, D. J. (1967). Essentials of implosive therapy: A learning-theory-based psychodynamic behavioral therapy. *Journal of Abnormal Psychology, 72,* 496–503.

Starr, M. D. (1978). An opponent-process theory of motivation: VI. Time and intensity variables in the development of separation-induced distress calling in ducklings. *Journal of Experimental Psychology: Animal Behavior Processes, 4,* 338–355.

Starr, M. D., & Mineka, S. (1977). Determinants of fear over the course of avoidance learning. *Learning and Motivation, 8,* 332–350.

Steinmetz, J. E. (1996). The brain substrates of classical eyeblink conditioning in rabbits. In J. Bloedel, T. Ebner, & S. Wise (Eds.), *Acquisition of motor behavior in vertebrates* (pp. 89–114). Cambridge, MA: MIT Press.

Steinmetz, J. E., Gluck, M. A., & Solomon, P. R. (Eds.). (2001). *Model systems and the neurobiology of associative learning.* Hillsdale, NJ: Lawrence Erlbaum Associates, Inc.

Stevenson-Hinde, J. (1973). Constraints on reinforcement. In R. A. Hinde & J. Stevenson-Hinde (Eds.), *Constraints on learning: Limitations and predispositions.* New York: Academic Press.

Stewart, J. (1992). Conditioned stimulus control of the expression of sensitization of the behavioral activating effects of opiate and stimulant drugs. In I. Gormezano & E. A. Wasserman (Eds.), *Learning and memory: The behavioral and biological substrates* (pp. 129–151). Hillsdale, NJ: Lawrence Erlbaum Associates, Inc.

Stewart, J., de Wit, H., & Eikelboom, R. (1984). Role of unconditioned and conditioned drug effects in the self-administration of opiates and stimulants. *Psychological Review, 91,* 251–268.

Stolerman, I. P. (1992). Drugs of abuse: Behavioral principles, methods and terms. *Trends in Pharmacological Sciences, 13,* 170–176.

Suarez, S. D., & Gallup, G. G. (1981). Predatory overtones of open-field testing in chickens. *Animal Learning & Behavior, 9,* 153–163.

Sunsay, C., Stetson, L., & Bouton, M. E. (2004). Memory priming and trial spacing effects in Pavlovian learning. *Learning & Behavior, 32,* 220–229.

Sutherland, R. J., Chew, G. L., & Linggard, R. C. (1987). Some limitations on the use of distal cues in place navigation by rats. *Psychobiology, 15,* 48–57.

Sutton, R. S., & Barto, A. G. (1981). Toward a modern theory of adaptive networks: Expectation and prediction. *Psychological Review, 88,* 135–170.

Suzuki, S., Augerinos, G., & Black, A. H. (1980). Stimulus control of spatial behavior on the eight-arm maze in rats. *Learning and Motivation, 11,* 1–18.

Swartzentruber, D. (1995). Modulatory mechanisms in Pavlovian conditioning. *Animal Learning & Behavior, 23,* 123–143.

Swartzentruber, D., & Bouton, M. E. (1986). Contextual control of negative transfer produced by prior CS-US pairings. *Learning and Motivation, 17,* 366–385.

Swartzentruber, D., & Rescorla, R. A. (1994). Modulation of trained and extinguished stimuli by facilitators and inhibitors. *Animal Learning & Behavior, 22,* 309–316.

Symonds, M., Hall, G., & Bailey, G. K. (2002). Perceptual learning with a sodium depletion procedure. *Journal of Experimental Psychology: Animal Behavior Processes, 28,* 190–199.

Tait, R. W., & Saladin, M. E. (1986). Concurrent development of excitatory and inhibitory associations during backward conditioning. *Animal Learning & Behavior, 14,* 133–137.

Tangen, J. M., & Allan, L. G. (2003). Cue interaction and judgments of causality: Contributions of causal and associative processes. *Memory and Cognition, 32:* 107–24.

Tarpy, R. M., & Sawabini, F. L. (1974). Reinforcement delay: A selective review of the last decade. *Psychological Bulletin, 81,* 984–997.

Terrace, H. S. (1963). Errorless transfer of a discrimination across two continua. *Journal of the Experimental Analysis of Behavior, 6,* 223–232.

Terry, W. S. (1976). Effects of priming unconditioned stimulus representation in short-term memory on Pavlovian conditioning. *Journal of Experimental Psychology: Animal Behavior Processes, 2,* 354–369.

Testa, T. J., Juraska, J. M., & Maier, S. F. (1974). Prior exposure to inescapable electric shock in rats affects extinction behavior after the successful acquisition of an escape response. *Learning and Motivation, 5,* 380–392.

Thewissen, R., Snijders, S. J. B. D., Havermans, R. C., van den Hout, M., & Jansen, A. (2006). Renewal of cue-elicited urge to smoke: Implications for cue exposure treatment. *Behaviour Research and Therapy,* in press.

Thomas, D. A. (1979). Retention of conditioned inhibition in a bar-press suppression paradigm. *Learning and Motivation, 10,* 161–177.

Thomas, D. R., & Barker, E. G. (1964). The effects of extinction and "central tendency" on stimulus generalization in pigeons. *Psychonomic Science, 1,* 119–121.

Thomas, D. R., & Lopez, L. J. (1962). The effects of delayed testing on generalization slope. *Journal of Comparative and Physiological Psychology, 55,* 541–544.

Thomas, D. R., Mood, K., Morrison, S., & Wiertelak, E. (1991). Peak shift revisited: A test of alternative interpretations. *Journal of Experimental Psychology: Animal Behavior Processes, 17,* 130–140.

Thomas, G. V., Robertson, D., & Lieberman, D. A. (1987). Marking effects in Pavlovian trace conditioning. *Journal of Experimental Psychology: Animal Behavior Processes, 13,* 126–135.

Thompson, R. F. (1986). The neurobiology of learning and memory. *Science, 233,* 941–947.

Thompson, R. F., & Krupa, D. J. (1994). Organization of memory traces in the mammalian brain. *Annual Review of Neuroscience, 17,* 519–549.

Thorndike, E. L. (1911). *Animal intelligence: Experimental studies.* New York: Macmillan.

Tiffany, S. T., Drobes, D. J., & Cepeda-Benito, A. (1992). Contribution of associative and nonassociative processes to the development of morphine tolerance. *Psychopharmacology, 109,* 185–190.

Timberlake, W. (1980). An equilibrium theory of learned performance. In G. H. Bower (Ed.), *Psychology of learning and motivation* (Vol. 14, pp. 1–58). New York: Academic Press.

Timberlake, W. (1983). The functional organization of appetitive behavior: Behavior systems and learning. In M. D. Zeiler & P. Harzen (Eds.), *Advances in the analysis of behavior, Vol. 3* (pp. 77–221). Chichester, UK: J. Wiley.

Timberlake, W. (1984). Behavior regulation and learned performance: Some misapprehensions and disagreements. *Journal of the Experimental Analysis of Behavior, 41,* 355–375.

Timberlake, W. (1994). Behavior systems, associationism, and Pavlovian conditioning. *Psychonomic Bulletin & Review, 1,* 405–420.

Timberlake, W. (2001). Motivational modes in behavior systems. In R. R. Mowrer & S. B. Klein (Eds.), *Handbook of contemporary learning theories* (pp. 155–210). Mahwah, NJ: Lawrence Erlbaum Associates, Inc.

Timberlake, W., & Allison, J. (1974). Response deprivation: An empirical approach to instrumental performance. *Psychological Review, 81,* 146–164.

Timberlake, W., & Farmer-Dougan, V. A. (1991). Reinforcement in applied settings: Figuring out ahead of time what will work. *Psychological Bulletin, 110,* 379–391.

Timberlake, W., & Grant, D. L. (1975). Auto-shaping in rats to the presentation of another rat predicting food. *Science, 190,* 690–692.

Timberlake, W., & Lucas, G. A. (1985). The basis of superstitious behavior: Chance contingency, stimulus substitution, or appetitive behavior? *Journal of the Experimental Analysis of Behavior, 44,* 279–299.

Timberlake, W., & Lucas, G. A. (1991). Periodic water, interwater interval, and adjunctive behavior in a 24-hour multiresponse environment. *Animal Learning & Behavior, 19,* 369–380.

Timberlake, W., & Silva, K. M. (1995). Appetitive behavior in ethology, psychology, and behavioral systems. In N. S. Thompson (Ed.), *Perspectives in ethology, Vol. 11: Behavioral design* (pp. 211–253). New York: Plenum Press.

Timberlake, W., Wahl, G., & King, D. (1982). Stimulus and response contingencies in the misbehavior of rats. *Journal of Experimental Psychology: Animal Behavior Processes, 8,* 62–85.

Tinbergen, L. (1960). The natural control of insects in pine woods: I. Facts influencing the intensity of predation by songbirds. *Archives Neerlandaises de Zoologie, 17,* 2–11.

Tinbergen, N. (1951). *The study of instinct.* London: Oxford University.

Tinbergen, N. (1963). The shell menace. *Natural History, 72,* 28–35.

Tinbergen, N., & Perdeck, A. C. (1950). On the stimulus situation releasing the begging response in the newly hatched Herring Gull chick (*Larus argentatus argentatus* Pont.). *Behaviour, 3,* 1–39.

Tinklepaugh, O. L. (1928). An experimental study of representative factors in monkeys. *Journal of Comparative Psychology, 8,* 197–236.

Tolman, E. C. (1932). *Purposive Behavior in Animals and Men.* New York: The Century Co.

Tolman, E. C. (1938). The determiners of behavior at a choice point. *Psychological Review, 45,* 1–41.

Tolman, E. C. (1945). A stimulus-expectancy need-cathexis psychology. *Science, 101,* 160–166.

Tolman, E. C. (1948). Cognitive maps in rats and men. *Psychological Review, 55,* 189–208.

Tolman, E. C. (1949). There is more than one kind of learning. *Psychological Review, 56,* 144–155.

Tolman, E. C., & Honzik, C. H. (1930). Introduction and removal of reward, and maze performance in rats. *University of California Publications in Psychology, 4,* 257–275.

Tolman, E. C., Ritchie, B. F., & Kalish, D. (1946a). Studies in spatial learning. I. Orientation and the short-cut. *Journal of Experimental Psychology, 36,* 13–24.

Tolman, E. C., Ritchie, B. F., & Kalish, D. (1946b). Studies in spatial learning. II. Place learning versus response learning. *Journal of Experimental Psychology, 36,* 221–229.

Tomarken, A. J., Mineka, S., & Cook, M. (1989). Fear-relevant selective associations and covariation bias. *Journal of Abnormal Psychology, 98,* 381–394.

Tomie, A. (1996). Locating reward cue at response manipulandum (CAM) induces symptoms of drug abuse. *Neuroscience and biobehavioral reviews, 20,* 505–535.

Tomie, A. (2001). Autoshaping and drug-taking. In R. R. Mowrer & S. B. Klein (Eds.), *Handbook of contemporary learning theories* (pp. 409–440). Mahwah, NJ: Lawrence Erlbaum Associates, Inc.

Trapold, M. A. (1970). Are expectancies based upon different positive reinforcing events discriminably different? *Learning and Motivation, 1,* 129–140.

Trapold, M. A., & Overmier, J. B. (1972). The second learning process in instrumental learning. In A. H. Black & W. F. Prokasy (Eds.), *Classical conditioning: Vol. 2. Current research and theory* (pp. 427–452). New York: Appleton-Century-Crofts.

Treisman, A. (1988). Features and objects: The fourteenth Bartlett Memorial lecture. *Quarterly Journal of Experimental Psychology, 12,* 97–136.

Trivers, R. L. (1972). Parental investment and sexual selection. In B. Campbell (Ed.), *Sexual selection and the descent of man.* Chicago, IL: Aldine.

Tryon, R. C. (1942). Individual differences. In F. A. Moss (Ed.), *Comparative psychology.* Englewood Cliffs, NJ: Prentice-Hall.

Tulving, E. (1972). Episodic and semantic memory. In E. Tulving & W. Donaldson (Eds.), *Organization of memory* (pp. 381–403). New York: Academic Press.

Urcelay, G. P., & Miller, R. R. (2006). Counteraction between overshadowing and degraded contingency treatments: support for the extended comparator hypothesis. *Journal of Experimental Psychology: Animal Behavior Processes, 32,* 21–32.

Urcuioli, P. J. (2001). Categorization and acquired equivalence. In R. G. Cook (Ed.), *Avian visual cognition* [On-line]. Available: www.pigeon.psy.tufts.edu/avc/urcuioli/

Urcuioli, P. J., & Zentall, T. R. (1986). Retrospective coding in pigeons' delayed matching-to-sample. *Journal of Experimental Psychology: Animal Behavior Processes, 12,* 69–77.

Urcuioli, P. J., Zentall, T. R., Jackson-Smith, P., & Steirn, J. N. (1989). Evidence for common coding in many-to-one matching: Retention, intertrial interference, and transfer. *Journal of Experimental Psychology: Animal Behavior Processes, 15,* 264–273.

Urushihara, K., Stout, S. C., & Miller, R. R. (2004). The basic laws of conditioning differ for elemental cues and cues trained in compound. *Psychological Science, 15,* 268–271.

Van Hamme, L. J., & Wasserman, E. A. (1994). Cue competition in causality judgments: The role of nonpresentation of compound stimulus elements. *Learning and Motivation, 25,* 127–151.

Van Hamme, L. J., Wasserman, E. A., & Biederman, I. (1992). Discrimination of contour-deleted images by pigeons. *Journal of Experimental Psychology: Animal Behavior Processes, 18,* 387–399.

Vaughan, W., & Greene, S. L. (1984). Pigeon visual memory capacity. *Journal of Experimental Psychology: Animal Behavior Processes, 10,* 256–271.

Vila, J. C. (1989). Protection from pentobarbital lethality mediated by Pavlovian conditioning. *Pharmacology, Biochemistry and Behavior, 32,* 365–366.

Visintainer, M. A., Volpicelli, J. R., & Seligman, M. E. (1982). Tumor rejection in rats after inescapable or escapable shock. *Science, 216,* 437–439.

von Fersen, L., & Lea, S. E. G. (1990). Category discrimination by pigeons using five polymorphous features. *Journal of the Experimental Analysis of Behavior, 54,* 69–84.

Vos, D. R., Prijs, J., & Cate, C. T. (1993). Sexual imprinting in zebra finch males: A differential effect of successive and simultaneous experience with two colour morphs. *Behaviour, 126,* 137–154.

Vreven, D., & Blough, P. M. (1998). Searching for one or many targets: Effects of extended experience on the runs advantage. *Journal of Experimental Psychology: Animal Behavior Processes, 24.*

Wagner, A. R. (1959). The role of reinforcement and nonreinforcement in an "apparent frustration effect." *Journal of Experimental Psychology, 57,* 130–136.

Wagner, A. R. (1961). Effects of amount and percentage of reinforcement and number of acquisition trials on conditioning and extinction. *Journal of Experimental Psychology, 62,* 234–242.

Wagner, A. R. (1971). Elementary associations. In H. H. Kendler & J. T. Spence (Eds.), *Essays in neobehaviorism: A memorial volume to Kenneth W. Spence* (pp. 187–213). New York: Appleton-Century-Crofts.

Wagner, A. R. (1976). Priming in STM: An information-processing mechanism for self-generated or retrieval-generated depression in performance. In T. J. Tighe & R. N. Leaton (Eds.), *Habituation: Perspectives from child development, animal behavior and neurophysiology* (pp. 95–128). Hillsdale, NJ: Lawrence Erlbaum Associates, Inc.

Wagner, A. R. (1978). Expectancies and the priming of STM. In S. H. Hulse, H. Fowler, & W. K. Honig (Eds.), *Cognitive processes in animal behavior* (pp. 177–209). Hillsdale, NJ: Lawrence Erlbaum Associates, Inc.

Wagner, A. R. (1981). SOP: A model of automatic memory processing in animal behavior. In N. E. Spear & R. R. Miller (Eds.), *Information processing in animals: Memory mechanisms* (pp. 5–47). Hillsdale, NJ: Lawrence Erlbaum Associates, Inc.

Wagner, A. R. (2003). Context-sensitive elemental theory. *Quarterly Journal of Experimental Psychology B: Comparative and Physiological Psychology, 56B,* 7–29.

Wagner, A. R., & Brandon, S. E. (1989). Evolution of a structured connectionist model of Pavlovian conditioning (AESOP). In S. B. Klein & R. R. Mowrer (Eds.), *Contemporary learning theories: Pavlovian conditioning and the status of traditional learning theory* (pp. 149–189). Hillsdale, NJ: Lawrence Erlbaum Associates, Inc.

Wagner, A. R., & Brandon, S. E. (2001). A componential theory of Pavlovian conditioning. In R. R. Mowrer & S. B. Klein (Eds.), *Handbook of contemporary learning theories.* (pp. 23–64). Hillsdale, NJ: Lawrence Erlbaum Associates, Inc.

Wagner, A. R., & Rescorla, R. A. (1972). Inhibition in Pavlovian conditioning: Application of a theory. In M. S. Halliday & R. A. Boakes (Eds.), *Inhibition and learning* (pp. 301–336). New York: Academic Press.

Wagner, A. R., Logan, F. A., Haberlandt, K., & Price, T. (1968). Stimulus selection in animal discrimination learning. *Journal of Experimental Psychology, 76,* 177–186.

Wagner, A. R., Rudy, J. W., & Whitlow, J. W. (1973). Rehearsal in animal conditioning. *Journal of Experimental Psychology, 97,* 407–426.

Waldmann, M. R. (1996). Knowledge-based causal induction. In D. R. Shanks, K. J. Holyoak, & D. L. Medin (Eds.), *The psychology of learning and motivation, Vol. 34: Causal learning* (pp. 47–88). San Diego, CA: Academic Press.

Waldmann, M. R. (2000). Competition among causes but not effects in predictive and diagnostic learning. *Journal of Experimental Psychology: Learning, Memory, and Cognition, 26,* 53–76.

Waldmann, M. R., & Holyoak, K. J. (1992). Predictive and diagnostic learning within causal models: Asymmetries in cue competition. *Journal of Experimental Psychology: General, 121,* 222–236.

Wall, P. L., Botly, L. C. P., Black, C. K., & Shettleworth, S. J. (2004). The geometric module in the rat: Independence of shape and feature learning in a food finding task. *Learning & Behavior, 32,* 289–298.

Warden, C. J. (1931). *Animal motivation: Experimental studies on the albino rat.* New York: Columbia University Press.

Wasserman, E. A. (1973). Pavlovian conditioning with heat reinforcement produces stimulus-directed pecking in chicks. *Science, 181,* 875–877.

Wasserman, E. A. (1974). Stimulus-reinforcer predictiveness and selective discrimination learning in pigeons. *Journal of Experimental Psychology, 103,* 284–297.

Wasserman, E. A. (1990). Attribution of causality to common and distinctive elements of compound stimuli. *Psychological Science, 1,* 298–302.

Wasserman, E. A. (1995). The conceptual abilities of pigeons. *American Scientist, 83,* 246–255.

Wasserman, E. A., & Bhatt, R. S. (1992). Conceptualization of natural and artificial stimuli by pigeons. In W.K. Honig & J. G. Fetterman (Eds.), *Cognitive aspects of stimulus control* (pp. 203–223). Hillsdale, NJ: Lawrence Erlbaum, Inc.

Wasserman, E. A., DeVolder, C. L., & Coppage, D. J. (1992). Non-similarity-based conceptualization in pigeons via secondary or mediated generalization. *Psychological Science, 3,* 374–379.

Wasserman, E. A., Elek, S. M., Chatlosh, D. L., & Baker, A. G. (1993). Rating causal relations: Role of probability in judgments of response-outcome contingency. *Journal of Experimental Psychology: Learning, Memory, and Cognition, 19,* 174–188.

Wasserman, E. A., Frank, A. J., & Young, M. E. (2002). Stimulus control by same-versus-different relations among multiple visual stimuli. *Journal of Experimental Psychology: Animal Behavior Processes, 28,* 347–357.

Wasserman, E. A., Hugart, J. A., & Kirkpatrick-Steger, K. (1995). Pigeons show same–different conceptualization after training with complex visual stimuli. *Journal of Experimental Psychology: Animal Behavior Processes, 21,* 248–252.

Wasserman, E. A., Kiedinger, R. E., & Bhatt, R. S. (1988). Conceptual behavior in pigeons: Categories, subcategories, and pseudocategories. *Journal of Experimental Psychology: Animal Behavior Processes, 14,* 235–246.

Wasserman, E. A., Young, M. E., & Cook, R. G. (2004). Variability discrimination in humans and animals: Implications for adaptive action. *American Psychologist, 59,* 879–890.

Watanabe, S., Sakamoto, J., & Wakita, M. (1995). Pigeons' discrimination of painting by Monet and Picasso. *Journal of the Experimental Analysis of Behavior, 63,* 165–174.

Watson, J. B. (1913). Psychology as the behaviourist views it. *Psychological Review, 20,* 158–177.

Watson, J. B. (1916). The place of the conditioned-reflex in psychology. *Psychological Review, 23,* 89–116.

Watson, J. B. (1924). *Behaviorism.* New York: Norton.

Watson, J. B., & Rayner, R. (1920). Conditioned emotional reactions. *Journal of Experimental Psychology, 3,* 1–14.

Wearden, J. H., & Doherty, M. F. (1995). Exploring and developing a connectionist model of animal timing: Peak procedure and fixed-interval simulations. *Journal of Experimental Psychology: Animal Behavior Processes, 21,* 99–115.

Weary, D. M., Guilford, T. C., & Weisman, R. G. (1992). A product of discriminative learning may lead to female preferences for elaborate males. *Evolution, 47,* 333–336.

Weidemann, G., & Kehoe, E. J. (2005). Stimulus specificity of concurrent recovery in the rabbit nictitating membrane response. *Learning & Behavior, 33,* 343–362.

Weingarten, H. P. (1983). Conditioned cues elicit feeding in sated rats: A role for learning in meal initiation. *Science, 220,* 431–433.

Weingarten, H. P. (1984). Meal initiation controlled by learned cues: Basic behavioral properties. *Appetite, 5,* 147–158.

Weingarten, H. P. (1985). Stimulus control of eating: Implications for a two-factor theory of hunger. *Appetite, 6,* 387–401.

Weingarten, H. P. (1990). Learning, homeostasis, and the control of feeding behavior. In E. D. Capaldi & T. L. Powley (Eds.), *Taste, experience, and feeding* (pp. 14–27). Washington DC: American Psychological Association.

Weinstock, S. (1954). Resistance to extinction of a running response following partial reinforcement under widely spaced trials. *Journal of Comparative and Physiological Psychology, 47,* 318–322.

Weisman, R. G., & Litner, J. S. (1969). Positive conditioned reinforcement of Sidman avoidance behavior in rats. *Journal of Comparative and Physiological Psychology, 68,* 597–603.

Weisman, R., Shackleton, S., Ratcliffe, L., Weary, D., & Boag, P. T. (1994). Sexual preferences of female zebra finches: Imprinting on beak colour. *Behaviour, 128,* 15–24.

Weiss, J. (1968). The effects of coping responses on stress. *Journal of Comparative and Physiological Psychology, 65,* 251–260.

Weiss, J. M., Goodman, P. A., Losito, B. G., Corrigan, S., Charry, J. M., & Bailey, W. H. (1981). Behavioral depression produced by an uncontrollable stressor: Relationship to norepinephrine, dopamine, and serotonin levels in various regions of the rat brain. *Brain Research Review, 3,* 167–205.

Weiss, S. J., & Weissman, R. D. (1992). Generalization peak shift for autoshaped and operant key pecks. *Journal of the Experimental Analysis of Behavior, 57,* 27–143.

White, K. G., Parkinson, A. E., Brown, G. S., & Wixted, J. T. (2004). Local proactive interference in delayed matching to sample: The role of reinforcement. *Journal of Experimental Psychology: Animal Behavior Processes, 30,* 83–95.

White, N. M., & McDonald, R. J. (2002). Multiple parallel memory systems in the brain of the rat. *Neurobiology of Learning and Memory, 77,* 125–184.

Whitehead, A. N. (1911). *An introduction to mathematics.* New York: Holt.

Whitlow, J. W. (1975). Short-term memory in habituation and dishabituation. *Journal of Experimental Psychology: Animal Behavior Processes, 1,* 189–206.

Wiens, S., & Öhman, A. (2002). Unawareness is more than a chance event: Comment on Lovibond and Shanks. *Journal of Experimental Psychology: Animal Behavior Processes, 28,* 27–31.

Wilcoxon, H. C., Dragoin, W. B., & Kral, P. A. (1971). Illness-induced aversions in rat and quail: Relative salience of visual and gustatory cues. *Science, 171,* 826–828.

Williams, B. A. (1988). Reinforcement, choice, and response strength. In R. C. Atkinson & R. J. Herrnstein (Eds.), *Stevens' handbook of experimental psychology, Vol. 1: Perception and motivation; Vol. 2: Learning and cognition* (2nd ed., pp. 167–244). New York: Wiley.

Williams, B. A. (1989). The effect of response contingency and reinforcement identity on response suppression by alternative reinforcement. *Learning and Motivation, 20,* 204–224.

Williams, B. A. (1994a). Conditioned reinforcement: Neglected or outmoded explanatory construct? *Psychonomic Bulletin & Review, 1,* 457–475.

Williams, B. A. (1994b). Reinforcement and choice. In N. J. Mackintosh (Ed.), *Animal learning and cognition. Handbook of perception and cognition series* (2nd ed., pp. 81–108). San Diego, CA: Academic Press.

Williams, D. A. (1995). Forms of inhibition in animal and human learning. *Journal of Experimental Psychology: Animal Behavior Processes, 21,* 129–142.

Williams, D. A., Overmier, J. B., & LoLordo, V. M. (1992). A reevaluation of Rescorla's early dictums about Pavlovian conditioned inhibition. *Psychological Bulletin, 111,* 275–290.

Williams, D. A., Sagness, K. E., & McPhee, J. E. (1994). Configural and elemental strategies in predictive learning. *Journal of Experimental Psychology: Learning, Memory, and Cognition, 20,* 694–709.

Williams, D. R. (1965). Classical conditioning and incentive motivation. In W. F. Prokasy (Ed.), *Classical conditioning: A symposium.* New York: Appleton Century Crofts.

Williams, D. R., & Williams, H. (1969). Auto-maintenance in the pigeon: Sustained pecking despite contingent non-reinforcement. *Journal of Experimental and Analytical Behavior, 12,* 511–520.

Williams, G. C. (1966). *Adaptation and natural selection.* Princeton, NJ: Princeton University Press.

Williams, J. L., & Maier, S. F. (1977). Transitional immunization and therapy of learned helplessness in the rat. *Journal of Experimental Psychology: Animal Behavior Processes, 3,* 240–252.

Williams, S. B. (1938). Resistance to extinction as a function of the number of reinforcements. *Journal of Experimental Psychology, 23,* 506–522.

Wilson, E. O. (1975). *Sociobiology: The new synthesis.* Cambridge, MA: Belknap Press.

Wilson, P. N., Boumphrey, P., & Pearce, J. M. (1992). Restoration of the orienting response to a light by a change in its predictive accuracy. *Quarterly Journal of Experimental Psychology B: Comparative and Physiological Psychology, 44B,* 17–36.

Witcher, E. S., & Ayres, J. J. (1984). A test of two methods for extinguishing Pavlovian conditioned inhibition. *Animal Learning & Behavior, 12,* 149–156.

Wolf, M. M., Risley, T., & Mees, H. (1964). Application of operant conditioning procedures to the behavior problems of an autistic child. *Behavior Research and Therapy, 1,* 305–312.

Wolpe, J. (1958). *Psychotherapy by reciprocal inhibition.* Stanford: Stanford University Press.

Woodbury, C. B. (1943). The learning of stimulus patterns by dogs. *Journal of Comparative Psychology, 35,* 29–40.

Woods, S. C. (1991). The eating paradox: How we tolerate food. *Psychological Review, 98,* 488–505.

Woods, S. C., & Shogren, R. E. (1972). Glycemic responses following conditioning with different doses of insulin in rats. *Journal of Comparative and Physiological Psychology, 81,* 220–225.

Woods, S. C., & Strubbe, J. H. (1994). The psychobiology of meals. *Psychonomic Bulletin & Review, 1,* 141–155.

Wyvell, C. L., & Berridge, K. C. (2000). Intra-accumbens amphetamine increases the conditioned incentive salience of sucrose reward: Enhancement of reward "wanting" without enhanced "liking" or response reinforcement. *Journal of Neuroscience, 20,* 8122–8130.

Young, A. M., & Herling, S. (1986). Drugs as reinforcers: Studies in laboratory animals. In S. R. Goldberg & I. P. Stolerman (Eds.), *Behavioral analysis of drug dependence.* Orlando, FL: Academic Press.

Young, M. E., & Wasserman, E. A. (1997). Entropy detection by pigeons: Response to mixed visual displays after same–different discrimination training. *Journal of Experimental Psychology: Animal Behavior Processes, 23,* 157–170.

Young, M. E., Wasserman, E. A., & Garner, K. L. (1997). Effects of number of items on the pigeon's discrimination of same from different visual displays. *Journal of Experimental Psychology: Animal Behavior Processes, 23,* 491–501.

Zach, R. (1978). Selection and dropping of whelks by Northwestern crows. *Behaviour, 67*(1-sup-2), 134–148.

Zach, R. (1979). Shell dropping: Decision-making and optimal foraging in northwestern crows. *Behaviour, 68*(1-sup-2), 106–117.

Zahorik, D. M., & Maier, S. F. (1969). Appetitive conditioning with recovery from thiamine deficiency as the unconditioned stimulus. *Psychonomic Science, 17,* 309–310.

Zentall, T. R. (1997). Animal memory: The role of "instructions." *Learning and Motivation, 28,* 280–308.

Zentall, T. R. (1998). Symbolic representations in animals: Emergent stimulus relations in conditional discrimination learning. *Animal Learning & Behavior, 26,* 363–377.

Zentall, T. R., Steirn, J. N., & Jackson-Smith, P. (1990). Memory strategies in pigeons' performance of a radial-arm-maze analog task. *Journal of Experimental Psychology: Animal Behavior Processes, 16,* 358–371.

Zentall, T. R., Steirn, J. N., Sherburne, L. M., & Urcuioli, P. J. (1991). Common coding in pigeons assessed through partial versus total reversals of many-to-one conditional and simple discriminations. *Journal of Experimental Psychology: Animal Behavior Processes, 17,* 194–201.

Zimmer-Hart, C. L., & Rescorla, R. A. (1974). Extinction of Pavlovian conditioned inhibition. *Journal of Comparative and Physiological Psychology, 86,* 837–845.

Author Index

Subject Index

a-process, 362
A1 state, 131–135, 172, *173*
A2 state, 131–135, 172, *173*
acquired drive experiment, 374
acquired equivalence, 289–292
acquired motivation, 342
acquisition
   extinction and, *352*
   of signals, 60
adaptation, 360
   in behavior, 40–42
   classical conditioning and, 27, 50–60
   instrumental conditioning and, 46–50
   learning and, 39–70
addiction
   motivation and, 358–359
   opponent-process theory and, 365–367
   withdrawal responses, 366
adjunctive behaviors, 398
adrenal glands, 330–331
AESOP (affective extension of standard operating procedures), *135*, 135–137, 169
affect, 135
affective dynamics, *360*, 361, *361*
affective extension, 356
affective extension of standard operating procedures (AESOP), *135*, 135–137, 169
after-images, 360
after-reactions, 360
aggression, territoriality and, 52–53
agoraphobia, 180, 374
Albert (infant), 15, 79
alcohol
   body-temperature effects, 171

complementarity, 250
instrumental action and, 358
loss of tolerance, 57
renewal effects, 156
almond odors, 196–197
ambiguity, paradigms involving, *158*
Amsel, Abram, *346*
analogous traits, 201
animal cognition, 269
animals, learning by, 25–27. *see also specific* animals; *specific* behaviors
antecedents, 18, 19
anticipation, 342–359, 367
antipredator behaviors, 41–42
anxiety disorders, 156, 374–375
appetitive conditioning, 196
appetitive learning, 395–403
artificial selection, 44
association
   after extinctions, *154*
   in animals, 209
   causal power and, 216–217
   in classical conditioning, *75*
   declarative memory and, 304
   formation, *162*
   generalization and, 291–292
   between ideas, 7
   laws of, 8
   learning and, 213
   memory nodes and, *130*
   modification of, 165
   partial reinforcement extinction effect and, 350
   procedural memory and, 304
   R-S* learning, 408
   stimulus-response, 225

strength of, 276
within-compound, 198
Associationists. *see* Empiricists
associative learning
   classical conditioning and, 73
   flavor aversion learning and, 186
   in honeybees, 205–207
   in humans, 188, 207–212
   imprinting and, 362–363
   inferential reasoning and, 213
   in insects, 203
   object learning and, 74
   predictions, 288
   trial order and, 217
associative strength, 105
assumptions, a priori, 8–9
asymptote, definition, 105
atomistic approach, definition, 7
atropine, 174
attachment, social, 362–365
attention
   conditioning and, 119–123
   habits and, 415
   information processing and, 296–298
   priming, 297–298, *298*
authority, introspection and, 14
automaintenance, negative, 399–400
automatized behaviors, 33–34
autoshaping, *81*, 81–82, 164–165, 199, 399, 400
aversions. *see also* taste aversions
   conditioning and, 88–89
   interval schedules and, 409
   learning of, 82–83
avoidance behavior
   expectancies and, 388, *389*